"A comprehensive collection of the main statements of faith of all Reformed communities considered as orthodox (Waldensian, Zwinglian, Calvinist, and Anglican). Many of these documents are translated into English for the first time. References to existing critical editions are provided systematically. The editor has rendered a great service to modern-day churches that identify with the Zwinglian and Calvinist Reformation and also to all students and scholars not just of theology but of the history of religious institutions and culture of the period. He is particularly to be commended for including the seventeenth century, thus enabling us to chart the diversity and the development of Reformation communities over nearly two centuries. A must for every library."

—Dr. Irena Backus, Professor, Institute of
Reformation History, University of Geneva

"James Dennison's introductions and comprehensive compilation of sixteenth and seventeenth century Reformed confessions is a magnificent achievement that witnesses powerfully to the rich development, harmony, and piety of the Reformed faith. With the Spirit's blessing, these volumes will help recover a robust and vital Reformed theology that informs minds, convicts hearts, and moves hands to live exclusively for God's glory. Every Reformed pastor, professor, seminary student, library, and thoughtful layman should buy and study this remarkable collection."

—Dr. Joel R. Beeke, President of
Puritan Reformed Theological Seminary

"This is an invaluable compilation that brings together in four volumes many Reformed confessions written from 1523–1693. The whole series is most useful both for bringing together what has previously been scattered and for making material available in English for the first time."

—Dr. Anthony N. S. Lane, Professor of Historical Theology
and Director of Research, London School of Theology

"This four-volume set is a highly significant collection of Reformed confessional documents, offering not only the confessions and catechisms found in the older collections but a host of important confessions and catechisms that belong to the history of the Reformed churches but have been either ignored or left untranslated. These documents will provide a substantial resource for the study of the rise and progress of the Reformed faith in the early modern era."

—Dr. Richard A. Muller, P. J. Zondervan Professor
of Historical Theology, Calvin Theological Seminary

"Through these volumes, James Dennison has provided an invaluable resource for those interested in the history of the Reformation. His compilation of statements of faith and doctrine from across Europe's Reformed churches includes many texts here translated into English for the first time. These volumes will greatly aid our understanding of the nature and development of the Reformed tradition in early modern Europe."

—Dr. Graeme Murdock, Lecturer in European History,
Trinity College, University of Dublin

Reformed Confessions
of the 16th and 17th Centuries in
English Translation: Volume 4, 1600–1693

Reformed Confessions
of the 16th and 17th Centuries in
English Translation: Volume 4, 1600–1693

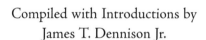

Compiled with Introductions by
James T. Dennison Jr.

REFORMATION HERITAGE BOOKS
Grand Rapids, Michigan

*Reformed Confessions of the 16th and 17th Centuries
in English Translation: Volume 4, 1600–1693*
© 2014 by James T. Dennison Jr.

Published by
Reformation Heritage Books
2965 Leonard St. NE
Grand Rapids, MI 49525
616-977-0889 / Fax 616-285-3246
e-mail: orders@heritagebooks.org
website: www.heritagebooks.org

Library of Congress Cataloging-in-Publication Data

Reformed confessions of the 16th and 17th centuries in English
translation : volume 1, 1523-1552 / compiled with introductions by James
T. Dennison.
    p. cm.
Includes bibliographical references.
ISBN 978-1-60178-044-7 (hardcover : alk. paper)
1. Reformed Church—Creeds. I. Dennison, James T., 1943-
BX9428.A1R445 2008
238'.4209031—dc22
                                        2008039005

TABLE OF CONTENTS

PERMISSIONS

The compiler and publisher wish to express our gratitude to the following for permission to reprint versions of the following confessions:

Reformed Fellowship, Inc., Wyoming, Michigan for The Counter Remonstrance (1611).

Northwest Theological Seminary, Lynnwood, Washington and *Kerux: The Journal of Northwest Theological Seminary* for The Bentheim Confession (1613/1617).

Christian Reformed Church of North America, Grand Rapids, Michigan for The Canons of Dort (1618–1619).

Free Presbyterian Church of Scotland for The Westminster Confession of Faith (1646), The Westminster Larger Catechism (1647), and The Westminster Shorter Catechism (1647).

John Cargill for his internet version of The Midlands Confession (1655).

Trinity Journal and Martin I. Klauber for his translation of the canons of The Formula Consensus Helvetica (1675).

ABBREVIATIONS

Müller   E. F. Karl Müller, ed. *Die Bekenntnisschriften der reformierten Kirche.* Waltrop: Hartmut Spenner, 1999 [1903].

Niemeyer   H. A. Niemeyer, *Collectio confessionum in ecclesiis reformatis publicatarum.* Lipsiae, 1840.

Schaff   Philip Schaff, *The Creeds of Christendom.* Grand Rapids: Baker Book House, 1966 [1877].

92
The Points of Difference (1603)

O n the death of Elizabeth I (1533–1603), the Puritan faction in the Church of England expectantly awaited the progress of James VI (to be James I, [1566–1625]) of Scotland from Edinburgh to London. Eagerly they presented the so-called 1603 Millenary Petition to the new monarch, hoping for some reform in the established church. Though trained under Scottish Presbyterians, James was in fact contemptuous of the lairds of the Kirk and sneered at the proposed petitioners. A year later, at the Hampton Court Conference, James reinforced the tenets of Anglican and monarchical supremacy and threatened to "harrie [the Puritans] out of the land or do worse."

The London-Amsterdam Separatists joined in the optimism of their Puritan (non-Separatist) brethren in England by presenting the king with a copy of their 1598 statement of faith (revised 1596 version). Francis Johnson (1562–1617/18) and Henry Ainsworth (1571–1622) were the bearers of this document to the court. Ignored by the crown, they persisted with the fourteen-point declaration below. This too was ignored, evidently; and when a third petition failed to elicit any response from the court, the Separatists realized that James was as hostile or indifferent to their principles as Elizabeth had been.

Our text is found in Williston Walker, *The Creeds and Platforms of Congregationalism* (1893), 77–80. Spelling and punctuation have been modified. The text is also found in Müller, 539–41.

THE POINTS OF DIFFERENCE

1. That Christ the Lord has by His last Testament given to His church, and set therein, sufficient ordinary offices, with the manner of calling or entrance, works, and maintenance, for the administration of His holy things, and for the sufficient ordinary instruction, guidance, and service of His church, to the end of the world.

2. That every particular church has like and full interest and power to enjoy and practice all the ordinances of Christ given by Him to His church to be observed therein perpetually.

3. That every true visible church is a company of people called and separated from the world by the Word of God, and joined together by voluntary profession of the faith of Christ, in the fellowship of the gospel. And that therefore no known atheist, unbeliever, heretic, or wicked liver is to be received or retained a member in the church of Christ, which is His body; God having in all ages appointed and made a separation of His people from the world, before the law, under the law, and now in the time of the gospel.

4. That discreet, faithful, and able men (though not yet in office of ministry) may be appointed to preach the gospel and whole truth of God, that men being first brought to knowledge, and converted to the Lord, may then be joined together in holy communion with Christ our Head and one with another.

5. That being thus joined, every church has power in Christ to choose and take unto themselves meet and sufficient persons into the offices and functions of pastors, teachers, elders, deacons, and helpers, as those which Christ has appointed in His Testament, for the feeding, governing, serving, and building up of His church. And that no anti-Christian hierarchy or ministry of popes, archbishops, lord-bishops, suffragans, deans, archdeacons, chancellors, parsons, vicars, priests, dumb-ministers, nor any such like are to be set over the spouse and church of Christ, nor retained therein.

6. That the ministers aforesaid being lawfully called by the church where they are to administer ought to continue in their functions according to

God's ordinance, and carefully to feed the flock of Christ committed unto them, being not enjoined or suffered to bear civil offices withal, neither burdened with the execution of civil affairs, as the celebration of marriage, burying the dead, etc., which things belong as well to those without as within the church.

7. That the due maintenance of the officers aforesaid should be of the free and voluntary contribution of the church, that according to Christ's ordinance, they which preach the gospel may live of the gospel: and not by popish lordships and livings, or Jewish tithes and offerings. And that therefore the lands and other like revenues of the prelates and clergy yet remaining (being still also baits to allure the Jesuits and seminaries into the land, and incitements unto them to plot and prosecute their wonted evil courses, hoping to enjoy them in time to come) may now by Your Highness be taken away, and converted to better use, as those of the abbeys and nunneries have been heretofore by Your Majesty's worthy predecessors, to the honor of God and great good of the Realm.

8. That all particular churches ought to be so constituted, as having their own peculiar officers, the whole body of every church may meet together in one place, and jointly perform their duties to God and one towards another. And that the censures of admonition and excommunication may be in due manner executed for sin, convicted and obstinately stood in. This power is also to be in the body of the church whereof the parties so offending and persisting are members.

9. That the church is not governed by popish canons, courts, classes, customs, or any human inventions, but by the laws and rules which Christ has appointed in His Testament. That no apocryphal writings, but only the canonical Scriptures, are to be used in the church. And that the Lord is to be worshipped and called upon in Spirit and truth, according to that form of prayer given by the Lord Jesus (Matt. 6) and after the liturgy of His own Testament, not by any other framed or imposed by men, much less by one translated from the popish liturgy, as the Book of Common Prayer, etc.

10. That the sacraments, being seals of God's covenant, ought to be administered only to the faithful, and baptism to their seed or those under

their government. And that according to the simplicity of the gospel, without any popish or other abuses, in either sacrament.

11. That the church is not to be urged to the observation of days and times, Jewish or popish, save only to sanctify the Lord's Day. Neither to be laden in things indifferent, with rites and ceremonies whatsoever invented by men; but that Christian liberty may be retained, and what God has left free, none are to make bound.

12. That all monuments of idolatry in garments or any other things, all temples, altars, chapels, and other places, dedicated heretofore by the heathen or anti-Christians to their false worship, ought by lawful authority to be razed and abolished—not suffered to remain, for nourishing superstition, much less employed to the true worship of God.

13. That popish degrees in theology, enforcement to single life in colleges, abuse of the study of profane heathen writers, with other like corruptions in schools and academies, should be removed and redressed, that so they may be the wellsprings and nurseries of true learning and godliness.

14. Finally that all churches and people (without exception) are bound in religion only to receive and submit unto that constitution, ministry, worship, and order, which Christ as Lord and King has appointed unto His church, and not to any other devised by man whatsoever.

93

Waldensian Confession (1603)

The following document, while not a formal confession of faith, attests to the Reformed character of the Waldensian Church at the turn of the seventeenth century. Here the Vaudois align themselves emphatically with the Reformed churches of Europe.

The general context of the declaration is the ongoing persecution of the Waldensians in the region of Saluzzo/Salusse/Saluces (so-called Marquisate of Saluzzo), south of Turin, Italy. Emmanuel Philibert (1528–1580) had regained the Duchy of Savoy-Piedmont from the French in 1559 and made Turin his capital in 1562. He was succeeded in 1580 by Charles Emmanuel I (the Great [1580–1630]), who repeatedly attempted to conquer and suppress Calvinism in his domain and beyond (twice he failed to attack and conquer Geneva, in 1588 and in 1602). The Waldensians were classified along with other *banditti* as outlaws and heretics. They responded with an appeal to Charles Emmanuel at a conference in the spring of 1603. On April 9, he issued a decree of general amnesty (a copy is reproduced in Morland, 466–71). The Waldensians gained a few brief years of tranquility by this decree.

Our translation is based on the French text found in Leger, *Histoire générale des églises évangeliques des Vallées de Piémont* (1669), 1:111–12, as compared with the English version in Samuel Morland, *The History of the Evangelical Churches of the Valleys of Piemont* (1658), 41–43.

A Declaration of the Waldenses of the Valleys of Meane, and of Maties and of the Marquisate of Saluzzo, presented in the year 1603, to the Duke of Savoy.

Whereas our predecessors from all time, and from father to son, have been instructed in the doctrine and religion which we have always openly professed from our childhood and in which we have instructed our families, as we have learned from our fathers, and which (while the king [of France] held the Marquisate of Saluzzo), we were permitted to profess without any disturbance no less than our brothers in the Valleys of Lucerne, who, by a treaty expressly made with their sovereign prince, have rejoiced with us in securing its continuation: and because His Highness, incited instead by persons of evil intentions than by his own will, has resolved to disturb us and to that end has brought forth an edict against us: that all the world may know that it is not for any crime which we have committed, either against the person of our prince, or to rebel against the laws, or that we have been guilty of murders, of thefts, etc.; that we have been tormented in that way, spoiled of our goods, and the possessions of our houses, etc. We declare that we are certain and persuaded that the doctrine and religion practiced by the Reformed Churches of France, Switzerland, Germany, England, Scotland, Geneva, Denmark, Sweden, Holland and other kingdoms, nations and dominions, of which we have before made open profession under the obedience of our princes and principal sovereigns, is the only doctrine and religion ordained of God, which alone is able to render us acceptable to God and to lead us to salvation. We have resolved to hold it at the peril of our lives, goods, and honor, and to continue in it up to the last breath of our life. And if anyone believes that we are in error, we very humbly beseech him that he show us our errors; we offer to renounce it without delay and to follow whatever would be shown to be more excellent, desiring nothing more than to render the obedience to God that we owe to Him, as poor creatures, and by this means obtain from Him true and eternal happiness. But if by violence, they wish to constrain us to abandon the way of salvation, to follow the errors and false doctrines invented by men, we choose rather to suffer the loss of our houses, goods, and lives, begging most humbly His Highness, whom we recognize as our lawful Prince and Sovereign, that he not permit us to be persecuted without cause, but rather that he allow us to continue all the rest of our life, and our children and posterity after us, in the same obedience which we have before inviolably rendered as his true and faithful subjects.

Since we request nothing else of him except the rendering whatever we ought according to the express commandment of God, we may also be allowed to give to God the service which is due to Him and which is required of us by His Word. And meanwhile in the midst of our calamities and banishment, we pray the Reformed churches to recognize us as true members of theirs, always ready to seal with our own blood, if God calls us to, the confession of faith which has been published, which we hold in every way agreeing with the doctrine of the holy apostles, wishing to live and die in it. And if for so doing we are persecuted, we return thanks to God, who has granted us the honor of suffering for Him, committing the outcome of our affairs and the justice of our cause into the hands of the providence of God, who will deliver us when and by the means which shall please Him. Most humbly praying that as He holds the hearts of kings and princes in His hand, He will be pleased to bend the heart of His Highness to have pity on us, who have never offended him, and have resolved not ever to offend him, that he may acknowledge us, he may recognize us to be most faithful subjects, than those who persuade him to persecute us severely, and for ourselves, that He will be pleased to strengthen us amid these temptations and give us constancy and patience to persevere in the profession of the truth until the end of our life and that of our posterity after us. Amen.

94

Confession of the Synod of Cassel (1607)

The conversion of Landgrave Maurice (Moritz) of Hesse-Kassel/Cassel (1572–1632) from Lutheranism to Calvinism was not altogether surprising. His father, William IV of Hesse-Kassel (1532–1592), had followed the moderately ecumenical (i.e., Lutheran, Zwinglian, and Reformed) sympathies of his father before him, Philip the Magnanimous (1504–1567). Philip had been integral to convening the Marburg Colloquy (1529), and his son, William IV, promoted a presbyterian organization of the church in his region under the influence of Martin Bucer (1491–1551).

Having been influenced by the Reformed theologians and nobles of Nassau, Maurice formally embraced the Reformed faith in 1605. On account of *cuius regio, eius religio* (Peace of Augsburg, 1555), the citizens of his duchy were obliged to follow suit. The synod that convened at Kassel on April 12, 1607, was an attempt to promote the unity of theology and doctrine throughout his formerly Lutheran domain. The five articles below were basic comments on essentials of worship and belief. One consequence of adopting these articles was the dismissal of Lutheran theologians from Marburg as well as the removal of numerous Lutheran pastors from their parishes. These men took refuge in nearby Hesse-Darmstadt, where they fueled feuds with their former liege that severely hampered the economic prosperity of Maurice's domain. Near financial ruin, Maurice abdicated in 1627 in favor of his son, William V (1601/02–1637).

Schaff calls this confession "The Hessian Confession." The German title is *Christliche und richtige Bekäntnis* (1607). Our translation is from the German text printed in Müller, 817–21. The text also appears in Heinrich Heppe, *Die Bekenntnisschriften reformirten Kirchen Deutschlands* (1860), 244–49.

THE CHRISTIAN AND ORTHODOX CONFESSION OF THE GENERAL SYNOD RECENTLY HELD IN THE YEAR 1607 AT CASSEL, REGARDING CURRENTLY CONTROVERTED ARTICLES

We believe from the heart and confess with the mouth, before God in heaven and His holy churches on the earth, that the Holy Scripture given from God is the only, the certain, and the infallible rule of conduct, the foundation and standard for everything in our Christianity that we believe and ought to do. Therefore, all that conforms to that standard is correct and good, but what runs counter to it is false and evil. For thus says the Lord, "Verily, to the law and the testimony: if they do not speak accordingly, they will not have the dawning of the day" (Isa. 8:20). Likewise: "Walk not in the statutes of your fathers, and observe not their judgments, nor defile yourselves with their idols. I am the Lord your God; you shall walk in my statutes, and keep my judgments, and do them" (Ezek. 20:18). Similarly, Christ sends us to the Scriptures when He says, "Search the Scriptures" (John 5:39). Also: "What is written in the law? How readest thou?" (Luke 10:26). Also: "They have Moses and the prophets; let them hear them" (Luke 16:29). To the same effect, Peter says, "We have a sure word of prophecy, and you do well to heed it" (2 Peter 1:19). Like St. Paul before the governor Felix, so we also confess and declare before the whole world that we "believe all things which are written in the law and in the prophets" (Acts 24:14). We "say none other things than those which the prophets did say" (Acts 26:22, and the apostles, on which foundation we are built into a habitation of God through the Spirit, Eph. 2:19).

I. The Ten Commandments

On this immutable foundation of divine truth, we believe and teach the holy Ten Commandments, word for word, to the letter, as God spoke them from His holy mouth, wrote them with His own finger on the tables of stone, and had Moses write them for us in the book of the covenant, with an accompanying earnest warning, "Ye shall not add unto the word which I command you, neither shall ye diminish aught from it, that ye may keep the commandments of the Lord thy God which I command you" (Deut. 4:2).

But with respect to the division of the Ten Commandments, because it is not expressly fixed by the Word of God, we do not wish to quarrel over this with other churches. Inasmuch as that division which was customary in the printed catechism of our churches beginning from the period of Count Philip is agreeable to Scripture and antiquity, we consider it to be not unreasonable that the same be uniformly and everywhere retained and made use of in our churches. We also are expecting that this division will give no one a reason to bring schism or rupture to our churches.

II. The Extirpation of Images

As then we are bound to teach and study the words of the holy Ten Commandments, so also we are pledged and obliged to obey them, as was said by Moses, the man of God: "Behold, I have taught you statutes and judgments, even as the Lord my God commanded me, that ye should do so, etc. Keep therefore and do them, etc." (Deut. 5[4]:5). Likewise: "What thing soever I command you, observe to do it. Ye shall not every man do whatsoever is right in his own eyes" (Deut. 12:33, 8). Further, God the Lord has said in His holy Ten Commandments: "Thou shalt not make unto thee any graven image or any likeness, etc." (Ex. 20:4). Also: "Take ye therefore good heed unto yourselves; for ye saw no manner of similitude on the day that the Lord spake unto you in Horeb out of the midst of the fire. Lest ye corrupt yourselves, and make you a graven image, the likeness of male or female, etc." (Deut. 4:15). Also: "Take heed then unto yourselves, lest ye forget the covenant of the Lord your God, which he made with you. Do not make unto you a graven image of any likeness, as the Lord your God has commanded. For the Lord thy God is a consuming fire, even a jealous God" (4:23). To the contrary, it is never written that God commanded and said, "Thou shalt make a picture of me; thou shalt make some graven image or likeness of me." Similarly, nowhere in the entire Bible is it written that either the patriarchs Noah, Abraham, Isaac, Jacob, Joseph, and David, or the prophets and apostles, or other saints of God, even once erected an image of God, of Christ, or of Mary, or other deceased patriarchs and saints. Much rather the Scripture testifies that they broke in pieces the images and idols erected by others, and put them out of the sight of the churches. Therefore we regard ourselves bound and engaged to remove from the eyes of God's congregation the superstitious images carried over from the papacy, which had been set up, consecrated, and used in our churches for no other end than idolatry.

III. The Articles of the Creed and the Person of Christ

Respecting God the Father, Son, and Holy Spirit, our faith is on the same lines as everything on this topic that has been compiled from the Word of God and drawn up in the articles of our Christian apostolic creed. Besides these we believe, teach, and declare nothing. Instead, we bring our reason captive in obedience to the Holy Scripture and the articles of the Christian creed. Accordingly, when Holy Scripture nowhere declares, neither in the Old nor in the New Testament, and neither by the evangelists nor by the apostles, that the humanity or the body of Christ, or the human nature in Christ's person, is physically present everywhere, at one and the same time in heaven, in the air, on the earth, in the water, in the fire, and in all creaturely things, we shall once again adhere to Scripture and part company with our old synodical decisions, refraining from ways of speaking that are unknown to Holy Scripture. Acknowledging ourselves to be under obedience to Holy Scripture, we only speak of the high mystery of the person of Christ to the extent that Scripture does, and we wish to remain silent insofar as it does. For the Lord says in Scripture, "I am with you always, even unto the end of the world" (Matt. 28:20). Likewise: "Where two or three are gathered together in my name, there am I in the midst of them" (Matt. 18:20). This is something we believe from the heart, and make it our highest comfort in all our trouble and concern. But we also console ourselves that the Lord has said, "I leave the world, and go to the Father" (John 16:28). Likewise: "I am no more in the world, but these are in the world, and I come to thee. Holy Father, keep them through thy name, that they may be one, as we are" (John 17:11). Also: "In my Father's house are many mansions: if it were not so, I would have told you. I go away to prepare a place for you. And if I go away to prepare a place for you, I will come again, and receive you unto myself: that you may be where I am" (John 14:2–3).

IV. Eternal Predestination

After the same fashion, we believe and teach with respect to the high mystery of eternal predestination all that is written about it in the Bible, and further than that we believe and teach nothing on the matter. We disavow in this regard all impertinent prying and disputing spun from human reason. We abstain from the harsh language which some may use and which might give occasion for the simple to fall into despair or into carnal security. Thus we handle this doctrine in a way that ministers to people an assured and steadfast comfort, and a godly life and walk. And that we may yet more expressly explain ourselves on this point, our confession is just that which Luther has taken from the Word of God (which at all times we make our only infallible foundation in this and all other matters), and in the Bible has written a preface to the epistle to the Romans, which reads verbatim as follows: "In chapters nine, ten and eleven, he (Paul) teaches about God's eternal predestination, from which originally proceeds who shall believe or not believe, who can get free from sin or not get free, so that whether we shall become godly is altogether taken out of our hands and placed in the hand of God alone. This is in the highest degree necessary. For we are so weak and doubtful that if it depended on us no one at all would be saved, and the devil would undoubtedly overwhelm them all. But since God is dependable, so that his predestination does not fail and no one can hinder him, we still have hope in the face of sin, etc." Thus far, Luther. And this precisely is also our confession regarding this high mystery of eternal election.

V. The Holy Lord's Supper

Respecting the most holy Lord's Supper of our Lord Jesus Christ, we believe and observe all that is written in the Holy Bible, but besides that we believe and teach nothing. The Scripture testifies that our Lord Jesus Christ, on the night in which He was betrayed, took quite genuine bread and wine (such as the host and all other Jews on the same occasion ate and drank during the meal at their tables), and broke into pieces the same bread with His hands at the table, in the sight of His disciples, and commanded them to take the broken bread itself and eat. And then He said, "This do," which word of command the apostles and early church understood to indicate that the Supper should be administered with actually nourishing bread and with the holy ceremony of breaking, and that this actual breaking of the bread has been prescribed to us (Acts 2, 4, 20; 1 Cor. 10, 11). Therefore we regard ourselves as bound to observe the Lord's Supper with quite genuine bread, and to practice a breaking of the bread. And we are certain that in this we act not improperly, but properly, and can with the holy apostle say, we have received of the Lord that which also we have delivered unto you. But if we did not practice this, how could we truthfully say that we have received of the Lord, since what we have received is indeed not without genuine bread or without such breaking (1 Cor. 10, 11)? Moreover, because the Lord says of that bread broken and appointed for use in the sacrament of His body, "Eat" (so that what is understood according to plain usage is that eating of bread with the mouth with which everyone is familiar), we believe and practice that this consecrated bread is to be received with our physical mouth, chewed with our teeth, tasted with our tongues, and should be taken into our stomachs; and this is all the same with the actual eating with the mouth with which everyone is familiar. However, this bread is called and is a sacrament of the body of Christ, and in accordance with this holy usage and rule is not straight common bread; and accordingly this eating is called and is, not a common but a sacramental eating. After all, the Lord says of the bread, "This is my body which is given for you"; and further, "This do in remembrance of me." By these words, He calls for faith, and will not only have us with the physical mouth eat the earthly bread, but also with the mouth of believing hearts eat and drink the heavenly food, which is His true body given for us, and His true blood on the cross poured out for us from His sides and wounds for the forgiveness of our sins. Thereby our hungering and thirsting souls will be fed, satiated, and revived unto everlasting life. Thus we believe that in the holy Lord's Supper, along with the physical use of the sacrament of the body of Christ, there is at the same time an actual partaking of the true body and blood of Jesus Christ Himself, and not a partaking that is imaginary or merely notional. Through such nurture Christ dwells in our hearts. On this account, the Lord Jesus Christ is not absent, but present truly to feed us in His holy Supper with His holy flesh, and makes us to drink of His blood. This use of the body and blood of Christ brings and yields strong consolation, life, and eternal salvation to all timid, distressed, but believing hearts, in accordance with the word and promise of the Lord, "Verily, verily, I say unto you, whoso eateth my flesh, and drinketh my blood, dwelleth in me, and I in him. He hath eternal life, and I will raise him up at the last day" (John 6:54–56). But woe to all who do not have this feeding, and gape after other things, for the Lord says: "Except ye eat the flesh of the Son of man, and drink his blood, ye have no life in you." If such be the case, we rightly pray in accordance with our church order: "O almighty God, give us to relish with true faith the body and blood of thy dear Son in the holy sacrament, that He should live in us, and we in Him." Likewise: "Give us to receive, with the appetite of true piety and in thankfulness, His body and blood in His holy Lord's Supper." Also: "Give us above all to eat and drink His body and blood in the holy sacrament unto everlasting life, in order that we may always live in Him and He in us." Both sorts of eating, namely eating with the mouth during the sacrament, and then the spiritual eating of the body of Christ, are set forth in Scripture in clear and distinct letters. But that beyond these two there is yet a third eating, in which with the physical mouth the body of Christ is eaten also by blasphemers, sorcerers, and other unbelievers, in an inexplicable and unfeeling manner, and indeed without any benefit or fruit, lacks any basis in the institution of the Supper or in any passage in the Holy Scriptures. For this reason, we adhere to the said two ways of eating that are expressly set forth in the Word of God, and leave to the side the third, as that which in Scripture is supported neither by a command nor a promise, though if churches believe or hold it we have no desire either to quarrel with them over this or to condemn them. This then is our simple and straightforward faith and confession respecting the above-mentioned articles, founded securely on the divine Word in clear and distinct letters, and in nothing contrary to the Augsburg Confession, its Apology, and our church order. We submit all to the judgment and understanding of each Christian and indeed to the entire Christian church, not doubting that to everyone from now on it will appear manifest and evident how invalid are the diverse accusations of frightful and detestable errors with which until now we have been loaded, but of which we are not at all aware. God be praised.

The God of all grace and mercy keep us in the true faith, and grant peace and truth to His dear churches. Amen.

(Translated by George Friesen; revised by R. Sherman Isbell)

95

Hessian Catechism (1607)

As part of the acts of the Synod of Cassel (see the previous document), a revision of the small Lutheran Catechism was authorized for use in the schools and churches of Hessia/Hesse (west-central Germany). An earlier draft of this document had been prepared in Cassel in 1605. The original 1607 version does not appear to have survived. Müller's text combines an 1897 edition (remarkably, the catechism was still in use at that time) with the 1736 Marburg version. The footnotes compare the current text with the catechism of the Marburg church order of 1566 — a catechism that departs slightly from Luther. Our translation is from Müller, 822–33.

THE HESSIAN CATECHISM OF 1607
Instruction of Children:
That Is, the Five Main Parts of Christian Doctrine Put into
Question and Answer Form for the Churches and Schools in Hessia

1. Are you a Christian? Yes, sir.

2. From whence do you know that? From this, that I have been baptized in the name of our Lord Jesus Christ, and that I know and believe the Christian doctrine.

3. Then what is this Christian doctrine?[1] That which is written and understood in the writings of Moses, the prophets, and the apostles.

---

1. 1566 inserts here: "That which God Himself in Paradise has given to the first parents, revealed to the fathers and patriarchs, through Moses, the prophets, His only

4. How many main parts does this Christian doctrine have? Five.

1. The Ten Commandments
2. The articles of Christian faith
3. The Lord's Prayer
4. The sacrament of holy baptism
5. The Lord's Supper, or the sacrament of the body and blood of our Lord Jesus Christ.

5. On the whole, how do these altogether serve us? That we recognize first, who we are, and how we stand with our Lord God; after that, who our Lord God is, and how we may be reconciled and become united with Him.

I. The First Main Part, of the Law of the Lord[2]

1. How is the law of the Lord divided? First, into ten words or commandments, and then once again into two tables. Therefore, God describes in the first table the commandments of His love; in the other, however, He describes the love of neighbors.

2. What then does the first commandment mean? I am the Lord your God; I have led you out of the land of Egypt, out of the house of servitude; you shall have no other gods besides Me.

3. What is that? We should, first of all, rightly know God, fear Him above all, love and trust Him alone.

4. What does the second commandment mean? You shall not make to yourself any image nor any likeness, neither of that which is above in heaven, nor that which is below in the earth, neither that which is in the water under the earth. Do not pray to them and serve them not, for I, the Lord, your God, am a jealous God, that afflicts the sins of the fathers

---

Son, Christ Jesus, declared to the apostles, and confirmed with manifold miracles, and that according to His Word has openly testified and shown. One could answer in a shorter manner."

2. 1566 gives here the Decalogue without explanation, in the form of the Lutheran Catechism: "Say here the Ten Commandments? The first commandment: You shall have no other gods. The other: You shall…the name. What does God now say about all of these commandments? He says, therefore: 'I am the Lord your God, I am a jealous God.…'" The agreement begins again at question 24.

on the children unto the third and fourth generation of those who hate Me, and show mercy on many thousands who love Me and hold to My commandments.

5. What is that? We shall fear and love God, so that we, in no way, make a likeness of Him; also [that we worship Him] through and in front of no images, or after our own folly or opinion, but serve and honor [Him] after His Word alone.

6. What does the third commandment mean? You shall not misuse the name of the Lord your God, because the Lord will not allow him to go unpunished, who misuses His name.

7. What is that? We shall fear and love God, so that we, by His name, do not curse, swear, practice magic, lie, or deceive, but in all needs call on Him, pray to Him, and praise and thank Him.

8. What does the fourth commandment mean? Remember the Sabbath day, to keep it holy; six days shall you work and put all things in order; however the Sabbath of the Lord, your God, is on the seventh day; you shall do no work, nor your son, nor your daughter, nor your manservant, nor your maid, nor your cattle, nor the stranger that is within your gates. For in six days the Lord made heaven and earth, and the sea, and all that is within, and rested on the seventh day. Therefore the Lord blessed the Sabbath day and made it holy.

9. What is that? We shall fear and love God, so that we do not despise preaching and His Word, but rather that we hold it as holy, gladly hear and learn it.

10. What does the fifth commandment mean? You shall honor your father and mother, that you may live long in the land that the Lord your God gives.

11. What is that? We shall fear and love God, so that we do not despise, nor anger, our parents and masters; rather that we hold them in respect, serve, obey, love, and honor them.

12. What does the sixth commandment mean? You shall not kill.

13. What is that? We shall fear and love God, so that we do no wrong or hurt to our neighbor or his body, but rather help and further him in all of his bodily needs.

14. What does the seventh commandment mean? You shall not break the bond of marriage.

15. What is that? We shall fear and love God, so that we live purely and modestly in words and in deeds, and that each one of us shall love and honor his spouse.

16. What does the eighth commandment mean? You shall not steal.

17. What is that? We shall fear and love God, so that we do not take our neighbor's money or property, nor bring with us false goods or business, but rather help, better, and preserve him in his property and livelihood.

18. What does the ninth commandment mean? You shall speak no false witness against your neighbor.

19. What is that? We shall fear and love God, so that we do not wrongly lie to, betray, slander, or make an evil reputation of our neighbor, but rather shall excuse him, speak good of him, and turn everything to his benefit.

20. What does the tenth commandment mean? You shall not covet your neighbor's house, you shall not covet your neighbor's wife, nor his manservant, nor his maid, nor his ox, nor his donkey, nor anything that your neighbor has.

21. What is that? We shall fear and love God, so that we do not stand toward our neighbor with cunning against his heritage or house, nor his wife, children, servants, or cattle, to alienate, to force away, or to entice away; rather [that we] restrain these things, so that they remain and do what they ought; yes, that we guard ourselves against all evil desires, longings, and thoughts against our neighbor and keep the commandments of the Lord.

22. What, now, does God say about all of these commandments? "Cursed is he who does not fulfill all of the words of the commandments, that he does them" (Deut. 27:26). However, "whatever person does these things, he will live through them" (Lev. 18:5).

23. What is that? God threatens to punish all those who transgress these commandments. Therefore, for that reason, we ourselves should also fear before His wrath and do nothing against such commandments. However, He promises grace and everything good to all who keep such commandments. For this reason, we shall love and trust Him and gladly act according to His commandments.

24. For what are these Ten Commandments to be used by us? In two ways: first, they show us our sins and reveal God's wrath toward our sins; and thereby, they produce in us [the desire] to seek forgiveness of sins by our Lord and Savior Jesus Christ, and to seek comfort over against God's wrath and everlasting death. Second, they teach us what good works are, in order to do them, as believers and the newborn are obligated; therewith, to prove their obedience and thankfulness to their gracious Father in heaven.

II. The Second Main Part: Of the Articles of the Christian Faith

They are these:

1. The first article: Of the creation. I believe in God, the Father Almighty, Creator of heaven and earth.

2. What is that? I believe that God has created me, together with all creatures; has given me body, soul, eyes, ears, and all members, intelligence and all understanding; and still upholds, provides clothes and shoes, food and drink, house and property, wife and child, field, cow, and all goods, with all necessity and sustenance of the body and life daily and richly; protects and defends against all danger, guards and preserves from all evil; and all that out of pure fatherly, godly goodness and mercy without any of my merit and worthiness; that I thank and praise Him in everything and therefore serve and am obliged to Him in obedience. That is certainly true.

3. The second article: Of redemption. And in Jesus Christ, His only begotten Son, our Lord, who was conceived by the Holy Ghost, born of the virgin Mary, suffered under Pontius Pilate, was crucified, died, and was buried, descended to hell; on the third day He arose from the dead, ascended into heaven, sits on the right hand of God, the Almighty Father; from thence He will come to judge the living and the dead.

4. What is that? I believe that Jesus Christ, true God, begotten from the Father in eternity, and also true man, born of the virgin Mary, is my Lord; who has redeemed lost and accursed man—gained, won from all sins, from death, from the power of the devil, not with gold or silver, but rather with His holy, dear blood and with His guiltless suffering and death; through which I am His and live in His kingdom under Him, and serve Him in everlasting righteousness, innocence, and blessedness, just as He is risen from the dead, lives, and reigns in eternity. That is certainly true.

5. The third article: Of sanctification. I believe in the Holy Ghost, a holy universal Christian church, the communion of the saints, forgiveness of sins, resurrection of the flesh, and an everlasting life.

6. What is that? I believe that I cannot, by my own reason or strength, believe on Jesus Christ, my Lord, or can come to Him; but rather the Holy Ghost has called me through the gospel, enlightened me with His gifts, made [me] holy and preserved [me] in true faith, just as He calls, gathers, enlightens, and makes holy all of Christendom on the earth and by Jesus Christ preserves [them] in true, singular faith; in which Christianity, He daily and abundantly forgives all of my sins and the sins of all of the faithful, and on the Judgment Day will raise me and all of the dead, and will give everlasting life to me and all of the faithful in Christ. That is certainly true.

7. To what end do these articles serve Christian faith? That out of them we might learn to know our God, who He is in His being and what His gracious will toward us is.

8. Who is God, then, in His Being?[3] He is God the Father, God the Son, God the Holy Ghost; three distinct persons in one single, eternal, inseparable Being.

---

3. 1566 inserts here: "He is God the Father, who has created all men and all creatures and the purpose of man; God the Son, who with His incarnation into man has suffered, died, and arisen, and has redeemed man from sins and everlasting death; and God the Holy Ghost, who has sanctified man, who rightly brings the service of the gospel; and thereby is preserved three distinct persons in one single, eternal, distinct being."

9. What is the gracious will of God?[4] That He will forgive our sins and impart everlasting, blessed life.

10. Of what use is the knowledge of God's being and will? That we receive therewith a right faith and through faith become blessed.

11. What is that faith that makes one blessed? It is not only a mere knowledge and approval, but rather a heartfelt trust in God, that He forgave my sins for the sake of the precious merit of Jesus Christ, our only Mediator, and through grace gives righteousness and everlasting happiness.

12. What is the source of such faith? It does not come from our own understanding or strength, but rather from the Holy Ghost, through whom the preaching of the gospel works and accomplishes.

III. The Third Main Part: The Lord's Prayer

1. How does the Lord's Prayer read? Our Father, who art in heaven. Hallowed be Thy name. Thy Kingdom come. Thy will be done, as in heaven, therefore also on earth. Give us today our daily bread. Forgive us our debts, as we also forgive our debtors. And lead us not into temptation, but deliver us from evil. For Thine is the kingdom, and the power, and the glory eternally. Amen!

2. How is the Lord's Prayer divided?
>Into three passages:
>>1. Into the introduction.
>>2. Into the seven requests.
>>3. Into the conclusion.

3. How does the introduction read? Our Father, who art in heaven.

4. What is that? God will draw us by it that we shall believe He is our lawful Father and we are His lawful children; on that we are confident and with all trust we shall ask Him, just as dear children [ask] of their dear father.

---

4. 1566 inserts here: "That we, whom He has created, He has redeemed through His only Son, and has made us altogether entirely holy; will forgive our sins, and after this miserable, fleeting life, place [us] in everlasting, blessed life."

5. How does the first request read? Hallowed be Thy name.

6. What is that? God's name is indeed holy about Himself alone; however, we ask in this prayer that He will also be holy among us.

7. How does that happen? Where the Word of God is clearly and purely taught; and we also live thereby, in a holy manner as children of God—so help us, dear Father in heaven. However, whoever teaches and lives [in a manner] other than the Word of God, profanes among us God's name—preserve us from that, dear heavenly Father.

8. How does the second request read? Thy kingdom come.

9. What is that? God's kingdom comes truly from Him Himself, without our prayer; however, we request in the prayer that it also comes to us.

10. How does that happen? When the heavenly Father gives us His Holy Ghost, that we believe His Holy Word through His grace and live in a godly manner, here temporally and there everlastingly.

11. How does the third request read? Thy will be done, as in heaven, so also on earth.

12. What is that? God's good, gracious will is done without our prayer; however, we request in this prayer that it is also done among us.

13. How does this happen? When God breaks and hinders all evil counsel and will (we do not hallow God's name and do not want His kingdom to come—what is of the devil, the world, and our fleshly will), but rather strengthens and keeps us fast in His Word and faith unto the end. That is His good, gracious will.

14. How does the fourth request read? Give us today our daily bread.

15. What is that? God truly gives daily bread (it is true even without our request) to all evil men; however, we request in this prayer that He allows us to understand such; and we receive our daily bread with thanksgiving.

16. What does daily bread mean then? Everything that belongs to life's sustenance and necessity: as food, drink, clothing, shoes, house, property, fields, cows, money, estates; pious spouses, pious children, pious servants,

pious and faithful overlords, good government, good weather, peace, health, cultivation, honor, good friends, good neighbors, and the like.

17. How does the fifth request read? And forgive us our debts as we also forgive our debtors.

18. What is that? We request in this prayer that the Father in heaven will not consider our sins, and of the same will not refuse our request, because we are not worthy of that which we request, also have not earned it; but rather He will give us everything out of grace; because we sin much daily and certainly deserve nothing but punishment; so we will indeed again heartily pardon and gladly do good to those that sin against us.

19. How does the sixth request read? And lead us not into temptation.

20. What is that? Indeed, God tempts no one; however in this prayer we ask that God will guard and preserve us, in that the devil, the world, and our flesh do not deceive, nor tempt [us] in unbelief, despair, and [any] other great shame and burden; and if we are thereby attacked, that we finally win and receive the victory.

21. How does the seventh request read? But deliver us from evil.

22. What is that? We ask in this prayer, as in the whole, that our Father in heaven deliver us from every kind of evil of the body and of the soul; redeem [us] to goodness and honor, and at last when our hour comes, to present a blessed end; and with grace take us out of this vale of tears into heaven. Amen!

23. How does the closing of the prayer of the Lord read? For Thine is the kingdom and the power and the glory eternally. Amen!

24. What is that? We realize herewith that God will give and is able to do everything which we ask, to the praise and glory of His magnificent name.

25. What is the meaning of "amen"? That it shall certainly be; such requests are received and heard by the Father in heaven; then He Himself has commanded us therefore to pray and promises that He will hear us. Amen, Amen; that means that it therefore will happen.

26. To what end does the Lord's Prayer serve us? That we recognize that everything that belongs to the content of this temporal [life] and the abode of everlasting life, one cannot obtain from any other place than from God; and for that reason we ask and obtain from Him with believing hearts.

IV. The Fourth Main Part: Of the Sacrament of Holy Baptism

1. What are the holy sacraments? They are godly acts, wherein God pictures to us, not alone with visible signs, but rather also seals and delivers invisible grace and the promised goodness.[5]

2. To what end are the sacraments instituted? To the confirmation of our faith in the godly promise.

3. How many sacraments are in the New Testament? Two: baptism and the Lord's Supper.

4. What is baptism? It is a godly act in which God washes and purifies us from all our sins with the visible water-bath in the Word, the invisible grace and promised goodness, namely the Holy Ghost and the blood of Jesus Christ; it not only pictures, but also seals and delivers.[6]

5. How do the words of the institution of holy baptism read? At the last part of Matthew: "Go forth into all of the world and teach all peoples; and baptize in the name of the Father, and of the Son, and of the Holy Ghost." And at the last part of Mark: "Who then believes and is baptized, the same is blessed, however who does not believe, the same is damned."

6. How does baptism serve to our advantage? That we are thereby assured God has taken us to be His children and will show Himself to be a gracious Father toward us in all things.

7. Where is this advantage written? In the third chapter of Titus: God blesses us after His mercy through the washing of rebirth and renewing

---

5. 1566: "They are godly acts, wherein God, with visible signs, promises and delivers the invisible, promised grace and goodness."

6. 1566: "It is a godly activity toward us in which God through the washing and the Word graciously forgives our sins, because of the purpose of Jesus Christ; takes us to be His children, and makes us heirs of all His heavenly goodness."

of the Holy Ghost, which, over us, He has poured out richly through Jesus Christ, our Savior; upon which, we are justified through this same grace and are heirs of everlasting life according to the hope that it is certainly true.

8. How can water do such great things? To be certain water does not do this, but rather the Word of God, which is with and in the water; and faith, the same relies upon the Word of God in the water. Then without God's Word the water is ill water and no baptism; however with the Word of God there is a baptism, that is, a water of life, rich with grace, and a washing of new birth in the Holy Ghost, as St. Paul says in the third chapter of Titus.

9. What is the meaning of baptism with such water? It means that the old Adam in us, through daily remorse and repentance, shall be drowned and die with all sins and evil desires; and daily anew, result in and arise from the dead, a new man who lives everlastingly in righteousness and purity before God.

10. Where is this written? St. Paul speaks to the Romans in the sixth chapter: "We are together with Christ, through baptism, buried in death, that just as Christ is risen from the dead through the glory of the Father, therefore shall we also walk in a new life."

V. The Fifth Main Part: Of Holy Communion

1. What is the Holy Communion of our Lord Jesus Christ? The Holy Communion of our Lord is a sacrament or godly act that the Lord Jesus, Himself present, with the visible bread and wine, namely, His real body broken for us and His real blood poured out for us for the forgiveness of our sins, not only pictures, but also seals and delivers the invisible grace and promised goodness.[7]

2. What are the words of the institution of the Lord's Supper? Our Lord Jesus Christ, the night in which He was betrayed, took the bread, gave thanks, broke it, and gave it to His disciples and spoke: "Take to yourselves and eat, this is My body that is given for you. Do this to My remembrance."

---

7. 1566: "The Communion of our Lord is a sacrament or godly act, that the Lord Christ is present and delivers to us with bread and wine His true body and blood, for a certain assurance that we have forgiveness of sins, and should live with Him everlastingly."

In a similar way, He took the cup after the supper, gave thanks and gave it to them and spoke, "Take to yourselves and drink all thereof; this cup is the new testament in My blood that is poured out for you and for many for the forgiveness of sins. Do this, as oft as you drink, to My memory."

3. How does the Lord's Supper serve us to advantage? We are assured thereby that if we have angered our Father in heaven, that He will as such still forgive, will be and remain our gracious Father. And Holy Communion, like baptism, is an assurance that God has taken us to be His children; but Holy Communion assures us that He will not allow us to be rewarded for our disobedience.[8]

4. Can then bodily eating and drinking do such a great thing? Eating and drinking surely do not do this, rather the Word, as it is written: "Given and poured out for you for the forgiveness of sins," which words are alongside the bodily eating and drinking as the main point in the sacrament; and whoever believes these same words, he has what they say, namely the forgiveness of sins.

5. Who, then, receives such a sacrament worthily? Fasting and preparing oneself bodily is a fine outward discipline; however, he is rightly worthy and well prepared, who has faith on these words: "Given and poured out for you for the forgiveness of sins." However, whoever does not believe these words or doubts by it, he is unworthy and careless; then the words "for you" call for hearts that believe vainly.

(Translated by Tom and Kirsten DeVries)

---

8. Here 1566 closes. And then follow immediately the confirmation questions: "Do you believe and recognize all of this from the heart which you have at the present stated from the Christian doctrine?"

96

Confession of the Heidelberg Theologians (1607)

The university town of Heidelberg was caught in the seesaw between Lutheran and Reformed shifts in Palatine Germany during the late sixteenth and early seventeenth centuries. Like a bouncing ball, the elector of the city controlled the religious emphasis endorsed by the university faculty. Hence the revolving door ushered out Lutherans and ushered in Calvinists, only to be reversed when the Calvinists were ushered out and the Lutherans ushered back in. By 1562, Elector Frederick III (1515–1576) had made his own theological shift—from Lutheran to Reformed. The Heidelberg Catechism (1563) was the result, and the oscillating political-theological game began.

Frederick's successor, Ludwig VI (1539–1583), returned the Palatinate to the Lutheran faith (he also introduced the Formula of Concord in 1580). Requiring an oath of allegiance to the Lutheran creeds, he ejected the Reformed professors from the university. Girolamo Zanchius (1516–1590) was one casualty of this reorganization in 1577, as was David Pareus (1548–1622). But when Ludwig died, his brother, Pfalsgrave Johann Casimir (1543–1592), a Calvinist and regent for the under-aged future elector, Frederick IV (1574–1610), ejected the Lutheran professors and installed Reformed men instead. It was the Calvinist Johann Jacob Grynaeus (1540–1617), former professor of Old Testament at the University of Basel (1575–1584), who reorganized the University of Heidelberg in 1584. He was joined by Franciscus Junius (1545–1602) and Daniel Toussain/Tossanus (1541–1602), among others.

Since the matter of the Lord's Supper was the chief bone of contention, the irenic tone of the confession below reflects that concern. This plea for peace had become a badge of honor to the Reformed faculty of Heidelberg with Pareus, Bartolomeus Pitiscus (1561–1613) and Tossanus publishing large tomes dedicated to proving that Luther himself was not always a hard-nosed ubiquitarian.

Our translation is based on the text in Heinrich Heppe, *Die Bekenntnischriften der reformirten Kirchen Deutschlands* (1860), 250–61.

CONFESSION OF THE HEIDELBERG THEOLOGIANS

A detailed affirmation of what the Reformed churches in Germany believe and do not believe; That is, what sacraments they either use or do not use, added to which are all the reasons why they either do or refrain from doing certain things. Published for the edification of the pure in heart in the Electorate of Heidelberg (1607).

Preface
Concerning the purpose and content of this document.

Dear Christian Reader,

It cannot be expressed what harm the controversy regarding the sacraments has inflicted, and still does inflict—and regretfully will increasingly do so in the Reformed churches.

Not only have we ourselves always been inclined to make peace, and, as becomes Christians, have made every conceivable effort in that regard, but there are also many honest and God-fearing people of every station of life who, when the opposite manifests itself, desire peace as much as we do and wish to do their utmost to facilitate this. They also acknowledge that the means we have used to that end are Christian in nature, and are in harmony with the word and will of God. In doing so, we recognize that though we are one when it comes to the fundamentals of Christianity, we may not condemn one another due to differing levels of understanding regarding secondary issues. In this life it cannot possibly be achieved that all the members of Christ will have a perfect and uniform understanding of all divine mysteries—as is confirmed by Scripture and the experience of all ages.

The only thing that holds them back is the fact that their ministers, some of whom they esteem, are both saying and writing that we are not merely dealing with some secondary issues, but rather, that there is a difference of opinion regarding the fundamentals of Christianity. Since they consider us guilty of so many dreadful errors, no Christian will therefore be able, in good conscience, to acknowledge us as brothers in Christ Jesus—and thus will neither be able to dwell with us in peace nor have fellowship with us.

In order that we may hereby also remove this obstacle, and that the upright may thoroughly know what they have on us, we desire to declare once more (though there should be no need for this) what we do and do not believe regarding all points of doctrine. Additionally, we also wish to inform you which sacraments we observe and do not observe in our churches, as well as the reasons why we either do or refrain from doing certain things.

May the merciful and faithful God and Father bestow His grace and blessing upon such labors, so that the eyes of many may be opened—to His glory and to the benefit of His church. Amen.

Chapter One
We do not have such dreadful beliefs as are attributed to us by those who oppose peace.

Chapter Two
What we truly do believe.

If someone were to ask us what we really do believe, which we are readily inclined to do, our answer will be as follows:

1. *Concerning God.* We believe that there is one true God, the Father of our Lord Jesus Christ, together with the Son and the Holy Ghost, and that therefore three distinct persons subsist in the one divine Being: the Father, the Son, and the Holy Ghost.

2. We believe furthermore that the same only true God is eternal and omnipotent, and is capable of creating whatever He pleases. He is also infinite and is consequently omnipresent—and He sees, hears, and knows everything. Moreover, He is just and will not punish anyone without cause. However, He is also merciful, and has no pleasure in the death of the sinner, but rather, that he would turn and live.

3. *Concerning creation.* We believe furthermore that the same only true God of heaven and earth has created all that is therein out of nothing.

4. *Concerning providence.* We believe furthermore that God holds all things which He has created in His hands in such a fashion that without His will not a creature can either stir or move. Consequently, nothing can happen without God's permission—whether good or evil. Furthermore, everything that God either presently does or intends to do, He has known from eternity—and He has decreed according to His determinate counsel that He would either act accordingly or make the necessary arrangements. Also He did not decree that He would permit evil to occur without being able and determined to direct it to a good end.

5. *Concerning the fall of angels and men; and concerning hereditary sin.* We also believe that even though God did initially create angels and men holy and good, and that He especially created man in His image and for blessed immortality, they—the angels for the largest part and both original human beings—fell away from God their Creator not long after having been created. By virtue of this fall, they not only have brought upon themselves the wrath of God, but have also contracted a corruption of their nature, which is such that they no longer either desire or are capable of any good. The fallen angels, as a body, have all at once become subject to this corruption, whereas human beings inherit such corruption from the one to the other, along with the guilt of temporal and eternal death. This corruption of man is therefore called hereditary sin.

6. *Concerning the cause of the fall.* We believe furthermore that though the dreadful fall of both angels and men could not have transpired outside of God's decree, and that He does not decree anything without purpose, the guilt of this fall can in no wise be attributed to Him. It must be observed that both angels and men were created in such a fashion that they were capable of exercising their free will toward good as well as evil.

7. We believe furthermore that as poor creatures we have no right to dispute with God why He created angels and men capable of falling, nor why He did not prevent such a fall—which He indeed could have done. He is the Lord, and His will is always right and good, even though we do not always understand this.

The apostle Paul states that God has concluded all things under unbelief (Rom. 11:32) or under sin (Gal. 3:22) in order that He might be merciful to all (that is, that no one would be saved apart from the mercy of God). See also Romans 9:22–23: "What if God, willing to show His wrath, and to make His power known, endured with much longsuffering the vessels of wrath fitted to destruction: and that He might make known the riches of His glory on the vessels of mercy, which He had before prepared unto glory." We should reasonably leave it at that.

8. *Concerning the condition of angels and men after the fall.* We believe furthermore that fallen angels and men by their grievous fall did not thwart the omnipotent government of God. Instead, the one as well as the other are in the hand of God, and their wickedness cannot manifest itself in any other way than which God has decreed concerning them. NB: This article of faith is our greatest comfort on earth. For if wicked angels and men could do as they please, what refuge could we find from them?

9. *Concerning the cause of sin after the fall.* We believe furthermore that though God has decreed all the sins of angels and men, He also often uses their sinful works to accomplish His holy works (such as Absalom's dreadful deeds for the chastisement of David, as well as the betrayal of Judas for the redemption of the human race, etc.). Moreover, though He often punishes sin with sin, and generally fully blinds and hardens those who with seeing eyes wish to be blind (which He did earlier to Pharaoh), nevertheless He Himself takes no pleasure in sin, and even less stimulates or compels anyone to that end. Rather, the actual cause of all committed sin is to be attributed solely to the free and uninhibited will of evil angels and men.

10. *Concerning the punishment of the fall.* We believe furthermore that God has condemned the fallen angels to eternal fire without there being any recourse to grace and mercy, thereby warning us that we should not take the wrath of God against sin lightly.

11. *Concerning the redemption of the human race.* We believe furthermore that God would have had the prerogative and power to also cast fallen man into the eternal fire without any recourse to grace and mercy. However, He did not do so, but rather promised man grace instead. And in order to enable Him to bestow grace upon them without compromising His justice, he

decreed that His only begotten Son would be our Surety and Mediator, and would take upon Himself the punishment which we deserve, and by His innocent death would deliver us from an eternal and well-deserved death.

12. In order to accomplish the will and council of God the heavenly Father, the Son of God, our Lord and Savior Jesus Christ, became man in the last days of the world, having been conceived of the Holy Ghost, born of the virgin Mary, and made like unto us in all things, sin excepted. And having reached His thirtieth year as a man, He began to teach and preach the gracious will of His heavenly Father concerning us poor, sinful men. In the fourth year thereafter, He was captured, crucified, put to death, buried, descended into hell, and on the third day arose from the dead. Forty days thereafter He ascended into heaven, and is seated at the right hand of God the Father Almighty. From thence He shall come to judge the quick and the dead.

13. *Concerning the person of Christ.* We believe therefore that Christ was not merely a man, but rather that He is the eternal, almighty Son of God who at a specific moment took upon Himself human nature and is now simultaneously both God and man—and who will remain so forever in one singular and indivisible person.

14. And since presently He is simultaneously both God and man in one singular and indivisible person, we believe furthermore that one can say concerning Him everything that pertains to God, and everything that pertains to man. We must make this distinction, however, that that which pertains to the divine must be viewed in terms of His divine nature, and that which is human must be viewed in terms of His human nature. For example, one can say concerning Him that He is from eternity, but also that He has been born during the last days. Both are true, but not according to both natures, for according to His human nature He is not from eternity. Therefore according to His divine nature, He has not been born during the last days, but rather He is from eternity according to His divine nature. It is only according to His human nature that He has been born in the last days.

15. Accordingly, we believe that He actually and truly died for us as the Son of God—however, not according to His Godhead, but rather according to His humanity, for His divinity is immortal.

16. Moreover, we believe that Christ actually and truly will remain with us until the end of the world—however, not according to His human nature, but rather, according to His divine nature. For according to His human nature, He has ascended to heaven. And Scripture is clear when it states that on the basis of His bodily sacrifice, He has entered into the heavens and could not remain on earth. Else He would not be our Priest (cf. Heb. 8, 9, 10).

17. *Concerning the efficacy of the death of Christ.* Concerning the efficacy of the death of Christ, we believe that the death of Christ (because He did not die as merely a man, but rather as the Son of God) is a perfect and sufficient atonement, not only for ours, but also for the sins of the whole world. Furthermore, by His death He not only merited the forgiveness of sins but also the renewal of the Holy Ghost, and finally eternal life itself.

18. However, we also believe that no one will be a partaker of these benefits of Christ without believing in Him. For Scripture is clear when it states, "He that believeth not shall be damned" (Mark 16:16), and that the wrath of God will abide on those who do not believe the Son of God (John 3:36).

19. *Concerning the nature of true, saving faith.* We believe furthermore that true, saving faith cannot exist apart from repentance and good works, for faith embraces the whole Christ, who has not only been made justification unto us by God, but also sanctification (1 Cor. 1:30).

20. *Concerning the justification of the sinner before God.* We believe further-more that even though there can be no true, saving faith without good works, man will nevertheless not be able to appeal to his good works before the judgment seat of God (that is, when he is assaulted about his sins), since they will always be imperfect. Rather, before the judgment seat of God, man should solely and exclusively appeal to the grace of God which He has promised us in Christ, and to receive this grace with a believing heart. God will then pardon his sins, and declare him righteous on the basis of the satisfaction of Christ. This is what we mean when we say that man can be righteous before God only by faith without the contribution of good works—that is, not that there should be no good works, but simply that man may not put his trust in them.

21. *Concerning the ministry.* We believe furthermore that God has ordained the preaching of His gospel to that end that He is pleased to work in us faith in Christ, and that God the Lord is not insincere in this preaching, but rather, that it is His sincere will and intent that all men who hear such preaching would believe it and turn to Christ.

22. *Concerning free will and the origin of faith.* We believe furthermore that man by virtue of the fall of our first parents has become so depraved that he can neither understand nor accept this preaching, unless God by His Spirit opens the understanding and inclines the heart toward Christ.

23. Therefore, not only is the gospel an extraordinary gift of God which God does not bestow on all peoples, but also the understanding and acceptance of the gospel, or to say it with one word, faith is an extraordinary gift of God (cf. Eph. 2:8; 2 Thess. 3:2).

24. No one is worthy of receiving this gift from God, for we are altogether sinners (Rom. 3:23). Rather, God grants this gift graciously to whomever He wills (Rom. 9:18).

25. However, whatever He wills presently, He has willed from eternity, for "known unto God are all His works from the beginning of the world" (Acts 15:18).

26. *Concerning eternal election.* It is therefore most certainly true that no one will believe in Christ without God, from eternity, having elected one to be the recipient of such grace—as Paul states, "but the election hath obtained it, and the rest were blinded" (Rom. 11:7). Luke speaks likewise: "and as many as were ordained to eternal life believed" (Acts 13:48).

27. However, it is also true that we may not pry into the secret will of God as to whether we are of the elect, for such prying is futile (2 Tim. 2:19). God has sealed the Book of Life, and He will not permit any creature to look into this book. Instead, we are to hold to the revealed Word of God, which states that God has chosen us in Christ; that is, we must be of a mindset that He is pleased to save us in no other way but through Christ (Eph. 1:3). We are therefore obliged to repent, to believe in Christ, and thus to seek salvation in Him. We are to submit to this divine command in proportion to the grace God has given us, and to pray without ceasing that

God would grant us more and more grace. When doing this, we may not continue to pry as to whether we have been elected to eternal life. For this is most certainly and infallibly true, that all who without hypocrisy repent and believe in Christ have been chosen unto eternal life.

28. It is therefore God's will not to reveal our election in any other way except through these signs, so that we would not be entangled in carnal security, but rather that we would work out our salvation with fear and trembling (Phil. 2:2).

29. When there is such fear, it will surely also be accompanied by the comfort that God is faithful, and that He "will not suffer you to be tempted above that ye are able" (1 Cor. 10:13). It is likewise true that "a bruised reed shall He not break, and the smoking flax shall He not quench" (Isa. 42:3), and that Christ will in no wise cast out anyone who comes to Him desiring to be saved by Him. We also read that no one will be able to pluck His sheep out of His hands (John 10:28). From this comfort, the believer derives a joy that passes all understanding. Therefore, the testimony of the Holy Scriptures that speaks of the immutable election and foreknowledge of God (Matt. 24:24; 2 Tim. 2:19, etc.) no longer frightens them, but rather is exceedingly lovely and encouraging. For it is from this that they conclude that nothing can separate them from the love of God which is in Christ Jesus our Lord (Rom. 8:38) — without which it would be impossible that anyone could say with heartfelt conviction, "I believe that I will be the recipient of eternal life." On the contrary, all people would have to doubt eternal life (1 Peter 1:2) if we did not have the comfort that the God who has graciously gifted us with faith in Christ would, by his power, preserve this same faith for eternal felicity. And indeed, we are far too weak to preserve ourselves in the face of the many assaults of Satan, the world, and our own flesh.

30. *Concerning the holy sacraments.* We believe furthermore that God, in addition to the daily repetition of His Word, has also ordained the holy sacraments to preserve and strengthen us in the faith. It is the preeminent purpose of the holy sacraments that God thereby wishes to display visibly the promises of the gospel (or our being a partaker of Christ and His benefits), so that we would not only hear, but also see, feel, and appropriate how He is disposed toward us — namely, that He desires to forgive our

sins, and to grant us the Holy Spirit and eternal life for the sake of the shed blood of Christ. Of this His commitment and promise, God desires to assure us by way of the holy sacrament.

31. However, by its use we are to reciprocate by obligating ourselves before God that we will steadfastly believe in Christ, and also honor Him by living a life beyond reproach.

32. *Concerning God's covenant.* And this is the new covenant between God and man of which such frequent mention is made in the Holy Scriptures (Jer. 31:31–34; Heb. 8:9–12; the institutional formula of the Lord's Supper, etc.), namely, that God desires to be gracious to us for Christ's sake, in response to which we are to obey Him and upon His command believe in Christ and love one another.

33. The old covenant consisted of God being gracious to man upon his perfect observance of His law. However, should they transgress this law to the smallest degree, they would be both cursed and damned. It is therefore impossible for a man to be faithful to this covenant.

34. God has therefore entered into a new covenant with us which He had already revealed to our believing fathers, who, as the apostle Peter testifies in Acts 15:11, reaped the benefits of this covenant unto salvation no less than we did. In this covenant, He promises us that He will be gracious to us for Christ's sake, though we do not keep the law perfectly, but rather are manifold transgressors of it. All we are required to do is to acknowledge His grace, embrace it with a believing heart, and, as a debt of gratitude, diligently seek to live a life that is beyond reproach. To this end, He is pleased to grant us the abundant help of His Spirit if we ask Him for it; and that which, due to our imperfection, is still lacking in us, He will cover with the perfect satisfaction of Jesus Christ.

This is the new covenant of God with man, for the confirmation of which He has instituted the holy sacraments. It is in the manner in which human beings transact business with one another that God also deals with us—namely, that covenants and contracts are not merely confirmed verbally, but rather that, by way of documentation and seals (or other public transactions), customs and ceremonies are ratified. Not only does He set before us this gracious covenant in words, nor has He merely caused it to be inscripturated, but He has also instituted certain ceremonies in connection with it, so that thereby His covenant between Him and us could be confirmed and certified before the eyes of the whole world, thereby sealing it at the same time.

Such is the proper purpose and benefit of the holy sacraments.

35. The two New Testament sacraments are baptism and the Lord's Supper—just as there were formerly two sacraments in the Old Testament, namely, circumcision and the Passover.

36. *Concerning holy baptism.* Baptism is the first sacrament of the New Testament. First, God has ordained it for the benefit of those who embrace the Christian faith, and thus desire to enter into covenant with Him. He hereby gives them a public confirmation whereby they can be reminded their entire lifetime that God has truly incorporated them into His covenant, and that according to the formula of this covenant they are surely washed with the blood and Spirit of Christ from the uncleanness of their souls (that is, that their sins are forgiven them for the sake of the shed blood of Christ)—and that by the Spirit of Christ they are increasingly restored unto a new creature; that is, as surely as they are externally sprinkled and washed with water whereby the uncleanness of the body is removed.

Second, by embracing this divine covenant sign, they reciprocate by publicly acknowledging before the entire world that they will fulfill their obligation toward God the Lord, which they own and confirm as covenant partners and members of Christ, desiring, by the enablement of the Spirit, to live a life that is beyond reproach.

37. It is for this purpose that God has instituted baptism, and it is therefore exceedingly comforting and edifying to the believer. The unbeliever, on the contrary, benefits as little from it as circumcision profited the disobedient Jew in former days.

38. Although baptism is referred to in Scripture as the washing of regeneration and the washing away of sins (Titus 3:5; Acts 22:16), this does not mean that the external washing with water brings about the washing away of sins and regeneration, regardless of whether one is a believer or unbeliever. Rather, it means that by these glorious and public ceremonies believers are received as children of God, and that the washing

away of sin, which is brought about by the blood (1 John 1:8) and Spirit of Christ (Titus 3:5; 1 Cor. 6:11) is signified and sealed to them. In one word: the water saves us—not, as Peter puts it, the putting away of the filth of the flesh, but the answer of a good conscience toward God (1 Peter 3:21).

39. *Concerning repentance after baptism.* Furthermore, if someone does transgress the covenant he has made with God in baptism and subsequently falls grievously, having been deceived by Satan, the world, and his own flesh, he should therefore not despair of God's grace and mercy. Rather, he should reflect on what he has obliged himself to do before God in baptism, and repent in light of this obligation; that is, to express heartfelt sorrow over the evil he has committed, and to beseech God to pardon him for Christ's sake—and to resolve never to commit this sin again. God will then, as He has promised in baptism, also be mindful of His obligation and pardon his sin, as well as give him the strength to resist Satan.

And thus the benefit, power, and efficacy of baptism will be experienced as long as a man lives on earth, and not merely at the hour when baptism is administered. And indeed, all the promises of God are sealed to the believer by means of baptism. Among these promises there is also this one, when God speaks, "As I live, saith the Lord God, I have no pleasure in the death of the wicked, but that the wicked turn from his way and live" (Ezek. 33:11). It is this very promise that God seals to us in baptism. We should therefore not yield to Satan, who will seek to bring us to despair (John 8:44). He is a liar and murderer from the beginning. God is, however, trustworthy, and has never deceived anyone who has put his trust in His promise (Ps. 25:1). It is in this way that a poor, grieving sinner can comfort himself.

40. *Concerning the Lord's Supper.* In order to strengthen oneself by way of such comfort, one should, among other means, frequently partake of the Holy Supper, which is the other sacrament of the New Testament. Christ primarily instituted it for the purpose of visibly and frequently setting His death before our eyes, in order to assure us increasingly of our participation in His death; that is, having blessed fellowship with His crucified body and shed blood. This is indeed what He has in mind when He takes the bread and breaks it, saying, "This is my body which is broken for you. Take, and eat, etc." It is as if Christ speaks to everyone individually,

> Behold, dear soul, I know that you are grieving because of your sins.
> Be of good comfort, however! For as surely as the bread is broken

before your eyes, and the wine is set apart from the bread, so surely has my body been broken or slain on the cross, and has my blood been extracted from my body and been shed for the forgiveness of your sins. Likewise, as surely as I am giving you the tokens of my body and blood in order that you might eat and drink them, being a partaker of them as much as others are, so sure it is that you are a true partaker of my body and blood which I have yielded unto death on the cross. This has also occurred for your benefit. Also you shall thereby be delivered from that eternal hunger and thirst which you would otherwise have had to suffer in hell. Therefore, take hold of this by a true faith. And when you place the holy tokens of my body and blood in your mouth, eating and drinking them, you should likewise embrace my crucified body and shed blood in your heart. In doing so, you shall neither hunger nor thirst to all eternity, for "whoso eateth my flesh, and drinketh my blood, hath eternal life; and I will raise him up at the last day" (John 6:35, 54–57). Yes, also in this life I will remain in him and he in me. I will always govern and comfort him by my Spirit. Therefore, be comforted dear soul, however weak you may be. "No man shall pluck you out of my hand. My Father, which gave you to me, is greater than all, etc." (John 10:28–29).

That is the primary and most significant benefit and use of the Lord's Supper, namely, that we, as stated, would thereby be increasingly assured in our hearts concerning the death of Christ and His blessed fellowship—that is, of the covenant of God's grace which is grounded in the death of Christ. It is thus that Christ speaks: "This is the new covenant in my blood," wishing to say thereby, "This shall be a sign and seal, or an affirmation and confirmation, of the new covenant that I have merited for you with my own blood."

41. The other benefit is that with these glorious ceremonies, we proclaim, magnify, and praise the death of Christ to the whole world. This is according to Christ's own words, "This do in remembrance of me." Paul speaks likewise, "For as often as ye eat this bread, and drink this cup, ye do show (i.e., magnify and praise) the Lord's death till he come" (1 Cor. 11:26).

42. The third benefit is that we thereby publicly align ourselves with the fellowship of Christ and His churches, and, as required by this fellowship, live a holy life, love one another as members of one body, and by renewal, promise and commit ourselves to this. The apostle Paul speaks accordingly: "The cup of blessing which we bless, is it not the communion of the blood

of Christ? The bread which we break, is it not the communion of the body of Christ? For we being many are one bread, and one body: for we are all partakers of that one bread" (1 Cor. 10:16–17). "Wherefore…flee from idolatry" (1 Cor. 10:14), "and I would not that ye should have fellowship with devils" (1 Cor. 10:20–21), etc. Likewise, "by one Spirit are we all baptized into one body [i.e., in holy baptism]…and have been all made to drink into one Spirit [i.e., at the Lord's Supper]" (1 Cor. 12:13). Therefore, as members of one body we should care for one another, and one member should have patience with and pity upon another (1 Cor. 12:12–27).

43. Finally, we believe that most of the time God subjects His church in this life to the cross, and only in the life hereafter will He redeem and glorify her fully in the likeness of the Son who by way of the cross and suffering had to enter into His glory.

(Translated by Bart Elshout)

97

The Remonstrance (1610)

James (Jacobus) Arminius (1560–1609) was the *agent provocateur* of the turmoil in Holland that eventually led to the Canons and Decrees of the Synod of Dort. He is the *cause célèbre* of the so-called *tertium genus Reformationis* (third kind of Reformation), as the Arminian party defined themselves. His nonconformist story begins with a sojourn in Geneva to study under Calvin's successor at the Academy, Theodore Beza (1519–1605). There he became a reactionary (1582–1583, 1584–1586), rejecting the predestinarian Reformed theology of the epigones. As Arminius's modern biographer, Carl Bangs, suggests, "he probably never had agreed with it." On his return to his native Holland, Arminius began a pastorate at Amsterdam in 1588. By 1603, he was appointed professor at the University of Leiden, where he joined Francis Gomarus (1563–1641). Sparks flew when Arminius presented sermons and lectures based on Paul's epistle to the Romans in which he deviated from the Calvinistic doctrine of predestination favored by the Church of Holland.

When Arminius died, his chair was awarded to Conrad Vorstius (1569–1622). Now the Arminian tendency to rationalistic Socinianism began to clearly manifest itself. Gomarus was disgusted and resigned from the faculty; he became a pastor in Middleburgh (1609–1615) before finally going to France and Germany as a professor of theology. Meanwhile, the agitation of the Arminian party under the leadership of Johannes Uytenbogaert (1557–1644) produced a document notorious for its semi-Pelagianism. The *Remonstrantia* of 1610 specified five points of opposition to the established Calvinism of the Reformed Church of Holland: partial depravity (the human will is free of any bias toward iniquity); conditional election (God's choice is conditioned on man's choosing to believe); universal atonement (the blood of Jesus purchases a universal ability/power for sinners to believe); resistible grace (even the regenerating grace of the Holy Spirit can be resisted by the sinner's will); conditional perseverance (achievement of final salvation, i.e., heaven, is dependent on completing the race—that is, salvation may be lost along the way and is only retained as long as the believer keeps himself faithful; if he falls, salvation and heaven are lost).

The orthodox Reformed party issued an answer to this Remonstrance a year later from the pen of Festus Hommius (1576–1642) of Leiden. Hence the terms "Remonstrants" and "Counter-Remonstrants" define the parties. The national church was divided by the controversy and after several futile attempts at reconciliation, a national synod was summoned to Dordrecht (1618–1619) by the Estates-General under Maurice of Orange (1567–1625). The theological rupture in the nation was reflected politically in Maurice (Counter-Remonstrant) and his nemesis, Johan van Oldenbarneveldt (1547–1619), Remonstrant supporter. Politically and militarily, Maurice and the Counter-Remonstrants had the upper hand.

Our translation is based on the Latin text found in Schaff 3:545–49. In three columns Schaff places the Dutch, the Latin, and an English translation that differs slightly from our own.

Article I

God, by an eternal and unchangeable decree in His Son, Christ Jesus, before laying the foundation of the world, determined, out of the human race fallen in sin, to save those in Christ, on account of Christ, and through Christ, who through the grace of the Holy Spirit, would believe on His same Son, and who would persevere in that very faith and obedience of faith, through the same grace without ceasing to the end; but on the other hand, to leave the obstinate and unbelieving under sin and wrath, and condemn them as alienated from Christ, according to the word of the gospel: "He that believes in the Son has eternal life; but he that does not obey the Son will not see life, but the wrath of God remains on him" (John 3:36). To which other expressions of Scripture correspond.

Article II

Accordingly Jesus Christ, Savior of the world, has died for each and every man, and through His death on the cross has merited reconciliation and forgiveness of sins for all; nevertheless so that no one in fact becomes a partaker of this forgiveness except believers, and that also according to the words of the gospel of John: "For God so loved the world that He gave His only begotten Son, that whoever believes in Him, should not perish, but have eternal life" (3:16). And in the first epistle of John: "He is the propitiation for our sins, and not for ours only, but also for the sins of the whole world" (2:2).

Article III

Man has no saving faith of himself, nor from the strength of his own free will, since in the state of apostasy and sin he is not able to think, will, or do anything good (what indeed is truly good, such as saving faith is in the first place); but it is necessary that he be regenerated and also renewed by God, in Christ, through His Holy Spirit in his intellect, affections, or will, and all his powers, that he may rightly understand, ponder, will, and also accomplish the true good as it is written: "Without me you are able to do nothing" (John 15:5).

Article IV

This grace is the beginning, the increase, and completion of every good thing; to be sure even that the regenerate person himself is not even able to think, will, or accomplish good, nor resist any temptation to evil apart from or preceding that prevenient, moving, accompanying, and cooperating grace, so that all good works and actions which are able to be conceived must be ascribed to the grace of God in Christ. As for the rest, what pertains to the manner of operation of this grace—that it is not irresistible, since indeed it is written about many that "they resisted the Holy Spirit," Acts 7:[51] and several other places.

Article V

Those who are ingrafted into Christ by true faith and as a consequence have been made participants of His life-giving Spirit, have been abundantly equipped by this power, by which they are able to fight against Satan, sin, the world, and their flesh, and therefore also obtain the victory over them; nevertheless always (because we wish to be careful) assisted in every temptation by the help of the grace of the Holy Spirit; and Jesus Christ Himself, through His Spirit, holds out His hand, and (if only they are prepared to fight themselves, and beseech His help, and do not desert Him themselves), secures and confirms them, so that they are seduced by no deceit or power of Satan, nor are able to be ripped out of the hands of Christ, according to the word of Christ: "No one takes my sheep out of my hand" (John 10:28). As for the rest, whether they themselves are not able through carelessness την αρχην της υποστασεως χριστου καταλειπειν (to abandon the beginning of their subjection to Christ), and embracing again this present world, to forsake the holy doctrine once delivered to them, to let a good conscience slip away, and to despise grace; must be more accurately sought from the sacred Scripture before we are able to teach others with πληροφορια (full persuasion) of our minds.

Therefore these articles thus proposed and delivered, the Remonstrants approve as conformed to the divine Word, fitting for edification, and in this argument to be sure sufficient for salvation; thus that it is not necessary, or serving for edification, either to climb higher or sink lower.

(Translated by James T. Dennison, Jr.)

98

The Counter Remonstrance (1611)

The gathering of the followers of James Arminius (1560–1609) at Gouda in 1610 brought to the press a document agreed upon by forty-three ministers who declared themselves "Remonstrants." Johannes Uytenbogaert (1557–1644), court preacher at The Hague, was the leader and champion of the Remonstrant cause. By December 1610, the States General of Holland urged the Remonstrants and the proto-Counter-Remonstrants (Gomarists) to meet so as to resolve the emerging doctrinal tensions.

On March 10, 1611, at The Hague, the famous *Collatio Hagensis* (Conference of the Hague) convened with six members of the Remonstrant party and six members of the opposition. Festus Hommius (1576–1642), pastor at Leiden, delivered his answer to the 1610 affirmation in "counter remonstrance." Over the next ten days (until March 20), each party labored to defend its position in two documents: one affirming their own interpretation of Scripture regarding the five points in dispute (Remonstrance versus Counter Remonstrance) and the other refuting the objections of the opposite party to their foundational declaration.

In 440 pages (the record of the conference as printed), the parties concluded that there was an irreconcilable division between them: Arminianism and Calvinism were immiscible. It would take a National Synod to resolve this matter, or at least determine the authority of the Reformed faith for the Netherlands. But Arminianism would garner the respite of toleration; by mid-century, Reformed theology no longer united Holland *de facto*. Arminius had achieved his goal of a "third variety of Reformation" and attenuated the Calvinism of the Lowlands. In the wings were Benedict Spinoza and the precursors of the Enlightenment. It must be acknowledged that Arminianism paved the way for this epistemological revolution.

The English translation of the Counter Remonstrance is taken from *Crisis in the Reformed Churches: Essays in Commemoration of the Great Synod of Dort, 1618–1619*, edited by Peter Y. DeJong (Grandville, Mich.: Reformed Fellowship, 2008), 248–50. It appears below with the permission of the publisher.

COUNTER REMONSTRANCE

1. As in Adam the whole human race, created in the image of God, has with Adam fallen into sin and thus become so corrupt that all men are conceived and born in sin and thus are by nature children of wrath, lying dead in their trespasses so that there is within them no more power to convert themselves truly unto God and to believe in Christ than a corpse has power to raise itself from the dead; so God draws out of this condemnation and delivers a certain number of men who in his eternal and immutable counsel He has chosen out of mere grace, according to the good pleasure of his will, unto salvation in Christ, passing by the others in his just judgment and leaving them in their sins.

2. That not only adults who believe in Christ and accordingly walk worthy of the gospel are to be reckoned as God's elect children, but also the children of the covenant so long as they do not in their conduct manifest the contrary; and that therefore believing parents, when their children die in infancy, have no reason to doubt the salvation of these their children.

3. That God in his election has not looked to the faith or conversion of his elect, nor to the right use of his gifts, as the grounds of election; but that on the contrary He in his eternal and immutable counsel has purposed and decreed to bestow faith and perseverance in godliness and thus to save those whom He according to his good pleasure has chosen to salvation.

4. That to this end He has first of all presented and given to them his only-begotten Son Jesus Christ, whom He delivered up to the death of the cross in order to save his elect, so that, although the suffering of Christ as that of the only-begotten and unique Son of God is sufficient unto the atonement

of the sins of all men, nevertheless the same, according to the counsel and decree of God, has its efficacy unto reconciliation and forgiveness of sins only in the elect and true believer.

5. That furthermore to the same end God the Lord has his holy gospel preached, and that the Holy Spirit externally through the preaching of that same gospel and internally through a special grace works so powerfully in the hearts of God's elect, that He illumines their minds, transforms and renews their wills, removing the heart of stone and giving them a heart of flesh, in such a manner that by these means they not only receive power to convert themselves and believe but also actually and willingly do repent and believe.

6. That those whom God has decreed to save are not only once so enlightened, regenerated and renewed in order to believe in Christ and convert themselves to God, but that they by the same power of the Holy Spirit by which they were converted to God without any contribution of themselves are in like manner continually supported and preserved; so that, although many weaknesses of the flesh cleave to them as long as they are in this life and are engaged in a continual struggle between flesh and Spirit and also sometimes fall into grievous sins, nevertheless this same Spirit prevails in this struggle, not permitting that God's elect by the corruption of the flesh should so resist the Spirit of sanctification that this would at any time be extinguished in them, and that in consequence they could completely or finally lose the true faith which was once bestowed on them and the Spirit of adoption as God's children which they had once received.

7. That nevertheless the true believers find no excuse in this teaching to pursue carelessly the lusts of the flesh, since it is impossible that those who by a true faith are ingrafted into Christ should not produce the fruits of thankfulness; but on the contrary the more they assure themselves and feel that God works in them both to will and to do according to his good pleasure, the more they persist in working their own salvation with fear and trembling, since they know that this is the only means by which it pleases God to keep them standing and to bring them to salvation. For this reason He also employs in his Word all manner of warnings and threatenings, not in order to cause them to despair or doubt their salvation but rather to

awaken in them a childlike fear by observing the weakness of their flesh in which they would surely perish, unless the Lord keep them standing in his undeserved grace, which is the sole cause and ground of their perseverance; so that, although He warns them in his Word to watch and pray, they nevertheless do not have this of themselves that they desire God's help and lack nothing, but only from the same Spirit who by a special grace prepares them for this and thus also powerfully keeps them standing.

99

The Bentheim Confession (1613/1617)

The Bentheim region (Grafschaft/Graafschap Bentheim) of Germany borders Overijsel in the Netherlands on the east. Noted for its Castle (erected by the Romans when the Tubanten people inhabited the region), its forest and therapeutic sulfur springs, Bentheim came into the Protestant camp in the sixteenth century and moved toward Calvinism by the seventeenth. The catalyst in this evolution was Anna of Tecklenburg (1532–1582), the wife of Everwin III (b. 1532), governor of Grafschaft Bentheim from 1553 until his premature death in 1562. Anna had become persuaded of more than the teachings of Martin Luther and Philip Melanchthon—she had discovered John Calvin.[1] Upon the death of her husband, Anna devoted her son Arnold (1554–1606) and daughter Walpurgis (1555–1628) to training in the Reformed faith. The son and future governor of Grafschaft Bentheim was sent to Strasbourg in 1571 to be educated in the academy of the city where John Calvin and Martin Bucer had labored. On his return to Bentheim to assume his role as governor, Count Arnold II called Johan Kemmener to be court preacher in 1576. Kemmener preached through the life of Jesus and the disciples in order to establish the biblical foundation for Reformed doctrine and worship.

Meanwhile, Count Arnold's mother had been advancing the Reformed faith in Tecklenburg since 1574. Most pastors there were Reformed in

---

1. Count Arnold (†1553) had governed Bentheim as a committed Roman Catholic until 1535. His court preacher, Johan van Loen, had devoured the works of Martin Luther. Van Loen provided Arnold with books by Luther and Melanchthon, urging him to compare them with the inspired Scriptures. Arnold then examined Luther's Catechism, the Smalkald Articles, and the Augsburg Confession. In 1544, he commanded van Loen that all the clerics of his region were to preach according to the Augsburg Confession. Bentheim was solidly Lutheran until 1587.

conviction but observed some Roman Catholic formalities in worship (i.e., the use of an altar and wafers instead of bread in communion). In 1587, Arnold II summoned an ecclesiastical conference for Tecklenburg and its neighboring cities, Schuttorf and Nordhorn. Arnold advanced a new Church Order declaring Reformed worship alone to be acceptable. Arnold's brother Adolf, Count of Neuenar, Meurs, and Limburg, had prepared the directory, and it had been submitted to the leaders of the church in Heidelberg for endorsement. When unanimously approved by the church conference in Tecklenburg, it became known as the Church Order of 1587. On Christmas Day 1587, the Lord's Supper was observed for the first time according to the Reformed rubric (i.e., at tables, not an altar). Bentheim and the other cities of Grafschaft Bentheim followed suit.

Arnold now applied the educational policy of his mother to his realm. A Latin school at Schuttorf was moved to Steinfort in 1591 in order to become a theological academy for ministerial training. But his choice of Conrad Vorstius (1569–1622) to serve as professor of theology (1596) was to prove disastrous. Vorstius had been trained at Heidelberg, Basel, and Geneva. He had impressed Theodore Beza during his sojourn in the latter city (1595–1596). But in 1599, the faculty at Heidelberg summoned him to defend his views on the Trinity. Suspected of Socinianism, Vorstius parried the accusation with a deft defense of his alleged orthodoxy. Count Arnold II rewarded him with appointment as court preacher in 1602. His influence in Steinfort was immense, and when he was appointed James Arminius's (1560–1609) successor at Leiden in 1610, his semi-Pelagian sympathies were evident. His translation of select works of Socinus, the notorious Unitarian, clearly indicated his own Socinian tendencies. Vigorously opposed by Francis Gomarus (1563–1641), Vorstius was forced to withdraw from Leiden in 1612. At the Synod of Dort (1618–1619), he was condemned as a heretic and forced into hiding until his death.

In 1604, Count Arnold II summoned a General Synod to convene in Schuttorf. Representatives from the provinces of Tecklenburg, Steinfort, and Bentheim were present. Reemphasizing that the Word of God alone was the foundation of the church, the Synod renewed the Church Order of 1587 and resolved to meet annually.

On his death in 1606, Arnold's five sons divided the territory over which he had ruled. Arnold Jost received Bentheim; he would govern from 1610–1643. This son, unlike his father, arrogated to himself control over the church. He formed a "High Consistory" on October 13, 1613, to which every congregation in Bentheim was responsible. This magisterial board appointed (and removed) all church officers. At the same time, Arnold Jost renewed his commitment to the Reformed faith by placing the Bentheim Confession alongside the Heidelberg Catechism. This was done to assure his people and the churches that in doctrine, the Calvinism of his grandmother remained. From 1617 to 1651, every parishioner was required to sign these twelve articles. But the future of the Bentheim church depended upon the ruler of Bentheim. And when Arnold Jost's son and successor, Ernst Willem (1623–1693), converted to Catholicism in 1668, it marked the inevitable downgrade to a hierarchical state church.

The twelve articles of the Bentheim Confession are a clear affirmation of Trinitarian and Calvinistic distinctives. In the context of Vorstius's anti-Trinitarianism as well as his Arminianism, the Bentheimers were formulating succinct statements of their orthodox and Reformed convictions. The controversy that was to peak at Dort over the Remonstrance and Counter-Remonstrance is also part of the larger context of this brief confession.

Sources

Background information for this introduction to the Bentheim Confession has been gathered from several encyclopedias and essays. Most important is the little booklet written by Geerhardus Vos's uncle, Dr. Hendrik Beuker, entitled *Tubantia: Church-State Conflicts in Graafschap Bentheim Germany*. This work was published in Dutch by J. H. Kok (Kampen) in 1897. An English edition was prepared by the Historical Library Committee of the Graafschap Christian Reformed Church in Holland, Michigan, in 1986.

I am particularly indebted to Hans-Jürgen Schmidt and his essay, "Die zwölf Bentheimer Artikel von 1613 und der arminianische Streit in den Niederlanden." Schmidt's essay is published in the *Bentheimer Jahrbuch 2006*. Pastor Gerrit Jan Beuker of Hoogstede, Germany, was also very helpful in providing German materials.

Finally, I wish to acknowledge the kindness of my son-in-law, Dr. Tucker McElroy, for translating several German documents into English for me, including Schmidt's German version of the Confession.

The following translation of the Bentheim Confession was part of a joint class assignment in the Ecclesiastical Latin course at Northwest Theological

Seminary during the academic year 2004–2005. The translation of the original Latin version was then compared with the English translation of the German document found in Schmidt.[2] Thus, the final version of our translation is indebted to both the Latin and the German editions, though we have focused on the Latin text primarily. This translation was first published in *Kerux: The Journal of Northwest Theological Seminary* 20/2 (September 2005): 3–9 and appears by permission.

BENTHEIM CONFESSION (1613/1617)

Articles proposed by the preachers in the ecclesiastical visitation of the Imperial Count of Bentheim in the year 1613 in the month of March and received again and approved in the solemn and also extraordinary assembly in the Castle at Bentheim in the year 1617 in the month of April.

It is asked

    I. Concerning the Unity of the Divine Essence

    Whether you believe that the divine essence is one and undivided or that Jehovah, our God, is one in number.

    II. Concerning the Trinity of Persons

    Whether you believe that in the unity of the divine essence or Godhead there are three distinct, equal and coessential persons — the Father, the Son and the Holy Spirit.

    III. Concerning the Person of Jesus Christ

    Whether you believe that Jesus Christ is true God in one person, begotten from eternity in an ineffable manner by the Father, and true man, born in time without sin from the virgin Mary.

    IV. Concerning the Office of Christ in General

    Whether you believe that Jesus Christ was given to us by God [and] was ordained as Prophet, Priest and King.

---

2. The Latin text is found in E. F. K. Müller, *Die Bekenntnisschriften der reformierten Kirche* (Leipzig, 1903) 833–34.

V. Concerning the Prophetic Office of Christ in Particular

Whether you believe that Christ [as] Prophet has declared to us salvation and His way, and therefore as Arbitrator and Internuncio, is our Mediator.

VI. Concerning the Priestly Office

Whether you believe that Christ as Priest has interceded for us not only in these earthly things, yet also intercedes with the Father in heavenly things; but that also by His suffering and death, as an all-sufficient sacrifice, He has freed us from our sins and eternal death; and so also by way of intercession and payment, is our Mediator.

VII. Concerning the Kingly Office

Whether you believe that Jesus Christ brought forth and established grace by His suffering, to apply it to true believers and penitents efficaciously by the Spirit, the Word and the Sacraments, and to keep them perseveringly in that grace; and likewise finally through this mode of application and preservation, is our Mediator.

VIII. Concerning the Efficacy of the Merit of Christ

Whether you believe that no salvation is able to be possessed and retained apart from Christ and therefore, the fathers of the Old Testament have been justified and saved no less by faith in Christ, at that time about to come, than we in the New Testament are justified and saved by faith in Christ now displayed.

IX. Concerning Infant Baptism

Whether you believe that infants, no less than adults, belong to the gracious covenant of God and the sign and seal of that covenant, namely baptism, is not to be denied them.

X. Concerning Election

Whether you believe that God before He laid the foundation of the world has chosen us in Christ Jesus; and has ordained us unto the adoption of sons, according to the good pleasure of His will, unto the praise of His glorious grace; and even for this [purpose], that we might live holy and blameless before Him in love.

XI. Concerning Salvation

Whether you believe that God wills that all believing and penitent persons be saved: but unbelievers and the impenitent, who obstinately persevere in impiety and unbelief to the end, certainly are going to be sentenced to eternal damnation.

XII. Concerning the Means of Salvation

Whether you believe that in the means of salvation, the beginning, middle and end ought to be altogether ascribed to God, but should not be granted by the powers and works of man and their merits, either completely or in part: notwithstanding God working unto salvation, the pious and faithful cooperate through the grace of God.

(Translated by James T. Dennison, Jr., Kuldip S. Gangar, Peter M. Gangar, Alice L. Hamstra, Adam D. King, Margaret A. Luckel, John W. Ming, and Samuel Son)

Confession of the Evangelical Church in Germany (1614)

When John Sigismund (1572–1619) received the Lord's Supper in accordance with the Reformed rubric on Christmas Day 1613, he not only made a formal break with Lutheranism and the Book of Concord, he also set in motion a vigorous reaction against his endorsement of Calvinism (cf. the full introduction to the Confession of John Sigismund [1614], which follows this document). That reaction labeled the "Second Reformation" (Lutheranism to Calvinism) a "deformation," and regarded the conversion of John Sigismund as virtual apostasy and heresy. Charges were openly made that Calvinism (1) repudiated the omnipotence of God (alleged from the non-ubiquitous presence of the glorified body of Christ); (2) affirmed that God was the author of evil (alleged from divine predestination of whatsoever comes to pass); (3) "Nestorianized" the union of the divine and human natures of Christ (denied a true hypostatic union and communion of the two natures; i.e., divided the natures); (4) advocated rank antinomianism (i.e., the elect are saved regardless of whether they live an immoral life). The confession below was drafted to answer these and other gross caricatures of the Reformed faith.

It was signed on May 10, 1614, at Cölln, a city of old Berlin located on an island in the Spree River. John Sigismund was joined in promoting this statement of the Reformed faith by his eldest son, George William (1595–1640), Margrave of Brandenburg (1619–1640) and his brother, John George (1577–1624).

Our translation is based on the German version printed in Heinrich Heppe, *Die Bekenntnisschriften der reformirten Kirchen Deutschlands* (1860), 262–83. Corrected Scripture citations are indicated by square brackets [ ].

Content of This Confession of Faith

What is treated in this confession of faith:

1. Of the Fundamentals of True Religion
2. Of God
3. Of the Creation
4. Of Providence
5. Of the Fall of Angels and Men, and the Origin of Sin
6. Of the Punishment (Resulting) from the Fall
7. Of the Redemption of the Human Race
8. Of the Person of Christ
9. Of the Office of Christ
10. Of the Present State of Christ
11. Of the Power of Christ's Death
12. Of Justification by Faith
13. Of the Marks of True Faith
14. Of the Origin of Faith
15. Of Gracious Election
16. Of the Sacraments
17. Of Baptism
18. Of the Lord's Supper
19. Of the External Ceremonies of the Sacraments
20. Of the Unreasonable Truncation of the Ten Commandments
21. Conclusion

CONFESSION OF FAITH

1. Of the Fundamentals of True Religion

I. First, we believe and are assured that regarding matters of faith one should not look to man but should be grounded solely upon the Word of God. For it is written: "You shall walk according to My statutes, not according to the statutes of your fathers" (Ezek. 20:18–19).

II. Second, we believe that no one can truly comprehend God's Word apart from God enlightening him through His Spirit. For it is written: "The natural man understands nothing of the Spirit of God (1 Cor. 2:14). But to us God revealed them through His Spirit" (1 Cor. 2:10).

III. Third, we believe that God does not refuse His Spirit to anyone who asks for it heartily and with certain trust. For it is written: "If you then, being evil, know how to give good gifts to your children, how much more will your heavenly Father give the Holy Spirit to those who ask Him?" (Luke 11:13). "And all things you ask in prayer, believing, you will receive" (Matt. 21:22). Yet such prayer must occur in the fear of God and with such a purpose that when God reveals His will to a man he will desire to follow it, may it redound in this world honor or shame, advantage or harm. For it is written: "Whoever is willing to do the will of Him who sent Me, he will know whether this teaching is of God" (John 7:17). But to those who look for earthly honor and do not want to cause themselves any insult amongst the people on behalf of their belief, it is written: "How can you believe, when you receive glory from one another and you do not seek the glory that is from the one and only God?" (John 5:44). And of those who disregard the fear of God, contradicting their conscience as they live in sin? "The world cannot receive the Spirit of truth" (John 14:17).

2. Of God

IV. Further, we confess to only one true God, the Father together with the Son and the Holy Spirit. For it is written: "Hear O Israel, the Lord our God is the only God" (Deut. 6:4). And moreover, this one Lord also revealed Himself to be the Father, the Son, and the Holy Spirit. As it is written: "Baptize in the name of the Father, and the Son, and the Holy Spirit" (Matt. 28:19). And John says expressly: "Whoever denies the Son (as the Jews and the Turks deny Him), he also does not have the Father" (1 John 2:23).

3. Of the Creation

V. We believe and confess that the one true God, the Father, Son, and Holy Spirit, created heaven and earth and all things out of nothing. For it is written: "In the beginning God created heaven and earth" (Gen. 1:1). "All things were made through the Word" (that is, through the Son of God) (John 1:3; Col. 1:16; Heb. 1:2). "The heavens were made by the Word of the Lord, and all His host by the breath of His mouth" (Ps. 33:6).

4. Of Providence

VI. We believe and confess that God, who created all things, also holds all things in His hand, preserves, and governs, as long and in the manner that pleases Him. For it is written: "In Him we live, move, and exist" (Acts 17:28). "Our God is in the heavens, He does whatever He pleases" (Ps. 115:3). And while He is able to do whatever He desires, so He can also prevent that which He does not want to allow to happen; therefore nothing occurs which God does not ordain. Again, as it is written: "Does one not buy two sparrows for one cent, yet not one of them falls to the ground apart from your Father?" (Matt. 10:29). For we know that no creature can harm us apart from the will of God, that nothing is ordained except what serves us best (Rom. 8:[28]).

VII. We believe and confess that whatever God ordains He foreknew from all eternity and purposed unto a good end. For it is written: "God's works are made known from long ago" (Acts 15:18). "God works all things after the counsel of His will" (Eph. 1:11). "You thought evil against me, but God thought it for good in order to bring about this present result, to preserve many people alive" (Gen. 50:20). "For truly in this city there were gathered together against your holy servant Jesus, whom you anointed, both Herod and Pontius Pilate, along with the heathen and the peoples of Israel, to do whatever your hand and your purpose predestined to occur" (Acts 4:27–[28]).

5. Of the Fall of Angels and Men, and the Origin of Sin

VIII. We believe and confess that the sin which is in the world, even though it does not occur without God's ordainment, does not come from God, but from the devil and his angels, whom God created good in the beginning: but in their rebellion they fell away from God and deceived our first parents, so that they also rebelled against God. With their free will they plunged themselves and their posterity into sin and death, even though God created them in the beginning after His image and unto a blessed immortality. For it is written: "And God saw all that He had made, and behold, it was very good" (Gen. 1:31). Of the devil: He does not stand in the truth. "When he speaks lies, he speaks from his own nature, for he is a liar and a father of lies" (John 8:44). But of man: "And God created man in His own image," that is, "in thorough righteousness and holiness" (Gen. 1:27; Col. 3:10; Eph. 4:[24]). Also, "the serpent deceived me," namely, the devil; for "the devil is the old serpent who deceives the whole world" (Gen. 3:13; Rev. 12:9). "By a man sin entered the world and death through sin" (Rom. 5:12, 16–19). "For man's intents and aims are evil from his youth, and we are all by nature children of wrath" (Gen. 6:5; 8:21; Eph. 2:3).

IX. In addition we believe and confess that after the devil and men brought sin into the world, the Lord our God out of righteous judgment has often used sin with sin, in that He punishes one wicked scoundrel with another; thus He also chastises His beloved children by the sins of evil men. Many such examples are to be found in the Scriptures; also as is spoken of the idolatrous heathen: "They exchanged the glory of the incorruptible God into an image resembling corruptible man and of birds and of four-footed animals and crawling creatures. Therefore God gave them over in the lusts of their hearts to impurity, to the dishonoring of their bodies among themselves" (Rom. 1:23–24). Of Shimei, who curses his king David: "The Lord commanded him" (2 Sam. [16:11]).

6. Of the Punishment (Resulting) from the Fall

X. We believe and confess that God has eternally cast out the devil and his angels on account of their wanton rebellion, and will never again receive them into His grace. For it is written: "Enter the eternal fire prepared for the devil and his angels" (Matt. 25:41).

XI. We believe and confess that God possessed the just authority to likewise cast out mankind, for we are as the evil angels, having fallen away from God and having transgressed His law, unmindful that He had adamantly warned us as He spoke: "On the day you eat from this tree, you shall die" (Gen. 2:17). Understand not merely the present but also the eternal death, which is the eternal torment and anguish "in the lake which burns with fire and brimstone" (Rev. 21:8).

7. Of the Redemption of the Human Race

XII. But God has not dealt with us according to what we deserve, but by His great mercy He has taken us unto Himself again; and before He allowed the entire human race to be destroyed, He gave His Son for us, as it is written: "For God so loved the world that He gave His only begotten Son, that whoever believes in Him shall not be lost, but have everlasting life" (John 3:16).

XIII. And such things God has done according to His eternal counsel and will, as once more it is written: "You are saved by the blood of Christ, as of an innocent, unblemished lamb who was foreknown before the foundation of the world was laid, but revealed in these last times" (1 Peter 1:19–20).

XIV. In time, as in God's gracious providence the Son of God was to become our Mediator, so He also had to become man, namely, He had to take on a human nature so that in His humanity He would suffer death and also atone and pay for our sins. As it is written: "Therefore, since the children share in flesh and blood, He Himself likewise also partook of the same, that through death He might render powerless him who had the power of death, that is, the devil: and delivered those who through fear of death were subject to slavery all their lives" (Heb. 2:14–[15]).

XV. And so that this should occur, God promised from the beginning, as it is written: the seed of the woman shall crush underfoot the head of the snake (Gen. 3:15).

XVI. But in the last days it was fulfilled, as it is written: "henceforth when the fullness of time came God sent forth His Son, born of a woman (namely, from the virgin Mary), born under the law, so that He might redeem those who were under the law" (Gal. 4:4–[5]).

8. Of the Person of Christ

XVII. We believe concerning the person of Christ, that He is not a mere man, as the Arians believe: but that He is the eternal, almighty Son of God, who in the last days of this world took on Himself a human nature; and since He previously was only God, now is both God and man unto all eternity. For it is written: "In the beginning was the Word" (that is, the Son of God), "and the Word became flesh" (John 1:1, 14). The Son of God "through whom God made the world," and who "upholds all things by His mighty Word," who took unto Himself "the seed of Abraham" (Heb. 1:2–3; 2:16). "Jesus Christ, although He existed in the form of God, did not conceive of it as robbery to be equal with God, but emptied Himself and took on the form of a servant and was made in the likeness of men: He humbled Himself and was obedient unto death, yes, to death on the cross" (Phil. 2:5–8). "He had to be made like unto His brethren in all things" (Heb. 2:17). "He was tempted in all things, as we are, yet without sin" (Heb. 4:15).

XVIII. Since Christ is God and man, we believe that we can say everything of Him that can be said of God, and everything that can be said of man. First, because He is God according to the Godhead: second, because He is man according to the manhood. For example: In Scripture this is said of Him: "His goings forth are from eternity" (Mic. 5:2). In another place: He was born in "the fullness of time" (Gal. [4:4]); or "in the last times" (1 Peter 1:20). Both are true, one according to the deity, the other according to humanity. As the apostles teach us discernment, just as Paul says: "He was born from the seed of David according to the flesh (that is, according to humanity), and was declared to be the almighty Son of God according to the Spirit (that is, according to the deity)" (Rom. 1:3–4). And Peter: "Who died according to the flesh, yet was resurrected according to the Spirit" (1 Peter 3:[18]).

9. *Of the Office of Christ*

XIX. Of the office of Christ we believe that He is our Savior who reconciles us to God through His death, and He makes such a reconciliation known to us, and allows this to be known; also, that He claims His faithful ones for His own and preserves and protects them unto eternity. For it is written: "Jesus Christ came into the world to save sinners" (1 Tim. 1:15). "Christ died for us" (Rom. 5:8). "God was in Christ reconciling the world to Himself, not counting their trespasses against them: and He has committed to us the word of reconciliation" (2 Cor. 5:19). "I give eternal life to My sheep, and they will never perish, and no one will snatch them out of My hand" (John 10:28).

10. *Of the Present State of Christ*

XX. Of the present state of Christ we believe that He no longer exists in bodily form on this earth: but that forty days after His resurrection He ascended up to heaven and in heaven sits at the right hand of God, where God has given Him all authority and governance over all the creatures in heaven and on earth (which is our comfort). And that He will in the last days come again to resurrect the living and the dead. For it is written: "I am leaving the world and am going to the Father" (John 16:28). "I am ascending to my Father" (John 20:17). "He parted from them and ascended to heaven" (Luke 24:[51]). "He entered heaven itself, now to appear in the presence of God for us" (Heb. 9:[24]). "You always have the poor with you, but you do not always have Me" (Matt. 26:11). "God seated Him at His right hand in heaven over all principalities, power, authority, and rule" (Eph. 1:[20]–21). "To Me is given all power in heaven and on earth" (Matt. 28:18). "Seek the things above, where Christ is seated at the right hand of God" (Col. 3:1). "This Jesus, who has been taken up from you into heaven, will come in just the same way as you have watched Him ascend into heaven" (Acts 1:11). "Whom heaven must receive until the time of restoration of all things about which God spoke by the mouth of His holy prophets from the beginning of the world" (Acts 3:21).

XXI. Additionally we believe that even though Christ is no longer with us according to His humanity, yet He is nevertheless with us, and will remain with us unto all eternity according to His divinity. As He spoke: "I am with you always, until the end of the age" (Matt. 28:20). "Where two or three are gathered in My name, there I am in their midst" (Matt. 18:20).

XXII. Thus His presence is useful and comforting to us. For when He is with us in His almighty and divine power, He can help us in all our needs, even though He is not present in the flesh: just as the centurion from Capernaum who trusted in Him spoke: "Lord, I am not worthy for You to come under my roof, but just say the word, and my servant will be healed" (Matt. 8:8). Whose faith Christ highly praised, and said: "Truly I say to you, I have not found such faith in Israel" (Matt. 8:10).

XXIII. Yet if we should believe that Christ is not able to help us unless He is with us in the flesh, that would not only diminish His almighty and divine power; but also, if we should believe that Christ, in the flesh, is still with us in this world, with such a belief we would be deprived of our supreme comfort. "For if I do not go away," says Christ, "the Comforter will not come to you" (John 16:7). And the apostle says to the Hebrews: "Now if He were on earth, He would not be a priest" (Heb. 8:4). That is, He would not be our Reconciler and Mediator with the Father. Woe to us wretched men! What if we should no longer have Christ as our Mediator and the Holy Spirit as our Comforter? Therefore Christ speaks with great seriousness to His disciples: "Because I have said these things to you (namely, that I am going to the Father), sorrow has filled your heart" (John 16:6). "But I tell you the truth, it is good that I go: for if I do not go, the Comforter will not come to you. But if I go, I will send Him to you so that He shall remain with you forever" (John [16:7]). And because He remains with us, we know that Christ abides with us; as it is written: "Thereby we know that He abides in us, by the Spirit whom He gave to us" ([1 John 3:24]).

XXIV. Therefore the personal union of both natures in Christ will not be separated, even though He is not omnipresent in His human nature as in His divine nature. For that does not accompany the personal union, namely, that the human nature must be eternal and conjointly omnipresent as the divine nature. Otherwise what must follow is that during the time Christ was still on earth, that is, throughout the thirty-four years, either the personal union of both natures in Christ did not occur, or the evangelists wrote falsely. And that according to His human nature He had not been everywhere, but had been: now in His mother's womb, now in the manger, now in Bethlehem, now in Egypt, now in Nazareth, now in Cana of Galilee, now in Capernaum, now in Bethany, now not in Bethany, now on the Mount of Olives, now in the temple, now on the cross, now taken from the cross, now in the grave, now not in the grave, now in the garden in Jerusalem, now in Galilee, now on the mountain, now leaving the mountain and ascending on high. In summary, Christ remains God and man in an undivided person, even if in His bodily form He is not omnipresent, as in His divine omnipotence.

11. Of the Power of Christ's Death

XXV. Of the power of Christ's death, we believe that although Christ's death is the atonement for the sins of the whole world, as is read in John, such reconciliation profits no one except those alone who believe on Him. For it is written: "That whoever believes in Him shall not be lost, but have everlasting life" (John 3:16). "Whoever does not believe, he will be condemned" (Mark 16:16). "The wrath of God abides on him" (John 3:36). Namely, that which by nature abides in all men; as the verse says, "We are all by nature children of wrath" (Eph. 2:3).

12. Of Justification by Faith

XXVI. So when someone believes in Christ and sincerely trusts in God, his sins will be forgiven on account of the shed blood of Christ; and he will be adopted as His child and will inherit eternal life. The same will be pardoned of all their sins and regarded as righteous, just as if he had never been guilty of sin nor had ever committed any sin. As it is written: "The righteousness of God comes through faith in Jesus Christ, to all who believe" (Rom. 3:22). And so it is fulfilled what is written: "That man is justified apart from the work of the law (that is, without merit and by pure grace), solely by faith" (Rom. 3:[28]).

13. Of the Marks of True Faith

XXVII. Whether one has such faith and trust in God (but not like the hypocrites who call upon Christ with a deceitful tongue)—that will be made known by the labor of love. For it is written: "In Christ Jesus neither circumcision nor uncircumcision is of any value, but faith working through love" (Gal. [5:6]). John says: "For this is the love of God, that we keep His commandments" (1 John 5:3). For this is love for our neighbor, that we do not harm our neighbor, but bless him according to our capability, as it is written: "Love does no wrong to a neighbor" (Rom. [13:10]). We should also lay down our life for our brethren (John 10:[15]).

XXVIII. And surely where faith in Christ is truly rooted in men's hearts and does not just drift off the tongue, it is revealed by their works of love. It is thus impossible for one who believes that God allowed His Son to die for him not to respond with love toward God and a desire to do what He loves. As it is written: "For the love of God controls us, having concluded this, that one died for all, therefore all died; and He died for all, so that they who live might no longer live for themselves, but for Him who died and rose again on their behalf" (2 Cor. 5:14–15). Therefore, when someone says he believes in Christ and hopes for his salvation through Christ, yet continues to live in sin, such hope and faith is useless. For it is written: "Everyone who hopes in Him cleanses himself, just as He is clean" ([1 John 3:3]). "If anyone is in Christ, he is a new creature" (2 Cor. 5:17). "Those who belong to Christ, they crucify their flesh with its lusts and desires" (Gal. 5:24).

XXIX. This is God's covenant with us men which is so often conveyed in Scripture; namely, that God desires to be merciful to us for Christ's sake, yet we are to acknowledge His grace with thankfulness and serve Him faithfully. For whoever does not set himself to this task with all diligence, to him God will withhold His offer of grace. Instead: The grace of God is "toward those who keep His covenant and remember His law, to do according to them" (Ps. 103:[18]). "But to the ungodly God says, 'Why do you take My covenant in your mouth since you hate discipline, and you cast My words behind you?'" (Ps. 50:16–17). Whoever performs that which he knows and is enabled to do through God's bestowal, God will not only be patient with his remaining weaknesses for Christ's sake, but He will continue to bless him through the granting of His Spirit, as it is written: "For to everyone who has, more shall be given, and he will have an abundance; but from the one who does not have, even what he does have shall be taken away" (Matt. 25:29).

14. *Of the Origin of Faith*

XXX. Furthermore, we believe that God so ordained the preaching of His Word to work in us a belief in Christ. For it is written: "How will they believe in Him whom they have not heard? And how will they hear without a preacher? How will they preach unless they are sent? So faith comes from preaching and preaching from the Word of God" (Rom. 10:14, 15, 17).

XXXI. We also believe, as we previously alluded, that man is corrupted by the fall so that he cannot comprehend nor acknowledge the preaching of the gospel of Christ unless God, by His Spirit, enlightens and guides the heart. For it is written: "No one can say 'Jesus is Lord' (that is, acknowledge Him as their Lord and Savior) except by the Holy Spirit" (1 Cor. 12:3). "No one can come to Me unless the Father draws him" (John 6:44).

XXXII. Therefore we hold as certain that faith is an extraordinary gift of God. For it is written: "For not all have faith" ([2 Thess. 3:2]). "For by grace you have been saved through faith; and that not of yourselves, it is a gift of God; not as a result of works, so that no one may boast" (Eph. 2:8).

XXXIII. God gives this gift to whomever He wills. For again, it is written: "He has mercy on whom He desires and hardens whom He desires" (Rom. 9:18).

XXXIV. Yet God does not act unjustly toward anyone, "for all have sinned" (Rom. 3:23) and therefore deserve to have their hearts hardened by God. And some are especially so stiff-necked that they do not want to see with their eyes; it serves them right when God completely blinds them. What is written is certain to befall them: "Because they did not receive the love of the truth so as to be saved, therefore God will send upon them a strong delusion so that they will believe the lie, in order that they all may be judged who did not believe the truth, but took pleasure in wickedness" (2 Thess. 2:[10]–12).

15. *Of Gracious Election*

XXXV. Furthermore, we believe that to whomever God gives faith, those He also chose to receive eternal life. For it is written: "As many as had been ordained to eternal life believed" (Acts 13:[48]).

XXXVI. And again, those whom God has chosen for eternal life He has given faith in Christ and a will and zeal for a godly life and walk. For it is written: "He chose us in Christ before the foundation of the world, that we should be holy and blameless before Him. In love He predestined us to adoption as sons through Jesus Christ to Himself, according to the good pleasure of His will, to the praise of the glory of His grace, which He freely bestowed on us in the Beloved" (Eph. 1:4–6).

XXXVII. Therefore it is wicked when those blasphemers say: If God has chosen me I will be saved and can do as I please; for if God has chosen you for salvation, He chose you so you would be "holy and blameless for Him in love" (Eph. 1:4).

Whomever God has chosen for eternal life He protects, so that they do not become entangled in damnable error or tenacious unbelief and unrepentance. For it is written: "Were it possible, even the elect would be misled into error" (Matt. 24:24). With which words Christ gives us a clear understanding that it is not possible.[1]

XXXIX. This is the reason the elect will not be lost. "They are protected by the power of God through faith for salvation" (1 Peter 1:5).

XL. Wherefore it is our and all elect children's greatest comfort, that we can say with the apostle Paul: "I am convinced that neither death, nor life, nor angels, nor principalities, nor powers, nor things present, nor things to come, nor height, nor depth, nor any other created thing, will be able to separate us from the love of God, which is in Christ Jesus our Lord" (Rom. 8:38–39).

---

1. To maintain consistency with the original, we have skipped paragraph numbering XXXVIII. However, one may assume that it would refer to this paragraph.

XLI. Furthermore, we believe that whoever desires to know if he is elected should not search in the secret counsel of God, otherwise he will never find it. But whoever desires to know if he is elected should believe in Christ, for then he will be assured. For all who believe are elected. As it is written: "The faith of those chosen of God" (Titus 1:1). And the promise remains infallible. "So that whoever believes in Him shall not perish, but have everlasting life" (John 3:16). Whoever desires to become more assured of his election must continue in holiness; for that is what the chosen do. This is Peter's warning as he says: "Therefore, brethren, be all the more diligent to make certain about His calling and choosing you" (2 Peter 1:10).

XLII. And even if our faith is very small, we should not doubt then: "A crushed reed He shall not smash, and a dimly burning wick He will not extinguish" (Isa. 42:3). "The one who comes to Me," says Christ, "I will not cast out" (John 6:37). But that also signifies coming to Christ; desiring salvation through Him. When you have the desire, He will not cast you out, however weak your faith is. But whoever does not have this desire, he will not trouble himself much about election. If we are overtaken by great sins, that should not cause us to doubt. Many elect have encountered many terrible temptations, as Peter himself denied Christ; yet he was and remained an elect of God, which he proved by his repentance. After whose example everyone who has sinned should do penance, that is, acknowledge their sins and repent; take refuge in Christ's mercy and not continue in sin. In this way God will not reject him. For it is written: "As I live, declares the Lord, I take no pleasure in the death of the wicked, but rather that the wicked turn from his way and live" (Ezek. 33:11). "If anyone sins, we have an advocate with the Father, Jesus Christ the righteous; and He Himself is the propitiation for our sins" (1 John [2:1–2]). "Where sin increased, grace abounded all the more" (Rom. 5:21).

16. Of the Sacraments

XLIII. Because God knew that in our nature we are inclined to doubt, He promised us His grace in Christ. And not only in distinct words, but also in visible signs, which are called sacraments, confirmed and sealed. These are not heard merely with the ears, but also seen with the eyes, and which speak through all our senses to feel, grasp, and perceive how God is disposed toward us.

17. *Of Baptism*

As to water baptism, He confirmed the promise that for the sake of Christ's shed blood, He beholds us as washed and cleansed of all of our sins; and through His Holy Spirit continues to renew us unto a pure, unstained way of life and to finally bring us to eternal salvation. That is the meaning of baptism, and therefore it is said of baptism that it is the bath of the rebirth which cleanses from sin and saves, while these gifts of God mold and reassure us; but not as if water baptism in and of itself washes away sin and saves us. This is why we believe this, for it is written: "Not the removal of the filth of the flesh which saves us, but the bond of a good conscience toward God" ([1 Peter 3:21]). Which is confirmed by baptism, as it was confirmed in ancient times by circumcision, and which was replaced by baptism, as it is written: "You are circumcised with the circumcision of Jesus Christ, in that you are buried with Him through baptism" (Col. 2:11–12).

XLIV. As in ancient times circumcision was named the covenant of God, it was a sign of the covenant of God and a seal of the righteous of faith, as it is written: "For that is My covenant" (Gen. 17:[10]). And soon thereafter: "That shall be a sign to you of the covenant" (Gen. 17:[11]). Abraham "received the sign of the circumcision as a seal of the righteousness of faith" (Rom. [4]:11). So now baptism is named the bath of rebirth and also the covenant and adoption of the children of God, while it is a sign and seal of the grace of God. As believers we are so assured of this grace, as certain as when we received baptism, according to the promise: "Whoever believes and is baptized will be saved. But whoever does not believe will be damned" (Mark 16:16).

XLV. Whoever has faith, namely with such a faith that works through love. For: "In Christ Jesus neither circumcision nor uncircumcision means anything (as also baptism or not to be baptized), but faith working through love" (Gal. 5:6).

XLVI. So in our baptism as thankful covenant friends of God, we are indebted and acknowledge our lifelong obligation, as it is written: "How shall we who died to sin still live in it: Do you not know that all of us who have been baptized into Jesus Christ have been baptized into His death? Therefore we have been buried with Him through baptism into death, so that as Christ was raised from the dead, so we too shall walk in a new life" (Rom. 6:2–4).

XLVII. And now whoever walks in such a manner is truly born again of God. But whoever does not walk in such a manner is not yet born of God, even if he is baptized. For it is written: "Whoever is born of God does not sin because His seed abides in him and he cannot sin, because he is born of God. By this it is revealed who the children of God and who the children of the devil are. Anyone who does not practice righteousness is not of God, nor the one who does not love his brother" (1 John 3:9–10).

XLVIII. Regarding the children of Christians, we believe that when they desire to be baptized according to the Christian order, one should not neglect to baptize them. For it is written: "For the promise is for you and your children" (Acts 2:39). Therefore Peter says: "Let each of you be baptized" (Acts 2:38).

XLIX. We call this the Christian order, when one can have a teacher or preacher who baptizes; for Christ commanded no one to baptize except those whom He also commanded to teach. As it is written: "Go and teach all people (nations), and baptize them" (Matt. 28:19).

L. In the case a child is overcome by death before one can bring him to a preacher, or bring a preacher to him, we believe that the child is not lost for this reason. For it is written: "I am God to you and to your seed after you" (Gen. 17:7). Throughout all time God will preserve such a promise toward all believers, if He has not already sealed their children; and He is able to keep such a promise. For what He did for John, He can accomplish for all children; of whom it is said: "He would be filled with the Holy Spirit while yet in his mother's womb" (Luke 1:[15]).

18. *Of the Lord's Supper*

LI. Now with baptism God has confirmed and sealed the promise unto us, has received us and our children into His covenant, and through the covenant has forgiven our sins, and desires to give us the gift of the Holy Spirit and eternal life on account of Christ's shed blood. In order for us to receive even greater comfort in this covenant and to be reminded of His continual grace, besides the preaching of His Word, He instituted and ordained the Lord's Supper, so that by this practice the suffering and death of Jesus Christ, wherein our covenant is grounded, would often be brought before our eyes and preserve in us a faithful remembrance, as it is written: "The Lord Jesus in the night in which He was betrayed took bread; and when He had given thanks, He broke it, and gave it to His disciples and said: Take, eat, this is My body which is broken for you, do this in remembrance of Me. In the same way He took the cup after supper and said: Drink, all of you; this is the cup of the new covenant in My blood, which is shed for you and many for the forgiveness of sins. As often as you do this, do this in remembrance of Me" (Matt. 26:26; Mark 14:22; Luke 22:19; 1 Cor. 11:23). In this way the Lord's Supper is a remembrance of the death of Christ and a renewal of God's covenant with us. As Christ says, "Do this in remembrance of Me." Also, in saying, "This cup is the new covenant," it is as if He wanted to say, "Therefore, keep this ceremony. First, that by this you are reminded and assured that I truly gave My body for you as I died on the cross and shed My blood for the forgiveness of your sins (Heb. 8:10–11; Jer. 31; etc.); or for the establishment of the new covenant wherein God promised you the forgiveness of sins, the spirit of sanctification, and eternal life (1 Cor. 10:15–16). Surely, as you eat of this bread and drink of this cup, you truly share these graces in common. Additionally, so that you announce, praise, and extol to the whole world My great love and faithfulness toward you (namely, that My body was given for you, and My blood was poured out for the forgiveness of your sins) by this public and glorious act of My death (1 Cor. 11:26). And as you commit to honor Me as you live holy lives and sincerely love one another; also, as you eat from one bread, you are bound to become one heart and one body, one spirit and altogether one mind (1 Cor. 10:16–17; 12:12–13, etc.)."

LII. To understand that this was instituted by Christ, and that therefore Christ named the bread His body, in that He established it as a remembrance of His body, not that the body was contained in it. Therefore we believe this: that the body of Christ is in the bread or ever was, is nowhere written in the entire Bible, but that Christ celebrated the first Lord's Supper with His disciples, so wrote the evangelists, that He sat at the table with them (Matt. 26:20; Mark 14:17; Luke 22:14). But not that He was concealed in the bread. But now that Christ ascended to heaven, the Scriptures testify that He is not on earth and therefore not in the bread. And Christ also never said: "Therein is My body" (Heb. 8:4). Otherwise we undoubtedly wanted to believe His omnipotence, but He took the bread and of it He says, "That is My body" (Matt. 26; Mark 14; Luke 22; 1 Cor. 11). Therefore the bread is the body of Christ, not something else in the bread.

Now every Christian knows that the bread is not naturally the body of Christ. For the bread is not born of the virgin Mary and crucified for us. Therefore the saying: "the bread is My body" does not provide complete understanding until there follows: "Do this in remembrance of Me" (Luke 22; 1 Cor. 11). Henceforth, every Christian understands why the Lord called the bread "His body," and how the bread is His body, namely, for a remembrance; or how one customarily speaks sacramentally, that is, in the custom of the sacraments. Then that is characteristic of the sacraments, that the signs or remembrances of God's blessings (the earthly or heavenly blessings) themselves take care to be named with the names of such good works (see XLIV). Just as circumcision is called the covenant of God, while it was a sign of God's covenant. Baptism is named the bath of rebirth while instead of circumcision it is a sign of regeneration and adoption into the covenant as a child of God (Ex. 12:12–15; 13:9). The Paschal Lamb is named the Passover or the passing over, because it was a sign and memorial of the passing of the angel of destruction over the houses of the children of Israel. In such a way as is otherwise customary in all sacraments, also in this sacrament the sign of the body of Christ is called the body of Christ. And the comparison of all words that were used in the establishment of the Paschal Lamb and the Lord's Supper reassures us in such a belief: as when Christ wanted to point with fingers to the Paschal Lamb and say: Just as in former times the Paschal Lamb was instituted as a remembrance of the deliverance from Egypt, so now I institute the Lord's Supper as a remembrance of the deliverance from hell. Then to be sure:

How God speaks of the sacrificial lamb	So Christ speaks of the bread in the Lord's Supper
Take	Take
Eat (Ex. 12:3, 5, 8, 11)	Eat
It is the Lord's Passover (that is, the passing over) (Ex. 12:12)	That is My Body
This day shall be a remembrance (Ex. 13:14)	Do this in remembrance of Me

And with the same understanding: "therefore this shall be a sign in your hand, and a memorial for your eyes" (Ex. [13]:9). This is why it is said of the cup: "This cup is the new testament in My blood" (Luke [22:20]; 1 Cor. [11:25]). Again, which words cannot be understood as they sound, but must be understood according to the following explanation: "Do this in remembrance of Me" (1 Cor. 11). For if the words are to be understood as they sound, the cup would have to be in the blood, not the blood in the cup; as well as the cup would have to be the new testament, that is, the forgiveness of sins themselves, which no Christian will say.

LIII. According to this it is undeniable that the words in the Lord's Supper: "This is My body, this is My blood," must not be understood as they sound concerning the words bread and blood, but in accordance with how the Lord explains them, (Luke 12; 1 Cor. 11). Namely, "Do this in remembrance of Me," as if He had said, "Take and eat, the bread is My body; that is, the bread shall be a remembrance to you of My body that I gave for you by My death." Which explanation, as Christ Himself gave, is comforting for all believers. For the Lord's Supper is instituted for a remembrance that Christ gave His body for us by His death and shed His blood for us for the forgiveness of our sins; and He would not remind us of such things and often declare them with so many memorials if it were not true; so we are assured and strengthened in our faith through the Lord's Supper that truly the Son of God died for us and earned eternal life for us by His death. Which faith is the true eating and drinking of the body and blood of Christ that work to our blessedness. For whoever eats and drinks Christ's body and blood, that is, whoever locks this comfort firmly in his heart and refreshes and edifies himself in that Christ gave His body for him by His death, that man (one) will no longer hunger or thirst, but will enter eternal life after this life. As Christ speaks of such eating and drinking: "He who comes to Me will not hunger, and he who believes in Me will never thirst" (John 6:35). "He who eats My flesh and drinks My blood has eternal life, and I will raise him up on the last day" (John [6]:54). "He who eats My flesh and drinks My blood abides in Me and I in him" (John 6:56). But of the eating of His flesh with the mouth Christ says: "The flesh profits nothing" (John 6:63). Because man becomes anxious over this to no avail, and is also directly rejected by Christ as he opposes the article (of faith) of His ascension to heaven with such fleshly thoughts, who says: "How then, when you shall see the Son of Man ascending to the place from which He came?" (John 6:[62]). As long as the article (of faith) remains true that Christ ascended to heaven, so also what He Himself concluded remains true, namely, that we cannot hold and eat Him with our mouth.

19. Of the External Ceremonies of the Sacraments

LIV. Of the visible ceremonies of the sacraments, we believe that no person has the power to change them, but one should follow Christ's commands, as He says: "If you love Me, so keep My commandments" (John 14:15). That is the reason we allow our children to be baptized in no other way than in the name of the Father, the Son, and the Holy Spirit. For in this way and no other Christ instituted it and commanded: "Go therefore and make disciples of all the nations and baptize them in the name of the Father, and the Son, and the Holy Spirit" (Matt. 28:19). But the words, "depart you unclean spirit," were not commanded by Christ for use in baptism. Therefore we will also not use it. There is also no need for it, for nowhere in Scripture is it found that children who were not baptized had the devil. But the children of believers, although they are unholy by nature nevertheless are holy by grace, as it is written: "Otherwise your children are unclean; but now they are holy" (1 Cor. 7:14). Also, in the Lord's Supper, we do not allow the host, as originated by the Papists; but partake of true bread, as it is written of Christ: "While they were eating, He took bread" (Matt. 26:26). In addition, we do not distribute all of the bread, as the Papists instituted the distribution of all the round hosts; instead we break the bread as Christ commanded, for: "He took the bread, broke it, and said, 'do this in remembrance'" that the temple of His body had been broken for us (Matt. 26:26ff.; 1 Cor. 11; John 2:19–21).

20. Of the Unreasonable Truncation of the Ten Commandments of God

LV. Just as we believe regarding the ceremonies of the sacraments that no one has the power to change them; so also we believe regarding God's laws, that no person has the power to change them, to add to or take away from them. For it is written: "You shall not add to what I command you, nor shall you take anything away from it" (Deut. 4:2). Therefore it is not fitting for a Christian that he cut out portions of the Ten Commandments of God, as the pope of Rome has removed portions of them and has scratched out the law regarding images, to his advantage, so that the common man would not notice that his images and idols are forbidden by God (Ex. [20]:4; Deut. 5:8).

21. *Conclusion*

This is our belief by which we are assured through God's Word and Spirit, that whoever has such a faith which he can prove by his deeds, cannot be lost. Therefore we wish from our heart that our faithful God and Father, who gave us such knowledge for which we can never sufficiently thank Him, desires to enlighten others who are still lost with the same understanding. It is His work: and surely he who fears God and considers these quoted passages, his own heart will drive and compel him to give honor to God and allow His Word to remain true. For it is written: "He who is of God hears God's Word" (John 8:[47]). "The Word of God is alive and powerful and sharper than a two-edged sword that cuts asunder soul and spirit, also marrow and bone, and is a judge of the thoughts" (Heb. [4:12]). "For judgment must be righteous, and all the upright in heart will follow it" (Ps. 94:[15]).

(Translated by Christina Munson; revisions by Tom and Kirsten DeVries)

101

The Confession of
John Sigismund (1614)

O n Christmas Day 1613, in Holy Trinity Cathedral of Berlin, Elector
John Sigismund (1572–1619) of Brandenburg joined about fifty other
members of his court and political entourage in receiving the Lord's Supper
in the Reformed manner (i.e., via the *fractio panis*, or "breaking of the bread").
The event inaugurates the Second Calvinistic Reformation in this region of
Germany. Regarded by its advocates as completing the Reformation begun
by Martin Luther (1483–1546), it joins similar movements of the sixteenth
and seventeenth centuries that found Calvinism to be the logical outcome
of *sola Scriptura*.

John Sigismund had become weary of Lutheran liturgical pomp (too
nearly Roman Catholic, in his opinion). But in 1607, when he and his
brother, John George, visited Heidelberg and the court of Palatine Elector
Frederick IV (1574–1610), they became convinced that the Lutheran view of
the Lord's Supper was erroneous, and were determined "to sweep the leftover
papal dung completely out of Christ's stable." By 1614, the two brothers
had designed a program to promote reform in the region by means of the
Joachimsthal Gymnasium and the University of Frankfort (an der Oder).

Abraham Scultetus (1566–1625) arrived in Berlin from Heidelberg
in 1614 to advance John Sigismund's plan. Lutherans charged the
elector with introducing a "deformation," and John Behm (1578–1648),
professor of theology at the University of Königsberg, took charge of
the anti-Calvinistic resistance. Christoph Pelargus (1565–1633), general
superintendent of the Mark (as the region around Brandenberg was called;
cf. the Latin *Marchicae*), was a vigorous leader of the Calvinist faction.
Samuel Dresemius (1578–1638), rector of the Joachimsthal, assisted the
Calvinist party. By the elector's decree, religious instruction was henceforth
to be based on the Heidelberg Catechism (1563).

In the summer of 1614, John Sigismund published his confession (*Confessio Sigismundi*, written by Martin Füssel). He followed this up by appointing Calvinists as professors at the University of Frankfort: John Bergius (1587–1658), who joined Pelargus and John Heidenreich (†1617) in 1614; Wolfgang Crell (1593–1664) in 1616; and Gregory Franck (1585–1651) in 1617.

This top-down Reformation did not commend itself to the third-generation Lutheran populace. The irruption of the Thirty Years' War (1618–1648) severely damaged the facilities at Joachimsthal and elector George William (1595–1640) settled for what Bodo Nischan calls "poly-confessionalism" (i.e., Calvinism at court, Lutheranism popularly in the streets; cf. Nischan, "The Schools of Brandenburg and the 'Second Reformation': Centers of Calvinist Learning and Propaganda," in *Calviniana: Ideas and Influence of John Calvin* [1988], 215–33). The Frankfort (an der Oder) University Calvinists drifted into "distinguished" irenicism, attempting to deemphasize the distinctives between Lutherans and Calvinists. They even moderated the classic Augustinian-Calvinist doctrine of predestination in the direction of foreknowledge (Lutheranism had long advocated a single predestination of those whom God foresaw would believe at a point in time). German Calvinism was being acculturated following the Arminian onslaught in Holland at the beginning of the century. Not coincidentally, Pelargus and Bergius adamantly refused to attend the Synod of Dort (1618–1619) because they feared relations with Lutherans would be damaged irreparably by the condemnations of the Arminians.

Hence, by 1630, the original plan of John Sigismund for the University of Frankfort (an der Oder) had been abandoned for confessional parity between Lutheran and Reformed groups. From 1641, an equal number of Calvinist and Lutheran faculty appointments were agreed upon. Moderatism in seventeenth-century German Protestantism would be the doorway through which the Enlightenment would incubate to burst upon the German university community with the importation of radically naturalistic, neo-pagan English deism in the eighteenth century by Sigmund J. Baumgarten (1706–1757).

Our text is from Müller, 835–43; cf. Neimeyer, 642–52, and the version found in Carl Friedrich Pauli, *Allgemeine preussische Staats-Geschichte des dazu gehörigen Königreichs, Fürstenthümer, Churfürstenthums Herzogthümer, Fürstenthümer, Graf- und Herrschaften aus bewährten Schriftstellern und*

Urkunden bis auf gegenwärtige Regierung (1762), 3:547–55. The proof texts are troublesome since, in the three versions of the text, they are not consistent. We have used brackets [ ] to indicate what we believe are the correct allusions.

THE CONFESSION OF FAITH OF JOHANN SIGISMUND, ELECTOR OF BRANDENBURG

By authority of the most luminous, high-born Prince and Lord, Johann Sigismund, Margrave of Brandenburg, Lord Chamberlain and Prince Elector of the Holy Roman Empire, Duke of Prussia, of Jülich, of Kleve and Berg, of Stettin in Pomerania, of the Kashubians, of the Wends, also of Silesia, and of Crossen and Jägerndorf, Baron of Nürnberg, Prince of Rügen, Count of Mark, Ravensberg and Moers, and Lord of Ravenstein. His Grace, the Elector, in gracious Christian piety recalls what the Holy Spirit recorded through the prophet Isaiah (Isa. 30[32]:8), "Princes will have purposes worthy of a prince and will persevere in them." He graciously ponders that among all the considerations and designs which preoccupy a prince, assuredly the chief and most necessary is that he seriously pursue the role which Almighty God has prescribed for kings, as guardians of His beloved churches, and for princes, as nurses of the churches (Isa. 49:23). In this way, the pure and clear Word of God from the fountain of Israel (Ps. 68:27 [65:9]) will be taught and preached in the churches and schools, freed of any human precepts (Matt. 15:9), and of any leaven of false and erring doctrine (Matt. 16:6; 1 Cor. 5:7), and of any addition or subtraction (Deut. 12:32; Prov. 30:6; Rev. 22:[18]–19). The holy sacraments will be dispensed as they were instituted by the Lord Christ, without any papistical superstition and idolatry, or ceremonies devised by human devotion. Thus the true worship of God will be ordered well and properly, in the mode and after the standard of the divine and Holy Scriptures, and conveyed to a beloved posterity (Isa. 8:10; John 5:39; 1 Cor. 1:6). His Grace, the Elector, is piously attentive to these things, for the God of tender mercy, who alone has authority over the kingdoms of men and gives them to whom He will (Dan. 4:14[17]), has committed so many principalities, territories, and people to His Grace, the Elector, and, as the Scripture says (Isa. 32:18), has paternally preserved them in splendid repose. This He has done in order that, in addition to temporal treasure, they might above all secure and retain the spiritual blessings and treasures. These will be obtained through the preaching of the pure Word of God, and a use of the holy sacrament which genuinely saves, issuing in everlasting blessedness. Therefore, his Grace, the Elector, by the impulse of the Holy Spirit, prefers nothing more than to make it his business in these territories, and especially in the beloved fatherland, the Electorate and Marches of Brandenburg, to remove from the churches and schools at an opportune time what is left over of papistical superstitions and other unsanctioned devotion of human origin, and to do everything, wherever it is possible and needful, in accord with the rule of conduct found in the divine Word and in accord with the apostolic primitive church. In order that no one should indulge evil thoughts or allow himself in hostility and acrimony to imagine that your Grace, the Elector, has arranged something novel or that is not expressly established by the Word of God, and then has resolved to convey things of that nature to his subjects, it is the desire of his Grace, the Elector, that a confession of faith be published under the Elector's auspices. By this it will be known and evident to all Christendom that his Grace, the Elector, has in these lands opened wide the gates to the King of Glory (Ps. 24:7, 9), and that to the Lord alone the glory is given (Pss. 115:1; 29:2). Recognized divine truth will be frankly and resolutely confessed, defended, and widely spread, by the strength and assistance of divine grace, and without timidity or fear in regard to those who have always borne the name of opponents and enemies to Christ. It will be undertaken with a gracious intention, for no other reason than compliance with the earnest command of God, and in accord with the laudable example of the pious kings and princes Jehoshaphat, Hezekiah, Josiah, Constantine, Theodosius, and many more, as well as from a debt of gratitude to God, who Himself is the truth, to the honor of His all-holy name, and for the eternal salvation and blessedness of our subjects (Ps. 2:11; 1 Kings 2:3; 2 Chron. 19:4; 29:5; 34:8; Eusebius, *Life of Constantine*, 4.3; Ambrose, *De obitu Theodosii*).

To begin with, his Grace, the Elector, confesses from the heart the true and infallible Word of God, which alone can save (2 Tim. 3:15–17; Ps. 119), as it is set down in the writings of the holy prophets and apostles in the Holy Bible, and which is and should be a rule of conduct for all pious people (Ps. 119:104). It is complete and sufficient for our salvation, and for discernment in all controversies in religion, and abides forever (Isa. 40:8; Matt. 24:35; Luke 21:33; 1 Peter 1:25). After this, he confesses also the principal Christian and universal creeds, as the Apostolic, the Athanasian, the Nicene, the Ephesian, and the Chalcedonian, in which the articles of the Christian faith are concisely and candidly handled, and sufficiently asserted and proved from Scripture, in refutation of old and new heresies. Then also, he confesses the Augsburg Confession, which the Emperor Charles V granted to the protesting princes and estates in the year 1530, and which subsequently required to be thoroughly examined and revised in several points.

As regards other writings, because they not only are conceived by men and thus can frequently err, but also contain much which is debatable and often what is contrary to or not always in exact accord with the Word of God, his Grace, the Elector, does not wish to distress consciences by binding either himself or his beloved subjects. Indeed all articles of faith must be grounded only and exclusively in the Word of God, and the writings of men should and can be received only insofar as they agree with the Word of God, as Luther himself confessed: "The Scripture alone is the proper teacher and master, superior to all writings and doctrine on the earth" (vol. 1, Jena edition, p. 369). Likewise, "This queen, the Holy Scripture, shall prevail and rule, and all others, regardless of what they are called, shall be submissive and obedient to her. They shall not be her master and judge; rather they are all only poor witnesses, pupils and confessors, whether it be the Pope, Luther, Augustine, Paul, or an angel from heaven. There is to be no other doctrine preached or heard in Christianity except the clear, unalloyed Word of God, else both teacher and hearer will be cursed and condemned" (vol. 1, Wittenberg edition, p. 33).

Touching several articles of Christian faith about which for a long time so much quarrelling and disputation has everywhere been aroused by the instigation of mischief-makers of a hellish spirit, as over the person of the Lord Christ, about baptism, the Lord's Supper, predestination, and election to everlasting life, your Grace, the Elector, hereby openly confesses as follows. With respect to the article concerning the person of Christ, you believe from the heart that in Christ are two distinct natures, the divine and the human, so personally united that not now nor ever afterwards may or can they be divided from one another, and that each nature possesses and retains its fixed and proper qualities even in the personal union. For all that, they have a true communion, so that one can well and properly attribute to Christ everything that may be said to belong to God, and everything that may be said to belong to true manhood. Thus the man Christ is from eternity, namely according to His divine nature (John 1:1; 5:8 [8:58]); the Son of God was born of the seed of David according to the flesh (Rom. 1:3); the Lord of glory was crucified (1 Cor. 2:8); God died in the flesh (1 Peter 3:18; 4:1). Likewise, Christ is with us and remains until the end of the world (Matt. 28:20) according to His infinite nature, supported by His divine majesty and strength, but not with respect to the nature in which He went into heaven (Mark 16:19) and from thence will come again (Acts 1:9; Phil. 3:20), which even in the highest exaltation cannot be everywhere present with respect to its essence, without the destruction of its own character (Augustine, Tractate 109, *On John*), since ubiquity is only attributable to the divine nature (Ps. 139:6–9[7–10]; Jer. 23:24; Acts 17:27). Likewise, it is confessed that He is and abides our Mediator, our High Priest, and our King according to both natures. Likewise, it is confessed that the Lord Christ, according to the human nature He assumed, was adorned and crowned with sublime and supernatural gifts, as referred to in Psalm 8:6[5], but nevertheless the human nature was not changed into deity, nor equalized with it, which was the Eutychian error.

His Grace, the Elector, wills that there be a suspension of the manner of speaking known as *Locutiones abstractivas* (abstract expressions), such as saying that the deity of Christ has suffered, or that the humanity of Christ is almighty or is present everywhere at the same time, and similarly the expression *extensionem, exaequationem et abolitionem naturaram et naturalium proprietatem*, that is, an expansion, equalization, and destruction of the natures and of the proper qualities of a nature. This quite dangerous and provocative use of words will be forced on no one, inasmuch as it cannot be discovered in the Holy Scriptures and is against the principal creeds. To the contrary, it should be noted that neither the orthodox church fathers nor Luther taught thus, and that through these and similar ways of speaking the articles of the Christian creed are largely darkened and rendered equivocal, if not entirely denied, and many eminent people till now are antagonized by them.

Respecting holy baptism as the first sacrament of the new testament, his Grace, the Elector, believes and confesses that it is truly a washing of regeneration and renewal by the Holy Spirit (Titus 3:5), and that no one can enter the kingdom of heaven except they be born again of water and the Spirit (John 3:5). It is not as though the outward washing is able to wash away sins and to regenerate, efficacious as well for unbelievers as for believers, but rather that in the holy sacrament believers are received as the children of God, are cleansed of their sins by the blood of Christ and by the Holy Spirit, and through these visible signs of the covenant of grace their salvation is certified as by an assured seal. Thus the apostle Peter said, "The water saves us in baptism, of which that (the ark of Noah) is a figure; not the putting away of the filth of the flesh, but the covenant of a good conscience toward God" (1 Peter 3:[20]–21). This is, according to Dr. Luther's own gloss in the margin (vol. 9, Wittenberg, p. 290), *stipulatio* (the "condition" of the covenant), meaning that God binds Himself to us by giving grace, and we receive it. Or, as Luther elsewhere says of baptism, it is not an empty sign, or merely a distinguishing mark among Christians, but rather a sign and work of God, in which faith is required of us, and through which we are regenerated. He writes in another place, "If I believe, baptism is of benefit to me" (vol. 2, Wittenberg, p. 461); and again, "if I do not believe, baptism is of no benefit to me," in eternity. Thus Christ spoke of "he who believes and is baptized" (Mark 16:16). This is the Word of God which therefore will endure, and in accord with this Word of God it is the belief of your Grace, the Elector, that holy baptism is of advantage and profit only to believers, who at all times find consolation in their covenant with God, and especially are helped in this way when passing through difficult circumstances. But the unbelieving are little profited by these signs of grace, as was the case for them in regard to circumcision. For this reason, when the children of believing Christians cannot obtain holy baptism on account of a swift and unforeseen approach of death, it is by no means to be believed that they are damned, because the Son of God says, "He that believeth and is baptized shall be saved; but he that believeth not shall be damned" (Mark 16:16). Luther in his *Church Postils* well writes: "It is at all times unanimously held that though a believer dies unbaptized, he will not on that account be damned, because it may sometimes happen that a believer who desires baptism will be suddenly overtaken by death. This extends to little children who die before, during, or soon after birth, but who were already offered and commended to Christ by the faith and prayers of their parents and others, and who doubtless will be received by

Him in accordance with His Word: 'Suffer the little children to come unto me.'" Thus far, Luther.

As regards exorcism, which in the rite of baptism was carried over from the papacy, his Grace, the Elector, holds that because it was neither commanded by Christ nor at any time used by the holy apostles in association with baptism, and is a superstitious ceremony, it detracts from the power and efficacy of holy baptism, and gives rise to vexatious thoughts among the simple on behalf of their children, as if they were physically possessed. But in the early church, when there were still gifts for the performance of miracles and in particular for casting out devils, it had quite a different use and effect. The Lord Christ expressly testified (Matt. 17:21) that the evil spirits were driven out through fasting and prayer, and not by exorcism or a man's admonition. Similarly, the holy apostle Paul (Eph. 6:13) and Peter (1 Peter 5:8), when they equip the Christian soldier with all kinds of weapons against Satan, have not a syllable's reflection about exorcism. For such causes and many more besides, it is now more profitable that it be discontinued, and altogether done away with among the orthodox.

With respect to the holy Lord's Supper, which is the other sacrament of the new testament, his Grace, the Elector, believes and confesses that as there are two things to consider (Irenaeus, *Against Heresies*, 4.24 [5.2]), namely both the outward signs of bread and wine, and also the true body of Christ given for us in death and His holy blood shed on the holy cross, so likewise there are two ways in which we feed upon them. The bread and wine are fed upon with the mouth, and in addition the true body and the true blood of Christ are really fed upon by faith; and therefore on account of the sacramental union both are present together in this holy action, and concurrently distributed and received. Thus, the spiritual manna or heavenly bread of the Word is spiritually eaten, for all things are spiritual in the kingdom of Christ, which is not of this world (John 18:36). His Grace, the Elector, believes that the holy Lord's Supper is a spiritual meal for souls, through which they will be refreshed, comforted and strengthened, and fed and kept unto immortality through union with Christ's body. With strictness, we abide in the holy words of institution, not adding anything to them. In them, it is declared that the bread is the true body of Christ and the wine is His holy blood; yet sacramentally, in the way that God instituted and ordained the holy sacraments in the old and new testaments to be visible and true signs of invisible grace. The Lord Christ Himself indicated that the holy Lord's Supper is a sign of the new covenant, but not a bare or empty one. It is instituted for the remembrance of Christ, or as the apostle Paul explains (1 Cor. 11:26), for a perpetual remembrance and proclamation of His death, so that it should be a consoling remembrance, a grateful remembrance, and a loving remembrance.

Inasmuch as faith is, as it were, the mouth by which the crucified body of the Lord Christ and His shed blood are received, his Grace, the Elector, constantly holds that the unbelieving and impenitent are not profited by such a sacrament. Neither do they partake of the true body and blood of Christ. For the Son of God, when He speaks in John 6:54 of the saving use of the Lord's Supper, roundly declares: "Whoso eateth my flesh, and drinketh my blood, hath eternal life," and previously at verse 47: "Verily, verily, I say unto you, He that believeth on me hath everlasting life," where He gives us to understand that it must be by faith that His holy flesh and blood are savingly fed upon. Luther testifies in his catechism for children that one is properly worthy and well prepared who has faith in this word, "given for you, shed for you," because that word "for you" requires only that we have believing hearts. Likewise, he elsewhere says that although the sacrament is an actual meal, yet he who does not in his heart receive it with faith obtains no benefit, because it constitutes no one a believer, but rather demands that he be already pious and believing.

As for the ceremonies associated with the holy Lord's Supper, it cannot be denied that the author of this sacrament took genuine, unleavened bread, such as was used at that time among the Jews in the Passover feast, and also that the holy apostles took common household bread in their assemblies, and not a special wafer, or host, as one calls it. This practice endured until the time of Alexander I around the year 119; or as others would have it until around the year 601[610], at the time of the murder of the Emperor Phocas. Therefore, it is reasonable to consider whether one ought not to have an eye much more for the original institution than for human alterations, and for God's wisdom more than for man's, and for the truth in the sign more than for the appearance; and whether one ought not to take and use genuine and real wine pressed from the vine, and therefore also genuine and true bread, especially in light of the significance specified by the ancients, and to which the apostle himself pointed in 1 Corinthians 10:17. For just as the genuine bread sustains the human body, and strengthens the heart of man (as is written in Psalm 104), so the body of Christ is a spiritual and heavenly meal by which the soul will be nourished, fed and sustained unto eternal life.

Let anyone with understanding judge for himself whether the wafer and the resemblance of bread would have the power and effect of genuine bread to satisfy and strengthen, and whether in that case the aforementioned significance would hold good. It can by no means be denied that the Lord Christ took bread and broke it; and only after first breaking it did He distribute it, as is not only expressly set down by the three Evangelists (Matt. 26:26; Mark 14:22; Luke 22:19), but is also recapitulated by the holy apostle (1 Cor. 11:23–24), when he testifies that in the third heaven he received from the Lord that He took the bread and broke it, and gave it to His disciples. It is no ταυτολογια (tautology), no reiteration of what had been stated, and much less a περισσολογια (superfluous word) or redundancy, an unnecessary or excessive word ascribed to the holy Evangelists and the holy apostle, and indeed to the Holy Spirit Himself, as if "to break" means nothing more than "to distribute." Indeed, elsewhere it is not to no purpose that it is written: "Break and give."

The breaking of bread in accord with the example of Christ and the apostle remained for many years in customary usage. The entire administration of the Lord's Supper was designated *fractio panis*, a "breaking of bread," by synecdoche or *excellentiam quandam* (a certain distinguishing feature), as can be seen in Acts 2:42. This is not even to speak of the special signification, that just as the bread is broken before the eyes of the communicants, so Christ had to be killed. For the sake of this perpetual depiction, the breaking of bread in the Holy Lord's Supper is to be retained, to which the apostle points when he says, "This is my body, which is broken for you" (1 Cor. 11:24).

Therefore, his Grace, the Elector, is of the opinion that here one ought to look neither to the Pope's inopportune cleverness, nor to long-established custom, nor to human authority, but more to the Lord Christ's unaltered, original institution. The performance of the Lord's Supper is to be ordered only after the mode and manner prescribed in plain words by the Lord Christ Himself and by the holy apostles, appealing to what He spoke. And although his Grace, the Elector, intends to urge no one with force, he would propose that every man piously consider which is better, to follow and yield to Christ or to the Antichrist, to the truth or to erroneous custom, to divine or to human wisdom, to the express mandate of Christ

(*Hoc facite*, "This do") or to the assured freedom of the world. In particular, Luther himself confesses: "There must be no sacrament observed if it diverges from the pattern of Christ's institution and example, and unless the sacramental element is broken and distributed among many by the priest" (vol. 7, Wittenberg ed., p. 297). Similarly, in that very place, he says: "Now compare the two, the antichrists and Christ. The latter, Christ, breaks the bread and gives of it to everyone. The former do not break it, and give of it to no one. They keep it for themselves alone, and have invented an illusion of breaking. What has become of the word of Christ, 'This do'? Why do they act differently, and against Christ?" And: "The words of Paul, 'This is my body, which is given for you,' are simply to be understood of the breaking and distributing at table, as he also says (1 Cor. 10): 'The bread which we break, is the distributed body of Christ'" (vol. 2, Wittenberg ed., folio 231).

With respect to the article concerning eternal predestination or election to eternal life, his Grace, the Elector, confesses and acknowledges this article to be one of the most comforting, and to be the principal foundation on which rests not only all else but even our salvation. Almighty God, of His mere grace and mercy, without any regard to human worthiness, apart from any merit or performance of ours and before the foundation of the world (Eph. 1:4), ordained to eternal life and chose all who steadfastly trust in Christ (Matt. 10:22; 24:13; Rom. 8:29–30). He knows and discerns full well His own (2 Tim. 2:19; John 10:14). As He has loved them from eternity, so also from His mere grace He bestows on them a solid and true faith and a powerful perseverance to the end (John 6:29; Rom. 9:18; 11:7, 29; Phil. 2:13). No one snatches them from the hand of Christ (John 10:28), none of them can be separated from His love, and for them all things, whether good or evil, must serve for the best, for these are called according to His purpose (Rom. 8:26, 38). So also God, in accordance with His strict justice, has from eternity passed over those who do not believe on Christ, and prepared for them everlasting hell fire (Matt. 13:42; 25:48[46]), as is expressly written: "He that believeth not the Son is condemned already. He that believeth not the Son shall not see life, but the wrath of God abideth (and ergo is already and to begin with) on Him" (John 3:18, 36; Isa. 13:9). It is not that God is a cause of man's ruin, nor that He desires the death of the sinner, nor that He is an author or instigator of sin, nor that He does not desire all to be saved, for we find the opposite throughout Holy Scripture (Ezek. 18:31–33[21–23]; 1 Tim.

2:4; 2 Peter 3:9; Matt. 10[?20]). Rather the cause of sin and of destruction is to be sought only in Satan and in the godless, whom God casts away to perdition on account of their unbelief and disobedience.

Likewise, we need not doubt anyone's salvation so long as the means of salvation are being used, for all men remain unaware of the time when God powerfully calls His own, or of who in the future will or will not believe. God is not tied to any time, and accomplishes everything in accord with His own pleasure. His Grace, the Elector, repudiates every opinion or way of speaking, to some extent blasphemous and to some extent dangerous, in which it is supposed that one with his reasoning must climb up to heaven and search a particular list or investigate God's secret chancellery and council chamber, to discover who is or is not chosen to eternal life, when indeed God has sealed the Book of Life, into which He wills that no creature shall peer (2 Tim. 2:19).

Likewise to be condemned is the opinion that God has elected some *propter fidem praevisam*, on account of a faith which he previously observed, which would be Pelagian; or that He grudges the largest number to have salvation, and damns them absolutely, unconditionally and without any cause, namely without regard to their sin, when in fact the just God determines no one to perdition except on account of sin. For this reason, the decree of reprobation to perdition is not to be regarded as an *absolutum decretum*, an unfettered and unencumbered decree, as the apostle testifies concerning the cast-off Jews: "They, the branches, were broken off because of their unbelief" (Rom. 11:20). Likewise to be condemned is the opinion that the elect may live as they wish; and that on the other hand those who are not elect are profited neither by the Word, nor by the sacrament, nor by piety. For it is obvious from the Word of God that a good tree does not bring forth rotten fruit (Matt. 7:18); and also that God chooses us in order that we should be holy, without blame before Him, in love, as is written in Ephesians 1:4. It is also written that as a true branch abides in Christ, the vine, and brings forth much fruit, so he who does not abide in Him is cast forth as a branch, and is withered, and men gather them and cast them into the fire, and they are burned, as Christ the Lord Himself has said (John 15:5–6).

In conclusion, his Grace, the Elector, embraces the Reformed Protestant churches with regard to these and other articles of religion, as those which are founded on the Word of God alone, and as far as possible have abolished all human traditions. Although his Grace, the Elector, is fully assured in heart and conscience that such a confession is sincere and altogether in conformity to God's Word, and would desire and like nothing better than to see God the Lord pleased, out of His mere grace and mercy, to bless and illumine our faithful subjects with the light of unerring truth, yet not all men have faith (2 Thess. 3:2), and faith is the work and gift of God (John 6:29; Phil. 1:29; Eph. 3:8). No man is left to rule over the conscience, or (as the apostle Paul says, 2 Cor. 1:24) would have dominion over your faith, which belongs only to the searcher of hearts. Therefore, his Grace, the Elector, does not wish to compel any of his subjects either publicly or secretly to embrace this confession in opposition to their own will. Instead, he sanctions a course and track only for the truth of God. It is not of him who runs and strives, but of God who shows mercy (Rom. 9:16). It is very much hoped, graciously requested, and gravely commanded, that our subjects and others, who either do not understand the disputed points in religion, or who have not yet been sufficiently informed about them, will refrain from slanders, revilings, and defamations directed against the orthodox and Reformed. Such are those who from unalloyed hatred and enmity for Calvinism make an outcry, as in past ages Tertullian wrote in his *Apologeticus* of what was said about Christians: *Oditur in innocuis innocuum nomen* (In innocent men, even an innocent name is hated). There is to be a patient bearing toward the weak in faith by those who think themselves to be strong, as the apostle Paul warned (Gal. 4[5]:1; Rom. 14:1). And what they do not themselves allow, or have not yet adequately comprehended, they should not quickly accuse and condemn as heresy, but rather diligently search the Scriptures (John 5:39), and commit the verdict to Him who judges righteously (1 Peter 2:23), who will bring to light the things hidden in darkness, and make manifest the counsels of the hearts; and then shall every man receive from God, etc. (1 Cor. 4:5).

(Translation by Christina Munson; revised translation by R. Sherman Isbell)

102

The Irish Articles (1615)

After the Protestant faith entered Ireland, the evangelical ministers formally adopted the Edwardian Book of Common Prayer (1552) in 1560. Although the Thirty-Nine Articles of the Church of England were available to the Irish clergy from 1562/63, they were never formally adopted in Ireland until 1635. In the meantime, a "Brief Declaration" (in twelve articles)—virtually synonymous with Archbishop Matthew Parker's (1504–1575) "XI Articles" of 1559/60—was adopted in 1566.

At the initial convocation of the Irish Episcopal Church (1613–1615), a set of 104 articles specific to Irish Calvinism was presented and adopted. The famous bishop of Armagh, James Ussher (1581–1656), is considered the author of these paragraphs. His Puritan sympathies, well documented in his *Body of Divinity* (1645), are reflected in the decidedly Reformed theology of the articles. Although approved in the name of James I (1566–1625) by the viceroy of Ireland, the articles were destined for the dustbin on the succession of King Charles I (1600–1649) and especially the elevation of William Laud (1573–1645) as archbishop of Canterbury. At the connivance of that other architect of Laudian "Thorough," Sir Thomas Wentworth, the earl of Strafford (1543–1641), and John Bramhall, bishop of Derry (1594–1663), the Irish Convocation of 1635 set them aside for the Thirty-Nine Articles. In fact, Laud and Bramhall had attacked the Irish Articles in the 1634 convocation. While alleged to bring the Church of Ireland into creedal harmony with the Church of England, the net effect was to deemphasize the Calvinism of the 1615 articles. Ussher acknowledged as much when he continued to require subscription to both documents. However, in spite of the good bishop of Armagh, they faded from practice and memory—they were not even acknowledged at the formation of the United Church of England and Ireland in the nineteenth century.

It cannot be doubted that the articles had a formative influence on the Westminster divines and their Standards. Ironically, out of loyalty to the crown and episcopacy, their author declined an invitation to sit at the Westminster Assembly (1643).

Our text is based on that found in Daniel Neal, *The History of the Puritans* (1844), 2:448–54, with slight modernization of expression, spelling, and capitalization; cf. also Müller, 526–39 (albeit slightly abbreviated) and Schaff, 3:526–44.

ARTICLES OF RELIGION AGREED UPON BY THE ARCHBISHOPS AND BISHOPS, AND THE REST OF THE CLERGY OF IRELAND, IN THE CONVOCATION HOLDEN AT DUBLIN, IN THE YEAR OF OUR LORD 1615, FOR THE AVOIDING OF DIVERSITIES OF OPINIONS, AND THE ESTABLISHING OF CONSENT TOUCHING TRUE RELIGION

Of the Holy Scripture and the Three Creeds

1. The ground of our religion, and rule of faith, and all saving truth, is the Word of God, contained in the Holy Scripture.

2. By the name of Holy Scripture we understand all the canonical books of the Old and New Testament, viz.,

Of the Old Testament:

The five books of Moses
Joshua
Judges
Ruth
The first and second of Samuel
The first and second of Kings
The first and second of Chronicles
Ezra
Nehemiah
Esther

Job

Psalms

Proverbs

Ecclesiastes

The Song of Solomon

Isaiah

Jeremiah, his prophecy and Lamentation

Ezekiel

Daniel

The twelve Minor Prophets

Of the New Testament:

The gospels according to Matthew, Mark, Luke, and John

The Acts of the apostles

The epistle of St. Paul to the Romans

The first and second epistle to the Corinthians

Galatians

Ephesians

Philippians

Colossians

The first and second epistle to the Thessalonians

The first and second epistle to Timothy

Titus

Philemon

Hebrews

The epistle of St. James

The two epistles of St. Peter

The three epistles of St. John

St. Jude

The Revelation of St. John

All which we acknowledge to be given by the inspiration of God, and in that regard to be of most certain credit and highest authority.

3. The other books, commonly called apocryphal, did not proceed from such inspiration, and therefore are not of sufficient authority to establish any point of doctrine; but the church reads them as books containing many worthy things for example of life and instruction of manners.

Such are these following:

The third book of Esdras
The fourth book of Esdras
The book of Tobias
The book of Judith
Additions to the book of Esther
The book of Wisdom
The book of Jesus the Son of Sirach, called Ecclesiasticus
Baruch, with the Epistle of Jeremiah
The Song of the Three Children
Susanna
Bel and the Dragon
The Prayer of Manasses
The first book of Maccabees
The second book of Maccabees

4. The Scriptures ought to be translated out of the original tongues into all languages for the common use of all men. Neither is any person to be discouraged from reading the Bible in a language he understands, but seriously exhorted to read the same with great humility and reverence, as a special means to bring him to the true knowledge of God, and of his own duty.

5. Although there are some hard things in the Scriptures (especially such as have proper relation to the times in which they were first uttered, and prophesies of things which were afterwards to be fulfilled), yet all things necessary to be known unto everlasting salvation are clearly delivered therein: and nothing of that kind is spoken under dark mysteries in one place, which is not in other places spoken more familiarly and plainly to the capacity of learned and unlearned.

6. The Holy Scriptures contain all things necessary to salvation, and are able to instruct sufficiently in all points of faith that we are bound to believe, and all duties that we are bound to practice.

7. All and every the articles contained in the Nicene Creed, the Creed of Athanasius, and that which is commonly called the Apostles' Creed, ought firmly to be received and believed, for they may be proved by most certain warrant of Holy Scripture.

Of Faith in the Holy Trinity

8. There is but one living and true God, everlasting, without body, parts, or passions, of infinite power, wisdom, and goodness; the Maker and Preserver of all things, both visible and invisible. And in unity of this Godhead there are three persons of one and the same substance, power, and eternity, the Father, the Son, and the Holy Ghost.

9. The essence of the Father does not beget the essence of the Son; but the person of the Father begetteth the person of the Son, by communicating His whole essence to the person begotten from eternity.

10. The Holy Ghost, proceeding from the Father and the Son, is of one substance, majesty, and glory with the Father and the Son, very and eternal God.

Of God's Eternal Decree, and Predestination

11. God from all eternity did, by His unchangeable counsel, ordain whatsoever in time should come to pass; yet so as thereby no violence is offered to the wills of the reasonable creatures, and neither the liberty nor the contingency of the second cause is taken away, but established rather.

12. By the same eternal counsel God has predestinated some unto life, and reprobated some unto death; of both which there is a certain number, known only to God, which can neither be increased nor diminished.

13. Predestination to life is the everlasting purpose of God, whereby, before the foundations of the world were laid, He has constantly decreed in His secret counsel to deliver from curse and damnation those whom He has chosen in Christ out of mankind, and to bring them by Christ unto everlasting salvation, as vessels made to honor.

14. The cause moving God to predestinate unto life is not the foreseeing of faith, or perseverance, or good works, or of anything which is in the person predestinated, but only the good pleasure of God Himself. For all things being ordained for the manifestation of His glory, and His glory being to appear both in the works of His mercy and of His justice, it seemed good to His heavenly wisdom to choose out a certain number, towards whom He would extend His undeserved mercy, leaving the rest to be spectacles of His justice.

15. Such as are predestinated unto life are called according unto God's purpose (His Spirit working in due season), and through grace they obey the calling; they are justified freely; they are made sons of God by adoption; they are made like the image of His only begotten Son Jesus Christ; they walk religiously in good works, and at length, by God's mercy, they attain to everlasting felicity. But such as are not predestinated to salvation shall finally be condemned for their sins.

16. The godly consideration of predestination, and our election in Christ, is full of sweet, pleasant, and unspeakable comfort to godly persons, and such as feel in themselves the working of the Spirit of Christ, mortifying the works of the flesh, and their earthly members, and drawing up their minds to high and heavenly things, as well because it greatly confirms and establishes their faith of eternal salvation to be enjoyed through Christ, as because it fervently kindles their love towards God; and on the contrary side, for curious and carnal persons lacking the spirit of Christ, to have continually before their eyes the sentence of God's predestination, is very dangerous.

17. We must receive God's promises in such wise as they are generally set forth unto us in Holy Scripture; and in our doings, that will of God is to be followed which we have expressly declared unto us in the Word of God.

Of the Creation and Government of All Things

18. In the beginning of time, when no creature had any being, God by His Word alone, in the space of six days, created all things; and afterwards by His providence continues, propagates, and orders them according to His own will.

19. The principal creatures are angels and men.

20. Of angels, some continued in that holy state wherein they were created, and are by God's grace forever established therein; others fell from the same, and are reserved in chains of darkness unto the judgment of the great day.

21. Man being at the beginning created according to the image of God (which consisted especially in the wisdom of his mind and the true holiness of his free will), had the covenant of the law ingrafted in his heart, whereby God did promise unto him everlasting life, upon condition that he performed entire and perfect obedience unto His commandments,

according to that measure of strength wherewith he was endued in his creation, and threatened death unto him if he did not perform the same.

Of the Fall of Man, Original Sin, and the State of Man before Justification

22. By one man sin entered into the world, and death by sin, and so death went over all men, for as much as all have sinned.

23. Original sin stands not in the imitation of Adam (as the Pelagians dream), but is the fault and corruption of the nature of every person that naturally is engendered and propagated from Adam, whereby it cometh to pass that man is deprived of original righteousness, and by nature is bent unto sin; and, therefore, in every person born into the world, it deserves God's wrath and damnation.

24. This corruption of nature remains even in those that are regenerated, whereby the flesh always lusts against the Spirit, and cannot be made subject to the law of God. And howsoever, for Christ's sake, there is no condemnation to such as are regenerate and do believe, yet the apostle acknowledges that in itself this concupiscence has the nature of sin.

25. The condition of man after the fall of Adam is such that he cannot turn and prepare himself, by his own natural strength and good works, to faith and calling upon God. Wherefore we have no power to do good works, pleasing and acceptable unto God, without the grace of God preventing us, that we may have a good will, and working with us, when we have that good will.

26. Works done before the grace of Christ and the inspiration of His Spirit are not pleasing unto God, for as much as they spring not of faith in Jesus Christ, neither do they make men meet to receive grace (or, as the school authors say, to deserve grace of congruity); yea, rather, for that they are not done in such sort as God has willed and commanded them to be done, we doubt not but they are sinful.

27. All sins are not equal, but some far more heinous than others: yet the very least is of its own nature mortal, and without God's mercy makes the offender liable unto everlasting damnation.

28. God is not the author of sin: however, He does not only permit, but also by His providence governs and orders the same, guiding it in such sort

by His infinite wisdom as it turns to the manifestation of His own glory, and to the good of His elect.

Of Christ, the Mediator of the Second Covenant

29. The Son, which is the Word of the Father, begotten from everlasting of the Father, the true and eternal God, of one substance with the Father, took man's nature in the womb of the blessed virgin, of her substance; so that two whole and perfect natures, that is to say, the Godhead and manhood, were inseparably joined in one person, making one Christ, very God and very man.

30. Christ, in the truth of our nature, was made like unto us in all things, sin only excepted, from which He was clearly void, both in His life and in His nature. He came as a lamb without spot to take away the sins of the world, by the sacrifice of Himself once made, and sin (as St. John says) was not in Him. He fulfilled the law for us perfectly; for our sakes He endured most grievous torments immediately in His soul, and most painful sufferings in His body. He was crucified, and died to reconcile His Father unto us; and to be a sacrifice not only for original guilt, but also for all our actual transgressions. He was buried, and descended into hell, and the third day rose from the dead, and took again His body, with flesh, bones, and all things appertaining to the perfection of man's nature, wherewith He ascended into heaven, and there sits at the right hand of His Father, until He returns to judge all men at the last day.

Of the Communicating of the Grace of Christ

31. They are to be condemned that presume to say that every man shall be saved by the law or sect which he professes, so that he is diligent to frame his life according to that law, and the light of nature; for Holy Scripture sets out unto us only the name of Jesus Christ whereby men must be saved.

32. None can come unto Christ unless it is given unto him, and unless He draws him. And all men are not so drawn by the Father that they may come unto the Son; neither is there such a sufficient measure of grace vouchsafed unto every man, whereby he is enabled to come unto everlasting life.

33. All God's elect are in their time inseparably united unto Christ, by the effectual and vital influence of the Holy Ghost, derived from Him, as from

the head, unto every true member of His mystical body. And being thus made one with Christ, they are truly regenerated, and made partakers of Him and all His benefits.

Of Justification and Faith

34. We are accounted righteous before God only for the merit of our Lord and Savior Jesus Christ, applied by faith, and not for our own works or merits. And this righteousness, which we so receive of God's mercy and Christ's merits, embraced by faith, is taken, accepted, and allowed of God for our perfect and full justification.

35. Although this justification is free unto us, yet it comes not so freely unto us that there is no ransom paid therefore at all. God showed His great mercy in delivering us from our former captivity, without requiring of any ransom to be paid, or amends to be made on our parts, which thing by us had been impossible to be done. And whereas all the world was not able of themselves to pay any part towards their ransom, it pleased our heavenly Father, of His infinite mercy, without any desert of ours, to provide for us the most precious merits of His own Son, whereby our ransom might be fully paid, the law fulfilled, and His justice fully satisfied; so that Christ is now the righteousness of all who truly believe in Him: He for them paid their ransom by His death; He for them fulfilled the law in His life; that now in Him, and by Him, every true Christian man may be called a fulfiller of the law; forasmuch as that which our infirmity was not able to effect, Christ's justice has performed; and thus the justice and mercy of God do embrace each other, the grace of God not shutting out the justice of God in the matter of our justification, but only shutting out the justice of man (that is to say, the justice of our own works) from being any cause of deserving our justification.

36. When we say that we are justified by faith only, we do not mean that the said justifying faith is alone in man without true repentance, hope, charity, and the fear of God (for such a faith is dead, and cannot justify); neither do we mean that this our act to believe in Christ, or this our faith in Christ, which is within us, does of itself justify us, nor cause us to deserve our justification (for that would be to account ourselves justified by the virtue or dignity of something that is within ourselves); but the true understanding and meaning thereof is, that although we have faith,

hope, charity, repentance, and the fear of God within us, and add never so many good works thereunto, yet we must renounce the merit of all our said virtues, of faith, hope, charity, and all our other virtues, and good deeds, which we either have done, shall do, or can do, as things that be far too weak, and imperfect, and insufficient to deserve remission of our sins, and our justification; and therefore we must trust only in God's mercy, and the merits of His most dearly beloved Son, our only Redeemer, Savior, and Justifier, Jesus Christ. Nevertheless, because faith directly sends us to Christ for our justification, and that by faith, given us of God, we embrace the promise of God's mercy and the remission of our sins (which thing none other of our virtues or works properly accomplishes), therefore the Scripture says that faith without works, and the ancient fathers of the church to the same purpose, that only faith justifies us.

37. By justifying faith we understand, not only the common belief of the articles of the Christian religion, and a persuasion of the truth of God's Word in general, but also a particular application of the gracious promises of the gospel to the comfort of our own souls, whereby we lay hold on Christ with all His benefits, having an earnest trust and confidence in God, that He will be merciful unto us for His only Son's sake. So that a true believer may be certain, by the assurance of faith, of the forgiveness of his sins, and of his everlasting salvation by Christ.

38. A true, lively, justifying faith, and the sanctifying Spirit of God, is not extinguished, nor vanishes away in the regenerate, either finally or totally.

Of Sanctification and Good Works

39. All that are justified are likewise sanctified, their faith being always accompanied with true repentance and good works.

40. Repentance is a gift of God, whereby a godly sorrow is wrought in the heart of the faithful for offending God, their merciful Father, by their former transgressions, together with a constant resolution for the time to come to cleave unto God and to lead a new life.

41. Albeit that good works, which are the fruits of faith, and follow after justification, cannot make satisfaction for our sins, and endure the severity of God's judgment; yet are they pleasing to God, and accepted of Him in

Christ, and do spring from a true and lively faith, which by them is to be discerned as a tree by the fruit.

42. The works which God would have His people to walk in are such as He has commanded in His Holy Scripture, and not such works as men have devised out of their own brain, of a blind zeal and devotion, without the warrant of the Word of God.

43. The regenerate cannot fulfill the law of God perfectly in this life, for in many things we offend all; and if we say we have no sin, we deceive ourselves, and the truth is not in us.

44. Not every heinous sin willingly committed after baptism is sin against the Holy Ghost and unpardonable; and, therefore, to such as fall into sin after baptism, place for repentance is not to be denied.

45. Voluntary works besides, over and above God's commandments, which they call works of supererogation, cannot be taught without arrogance and impiety; for by them men do declare that they not only render unto God as much as they are bound to do, but that they do more for His sake than of bounden duty is required.

Of the Service of God

46. Our duty towards God is to believe in Him, to fear Him, and to love Him with all our heart, with all our mind, with all our soul, and with all our strength: to worship Him, and to give Him thanks, to put our whole trust in Him, to call upon Him, to honor His holy name and His Word, and to serve Him truly all the days of our life.

47. In all our necessities we ought to have recourse unto God by prayer, assuring ourselves that whatsoever we ask of the Father in the name of His Son (our only Mediator and Intercessor) Christ Jesus, and according to His will, He will undoubtedly grant it.

48. We ought to prepare our hearts before we pray, and understand the things that we ask when we pray, that both our hearts and voices may together sound in the ears of God's majesty.

49. When Almighty God smites us with affliction, or some great calamity hangs over us, or any other weighty cause so requires, it is our duty to

humble ourselves in fasting, to bewail our sins with a sorrowful heart, and to addict ourselves to earnest prayer, that it might please God to turn his wrath from us, or supply us with such graces as we greatly stand in need of.

50. Fasting is a withholding of meat, drink, and all natural food, with other outward delights, from the body, for the determined time of fasting. As for those abstinences which are appointed by public order of our state for eating of fish, and forbearing of flesh at certain times and days appointed, they are in no way meant to be religious fasts, nor intended for the maintenance of any superstition in the choice of meats, but are grounded merely upon politic considerations, for provision of things tending to the better preservation of the commonwealth.

51. We must not fast with this persuasion of mind, that our fasting can bring us to heaven, or ascribe outward holiness to the work wrought; for God allows not our fast for the work's sake (which of itself is a thing merely indifferent), but chiefly respects the heart, how it is affected therein; it is therefore requisite that first, before all things, we cleanse our hearts from sin, and then direct our fast to such ends as God will allow to be good; that the flesh may thereby be chastened, the spirit may be more fervent in prayer, and that our fasting may be a testimony of our humble submission to God's majesty when we acknowledge our sins unto Him, and are inwardly touched with sorrowfulness of heart, bewailing the same in the affliction of our bodies.

52. All worship devised by man's fantasy, besides or contrary to the Scriptures (as wandering on pilgrimages, setting up of candles, stations, and jubilees, pharisaical sects, and feigned religions, praying upon beads, and such like superstition), has not only no promise of reward in Scripture, but contrariwise, threatenings and maledictions.

53. All manner of expressing God the Father, the Son, and the Holy Ghost in an outward form, is utterly unlawful; as also all other images devised or made by man to the use of religion.

54. All religious worship ought to be given to God alone, from whom all goodness, health, and grace ought to be both asked and looked for, as from the very author and giver of the same, and from none other.

55. The name of God is to be used with all reverence and holy respect, and therefore all vain and rash swearing is utterly to be condemned; yet notwithstanding, upon lawful occasions, an oath may be given and taken, according to the Word of God, justice, judgment, and truth.

56. The first day of the week, which is the Lord's Day, is wholly to be dedicated unto the service of God, and therefore we are bound therein to rest from our common and daily business, and to bestow that leisure upon holy exercises, both public and private.

Of the Civil Magistrate

57. The king's majesty under God has the sovereign and chief power, within his realms and dominions, over all manner of persons, of what estate, either ecclesiastical or civil, whoever they are, so as no other foreign power has or ought to have any superiority over them.

58. We do profess that the supreme government of all estates within the said realms and dominions, in all causes, as well ecclesiastical as temporal, of right appertains to the king's highness. Neither do we give unto him hereby the administration of the Word and sacraments, or the power of the keys, but that prerogative only which we see to have been always given unto all godly princes in Holy Scripture by God Himself; that is, that he should contain all estates and degrees committed to his charge by God, whether ecclesiastical or civil, within their duty, and restrain the stubborn and evildoers with the power of the civil sword.

59. The pope neither of himself, nor by any authority of the Church or See of Rome, nor by any other means with any other, has any power or authority to depose the king, or dispose of any of his kingdoms or dominions, or to authorize any other prince to invade or annoy him or his countries, or to discharge any of his subjects of their allegiance and obedience to his majesty, or to give license or leave to any of them to bear arms, raise tumult, or to offer any violence of hurt to his royal person, state, or government, or to any of his subjects within his majesty's dominions.

60. That princes which be excommunicated or deprived by the pope may be deposed or murdered by their subjects, or any other whatsoever, is impious doctrine.

61. The laws of the realm may punish Christian men with death for heinous and grievous offences.

62. It is lawful for Christian men, at the commandment of the magistrate, to bear arms, and to serve in just wars.

Of Our Duty towards Our Neighbors

63. Our duty towards our neighbors is to love them as ourselves, and to do to all men as we would they should do to us; to honor and obey our superiors, to preserve the safety to men's persons, as also their chastity, goods, and good names; to bear no malice nor hatred in our hearts; to keep our bodies in temperance, soberness, and chastity; to be true and just in all our doings; not to covet other men's goods, but labor truly to get our own living, and to do our duty in that estate of life unto which it pleases God to call us.

64. For the preservation of the chastity of men's persons, wedlock is commanded unto all men that stand in need thereof. Neither is there any prohibition by the Word of God, but that the ministers of the church may enter into the state of matrimony, they being nowhere commanded by God's law either to vow the estate of single life, or to abstain from marriage; therefore it is lawful also for them, as well as for all other Christian men, to marry at their own discretion, as they shall judge the same to serve better to godliness.

65. The riches and goods of Christians are not common, as touching the right, title, and possession of the same, as certain Anabaptists falsely affirm; notwithstanding, every man ought, of such things as he possesses, liberally to give alms to the poor, according to his ability.

66. Faith given is to be kept, even with heretics and infidels.

67. The popish doctrine of equivocation and mental reservation is most ungodly, and tends plainly to the subversion of all human society.

Of the Church and Outward Ministry of the Gospel

68. There is but one catholic church (outside of which there is no salvation), containing the universal company of all the saints that ever were, are, or shall be gathered together in one body, under one head, Christ Jesus; part whereof is already in heaven triumphant, part as yet militant here upon earth. And because this church consists of all those, and those alone, which

are elected by God unto salvation, and regenerated by the power of His Spirit, the number of whom is known only unto God Himself, therefore it is called catholic or universal, and the invisible church.

69. But particular and visible churches (consisting of those who make profession of the faith of Christ, and live under the outward means of salvation) are many in number; wherein, the more or less sincerely, according to Christ's institution, the Word of God is taught, the sacraments are administered, and the authority of the keys is used, the more or less pure are such churches to be accounted.

70. Although in the visible church the evil is ever mingled with the good; and sometimes the evil has chief authority in the ministration of the Word and sacraments, yet, forasmuch as they do not the same in their own name, but in Christ's, and minister by His own commission and authority, we may use their ministry both in hearing the Word and in receiving the sacraments. Neither is the effect of Christ's ordinance taken away by their wickedness, nor the grace of God's gifts diminished from such as by faith do rightly receive the sacraments ministered unto them, which are effectual, because of Christ's institution and promise, although they are ministered by evil men. Nevertheless, it appertains to the discipline of the church that inquiry be made of evil ministers, and that they be accused by those that have knowledge of their offences, and finally, being found guilty by just judgment, be deposed.

71. It is not lawful for any man to take upon him the office of public preaching, or ministering the sacraments in the church, unless he is first lawfully called, and sent to execute the same. And those we ought to judge lawfully called and sent are chosen and called to this work by men who have public authority given them in the church to call and send ministers into the Lord's vineyard.

72. To have public prayer in the church, or to administer the sacraments in a tongue not understood of the people, is a thing plainly repugnant to the Word of God and the custom of the primitive church.

73. That person who, by public denunciation of the church, is rightly cut off from the unity of the church, and excommunicate, ought to be taken of the whole multitude of the faithful as a heathen and publican, until,

by repentance, he is openly reconciled and received into the church by the judgment of such as have authority in that behalf.

74. God has given power to His ministers not simply to forgive sins (which prerogative He has reserved only to Himself), but in His name to declare and pronounce unto such as truly repent, and unfeignedly believe His holy gospel, the absolution and forgiveness of sins. Neither is it God's pleasure that His people should be tied to make a particular confession of all their known sins unto any mortal man; howsoever, any person grieved in his conscience upon any special cause, may well resort unto any godly and learned minister, to receive advice and comfort at his hands.

Of the Authority of the Church, General Councils, and Bishop of Rome

75. It is not lawful for the church to ordain anything that is contrary to God's Word; neither may it so expound one place of Scripture that it is repugnant to another. Wherefore, although the church is a witness, and a keeper of holy writ, yet as it ought not to decree anything against the same, so besides the same ought it not enforce anything to be believed upon necessity of salvation.

76. General councils may not be gathered together without the commandment and will of princes; and when they are gathered together (forasmuch as they are an assembly of men and not always governed with the Spirit and Word of God), they may err, and sometimes have erred, even in things pertaining to the rule of piety; wherefore things ordained by them as necessary to salvation have neither strength nor authority, unless it may be shown that they are taken out of Holy Scriptures.

77. Every particular church has authority to institute, to change, and clean to put away ceremonies and other ecclesiastical rites, as they are found to be superfluous, or abused, and to constitute other, making more to seemliness, to order, or edification.

78. As the churches of Jerusalem, Alexandria, and Antioch have erred, so also the Church of Rome has erred, not only in those things which concern matter of practice and point of ceremonies, but also in matters of faith.

79. The power which the Bishop of Rome now challenges, to be supreme head of the universal Church of Christ, and to be above all emperors, kings, and princes, is a usurped power, contrary to the Scriptures and Word of

God, and contrary to the example of the primitive Church, and therefore is, for most just causes, taken away and abolished within the king's majesty's realms and dominions.

80. The bishop of Rome is so far from being the supreme head of the universal church of Christ, that his works and doctrine do plainly discover him to be that man of sin foretold in the Holy Scriptures, "whom the Lord shall consume with the spirit of His mouth, and abolish with the brightness of His coming."

Of the State of the Old and New Testament

81. In the Old Testament the commandments of the law were more largely, and the promises of Christ more sparingly and darkly, propounded; shadowed with a multitude of types and figures, and so much more generally and obscurely delivered, as the manifesting of them was farther off.

82. The Old Testament is not contrary to the New; for both in the Old and New Testament everlasting life is offered to mankind by Christ, Who is the only Mediator between God and man, being both God and man; wherefore they are not to be heard which feign that the old fathers did look only for transitory promises, for they looked for all benefits of God the Father, through the merits of His Son Jesus Christ, as we now do; only they believed in Christ Who should come, we in Christ already come.

83. The New Testament is full of grace and truth, bringing joyful tidings unto mankind, that whatsoever formerly was promised of Christ is now accomplished; and so instead of the ancient types and ceremonies, exhibit the things themselves, with a large and clear declaration of all the benefits of the gospel. Neither is the ministry thereof restrained any longer to one circumcised nation, but is indifferently propounded unto all people, whether they are Jews or Gentiles: so that there is now no nation which can truly complain that they are shut forth from the communion of saints, and the liberties of the people of God.

84. Although the law given from God by Moses, as touching ceremonies and rites, is abolished, and the civil precepts thereof are not of necessity to be received in any commonwealth, yet notwithstanding, no Christian man whatsoever is freed from the obedience of the commandments which are called moral.

Of the Sacraments of the New Testament

85. The sacraments ordained by Christ are not only badges or tokens of Christian men's profession, but rather certain sure witnesses, and effectual or powerful signs, of grace and God's goodwill towards us, by which He works invisibly in us, and not only quicken, but also strengthen and confirm, our faith in Him.

86. There are two sacraments ordained of Christ our Lord in the gospel, that is to say, baptism and the Lord's Supper.

87. Those five which by the Church of Rome are called sacraments, to wit, confirmation, penance, orders, matrimony, and extreme unction, are not to be accounted sacraments of the gospel, being such as have partly grown from corrupt imitation of the apostles, partly are states of life allowed in the Scriptures, but yet have not like nature of sacraments with baptism and the Lord's Supper, for that they have not any visible sign or ceremony ordained of God, together with a promise of saving grace annexed thereunto.

88. The sacraments were not ordained of Christ to be gazed upon, or to be carried about, but that we should duly use them. And in such only as worthily receive the same, they have a wholesome effect and operation; but they that receive them unworthily, thereby draw judgment upon themselves.

Of Baptism

89. Baptism is not only an outward sign of our profession, and a note of difference, whereby Christians are discerned from such as are no Christians; but much more, a sacrament of our admission into the church, sealing unto us our new birth (and, consequently, our justification, adoption, and sanctification) by the communion which we have with Jesus Christ.

90. The baptism of infants is to be retained in the church, as agreeable to the Word of God.

91. In the administration of baptism, exorcism, oil, salt, spittle, and superstitious hallowing of the water, are for just causes abolished; and without them the sacrament is fully and perfectly administered to all intents and purposes, agreeably to the institution of our Savior Christ.

Of the Lord's Supper

92. The Lord's Supper is not only a sign of the mutual love which Christians ought to bear one towards another, but much more, a sacrament of our preservation in the church, sealing unto us our spiritual nourishment, and continual growth in Christ.

93. The change of the substance of bread and wine into the substance of the body and blood of Christ, commonly called transubstantiation, cannot be proved by holy writ, but is repugnant to plain testimonies of the Scripture, overthrows the nature of a sacrament, and has given occasion to most gross idolatry and manifold superstitions.

94. In the outward part of the Holy Communion, the body and blood of Christ is in a most lively manner represented, being no otherwise present with the visible elements than things signified and sealed are present with the signs and seals; that is to say, symbolically and relatively. But in the inward and spiritual part, the same body and blood is really and substantially presented unto all those who have grace to receive the Son of God, even to all those that believe in His name. And unto such as in this manner do worthily and with faith repair unto the Lord's Table, the body and blood of Christ is not only signified and offered, but also truly exhibited and communicated.

95. The body of Christ is given, taken, and eaten, in the Lord's Supper, only after a heavenly and spiritual manner; and the mean whereby the body of Christ is thus received and eaten is faith.

96. The wicked, and such as want a lively faith, although they do carnally and visibly, as St. Augustine says, press with their teeth the sacrament of the body and blood of Christ, yet in nowise are they made partakers of Christ, but rather to their condemnation do eat and drink the sign or sacrament of so great a thing.

97. Both the parts of the Lord's sacrament, according to Christ's institution and the practice of the ancient church, ought to be ministered unto God's people; and it is plain sacrilege to rob them of the mystical cup, for whom Christ has shed His most precious blood.

98. The sacrament of the Lord's Supper was not by Christ's ordinance reserved, carried about, lifted up, or worshipped.

99. The sacrifice of the mass, wherein the priest is said to offer up Christ for obtaining the remission of pain or guilt for the quick and the dead, is neither agreeable to Christ's ordinance, nor grounded upon doctrine apostolic; but on the contrary, most ungodly and most injurious to that all-sufficient sacrifice of our Savior Christ, offered once forever upon the cross, which is the only propitiation and satisfaction for all our sins.

100. Private mass, that is, the receiving of the Eucharist by the priest alone, without a competent number of communicants, is contrary to the institution of Christ.

Of the State of the Souls of Men after They Are Departed out of This Life, Together with the General Resurrection, and the Last Judgment

101. After this life is ended, the souls of God's children are presently received into heaven, there to enjoy unspeakable comforts; the souls of the wicked are cast into hell, there to endure endless torments.

102. The doctrine of the Church of Rome, concerning *limbus patrum, limbus puerorum,* purgatory, prayer for the dead, pardons, adoration of images and relics, and also invocation of saints, is vainly invented, without all warrant of Holy Scripture, yea, and is contrary to the same.

103. At the end of this world the Lord Jesus shall come in the clouds with the glory of His Father, at which time, by the almighty power of God, the living shall be changed, and the dead shall be raised, and all shall appear both in body and soul before His judgment seat, to receive according to that which they have done in their bodies, whether good or evil.

104. When the last judgment is finished, Christ shall deliver up the kingdom to His Father, and God shall be all in all.

The Decree of the Synod

If any minister, of whatever degree of quality, shall publicly teach any doctrine contrary to these articles agreed upon, if after due admonition, he does not conform himself, and cease to disturb the peace of the church, let him be silenced and deprived of all spiritual promotions he enjoys.

103

Scottish Confession (1616)

James VI (1566–1625), king of Scotland (1567–1603), reintroduced bishops into the Presbyterian Church of Scotland in 1599. He capitalized on the so-called Golden Act of 1592, which had transferred prelatic functions to the presbyteries. These bishops were initially parliamentary commissioners, but, as all power-hungry ecclesiastical tyrants do, they augmented their civil and church power incrementally. In 1610, they succeeded in consecrating Archbishop John Spottiswoode (1565–1639) as archbishop of Glasgow together with his clerical minions. These cronies would hold sway over the Kirk until James's son, the imperious Charles I (1600–1649), would launch the debacle known as the Bishops' Wars (1637), compelling the Scots Covenanters to rebel against prelacy and monarchy.

One beneficiary of James's royal and episcopal favor was Robert Howie (1568–ca. 1646). When he landed the prestigious role of principal at St. Mary's College, St. Andrews, Howie replaced the troublesome Andrew Melville (1545–1622) in 1607. Melville, who had rebuked James with his famous 1596 "two kingdoms" speech, had also had the audacity to criticize episcopacy openly in 1606; for this daring anti-prelacy, James called him to Hampton Court only to lock him in the Tower of London for four years. On the other hand, Howie, obliging his royal benefactor, began to preach and teach episcopal polity from his university office. The Presbytery of St. Andrews was not amused and censored him for his troubles. His subsequent change of heart regarding advocacy of prelacy did not cost him his position as principal, so it must be adjudged a very cautious reconsideration. After all, these were the days in which the members of the Aberdeen Assembly (1605) were arrested and banished by order of the king. And the hated Perth Articles (1618), in which James contrived to impose episcopal worship on the Church of Scotland, were in the offing.

Howie steered his career through all these shoals and is regarded as the primary (if not exclusive) author of the confession below.

Our text is taken from the version in David Calderwood, *The History of the Church of Scotland* (edited by Thomas Thomson, 1845), 7:233–42. We have rewritten the confession to conform to modern canons of spelling and pronunciation, and have added Scripture proofs where appropriate.

THE NEW CONFESSION OF FAITH

We believe with our hearts, and confess with our mouths, these articles of religion following:

That God is a Spirit, immutable, eternal, and infinite, in power, in wisdom, in goodness, in glory; from whom, by whom, to whom, are all things; in whom we live, in whom we have our being; who is one only God: and three persons, who are coessential, coeternal, and coequal. The first is the Father, who is of none: the second is the Son, who from all eternity is begotten of the Father: the third is the Holy Ghost, who from all eternity proceeds from the Father and the Son. This glorious God, from all eternity, out of His wisdom infinite, and knowledge, who knew and decreed all things that were after to be done; this God, before the foundation of the world was laid, according to the good pleasure of His will, for the praise of the glory of His grace, did predestinate and elect in Christ some men and angels unto eternal felicity, and others He did appoint for eternal condemnation, according to the counsel of His most free, most just, and holy will, and that to the praise and glory of His justice.

In the beginning of time, when God created of nothing all things in heaven and in earth, visible and invisible, He made them very good; and above all things, He made men and angels according to His own image, in righteousness and true holiness. But some of the angels, of their own free motive, sinned against God, left their original, forsook their habitation, and abode not in the truth; and thereby became damned devils.

Then Satan abused the crafty serpent for his instrument, seducing our mother Eve: she tempted her husband Adam; so both disobeyed the commandment of God, and thereby made themselves and their whole posterity the bondmen of Satan, slaves of sin, and heirs of eternal condemnation.

By this fall of Adam, all his posterity are so corrupted, from their conception and nativity, that not one of them can do or will anything truly acceptable to God, till they be renewed by the will and Spirit of God, and by faith ingrafted in Jesus Christ.

This our original and native corruption, by regeneration in a part is weakened and mortified; yet it is sin indeed remaining in us always, lusting against the Spirit, and tempting us to sin actually as long as we live.

Albeit all mankind are fallen in Adam, yet only these who are elected before all time are in time redeemed, restored, raised, and quickened again; not of themselves or of their works, least any man should glory, but only of the mercy of God, through faith in Jesus Christ, who of God is made unto us wisdom, and righteousness, sanctification, and redemption; that according as is written, "He that glorieth, let him glory in the Lord" (1 Cor. 1:31; 2 Cor. 10:17).

This then is life eternal, to know the true God, and whom He has sent, Jesus Christ (cf. John 17:3); whereas vengeance shall be taken of them that know not God, and do not subject themselves to the gospel of the Lord Jesus Christ, by the obedience of faith.

We believe that the rule of this knowledge, faith, and obedience, yea, and of the whole worship of God, and of all Christian conversation, is not the wit or will of man, nor unwritten traditions whatsoever; but the wisdom and will of God, which is sufficiently revealed in the canonical Scriptures of the Old and New Testament, which are Genesis, Exodus, etc., excluding the Apocrypha.

We believe that the authority of the Holy Scriptures is divine; for they are all of divine inspiration, and has God for their Author. Their authority depends upon God, and not upon man. They have power over all flesh, and no creature has power over them. We are absolutely bound to believe them for their own testimony, which is the testimony of God Himself speaking in the external testimony of the kirk witnessing of them. All things necessary to salvation are contained therein. All the doctrine of the kirk must be warranted by them. All controversies of the kirk must be decided by them, as the lively and plain voice of God, who is supreme Judge in matters of faith and worship.

We believe that all points of faith and worship are so set down in the Word of God, that what is obscurely propounded in one place is most clearly expounded in other places. Neither receive we any interpretation of any Scripture in these matters which is not warranted by other Scriptures.

These holy writs are delivered by God to His kirk to make us wise to salvation by faith in Jesus Christ, whose person, office, and benefits, they most clearly and fully set forth unto us.

The Lord Jesus Christ is declared in Scripture to be the eternal Son of God, begotten from all eternity of the Father; by whom He created the world, by whom also He does govern and sustain all things that He has made; and this eternal Son of God, when the fullness of time was come, was made man of the woman of the tribe of Judah, and of the seed of David and Abraham; even of the blessed virgin Mary, by the Holy Ghost coming upon her, and the power of the Most High overshadowing her; by whose marvelous and divine operation the Son of God was made man of a human body and soul, and in all things like unto us, sin only excepted. And yet, so He was made man that He ceased not to be God; and so is God that He is also man; having both the natures divine and human united together in a personal union. So that in one admirable person the two natures are distinct and not confounded, in respect of their essence, their essential properties, and proper operations.

And because of the union of the nature of man in one person with the Son of God, Christ, God and man, is to be adored and worshiped of us; for to Christ, God and man, all power in heaven and earth is given; and He hath gotten a name above every name, that at the name of Jesus every knee should bow.

The purity of the human nature of Christ is to be ascribed to the supernatural operation of the Holy Ghost, who separated the seed of the woman from the natural corruption; and not to the purity of the virgin mother; for she doubtless was conceived and borne in sin, and had need of her son to be her Savior as well as other women.

The Lord Jesus Christ, as God and man, is the Savior of His kirk, which is His body; and the fullness of Him fills all things, neither is there salvation in any other thing.

This blessed Lord has fulfilled the whole law for us to our benefit; both doing all that the law requires of us, and suffering the punishment due to our disobedience, even to the curse of the law and death of the cross; where, by the fulfilling of the law, our redemption was sealed and consummated.

We believe that as He died for our sin and rose for our righteousness, so He ascended to heaven to prepare a place for us, and sits at the right hand of God to make intercession for us, and is able perfectly to save them that come to God by Him: who, albeit in His manhood He is so in the heaven that He is no more in the earth, for the heavens must contain Him till He comes to judge the quick and the dead; yet, in His Godhead He is so present everywhere, by His power sustaining all things, and by His gracious Spirit directing and governing His kirk militant on earth.

We believe that the Lord Jesus Christ was appointed and anointed of His Father to be the King, the High Priest, and Supreme Teacher of His kirk.

We believe concerning the prophetic office that He is the only Master and Teacher of His kirk, whom God by His own voice from heaven commanded us to hear: who has revealed the whole will of His Father touching our salvation, and what He has heard of the Father He has made known to us; speaking nothing to His kirk which He did not before hear of His Father, that His kirk might learn to receive nothing in faith and worship which she has not heard of Him.

As concerning His priestly office: We believe that He is our only Mediator, both of redemption and intercession; and that by the sacrifice of Himself once offered on the cross, He has made a full satisfaction for all our sins, and does continually make intercession for us to God. And therefore we abhor that supposed reiterating of the sacrifice of Christ in the mass. And we renounce all kinds of intercession of saints and angels.

As concerning the kingdom of Christ, beside His absolute empire, whereby He rules all things, we believe Him to be our eternal King, and only Head of His kirk universal. Neither He nor His kirk has any need of a lieutenant deputy in His place, seeing He is present in His kirk always by His Spirit, powerfully working therein; calling, collecting, quickening, and graciously ruling her, by the ministry of the Word and sacraments, to the consummation of the world.

We believe that our communion with Christ our Head is spiritual, by that Holy Spirit which dwells powerfully both in the body and in the Head, making the members conform to the Head; and it is no way corporeal, or by any fleshly receiving of His body.

We believe that by virtue of this communion, Christ is ours, and we are Christ's; and His suffering is our satisfaction, and by it we have right, title, and interest to all the benefits which He did promerit, and purchase to us by His sufferings.

We believe that God justifies sinners, by remitting of their sins, and by imputing to them the righteousness and obedience of Christ, whereby

He fulfilled the whole law in our place, both in doing the commandments thereof, and in suffering the curse thereof, which was due to us because of our disobedience.

We believe that that righteousness whereby we are justified before God is not inherent in us, but in Jesus Christ; and that it is freely given to us of God's free grace, through our faith in Jesus Christ.

We believe that we are justified by faith, as it is an instrument apprehending and applying the righteousness of Christ to us; and not as it is a quality, and virtue inherent in us. So that the meritorious cause of our justification is not in the faith which apprehends, but in the righteousness of Christ by faith apprehended.

We believe that albeit we are not justified by good works before God, and can merit nothing at God's hand, yet they are the way to the kingdom of God, and are of necessity to be done for obedience to God, for glorifying of His name, for confirming ourselves anent our election, and for a good example to others; and constantly we affirm, that faith which brings not forth good works is dead, and avails nothing to justification or sanctification.

We believe that the elect being renewed, or sealed with the Holy Spirit of promise in such sort, that albeit they bear about in their flesh the remnants of that original corruption, and albeit they offend through infirmity, and through the enticements thereof, sin grievously, to the great offence of God, yet they cannot altogether fall from grace, but are raised again through the mercy of God, and kept unto salvation.

Concerning the certainty of our salvation, we believe that every one of us in particular ought to be fully persuaded thereof, giving credit both to the external promise of the Word, and internal witness of the Spirit. And as for the doubtings thereof, which we often find in ourselves, we do not allow, but contrariwise damn them, as the fruits of the flesh fighting against our faith.

We believe that God has appointed His Word and sacraments, as instruments of the Holy Ghost, to work and confirm faith in man.

We believe that the Word of God ought to be preached, and the sacraments administered, and all divine service, as praying and praising, in all languages known and understood by the people.

We believe that the sacraments are certain visible seals of God's eternal covenant, ordained by God to represent unto us Christ crucified, and to scale up our spiritual communion with Him.

We believe that the sacraments are to be ministered only by them who are lawfully called thereto by the kirk of God.

We believe that the sacraments have power to confirm faith, and confer grace, not of themselves, or *ex opere operato*, or force of the external action; but only by the powerful operation of the Holy Ghost.

We believe that there are only two sacraments appointed by Christ under the New Testament, baptism and the Lord's Supper.

We believe that baptism is necessary to salvation, if it can be orderly had, and, therefore, that not the want of it, but the contempt of it, doth damn.

We believe that baptism seals up unto us the remission of all our sins, whereof we are guilty, either before or after our baptism.

We believe that baptism is to be ministered simply in the element of water, with the rite of dipping, washing, or sprinkling, in the name of the Father, Son, and Holy Ghost, according to Christ's institution, without other elemental rites devised by man.

We believe that the Lord's Supper is to be given to all communicants under the elements of bread and wine, according to Christ's institution.

We believe that the elements of bread and wine in the Lord's Supper are not transubstantiated, or changed into the substance of the body and blood of Christ; but that they are sacraments of His body and blood, thus changing their use and not their substance.

We believe that the body and blood of Jesus Christ are truly present in the holy Supper; that they are truly exhibited unto us, and that we in very truth do participate of them, albeit only spiritually, and by faith, not carnally or corporally.

We believe that the Lord's Supper is a commemoration of the sacrifice of Christ, which once offered did fully expiate our sins. With His one sacrifice once offered, we are all fully content; neither do we seek any other expiatory or propitiatory sacrifice; but as for sacrifices of praise and thanksgiving, the sacrifice of a contrite heart, alms, and charitable deeds, these we ought daily to offer, as acceptable to God in Jesus Christ.

We believe that the sacrifice and merit of Christ is not applied to us by the work of the sacrificing mass-priest; but that faith, which is wrought in our souls by the Holy Ghost, is the means whereby the sacrifice and merit of Christ is applied to us, and being applied, becomes our satisfaction, atonement, and merit.

We believe that the souls of God's children which depart out of this present life in the faith of Jesus Christ, after the separating from their bodies, immediately pass to heaven, and there rest from their labors until the day of judgment; at which time, they shall be reunited with their bodies, to enjoy life everlasting with Christ. Likewise, the souls of the wicked immediately pass to hell, there to remain until the day of judgment; which day, being conjoined with their bodies, they shall sustain the judgment of everlasting fire. And beside these two, a third place for souls we do not acknowledge.

We believe that there is one holy catholic or universal kirk, which is the holy company of all these who according to the purpose of God's eternal election, since the beginning of the world, were called, and to the end of the world shall be called, to the kingdom of Christ, and to the communion of eternal life in Him.

We believe that the true members of His kirk are only the faithful, who are chosen to life everlasting.

This kirk we believe to be but one, and that out of it there is no remission of sins to salvation.

We believe that this kirk is partly triumphant in heaven, partly militant on earth. The whole militant kirk on earth is divided in many and diverse particular kirks, which are visible and conspicuous to the eyes of men.

We believe not that all these particular kirks on earth are pure; but these only which continue in the doctrine of the prophets and apostles, according to the holy canonical Scripture, ministering the sacraments, and worshipping God purely according to the same; and these be the true marks whereby a true visible kirk on earth may be discerned and known.

As concerning the worship of God, we confess and affirm that all religious worship or service is only to be given to God, as His proper due and glory, which He will communicate to no other; believing firmly that God is to be worshipped only according to His own will, revealed in His word.

And, therefore, we abhor all will-worship, all invocation of saints or angels, all worshiping of images, crucifixes, relics, and all other things which are beside the true God.

We believe and confess that God has ordained kings, princes, and magistrates for the good of the commonwealth, for the better governing in the kirk, and to be nursing fathers of the same. And, therefore, that all their subjects are bound in duty to obey them in all things they command lawfully, not repugnant to the will of God; and that they are obliged to pray for them daily, that under them they may lead a godly and a peaceable life.

We believe, and constantly affirm, that the Kirk of Scotland, through the abundant grace of our God, is one of the most pure kirks under heaven this day, both in respect of truth in doctrine, and purity in worship; and, therefore, with all our hearts we adjoin ourselves thereto, and to the religion publicly professed therein by the King's Majesty, and all his true subjects, and authorized by His Majesty's laws; promising, by the grace of God, to continue therein to the end of our life, according to all the articles which are here set down; which as we believe with our hearts, so we confess with our mouths, and subscribe with our hands, understanding them plainly as they are here conceived, without equivocation or mental reservation whatsoever: So may God help us in the great day of judgment.

Seven Articles of the
Church of Leiden (1617)

"Separating Puritans" formed the English church in Leiden, the Netherlands—they had abandoned the Church of England for independency or congregationalism in the early seventeenth century. Increasingly frustrated by the national church's hesitancy to proceed with a more "thorough Reformation," these Puritans determined to covenant together as independent assemblies (i.e., independent of the established Church of England). But England was too hot for them: King James I (1566–1625) had threatened to "harry them" out of the land or do worse. Thus they crossed the Channel to Holland and availed themselves of the toleration found among the Dutch Calvinists.

Two prominent groups crossed over, one from Gainsborough and the other from Scrooby. The Gainsborough group migrated to Amsterdam in 1606, with John Smyth (ca. 1554–1612) as pastor. The Scrooby group, with officers Richard Clyfton/Clifton (†1616) and John Robinson (ca. 1575–1625), crossed over to Amsterdam in 1607–1608. But Smyth had already rejected infant baptism, rebaptized himself and others (making him a Se-baptist), and embraced the Dutch Mennonites. This induced Robinson to move with his group to Leiden (Clyfton chose to remain in Amsterdam). William Brewster (ca. 1564–1644) was chosen to fill the vacancy left by Clyfton.

In 1617, the Virginia Company of London received an application from the Leiden group to settle on the coast of America. Two deacons, John Carver (ca. 1575–1621) and Robert Cushman (ca. 1580–1625), were delegated to present seven articles of conviction in order to assure King James and the Virginia Company of their good faith and loyalty. But the king and George Abbot (1562–1633), archbishop of Canterbury (1611–1633), rejected the charter application. It would not be until 1620 that the group would finally be approved for sailing to the New World. Boarding the Mayflower in Plymouth, England, in September 1620, a portion of the Leiden congregation entered Massachusetts Bay on November 15, 1620. Eventually they would disembark at what is today Plymouth Rock on December 21, 1620. The drafters of the Leiden Articles therefore prepared the way for the Pilgrim Fathers, Mothers, and Children of New England.

The articles are virtually a-theological, though article one acknowledges the Reformed faith as stated in the Thirty-Nine Articles and in other Reformed churches. Because of the nature of the case, the articles emphasize loyalty to the crown and recognize of the role of the clergy of the Church of England *de facto*.

For a facsimile seventeenth-century version, see Williston Walker, *The Creeds and Platforms of Congregationalism* (1893), 89–90. Our text has been updated for modern spelling.

SEVEN ARTICLES WHICH THE CHURCH OF LEIDEN SENT TO THE COUNCIL OF ENGLAND TO BE CONSIDERED IN RESPECT OF THEIR JUDGMENTS OCCASIONED ABOUT THEIR GOING TO VIRGINIA ANNO 1618

1. To the confession of faith published in the name of the Church of England and to every article thereof we do, with the Reformed churches where we live, and also elsewhere, wholly assent.

2. As we acknowledge the doctrine of faith there taught, so do we the fruits and effects of the same doctrine to the begetting of saving faith in the land (conformists and reformists) as they are called, with whom also, as with our brethren, we do desire to keep spiritual communion in peace, and will practice in our parts all lawful things.

3. The King's Majesty we acknowledge for Supreme Governor in his dominion in all causes and over all persons, and that none may decline or appeal from his authority or judgment in any case whatsoever, but in all things obedience is due unto him, either active, if the thing commanded be not against God's Word, or passive if it be, except pardon can be obtained.

4. We judge it lawful for His Majesty to appoint bishops, civil overseers, or officers in authority under him, in the several provinces, dioceses, congregations, or parishes to oversee the churches and govern them civilly according to the laws of the land, unto whom they are in all things to give an account, and by them to be ordered according to godliness.

5. The authority of the present bishops in the land we do acknowledge so far forth as the same is indeed derived from His Majesty unto them, and as they proceed in his name, whom we will also therein honor in all things and him in them.

6. We believe that no synod, classes, convocation, or assembly of ecclesiastical officers hath any power or authority at all, but as the same by the magistrate is given unto them.

7. Lastly, we desire to give unto all superiors due honor, to preserve the unity of the spirit with all that fear God, to have peace with all men what in us lies, and wherein we err to be instructed by any.

Subscribed by John Robinson and William Brewster.

105

The Canons of Dort (1618–1619)

The national church of Holland was divided by the controversy between the Remonstrants (1610) and the Counter-Remonstrants (1611). After several futile attempts at reconciliation, a national synod was summoned to Dordrecht (Dort) by the estates-general under Maurice of Orange (1567–1625). The theological rupture in the nation was reflected politically in Maurice, a Counter-Remonstrant, and his nemesis, Johan van Oldenbarneveldt (1547–1619), a Remonstrant supporter. Politically and militarily, Maurice and the Counter-Remonstrants had the upper hand.

Fifty-six delegates, five professors, eighteen political advisors, and twenty-six delegates from foreign churches (England, Germany, Switzerland, and others) gathered at Dort in 1618. Johannes Bogerman (1576–1637) was the chairman and author of the early draft of the canons. A committee composed of George Carleton (1559–1628), Abraham Scultetus (1556–1625), John Diodati (1576–1649), Johann Polyander (1568–1646), Antonius Walaeus (1573–1639), and Jacob Trigland (1583–1654) redacted Bogerman's efforts. They decided to present the orthodox propositions (canons) followed by a list of the rejection of errors under that specific head of doctrine.

On April 23, 1619, each member of the synod signed the completed articles. In addition to the canons, the *Acta Synodalia* were offered to the estates-general on May 30, 1619. The so-called five points of Calvinism (T.U.L.I.P.: total depravity, unconditional election, limited atonement, irresistible grace, perseverance of the saints) are traced to these canons, although the document merely summarizes historic biblical orthodoxy on these matters.

Our text is taken from the 1976 *Psalter Hymnal* with the permission of the publisher (pp. 92–116), the Christian Reformed Church of North America, Grand Rapids, Michigan. Schaff provides the canons in Latin and English, 3:550–97. Müller has the Latin version of the canons on pages 843–61.

CANONS OF DORT

FIRST HEAD OF DOCTRINE
DIVINE ELECTION AND REPROBATION

Article 1

As all men have sinned in Adam, lie under the curse, and are deserving of eternal death, God would have done no injustice by leaving them all to perish and delivering them over to condemnation on account of sin, according to the words of the apostle: *That every mouth may be stopped, and all the world may be brought under the judgment of God* (Rom. 3:19). And: *For all have sinned, and fall short of the glory of God* (Rom. 3:23). And: *For the wages of sin is death* (Rom. 6:23).

Article 2

But in this the love of God was manifested, that He *sent his only begotten Son into the world, that whosoever believeth on him should not perish, but have eternal life* (1 John 4:9; John 3:16).

Article 3

And that men may be brought to believe, God mercifully sends the messengers of these most joyful tidings to whom He will and at what time He pleases; by whose ministry men are called to repentance and faith in Christ crucified. *How then shall they call on him in whom they have not believed? And how shall they believe in him whom they have not heard? And how shall they hear without a preacher? And how shall they preach except they be sent?* (Rom. 10:14, 15).

Article 4

The wrath of God abides upon those who believe not this gospel. But such as receive it and embrace Jesus the Savior by a true and living faith are by Him delivered from the wrath of God and from destruction, and have the gift of eternal life conferred upon them.

Article 5

The cause or guilt of this unbelief as well as of all other sins is no wise in God, but in man himself; whereas faith in Jesus Christ and salvation through Him is the free gift of God, as it is written: *By grace have ye been saved through faith; and that not of yourselves, it is the gift of God* (Eph. 2:8). Likewise: *To you it hath been granted in the behalf of Christ, not only to believe on him,* etc. (Phil. 1:29).

Article 6

That some receive the gift of faith from God, and others do not receive it, proceeds from God's eternal decree. *For known unto God are all his works from the beginning of the world* (Acts 15:18, A.V.). *Who worketh all things after the counsel of his will* (Eph. 1:11). According to which decree He graciously softens the hearts of the elect, however obstinate, and inclines them to believe; while He leaves the non-elect in His just judgment to their own wickedness and obduracy. And herein is especially displayed the profound, the merciful, and at the same time the righteous discrimination between men equally involved in ruin; or that decree of election and reprobation, revealed in the Word of God, which, though men of perverse, impure, and unstable minds wrest it to their own destruction, yet to holy and pious souls affords unspeakable consolation.

Article 7

Election is the unchangeable purpose of God, whereby, before the foundation of the world, He has out of mere grace, according to the sovereign good pleasure of His own will, chosen from the whole human race, which had fallen through their own fault from their primitive state of rectitude into sin and destruction, a certain number of persons to redemption in Christ, whom He from eternity appointed the Mediator and Head of the elect and the foundation of salvation. This elect number, though by nature neither better nor more deserving than others, but with them involved in one common misery, God has decreed to give to Christ to be saved by Him, and effectually to call and draw them to His communion by His Word and Spirit; to bestow upon them true faith, justification, and sanctification; and having powerfully preserved them in the fellowship of His Son, finally to glorify them for the demonstration of His mercy, and for the praise of the riches of His glorious grace; as it is written: *Even as he chose us in him before the foundation of the world, that we should be holy and without blemish before him in love: having foreordained us unto adoption as sons through Jesus Christ unto himself, according to the good pleasure of his will, to the praise of the glory of his grace, which he freely bestowed on us in the Beloved* (Eph. 1:4, 5, 6). And elsewhere: *Whom he foreordained, them he also called: and whom he called, them he also justified: and whom he justified, them he also glorified* (Rom. 8:30).

Article 8

There are not various decrees of election, but one and the same decree respecting all those who shall be saved, both under the Old and the New Testament; since the Scripture declares the good pleasure, purpose, and counsel of the divine will to be one, according to which He has chosen us from eternity, both to grace and to glory, to salvation and to the way of salvation, which He has ordained that we should walk therein (Eph. 1:4, 5; 2:10).

Article 9

This election was not founded upon foreseen faith and the obedience of faith, holiness, or any other good quality or disposition in man, as the prerequisite, cause, or condition on which it depended; but men are chosen to faith and to the obedience of faith, holiness, etc. Therefore election is the fountain of every saving good, from which proceed faith, holiness, and the other gifts of salvation, and finally eternal life itself, as its fruits and effects, according to the testimony of the apostle: *He hath chosen us* (not because we were, but) *that we should be holy, and without blemish before him in love* (Eph. 1:4).

Article 10

The good pleasure of God is the sole cause of this gracious election; which does not consist herein that out of all possible qualities and actions of men God has chosen some as a condition of salvation, but that He was pleased out of the common mass of sinners to adopt some certain persons as a peculiar people to Himself, as it is written: *For the children being not yet born, neither having done anything good or bad, etc., it was said unto her* (namely, to Rebekah), *The elder shall serve the younger. Even as it is written, Jacob I loved, but Esau I hated* (Rom. 9:11, 12, 13). *And as many as were ordained to eternal life believed* (Acts 13:48).

Article 11

And as God Himself is most wise, unchangeable, omniscient, and omnipotent, so the election made by Him can neither he interrupted nor changed, recalled, or annulled; neither can the elect be cast away, nor their number diminished.

Article 12

The elect in due time, though in various degrees and in different measures, attain the assurance of this their eternal and unchangeable election, not by inquisitively prying into the secret and deep things of God, but by observing in themselves with a spiritual joy and holy pleasure the infallible fruits of election pointed out in the Word of God—such as, a true faith in Christ, filial fear, a godly sorrow for sin, a hungering and thirsting after righteousness, etc.

Article 13

The sense and certainty of this election afford to the children of God additional matter for daily humiliation before Him, for adoring the depth of His mercies, for cleansing themselves, and rendering grateful returns of ardent love to Him who first manifested so great love towards them. The consideration of this doctrine of election is so far from encouraging remissness in the observance of the divine commands or from sinking men in carnal security, that these, in the just judgment of God, are the usual effects of rash presumption or of idle and wanton trifling with the grace of election, in those who refuse to walk in the ways of the elect.

Article 14

As the doctrine of divine election by the most wise counsel of God was declared by the prophets, by Christ Himself, and by the apostles, and is clearly revealed in the Scriptures both of the Old and the New Testament, so it is still to be published in due time and place in the Church of God, for which it was peculiarly designed, provided it be done with reverence, in the spirit of discretion and piety, for the glory of God's most holy Name, and for enlivening and comforting His people, without vainly attempting to investigate the secret ways of the Most High (Acts 20:27; Rom. 11:33, 34; 12:3; Heb. 6:17, 18).

Article 15

What peculiarly tends to illustrate and recommend to us the eternal and unmerited grace of election is the express testimony of sacred Scripture that not all, but some only, are elected, while others are passed by in the eternal decree; whom God, out of His sovereign, most just, irreprehensible, and unchangeable good pleasure, has decreed to leave in the common misery into which they have wilfully plunged themselves, and not to bestow upon them saving faith and the grace of conversion; but, permitting them in His just judgment to follow their own ways, at last, for the declaration of His justice, to condemn and punish them forever, not only on account of their unbelief, but also for all their other sins. And this is the decree of reprobation, which by no means makes God the Author of sin (the very thought of which is blasphemy), but declares Him to be an awful, irreprehensible, and righteous Judge and Avenger thereof.

Article 16

Those in whom a living faith in Christ, an assured confidence of soul, peace of conscience, an earnest endeavor after filial obedience, a glorying in God through Christ, is not as yet strongly felt, and who nevertheless make use of the means which God has appointed for working these graces in us, ought not to be alarmed at the mention of reprobation, nor to rank themselves among the reprobate, but diligently to persevere in the use of means, and with ardent desires devoutly and humbly to wait for a season of richer grace. Much less cause to be terrified by the doctrine of reprobation have they who, though they seriously desire to be turned to God, to please Him only, and to be delivered from the body of death, cannot yet reach that measure of holiness and faith to which they aspire; since a merciful God has promised that He will not quench the smoking flax, nor break the bruised reed. But this doctrine is justly terrible to those who, regardless of God and of the Savior Jesus Christ, have wholly given themselves up to the cares of the world and the pleasures of the flesh, so long as they are not seriously converted to God.

Article 17

Since we are to judge of the will of God from His Word, which testifies that the children of believers are holy, not by nature, but in virtue of the covenant of grace, in which they together with the parents are comprehended, godly parents ought not to doubt the election and salvation of their children whom it pleases God to call out of this life in their infancy (Gen. 17:7; Acts 2:39; 1 Cor. 7:14).

Article 18

To those who murmur at the free grace of election and the just severity of reprobation we answer with the apostle: *Nay but, O man, who art thou that repliest against God?* (Rom. 9:20), and quote the language of our Savior: *Is it not lawful for me to do what I will with mine own?* (Matt. 20:15). And therefore, with holy adoration of these mysteries, we exclaim in the words of the apostle: *O the depth of the riches both of the wisdom and the knowledge of God! how unsearchable are his judgments, and his ways past tracing out! For who hath known the mind of the Lord, or who hath been his counsellor? or who hath first given to him, and it shall be recompensed unto him again? For of him, and through him, and unto him are all things. To him be glory for ever. Amen.* (Rom. 11:33–36).

REJECTION OF ERRORS

The true doctrine concerning election and reprobation having been explained, the Synod rejects the errors of those:

Paragraph 1

Who teach: That the will of God to save those who would believe and would persevere in faith and in the obedience of faith is the whole and entire decree of election unto salvation, and that nothing else concerning this decree has been revealed in God's Word.

For these deceive the simple and plainly contradict the Scriptures, which declare that God will not only save those who will believe, but that He has also from eternity chosen certain particular persons to whom, above others, He will grant, in time, both faith in Christ and perseverance; as it is written: *I manifested thy name unto the men whom thou gavest me out of the world* (John 17:6). *And as many as were ordained to eternal life believed* (Acts 13:48). And: *Even as he chose us in him before the foundation of the world, that we should be holy and without blemish before him in love* (Eph. 1:4).

Paragraph 2

Who teach: That there are various kinds of election of God unto eternal life: the one general and indefinite, the other particular and definite; and that the latter in turn is either incomplete, revocable, non-decisive, and conditional, or complete, irrevocable, decisive, and absolute. Likewise: That there is one election unto faith and another unto salvation, so that election can be unto justifying faith, without being a decisive election unto salvation.

For this is a fancy of men's minds, invented regardless of the Scriptures, whereby the doctrine of election is corrupted, and this golden chain of our salvation is broken: *And whom he foreordained, them he also called: and whom he called, them he also justified: and whom he justified, them he also glorified* (Rom. 8:30).

Paragraph 3

Who teach: That the good pleasure and purpose of God, of which Scripture makes mention in the doctrine of election, does not consist in this, that God chose certain persons rather than others, but in this, that He chose out of all possible conditions (among which are also the works of the law), or out of the whole order of things, the act of faith which from its very nature is undeserving, as well as its incomplete obedience, as a condition of salvation, and that He would graciously consider this in itself as a complete obedience and count it worthy of the reward of eternal life.

For by this injurious error the pleasure of God and the merits of Christ are made of none effect, and men are drawn away by useless questions from the truth of gracious justification and from the simplicity of Scripture, and this declaration of the apostle is charged as untrue: *Who saved us, and called us with a holy calling, not according to our works, but according to his own purpose and grace, which was given us in Christ Jesus before times eternal* (2 Tim. 1:9).

Paragraph 4

Who teach: That in the election unto faith this condition is beforehand demanded that man should use the light of nature aright, be pious, humble, meek, and fit for eternal life, as if on these things election were in any way dependent.

For this savors of the teaching of Pelagius, and is opposed to the doctrine of the apostle when he writes: *Among whom we also all once lived in the lusts of our flesh, doing the desires of the flesh and of the mind, and were by nature children of wrath, even as the rest; but God, being rich in mercy, for his great love wherewith he loved us, even when we were dead through our trespasses, made us alive together with Christ (by grace have ye been saved), and raised us up with him, and made us to sit with him in the heavenly places, in Christ Jesus; that in the ages to come he might show the exceeding riches of his grace in kindness towards us in Christ Jesus; for by grace have ye been saved through faith; and that not of yourselves, it is the gift of God; not of works, that no man should glory* (Eph. 2:3–9).

Paragraph 5

Who teach: That the incomplete and non-decisive election of particular persons to salvation occurred because of a foreseen faith, conversion, holiness, godliness, which either began or continued for some time; but that the complete and decisive election occurred because of foreseen perseverance unto the end in faith, conversion, holiness, and godliness; and that this is the gracious and evangelical worthiness, for the sake of which he who is chosen is more worthy than he who is not chosen; and that therefore faith, the obedience of faith, holiness, godliness, and perseverance are not fruits of the unchangeable election unto glory, but are conditions which, being required beforehand, were foreseen as being met by those who will be fully elected, and are causes without which the unchangeable election to glory does not occur.

This is repugnant to the entire Scripture, which constantly inculcates this and similar declarations: Election is *not of works, but of him that calleth* (Rom. 9:11). *And as many as were ordained to eternal life believed* (Acts 13:48). *He chose us in him before the foundation of the world, that we should be holy* (Eph. 1:4). *Ye did not choose me, but I chose you* (John 15:16). *But if it is by grace, it is no more of works* (Rom. 11:6). *Herein is love, not that we loved God, but that he loved us, and sent his Son* (1 John 4:10).

Paragraph 6

Who teach: That not every election unto salvation is unchangeable, but that some of the elect, any decree of God notwithstanding, can yet perish and do indeed perish.

By this gross error they make God to be changeable, and destroy the comfort which the godly obtain out of the firmness of their election, and contradict the Holy Scripture, which teaches that *the elect can not be led astray* (Matt. 24:24), that Christ *does not lose those whom the Father gave him* (John 6:39), and that *God also glorified those whom he foreordained, called, and justified* (Rom. 8:30).

Paragraph 7

Who teach: That there is in this life no fruit and no consciousness of the unchangeable election to glory, nor any certainty, except that which depends on a changeable and uncertain condition.

For not only is it absurd to speak of an uncertain certainty, but also contrary to the experience of the saints, who by virtue of the consciousness of their election rejoice with the apostle and praise this favor of God (Eph. 1); who according to Christ's admonition rejoice with his disciples that *their names are written in heaven* (Luke 10:20); who also place the consciousness of their election over against the fiery darts of the devil, asking: *Who shall lay anything to the charge of God's elect?* (Rom. 8:33).

Paragraph 8

Who teach: That God, simply by virtue of His righteous will, did not decide either to leave anyone in the fall of Adam and in the common state of sin and condemnation, or to pass anyone by in the communication of grace which is necessary for faith and conversion.

For this is firmly decreed: *He hath mercy on whom he will, and whom he will he hardeneth* (Rom. 9:18). And also this: *Unto you it is given to know the mysteries of the kingdom of heaven, but to them it is not given* (Matt. 13:11). Likewise: *I thank thee, O Father, Lord of heaven and earth, that thou didst hide these things from the wise and understanding, and didst reveal them unto babes; yea, Father, for so it was well-pleasing in thy sight* (Matt. 11:25, 26).

Paragraph 9

Who teach: That the reason why God sends the gospel to one people rather than to another is not merely and solely the good pleasure of God, but rather the fact that one people is better and worthier than another to which the gospel is not communicated.

For this Moses denies, addressing the people of Israel as follows: *Behold, unto Jehovah thy God belongeth heaven and the heaven of heavens, the earth, with all that is therein. Only Jehovah had a delight in thy fathers to love them, and he chose their seed after them, even you above all peoples, as at this day* (Deut. 10:14, 15). And Christ said: *Woe unto thee, Chorazin! woe unto thee, Bethsaida!*

for if the mighty works had been done in Tyre and Sidon which were done in you, they would have repented long ago in sackcloth and ashes (Matt. 11:21).

SECOND HEAD OF DOCTRINE
THE DEATH OF CHRIST, AND THE
REDEMPTION OF MEN THEREBY

Article 1

God is not only supremely merciful, but also supremely just. And His justice requires (as He has revealed Himself in His Word) that our sins committed against His infinite majesty should be punished, not only with temporal but with eternal punishments, both in body and soul; which we cannot escape, unless satisfaction be made to the justice of God.

Article 2

Since, therefore, we are unable to make that satisfaction in our own persons, or to deliver ourselves from the wrath of God, He has been pleased of His infinite mercy to give His only begotten Son for our Surety, who was made sin, and became a curse for us and in our stead, that He might make satisfaction to divine justice on our behalf.

Article 3

The death of the Son of God is the only and most perfect sacrifice and satisfaction for sin, and is of infinite worth and value, abundantly sufficient to expiate the sins of the whole world.

Article 4

This death is of such infinite value and dignity because the person who submitted to it was not only really man and perfectly holy, but also the only begotten Son of God, of the same eternal and infinite essence with the Father and the Holy Spirit, which qualifications were necessary to constitute Him a Savior for us; and, moreover, because it was attended with a sense of the wrath and curse of God due to us for sin.

Article 5

Moreover, the promise of the gospel is that whosoever believes in Christ crucified shall not perish, but have eternal life. This promise, together with the command to repent and believe, ought to be declared and published to all nations, and to all persons promiscuously and without distinction, to whom God out of His good pleasure sends the gospel.

Article 6

And, whereas many who are called by the gospel do not repent nor believe in Christ, but perish in unbelief, this is not owing to any defect or insufficiency in the sacrifice offered by Christ upon the cross, but is wholly to be imputed to themselves.

Article 7

But as many as truly believe, and are delivered and saved from sin and destruction through the death of Christ, are indebted for this benefit solely to the grace of God given them in Christ from everlasting, and not to any merit of their own.

Article 8

For this was the sovereign counsel and most gracious will and purpose of God the Father that the quickening and saving efficacy of the most precious death of' His Son should extend to all the elect, for bestowing upon them alone the gift of justifying faith, thereby to bring them infallibly to salvation; that is, it was the will of God that Christ by the blood of the cross, whereby He confirmed the new covenant, should effectually redeem out of every people, tribe, nation, and language, all those, and those only, who were from eternity chosen to salvation and given to Him by the Father; that He should confer upon them faith, which, together with all the other saving gifts of the Holy Spirit, He purchased for them by His death; should purge them from all sin, both original and actual, whether committed before or after believing; and having faithfully preserved them even to the end, should at last bring them, free from every spot and blemish, to the enjoyment of glory in His own presence forever.

Article 9

This purpose, proceeding from everlasting love towards the elect, has from the beginning of the world to this day been powerfully accomplished, and will hence-forward still continue to be accomplished, notwithstanding all the ineffectual opposition of the gates of hell; so that the elect in due time may be gathered together into one, and that there never may be wanting a Church composed of believers, the foundation of which is laid in the blood of Christ; which may stedfastly love and faithfully serve Him as its Savior (who, as a bridegroom for his bride, laid down His life for them upon the cross); and which may celebrate His praises here and through all eternity.

REJECTION OF ERRORS

The true doctrine having been explained, the Synod rejects the errors of those:

Paragraph 1

Who teach: That God the Father has ordained His Son to the death of the cross without a certain and definite decree to save any, so that the necessity, profitableness, and worth of what Christ merited by His death might have existed, and might remain in all its parts complete, perfect, and intact, even if the merited redemption had never in fact been applied to any person.

For this doctrine tends to the despising of the wisdom of the Father and of the merits of Jesus Christ, and is contrary to Scripture. For thus says our Savior: *I lay down my life for the sheep, and I know them* (John 10:15, 27). And the prophet Isaiah says concerning the Savior: *When thou shalt make his soul an offering for sin, he shall see his seed, he shall prolong his days, and the pleasure of Jehovah shall prosper in his hand* (Isa. 53:10). Finally, this contradicts the article of faith according to which we believe the catholic Christian Church.

Paragraph 2

Who teach: That it was not the purpose of the death of Christ that He should confirm the new covenant of grace through His blood, but only that He should acquire for the Father the mere right to establish with man such a covenant as He might please, whether of grace or of works.

For this is repugnant to Scripture which teaches that *Christ hath become the surety and mediator of a better, that is, the new covenant,* and that *a testament is of force where there hath been death* (Heb. 7:22; 9:15, 17).

Paragraph 3

Who teach: That Christ by His satisfaction merited neither salvation itself for anyone, nor faith, whereby this satisfaction of Christ unto salvation is effectually appropriated; but that He merited for the Father only the authority or the perfect will to deal again with man, and to prescribe new conditions as He might desire, obedience to which, however, depended on the free will of man, so that it therefore might have come to pass that either none or all should fulfil these conditions.

For these adjudge too contemptuously of the death of Christ, in no wise acknowledge the most important fruit or benefit thereby gained, and bring again out of hell the Pelagian error.

Paragraph 4

Who teach: That the new covenant of grace, which God the Father, through the mediation of the death of Christ, made with man, does not herein consist that we by faith, in as much as it accepts the merits of Christ, are justified before God and saved, but in the fact that God, having revoked the demand of perfect obedience of faith, regards faith itself and the obedience of faith, although imperfect, as the perfect obedience of the law, and does esteem it worthy of the reward of eternal life through grace.

For these contradict the Scriptures: *Being justified freely by his grace through the redemption that is in Christ Jesus; whom God set forth* to be *a propitiation, through faith, in his blood* (Rom. 3:24, 25). And these proclaim, as did the wicked Socinus, a new and strange justification of man before God, against the consensus of the whole Church.

Paragraph 5

Who teach: That all men have been accepted unto the state of reconciliation and unto the grace of the covenant, so that no one is worthy of condemnation on account of original sin, and that no one shall be condemned because of it, but that all are free from the guilt of original sin.

For this opinion is repugnant to Scripture which teaches that we are *by nature children of wrath* (Eph. 2:3).

Paragraph 6

Who use the difference between meriting and appropriating, to the end that they may instil into the minds of the imprudent and inexperienced this teaching that God, as far as He is concerned, has been minded to apply to all equally the benefits gained by the death of Christ; but that, while some obtain the pardon of sin and eternal life, and others do not, this difference depends on their own free will, which joins itself to the grace that is offered without exception, and that it is not dependent on the special gift of mercy, which powerfully works in them, that they rather than others should appropriate unto themselves this grace.

For these, while they feign that they present this distinction in a sound sense, seek to instil into the people the destructive poison of the Pelagian errors.

Paragraph 7

Who teach: That Christ neither could die, nor needed to die, and also did not die, for those whom God loved in the highest degree and elected to eternal life, since these do not need the death of Christ.

For they contradict the apostle, who declares: *Christ loved me, and gave himself up for me* (Gal. 2:20). Likewise: *Who shall lay anything to the charge of God's elect? It is God that justifieth; who is he that condemneth? It is Christ Jesus that died* (Rom. 8:33, 34), namely, for them; and the Savior who says: *I lay down my life for the sheep* (John 10:15). And: *This is my commandment, that ye love one another, even as I have loved you. Greater love hath no man than this, that a man lay down his life for his friends* (John 15:12, 13).

THIRD AND FOURTH HEADS OF DOCTRINE
THE CORRUPTION OF MAN, HIS CONVERSION
TO GOD, AND THE MANNER THEREOF

Article 1

Man was originally formed after the image of God. His understanding was adorned with a true and saving knowledge of his Creator, and of spiritual things; his heart and will were upright, all his affections pure, and the whole man was holy. But, revolting from God by the instigation of the devil and by his own free will, he forfeited these excellent gifts; and in the place thereof became involved in blindness of mind, horrible darkness, vanity, and perverseness of judgment; became wicked, rebellious, and obdurate in heart and will, and impure in his affections.

Article 2

Man after the fall begat children in his own likeness. A corrupt stock produced a corrupt offspring. Hence all the posterity of Adam, Christ only excepted, have derived corruption from their original parent, not by imitation, as the Pelagians of old asserted, but by the propagation of a vicious nature, in consequence of the just judgment of God.

Article 3

Therefore all men are conceived in sin, and are by nature children of wrath, incapable of saving good, prone to evil, dead in sin, and in bondage thereto; and without the regenerating grace of the Holy Spirit, they are neither able nor willing to return to God, to reform the depravity of their nature, or to dispose themselves to reformation.

Article 4

There remain, however, in man since the fall, the glimmerings of natural light, whereby he retains some knowledge of God, of natural things, and of the difference between good and evil, and shows some regard for virtue and for good outward behavior. But so far is this light of nature from being sufficient to bring him to a saving knowledge of God and to true conversion that he is incapable of using it aright even in things natural and civil. Nay further, this light, such as it is, man in various ways renders wholly polluted, and hinders in unrighteousness, by doing which he becomes inexcusable before God.

Article 5

In the same light are we to consider the law of the decalogue, delivered by God to His peculiar people, the Jews, by the hands of Moses. For though it reveals the greatness of sin, and more and more convinces man thereof, yet, as it neither points out a remedy nor imparts strength to extricate him from this misery, but, being weak through the flesh, leaves the transgressor under the curse, man cannot by this law obtain saving grace.

Article 6

What, therefore, neither the light of nature nor the law could do, that God performs by the operation of the Holy Spirit through the word or ministry of reconciliation; which is the glad tidings concerning the Messiah, by means whereof it has pleased God to save such as believe, as well under the Old as under the New Testament.

Article 7

This mystery of His will God revealed to but a small number under the Old Testament; under the New Testament (the distinction between various peoples having been removed) He reveals it to many. The cause of this dispensation is not to be ascribed to the superior worth of one nation above another, nor to their better use of the light of nature, but results wholly from the sovereign good pleasure and unmerited love of God. Hence they to whom so great and so gracious a blessing is communicated, above their desert, or rather notwithstanding their demerits, are bound to acknowledge it with humble and grateful hearts, and with the apostle to adore, but in no wise curiously to pry into, the severity and justice of God's judgments displayed in others to whom this grace is not given.

Article 8

As many as are called by the gospel are unfeignedly called. For God has most earnestly and truly declared in His Word what is acceptable to Him, namely, that those who are called should come unto Him. He also seriously promises rest of soul and eternal life to all who come to Him and believe.

Article 9

It is not the fault of the gospel, nor of Christ offered therein, nor of God, who calls men by the gospel and confers upon them various gifts, that those who are called by the ministry of the Word refuse to come and be converted. The fault lies in themselves; some of whom when called, regardless of their danger, reject the Word of life; others, though they receive it, suffer it not to make a lasting impression on their heart; therefore, their joy, arising only from a temporary faith, soon vanishes, and they fall away; while others choke the seed of the Word by perplexing cares and the pleasures of this world, and produce no fruit. This our Savior teaches in the parable of the sower (Matt. 13).

Article 10

But that others who are called by the gospel obey the call and are converted is not to be ascribed to the proper exercise of free will, whereby one distinguishes himself above others equally furnished with grace sufficient for faith and conversion (as the proud heresy of Pelagius maintains); but it must be wholly ascribed to God, who, as He has chosen His own from eternity in Christ, so He calls them effectually in time, confers upon them faith and repentance, rescues them from the power of darkness, and translates them into the kingdom of His own Son; that they may show forth the praises of Him who has called them out of darkness into His marvelous light, and may glory not in themselves but in the Lord, according to the testimony of the apostles in various places.

Article 11

But when God accomplishes His good pleasure in the elect, or works in them true conversion, He not only causes the gospel to be externally preached to them, and powerfully illuminates their minds by His Holy Spirit, that they may rightly understand and discern the things of the Spirit of God; but by the efficacy of the same regenerating Spirit He pervades the inmost recesses of man; He opens the closed and softens the hardened heart, and circumcises that which was uncircumcised; infuses new qualities into the will, which, though heretofore dead, He quickens; from being evil, disobedient, and refractory, He renders it good, obedient, and pliable; actuates and strengthens it, that like a good tree, it may bring forth the fruits of good actions.

Article 12

And this is that regeneration so highly extolled in Scripture, that renewal, new creation, resurrection from the dead, making alive, which God works in us without our aid. But this is in no wise effected merely by the external preaching of the gospel, by moral suasion, or such a mode of operation that, after God has performed His part, it still remains in the power of man to be regenerated or not, to be converted or to continue unconverted; but it is evidently a supernatural work, most powerful, and at the same time most delightful, astonishing, mysterious, and ineffable; not inferior in efficacy to creation or the resurrection from the dead, as the Scripture inspired by the Author of this work declares; so that all in whose heart God works in this marvelous manner are certainly, infallibly, and effectually regenerated, and do actually believe. Whereupon the will thus renewed is not only actuated and influenced by God, but in consequence of this influence becomes itself active. Wherefore also man himself is rightly said to believe and repent by virtue of that grace received.

Article 13

The manner of this operation cannot be fully comprehended by believers in this life. Nevertheless, they are satisfied to know and experience that by this grace of God they are enabled to believe with the heart and to love their Savior.

Article 14

Faith is therefore to be considered as the gift of God, not on account of its being offered by God to man, to be accepted or rejected at his pleasure, but because it is in reality conferred upon him, breathed and infused into him; nor even because God bestows the power or ability to believe, and then expects that man should by the exercise of his own free will consent to the terms of salvation and actually believe in Christ, but because He who works in man both to will and to work, and indeed all things in all, produces both the will to believe and the act of believing also.

Article 15

God is under no obligation to confer this grace upon any; for how can He be indebted to one who had no previous gifts to bestow as a foundation for such recompense? Nay, how can He be indebted to one who has nothing of his own but sin and falsehood? He, therefore, who becomes the subject of this grace owes eternal gratitude to God, and gives Him thanks forever. Whoever is not made partaker thereof is either altogether regardless of these spiritual gifts and satisfied with his own condition, or is in no apprehension of danger, and vainly boasts the possession of that which he has not. Further, with respect to those who outwardly profess their faith and amend their lives, we are bound, after the example of the apostle, to judge and speak of them in the most favorable manner; for the secret recesses of the heart are unknown to us. And as to others who have not yet been called, it is our duty to pray for them to God, who calls the things that are not as if they were. But we are in no wise to conduct ourselves towards them with haughtiness, as if we had made ourselves to differ.

Article 16

But as man by the fall did not cease to be a creature endowed with understanding and will, nor did sin which pervaded the whole race of mankind deprive him of the human nature, but brought upon him depravity and spiritual death; so also this grace of regeneration does not treat men as senseless stocks and blocks, nor take away their will and its properties, or do violence thereto; but it spiritually quickens, heals, corrects, and at the same time sweetly and powerfully bends it, that where carnal rebellion and resistance formerly prevailed, a ready and sincere spiritual obedience begins to reign; in which the true and spiritual restoration and freedom of our will consist. Wherefore, unless the admirable Author of every good work so deal with us, man can have no hope of being able to rise from his fall by his own free will, by which, in a state of innocence, he plunged himself into ruin.

Article 17

As the almighty operation of God whereby He brings forth and supports this our natural life does not exclude but require the use of means by which God, of His infinite mercy and goodness, has chosen to exert His influence, so also the aforementioned supernatural operation of God by which we are regenerated in no wise excludes or subverts the use of the gospel, which the most wise God has ordained to be the seed of regeneration and food of the soul. Wherefore, as the apostles and the teachers who succeeded them piously instructed the people concerning this grace of God, to His glory and to the abasement of all pride, and in the meantime, however, neglected not to keep them, by the holy admonitions of the gospel, under the influence of the Word, the sacraments, and ecclesiastical discipline; so even now it should be far from those who give or receive instruction in the Church to presume to tempt God by separating what He of His good pleasure has most intimately joined together. For grace is conferred by means of admonitions; and the more readily we perform our duty, the more clearly this favor of God, working in us, usually manifests itself, and the more directly His work is advanced; to whom alone all the glory, both for the means and for their saving fruit and efficacy, is forever due. Amen.

REJECTION OF ERRORS

The true doctrine having been explained, the Synod rejects the errors of those:

Paragraph 1

Who teach: That it cannot properly be said that original sin in itself suffices to condemn the whole human race or to deserve temporal and eternal punishment.

For these contradict the apostle who declares: *Therefore, as through one man sin entered into the world, and death through sin; and so death passed unto all men, for that all sinned* (Rom. 5:12). And: *The judgment came of one unto condemnation* (Rom. 5:16). And: *The wages of sin is death* (Rom. 6:23).

Paragraph 2

Who teach: That the spiritual gifts or the good qualities and virtues, such as goodness, holiness, righteousness, could not belong to the will of man when he was first created, and that these, therefore, cannot have been separated therefrom in the fall.

For such is contrary to the description of the image of God which the apostle gives in Eph. 4:24, where he declares that it consists in righteousness and holiness, which undoubtedly belong to the will.

Paragraph 3

Who teach: That in spiritual death the spiritual gifts are not separate from the will of man, since the will in itself has never been corrupted, but only hindered through the darkness of the understanding and the irregularity of the affections; and that, these hindrances having been removed, the will can then bring into operation its native powers, that is, that the will of itself is able to will and to choose, or not to will and not to choose, all manner of good which may be presented to it.

This is an innovation and an error, and tends to elevate the powers of the free will, contrary to the declaration of the prophet: *The heart is deceitful above all things, and it is exceedingly corrupt* (Jer. 17:9); and of the apostle: *Among whom* (sons of disobedience) *we also all once lived in the lusts of our flesh, doing the desires of the flesh and of the mind* (Eph. 2:3).

Paragraph 4

Who teach: That the unregenerate man is not really nor utterly dead in sin, nor destitute of all powers unto spiritual good, but that he can yet hunger and thirst after righteousness and life, and offer the sacrifice of a contrite and broken spirit, which is pleasing to God.

For these things are contrary to the express testimony of Scripture: *Ye were dead through your trespasses and sins* (Eph. 2:1, 5). And: *Every imagination of the thoughts of his heart was only evil continually* (Gen. 6:5; 8:21). Moreover, to hunger and thirst after deliverance from misery and after life, and to offer unto God the sacrifice of a broken spirit, is peculiar to the regenerate and those that are called blessed (Ps. 51:17; Matt. 5:6).

Paragraph 5

Who teach: That the corrupt and natural man can so well use the common grace (by which they understand the light of nature), or the gifts still left him after the fall, that he can gradually gain by their good use a greater, that is, the evangelical or saving grace, and salvation itself; and that in this way God on His part shows Himself ready to reveal Christ unto all men, since He applies to all sufficiently and efficiently the means necessary to conversion.

For both the experience of all ages and the Scriptures testify that this is untrue. *He showeth his word unto Jacob, his statutes and his ordinances unto Israel. He hath not dealt so with any nation; and as for his ordinances, they have not known them* (Ps. 147:19, 20). *Who in the generations gone by suffered all the nations to walk in their own way* (Acts 14:16). And: *And they* (Paul and his companions) *having been forbidden of the Holy Spirit to speak the word in Asia, when they were come over against Mysia, they assayed to go into Bithynia, and the Spirit of Jesus suffered them not* (Acts 16:6, 7).

Paragraph 6

Who teach: That in the true conversion of man no new qualities, powers, or gifts can be infused by God into the will, and that therefore faith, through which we are first converted and because of which we are called believers, is not a quality or gift infused by God but only an act of man, and that it cannot be said to be a gift, except in respect of the power to attain to this faith.

For thereby they contradict the Holy Scriptures, which declare that God infuses new qualities of faith, of obedience, and of the consciousness of His love into our hearts: *I will put my law in their inward parts, and in their heart I will write it* (Jer. 31:33). And: *I will pour water upon him that is thirsty, and streams upon the dry ground; I will pour my Spirit upon thy seed* (Isa. 44:3). And: *The love of God hath been shed abroad in our hearts through the Holy Spirit which was given unto us* (Rom. 5:5). This is also repugnant to the constant practice of the Church, which prays by the mouth of the prophet thus: *Turn thou me, and I shall be turned* (Jer. 31:18).

Paragraph 7

Who teach: That the grace whereby we are converted to God is only a gentle advising, or (as others explain it) that this is the noblest manner of working in the conversion of man, and that this manner of working, which consists in advising, is most in harmony with man's nature; and that there is no reason why this advising grace alone should not be sufficient to make the natural man spiritual; indeed, that God does not produce the consent of the will except through this manner of advising; and that the power of the divine working, whereby it surpasses the working of Satan, consists in this that God promises eternal, while Satan promises only temporal goods.

But this is altogether Pelagian and contrary to the whole Scripture, which, besides this, teaches yet another and far more powerful and divine manner of the Holy Spirit's working in the conversion of man, as in Ezekiel: *A new heart also will I give you, and a new spirit will I put within you; and I will take away the stony heart out of your flesh, and I will give you a heart of flesh* (Ezek. 36:26).

Paragraph 8

Who teach: That God in the regeneration of man does not use such powers of His omnipotence as potently and infallibly bend man's will to faith and conversion; but that all the works of grace having been accomplished, which God employs to convert man, man may yet so resist God and the Holy Spirit, when God intends man's regeneration and wills to regenerate him, and indeed that man often does so resist that he prevents entirely his regeneration and that it therefore remains in man's power to be regenerated or not.

For this is nothing less than the denial of all the efficiency of God's grace in our conversion, and the subjecting of the working of Almighty God to the will of man, which is contrary to the apostles, who teach that *we believe according to the working of the strength of his might* (Eph. 1:19); and that *God fulfils every desire of goodness and every work of faith with power* (2 Thess. 1:11). And that *his divine power hath granted unto us all things that pertain unto life and godliness* (2 Peter 1:3).

Paragraph 9

Who teach: That grace and free will are partial causes which together work the beginning of conversion, and that grace, in order of working, does not precede the working of the will; that is, that God does not efficiently help the will of man unto conversion until the will of man moves and determines to do this.

For the ancient Church has long ago condemned this doctrine of the Pelagians according to the words of the apostle: *So then it is not of him that willeth, nor of him that runneth, but of God that hath mercy* (Rom. 9:16). Likewise: *For who maketh thee to differ? And what hast thou that thou didst not receive?* (1 Cor. 4:7). And: *For it is God who worketh in you both to will and to work, for his good pleasure* (Phil. 2:13).

FIFTH HEAD OF DOCTRINE
THE PERSEVERANCE OF THE SAINTS

Article 1

Those whom God, according to His purpose, calls to the communion of His Son, our Lord Jesus Christ, and regenerates by the Holy Spirit, He also delivers from the dominion and slavery of sin, though in this life He does not deliver them altogether from the body of sin and from the infirmities of the flesh.

Article 2

Hence spring forth the daily sins of infirmity, and blemishes cleave even to the best works of the saints. These are to them a perpetual reason to humiliate themselves before God and to flee for refuge to Christ crucified; to mortify the flesh more and more by the spirit of prayer and by holy exercises of piety; and to press forward to the goal of perfection, until at length, delivered from this body of death, they shall reign with the Lamb of God in heaven.

Article 3

By reason of these remains of indwelling sin, and also because of the temptations of the world and of Satan, those who are converted could not persevere in that grace if left to their own strength. But God is faithful, who, having conferred grace, mercifully confirms and powerfully preserves them therein, even to the end.

Article 4

Although the weakness of the flesh cannot prevail against the power of God, who confirms and preserves true believers in a state of grace, yet converts are not always so influenced and actuated by the Spirit of God as not in some particular instances sinfully to deviate from the guidance of divine grace, so as to be seduced by and to comply with the lusts of the flesh; they must, therefore, be constant in watching and prayer, that they may not be led into temptation. When these are neglected, they are not only liable to be drawn into great and heinous sins by the flesh, the world, and Satan, but sometimes by the righteous permission of God actually are drawn into these evils. This, the lamentable fall of David, Peter, and other saints described in Holy Scripture, demonstrates.

Article 5

By such enormous sins, however, they very highly offend God, incur a deadly guilt, grieve the Holy Spirit, interrupt the exercise of faith, very grievously wound their consciences, and sometimes for a while lose the sense of God's favor, until, when they change their course by serious repentance, the light of God's fatherly countenance again shines upon them.

Article 6

But God, who is rich in mercy, according to His unchangeable purpose of election, does not wholly withdraw the Holy Spirit from His own people even in their grievous falls; nor suffers them to proceed so far as to lose the grace of adoption and forfeit the state of justification, or to commit the sin unto death or against the Holy Spirit; nor does He permit them to be totally deserted, and to plunge themselves into everlasting destruction.

Article 7

For in the first place, in these falls He preserves in them the incorruptible seed of regeneration from perishing or being totally lost; and again, by His Word and Spirit He certainly and effectually renews them to repentance, to a sincere and godly sorrow for their sins, that they may seek and obtain remission in the blood of the Mediator, may again experience the favor of a reconciled God, through faith adore His mercies, and henceforward more diligently work out their own salvation with fear and trembling.

Article 8

Thus it is not in consequence of their own merits or strength, but of God's free mercy, that they neither totally fall from faith and grace nor continue and perish finally in their backslidings; which, with respect to themselves is not only possible, but would undoubtedly happen; but with respect to God, it is utterly impossible, since His counsel cannot be changed nor His promise fail; neither can the call according to His purpose be revoked, nor the merit, intercession, and preservation of Christ be rendered ineffectual, nor the sealing of the Holy Spirit be frustrated or obliterated.

Article 9

Of this preservation of the elect to salvation and of their perseverance in the faith, true believers themselves may and do obtain assurance according to the measure of their faith, whereby they surely believe that they are and ever will continue true and living members of the Church, and that they have the forgiveness of sins and life eternal.

Article 10

This assurance, however, is not produced by any peculiar revelation contrary to or independent of the Word of God, but springs from faith in God's promises, which He has most abundantly revealed in His Word for our comfort; from the testimony of the Holy Spirit, witnessing with our spirit that we are children and heirs of God (Rom. 8:16); and lastly, from a serious and holy desire to preserve a good conscience and to perform good works. And if the elect of God were deprived of this solid comfort that they shall finally obtain the victory, and of this infallible pledge of eternal glory, they would be of all men the most miserable.

Article 11

The Scripture moreover testifies that believers in this life have to struggle with various carnal doubts, and that under grievous temptations they do not always feel this full assurance of faith and certainty of persevering. But God, who is the Father of all consolation, does not suffer them to be tempted above that they are able, but will with the temptation make also the way of escape, that they may be able to endure it (1 Cor. 10:13), and by the Holy Spirit again inspires them with the comfortable assurance of persevering.

Article 12

This certainty of perseverance, however, is so far from exciting in believers a spirit of pride, or of rendering them carnally secure, that on the contrary it is the real source of humility, filial reverence, true piety, patience in every tribulation, fervent in prayers, constancy in suffering and in confessing the truth, and of solid rejoicing in God; so that the consideration of this benefit should serve as an incentive to the serious and constant practice of gratitude and good works, as appears from the testimonies of Scripture and the examples of the saints.

Article 13

Neither does renewed confidence of persevering produce licentiousness or a disregard of piety in those who are recovered from backsliding; but it renders them much more careful and solicitous to continue in the ways of the Lord, which He has ordained, that they who walk therein may keep the assurance of persevering; lest, on account of their abuse of His fatherly kindness, God should turn away His gracious countenance from them (to behold which is to the godly dearer than life, and the withdrawal of which is more bitter than death) and they in consequence thereof should fall into more grievous torments of conscience.

Article 14

And as it has pleased God, by the preaching of the gospel, to begin this work of grace in us, so He preserves, continues, and perfects it by the hearing and reading of His Word, by meditation thereon, and by the exhortations, threatenings, and promises thereof, and by the use of the sacraments.

Article 15

The carnal mind is unable to comprehend this doctrine of the perseverance of the saints and the certainty thereof, which God has most abundantly revealed in His Word, for the glory of His Name and the consolation of pious souls, and which He impresses upon the hearts of the believers. Satan abhors it, the world ridicules it, the ignorant and hypocritical abuse it, and heretics oppose it. But the bride of Christ has always most tenderly loved and constantly defended it as an inestimable treasure; and God, against whom neither counsel nor strength can prevail, will dispose her so to continue to the end. Now to this one God, Father, Son, and Holy Spirit, be honor and glory forever. Amen.

REJECTION OF ERRORS

The true doctrine having been explained, the Synod rejects the errors of those:

Paragraph 1

Who teach: That the perseverance of the true believers is not a fruit of election, or a gift of God gained by the death of Christ, but a condition of the new covenant, which (as they declare) man before his decisive election and justification must fulfil through his free will.

For the Holy Scripture testifies that this follows out of election, and is given the elect in virtue of the death, the resurrection, and intercession of Christ: *But the election obtained it, and the rest were hardened* (Rom. 11:7). Likewise: *He that spared not his own Son, but delivered him up for us all, how shall he not also with him freely give us all things? Who shall lay anything to the charge of God's elect? It is God that justifieth; who is he that condemneth? It is Christ Jesus that died, yea rather, that was raised from the dead, who is at the right hand of God, who also maketh intercession for us. Who shall separate us from the love of Christ?* (Rom. 8:32–35).

Paragraph 2

Who teach: That God does indeed provide the believer with sufficient powers to persevere, and is ever ready to preserve these in him if he will do his duty; but that, though all things which are necessary to persevere in faith and which God will use to preserve faith are made use of, even then it ever depends on the pleasure of the will whether it will persevere or not.

For this idea contains an outspoken Pelagianism, and while it would make men free, it makes them robbers of God's honor, contrary to the prevailing agreement of the evangelical doctrine, which takes from man all cause of boasting, and ascribes all the praise for this favor to the grace of God alone; and contrary to the apostle, who declares that it is God, *who shall also confirm you unto the end, that ye be unreprovable in the day of our Lord Jesus Christ* (1 Cor. 1:8).

Paragraph 3

Who teach: That the true believers and regenerate not only can fall from justifying faith and likewise from grace and salvation wholly and to the end, but indeed often do fall from this and are lost forever.

For this conception makes powerless the grace, justification, regeneration, and continued preservation by Christ, contrary to the expressed words of the apostle Paul: *That, while we were yet sinners, Christ died for us. Much more then, being now justified by his blood, shall we be saved from the wrath of God through him* (Rom. 5:8, 9). And contrary to the apostle John: *Whosoever is begotten of God doeth no sin, because his seed abideth in him; and he can not sin, because he is begotten of God* (1 John 3:9). And also contrary to the words of Jesus Christ: *I give unto them eternal life; and they shall never perish, and no one shall snatch them out of my hand. My Father, who hath given* them *to me, is greater than all; and no one is able to snatch* them *out of the Father's hand* (John 10:28, 29).

Paragraph 4

Who teach: That true believers and regenerate can sin the sin unto death or against the Holy Spirit.

Since the same apostle John, after having spoken in the fifth chapter of his first epistle, vs. 16 and 17, of those who sin unto death and having forbidden to pray for them, immediately adds to this in vs. 18: *We know that whosoever is begotten of God sinneth not* (meaning a sin of that character), *but he that was begotten of God keepeth himself, and the evil one toucheth him not* (1 John 5:18).

Paragraph 5

Who teach: That without a special revelation we can have no certainty of future perseverance in this life.

For by this doctrine the sure comfort of the true believers is taken away in this life, and the doubts of the papist are again introduced into the Church, while the Holy Scriptures constantly deduce this assurance, not from a special and extraordinary revelation, but from the marks proper to the children of God and from the very constant promises of God. So especially the apostle Paul: *No creature shall be able to separate us from the love of God, which is in Christ Jesus our Lord* (Rom. 8:39). And John declares: *And he that keepeth his commandments abideth in him, and he in him. And hereby we know that he abideth in us, by the Spirit which he gave us* (1 John 3:24).

Paragraph 6

Who teach: That the doctrine of the certainty of perseverance and of salvation from its own character and nature is a cause of indolence and is injurious to godliness, good morals, prayers, and other holy exercises, but that on the contrary it is praiseworthy to doubt.

For these show that they do not know the power of divine grace and the working of the indwelling Holy Spirit. And they contradict the apostle John, who teaches the opposite with express words in his first epistle: *Beloved, now are we children of God, and it is not yet made manifest what we shall be. We know that, if he shall be manifested, we shall be like him; for we shall see him even as he is. And every one that hath this hope set on him purifieth himself, even as he is pure* (1 John 3:2, 3). Furthermore, these are contradicted by the example of the saints, both of the Old and the New Testament, who though they were assured of their perseverance and salvation, were nevertheless constant in prayers and other exercises of godliness.

Paragraph 7

Who teach: That the faith of those who believe for a time does not differ from justifying and saving faith except only in duration.

For Christ Himself, in Matt. 13:20, Luke 8:13, and in other places, evidently notes, besides this duration, a threefold difference between those who believe only for a time and true believers, when He declares that the former receive the seed in stony ground, but the latter in the good ground or heart; that the former are without root, but the latter have a firm root; that the former are without fruit, but that the latter bring forth their fruit in various measure, with constancy and stedfastness.

Paragraph 8

Who teach: That it is not absurd that one having lost his first regeneration is again and even often born anew.

For these deny by this doctrine the incorruptibleness of the seed of God, whereby we are born again; contrary to the testimony of the apostle Peter: *Having been begotten again, not of corruptible seed, but of incorruptible* (1 Peter 1:23).

Paragraph 9

Who teach: That Christ has in no place prayed that believers should infallibly continue in faith.

For they contradict Christ Himself, who says: *I made supplication for thee* (Simon), *that thy faith fail not* (Luke 22:32), and the evangelist John, who declares that Christ has not prayed for the apostles only, but also for those who through their word would believe: *Holy Father, keep them in thy name,* and: *I pray not that thou shouldest take them from the world, but that thou shouldest keep them from the evil one* (John 17:11, 15, 20).

CONCLUSION

And this is the perspicuous, simple, and ingenuous declaration of the orthodox doctrine respecting the five articles which have been controverted in the Belgic Churches; and the rejection of the errors, with which they have for some time been troubled. This doctrine the Synod judges to be drawn from the Word of God, and to be agreeable to the confession of the Reformed Churches. Whence it clearly appears that some, whom such conduct by no means became, have violated all truth, equity, and charity, in wishing to persuade the public:

> That the doctrine of the Reformed Churches concerning predestination, and the points annexed to it, by its own genius and necessary tendency, leads off the minds of men from all piety and religion; that it is an opiate administered by the flesh and the devil; and the stronghold of Satan, where he lies in wait for all, and from which he wounds multitudes, and mortally strikes through many with the darts both of despair and security; that it makes God the author of sin, unjust, tyrannical, hypocritical; that it is nothing more than an interpolated Stoicism, Manicheism, Libertinism, Turcism; that it renders men carnally secure, since

they are persuaded by it that nothing can hinder the salvation of the elect, let them live as they please; and, therefore, that they may safely perpetrate every species of the most atrocious crimes; and that, if the reprobate should even perform truly all the works of the saints, their obedience would not in the least contribute to their salvation; that the same doctrine teaches that God, by a mere arbitrary act of his will, without the least respect or view to any sin, has predestinated the greatest part of the world to eternal damnation, and has created them for this very purpose; that in the same manner in which the election is the fountain and cause of faith and good works, reprobation is the cause of unbelief and impiety; that many children of the faithful are torn, guiltless, from their mothers' breasts, and tyrannically plunged into hell: so that neither baptism nor the prayers of the Church at their baptism can at all profit them;' and many other things of the same kind which the Reformed Churches not only do not acknowledge, but even detest with their whole soul.

Wherefore, this Synod of Dort, in the name of the Lord, conjures as many as piously call upon the name of our Savior Jesus Christ to judge of the faith of the Reformed Churches, not from the calumnies which on every side are heaped upon it, nor from the private expressions of a few among ancient and modern teachers, often dishonestly quoted, or corrupted and wrested to a meaning quite foreign to their intention; but from the public confessions of the Churches themselves, and from this declaration of the orthodox doctrine, confirmed by the unanimous consent of all and each of the members of the whole Synod. Moreover, the Synod warns calumniators themselves to consider the terrible judgment of God which awaits them, for bearing false witness against the confessions of so many Churches; for distressing the consciences of the weak; and for laboring to render suspected the society of the truly faithful.

Finally, this Synod exhorts all their brethren in the gospel of Christ to conduct themselves piously and religiously in handling this doctrine, both in the universities and churches; to direct it, as well in discourse as in writing, to the glory of the Divine name, to holiness of life, and to the consolation of afflicted souls; to regulate, by the Scripture, according to the analogy of faith, not only their sentiments, but also their language, and to abstain from all those phrases which exceed the limits necessary to be observed in ascertaining the genuine sense of the Holy Scriptures, and may furnish insolent sophists with a just pretext for violently assailing, or even vilifying, the doctrine of the Reformed Churches.

May Jesus Christ, the Son of God, who, seated at the Father's right hand, gives gifts to men, sanctify us in the truth; bring to the truth those who err; shut the mouths of the calumniators of sound doctrine, and endue the faithful ministers of his Word with the spirit of wisdom and discretion, that all their discourses may tend to the glory of God, and the edification of those who hear them. Amen.

The Confession of
Cyril Lukaris (1629/1631)

A brief review of the remarkable life of Cyril Lukaris (Cyrillus Lucar/ Lukar, 1572–1638) is essential to understanding his remarkable confession. Lukaris was born in Crete, studied in Vienna and Padua, and became a Greek Orthodox priest (date uncertain; perhaps 1593, but before 1596). He was patriarch of Alexandria from 1602 to 1620, and patriarch of Constantinople from 1620 until his death. Through correspondence with European Protestants, he became familiar with evangelical doctrine. Among his correspondents were: George Abbot (1562–1633), archbishop of Canterbury (1611–1633); Gustavus Adolphus, king of Sweden (1594–1632); and Johannes Uytenbogaert, a Dutch Remonstrant minister (1557–1644). In addition to the letters, Protestant books were dispatched to Cyril in Alexandria—perhaps as early as 1602—from his contacts with a traveling Dutchman named Cornelius van Haga (1578–1654). By 1619, he was concentrating on the vexed question of predestination and free will.

England and Holland were eager to counter French influence in the Levant during Cyril's patriarchate in Constantinople. England commissioned Sir Thomas Roe (1580/81–1644) ambassador to the court of Sultan Murad IV (ca. 1612–1640) from 1621 to 1628. The Dutch ambassador to Constantinople from 1612 to 1639 was the previously mentioned Cornelius van Haga. Both of these diplomats acted to protect Cyril from intrigues advanced by the French and their Jesuit allies. Nonetheless, the patriarch was exiled from Constantinople on several occasions, notably 1622–1623, 1634, and 1635–1636.

However, it was the arrival of Antoine Leger (1594–1661) in the fall of 1628 that completed Lukaris's odyssey to Calvinism. Leger had been pastor of the Church of St. Martin's in the valleys of the Piedmont (Italian Alps). In 1628, the Venerable Company of Pastors in Geneva suggested that he go to Constantinople as chaplain to the Dutch embassy. Soon after his arrival, Leger became an intimate friend of Cyril and was welcomed as a theological kindred spirit.

But Cyril's enemies, assisted by the intrigues of the Jesuits and the French ambassador, accused him of treason against Murad IV. Specifically, Cyril was alleged to have encouraged the Cossacks in the sack of Asak (Asov) in 1638. Cyril was seized and taken by boat across the Bosporus to a place near St. Stephanos where he was strangled by rope on June 27, 1638. His body was buried near the shore, but later disinterred and dumped into the sea. When it later washed up on shore, it was buried by some fisherman on the small island of St. Andrew near Constantinople.

Cyril was one of the greatest benefactors of the textual criticism of the Bible. In 1628, he sent *Codex Alexandrinus* to King Charles I (1600–1649) and the British Museum.

Cyril's views as expressed in his confession were roundly anathematized by the Orthodox Church at the Synod of Constantinople (1638 and 1642), Jassy (Moldavia/Rumania, 1640), and the Council of Jerusalem and Bethlehem presided over by Dositheus (1641–1707) in 1672.

Our text is based upon the version found in *The Acts and Decrees of the Synod of Jerusalem*, edited by J. N. W. B. Robertson (1899), 185–207. Where possible, we have cited the proof texts in accordance with the numbering of the New American Standard Bible. Obvious corrections are in italics.

THE EASTERN CONFESSION OF THE CHRISTIAN FAITH.

In the name of the Father, and of the Son, and of the Holy Spirit.

Cyril, Patriarch of Constantinople, to those that ask and inquire concerning the faith and worship of the Church of the Greeks, that is, of the Eastern Church, how it thinks concerning the Orthodox faith, in the common name of all Christians publishes this concise Confession for a testimony both before God and before man, with a sincere conscience, and devoid of all dissimulation.

Chapter I

We believe in one God, true, almighty, and infinite, tri-personal, the Father, the Son, and the Holy Spirit: the Father unbegotten; the Son begotten of the Father before the ages, and consubstantial with Him; and the Holy Spirit proceeding from the Father through the Son, and consubstantial with the Father and the Son. These three persons in one essence we call the All-holy Trinity—by all creation to be ever blessed, glorified, and adored.

(Deut. 4:35; 6:4; 1 Cor. 8:4, 6; Matt. 19:26; Jer. 23:24; Rom. 11:33; Gen. 1:26; 3:12; Matt. 28:19; Eph. 4:4–6; Gal. 4:6; Isa. 40:4, 6; 46:9; Luke 1:37; Rev. 1:20; 1 Kings 8:27; 1 Tim. 1:17; 1 John 5:7; 1 Cor. 12:4; John 15:26; 2 Cor. 13:13.)

Chapter II

We believe the Sacred Scriptures to be God-taught; whose author is the Holy Spirit, and none other. Which we ought to believe without doubting; for it is written: "We have [as] more sure the prophetical word, whereunto ye do well to take heed, as unto a lamp shining in a darksome place." And so the witness of the Sacred Scriptures is of higher authority than that of the Church. For it is not the same for us to be taught by the All-holy Spirit, and [to be taught] by man; for man by reason of his ignorance, is liable to err, and to deceive, and to be deceived, but the Sacred Scriptures, neither deceive, nor are deceived, nor are subject to error; but are infallible and have perpetual authority.

(2 Tim. 3:16; John 16:13; Acts 15:28; 1 Thess. 2:13; 1 Cor. 3:10; John 3:31; Ps. 116; Acts 5:29; Matt. 15:9; Gal. 1:8; Ps. 12:6; Ps. 119:86, 104, 142; Rom. 1:17; 15:4; Matt. 5:18; 24:35; 2 Peter 1:8; Matt. 10:20; Gal. 1:11; Eph. 2:20; Jer. 23:28; Ps. 61:8; Rom. 3:4; Col. 2:8; Ezek. 20:18; Prov. 30:5; Ps. 19:8; Heb. 4:12; John 20:31; 10:35; Isa. 40:7; 1 Peter 1:23–25.)

Chapter III

We believe the most good God to have, before the foundation of the world, predestinated unto glory those whom He has chosen, without having in any wise regard to their works, and having no actuating cause for this election, except His good pleasure, the divine mercy. In like manner to have, before the world was, rejected those whom He has rejected; and of this rejection, if any one will look to the absolute power and authority of God, he will find the undoubted cause to be the divine will; and, if again any one will turn to the laws and rules of good order which the providence above uses in the governing of the world, he will perceive the cause to be His righteousness. For God is merciful and withal righteous.

(Eph. 1:4; Rom. 9:11–12; 3:9; 5:12; Eph. 2:3; John 17:6, 9; Acts 13:48; Titus 1:1; Matt. 13:10; John 6:37, 44; 12:37; 2 Tim. 2:19; Matt. 15:13; Rev. 13:20; Rom. 9:13, 18; Ps. 147:20; 2 Tim. 1:9; 1 Cor. 4:7; Titus 3:3; Rom. 8:28–29; 2 Thess. 3:2; Luke 10:21; Mark 4:11; Rom. 11:7; John 1:27; 1 John 2:19; Matt. 20:16; Deut. 10:14; 7:6; Acts 14:6; Rom. 11:33–36.)

Chapter IV

We believe the tri-personal God, the Father, the Son, and the Holy Spirit, to be the Maker of visible and invisible creatures. And by invisible we mean the angelic powers, but by visible, heaven and what is under heaven. And because the Maker is good by nature, He made all things good whatsoever He has made; nor can He ever be the Maker of evil. But if there is any evil in nature, it is either of the devil or of man. For it is a true and infallible rule that God is in no wise the author of evil, nor can any such by just reasoning be attributed to God.

(Gen. 1:1; Col. 1:16; Acts 17:24; Eccl. 7:30; James 1:13; Deut. 32:4; John 1:1; Ps. 33:6; Gen. 1:27; Ps. 8:4; John 8:44; 1 John 2:16.)

Chapter V

We believe all things to be governed by the providence of God, which we ought to adore, but not to curiously pry into, as being above our comprehension; nor are we able of ourselves to accurately attain unto the comprehension of the reasons thereof. Wherefore, concerning this matter, we feel we ought rather in humility to observe silence than to indulge unedifyingly in vain discourse.

(Ps. 115:3; Heb. 1:3; Ex. 7:3; 1 Chron. 21:1; John 1:12, 21; 19:11; Rom. 1:24; 11:33; Eph. 1:9; Matt. 1:29; 2 Sam. 12:11; 24:1; 1 Kings 3:22–23; Isa. 10:5; Acts 2:23; 4:27; Jer. 32:19; Deut. 29:29.)

Chapter VI

We believe the first man created by God to have fallen in Paradise, when, disregarding the divine commandment, he yielded to the deceitful counsel of the serpent. And hence hereditary sin flowed to his posterity; so that none is born after the flesh, who bears not this burden, and experiences not the fruits thereof in this present world.

(Eccl. 7:30; Ps. 51:5; John 3:6; Gen. 8:21; Gal. 3:22; John 3:3; Rom. 3:12; 1 John 1:8; Prov. 20:9; Rom. 5:12, 15, 19; Job 14:4; 5:14; Eph. 2:3; Rom. 8:7; 3:9, 26; Eccl. 7:21; 1 Kings 8:46; James 3:2; Rom. 7:7; 6:23.)

Chapter VII

We believe the Son of God, our Lord Jesus Christ, to have emptied Himself, that is, to have taken into His own person human flesh, being conceived of the Holy Spirit in the womb of the ever-virgin Mary; and becoming man, to have been born, to have suffered, to have been buried, and to have risen again in glory, and so to have procured for all believers salvation and glory. Whom also we look for to come to judge the living and the dead.

(Phil. 2:6; Luke 1:35; Rom. 1:3; Heb. 2:14; Rom. 4:25; Matt. 1:22; Gal. 4:4; John 1:14; 1 Cor. 15:3; 1 Tim. 3:16; 2 Tim. 4:1.)

Chapter VIII

We believe our Lord Jesus Christ, seated at the right hand of the Father, to be a mediator there, and to intercede for us, alone exercising the office of a true and genuine high priest and mediator; wherefore also He alone is solicitous for His own, and presides over the Church, adorning her with all variety of blessings, and ever enriching her.

(1 John 2:1; 1 Tim. 3:5; Matt. 11:28; 18:19; Acts 4:12; Eph. 2:18; 3:12; Rom. 8:34; John 14:6; 10:9; John 16:23; 14:13; Rom. 5:1, 5, 9; Heb. 4:15; 5:4; 12:22; 7:24; 10:12, 18.)

Chapter IX

We believe no one to be saved without faith. And that we call faith which justifies in Christ Jesus, which the life and death of our Lord Jesus Christ has procured for us, and the Gospel proclaims, and without which it is impossible to please God.

(Heb. 11:6; 11:1; John 5:24; 20:31; Gal. 5:6; Eph. 2:8; Rom. 5:2; 8:16; Heb. 10:22; James 1:6; Rom. 14:23; 10:17; Luke 8:11; James 2:14, 17, 22; Phil. 1:29; Eph. 3:12; 1:13; 1 John 4:13; 3:19; Rom. 14:5; John 3:18.)

Chapter X

We believe that what is called the Catholic Church contains generally the faithful in Christ, whether fallen asleep and in their home in the Fatherland, or yet pilgrims on their journey; of which Church, since a mortal man can in no wise be head, our Lord Jesus Christ is Himself sole head, and Himself holding the rudder, is at the helm in the governing of the Church: yet, nevertheless, because the particular Churches sojourning here are visible, and for order each have their President, he is not properly called the head of that particular church, but by abuse, because he is the leading member therein.

(Gal. 4:26; Eph. 2:14; 1:10; 4:4; Gal. 3:26; Acts 4:32; 2:42; Matt. 18:20; 28:20; Eph. 4:5; Heb. 5:4; Eph. 5:23; Col. 1:18; Matt. 16:18; Ps. 118:20; 1 Cor. 3:11; Matt. 23:8; 1 Tim. 3:1; 1 Cor. 14:32; Heb. 13:17; 2 Cor. 5:20; 12:11; Heb. 12:23; Col. 3:11; 1 Cor. 12:12; Heb. 10:24; John 10:24; James 4:12; John 3:27; 1 Cor. 11:3; Eph. 1:22; 4:15; 2:19; 1 Peter 2:6; Acts 4:11–12; Matt. 20:25; Luke 22:25; 1 Peter 5:2; 2 Cor. 1:24; 1 Cor. 4:1; Gal. 2:16.)

Chapter XI

We believe that the members of the Catholic Church are the saints that are elected unto eternal life; from whose lot and fellowship hypocrites are excluded; though we perceive and see that in particular churches the chaff is mingled with the wheat.

(Rom. 8:29; 9:23; Acts 2:39; 13:48; Matt. 7:21; Rom. 2:18; Rev. 21:27; Gal. 4:26; Rom. 9:19; John 5:35–36; 12:32; Matt. 20:16; 13:24, 47; Luke 13:26; Isa. 4:7; Heb. 12:22; John 17:6, 10, 28; 1 John 2:19; 2 Tim. 2:19.)

Chapter XII

We believe that during its sojourn here the Church is hallowed and taught by the All-holy Spirit. For He is the true Paraclete whom Christ sends from the Father to teach the truth, and to drive away darkness from the minds of the faithful. For it is true and certain, that the Church while on its way is liable to err, and, instead of truth, to choose falsehood. From which error and deception the teaching and light of the All-holy Spirit alone delivers us, not that of a mortal man; though this may be wrought through the instrumentality of such as faithfully minister in the Church.

(1 Cor. 3:16; 6:11; John 17:17; 6:45; Jer. 31:32; Eph. 1:13; Joel 2; 1 Cor. 2:10; Rom. 8:9; Eph. 4:4; Judg. 2:12; 2 Chron. 29:6; Dan. 9:11; Jer. 18:18; Jer. 23:11; 2:8; 1 Tim. 4:3; 1 John 2:18; Rom. 11:22; Rev. 2:2; Acts 5:29; Hos. 2:2; 1 Thess. 5:19; Matt. 22:29; Gal. 1:8; 2 Thess. 2:13; Isa. 54:13; Ezek. 11:19; John 14:16; 16:13; Acts 2:16; 10:44; 13:2; 15:28; 1 John 2:27; 1 Cor. 12:7; 2 Chron. 15:3; 1 Kings 19:10; Jer. 11:10; Isa. 1:21; Ezek. 7:26; 1 Tim. 4:1; Acts 20:30; 2 Thess. 2:3; 1 John 4:1; Rom. 3:4; Ezek. 2:18; Matt. 7:5; Acts 17:11; John 5:39; 2 John 9; John 8:31.)

Chapter XIII

We believe that man is justified by faith, not by works. But when we say by faith, we mean the correlative of faith, which is the righteousness of Christ; on which faith, as it were, fulfilling the function of a hand, lays hold, and applies the same unto us for salvation; which we declare to be for the sustaining, and not for the detriment, of works. And that works are not to be neglected, since they are necessary means for a witness to faith, and for certification of our calling, the truth itself teaches us. But withal they are of themselves in no wise sufficient to give boldness at the tribunal of Christ, and to claim a recompense as by merit of condignity, and to save the possessor; and that this is so human frailty testifies. But the righteousness of Christ applied to such as repent and imputed unto them alone justifies and saves the believer.

(Gal. 2:16; 1 Cor. 1:30; 6:11; Isa. 53:4–6; John 1:29; 6:11; Acts 4:12; Eph. 1:7; Gal. 3:10; 3:13, 22, 24; Rom. 9:31; 10:3; 11:6; Titus 2:11; Rom. 8:13; 6:1; 3:31; Phil. 3:8; Prov. 29; Dan. 9:18; Luke 15:21; 17:10; 18:9; Rom. 3:20; 4:2; 2 Cor. 5:21; 1 Peter 2:24; Matt. 20:29; Heb. 9:12; 1 John 1:7; Rom. 5:9; 10:4; James 2:10; Acts 13:38; Titus 3:5; Eph. 2:8; James 2:14, 17, 20; 1 Cor. 4:4; Pss. 130, 143, 32:1–2; Isa. 53:6; 64:6; Matt. 8:8; Rom. 8:8; 5:20; 6:23.)

Chapter XIV

We believe that in those that are not regenerated free will is dead; they being in no wise able to do what is good; and whatever they do is sin; but in those that are regenerated by the All-holy Spirit, free will is revived, and operates, yet not without the assistance of grace. So, therefore, for a regenerated man to do what is good, it is necessary that he be guided and prevented by grace, without which he is wounded, and has as many stripes as he received from the robbers who went down from Jerusalem to Jericho; so that he is of himself powerless, and able to do nothing.

(Matt. 7:18; John 15:5; 1 Cor. 2:11, 14; 12:3; Eph. 2:1; Rom. 3:9; John 1:5; 6:44; Rom. 6:17; 14:23; John 3:3; 8:34; Col. 1:12; 2:13; 2 Cor. 3:5; Eph. 2:10; Phil. 2:13; 1:29; Ezek. 11:19; 36:26; 1 Cor. 12:2; 2 Peter 1:3; Acts 16:14; 2 Cor. 4:16; Rom. 7:14ff.; Mark 9:24; Rom. 11:24; 8:7; 2 Cor. 3:5; Col. 1:21; Matt. 16:17; Eph. 5:7; 1 Peter 2:19; Eph. 2:8; 1 Peter 1:3; Rom. 6:18; 8:2; Eph. 2:5; Ps. 100; 2 Cor. 5:17; Deut. 30:6; Jer. 31:33; 32:39; James 1:17; 1 Cor. 15:10; 2 Tim. 2:25; 1 Cor. 1:8; Gal. 5:17; Ps. 119:34, 36–37; Pss. 143:11–12; 86:10; 103:2–3.)

Chapter XV

We believe that there are in the Church Evangelical Mysteries, which the Lord delivered in the gospel, and that these are two. For so many were delivered unto us; and the Institutor delivered no more. And that these consist of a word and of an element; and that they are the seals of God's promises, and procure grace, we hold firmly. But that the Mystery be perfect and entire, it is necessary that an earthly matter and the external act concur with the use of that earthly thing, which was instituted by our Lord Jesus Christ, united with sincere faith; for when faith is wanting in the receivers the entirety of the Mystery is not preserved.

(Matt. 28:19–20; 1 Cor. 11:13; 10:23; 12:13; Eph. 5:25; 1 Cor. 11:23; Ex. 12:11; 13:9; Col. 2:11; Acts 8:36; Mark 16:16; Luke 22:19; Gal. 3:15; Mark 1:4; Rom. 4:11; 1 Peter 3:21; Rom. 2:28–29; John 3:5; Heb. 10:22; 1 Cor. 11:27.)

Chapter XVI

We believe that Baptism is a Mystery instituted by the Lord, which, except any one receive, he has no communion with Christ, from whose death, burial, and glorious resurrection, flow all the virtue and efficacy of Baptism; wherefore, as to those that are so baptized, as is commanded in the Gospel, we doubt not that their sins are forgiven, whether hereditary, or any such as the baptized have committed; so that those who are washed in the name of the Father, and of the Son, and of the Holy Spirit, are regenerated, cleansed, and justified. But concerning a second repetition of Baptism, we have no commandment, so as to reiterate Baptism. Therefore we ought to refrain from this irregularity.

(Mark 1:4; Matt. 28:19; Rom. 6:3; Gal. 3:12; Luke 3:13; Titus 3:5; John 1:6, 33; 3:32; Mark 16:16; Col. 2:12; Gal. 3:26; Acts 2:38; 10:47; 22:16; Eph. 4:5; Heb. 6:4.)

Chapter XVII

We believe the other Mystery instituted by the Lord to be what we call the Eucharist. For in the night wherein the Lord gave Himself up, taking bread and blessing, He said to His Apostles, "Take, eat ye; This is my body." And taking the chalice and giving thanks, He said, "Drink ye all of it, This is my blood which for you is poured out; this do ye for my memorial." And Paul adds, "For as often as ye eat this bread and drink this chalice, ye proclaim the death of the Lord." This is the simple, true, and genuine tradition of this wondrous Mystery, in the performance and administration of which we acknowledge and believe is the true and real presence of our Lord Jesus Christ; nevertheless, such as our faith presents and offers unto us, not such as transubstantiation vainly invented teaches. For we believe the faithful that partake in the supper eat the body of our Lord Jesus Christ, not by perceptively pressing and dissolving the communion with the teeth, but by the soul realizing communion. For the body of the Lord is not what is seen in the Mystery with the eyes and received, but what faith spiritually apprehending presents unto us and bestows. Whence it is true that we eat, and partake, and have communion, if we believe. If we believe not, we are deprived of all benefit of the Mystery; consequently to drink the chalice in the Mystery is to really drink the blood of our Lord Jesus Christ, in the same manner as is said of the body. For as the Institutor gave commandment concerning His own body, so also did He concerning His own blood, which commandment ought not to be mutilated according to the fancy of every one; but rather the tradition of the institution should be preserved entire.

When, therefore, we worthily partake, and entirely communicate in the Mystery of the body and blood of the Lord Jesus Christ, we are already, we confess, reconciled to our Head, and united with Him, and one body with Him, with certain hope of also being co-heirs with Him in the Kingdom.

(Matt. 26:26; Luke 22:19; Acts 1:9; 3:21; Eph. 3:17; 1 Cor. 12:13; Heb. 11:1; Mark 14:22; 1 Cor. 11:23; 10:16; Col. 3:1; Gal. 2:30; 2 Cor. 5:7; John 6:35, 53, 56–58, 60.)

Chapter XVIII

We believe that the souls of those that have fallen asleep are either in blessedness, or in condemnation, according to what each one has wrought. For when they depart from their bodies, they depart immediately either to Christ, or to condemnation. For as any one is found in death, he receives the corresponding talent, there being no repentance after death. For the time of grace is the present life. Therefore, they that are justified here, will hereafter in no wise be subject to condemnation. And again as many as are not justified when they fall asleep, will inherit eternal condemnation. From which it is evident, we ought not to admit the fable of Purgatory; but to maintain in truth, that each one ought to repent in the present life, and seek forgiveness of sin through our Lord Jesus Christ, if he would be saved. And this is so.

(Heb. 9:27; Eccl. 11:3; Isa. 57:1; Rom. 14:8; Phil. 1:21–22; Luke 2:25; 23:42; Ps. 32:6; John 9:4; 11:9–10; 12:35; Eccl. 9:6; Heb. 3:7; 4:1; 10:26; 2 Cor. 5:10; Ezek. 18:4; 1 Peter 1:18; 1 John 1:7; 2:1; Heb. 9:12, 22, 25; 10:10; 1 Cor. 6:11; Eph. 5:25; 1 Cor. 1:30; Acts 15:9; Isa. 43:25; Col. 2:13; Luke 16:22; Rev. 14:13; 1 Thess. 4:13; 2 Cor. 5:1; 2 Tim. 4:6; Isa. 55:6; 2 Cor. 6; Matt. 25:1; 25:19; 24:42; Gal. 6:5; Matt. 16:26; Ps. 49:6; Hab. 2:4; Heb. 1:3; 7:25; Titus 2:13; Rom. 3:24; Rev. 1:5; John 15:3; Pss. 32; 103:12; Ezek. 18:21; 36:25; Rom. 5:1; 8:1, 30, 38; John 3:16, 36; 5:24.)

This, our concise Confession, will, we conjecture, be for a sign to be spoken against by those that love to unjustly calumniate and persecute us. But we, taking courage in the Lord, are sure that He will not neglect His own, nor forsake them, nor will He altogether leave the rod of the malignant upon the lot of the righteous.

Dated in Constantinople in the month of March, 1629. Cyril, Patriarch of Constantinople.

107

Leipzig Colloquy (1631)

The second of the three *Confessiones Marchicae* (John Sigismund's of 1614 is the first and the 1645 Colloquy of Thorn is the last) was drafted at a gathering of Lutheran and Reformed theologians summoned by Elector Christian William (1587–1665) of Brandenburg. Nearly halfway through the devastating Thirty Years' War (1618–1648), Holy Roman Emperor Ferdinand II (1578–1637), friend of the Jesuits, issued an edict for the eradication of Protestantism in Germany (the so-called Edict of Restitution, 1629). However, the landing of King Gustavus Adolphus (1594–1632) of Sweden preserved Protestantism in Germany. Caught between the Swedish invader to the north and the Roman Catholic Ferdinand in the south, John George of Saxony (1585–1666), at the urging of George William of Brandenburg (1595–1640), invited some 160 Protestant princes to meet for the Leipzig Convention on February 16, 1631. At the conclusion of this political gathering (April 12), the *Leipziger Bund* (defensive association) was established in order to cooperate in raising an army of 40,000 men for defense against Wallenstein's Roman Catholic troops.

In the context of this convention, Lutheran and Reformed theologians gathered in Leipzig on March 3, 1631 (cf. Bodo Nischan, "Reformed Irenicism and the Leipzig Colloquy of 1631," *Central European History* 9 [1996]: 3–26). The Lutherans were represented by Matthias Hoë von Hoënegg (1580–1645), Polycarp Leyser (1586–1633), and Henry Höpfner. The Reformed were represented by John Bergius (1587–1658), John Crocius, and Theophilus Neuberger (1593–1656).

Using the Augustana (Invariata of the 1530 Augsburg Confession), these theologians agreed on twenty-six of the confession's twenty-eight articles. The sticking points were article three (*communicatio idiomatum*) and article ten (ubiquity of Christ's physical presence in the Lord's Supper). Though the Reformed granted a concession on the Supper (Christ's "true body...and true blood...were truly and physically offered, distributed and taken"), the implications of this apparent *manducatio oralis* (oral partaking/ eating) was fiercely disputed after the colloquy concluded on March 23.

Our text is from E. G. A. Böckel's *Die Bekenntnissschriften der evangelisch-reformirten Kirche* (1847), 443–56; cf. Niemeyer, 653–68.

THE LEIPZIG COLLOQUY

That is, the discussion at Leipzig in the year 1631 between theologians of Electoral Saxony, Electoral Brandenburg, and the Principality of Hessia of points of religion which have been contested among the Protestants.

As by special providence of the almighty God, the venerable evangelical and protesting electors and princes were gathered in especially strong numbers in Leipzig for the arranged meeting: with Doctor Johann Bergius, theologian and court chaplain of His Electoral Highness of Brandenburg, our most gracious Elector and Lord Count; as also with the court theologian, Doctor Johann Crocius; and with the court chaplain, Mr. Theophilus Neuberger, of his Princely Grace, Lord Landgrave Wilhelm of Hessia, our most gracious prince and lord. These same conferred with Doctor Matthias Hoë von Hoënegg, chief court chaplain of his Electoral Highness of Saxony, our most gracious elector and lord; and with the two gentlemen, principal professors of theology at Leipzig, Dr. Polycarp Leyser, superintendent, and Doctor Heinrich Höpfner. All acknowledged one other with a peace-loving disposition and mourned that up until then such vigorous strife had taken place between the theologians of both religions and that this strife had been the occasion of no small rejoicing among the papists. They also recognized what trouble arose from this and how the papacy has used such division between us of both sides to its powerful advantage; and how now not only to themselves alone, but also to their most gracious electoral and princely lords, nothing more desirous or pleasant could befall than that either the present strife might be completely settled or that it might be in the least bit mitigated or reduced. So they entreated the Saxon electors whether they would be inclined to take part with them in a colloquy and to discover how far both sides could come and achieve (with the present opportunity) such a good and beneficial purpose for the Protestant churches—with the attendant condition that this conference (and completely private activity) should take place without any harm or prejudice to the respective parties. They were inclined to agree to and to do everything that they could to facilitate and advance the avowed purpose without harm to their consciences, acknowledging also that with this effort they were not to damage the interests of their electoral and princely lords, but rather conduct this business in their most gracious favor.

To which, the above-mentioned three electoral Saxon theologians declared themselves to be completely open, and likewise deplored greatly that enormous strife that had grown up and increased to the present day, to the great damage of the Protestant churches. On their part, they desired from their hearts that God would grant wholesome means to reach agreement and declared that as they were able to seek unity in the proper manner with their own life's blood and seek the truth of God without hindrance, they thus desired most willingly to give themselves to this work.

They were in doubt, however, whether in such a restricted time and between so few persons, something fruitful could be accomplished because the work was of great importance and concerned both denominations and all of the theologians of both sides (none of whom wanted to see anything decided, which was to their disadvantage). It was made known to the electoral Brandenburg and Hessian theologians that the entire matter had to do with *quod omnes tangit, ab omnibus curari debet* (that which touches everyone must be done with the consent of all); and further *quot capita, tot sensus* (many heads, many opinions). The Saxons were obliged to assure their Electoral Highness of Saxony, their most gracious Lord, and his esteemed gentlemen of the privy council that nothing would be promised on their behalf (much less anything undertaken) without their foreknowledge because these matters were closely tied to affairs of state. This concern, the electoral Brandenburg and Hessian theologians marked well and replied that they did not doubt that as they together here made a beginning and likewise attempted to lay a good ground, so it would become ever easier for the other theologians in Germany hereafter also in other kingdoms and lands (at least concerning the principal task) to attempt to advance this most important work (the approval of men certainly ensuing, as well as, in time, that of the lords and princes). Because their own most gracious electoral and princely lords consented willingly and eagerly to support this work, they lived in the firm confidence that since they sought nothing which was captious or dangerous (rather they wanted from their hearts only to apply themselves diligently to heal the disastrous division of the Protestant churches), that His Electoral Highness of Saxony would also not set himself against their effort.

And thereafter, His Electoral Highness of Saxony, with his privy counsel and according to the information previously received, finally announced his acceptance of the intention that this should be nothing more than a one-time, private, and altogether harmless conference, whose purpose was solely to examine, to hear, and to consider whether and how far unity in the Augsburg Confession could be found; or whether and how men of both sides might move closer together. And so the theologians of both sides came together for the first time in the name of the most Holy Trinity on the morning of the third of March in the apartments which at the time were occupied by the primary court chaplain of Electoral Saxony. At the opening of the conference, the electoral Brandenburg and Hessian theologians freely declared that they confess with mouth and heart the confession that was presented by the Protestant princes and nobility at the Reichstag on June 25 in the year 1530 to Emperor Charles V (of most laudable memory); and if and where it was desired, they would sign the same without any reservations; also that they were not opposed to witnessing with their signatures their agreement to that copy of the confession which is found in *The Apple of the Electoral Eye*[1]; and so much the more did they want to do so because they had not only fulfilled their duty to the Augsburg Confession in their own places, but also because, as their most gracious Lords of Brandenburg and of

---

1. This apparently refers to the printing arranged by order of Elector Johann Georg I of Saxony of the original, which was kept in Mainz. The ensuing volume contained this quote: "Necessary Defense of the Apple of the Eye of the Protestant Electors and Princes of the Holy Roman Empire, namely the true, pure, unaltered Augsburg Confession, presented to Emperor Charles V in the year 1530, and of the Religious Peace which was directed to the same; with thorough explanation that neither the Electors and Princes nor their faithful theologians turned away from a single article of the commemorated true Augsburg Confession and also of the salutary Religious Peace and thus did not subject themselves to forfeiture; compiled by a special gracious order as well as for the rejection of scurrilous libel and smears now and again brought up by those of the Jesuits; set in print by theologians appointed thereto" (Leipzig, 1628).

Hessia officially and oftentimes acknowledged, they taught the confession in their churches and schools.

Concerning the edition which was presented in the year 1540 at Worms and in the year 1541 at Regensburg on the side of the Protestants in their disputation with the papists, they neither could nor desired to rule it out. Rather they adhered to the "Explanation" of the Protestant electors and princes of this edition of the Augsburg Confession which was presented at the Diet at Naumburg in the year 1561 to the Emperor Ferdinand I, of most glorious memory. On this the electoral Saxons had, to be sure, been undecided; but for their part declared themselves against it because of the Diet of Naumburg's decision on the "Explanation" which the Protestant electors and princes included in the introduction to the Book of Concord.

Thereafter, the theologians of both sides did most carefully, with a good heart, go through each of the articles of the Augsburg Confession one by one, thereby making known their respective opinions. Being called to examine the first article concerning God carefully and word by word, the electoral Brandenburg and Hessian theologians clearly stated: they firmly believe along with the electoral Saxons that God is one in being and three in persons; also that the doctrine of the unity of the divine being and the mystery of the three distinct persons in the Godhead are powerfully and irrefutably grounded in the Old and the New Testaments, regardless of some pronouncements of contrary interpretations that have appeared in the writings of certain teachers. They believe from the heart, as did the electoral Saxons, that God is a simple and an eternal, incorporeal, and indivisible being, without end and without any limits, and so is all-powerful; that He can do all things which He wills to do, and that nothing at all is impossible to Him, except only that which is declared by His Word to be contrary to His nature and counsel. In all the remaining points which are comprehended in the first article as also in those which are thereby refuted, they were completely of one mind and voice.

Concerning the next article, the theologians of both sides declared that they believe that after the fall of Adam all men who are naturally born, including the children of believers, are truly conceived and born in sin; that also this same pestilence and original sin is truly sin in them; and all those are condemned under the eternal wrath of God who are not born again through baptism and the Holy Spirit. Therewith, the first conference came to an end.

On the afternoon of the third (as also of the fourth of March), the third article of the Augsburg Confession was subjected to careful deliberation. And indeed the electoral Brandenburg and the Hessian theologians declared that they accept and hold true, according to the very letters and words, everything contained in the article. For they, no less than the electoral Saxons, believe without doubt that God the Son has become very man, born of the virgin Mary, who before, during, and after Christ's birth remained a pure virgin, and who was not only a bearer of the humanity and not only a Χριστοτόκος (*Christotokos*, or bearer of Christ), but rather was truly a Θεοτόκος (*Theotokos*, or bearer of God). This true God and man is truly born in one, undivided person. He truly suffered. He was crucified, died, was buried; truly arose on the third day, ascended into heaven and sits at the right hand of God; that He truly governs and reigns over all creatures; that He, through the Holy Spirit, saves all who believe on Him; purifies, strengthens, comforts, and gives to them life and all blessings; and protects and guards them against the devil and against all sins, as the words of the article further declare. They also wished that they might be allowed to hold this confession in just such a simple form.

However, because they were not in agreement, and the words of the third article were not understood in the same way by the electoral Saxons and the electoral Brandenburg and Hessian theologians, and because much hard and intense strife had taken place on varying points up to the present time, they did not set themselves against each other to any great extent, so that further discussion of such advanced and important points might continue between themselves. And after deliberating back and forth, it was finally decided that the electoral Saxons and also the electoral Brandenburg and Hessian theologians who were present agreed among themselves on the following points:

1. That the Son of God in the body of the virgin Mary took a complete human nature, consisting in soul and body, into the unity of His divine person. Thus, that in the power of the personal union, the Son of God, not only according to the expression but truly and in fact, is man; and concerning the manhood, is not only according to the expression, but truly is the Son of God; and that this same person has all of the attributes of both natures which can be ascribed to each.

2. That the two natures of Christ (the divine and the human) thus are united indissolubly and indivisibly with each other, and that at no time

and in no place, whether in the state of humiliation or of exaltation, did any separation or division occur between the natures; and neither was ever separated from the other, not even in death. For although at that time, the bond between the body and the soul was severed, the bond of the personal union of both natures remained unseparated and indissoluble, by the power of which even while the Son of God was outside of (that is, without) His flesh and cut off from the same, He was neither at that time nor at any other time after His conception, without the flesh which He had taken on Himself and never will be.

3. That both natures are not only inseparably, indissolubly and completely united together, but are also united without confusion or inward mixing, amalgamation or equalization. This is as true of the natures as of their attributes. For as the divine nature did not become the human nature through the personal union, nor the human the divine nature (rather it remained divine), the human also is a true human nature and remains so in eternity. Thus also the divine attributes remain attributes of the divine nature and never become attributes of the humanity; in the same way, the humanity retains its attributes and these did not become attributes of the divine nature.

4. Both sides are united in this—that although suffering and death are attributes of the human nature alone, nevertheless a mere humanity alone did not suffer. Rather the Son of God Himself, "the Lord of Glory" (1 Cor. 2:8), "the Prince of Life" (Acts 3:15), the most holy God from eternity suffered after the flesh, and appropriated and took to Himself the suffering of His "flesh" (Rom. 9:5; 1 Peter 4:1); and the blood shed for us is not only mere human blood, but also the "blood" of the Son of God (1 John 1:7) or God's own "blood," as Paul says (Acts 20:28).

5. That the saying—the divinity alone suffered; or otherwise, the humanity alone did suffer—are both unscriptural. Therefore, one must properly eschew each of them.

6. The theologians of both sides were in agreement that in Christ (not only according to the words but in fact), the entire "fullness of the Godhead dwells bodily" (Col. 2:9); and that the entire Christ is, without separation of the natures, all-knowing, all-powerful, and everywhere present; not, to be sure, as if the omniscience, omnipotence, and omnipresence were also attributes of the human nature, or contained in, on, or out of the humanity itself, much less as if these attributes

adhered to the flesh of Christ. Rather they are and remain attributes of the divine nature and are attributed to the entire person, God and man, on account of the inward personal union of both natures.

7. Both sides agree that the entire Christ in one undivided person, as God and man, without any exclusion or dissociation of the flesh, is to be called upon and that trust is to be set upon Him and on His most holy merit, all of which was established by the Council of Ephesus (431 A.D.).

8. Both sides confess that the complete Jesus in one undivided person (God and man) in omnipresence (but without a bodily spatiality) reigns over and governs all things from "sea to sea" (Ps. 72:8); that "all things are subjected under His feet" (Ps. 8:6); that He has one "foot on the sea and the other on earth" (Rev. 10:2); that He is and will remain with us until "the end of the world" (Matt. 28:20); that "where two or three are gathered together in His name, that He is there in their midst" (Matt. 18:20); that He fills all in all (Eph. 4:10); and that according to the saying of the apostle Paul, God the Father did raise the Lord Jesus "from the dead, that He did set Him at His right hand in heaven over all principalities, authority, power, lordship, and everything that can be named, not only in this world, but also in the world to come" (Eph. 1:20–21).

9. Further, the theologians of both sides let stand the Lord's descending to hell as a weighty and important article of faith, which can no more be attained unto and grasped by human reason than can the article on the sitting at the right hand of the Father; and confess that the whole Christ, God and man, descended to hell, overcame the devil, destroyed the might of hell, and took away from the devil all his power.

10. Both sides are in agreement that the Lord Christ did not ascend to heaven already in the womb[2], but precisely on the fortieth day after His resurrection. And although He truly, spatially, visibly, and not in some manner by merely disappearing, ascended to heaven; and that heaven into which He ascended and in which are the blessed of the heavenly

---

2. *Mutterleibe* (German) which refers to the strange notion that, because of the ubiquity of the human nature and divine nature of Christ (Lutheran ubiquitarians), Jesus' body was present in Mary's womb and also at the same time in heaven; i.e., He had ascended into heaven already when He was in His mother's womb. The above represents a Lutheran concession at Leipzig.

Father is a corporeal home and a specific place which is outside of this world, exists in the heights, is created and governed by the Father, and is where we will have our home (John 14:2); nevertheless the Lord is not enclosed within heaven.

11. Both sides agreed that the right hand of the almighty Father cannot be understood as a specific or created place, just as that the sitting at the right hand of God cannot be understood as a bodily or spatial sitting. That rather the right hand of God means no less than the majesty, power, and omnipotence of God; hence it is called "the right hand of God's power" (Luke 22:69), also "the right hand" of the Majesty on high (Heb. 8:1), the right hand which gains the victory (Ps. 118:16), and "the right hand" from which no one can hide or steal himself away (Ps. 139:7). But that sitting at the right hand of God means that Christ reigns and governs eternally, which He does after His ascension to heaven, perfectly and gloriously, according to both natures over all creatures. But especially, He reigns over His church as her head, through which head the Father governs all things, and through whom He desires to be honored and called upon in prayer by men.

12. And the theologians of both sides were in agreement concerning the office of the Lord Jesus Christ—that the Lord Christ performed the holy office of mediator and redeemer according to both natures. God's Son accomplished (His work) in, with, and through the most holy flesh which He assumed, and is, in that assumed humanity, not at all excluded from the actual performance of and powerful working out of the Lord's offices (that is, from the regeneration, justification, and sanctification of man and such like). Hence, the body of the Son of God is called a regenerating body (John 6:54), and the blood of the Son of God has the power to purify all men from their sins (1 John 1:7).

Over and above this, the electoral Saxons further confessed the infallible and important truth that the Lord Jesus is truly omniscient, omnipotent, and omnipresent not only according to the divine nature, but also according to the human nature. However, that the omniscience, omnipotence, and omnipresence of the human nature are not natural attributes, but are communicated thereto through the personal union and through the exaltation to the right hand of God. They are also attributed within the person and not outside of the same in some peculiar fashion. So also the electoral Saxons remained unmoved in the teaching that everything that is said of Christ—what He received in time of glory, power, majesty, and honor—that such is not to be understood as referring to the divine nature, but only to the human nature, according to which Christ could be exalted and by grace "given a name which is above every name" (Phil. 2:9). As the rule states: He who is already God according to His nature, yes, who is the All Highest, cannot be exalted for the first time in time. But the flesh of the All Highest is raised to the infinite divine majesty, honor, and glory in time, not outside of the person, but rather within the person.

To this the electoral Brandenburg and Hessian theologians further declared their ready agreement that the divinity of Christ (or Christ according to His divine nature) was not actually exalted, that He did not receive any new inner glory, power, majesty, or honor according to the divine nature in itself. For according to the same, He is and remains from eternity the Most High, Most Powerful, and Most Perfect. Also, that the human nature did not suffer peculiarly and in itself alone, but that the person of the Son of God in the flesh is exalted through His resurrection, ascension, and sitting at the right hand of God, through which exaltation the human nature is glorified and lifted up above all creatures. However, the divine nature in itself is not, but is only to us men more perfectly glorified and revealed. That also the office of mediator and all of the authority and honor of the office is not given by the Father exclusively to one nature, but to the whole person, the Son of God in the flesh; which office, as has been explained before, He performs according to both natures alike. They confess further that Christ certainly (not only according to the divinity, but also according to His manhood through enlightenment and cooperation of the divinity) knows all things and is able to do all things which in any respect belong to His office of mediator; that He also is always present with His church on earth with His powerful work, grace, and help not only according to His divinity, but also in His manhood—powerfully protecting, maintaining, and governing the same in the midst of His enemies according to the promise: "I am with you unto the end of the world" (Matt. 28:20); and "where two or three are gathered in my name, there will I be in the midst of them" (Matt. 18:20).

One thing only they steadfastly deny and hold to be contrary to the Holy Scripture—that Christ, according to the manhood (or according to His human nature and being; or the body of Christ according to its substance and being in some invisible manner) is in all places and with all creatures, either in the state of humiliation or in the state of exaltation, either because of the personal union or because of the session on the right hand of God. They deny also that the other divine attributes (omniscience and omnipotence) are thus communicated to the human nature; that these same become any sort of infinite power and knowledge along with the divine omniscience and omnipotence, and that such can rightly be attributed to it as the scholastics speak *in abstracto* (i.e., in and for itself as the human nature).

Finally, they hold that there is no better means toward understanding on these points than that men should keep themselves in these great mysteries to those expressions alone which are specifically used in the Holy Scripture, by the ancient general councils and in the Augsburg Confession (as they for their part desire to bind themselves to no other words). Concerning which efforts toward understanding, the electoral Saxons were undecided on the question of future, continued discussion. And thus far with the third article, to which the theologians of both sides appended that they condemn and reject from the heart all the errors of ancient and contemporary Arians, Nestorians, Eutychians, Monothelites, Marcionites, Photinians, and those of whatever names they may have. In opposition thereto, they confess the Apostolic, Nicene, and Athanasian Creeds with mouth and heart.

On the fourth article, the theologians of both sides are of one accord (and the electoral Brandenburg and Hessian theologians declare) that the fourth article is likewise loved by them and taught on every occasion. That Christ the Lord and Savior died for all men and with His death had acted for the sins of the whole world completely, perfectly, and, in His death in and of itself, powerfully and sufficiently. That it is also not mere appearance, but that it is His actual, earnest will and command that all men should believe on Him, and be saved through faith; thus that no one is shut out from the power and benefit of the sufficiency of Christ but he who shuts himself out through unbelief.

The fifth, sixth, seventh, and eighth articles they accepted word for word without any exception in the same way as the electoral Saxons, for these have in every time been taught in their own churches.

The ninth likewise; and they therewith declared that holy baptism, according to the divine ordinance, is necessary as an ordained means of salvation; and although the grace of God does not work through baptism *ex opera operato*, that is, for the sake of the mere work (as also not through the mere outward washing), salvation does work in the power of the Word of the institution of the sacrament and of the promise which is conveyed by baptism. With the electoral Saxons, they also believe that it is right and necessary to baptize the children; and that when they are presented to God in baptism, they are then by the grace of God and according to God's ordinance, accepted and included.

On the seventh of March, during both morning and afternoon, they came to the remaining articles and these were deliberated. Thus the electoral Brandenburg and Hessian theologians accept and confess each word of the tenth article on the Holy Supper, as it is stated in the confession that was presented in the year 1530. Moreover, they (with the electoral Saxons) condemn the papist perversions; likewise the concomitance, the constant sacramental presence of the body and blood of Christ contrary to the instituted manner; the coexistence (*coexistentiam*), the inexistence (*inexistentiam*), any spatial and bodily manner of the presence of Christ, and praying which is directed to the bread or to the form of bread.

They confessed further that in the Holy Supper, not only the outward elements of the bread and wine are truly present (and not only the power and effectiveness or the mere signs of the body and blood), but that the true, essential body which was broken for us, and the true, essential blood of Jesus Christ Himself which is poured out for us are present. These are conveyed by means of the blessed bread and wine, and are truly and presently given, communicated, and partaken in the power of the sacramental union, which does not consist in the mere meaning or in the sealing, but rather in the entire, undivided administration of the earthly elements and of the true body and blood of Jesus Christ. However, this sacramental union does not take place outside of that operation which was ordained by Christ, but only in the same.

Further, they agreed that also in the spiritual partaking not only the power, benefit, and effect, but also the being and the substance of the body and blood of Jesus Christ are partaken in the Lord's Supper as it takes place here in the world (that is, when it is eaten and drunk in a spiritual manner through true faith); and that this spiritual partaking is most necessary to blessed enjoyment of the most worthy supper.

No less were both sides of one voice that in the sacramental partaking, the earthly elements and the body and blood of Christ are enjoyed alike and together. However, the electoral Brandenburg and the Hessian theologians did not want to concede the point that such enjoyment does not take place with the *organo oris* (or orally), by the unworthy as well as by the worthy. To be sure, they confessed that by means of the blessed bread and wine the actual body and blood of Christ are received at the same time; not with the mouth, but through faith alone through which the body and the blood of the Lord becomes one in a spiritual manner with those who worthily partake of the supper. To the unworthy, however, the body and blood is only offered, but because of their unbelief is not received and enjoyed, but rather cast out and rejected.

Over against this, the electoral Saxons were adamant that in the Holy Supper, by means of the blessed elements, the actual body and blood of the Lord Jesus Christ are eaten and drunk with the mouth, as the words say, "Eat" and "Drink". And although the blessed bread and the body of the Lord are received by all communicants *uno et eodem organo oris*, that is, with the bodily mouth, that nevertheless the partaking (as far as concerns the mode) takes place in different ways, in that one partakes of the bread and wine with the mouth without means and in an organic way; however, one partakes of the body and blood of Jesus Christ not without means, but in the power of the blessed elements in a heavenly and super-natural manner, known by God alone, and thus receives the elements with the mouth without any bodily, natural swallowing or chewing or consumption of the body and blood.

Although time could permit of no agreement on the tenth article on the matter of the oral partaking, but instead the same must be abandoned as it had been at Marburg in the year 1529, the electoral Brandenburg and Hessian theologians reckoned that there could nevertheless be a Christian unity or at least that tolerance could ensue. They asked of the others, concerning this point, that as they do not condemn, nor yet desire to impose their opinion on them as a necessary article of faith, so they should not condemn. And (the electoral Brandenburg and Hessians) did not doubt that because they were in agreement on the principal points of this article that they could stand against the papacy as one man. After which, the electoral Saxons considered the suggestion that the issue should be deliberated further in the fear of God and that further Christian discussions with a larger number of theologians should be fostered. The matter was left undecided at this time.

Concerning the eleventh article of the Augsburg Confession, the electoral Brandenburg and Hessian theologians declared that they held the form of confession which is customary in some Protestant churches, when it is conducted without misuse and as a thing in which Christians have freedom—as a free, Christian, and good ceremony which could be used with benefit in the church of God; and where it already is in use, may well be continued. The forced and obligatory confession of the papists, however, as well as other continued abuses, are entirely wrong and to be condemned.

On the twelfth, thirteenth, fourteenth, fifteenth, sixteenth, seventeenth, eighteenth, nineteenth, twentieth, twenty-first, twenty-second, twenty-third, twenty-fourth, twenty-fifth, twenty-sixth, twenty-seventh, and twenty-eighth articles, they were thoroughly and without exception in agreement; and the electoral Brandenburg and Hessian theologians declared concerning the nineteenth article in particular that God is not the cause nor the perpetrator of sins, created no man to sin or to perdition, nor ordained any one to sin or damnation in or out of a mere decree of His counsel.

And although the doctrine of the eternal election is not expressly stated in the Augsburg Confession, nevertheless the theologians of both sides considered it advisable (also in these points on which there has been so much strife) to declare their teaching and belief. Thus, the electoral Brandenburg and Hessian theologians confess the following as their unanimous doctrine and faith:

That God from eternity in Jesus Christ has elected out of the corrupt race of men not all, but some persons whose number and names are known to Him alone; whom He in His time, through the power and means of His Word and Spirit, enlightens and renews to faith in Christ. He also preserves the same to the end and finally saves them through faith unto eternity.

That He found or foresaw no cause or occasion or preceding means or condition of such election in the elect themselves, neither their good works nor their faith, or either the first saving inclination, movement, or consent to faith. Rather that everything good that is in them is ordained and given in eternity in Jesus Christ and flows only out of the pure, freely given grace of God to them rather than to others.

Also that God did not from eternity foreordain or cast out those who persist in their sins and unbelief out of any *absoluto decreto* or mere will and counsel—as if God foreordained in eternity or created in time the greatest part of the world nor even some men to eternal damnation or to the cause of the same without consideration of their sins and their unbelief. Rather the casting out as well as the condemnation occurs out of His righteous judgment, whose cause is in the people themselves—namely in their sins, impenitence, and unbelief. That thus the entire fault and cause of the casting out and condemnation of unbelievers is in themselves, while the entire cause of the election and salvation of believers is only in the pure grace of God in Jesus Christ according to the word of the Lord: "Israel, thou hast destroyed thyself, but in me is thine help" (Hos. 13:9).

That therefore also everyone should and can be certain of his election and salvation, not *a priori*, out of the hidden counsel of God, but only *a posteriori*, out of the revealed Word of God, and from his faith and the fruit of faith in Christ. And it does not follow (as the careless world derisively misuses this article, much less can it thus be taught) that whoever is elect may persist in his ungodliness as long as he wants and he must still be saved, or that whoever is not elect, if he truly believes and lives holily, must nevertheless be damned.

If, however, someone wants to search further and delve into this great mystery and desires to seek other causes beside God's free, gracious, and righteous counsel; why God the Father makes men who were by nature the same, whom He is able, in His omnipotence, to make all alike to believe and be saved, nevertheless actually made some rather than others to believe, and left the others in their sins and self-willed, hard-necked impenitence and unbelief, in the same way men spoke with the apostle: "O man, who art thou that repliest against God?... Hath not the potter power from one impure lump of clay to make one vessel unto honor, out of pure grace, and another unto dishonor out of righteous judgment?" (Rom. 9:20–21). "O the depth of the riches and wisdom of God! How unknowable are His judgments and unsearchable His ways! Who has been His counselor? Or who has known His mind? Or who hath first given to Him or it has been recompensed unto him again?" (Rom. 11:33–35).

To this, the electoral Saxons replied:

1. That God from eternity and before the foundation of the world was laid, chose in Christ not all but some to salvation.

2. That the number and names of the elect are known only to God; as the Lord speaks, He "knows" His sheep (John 10:14); and as St. Paul says, "He knows His own" (2 Tim. 2:19).

3. That God has chosen from eternity those whom He foresaw would in time, by the power and working of His Spirit, believe in Christ

and would persevere in the same unto the end; and although the elect can for a time fall from the grace of God, it is yet impossible that this should happen persistently and unto finality.

4. That in election, God found no cause or occasion for such choice in the elect themselves; also no first, saving inclination, movement, or consent to believe. Rather that all of the good which is in the elect flows first out of the pure, free grace of God which is given them in eternity in Jesus Christ.

5. That God has from eternity foreordained to condemnation and casting out those only whom He knew would persist in their sins and unbelief.

6. That this casting out did not occur because of an *absoluto decreto* or mere counsel and will, as if God has damned any one without consideration of his unbelief, merely according to His pleasure; that there is in God no mere counsel according to which He has either foreordained from eternity or created in time to eternal damnation or to the cause of the same, the largest part of men or even a single person.

7. That however as many men as are eternally lost and damned, this certainly happens out of the righteous judgment of God; but the cause of this condemnation lies in the people themselves, particularly in their besetting sins, their unbelief, and their impenitence. That thus the entire guilt and cause of the casting out and damnation of unbelievers is in themselves; however the entire cause of the election and salvation of the believers is the pure grace of God in Jesus Christ, according to the word of the Lord: "Israel thou hast destroyed thyself, but in me is thine help" (Hos. 13:9).

8. That each one can and should be certain of his salvation and election not *a priori*, out of the hidden counsel of God, but rather only *a posteriori*, out of the revealed Word of God and out of his faith in Christ; and it does not at all follow, as sometimes the careless world derisively misuses this important article, much less can it or should it thus be taught that whoever is elect may persist in his godlessness as long as he wants and he must and will nevertheless be saved. Or whoever is not elect must be damned regardless of whether he believes ever so firmly in Christ or lives ever so godly.

9. That in this great mystery of election men are aroused to many questions, which we will not understand in this mortal life, but can

be understood in no other way than as St. Paul writes: "O man, who art thou that repliest against God?" (Rom. 9:20); and further: "O the depth of the riches and wisdom of God! How unknowable are His judgments and unsearchable His ways! Who has been His counselor? Or who has known His mind? Or who hath first given to Him or it has been recompensed unto him again?" (Rom. 11:33–35).

10. Regarding all this the electoral Saxon theologians declared that they hold for right and consistent with the Holy Scriptures everything which is taught in the Book of Concord concerning this article on election; namely that God certainly elects us in Christ out of grace, but in such a way that He foresaw those who would persistently and truly believe in Christ; and those whom He foresaw would believe, these He also elected to save and to glorify.

Thus did this amicable and unoffending private conference end on the twenty-third of March. It was once again emphasized that men of neither side desired in the least to prejudice either the high princes and authorities nor other interested theologians, and least of all their respective denominations. Rather that it was only meant to make a summary beginning, to discover whether and how far both sides could find unity in the twenty-eight articles of the Augsburg Confession; and whether it might not be hoped and attempted by further conference of the more peace-loving theologians (and first and foremost through the authority of Christian high officials) that a closer unity might be established, and by such means the true church advanced and increase, and also some of the hopes taken away from the papists which they have had up to the present day because of the ongoing division.

In the meantime and before that should follow, everything that has occurred in the present conference should be as if nothing had taken place; and neither party should undertake without the express agreement of the other side to improperly disperse or to prematurely disseminate the contents of this meeting and consignation. The theologians of both sides desire to show each other Christian love in the future—everything in trust and without jeopardy to each other.

May the God of truth and peace give grace that we may all be one in Him, and be perfect in one as He and the Son are one (John 17:21). Amen! Amen! In the name of Jesus Christ, Amen!

Done at Leipzig in most eminent gathering in the presence of the most venerable evangelical and protesting electors and princes in the month of March, the year 1631.

Dr. Matthias Hoë von Hoënegg, by his own hand
Dr. Polycarpus Leyser, by his own hand
Dr. Henricus Höpfner, by his own hand
Dr. Johannes Bergius, by his own hand
Dr. Johannes Crocius, by his own hand
Theophilus Neuberger, court preacher at Hessia Cassel, by his own hand

(Translated by Peter Van Der Schaaf)

108

The London Baptist Confession (1644)

English Royalists and Laudians dreaded the ferment of not only the political clashes of the Civil War (or War of the Three Kingdoms, 1642–1651), but they also feared the rise of the "sectaries." Besides the colorful ones of this ilk, such as the Ranters, Muggletonians, Seekers, and Levellers, were the Baptists (or Anabaptists, as they were wont to be called in the seventeenth century). The British phase of the anti-paedobaptist movement arose from the English Puritan Separatists, first divulged in the congregational or independent movement of the early seventeenth century (the debt to sixteenth-century Brownists is still debated).

Pastor John Smyth (ca. 1554–1612) led the Gainsborough congregation of independent-minded migrants to Amsterdam in 1608, where he fell in with the Mennonites and proceeded to (re)baptize himself (earning the moniker "John the Se-baptist"—or "self-baptizer"). Smyth subsequently crossed over completely to Mennonitism, but in 1612 a tiny band from his Amsterdam church followed Thomas Helwys (ca. 1550–ca. 1616) back across the Channel. Near London, at Spitalfields, they organized the first Baptist congregation in England. Because of their Arminian sympathies (universal atonement, or general redemption), they became known as General Baptists.

From the same English Separatist soil, another branch of Baptists sprang up. These were decidedly Calvinistic in soteriology and followed the lead of Pastor Henry Jacob (1563–1624). The independent congregation thus established in London was known as the Jacob-Lathrop-Jessey Church for its successive pastors: Henry Jacob, John Lathrop (†1653), and Henry Jessey (1601–1663). Organized originally in Southwark in 1616 as a "non-separating" congregational body of the Church of England, the group divided in 1619 when Jacob withdrew as pastor. In 1624, Lathrop succeeded him, and served until he moved to New England ten years later. In 1633, a division in the church focused on whether the Church of England was a "true" church. Those who argued the negative followed Samuel Eaton to a new congregation, which he pastored from 1634 until his death in 1639. The Jacob-Lathrop church called Henry Jessey in 1637. By 1642, the congregation was convulsed by a debate over infant versus believer's baptism. Hanserd Knollys (ca. 1599–1691), who had previously been a minister in New England, asked that his child remain unbaptized. William Kiffin (1616–1701) joined him in this opinion. A London gathering or conference of independent churches in 1644 resulted in Kiffin establishing a new church with Calvinistic Baptist sentiments (limited atonement or particular redemption). Kiffin was to be the organizing spirit behind the congregation's 1643 First Confession of Faith, published in 1644 as the First London Confession of Faith. The reader will observe that this confession borrowed elements from the Second Confession of the London-Amsterdam Church (1596; cf. volume three of our series, pages 748–64), the Points of Difference (1603; above, pages 1–4); and the Scottish Confession (1616; above, pages 108–116). The final draft of the confession was signed by John Spilsbury (1593–ca. 1668), William Kiffin, and Thomas Killcop, among others.

Our text is based upon the 1644 edition published in London. We have modernized some spelling and inserted the proof texts in the body of the confession. Many of these have been corrected, several from the numbering of the texts in the Geneva Bible; others baffle us, and we have left them as they stand in the original.

THE CONFESSION OF FAITH,

Of those churches which are commonly (though falsely) called Anabaptists; presented to the view of all that fear God, to examine by the touchstone of the Word of Truth: As likewise for the taking off those aspersions which are frequently both in pulpit and print (although unjustly) cast upon them.

I.

That God as He is in Himself, cannot be comprehended of any but Himself, dwelling in that inaccessible light (1 Tim. 6:16), that no eye can attain unto, whom never man saw, nor can see; that there is but one God, one Christ, one Spirit, one faith, one baptism (1 Tim. 2:5; Eph. 4:4–6; 1 Cor. 12: 4–6, 13; John 14); one rule of holiness and obedience for all saints, at all times, in all places to be observed (1 Tim. 6:3, 13, 14; Gal. 1:8–9; 2 Tim. 3:15).

II.

That God is of Himself (Isa. 43:11; 46:9), that is, neither from another, nor of another, nor by another, nor for another: But is a Spirit (John 4:24), who as His being is of Himself (Ex. 3:14), so He gives being, moving, and preservation to all other things, being in Himself eternal, most holy, every way infinite in greatness, wisdom, power, justice, goodness, truth, etc. (Rom. 11:36; Acts 17:28). In this Godhead, there is the Father, the Son, and the Spirit; being every one of them one and the same God; and therefore not divided, but distinguished one from another by their several properties; the Father being from Himself (1 Cor. 8:6), the Son of the Father from everlasting (Prov. 8:22–23), the Holy Spirit proceeding from the Father and the Son (John 15:26; Gal. 4:6).

III.

That God has decreed in Himself from everlasting touching all things (Isa. 46:10; Rom. 11:34–36; Matt. 10:29–30), effectually to work and dispose them according to the counsel of His own will (Eph. 1:11), to the glory of His name; in which decree appears His wisdom, constancy, truth, and faithfulness; wisdom is that whereby He contrives all things (Col. 2:3); constancy is that whereby the decree of God remains always immutable (Num. 23:19–20); truth is that whereby He declares that alone which He has decreed (Jer. 10:10; Rom. 3:4), and though His sayings may seem to sound sometimes another thing, yet the sense of them does always agree with the decree; faithfulness is that whereby He effects that He has decreed, as He has decreed (Isa. 44[sic 46]:10). And touching His creature man, God had in Christ before the foundation of the world, according to the good pleasure of His will, foreordained some men to eternal life through Jesus Christ, to the praise and glory of His grace (Eph. 1:3–7; 2 Tim. 1:9; Acts 13:48; Rom. 8:29–30), leaving the rest in their sin to their just condemnation, to the praise of His justice (Jude 4, 6; Rom. 9:11–13; Prov. 16:4).

IV.

In the beginning God made all things very good (Gen. 1; Col. 1:16; Heb. 11:3; Isa. 45:12), created man after His own image and likeness (Gen. 1:26; 1 Cor. 15:45–46; Eccl. 7:31[sic 29]), filling Him with all perfection of all natural excellence and uprightness, free from all sin (Ps. 49:20). But long he abode not in this honor, but by the subtlety of the serpent (Gen. 3:1, 4, 5; 2 Cor. 11:3), which Satan used as his instrument, himself with his angels having sinned before, and not kept their first estate (2 Peter 2:4; Jude 6; John 8:44), but left their own habitation; first Eve, then Adam, being seduced did wittingly and willingly fall into disobedience and transgression of the commandment of their great Creator (Gen. 3:1, 2, 6; 1 Tim. 2:14; Eccl. 7:31[sic 29]; Gal. 3:22), for the which death came upon all, and reigned over all, so that all since the fall are conceived in sin, and brought forth in iniquity, and so by nature children of wrath, and servants of sin, subjects of death, and all other calamities due to sin in this world and for ever (Rom. 5:12, 18, 19; 6:23; Eph. 2:3), being considered in the state of nature, without relation to Christ.

V.

All mankind being thus fallen, and become altogether dead in sins and trespasses, and subject to the eternal wrath of the great God by transgression; yet the elect, which God has loved with an everlasting love (Jer. 31:2[sic 3]), are redeemed, quickened, and saved, not by themselves, neither by their own works, lest any man should boast himself (Gen. 3:15; Eph. 1:3, 7; 2:4, 9; 1 Thess. 5:9; Acts 13:38), but wholly and only by God of His free grace and mercy through Jesus Christ, who of God is made unto us wisdom, righteousness, sanctification, and redemption (1 Cor. 1:30–31; 2 Cor. 5:21; Jer. 9:23, 24), that as it is written, He that rejoices, let him rejoice in the Lord.

VI.

This therefore is life eternal, to know the only true God, and whom He has sent, Jesus Christ (John 17:3; Heb. 5:9; Jer. 23:5, 6). And on the contrary, the Lord will render vengeance in flaming fire to them that know not God, and obey not the gospel of our Lord Jesus Christ (2 Thess. 1:8; John 3:36).

VII.

The rule of this knowledge, faith, and obedience, concerning the worship and service of God, and all other Christian duties, is not man's inventions, opinions, devices, laws, constitutions, or traditions unwritten whatsoever, but only the Word of God contained in the canonical Scriptures (John 5:39; 2 Tim. 3:15–17; Col. 2:18, 23; Matt. 15:9).

VIII.

In this written Word God has plainly revealed whatsoever He has thought needful for us to know, believe, and acknowledge, touching the nature and office of Christ, in whom all the promises are yea and amen to the praise of God (Acts 3:22, 23; Heb. 1:1, 2; 2 Tim. 3:15–17; 2 Cor. 1:20).

IX.

Touching the Lord Jesus, of whom Moses and the prophets wrote (Gen. 3:15; 22:18; 49:10; Dan. 7:13; 9:24–26), and whom the apostles preached, is the Son of God the Father, the brightness of His glory, the ingraven form of His being (Prov. 8:23; John 1:1–3; Col. 1:1, 15–17), God with Him and with His Holy Spirit, by whom He made the world, by whom He upholds and governs all the works He has made, who also when the fullness of time was come was (Gal. 4:4), was made man of a woman, of the tribe of Judah (Heb. 7:14; Rev. 5:5; Gen. 49:9–10), of the seed of Abraham and David, to wit, of Mary, that blessed virgin, by the Holy Spirit coming upon her, and the power of the Most High overshadowing her (Rom. 1:3; 9:5; Matt. 1:16; Luke 3:23, 26; Heb. 2:16), and was also in all things like unto us (Isa. 53:3–5; Phil. 2:8), sin only excepted.

X.

Touching His office, Jesus Christ only is made the mediator of the new covenant (2 Tim. 2:15[sic 1 Tim. 2:5]; Heb. 9:15; John 14:6), even the everlasting covenant of grace between God and man, to be perfectly and fully the prophet, priest, and king of the church of God for evermore (Heb. 1:2; 3:1, 2; 7:24; Isa. 9:6–7; Acts 5:31).

XI.

Unto this office He was foreordained from everlasting, by the authority of the Father, and in respect of His manhood (Prov. 8:23; Isa. 42:6; 49:1, 5), from the womb called and separated, and anointed also most fully and abundantly with all gifts necessary, God having without measure poured the Spirit upon Him (Isa. 11:2–5; 61:1–3; Luke 4:17, 22; John 1:14, 16; 3:34).

XII.

In this call the Scripture holds forth two special things considerable; first, the call to the office; secondly, the office itself. First, that none takes this honor but he that is called of God (Heb. 5:4–6), as was Aaron, so also Christ, it being an action especially of God the Father, whereby a special covenant being made, He ordains His Son to this office: which covenant is, that Christ should be made a sacrifice for sin, that He shall see His seed, and prolong His days, and the pleasure of the Lord shall prosper in His hand (Isa. 53:10); which calling therefore contains in itself choosing (Isa. 42:13), foreordaining (1 Peter 1:20), sending (John 3:17; 9:27[*sic* 7:29]; 10:36). Choosing respects the end, foreordaining the means, sending the execution itself, all of mere grace, without any condition foreseen either in men (Rom. 8:32), or in Christ Himself.

XIII.

So that this office to be mediator, that is, to be, priest, and king of the church of God, is so proper to Christ, as neither in the whole, nor in any part thereof, can it be transferred from Him to any other (1 Tim. 2:5; Heb. 7:24; Dan. 5:14; Acts 4:12; Luke 1:33; John 14:6).

XIV.

This office itself to which Christ was called, is threefold, of a prophet (Deut. 18:15; Acts 3:22–23), of priest (Ps. 110:3[*sic* 4]; Heb. 3:1; 4:14–15; 5:6), and of king (Ps. 2:6): this number and order of offices is showed; first, by men's necessities grievously laboring under ignorance (Acts 26:18; Col. 1:3[*sic* 2]), by reason whereof they stand in infinite necessity of the prophetical office of Christ to relieve them. Secondly, alienation from God (Col. 1:21; Eph. 2:12), wherein they stand in need of the priestly office to reconcile them. Thirdly, our utter disability to return to Him (Song 1:3[*sic* 4]; John 6:44), by which they stand in need of the power of Christ in His kingly office to assist and govern them.

XV.

Touching the prophecy of Christ, it is that whereby He has perfectly revealed the whole will of God out of the bosom of the Father (John 1:18; 12:49–50; 15; 17:8; Deut. 18:15), that is needful for His servants to know, believe, and obey; and therefore is called not only a prophet and a doctor (Matt. 23:10), and the apostle of our profession (Heb. 3:1), and the angel of the covenant (Mal. 4:15[sic 3:1]); but also the very wisdom of God (1 Cor. 1:24), and the treasures of wisdom and understanding (Col. 2:3).

XVI.

That He might be such a prophet as thereby to every way complete, it was necessary that He should be God (John 1:18; 3:13), and withall also that He should be man; for unless He had been God, He could have never perfectly understood the will of God, neither had He been able to reveal it throughout all ages (1 Cor. 2:11, 16); and unless He had been man, He could not fitly have unfolded it in His own person to man (Acts 3:22; Deut. 18:15; Heb. 1:1).

XVII.

Touching His priesthood, Christ being consecrated, has appeared once to put away sin by the offering and sacrifice of Himself (John 17:19; Heb. 5:7–9; 9:26; Rom. 5:19; Eph. 5:2; Col. 1:20), and to this end has fully performed and suffered all those things by which God, through the blood of His cross in an acceptable sacrifice, might reconcile His elect only; and having broken down the partition wall (Eph. 2:14–16; Rom. 8:34), and therewith finished and removed all the rites, shadows, and ceremonies, is now entered within the veil, into the Holy of Holiest, that is, to the very heavens, and presence of God, where He forever lives and sits at the right hand of majesty, appearing before the face of His Father to make intercession for such as come to the throne of grace by that new and living way; and not that only, but makes His people a spiritual house, an holy priesthood (1 Peter 2:5; John 4:23, 24), to offer up spiritual sacrifice acceptable to God through Him; neither does the Father accept, or Christ offer to the Father any other worship or worshipers.

XVIII.

This priesthood was not legal, or temporary, but according to the order of Melchizedek (Heb. 7:17); not by a carnal commandment, but by the power of endless life (Heb. 7:16); not by an order that is weak and lame, but stable and perfect (Heb. 7:18–21), not for a time, but forever (Heb. 7:24–25), admitting no successor, but perpetual and proper to Christ, and of Him that ever lives. Christ Himself was the priest, sacrifice, and altar: He was priest (Heb. 5:6), according to both natures, He was a sacrifice most properly according to His human nature: whence in the Scripture it is wont to be attributed to His body, to His blood (Heb. 10:10; 1 Peter 1:18–19; Col. 1:20–21; Isa. 53: 10; Matt. 20:28); yet the chief force whereby this sacrifice was made effectual, did depend upon His divine nature (Acts 20:28; Rom. 8:3), namely, that the Son of God did offer Himself for us: He was the altar properly according to His divine nature, it belonging to the altar to sanctify that which is offered upon it (Heb. 9:14; 13:10, 12, 15; Matt. 23:17; John 17:19), and so it ought to be of greater dignity than the sacrifice itself.

XIX.

Touching His kingdom, Christ being risen from the dead, ascended into heaven, sat on the right hand of God the Father, having all power in heaven and earth given unto Him (1 Cor. 15:4; 1 Peter 3:21–22; Matt. 28:18–20; Luke 24:51; Acts 1:11; 5:30–31; John 19:36; Rom. 14:17), He spiritually governs His church, exercising His power over all angels and men (Mark 1:27; Heb. 1:14; John 16:7, 15), good and bad, to the preservation and salvation of the elect, to the overruling and destruction of His enemies, which are reprobates, communicating and applying the benefits, virtue, and fruit of His prophecy and priesthood to His elect (John 5:26–27; Rom. 5:6–8; 14:17; Gal. 5:22–23; John 1:4, 13), namely, to the subduing and taking away of their sins, to their justification and adoption of sons, regeneration, sanctification, preservation, and strengthening in all their conflicts against Satan, the world, the flesh, and the temptations of them, continually dwelling in, governing, and keeping their hearts in faith and filial fear by His Spirit, which having given it, He never takes it away from them (John 13:1; 10:28–29; 14:16–17; Rom. 11:29; Ps. 51:10–11; Job 33:29–30; 2 Cor. 12:7, 9), but by it still begets and nourishes in them faith, repentance, love, joy, hope, and all heavenly light in the soul unto immortality, notwithstanding through our own unbelief, and the temptations of Satan, the sensible sight of this light and love are clouded and overwhelmed for the time. And on the contrary, ruling in the world over His enemies, Satan, and all the vessels of wrath (Job 1, 2; Rom. 1:21; 2:4–6; 9:17–18; 2 Peter 2), limiting, using, restraining them by His mighty power, as seems good in His divine wisdom and justice to the execution of His determinate counsel, delivering them up to a reprobate mind, to be kept through their own deserts, in darkness and sensuality unto judgment.

XX.

This kingdom shall be then fully perfected when He shall the second time come in glory to reign among His saints, and to be admired of all them which do believe, when He shall put down all rule and authority under His feet, that the glory of the Father may be full and perfectly manifested in His Son, and the glory of the Father and the Son in all His members (1 Cor. 15:24, 28; Heb. 9:28; 2 Thess. 1:9, 10; 1 Thess. 4:15–17; John 17:21, 26).

XXI.

That Christ Jesus by His death did bring forth salvation and reconciliation only for the elect (John 15:13; Rom. 8:32–34; 5:11; 3:25), which were those which God the Father gave Him (Job 17:2; 6; 37); and that the gospel which is to be preached to all men as the ground of faith, is, that Jesus is the Christ, the Son of the ever-blessed God (Matt. 16:16; Luke 2:26; John 6:9; 7:3; 20:31; 1 John 5:11), filled with the perfection of all heavenly and spiritual excellencies, and that salvation is only and alone to be had through believing in His name.

XXII.

That faith is the gift of God wrought in the hearts of the elect by the Spirit of God (Eph. 2:8; John 6:29; 4:10; Phil. 1:29; Gal. 5:22), whereby they come to see, know, and believe the truth of the Scriptures (John 17:17; Heb. 4:11–12; John 6:63), and not only so, but the excellence of them above all other writing and things in the world, as they hold forth the glory of God in His attributes, the excellence of Christ in His nature and offices, and the power of the fullness of the Spirit in His workings and operations; and thereupon are enabled to cast the weight of their souls upon this truth thus believed.

XXIII.

Those that have this precious faith wrought in them by the Spirit, can never finally nor totally fall away; and though many storms and floods do arise and beat against them, yet they shall never be able to take them off that foundation and rock which by faith they are fastened upon, but shall be kept by the power of God to salvation, where they shall enjoy their purchased possession, they being formerly engraved upon the palms of God's hands (Matt. 7:24–25; John 13:1; 1 Peter 1:4–6; Isa. 49:13–16).

XXIV.

That faith is ordinarily begotten by the preaching of the gospel, or word of Christ (Rom. 10:17; 1 Cor. 1:21), without respect to any power or capacity in the creature (Rom. 9:16), but it is wholly passive, being dead in sins and trespasses (Rom. 2:1–2; Ezek. 16:6; Rom. 3:12), does believe, and is converted by no less power, than that which raised Christ from the dead (Rom. 1:16; Eph. 1:19; Col 2:12).

XXV.

That the tender of the gospel to the conversion of sinners, is absolutely free (John 3:14–15; 1:12; Isa. 55:1; John 7:37), no way requiring, as absolutely necessary, any qualifications, preparations, terrors of the law, or preceding ministry of the law, but only and alone the naked soul, as a sinner and ungodly to receive Christ (1 Tim. 1:15; Rom. 4:5; 5:8), as crucified, dead, and buried, and risen again, being made a prince and a Savior for such sinners (Acts 5:30–31; 2:36; 1 Cor. 1:22–24).

XXVI.

That the same power that converts to faith in Christ, the same power carries on the soul still through all duties, temptations, conflicts, sufferings, and continually whatever a Christian is (1 Peter 1:5; 2 Cor. 12:9), he is by grace (1 Cor. 15:10), and by a constant renewed operation from God (Phil. 2:12–13; John 15:5; Gal. 2:19–20), without which he cannot perform any duty to God, or undergo any temptations from Satan, the world, or men.

XXVII.

That God the Father, and Son, and Spirit, is one with all believers (1 Thess. 1:1; John 14:10, 20; 17:21), in their fullness (Col. 2:9–10; 1:19; John 1:17[sic 16]), in relations (John 20:17; Heb. 2:11), as head and members (Col. 1:18; Eph. 5:30), as house and inhabitants (Eph. 2:22; 1 Cor. 3:16–17), as husband and wife (Isa. 16:5; 2 Cor. 11:3), one with Him, as light and love (Gal. 3:26), and one with Him in His inheritance, and in all His glory (John 17:24); and that all believers by virtue of this union and oneness with God, are the adopted sons of God, and heirs of Christ, co-heirs and joint heirs with Him of the inheritance of all the promises of this life, and that which is to come.

XXVIII.

That those which have union with Christ, are justified from all their sins, past, present, and to come (John 1:7; Heb. 10:14; 9:26; 2 Cor. 5:19; Rom. 3:23), by the blood of Christ; which justification we conceive to be a gracious and free acquittal of a guilty, sinful creature, from all sin by God, through the satisfaction that Christ has made by His death (Acts 13:38–39; Rom. 5:1; 3:25, 30); and this applied in the manifestation of it through faith.

XXIX.

That all believers are a holy and sanctified people (1 Cor. 1:1[sic 2]; 1 Peter 2:9), and that sanctification is a spiritual grace of the new covenant (Eph. 1:4), and effect of the love of God (1 John 4:16), manifested to the soul, whereby the believer is in truth and reality separated, both in soul and body, from all sin and dead works (Eph. 4:24), through the blood of the everlasting covenant (Phil. 3:15[sic Heb. 13:20]), whereby he also presents after a heavenly and evangelical perfection, in obedience to all the commands (Matt. 28:20), which Christ as head and king in this new covenant has prescribed to him.

XXX.

All believers through the knowledge of that justification of life given by the Father, and brought forth by the blood of Christ (2 Cor. 5:19; Rom. 5:9–10), have this as their great privilege of that new covenant, peace with God (Isa. 54:10; 26:12), and reconciliation, whereby they that were afar off, were brought nigh by that blood (Eph. 2:13–14), and have (as the Scripture speaks) peace passing all understanding (Phil. 4:7), yea, joy in God, through our Lord Jesus Christ, by whom we have received the atonement (Rom. 5:10–11).

XXXI.

That all believers in the time of this life, are in a continual warfare, combat, and opposition against sin, self, the world, and the devil, and liable to all manner of afflictions, tribulations, and persecutions, and so shall continue until Christ comes in His kingdom, being predestined and appointed thereunto; and whatsoever the saints, any of them possess or enjoy of God in this life, is only by faith (Eph. 6:10–13; 2 Cor. 10:3; Rev. 2:9–10).

XXXII.

That the only strength by which the saints are enabled to encounter with all opposition, and to overcome all afflictions, temptations, persecutions, and trials, is only by Jesus Christ, who is the captain of their salvation, being made perfect through sufferings, who has engaged His strength to assist them in all their afflictions, and to uphold them under all their temptations, and to preserve them by His power to His everlasting kingdom (John 16:33; Heb. 2:9–10; John 15:5).

XXXIII.

That Christ has here on earth a spiritual kingdom, which is the church, which He has purchased and redeemed to Himself, as a particular inheritance: which church, as it is visible to us, is a company of visible saints (1 Cor. 1:1[*sic* 2]; Eph. 1:1), called and separated from the world (Rom. 1:7; Acts 26:18; 1 Thess. 1:9; 2 Cor. 6:17; Rev. 18:18), by the Word and the Spirit of God (Acts 2:37; 10:37), to the visible profession of the faith of the gospel, being baptized into the faith, and joined to the Lord, and each other, by mutual agreement, in the practical enjoyment of the ordinances, commanded by Christ, their head and king (Rom. 10:10; Acts 2:42; 20:21; Matt. 18:19–20; 1 Peter 2:5).

XXXIV.

To this church He has made His promises, and given the signs of His covenant, presence, love, blessing, and protection (Matt. 28:18–20; 2 Cor.

6:18): here are the fountains and springs of His heavenly grace continually flowing forth; thither ought all men to come, of all estates, that acknowledge Him to be their prophet, priest, and king, to be enrolled among His household servants, to be under His heavenly conduct and government, to lead their lives in His walled sheepfold, and watered garden, to have communion here with the saints, that they may be made to be partakers of their inheritance in the kingdom of God (Isa. 8:16; 1 Tim. 3:15; 4:16; 6:3, 5; Acts 2:41, 47; Song 4:12; Gal. 6:10; Eph. 2:19).

XXXV.

And all His servants are called thither, to present their bodies and souls, and to bring their gifts God has given them; so being come, they are here by Himself bestowed in their several order, peculiar place, due use, being fitly compact and knit together, according to the effectual working of every part, to the edification of itself in love (1 Cor. 12:6, 7, 12, 18; Rom. 12:4–6; 1 Peter 4:10; Eph. 4:16; Col. 2:5, 6, 19; 1 Cor. 12:12–31).

XXXVI.

That being thus joined, every church has power given them from Christ for their better well-being (Acts 1:2; 6:3; 15:22, 25; 1 Cor. 16:3), to choose to themselves fitting persons into the office of pastors, teachers, elders, deacons, being qualified according to the Word (Rom. 12:7–8; 16:1; 1 Cor. 12:8, 28; 1 Tim. 3; Heb. 13:7; 1 Peter 5:1–3), as those which Christ has appointed in His Testament, for the feeding, governing, serving, and building up of His church, and that none other have power to impose them, either these or any other.

XXXVII.

That the ministers aforesaid, lawfully called by the church, where they are to administer, ought to continue in their calling, according to God's ordinance, and carefully to feed the flock of Christ committed to them, not for filthy lucre, but of a ready mind (Heb. 5:4; Acts 4:23; 1 Tim. 4:14; John 10:3–4; Acts 20:28; Rom. 12:7–8; Heb. 13:7, 17).

XXXVIII.

That the due maintenance of the officers aforesaid, should be the free and voluntary communication of the church, that according to Christ's ordinance, they that preach the gospel, should live on the gospel and not by constraint to be compelled from the people by a forced law (1 Cor. 9:7, 14; Gal. 6:6; 1 Thess. 5:13; 1 Tim. 5:17–18; Phil. 4:15–16).

XXXIX.

That baptism is an ordinance of the New Testament, given by Christ, to be dispensed only upon persons professing faith, or that are disciples, or taught, who upon a profession of faith, ought to be baptized (Acts 2:37–38; 8:36–38; 18:8).

XL.

The way and manner of the dispensing of this ordinance the Scripture holds out to be dipping or plunging the whole body under water (Matt. 3:16; John 3:23; Acts 8:38): it being a sign, must answer the thing signified, which are these: first, the washing the whole soul in the blood of Christ (Rev. 1:5; 7:14; Heb. 10:22); secondly, that interest the saints have in the death, burial, and resurrection (Rom. 6:3–5); thirdly, together with a confirmation of our faith, that as certainly as the body is buried under water, and rises again, so certainly shall the bodies of the saints be raised by the power of Christ, in the day of the resurrection, to reign with Christ (1 Cor. 15:28–29).

XLI.

The persons designed by Christ, to dispense this ordinance, the Scriptures hold forth to be a preaching disciple, it being nowhere tied to a particular church, officer, or person extraordinarily sent, the commission enjoining the administration, being given to them under no other consideration, but as considered disciples (Isa. 8:16; Matt. 28:16–19; John 4:1–2; Acts 20:7; Matt. 26:26).

XLII.

Christ has likewise given power to His whole church to receive in and cast out, by way of excommunication, any member; and this power is given to every particular congregation, and not one particular person, either member or officer, but the whole (Acts 2:47; Rom. 16:2; Matt. 18:17; 1 Cor. 5:4; 2 Cor. 2:6–8).

XLIII.

And every particular member of each church, how excellent, great, or learned soever, ought to be subject to this censor and judgment of Christ; and the church ought with great care and tenderness, with due advice to proceed against her members (Matt. 18:16–18; Acts 11:2–3; 1 Tim. 5:19–21).

XLIV.

And as Christ for the keeping of this church in holy and orderly communion, places some special men over the church (Acts 20:27–28; Heb. 13:17, 24; Matt. 24:25; 1 Thess. 5:14), who by their office are to govern, oversee, visit, watch; so likewise for the better keeping thereof in all places, by the members, He has given authority, and laid duty upon all, to watch over one another (Mark 13:34, 37; Gal. 6:1; 1 Thess. 5:11; Jude 3, 20; Heb. 10:34–35; 12:15).

XLV.

That also such to whom God has given gifts, being tried in the church, may and ought by the appointment of the congregation, to prophesy, according to the proportion of faith, and so teach publicly the Word of God, for the edification, exhortation, and comfort of the church (1 Cor. 14; Rom. 12:6; 1 Peter 4:10–11; 1 Cor. 12:7; 1 Thess. 5:17–19).

XLVI.

Thus being rightly gathered, established, and still proceeding in Christian communion, and obedience of the gospel of Christ, none ought to separate for faults and corruptions, which may, and as long as the church consists of men subject to failings, will fall out and arise amongst them, even in true constituted churches, until they have in due order sought redress thereof (Rev. 2, 3; Acts 15:12; 1 Cor. 1:10; Eph. 2:16; 3:15–16; Heb. 10:25; Jude 15; Matt. 18:17; 1 Cor. 5:4–5).

XLVII.

And although the particular congregations be distinct and several bodies, every one a compact and knit city in itself; yet are they all to walk by one and the same rule, and by all means convenient to have the counsel and help one of another in all needful affairs of the church, as members of one body in the common faith under Christ, their only Head (1 Cor. 4:17; 14:33, 36; 16:1; Matt. 28:20; 1 Tim. 3:15; 6:13–14; Rev. 22:18–19; Col. 2:6, 19; 4:16).

XLVIII.

That a civil magistrate is an ordinance of God set up by God for the punishment of evildoers, and for the praise of them that do well; and that all lawful things commanded by them, subjection ought to be given by us in the Lord: and that we are to make supplication and prayer for kings, and all that are in authority, that under them we may live a peaceable and quiet life in all godliness and honesty (Rom. 13:1–4; 1 Peter 2:13–14; 1 Tim. 2:2).

XLIX.

The supreme magistrate of this kingdom we believe to be the king and parliament freely chosen by the kingdom, and that in all those civil laws which have been acted by them, or for the present is or shall be ordained, we are bound to yield subjection and obedience unto in the Lord, as conceiving ourselves bound to defend both the persons of those thus chosen, and all civil laws made by them, with our persons, liberties, and estates, with all that is called ours, although we should suffer never so much from them in not actively submitting to some ecclesiastical laws, which might be conceived by them to be their duties to establish which we for the present could not see, nor our consciences could submit unto; yet are we bound to yield our persons to their pleasures.

L.

And if God should provide such a mercy for us, as to incline the magistrates' hearts so far to tender our consciences, as that we might be protected by them from wrong, injury, oppression, and molestation, which long we formerly have groaned under by the tyranny and oppression of the prelatical hierarchy, which God through mercy has made this present king and parliament wonderfully honorable; as an instrument is His hand, to throw down; and we thereby have had some breathing time, we shall, we hope, look at it as a mercy beyond our expectation, and conceive ourselves further engaged forever to bless God for it (1 Tim. 1:2–4; Ps. 126:1; Acts 9:31).

LI.

But if God withhold the magistrate's allowance and furtherance herein; yet we must notwithstanding proceed together in Christian communion, not daring to give place to suspend our practice, but to walk in obedience to Christ in the profession and holding forth this faith before mentioned (Acts 2:40–41; 4:19; 5:28–29, 41; 20:23; 1 Thess. 3:3; Phil. 1:27–29; Dan. 3:16–17; 6:7, 10, 22, 23), even in the midst of all trials and afflictions, not accounting our goods, lands, wives, children, fathers, mothers, brethren, sisters, yea, and our own lives dear unto us, so we may finish our course with joy: remembering always we ought to obey God rather then men, and grounding upon the commandment, commission, and promise of our Lord and Master Jesus Christ, who as He has all power in heaven and earth, so also has promised, if we keep His commandments which He has given us, to be with us to the end of the world (Matt. 28:18–20; 1 Tim. 6:13–15; Rom. 12:1, 8; 1 Cor. 14:37; 2 Tim. 4:7–8; Rev. 2:10; Gal. 2:4–5): And when we have finished our course, and kept the faith, to give us the crown of righteousness, which is laid up for all that love His appearing, and to whom we must give an account of all our actions, no man being able to discharge us of the same.

LII.

And likewise unto all men is to be given whatsoever is their due; tributes, customs, and all such lawful duties, ought willingly to be by us paid and performed, our lands, goods, and bodies, to submit to the magistrate in the Lord, and the magistrate every way to be acknowledged, reverenced, and obeyed, according to godliness; not because of wrath only but for conscience sake. And finally, all men so to be esteemed and regarded, as is due and meet for their place, age, estate, and condition (Rom. 13:5–7; Matt. 22:21; Titus 3; 1 Peter 2:13; 5:5; Eph. 5:21–22; 6:1, 9).

LIII.

And thus we desire to give God that which is God's, and unto Caesar that which is Caesar's, and unto all men that which belongs unto them, endeavoring ourselves to have always a clear conscience void of offense towards God, and towards man. And if any take this that we have said to be heresy, then do we with the apostle freely confess that after the way which they call heresy, worship we the God of our fathers, believing all things which are written in the Law and in the Prophets and apostles, desiring from our souls to disclaim all heresies and opinions which are not after Christ, and to be steadfast, unmovable, always abounding in the work of the Lord, as knowing our labor shall not be in vain in the Lord (Matt. 22:21; Acts 24:14–16; John 5:28; 2 Cor. 4:17; 1 Tim. 6:3–5; 1 Cor. 15:58, 59[*sic*]).

1 [*sic*] 2 Corinthians 1:24

Not that we have dominion over your faith, but are helpers of your joy: for by faith we stand.

109

Brief Confession of the Westminster Assembly (1645)

In April 1645, the Westminster divines reported to the Parliament of Great Britain that they had "resolved" upon terms of admission to the Lord's Supper.[1] These terms were presented to Parliament on April 1 and April 17. In 1647, Robert Austin published the propositions in a pamphlet originally titled *The Parliaments Rules and Directions concerning Sacramentall Knowledge*. We present both the version reported in the *Commons Journals* and Austin's rendition. The source of the former is *Journals of the House of Commons: From December the 25th, 1644...to December the 4th, 1646* (1803), 95, 113–14.[2] The latter is located in Alexander F. Mitchell, *Catechisms of the Second Reformation* (1886), 151–54. Our texts have been modernized in spelling and capitalization.

TERMS OF ADMISSION TO THE LORD'S SUPPER

It is resolved upon the question, that all such persons, who shall be admitted to the sacrament of the Lord's Supper, ought to know, first, that there is a God: secondly, that there is but one ever-living and true God, Maker of heaven and earth, and Governor of all things: thirdly, that this only true God is the God whom we worship: fourthly, that this God is but one; yet three distinct persons, the Father, Son, and Holy Ghost, all equally God.

Resolved [that those shall not be admitted to the sacrament of the Lord's Supper] that they have not a competent measure of understanding,

---

1. I owe this reference to Chad Van Dixhoorn.
2. My thanks to Adam King for retrieving the pages of this document for me.

concerning the state of man by creation, and by his fall, who do not know, that God created man after His own image, in knowledge, righteousness, and true holiness: that, by one man, sin came into the world, and death by sin; and so death passed upon all men, for that all have sinned: that thereby they are all dead in trespasses and sins; and are, by nature, the children of wrath; and so are liable to eternal death, the wages of every sin.

Resolved, etc. that they have not a competent measure of understanding, concerning the redemption by Jesus Christ, who do not know, that there is but one Mediator between God and Man, the man Christ Jesus, who is also, over all, God blessed for ever; neither is there salvation in any other: that He was conceived by the Holy Ghost, and born of the virgin Mary: that He died upon the cross, to save His people from their sins: that He rose again the third day from the dead; ascended into heaven; sits at the right hand of God; and makes continual intercession for us; of whose fullness we receive all grace necessary to salvation.

Resolved, etc. that they have not a competent measure of understanding, concerning the way and means to apply Christ, and His benefits, who do not know, that Christ, and His benefits, are applied only by faith: that faith is the gift of God; and that we have it not of ourselves; but it is wrought in us by the Word and Spirit of God.

Resolved, etc. that they have not a competent measure of understanding in the nature and necessity of faith, who do not know, that faith is that grace, whereby we believe and trust in Christ for remission of sins, and life everlasting, according to the promises of the gospel: that whosoever believes not on the Son of God, shall not see life, but shall perish eternally.

Resolved, etc. that they have not a competent measure of the knowledge of repentance, who do not know, that they who truly repent of their sins, do see them, sorrow for them, and turn from them to the Lord; and that, except men repent, they shall surely perish.

Resolved, etc. that they have not a competent measure of knowledge concerning a godly life, who do not know, that a godly life is a life conscionably ordered according to the Word of God, in holiness and righteousness, without which no man shall see God.

Resolved, etc. that they have not a competent measure of understanding in the nature and use of the sacrament, who know not, that the sacraments are seals of the covenant of grace in the blood of Christ: that the sacraments of the New Testament are baptism, and the Lord's Supper: that the outward elements in the Lord's Supper are bread and wine, and do signify the body and blood of Christ crucified; which the worthy receiver by faith doth partake of in this sacrament; which Christ hath likewise ordained for a remembrance of His death: that whosoever eats and drinks unworthily, is guilty of the body and blood of the Lord: and therefore, that everyone is to examine himself, lest he eat and drink judgment to himself; not discerning the Lord's body.

Resolved, etc. that they have not a competent measure of understanding, concerning the condition of man after this life, who do not know, that the souls of the faithful, after death, do immediately live with Christ in blessedness; and that the souls of the wicked do immediately go into hell torments; that there shall be a resurrection of the bodies, both of the just and the unjust, at the last day; at which time all shall appear before the judgment seat of Christ, to receive according to what they have done in the body, whether it be good or evil: and that the righteous shall go into life eternal; and the wicked into everlasting punishment.

Resolved, etc. that those who have a competent measure of understanding, concerning the matters contained in these eight articles, shall not be kept back from the sacrament of the Lord's Supper, for ignorance.

Resolved, etc. that the examination and judgment of such persons as shall, for their ignorance of the aforesaid points of religion as have been voted by this committee not to be admitted to the sacrament of the Lord's Supper, is to be in the power of the eldership of every congregation.

THE PARLIAMENT'S RULES AND DIRECTIONS (ROBERT AUSTIN)

All such persons who shall be admitted to the sacrament of the Lord's Supper ought to know:

1. Of One God in Three Persons

That there is a God, that there is but one ever-living and true God, Maker of heaven and earth, and Governor of all things; that this only true God, is the God whom we worship; that this God is but one, yet three distinct persons, the Father, Son and Holy Ghost, all equally God;

2. Of Man's Creation and Fall

That God created man after His own image, in knowledge, righteousness, and true holiness: that by one man sin came into the world, and death by sin, and so death passed upon all men, for that all have sinned; that thereby they are all dead in trespasses and sins, and are by nature the children of wrath, and so liable to eternal death, the wages of every sin;

3. Of Christ [the Mediator]

That there is but one Mediator between God and man, the man Christ Jesus, who is also over all, God blessed for ever, neither is there salvation in any other; that He was conceived by the Holy Ghost, and born of the virgin Mary; that He died upon the cross, to save His people from their sins; that He rose again the third day from the dead, ascended into heaven, sits at the right hand of God, and makes continual intercession for us, of whose fullness we receive all grace necessary to salvation;

4. Of Faith, Repentance, and Holy Life

That Christ and His benefits are applied only by Faith; that faith is the gift of God, and that we have it not of ourselves, but it is wrought in us by the Word and Spirit of God. That faith is that grace whereby we believe and trust in Christ for remission of sins and life everlasting, according to the promise of the gospel, that whosoever believes not on the Son of God, shall not see life, but shall perish eternally. That all they, who truly repent of their sins, do see them, sorrow for them, and turn from them to the Lord, and that except men repent they shall surely perish. That a godly life is conscionably ordered according to the Word of God, in holiness and righteousness, without which no man shall see God.

5. Of the Sacraments

That the sacraments are seals of the covenant of grace in the blood of Christ; that the sacraments of the New Testament are baptism and the Lord's Supper; that the outward elements in the Lord's Supper are bread and wine, and do signify the body and blood of Christ crucified, which the worthy receiver by faith doth partake of in this sacrament, which Christ hath likewise ordained for a remembrance of His death; that whosoever eats and drinks unworthily is guilty of the body and blood of the Lord, and therefore that every one is to examine himself lest he eat and drink judgment to himself, not discerning the Lord's body.

6. Of the Souls and Bodies of Men after Death

That the souls of the faithful after death do immediately live with Christ in blessedness, and that the souls of the wicked do immediately go into hell torments. That there shall be a resurrection of the bodies both of the just and the unjust at the last day, at which time all shall appear before the judgment seat of Christ, to receive according to what they have done in the body, whether it be good or evil; and that the righteous shall go into life eternal, and the wicked into everlasting punishment.

And it is further ordained by the lords and commons, that they have a competent measure of understanding concerning the matters contained in these articles shall not be kept back from the sacrament of the Lord's Supper for ignorance; and that the examination and judgment of such persons as shall for their ignorance of the aforesaid points of religion not be admitted to the sacrament of the Lord's Supper, is to be in the power of the eldership of every congregation.

110

The Colloquy of Thorn (1645)

Begun as a proposal to King Vladislaus (Władysław) IV Vasa (1595–1648) of Poland, the Colloquy of Thorn/Toruń (western Prussia) was an ambitious attempt at rapprochement in the seventeenth century. Vladislaus was joined by his chancellor, George/Jerzy Ossoliński (1595–1650), and Bartholomew Nigrinus (1594–1646), a Roman Catholic visionary from Danzig/Gdańsk. Union of all Christians (Protestant and Roman Catholic) in Poland was the goal. To accomplish this, the *Colloquium Charitativum*, a "friendly conversation" involving all parties, was scheduled for October 1644. However, a Reformed synod in Orła/Podlachia (Poland) in August 1644 petitioned the monarch for more time to prepare for the joint discussions. The king rescheduled the gathering for August 28, 1645.

Before the appointed day, the synod of the Reformed-Bohemian churches of Major Poland met at Leszno/Lissa (Poland) on April 23, 1645, in order to choose delegates for the Thorn Colloquy. The Lutherans were also meeting in Leszno at the same time. The Reformed-Bohemian synod then appealed to the Lutherans to join them in unity against the "common enemy" (Catholicism) at Thorn. The Lutherans submitted the matter to the theologians at the University of Wittenberg, who informed them that cooperation with the Bohemian and Reformed brethren was impossible. The differences between the Bohemian and Reformed communions and the Augustana posed an insurmountable obstacle to joint cooperation. The Polish Lutherans, however, did send a delegation to the colloquy despite the advice from Germany.

On August 28, seventy-six theologians representing Roman Catholic, Lutheran, Bohemian, and Reformed churches gathered at Thorn. The king was present at the outset, but his chancellor, George Ossoliński, presided.

He was assisted by the royal deputy, John Leszczyński of Gniezno/Gnesen (Poland). The Catholic delegation was led by Bishop George Tyszkiewicz (1596–1656) of Samogitia (western Lithuania). The Bohemian (Czech) and Reformed (Helvetian) representatives sat together under Zbigniew Gorajski (1596–1655) of Chełm (eastern Poland). The chief spokesman of this united group was to be the famous educator, John Amos Comenius (Komenský, 1592–1670). The Lutherans were initially led by Sigismund Guldenstein of Sztum (Poland), but he became sick and was replaced by the theologian, John Hüsselmann/Hülsemann (1602–1661) of Wittenberg. The Dutch Remonstrant (Arminian) Hugo Grotius (1583–1645) was to be present, but he died en route at Rostock.

The initial decision was to read a clear and precise (*liquidation*) version of the confession of each group. The Roman Catholic confession was read on September 16. The Reformed confession, titled *Declaratio doctrinae ecclesiarum Reformatarum catholicae*, was also read on September 16. The Lutheran confession was prepared for presentation by September 20, but was never read. What was to be an irenic reading turned into a rhubarb. The confessions, of course, contained some strong language about the theological and liturgical positions of the other bodies. The result was months of haggling over procedural matters and the colloquy became most unfriendly (*colloquium irratativum*). The colloquy dissolved on November 21, 1645, without accomplishing the reconciliation envisioned by its original proponents (if, in fact, such living-in-denial were even actually possible).

Our translation is from the German version printed in E. G. A. Böckel, *Die Bekenntnisschriften der evangelisch-reformirten Kirche* (1847), 864–84, as clarified by the Latin text in Niemeyer, 669–89. We have also examined the English translation of pages 870–74 of Böckel as it appears in B. B. Warfield's article "Predestination in the Reformed Confessions," *The Presbyterian and Reformed Review* 12 (1901): 49–128; cf. 84–87 for the Böckel material.

I. COMMON CONFESSION OF THE DOCTRINE OF THE REFORMED CHURCH IN THE KINGDOM OF POLAND, IN THE GRAND DUCHY OF LITHUANIA AND THE RESPECTIVE PROVINCES OF THE KINGDOM, FOR THE CLARIFICATION OF DISPUTED POINTS AT THE COLLOQUY AT THORN IN 1645, PRESENTED ON SEPTEMBER 1

We thus profess, above all else, that we accept the sacred canonical Scriptures of the Old and New Testaments, originally written in Hebrew in the Old and in Greek in the New by the prophets and apostles by the inspiration of the Holy Spirit; which we acknowledge as the only perfect rule of our faith and worship; wherein one finds clearly expounded all that is necessary for salvation; or, as the blessed Augustine says, which contains the faith and the way of life, that is to say, hope and love.

This is, as it were, a compendium regarding what we are to believe: the Apostles' Creed, into which we all have been baptized; regarding what we should do, the Ten Commandments, whose chief content consists in the love of God and of neighbor; and regarding that for which we ought to pray and hope, contained in the Lord's Prayer. This faith is also confirmed by our Lord Jesus Christ through the institution of baptism as the sacrament of initiation or rebirth, and through the Lord's Supper as the sacrament of spiritual nourishment.

Thus we believe that the saving doctrine is contained in these principal points, for whose spread and preservation in the church, our Lord has also instituted the sacred ministry (which must preach the gospel and administer the sacraments) and armed it with the spiritual power of the keys against the unbelieving and disobedient.

However, if in these principal heads of Christian doctrine, a doubt or dispute over their actual sense should develop, then we profess further that we accept the Nicene and Constantinopolitan Creeds as sure and undoubted expositions of Scripture (entirely with the same words in which it is explained in the third session of the Council of Trent) as the foundation on which all who profess faith in Christ essentially agree, and as the firm and only foundation which the gates of hell will never overcome.

We also confess that the so-called Athanasian Creed agrees therewith as well, no less than do the confessions of the first Council of Ephesus and the Council of Chalcedon, and that which in the fifth and sixth councils were set over against the Nestorians and Eutychians; as well as that which the first council at Mileve and the second council at Orange taught from Scripture against the Pelagians. And further, that which the early church from the times of the apostles onward has with one accord and in well-known agreement believed and taught as a necessary article of faith, we likewise profess to believe and teach according to the Scriptures.

By this confession of our faith, we, as true catholic Christians, dissociate ourselves from all old and new heresies, which the ancient universal church unanimously rejected and condemned according to Scripture.

That which otherwise concerns the controversies which in the memories of our fathers have divided the churches of the west by a grievous schism, we profess that we hold the opinion, which is also in the Augsburg Confession (which was presented to Emperor Charles V in the year 1530 by the Protestant princes and cities of this kingdom, that is declared to be the unaltered [*invariata*] or the renewed and rectified faith), as also according to the Scriptures; in the Bohemian and Sendomir [Sandomierz] Confessions, and which has held sway in the Reformed congregations of this kingdom for nearly an entire century. For these three confessions, although differing from each other somewhat in expression, but in the substance itself agreeing with Scriptures and, among themselves, in the necessary principal points of the faith, according to the Consensus of Sendomir, which was accepted and incorporated into our churches in the year 1570, and through an alliance of peace and public security established and confirmed in this kingdom.

II. OUR DECLARATION IN ITS PARTICULARS

1. Of the Rule of Faith and Worship

1) The Holy Scripture, given by God in the books of the Old Testament through Moses and the prophets, and in the books of the New Testament through the evangelists and apostles, is the only infallible and absolute guide and rule of Christian faith and worship, enjoined to ministers of both church and state. In her is so much that is clearly and openly expounded, that one finds therein all that encompasses the faith and conduct of life, or all that is necessary for salvation, as it is declared in our recent declaration with others concerning the Word of God.

2) Those books which are not in the Hebrew canon of the Old Testament, but exist merely in Greek text, are called apocryphal and therefore may not be numbered in the divine canon, expressly under pain of anathema, even though they may be read with benefit for the edification of the church.

3) The reading of Scripture in the mother tongue is by no means to be refused to the laity, or counseled against as dangerous or harmful, but is rather to be allowed as free and useful; indeed, it is to be recommended.

4) Translations of the Scriptures are allowed, although they require the common judgment of the church for their acceptance. However, no one at all is to use, prefer, or consider, much less declare, as the original source the Latin Vulgate, under threat of anathema. But it should be referred to only where it agrees with the original texts, the Hebrew and Greek of the Old and New Testaments. These translations can be interpreted by every believer in the clear and easily understandable texts out of the consensus of the different translations, although the more difficult texts should only be expounded by the learned.

5) Concerning the doctrines of the faith or the regulations of life necessary to salvation, there is no Word of God in existence, or which can be shown to be such with certainty, which is not written or grounded in the Scripture, but is only commended by the unwritten traditions of the church.

6) No pope, bishop, or council of bishops on earth, neither as a higher and more infallible judge, nor through judicial authority, or under pain of anathema, can dictate as an article of faith that which is not openly taught in Scripture, or cannot be derived from certain necessary and evident deduction from Scripture, and cannot be confirmed through the approval of the early church.

7) Much less do we accept that the particular spirit of the believer himself is the judge of the Scripture or a rule of faith. Rather we profess that the believing as well as the teaching spirit, and every judgment, is to be guided and to be judged by the church and her pastors according to the Scripture as the only rule and infallible law for the highest of earthly judges.

2. Of the Most Holy Trinity, and of the Person and the Office of Christ

1) We confess the article of the most Holy Trinity and the person of our Lord Jesus Christ, the God-Man, as the actual foundation of the entire Christian faith and we believe it most certainly. But we now include a

declaration of the article because no dissension occurs over it between our church and the Roman church, even though with justification we despise the majority of the questions and disputes of some learned men over so sublime a mystery, which should be believed in its noble simplicity more according to Scripture rather than probed with excessive curiosity, because they are more captious and meddlesome than useful.

2) We likewise believe the article on the office of our Lord Jesus Christ as a fundamental article, namely that the only begotten Son of the Father became flesh through Mary (who remained always a virgin) is our sole Redeemer and Mediator, and through this alone is the Foundation, the Head, the High Priest, and the Prophet, and likewise the sole King and Bridegroom of the church, in whom alone, the fullness of power, grace, and life resides, which from Him, as the head through the same Spirit, is poured out into all members according to the measure of each believer.

3) As Christ alone is our mediator and redeemer, none of the saints nor even the most blessed virgin Mary (even though we recognize her as the most blessed among women and praiseworthy above all others as the mother of God) may be called mediators between God and men. Nor is it to be assigned to Mary to be the queen of heaven with lordship over all creatures, which is the province of Christ alone. And outside our obligation to Christ, our Redeemer, no one may be committed or ordained to her special service.

4) Much less may anyone assign to a bishop or pope on earth that name or the power that belongs to Christ alone; that he is the Foundation, the Head, the Bridegroom, the sole King of the entire church; or that he, as the vicar of God and Christ, has full power both in spiritual and temporal things, be it direct or indirect, so that he can overthrow kings from their lordship, absolve subjects from the oath of loyalty taken before God and from other vows taken before those in God's stead, make saints and raise them to heaven, free souls from purgatory, and give precedence to others, and thus expand to such an extent his authority not only over all lands, but also into heaven and hell.

3. Of Sin

1) God is not at all the author of any sin, but rather the source and author of all good things; by contrast, the hater and avenger of all that is evil.

2) It is therefore outright calumny when that horrible blasphemy impugns our church—that we make God the author of sin. We abhor this profanity with all our hearts. Instead, we confess the providence of God in regard to sin and over the sinner himself, in the same way that it is taught by most theologians of the Roman church.

3) No less grave a calumny is it that we teach that Christ Himself may have sinned or may have despaired on the cross. This blasphemy we also reject with all our soul.

4) All men, Christ alone excepted, are conceived and born in original sin, even the most holy virgin Mary herself.

5) Original sin consists not only in the simple absence of righteousness, but also in depravity or inclination to evil which was propagated from Adam to all mankind.

6) Even though the natural faculty of free will remains after the fall in natural and civil things, one has, however, no ability to recognize, or to will, or to do supernatural and spiritual good, or to fulfill the law in its substance. In this respect, it is rightly called not so much a free will as a will that is a slave of sin and dead in sin, until it is awakened and freed through the grace of Christ.

7) Although in the regenerated, original sin, that which concerns the debt is abolished through the gracious remission, and concerning the depravity is more and more put to death through the grace of Christ, yet there remains in them (as long as they are in the flesh) the remnants of that depravity, particularly the evil inclinations and the stirrings of concupiscence which are therefore called in truth real sins, not only insofar as they are the punishment and origin of sin but also insofar as they strive against the law of God was well as against the Spirit of grace. This doctrine, because it is taught by the apostle himself, cannot be rejected as in error, much less condemned by anathema as heretical.

8) Each particular sin is by its nature mortal because it is contrary to the law and therefore deserves the curse of the law. Nonetheless, although not all sins are alike, none according to its nature is pardoned without the grace of Christ.

9) But in the reborn, the sins of ignorance and weakness, even though in themselves and according to their nature (if God were to deal with them according to the strictness of the law) are mortal sins, but as long

as they do not nullify faith, love, and good intent, and are washed away through daily repentance, they are through God's grace not mortal sins, but pardoned, because they are not imputed unto death, but rather for the sake of Christ are remitted to those who have faith in Him.

4. Of Grace

1) From sin and death, there is no salvation or justification by the power of nature or through the righteousness of the law, but only through the grace of God in Christ, who redeemed us from wrath and the curse who were dead in sins through that only sacrifice of His death and through the merit of His perfect obedience in which He worked sufficiently for our, and not only for our, but also for the sins of the entire world.

2) Who has efficaciously through the Word of the gospel and Spirit of grace called the saved out of the kingdom of sin and death into the kingdom of grace and life and sealed them through the sacraments of grace.

3) Who justifies, or absolves from sin and accepts as children, the elect and truly repentant only for the sake of the merit of Christ, which they lay hold of by faith, and which is imputed to believers, purely out of grace, as members of Christ.

4) Who at the same time, from day to day, more and more renews and sanctifies them by the Spirit of love who is poured out into our hearts, unto sincere zeal in holiness and new obedience, that is to say makes them righteous and holy.

5) Who will finally eternally glorify those who persevere in faith and in love by means of His grace unto the end of this life as heirs of the kingdom of heaven, not out of any merit, but only out of the grace that is promised in Christ.

6) And so also in a fatherly manner rewards their good works which are done in faith in Christ and in love for Him through the grace of the Holy Spirit, without and beyond merit, with abundantly rich and unending reward for the sake of Christ.

7) He has chosen them from eternity in Christ, not on account of foreseen faith or any merit of works or of any condition, but rather out of pure and unearned grace, unto the grace of redemption that is given to them in time, unto calling, justification, adoption unto children, and

persevering sanctification as well as unto the crown and glory of eternal life which can be attained through these means.

8) Meanwhile, those who remain, resisting the truth with their unrighteousness and defiantly scorning the offered grace of Christ, will be damned in a just judgment.

From this doctrine of grace, which we have stated in its most important points, wherein the entire foundation of our salvation is contained:

1) It will hopefully be manifest that we absolutely disagree with Socinus, who in a godless manner denies and disputes the satisfaction and merit of Christ, even the salvation itself that is achieved through Christ's blood.

2) We deny that outside of the death of Christ the smallest part of our redemption or salvation can be attributed to a sacrifice, a merit, or to a satisfaction, whether it be from saints or from ourselves.

3) We also deny that the unregenerate, if they do that which is in themselves to do, make themselves capable through any claim on the first grace of calling (merit of congruity).

4) Also, we do not make the efficacy of calling grace dependent upon the free will of man, as if he through his own will, and not God through special grace, would finally decide.

5) We are falsely accused, however, as if we deny that the death and merit of Christ suffices for all, or as if we diminish His power. For we teach much the same as that which the Council of Trent taught in its sixth session, in the third chapter, namely: "Although Christ died for all, yet not all enjoy the benefit of His death; rather only they to whom the merit of His suffering is imparted." We profess also that the cause or blame for this, whereby it is not imparted to all, lies in men themselves and in no way in the death and merit of Christ.

6) We are also falsely accused, as if we teach that not all those called through the Word of the gospel are earnestly, sincerely, or sufficiently called to repentance and blessedness by God, but rather that most are only seemingly and deceitfully called, only by signs through the revealed will, whereas the inner will of God's counsel is lacking and He does not therein wish blessedness for all. We profess that we are far removed from this notion, for which people have charged us, either through false understanding or by the untoward words of a few; and

that in God we attribute the highest truth and fidelity to all of His words and works, but in particular to those words which accompany the grace which calls to salvation, we do not attribute to Him a will which stands in constant contradiction to itself.

7) Wrongly we are accused as if we deny that righteousness which lives within all believers, and claim that they are justified only through the external imputation of the righteousness of Christ, which occurs without any inner regeneration. For we teach that righteousness is imputed only to those who are repentant and have a lively faith in Christ. Likewise, through this faith, the Holy Spirit animates the contrite heart unto burning love for Christ, awakens zeal for the new obedience, cleanses one of evil affections, and thus commences the righteousness and sanctification of new life and perfects it from day to day. Here we add only this: that through one's own inherent righteousness (because it is imperfect in this life), no one can be confident in it or stand before the stern judgment of God. One does not become justified or absolved from the guilt of death through this righteousness, but rather only by means of the perfect righteousness of Christ and His merit, taken hold of by living faith.

8) Falsely we are accused as if we believe that one is justified through that faith alone which is without works and which consists only in trust; and that the sins of a man are forgiven him for the sake of Christ, even though he persists in all impenitence. For indeed we freely profess that such a faith is completely false and that not only is man not justified through it, but he also is much more grievously damned because he sinfully abuses that grace of God which is meant for freedom. Rather we call true, justifying faith only that which actively and confidently embraces the promise of the gospel, through which forgiveness and life in Christ is offered to the penitent, which consecrates itself with a true, contrite heart, and which works in love. We do not assert that this justifies because it is this alone, but because it alone takes hold of the promise of the gospel and so also the righteousness of Christ itself, and by means of and because of this faith alone, without any of our own merit, we become righteous.

9) Wrongly we are accused that through this doctrine, we remove the zeal for good works and deny their necessity. For from the aforementioned, it is obvious that neither justifying faith nor justification itself can have any place among adult believers without sanctification and

zeal for good works. In this sense, we also recognize that they are indeed necessary for salvation, although not as meritorious causes of justification and salvation.

10) Wrongly we are accused as if we assert that the commandments of Christ can in no way be upheld by the faithful. For we teach that not by our own strength, but through the grace of the Holy Spirit, the commandments not only can be upheld, but indeed *must* be upheld by all; and certainly not by a mere desire alone or through an ineffectual resolution, but in true deed, and a true, sincere, and lasting zeal in all of life. They are not and cannot be kept so completely by any one in this life, with the result that we cannot satisfy the law of God through our ways and fulfill it altogether. Rather, from the feeling of our own imperfection and weakness, we must daily pray to God in humility for forgiveness of many errors and trespasses.

11) Wrongly we are accused that we assert that the justified cannot lose the grace or assurance of God and the Holy Spirit, even though they freely live in sin. For we teach much to the contrary that the reborn themselves, as often as they fall back into sin against their consciences and persist there for a long time, retain for that time neither the living faith nor the justifying grace of God, much less the assurance thereof and the Holy Spirit. Rather they burden themselves with a new debt of wrath and eternal death, and therefore, if they are not awakened by the special grace of God (which we do not doubt in the elect) and renewed in repentance again, naturally they too must be damned.

12) We further deny that faith in Christ justifies only in an awakening, preparatory, introductory manner, because faith awakens particularly to love and to other virtues, such as indwelling righteousness.

13) We deny also that we become justified through an inherent righteousness, so that by virtue of it we are exculpated from the debt of death before the judgment of God, accepted as His children and declared worthy of eternal life. For in this juridical sense the term "justified by the Holy Spirit" is used in this doctrine. For in this proper sense, it can also be said that the faithful are justified, that is to say, made just and holy through love and other virtues affected in them. But this righteousness is imperfect in this life, and therefore, as mentioned above, it cannot by any means stand before the stern judgment of God. And this is principally observed in this doctrine.

14) Hence, we also disagree with those who teach that the reborn satisfy the justice of God for their sins through their good work and actually earn forgiveness or life—indeed through legal actions or because of the inner worth of their works or because they have balanced out their rewards. From this, a covenant or promise cannot be assumed, as some desire it.

15) We also disagree with those who teach that the reborn can perfectly fulfill the law of God in this life, not only the part in perfection, but also its standard, so that they live without any sin, which would be in itself and according to its nature mortal sin; indeed they are even able to perform works that are beyond what is required and go beyond legal perfection and thereby acquire merit not only for themselves, but also for others.

16) Also, we disagree with those who teach that without special revelation, no one can know that he has acquired the grace of God with that certainty which no deception can destroy, and therefore all must always doubt of grace. But even though we profess that the faithful and justified cannot overconfidently and carelessly count on the grace of God and often struggle with anxieties and doubts, they nevertheless can and should (as we teach according to Scripture) struggle for certainty in this life with the help of the grace of God and achieve that certainty by which the Holy Spirit witnesses with our spirits that we are children and heirs of God. This witness can no deception destroy, even though not all who boast of the Spirit of God have this witness in truth.

17) Finally, we teach that not all people are elected, and that the elect are chosen not because of the foreseen merit of their works, or because of a foreseen disposition in them towards faith, or because of the assent of their wills, but from the simple grace which is in Christ. And thus the number of those who are elected by God and who are to be saved remains constant.

18) Meanwhile, we declare that a completely foreign notion is attributed to us by those who accuse us of teaching that eternal election and reprobation are unconditional, without any regard to faith or faithlessness, or to the good and evil works which are done. For we assert much more that in election, faith and obedience are foreseen in those to be elected, certainly not as the origin or ground of election itself but rather as means of salvation which are predestined to them

by God. In reprobation, not only original sin, but also, with respect to adults, faithlessness and obstinate impenitence are not actually predestined by God, but foreseen and permitted in the reprobate themselves as the proper ground of rejection and damnation; and they are rejected in that most just judgment.

Therefore, we hold fast to the conception of this deep mystery of election by grace, which, according to Scripture, Augustine defended in ancient times against Pelagius, and to which the most excellent teachers of the Roman Church themselves hold even today, especially the followers of Thomas Aquinas.

5. Of the Worship Service

1) The sole true God, is one in being and threefold in persons; the all-knowing, almighty, omnipresent, Creator and Giver of all good things, who turns away evil, and is the all-sufficient, most merciful Savior who should be honored by us in private and in public worship, and certainly in the manner which He Himself has prescribed in His Word.

2) To honor any other person or thing that is not God in a religious or divine manner is idolatry; but to honor the true God in ways not prescribed or established by His Word is superstitious and vain and sometimes idolatrous.

3) Reverence which is fitting to God consists first in pious worship, as well and especially in that inward worship, given through the deepest humility of the soul and submission before God as the highest and most holy Lord of all things, and as the everywhere present Searcher and Judge of the hearts and reins; as well as by the external worship, through bowing and prostration of the body, lifting up of the hands, and other similar gestures, which are rooted in inner reverence and will be judged according to it. For these can also be used as civil gestures which show civil honor.

4) So also in prayer, by which we ask God to bestow bodily as well as spiritual gifts and the turning away of evil, in order for it to be pleasing to Him, must be conducted in the name of and in the confidence in our only Mediator, Jesus Christ.

5) Thereto pertains also the singing of God's praise through psalms and hymns of praise; the giving of thanks for received blessings, as well

as the worshipful hearing of the divine Word; the participation in the sacraments in faith and likewise the permissible oath, by which we invoke God, the Lord of the heart, as the witness of truth and the avenger of deception. Finally, also the holy vow, whereby we sanctify and consecrate ourselves and all of our dealings and actions as spiritual offerings to God.

6) Outward sacrifices, modeled and decreed in the law, are characteristics of the Old Testament, and are fulfilled and superseded through the one sacrifice of Christ on the cross.

7) We recognize that each and every part of the worship service we have discussed cannot simply be performed in private, at any place or time, but is also or especially to be performed publicly or in the public congregation of the church; and also certain places, namely the temple and holy building, if one can have them, are to be designated.

8) At the public or official worship service, it is befitting to use a language familiar to all the people, so that each of the faithful can say Amen to the prayers, to the hymns of praise, and to the preaching.

9) Certain times are also to be named for public worship. We observe the day of the Lord throughout the entire year, as well as certain feast days, such as the birth, circumcision, passion and resurrection, the ascension, Pentecost, and so forth.

10) Some of the days are consecrated to the remembrance of saints, such as the blessed virgin Mary, the archangel Michael, and the apostle. We celebrate, not actually to confer worshipful veneration on them in themselves, but rather in order to exalt in grateful memory the grace of God demonstrated through them and to move ourselves to emulate them.

11) Moreover, we believe that it is permissible for Christian magistrates, in collaboration with the overseers of the church, to arrange from time to time either thanksgivings for a particular blessing or fast and prayer days for a great danger or a pressing concern.

We believe that these teachings are opposed to true worship in the manner that is prescribed in the New Testament:

1) When one believes that after the sacrifice of Christ performed once on the cross, yet another bloodless, so-called sacrifice of atonement for

the living and dead, must be offered daily. We assert that it is neither ordered nor used nor approved in the New Testament.

2) When the consecrated host is elevated or brought forth for adoration in the name of Christ;

3) When adoration or invocation, whether outwardly or inwardly, are directed towards created things or persons, be they angels or deceased saints, as intercessors or as helpers and givers of gifts; and psalms and hymns of praise that ought to be dedicated to God alone are applied to them;

4) When one worships either the invisible or incomprehensible God Himself or Christ or deceased saints in graven, cast and painted images; and teaches that the images themselves are not only in an accidental and figurative manner representatives of the original, but also are to be revered actually and in themselves by the congregation.

5) When one demonstrates veneration for or places faith in relics of saints, be they authentic or dubious and suspicious.

6) When one dedicates feasts to the saints, sanctifies a temple, presents vows, or makes vows or oaths in their name.

7) When one repeats a certain number of times the Lord's Prayer and the angelic salutation or other prayer formulas, directed either to God Himself or to the most holy virgin and other saints with the notion of this as a merit or work of satisfaction for sins.

8) When one reckons monks' vows as meritorious and works of supererogation in the worship of God.

9) When one believes that the state and the chastity of clerics, undertaken in the absence of the special gift of abstinence and not without the danger of incontinences, is not only commendable or, at least, to be excused, but is also a meritorious service of God.

10) When one goes on pilgrimages to holy places (principally during so-called jubilee years) with the notion of acquiring a special grace of God or forgiveness of sins.

11) When one employs creatures of God such as water, salt, oil, wax candles, and other things not only in the natural uses ordained by God, but also consecrates them to spiritual or supernatural uses, so that one sets by them a certain power to turn away devilish sorceries or for the safety of the soul and the body.

12) And finally, when one believes that fasts (in particular during the forty days before Easter) are in themselves pleasing and meritorious or satisfying to God; and indeed believes not only in true fasts, such as were the custom in the first church, as useful exercises in repentance, but also in such fasts that consist more in the selection rather than the lack of food, and are more often spent by many in the enjoyment of delicacies than in the abstention from food.

13) If these and similar things which are too numerous to count are too far removed from the true worship of God, then we are of the opinion that one can quickly do away with those things that remain in the church that are not without danger of giving offence, which are found in customs and ceremonies which were introduced only through long or ancient usage, which either militate against God's Word or lack a sound foundation, or which finally by their performance, according to experience, work more to the ruin and deterioration than to the advantage and edification of the church.

6. Of the Sacraments

1) Sacraments are outward and clear signs, seals, and witnesses of God's will, through the Word which is joined to the elements, instituted by God Himself to show forth the invisible grace which is promised in the Word of the covenant to seal it by means of these signs.

2) There are in truth actually only two sacraments in the New Testament: baptism and the Lord's Supper. These differentiate themselves from the sacraments of the Old Testament for the most part in that those testify to the future appearance of Christ while these witness to Christ's accomplished work.

3) The truth or authenticity of the sacrament is not to be judged according to the worthiness or unworthiness of those who dispense them or those who receive them, but alone according to the truth and will of God, who has instituted them.

4) Therefore, they also do not work or confer grace through the mere action without any good inclination toward God in their use, but rather through the power of the promise, which must be accepted with true faith.

5) And so the efficacy of the sacrament depends not upon the intent of the minister, if only the divinely instituted form itself is observed with respect to its performance or administration.

6) Although those customs which belong to good order are left to the freedom of the church, nevertheless no customs except those which Christ Himself has ordained may be made compulsory under threat of excommunication, as belonging to the nature or the validity of the sacrament by any church or by her pastors. But those that have crept in through abuse or superstition are properly done away with.

7) Out of the law, it is also clear that we do not accept mere empty and ineffectual signs or mere earmarks of an outward confession. For in addition to the mysterious signs, we attribute (according to the divine ordinance) a certain sealing of the divine promises, at the same time a true and infallible presentation of that which is promised, all which occurs in a manner which is fitting and peculiar to them and which must be received with a living faith.

8) So we believe, in conclusion, that only those who truly believe are truly made partakers of the gifts which are presented through signs and the Word, but unbelievers and hypocrites, because they partake of the signs in an unworthy manner and do not receive that which is signified with a true faith, incur to themselves guilt and judgment.

7. Of Baptism

1) Baptism is a sacrament of the New Testament, instituted by Christ the Lord, which must be administered by servants of the Word as well to children born in the church as to those adults joining the church through the profession of their faith, by washing with water along with prayers to the most Holy Trinity, in order to signify and testify to the inward washing or forgiveness of sins achieved through the blood of Christ; and likewise to testify to the beginning of renewal through the Holy Spirit or regeneration.

2) That this sacrament, because of the institution of Christ, is completely necessary as a well-ordained means of salvation, we profess in faith. Although we do not hold its importance to be so absolute that whoever should depart this life without outward baptism, be he a child or adult, through whatever accident that may happen, but without any contempt of the sacrament, is thereby of necessity damned. We much more believe here that the rule governs that it is not deprivation but contempt of the sacrament which condemns.

8. Of the Holy Supper

1) Just as baptism is the sacrament of our spiritual rebirth in Christ, so is the Holy Supper the sacrament of our spiritual nourishment in Christ, through which Christ Himself presents and communicates to us His body given for us and the blood of the New Testament which is poured out for us through the symbols of bread and wine, sanctified by the sovereign power of His Word, which He has commanded us to eat bodily and visibly in remembrance of His sacrifice.

2) Thus, this sacrament consists in earthly things (in the bread and wine), as well as in heavenly things (the body and blood of the Lord). Both these things are indeed offered to us in different yet in the truest, most substantial and real manners. Namely, we lay hold of the earthly things in a natural, corporeal, and earthly manner, but lay hold of the heavenly things in a spiritual, mysterious, and heavenly manner, as inscrutable to reason and perception and with faith alone, by means of which we apprehend the words of the promise and that which is promised itself, namely Christ crucified, with all His benefits.

3) Therefore, the earthly elements, bread and wine, both in name and in truth are the body and blood of Christ, certainly not communicated in essence or corporally but sacramentally and mysteriously and by means of the sacramental union, which does not consist in the mere signification nor only in the sealing, but in the combined and simultaneous administration and imparting of the earthly and heavenly elements.

4) In the same sense, the ancients say (and we with them) that bread and wine change into the body and the blood, certainly not according to the being and nature, but according to the use and service, and not by name or by that which is perceived by the senses, as by that which faith sees and receives in them by the power of the promise.

5) Therefore, the entire operation of the holy communion is called an offering by the ancients and specifically, with good reason, an offering of thanks; for these holy symbols, which are in a mysterious way the body and blood of Christ, are offered by prayer of thanksgiving to God and imparted to us in thankful commemoration and appropriation in faith of that single sacrifice which is the true and real sacrifice of atonement accomplished once on the cross.

6) Albeit, we do not accept a transubstantiation, whereby the elements of bread and wine would be annihilated in their essence or essentially transformed into the body of Christ;

7) Nor any inclusion, inner or accompanying presence, local or bodily presence, or any such union of the elements with the body of Christ whereby the same is eaten with the mouth by the unbelieving and godless as well as by believers.

8) Nor yet a true and actual sacrifice of atonement of the body and blood in the Lord's Supper.

9) Albeit, we also do not direct the worship of Christ (which we unconditionally profess is most necessary in the administration of the Holy Supper) to the elements or to an invisible body hidden in them, but rather to Christ Himself, who reigns at the right hand of the Father.

10) So we absolutely refuse mere, empty, and idle signs, and moreover, that which they signify, seal, and minister, we receive as the most certain means and efficacious instruments by which the body and blood of Christ (indeed Christ Himself with all His good gifts) is offered to each participant, but distributed to the faithful, granted to and received by them as saving and regenerating food of the soul.

11) Also, we most certainly do not deny the true presence of the body and blood of Christ in the Lord's Supper, but only the local and corporeal manner of presence and its essential union with the elements. But we believe His presence with us to be holy and indeed not an imagined, but rather the truest, most essential and actual presence. Namely, it is that mysterious union of Christ with us which He Himself promises in His Word, presents in the symbols and so effects through the Spirit, which we accept in faith and perceive through love, according to that old expression: "The notion we perceive, the type and manner we do not know, in the presence we believe" (*Motum sentimus, modum mescimus, praesentiam credimus*).

12) Thence, it is also clear that not only the strength, the ability and force, or good gifts of Christ are offered and imparted, but principally the essence of the body and blood of Christ Himself or the sacrifice which was given and slaughtered on the cross for the life of the world. We receive our part in this sacrifice and union with Christ Himself, as thereby also in the merits and benefits which His sacrifice gained by faith. And as He abides in us, so too we abide in Him;

13) And indeed, not merely with respect to our souls, but also with respect to our bodies. For although we receive the earthly things with our bodily mouth, so in the faith of our hearts, we receive it as the actual instrument, the heavenly thing, according to that old verse: "That which the teeth chew is only enjoyed by the body; but the soul enjoys that which it apprehends in faith" (German: *Was die Zähne zerkaun, nur das wird leiblich genossen; Aber die Seele geniesst, was sie im Glauben ergreift*. Latin: *Ventrem, quod terminus, mentem, quod credimus, intrat*; lit., "We chew that which enters the stomach and believe that which enters the mind"). So by means of this faith, not only our spirits, but also our bodies themselves, are united and bound to the body of Christ through His Spirit in the hope of the resurrection and of eternal life. Thus, we are flesh of His flesh and bone of His bones, and are one body with Him in a mysterious manner. Whereof the apostle says with good reason: "the mystery is great" (Eph. 5:32).

14) Finally, concerning the usages which are parts of this sacrament, we add at least this: that Christ Himself bade all no less to drink from the chalice than to eat the bread, and that the power to do away with the customs which He Himself ordained, either in part or completely, or to transfer a usage to another purpose or intent, or to add another custom as obligatory under threat of excommunication, belongs to no mortal.

9. Of Confirmation

1) We believe that it merits approval that the doctrine of the laying on of hands (which in Hebrews 6:12 is bound together with the doctrine of baptism) relates to that ordinance of the church, according to which children who have been instructed in the catechism should be presented to the congregation before one allows them to partake in the Lord's Supper, in order for them to give an account of their faith and to be commended to God with prayers, along with the application of the custom of the laying on of hands, a practice, alongside of prayer and blessing, which was common in the time of the patriarchs and thereafter. We gladly permit this intercession and commendation to God on the part of the adult believers, followed by the customary examination, to be called "confirmation," as this custom is also observed in an orderly manner in our congregations.

2) We deny however:

   a. That confirmation is in truth a sacrament of the New Testament.

   b. That it impresses an indelible mark onto the soul.

   c. That both of these must be believed under punishment of excommunication.

   d. That confirmation is not only to be compared with baptism, but also to be preferred to it on two points: namely because of the dignity of the minister, who is the bishop alone; and because of the completeness of the effect.

10. Of Penitence

1) Here it is not disputed whether conversion of the heart toward God and an inner abhorrence for sins that is combined with anguish is required for the forgiveness of sins. For we assert that such repentance has been demanded in both Testaments as a standing condition for the forgiveness of sin, which the sinner however does not merit (for the merit and satisfaction made by Christ alone accomplishes this when we dedicate ourselves in living faith). But it is fulfilled through the aforementioned condition, whereby it is given to desire the divine mercy. This inner penitence, we assert, suffices for secret sins of which the sinner is conscious and which are known only to God.

2) However, we consider it to be permissible and very valuable to anxious consciences to seek shelter in the counsel of those who because of their office better understand the nature and characteristics of sin; and to seek solace from one's own pastor through a confession of the sin which disturbs the troubled heart. For this reason, in our opinion, private absolution can be retained as useful.

3) Regarding graver sins, however, which have caused offense in the congregation and are known to a number of people, we demand outward and public repentance and assert that against such sins the church and its leaders can and should use the authority of the keys, so as to bind them by means of the authority of the church; and when they have produced the fruits of penitence, loosen them again by the authority of the office which God has conferred upon them for this purpose.

4) We deny, however:

   a. That any outward penitence, be it private or official, whether in penance or in the actions of the clergy, considered individually or together, is a true sacrament of the New Testament and that it must be considered as such under punishment of excommunication.

b. That a confession by enumeration of each and every mortal sin which one recalls after dutiful and careful meditation, as well as of those hidden sins and of those which are against the last of the Ten Commandments, is necessary for the forgiveness of sins according to divine law, so that it must be made secretly and before a priest alone and that this must be believed under pain of excommunication.

c. Since the satisfaction and merit of Christ alone makes us free, not only from debt, but also from all intrinsic satisfaction-making punishments, we deny that they are necessary for redemption from eternal or temporal punishment, in part in this life by ecclesiastical satisfaction or in part after this life by the satisfaction-making penance of purgatory.

d. We deny also that indulgences, as they are in use in our day, have any value.

e. Wrongly, it is ascribed to us that we reject all repentance and that we promise atonement to sinners without contrition and abhorrence of the life that has previously been led and without a vow of sincere improvement.

11. Of Extreme Unction

1) We confess that the apostle anointed the sick with oil, whereby they were also healed in body. We profess also that the epistle of James commands that the elders of the congregation are to call on the sick in order to anoint them with oil and they are to pray for them, for the recovery of health. Also, we profess that in our day the office of the minister demands that they visit the sick and that they comfort them both through the preaching of the gospel and through the distribution of Holy Communion, and that they pray along with the congregation for their welfare.

2) We deny, however:

a. That, as the gift of miraculous healing has ended, this custom of oil remains of use in the church.

b. That it is instituted as a true sacrament of the New Testament by Christ, and that it must be believed to be such under pain of excommunication.

12. Of Ordination

1) We acknowledge that everything must take place in the church in an orderly and decent manner and that no one is legally authorized to exercise the office of preacher in the church except he be called to the teaching office, be it through a direct and extraordinary call or be it a usual call which uses means, not only on the basis of an inner incitement of the Holy Spirit and with the preceding granting of sufficient gifts, but also in the effective, outward consent of the congregation and especially of its leaders, through the election of the congregation and confirmed through ordination, that is, the laying on of hands by the elders. And we acknowledge that also among the ministers of the divine Word, there are certain degrees of office and gifts that are granted by God.

2) We deny, however:
   a. That ordination is a sacrament of the New Testament.
   b. That ordination confers grace simply through the action itself and impresses a mark upon the soul of the ordained.
   c. That one must believe both under pain of excommunication.
   d. That the pastors of our congregations have lacked or lack a legitimate sending, calling, and ordination which accord with the Word of God.

13. Of Marriage

1) We assert that marriage is a holy and divine institution; and we are therefore of a different opinion, with the apostle (1 Tim. 4:3), from those who prohibit marriage, either openly reproving it or depreciating it in a covert way as if it were not holy, but rather impure.

2) Meanwhile, we deny:
   a. That it is truly a sacrament of the New Testament and must be considered such under pain of excommunication.
   b. That marriage was forbidden to the clergy by Christ or by the early church.

14. Of the Church

1) From that which is spoken by the Word of God, of Christ, the Head of the church, and further of the sacraments and divine worship, it is easy to discover how we should think of the true and false church, as

well as the common and the particular church. For the true church is nothing other than the congregation of believers, who under one head, Christ, are called by the same Spirit of grace from the power of darkness to the kingdom of God by the Word of the gospel. And they are bound both by the inner communion of faith, of love, and of hope, as well as by the external communion of the sacraments and the entire worship service, and by church discipline.

2) Therefore, although those true and living members of the church are only those who are both inwardly and outwardly bound in communion with Christ as the head of the church and with the church as His spiritual body, but because the inward communion and union with the church are things that are invisible, according to the judgment of love all of those who remain in the outward, visible confession of saving faith and in the communion of the true worship of God and of church discipline must be considered members of the church, even if some of them may be hypocrites before God.

3) The universal church is therefore the community of believers who are scattered across the earth. And they all are and remain a single catholic (or universal) church, so long as they remain united under a single head in heaven, Christ, and through a single spirit of saving faith and love, and a single confession, even if they are not and cannot be bound together in a common, external government on this earth, but are scattered from each other in ever so diverse and even hostile nations, kingdoms or free states; and as concerns the outward communion or government of the church are completely separated from each other.

4) But particular churches are those which are also bound by the outward ecclesiastical rule of a city or of a people in an ordered communion of saints.

5) Therefore, these can and must be judged by those same marks whether they are true or false churches; namely, by their profession of the same saving faith, by the indisputable Word of God, by the pure administration of those sacraments which are instituted by Christ, by the communion of the worship which is commanded by God and by ecclesiastical discipline. By these are all other accidental marks that man can put forward to be restricted and judged.

6) Meanwhile, we do not deny that there are among these churches varying degrees of purity and perfection; and that they do not immediately

cease to be a true church of Christ if there is something which is not pure in all its parts, either in doctrine or in administration of the sacraments or in the other portions of the worship service, usages and church discipline; but instead some errors are mingled into the saving faith or troublesome liberties into church discipline, if meanwhile it retains at least the foundation of the saving doctrine, the exercise of faith and worship of God, and does not completely dissolve the bond of Christian and brotherly love with other churches.

7) But if any church destroys the foundation of saving faith and divine worship, and obstinately breaks the bond of Christian love with other churches which hold fast to the foundation, we consider her no longer as a true church, but rather as a false church.

8) Whereas we do not at all deny that it sometimes happens or can happen in the universal church in the whole world that she may entirely fall away from the saving faith and worship of God, so we do not acknowledge that any particular church, whichever it may be, is given this primacy by Christ that she can never err in faith or leave it; and that although she may be susceptible in church discipline to various scandals, just as much as other churches, but in the doctrine of the faith and the practice of worship is always free from every error and the possibility to err, and remains pure.

9) Concerning government of the church, we believe that although she is in truth monarchial in relation unto Christ (the one king and monarch of the entire universal church), yet the outward government of particular churches on earth (according to the ordinance of Christ) is aristocratic; however, in such a way that we do not deny to the bishops or superintendents or inspectors a certain precedence of rank and rule over the other elders.

10) We deny, however, that there is any single head or monarch on earth invested by divine right to whom each and every church in the world, their bishops and individual believers must be subject as a requirement of salvation, under pain of excommunication, so that without this subjection, they can neither be true members of Christ nor of the catholic church.

And this is now the declaration of the specific doctrines of the Reformed Church of this kingdom concerning disputed points which had earlier been set before the Lords of the Roman Catholic Church and were read in public meeting on September 16. Because we noted, however, that their tempers were somewhat aroused by some expressions so that they solemnly declared themselves to be against their adoption in the conference, so we were of a mind, after mature consideration of the matter, to once again relent so that it would not seem as if we through our fault had given occasion for the breaking off of this friendly conference. And that is why we changed some things which appeared in their manner of expression to be displeasing to them or which seemed more properly to belong in a second conference, such as the proofs of the disputed points and the elucidation of the same. This is a power which we had already freely and unrestrainedly reserved for ourselves in the first clause of this declaration; then as now, we voluntarily reserved for ourselves the right to clarify those points which still may appear obscure. And we wish to reserve for ourselves this freedom to declare our beliefs further, and hope that the Lords of the Roman Catholic Church will ungrudgingly grant this to us, as the rules of this colloquy have it.

(Here follow the signatures of seven noblemen and twenty clergy.) [The signatures are not included in Böckel's text. However, they do appear in Niemeyer's Latin edition, pp. 687–89.]

(Translated by Jacob Baum; revisions by Peter VanDer Schaaf)

111

The Westminster Confession
of Faith (1646)

What many regard as the queen of the Reformed Confessions, namely the Westminster Confession and Catechisms, was forged in the heat of a bloody Civil War (1642–1651). This conflict, which pitted Royalist sympathizers of the Crown (Charles I, 1600–1649) and the Anglican establishment (especially the archbishop of Canterbury, William Laud, 1573–1645) against Cavalier supporters of Parliament (led by John Pym, 1584–1643) and the Puritans, altered (for a time) the ecclesiastical and political landscape of Britain. The Civil War itself—or the War of the Three Kingdoms, as it is now known—impacted not only England, but Scotland and Ireland as well. The defining alteration of this struggle was that no absolute or divine right (*jure divino*) monarch would occupy the British throne after 1649; and Protestant nonconformity (Puritan in the seventeenth century) would leave an indelible mark on Scotch, Irish, and English evangelicalism. The Westminster Standards have been the confessional bedrock of Scotch-Irish Presbyterianism in the Old World as well as the New ever since.

When Charles I was compelled to summon Parliament on April 13, 1640, after the "Eleven Years Tyranny" (no Parliament had sat since 1629—the so-called era of "Personal Rule"), Parliament turned its attention to "grievances." Charles's temperament was to allow no dallying with his divine right period, so he closed that Short Parliament down on May 5, 1640. But the nagging question of funding his blundered, ill-advised war with the Scots—precipitated in 1637 by his attempt to impose the Anglican Prayer Book on the Scottish Presbyterian Kirk (the so-called Bishops' Wars of 1638–1640)—compelled him to summon Parliament once again on November 3, 1640. This time Parliament's dander was up, and they refused to allow themselves to be dissolved again until they had redressed grievances which so disturbed the body political and theological in the Three Realms.

Thus the Long Parliament (1640–1653) was born. This faithful assembly would lay the foundation for a constitutional monarchy in which the power of the Crown was limited (in theory) by Parliament. It would also demand the disestablishment of Anglican Arminian theology together with the limitation of power in the prelatic bishops of the Church of England.

Parliament got to work on reformation in church and state, even at the force of arms (raising an army to oppose the king in civil war). Parliament's unprecedented step to refuse permission to the Crown to dissolve its *sederunt* produced Charles's breach of privilege in which he invaded Parliament with armed guards in order to arrest five members (John Pym, John Hamden [1594–1643], Denzil Holles [1599–1680], Arthur Haselrig [1601–1661], and William Strode [1598–1645]). This foolish act but incensed opposition to the Crown the more and produced the First Civil War (1642–1648) between the king and Parliament.

Part of Parliament's goal was the reformation of the Church of England. Since the late sixteenth century, Puritan Calvinists had been alleging that the Church of England was but "halfly reformed" (the famous Anglican *via media*), and needed a thorough alteration on the model of Calvin's Geneva and the best Reformed churches on the Continent. Thus Parliament appointed 135 clergy to an "assembly of divines" (or theologians). They were to convene on July 1, 1643, in order to draft the constitution of a new, thoroughly Reformed church in England. The divines gathered in the Chapel of Henry VII (1457–1509) in Westminster Abbey on that inaugural day. Subsequently, on October 2, 1643, they moved to the Jerusalem Chamber for their daily deliberations.

The divines were first charged by Parliament with a revision of the Anglican Thirty-Nine Articles (1562/63) in a more consistently Calvinistic direction. The work began on July 10, 1643. By October 12, they had completed a review of fifteen of the Thirty-Nine Articles. But the entrance of the Scots into the Civil War as allies of Parliament (via the Solemn League and Covenant of September 25) shifted the focus of the assembly from theology to polity. The Scots wanted Presbyterianism as a condition of their joining Parliament against the king and his Anglican compatriots. On October 12, Parliament asked the assembly to produce a form of government and directory for worship. The effect was the disestablishment of episcopacy. In its place, the assembly drafted a "Directory for Worship of God" (completed January 3, 1645), which supplanted the Anglican Book of Common Prayer (1552). The "Form of Government" endorsing *jure divino*

Presbyterianism was drafted during 1644–1645, submitted to Parliament in 1647, and approved with modification in 1648 (the alteration required by Parliament was that Presbyterianism be regarded as "agreeable to the Word of God," not necessarily *jure divino*).

The Confession of Faith was completed November 26, 1646, and approved by Parliament in 1648. The Larger Catechism was completed on October 15, 1647, and was followed by the Shorter Catechism on November 25, 1647. Both were approved by Parliament in 1648 (though the House of Lords never approved the Larger Catechism). With the assembly's substantive theological and ecclesiastical work completed, the Westminster divines became a committee to examine and ordain ministers (1648–1652). The last entry in the minutes of the assembly is dated March 25, 1652. There is no record that the assembly was ever closed or dissolved, either internally or by Parliament.

Our text is from the original edition of the Standards published by the Free Presbyterian Church of Scotland (1970) and is printed here with their kind permission. We have inserted the prooftexts in the body of the Confession and Catechisms, but to save space, we have not included the full text of the biblical passages as found in the Free Church version.

THE CONFESSION OF FAITH,

Agreed upon by the ASSEMBLY OF DIVINES at Westminster:
Examined and approved, *Anno* 1647, by the GENERAL
ASSEMBLY of the CHURCH OF SCOTLAND; and ratified
By ACTS OF PARLIAMENT 1649 and 1690.

CHAP. I.— *Of the Holy Scripture.*

I. ALTHOUGH the light of nature and the works of creation and providence do so far manifest the goodness, wisdom, and power of God, as to leave men inexcusable (Rom. 2:14–15; 1:19–20; Ps. 19:1–3; Rom. 1:32; 2:1); yet are they not sufficient to give that knowledge of God, and of His will, which is necessary unto salvation (1 Cor. 1:21; 2:13–14). Therefore it pleased the Lord, at sundry times, and in divers manners, to reveal Himself, and to declare that His will unto His Church (Heb. 1:1); and afterwards, for the better preserving and propagating of the truth, and for the more sure establishment and comfort of the Church against the corruption of the flesh, and the malice of Satan and of the world, to commit the same wholly unto writing (Prov. 22:19–21; Luke 1:3–4; Rom. 15:4; Matt. 4:4, 7, 10; Isa. 8:19–20): which maketh the Holy Scripture to be most necessary (2 Tim. 3:15; 2 Peter 1:19); those former ways of God's revealing His will unto His people being now ceased (Heb. 1:1–2).

II. Under the name of Holy Scripture, or the Word of God written, are now contained all the books of the Old and New Testaments, which are these,

OF THE OLD TESTAMENT.

Genesis	Ezra	Hosea
Exodus	Nehemiah	Joel
Leviticus	Esther	Amos
Numbers	Job	Obadiah
Deuteronomy	Psalms	Jonah
Joshua	Proverbs	Micah
Judges	Ecclesiastes	Nahum
Ruth	The Song of	Habakkuk
1 Samuel	Songs	Zephaniah
2 Samuel	Isaiah	Haggai
1 Kings	Jeremiah	Zechariah
2 Kings	Lamentations	Malachi
1 Chronicles	Ezekiel	
2 Chronicles	Daniel	

OF THE NEW TESTAMENT.

The Gospels according to	Galatians	The Epistle of James
Matthew	Ephesians	The First and
Mark	Philippians	The First and second Epistles
Luke	Colossians	of Peter
John	Thessalonians 1	The first, second,
The Acts of the Apostles	Thessalonians 2	and third Epistles of John
Paul's Epistles to the Romans	To Timothy 1	The Epistle of Jude
Corinthians 1	To Titus	The Revelation of John
Corinthians 2	To Philemon	
	The Epistle to the Hebrews	

All which are given by inspiration of God to be the rule of faith and life (Luke 16:29, 31; Eph. 2:20; Rev. 22:18–19; 2 Tim. 3:16).

III. The books commonly called Apocrypha, not being of divine inspiration, are no part of the canon of the Scripture, and therefore are of no authority in the Church of God, nor to be any otherwise approved, or made use of, than other human writings (Luke 24:27, 44; Rom. 3:2; 2 Peter 1:21).

IV. The authority of the Holy Scripture, for which it ought to be believed, and obeyed, dependeth not upon the testimony of any man, or Church; but wholly upon God (who is truth itself) the author thereof: and therefore it is to be received, because it is the Word of God (2 Peter 1:19, 21; 2 Tim. 3:16; 1 John 5:9; 1 Thess. 2:13).

V. We may be moved and induced by the testimony of the Church to a high and reverend esteem of the Holy Scripture (1 Tim. 3:15). And the heavenliness of the matter, the efficacy of the doctrine, the majesty of the style, the consent of all the parts, the scope of the whole (which is, to give all glory to God), the full discovery it makes of the only way of man's salvation, the many other incomparable excellencies, and the entire perfection thereof, are arguments whereby it doth abundantly evidence itself to be the Word of God: yet notwithstanding, our full persuasion and assurance of the infallible truth and divine authority thereof, is from the inward work of the Holy Spirit bearing witness by and with the Word in our hearts (1 John 2:20, 27; John 16:13–14; 1 Cor. 2:10–12; Isa. 59:21).

VI. The whole counsel of God concerning all things necessary for His own glory, man's salvation, faith and life, is either expressly set down in Scripture, or by good and necessary consequence may be deduced from Scripture: unto which nothing at any time is to be added, whether by new revelations of the Spirit or traditions of men (2 Tim. 3:15–17; Gal. 1:8–9; 2 Thess. 2:2). Nevertheless, we acknowledge the inward illumination of the Spirit of God to be necessary for the saving understanding of such things as are revealed in the Word (John 6:45; 1 Cor. 2:9–12): and that there are some circumstances concerning the worship of God, and government of the Church, common to human actions and societies, which are to be ordered by the light of nature, and Christian prudence, according to the general rules of the Word, which are always to be observed (1 Cor. 11:13–14; 14:26, 40).

VII. All things in Scripture are not alike plain in themselves, nor alike clear unto all (2 Peter 3:16): yet those things which are necessary to be known, believed, and observed for salvation, are so clearly propounded, and opened in some place of Scripture or other, that not only the learned, but the unlearned, in a due use of the ordinary means, may attain unto a sufficient understanding of them (Ps. 119:105, 130).

VIII. The Old Testament in Hebrew (which was the native language of the people of God of old), and the New Testament in Greek (which, at the time of the writing of it, was most generally known to the nations), being immediately inspired by God, and, by His singular care and providence, kept pure in all ages, are therefore authentical (Matt. 5:18); so as, in all controversies of religion, the Church is finally to appeal unto them (Isa. 8:20; Acts 15:15; John 5:39, 46). But, because these original tongues are not known to all the people of God, who have right unto, and interest in the Scriptures, and are commanded, in the fear of God, to read and search them (John 5:39), therefore they are to be translated into the vulgar language of every nation unto which they come (1 Cor. 14:6, 9, 11–12, 24, 27–28), that, the Word of God dwelling plentifully in all, they may worship Him in an acceptable manner (Col. 3:16); and, through patience and comfort of the Scriptures, may have hope (Rom. 15:4).

IX. The infallible rule of interpretation of Scripture is the Scripture itself: and therefore, when there is a question about the true and full sense of any Scripture (which is not manifold, but one), it must be searched and known by other places that speak more clearly (2 Peter 1:20–21; Acts 15:15–16).

X. The supreme judge by which all controversies of religion are to be determined, and all decrees of councils, opinions of ancient writers, doctrines of men, and private spirits, are to be examined, and in whose sentence we are to rest, can be no other but the Holy Spirit speaking in the Scripture (Matt. 22:29, 31; Eph. 2:20; Acts 28:25).

CHAP. II.— *Of God, and of the Holy Trinity.*

I. THERE is but one only (Deut. 6:4; 1 Cor. 8:4, 6), living, and true God (1 Thess. 1:9; Jer. 10:10), who is infinite in being and perfection (Job 11:7– 9; 26:14), a most pure spirit (John 4:24), invisible (1 Tim. 1:17), without body, parts (Deut. 4:15–16; John 4:24; Luke 24:39), or passions (Acts 14:11, 15); immutable (James 1:17; Mal. 3:6), immense (1 Kings 8:27; Jer. 23:23–24), eternal (Ps. 90:2; 1 Tim. 1:17), incomprehensible (Ps. 145:3), almighty (Gen. 17:1; Rev. 4:8), most wise (Rom. 16:27), most holy (Isa. 6:3; Rev. 4:8), most free (Ps. 115:3), most absolute (Ex. 3:14), working all things according to the counsel of His own immutable and most righteous will (Eph. 1:11), for His own glory (Prov. 16:4; Rom. 11:36); most loving (1 John 4:8, 16), gracious, merciful, long-suffering, abundant in goodness and truth, forgiving iniquity, transgression, and sin (Ex. 34:6–7); the rewarder of them that diligently seek Him (Heb. 11:6); and withal, most just, and terrible in His judgments (Neh. 9:32–33), hating all sin (Ps. 5:5–6), and who will by no means clear the guilty (Nah. 1:2–3; Ex. 34:7).

II. God hath all life (John 5:26), glory (Acts 7:2), goodness (Ps. 119:68), blessedness (1 Tim. 6:15; Rom. 9:5), in and of Himself; and is alone in and unto Himself all-sufficient, not standing in need of any creatures which He hath made (Acts 17:24–25), nor deriving any glory from them (Job 22:2–3), but only manifesting His own glory in, by, unto, and upon them. He is the alone fountain of all being, of whom, through whom, and to whom are all things (Rom. 11:36); and hath most sovereign dominion over them, to do by them, for them, or upon them whatsoever Himself pleaseth (Rev. 4:11; 1 Tim. 6:15; Dan. 4:25, 35). In His sight all things are open and manifest (Heb. 4:13), His knowledge is infinite, infallible, and independent upon the creature (Rom. 11:33–34; Ps. 147:5), so as nothing is to Him contingent, or uncertain (Acts 15:18; Ezek. 11:5). He is most holy in all His counsels, in all His works, and in all His commands (Ps. 145:17; Rom. 7:12). To Him is due from angels and men, and every other creature, whatsoever worship, service, or obedience He is pleased to require of them (Rev. 5:12–14).

III. In the unity of the Godhead there be three persons, of one substance, power, and eternity: God the Father, God the Son, and God the Holy Ghost (1 John 5:7; Matt. 3:16–17; 28:19; 2 Cor. 13:14): the Father is of none, neither begotten, nor proceeding; the Son is eternally begotten of the Father (John 1:14, 18); the Holy Ghost eternally proceeding from the Father and the Son (John 15:26; Gal. 4:6).

CHAP. III.—*Of God's Eternal Decree.*

I. GOD from all eternity, did, by the most wise and holy counsel of His own will, freely, and unchangeably ordain whatsoever comes to pass (Eph. 1:11; Rom. 11:33; Heb. 6:17; Rom. 9:15, 18): yet so, as thereby neither is God the author of sin (James 1:13, 17; 1 John 1:5), nor is violence offered to the will of the creatures; nor is the liberty or contingency of second causes taken away, but rather established (Acts 2:23; Matt. 17:12; Acts 4:27–28; John 19:11; Prov. 16:33).

II. Although God knows whatsoever may or can come to pass upon all supposed conditions (Acts 15:18; 1 Sam. 23:11–12; Matt. 11:21, 23), yet hath He not decreed any thing because He foresaw it as future, or as that which would come to pass upon such conditions (Rom. 9:11, 13, 16, 18).

III. By the decree of God, for the manifestation of His glory, some men and angels (1 Tim. 5:21; Matt. 25:41) are predestinated unto everlasting life; and others foreordained to everlasting death (Rom. 9:22–23; Eph. 1:5–6; Prov. 16:4).

IV. These angels and men, thus predestinated, and foreordained, are particularly and unchangeably designed, and their number is so certain and definite, that it cannot be either increased or diminished (2 Tim. 2:19; John 13:18).

V. Those of mankind that are predestinated unto life, God, before the foundation of the world was laid, according to His eternal and immutable purpose, and the secret counsel and good pleasure of His will, hath chosen, in Christ, unto everlasting glory (Eph. 1:4, 9, 11; Rom. 8:30; 2 Tim. 1:9; 1 Thess. 5:9), out of His mere free grace and love, without any foresight of faith, or good works, or perseverance in either of them, or any other thing in the creature, as conditions, or causes moving Him thereunto (Rom. 9:11, 13, 16; Eph. 1:4, 9): and all to the praise of His glorious grace (Eph. 1:6, 12).

VI. As God hath appointed the elect unto glory, so hath He, by the eternal and most free purpose of His will, foreordained all the means thereunto (1 Peter 1:2; Eph. 1:4–5; 2:10; 2 Thess. 2:13). Wherefore, they who are elected, being fallen in Adam, are redeemed by Christ (1 Thess. 5:9–10; Titus 2:14), are effectually called unto faith in Christ by His Spirit working in due season, are justified, adopted, sanctified (Rom. 8:30; Eph. 1:5;

2 Thess. 2:13), and kept by His power, through faith, unto salvation (1 Peter 1:5). Neither are any other redeemed by Christ, effectually called, justified, adopted, sanctified, and saved, but the elect only (John 17:9; Rom. 8:28–39; John 6:64–65; 10:26; 8:47; 1 John 2:19).

VII. The rest of mankind God was pleased, according to the unsearchable counsel of His own will, whereby He extendeth or withholdeth mercy, as He pleaseth, for the glory of His sovereign power over His creatures, to pass by; and to ordain them to dishonour and wrath for their sin, to the praise of His glorious justice (Matt. 11:25–26; Rom. 9:17–18, 21–22; 2 Tim. 2:19–20; Jude 4; 1 Peter 2:8).

VIII. The doctrine of this high mystery of predestination is to be handled with special prudence and care (Rom. 9:20; 11:33; Deut. 29:29), that men, attending the will of God revealed in His Word, and yielding obedience thereunto, may, from the certainty of their effectual vocation, be assured of their eternal election (2 Peter 1:10). So shall this doctrine afford matter of praise, reverence, and admiration of God (Eph. 1:6; Rom. 11:33); and of humility, diligence, and abundant consolation to all that sincerely obey the Gospel (Rom. 11:5–6, 20; 2 Peter 1:10; Rom. 8:33; Luke 10:20).

CHAP. IV.— *Of Creation.*

1. IT pleased God the Father, Son, and Holy Ghost (Heb. 1:2; John 1:2–3; Gen. 1:2; Job 26:13; 33:4), for the manifestation of the glory of His eternal power, wisdom, and goodness (Rom. 1:20; Jer. 10:12; Ps. 104:24; 33:5–6), in the beginning, to create, or make of nothing, the world, and all things therein whether visible or invisible, in the space of six days; and all very good (Gen. 1; Heb. 11:3; Col. 1:16; Acts 17:24).

II. After God had made all other creatures, He created man, male and female (Gen. 1:27), with reasonable and immortal souls (Gen. 2:7; Eccl. 12:7; Luke 23:43; Matt. 10:28), endued with knowledge, righteousness, and true holiness, after His own image (Gen. 1:26; Col. 3:10; Eph. 4:24); having the law of God written in their hearts (Rom. 2:14–15), and power to fulfil it (Eccl. 7:29): and yet under a possibility of transgressing, being left to the liberty of their own will, which was subject unto change (Gen. 3:6; Eccl. 7:29). Beside this law written in their hearts, they received a command, not to eat of the tree of the knowledge of good and evil (Gen. 2:17; 3:8–11, 23);

which while they kept, they were happy in their communion with God, and had dominion over the creatures (Gen. 1:26, 28).

CHAP. V.— *Of Providence.*

I. GOD the great Creator of all things doth uphold (Heb. 1:3), direct, dispose, and govern all creatures, actions, and things (Dan. 4:34–35; Ps. 135:6; Acts 17:25–26, 28; Job 38-41), from the greatest even to the least (Matt. 10:29–31), by His most wise and holy providence (Prov. 15:3; Ps. 104:24; 145:17), according to His infallible foreknowledge (Acts 15:18; Ps. 94:8–11), and the free and immutable counsel of His own will (Eph. 1:11; Ps. 33:10–11), to the praise of the glory of His wisdom, power, justice, goodness, and mercy (Isa. 63:14; Eph. 3:10; Rom. 9:17; Gen. 45:7; Ps. 145:7).

II. Although, in relation to the foreknowledge and decree of God, the first Cause, all things come to pass immutably, and infallibly (Acts 2:23); yet, by the same providence, He ordereth them to fall out, according to the nature of second causes, either necessarily, freely, or contingently (Gen. 8:22; Jer. 31:35; Ex. 21:13; Deut. 19:5; 1 Kings 22:28, 34; Isa. 10:6–7).

III. God, in his ordinary providence, maketh use of means (Acts 27:31, 44; Isa. 55:10–11; Hos. 2:21–22), yet is free to work without (Hos. 1:7; Matt. 4:4; Job 34:10), above (Rom. 4:19–21), and against them (2 Kings 6:6; Dan. 3:27), at His pleasure.

IV. The almighty power, unsearchable wisdom, and infinite goodness of God so far manifest themselves in His providence, that it extendeth itself even to the first fall, and all other sins of angels and men (Rom. 11:32–34; 2 Sam. 24:1; 1 Chron. 21:1; 1 Kings 22:22–23; 1 Chron. 10:4, 13–14; 2 Sam. 16:10; Acts 2:23; 4:27–28); and that not by a bare permission (Acts 14:16), but such as hath joined with it a most wise and powerful bounding (Ps. 76:10; 2 Kings 19:28), and otherwise ordering, and governing of them, in a manifold dispensation, to His own holy ends (Gen. 1:20; Isa. 10:6–7, 12); yet so, as the sinfulness thereof proceedeth only from the creature, and not from God, who, being most holy and righteous, neither is nor can be the author or approver of sin (James 1:13–14, 17; 1 John 2:16; Ps. 50:21).

V. The most wise, righteous, and gracious God doth oftentimes leave, for a season, His own children to manifold temptations, and the corruption of their own hearts, to chastise them for their former sins, or to discover unto them the hidden strength of corruption and deceitfulness of their hearts, that they may be humbled (2 Chron. 32:25–26, 31; 2 Sam. 24:1); and, to raise them to a more close and constant dependence for their support upon Himself, and to make them more watchful against all future occasions of sin, and for sundry other just and holy ends (2 Cor. 12:7–9; Ps. 73; 77:1, 10, 12; Mark 14:66–72; John 21:15–17).

VI. As for those wicked and ungodly men whom God, as a righteous Judge, for former sins, doth blind and harden (Rom. 1:24, 26, 28; 11:7–8), from them He not only withholdeth His grace whereby they might have been enlightened in their understandings, and wrought upon in their hearts (Deut. 29:4); but sometimes also withdraweth the gifts which they had (Matt. 13:12; 25:29), and exposeth them to such objects as their corruption makes occasions of sin (Deut. 2:30; 2 Kings 8:12–13); and, withal, gives them over to their own lusts, the temptations of the world, and the power of Satan (Ps. 81:11–12; 2 Thess. 2:10–12), whereby it comes to pass that they harden themselves, even under those means which God useth for the softening of others (Ex. 7:3; 8:15, 32; 2 Cor. 2:15–16; Isa. 8:14; 1 Peter 2:7–10; Acts 28:26–27).

VII. As the providence of God doth, in general, reach to all creatures; so, after a most special manner, it taketh care of His Church, and disposeth all things to the good thereof (1 Tim. 4:10; Amos 9:8–9; Rom. 8:28; Isa. 43:3–5, 14).

CHAP. VI.—*Of the Fall of Man, of Sin,*
and of the Punishment thereof.

I. OUR first parents, being seduced by the subtilty and temptation of Satan, sinned, in eating the forbidden fruit (Gen. 3:13; 2 Cor. 11:3). This their sin, God was pleased, according to His wise and holy counsel, to permit, having purposed to order it to His own glory (Rom. 11:32).

II. By this sin they fell from their original righteousness and communion (Gen. 3:6–8; Eccl. 7:29; Rom. 3:23), with God, and so became dead in sin (Gen. 2:17; Eph. 2:1), and wholly defiled in all the faculties and parts of soul and body (Titus 1:15; Gen. 6:5; Jer. 17:9; Rom. 3:10–18).

III. They being the root of all mankind, the guilt of this sin was imputed (Gen. 1:27–28; 2:16–17; Acts 17:26; Rom. 5:12, 15–19; 1 Cor. 15:21–22, 45, 49); and the same death in sin, and corrupted nature, conveyed to all their posterity descending from them by ordinary generation (Ps. 51:5; Gen. 5:3; Job 14:4; 15:14).

IV. From this original corruption, whereby we are utterly indisposed, disabled, and made opposite to all good (Rom. 5:6; 8:7; 7:18; Col. 1:21), and wholly inclined to all evil (Gen. 6:5; 8:21; Rom. 3:10–12), do proceed all actual transgressions (James 1:14–15; Eph. 2:2–3; Matt. 15:19).

V. This corruption of nature, during this life, doth remain in those that are regenerated (1 John 1:8, 10; Rom. 7:14, 17–18, 23; James 3:2; Prov. 20:9; Eccl. 7:20); and although it be, through Christ, pardoned and mortified; yet both itself, and all the motions thereof, are truly and properly sin (Rom. 7:5, 7–8, 25; Gal. 5:17).

VI. Every sin, both original and actual, being a transgression of the righteous law of God, and contrary thereunto (1 John 3:4), doth, in its own nature, bring guilt upon the sinner (Rom. 2:15; 3:9, 19); whereby he is bound over to the wrath of God (Eph. 2:3), and curse of the law (Gal. 3:10), and so made subject to death (Rom. 6:23), with all miseries spiritual (Eph. 4:18), temporal (Rom. 8:20; Lam. 3:39), and eternal (Matt. 25:41; 2 Thess. 1:9).

CHAP. VII.— *Of God's Covenant with Man.*

I. THE distance between God and the creature is so great, that although reasonable creatures do owe obedience unto Him as their Creator, yet they could never have any fruition of Him as their blessedness and reward, but by some voluntary condescension on God's part, which He hath been pleased to express by way of covenant (Isa. 40:13–17; Job 9:32–33; 1 Sam. 2:25; Ps. 113:5–6; 100:2–3; Job 22:2–3; 35:7–8; Luke 17:10; Acts 17:24–25).

II. The first covenant made with man was a covenant of works (Gal. 3:12), wherein life was promised to Adam; and in him to his posterity (Rom. 10:5; 5:12–20), upon condition of perfect and personal obedience (Gen. 2:17; Gal. 3:10).

III. Man, by his fall, having made himself incapable of life by that covenant, the Lord was pleased to make a second (Gal. 3:21; Rom. 8:3; 3:20–21; Gen.

3:15; Isa. 42:6), commonly called the covenant of grace; wherein He freely offereth unto sinners life and salvation by Jesus Christ; requiring of them faith in Him, that they may be saved (Mark 16:15–16; John 3:16; Rom. 10:6, 9; Gal. 3:11), and promising to give unto all those that are ordained unto life His Holy Spirit, to make them willing, and able to believe (Ezek. 36:26–27; John 6:44–45)

IV. This covenant of grace is frequently set forth in Scripture by the name of a testament, in reference to the death of Jesus Christ the Testator, and to the everlasting inheritance, with all things belonging to it, therein bequeathed (Heb. 9:15–17; 7:22; Luke 22:20; 1 Cor. 11:25).

V. This covenant was differently administered in the time of the law, and in the time of the gospel (2 Cor. 3:6–9): under the law it was administered by promises, prophecies, sacrifices, circumcision, the paschal lamb, and other types and ordinances delivered to the people of the Jews, all foresignifying Christ to come (Heb. 8–10; Rom. 4:11; Col. 2:11–12; 1 Cor. 5:7); which were, for that time, sufficient and efficacious, through the operation of the Spirit, to instruct and build up the elect in faith in the promised Messiah (1 Cor. 10:1–4; Heb. 11:13; John 8:56), by whom they had full remission of sins, and eternal salvation; and is called, the old Testament (Gal. 3:7–9, 14).

VI. Under the gospel, when Christ, the substance (Col. 2:17), was exhibited, the ordinances in which this covenant is dispensed are the preaching of the Word, and the administration of the sacraments of Baptism and the Lord's Supper (Matt. 28:19–20; 1 Cor. 11:23–25): which, though fewer in number, and administered with more simplicity, and less outward glory, yet, in them, it is held forth in more fulness, evidence, and spiritual efficacy (Heb. 12:22–27; Jer. 31:33–34), to all nations, both Jews and Gentiles (Matt. 28:19; Eph. 2:15–19); and is called the new Testament (Luke 22:20). There are not therefore two covenants of grace, differing in substance, but one and the same, under various dispensations (Gal. 3:14, 16; Acts 15:11; Rom. 3:21–23, 30; Ps. 32:1; Rom. 4:3, 6, 16–17, 23–24; Heb. 13:8).

CHAP. VIII.— Of Christ the Mediator.

I. IT pleased God, in His eternal purpose, to choose and ordain the Lord Jesus, His only begotten Son, to be the Mediator between God and man (Isa. 42:1; 1 Peter 1:19–20; John 3:16; 1 Tim. 2:5), the Prophet (Acts 3:22), Priest

(Heb. 5:5–6), and King (Ps. 2:6; Luke 1:33), the Head and Saviour of His Church (Eph. 5:23), the Heir of all things (Heb. 1:2), and Judge of the world (Acts 17:31): unto whom He did from all eternity give a people, to be His seed (John 17:6; Ps. 22:30; Isa. 53:10), and to be by Him in time redeemed, called, justified, sanctified, and glorified (1 Tim. 2:6; Isa. 55:4–5; 1 Cor. 1:30).

II. The Son of God, the second person in the Trinity, being very and eternal God, of one substance and equal with the Father, did, when the fulness of time was come, take upon Him man's nature (John 1:1, 14; 1 John 5:20; Phil. 2:6; Gal. 4:4), with all the essential properties, and common infirmities thereof, yet without sin (Heb. 2:14, 16–17; 4:15); being conceived by the power of the Holy Ghost, in the womb of the virgin Mary, of her substance (Luke 1:27, 31, 35; Gal. 4:4). So that two whole, perfect, and distinct natures, the Godhead and the manhood, were separately joined together in one person, without conversion, composition, or confusion (Luke 1:35; Col. 2:9; Rom. 9:5; 1 Peter 3:18; 1 Tim. 3:16). Which person is very God, and very man, yet one Christ, the only Mediator between God and man (Rom. 1:3–4; 1 Tim. 2:5).

III. The Lord Jesus, in His human nature thus united to the divine, was sanctified, and anointed with the Holy Spirit, above measure (Ps. 45:7; John 3:34), having in Him all the treasures of wisdom and knowledge (Col. 2:3); in whom it pleased the Father that all fulness should dwell (Col. 1:19); to the end that, being holy, harmless, undefiled, and full of grace and truth (Heb. 7:26; John 1:14), He might be thoroughly furnished to execute the office of a Mediator and Surety (Acts 10:38; Heb. 12:24; 7:22). Which office He took not unto Himself, but was thereunto called by His Father (Heb. 5:4–5), who put all power and judgment into His hand, and gave Him commandment to execute the same (John 5:22, 27; Matt. 28:18; Acts 2:36).

IV. This office the Lord Jesus did most willingly undertake (Ps. 40:7–8; Heb. 10:5–10; John 10:18; Phil. 2:8); which that He might discharge, He was made under the law (Gal. 4:4), and did perfectly fulfil it (Matt. 3:15; 5:17); endured most grievous torments immediately in His soul (Matt. 26:37–38; Luke 22:44; Matt. 27:46), and most painful sufferings in His body (Matt. 26–27); was crucified, and died (Phil. 2:8), was buried, and remained under the power of death, yet saw no corruption (Acts 2:23–24, 27; 13:37; Rom. 6:9). On the third day He arose from the dead (1 Cor.

15:3–5), with the same body in which He suffered (John 20:25, 27), with which also he ascended into heaven, and there sitteth at the right hand of His Father (Mark 16:19), making intercession (Rom. 8:34; Heb. 9:24; 7:25), and shall return, to judge men and angels, at the end of the world (Rom. 14:9–10; Acts 1:11; 10:42; Matt. 13:40–42; Jude 6; 2 Peter 2:4).

V. The Lord Jesus, by His perfect obedience, and sacrifice of Himself, which He through the eternal Spirit, once offered up unto God, hath fully satisfied the justice of His Father (Rom. 5:19; Heb. 9:14, 16; 10:14; Eph. 5:2; Rom. 3:25–26); and purchased, not only reconciliation, but an everlasting inheritance in the kingdom of heaven, for all those whom the Father hath given unto Him (Dan. 9:24, 26; Col. 1:19–20; Eph. 1:11, 14; John 17:2; Heb. 9:12, 15).

VI. Although the work of redemption was not actually wrought by Christ till after His incarnation, yet the virtue, efficacy, and benefits thereof were communicated unto the elect, in all ages successively from the beginning of the world, in and by those promises, types, and sacrifices, wherein He was revealed, and signified to be the seed of the woman which should bruise the serpent's head; and the Lamb slain from the beginning of the world; being yesterday and today the same, and for ever (Gal. 4:4–5; Gen. 3:15; Rev. 13:8; Heb. 13:8).

VII. Christ, in the work of mediation, acts according to both natures, by each nature doing that which is proper to itself (Heb. 9:14; 1 Peter 3:18); yet, by reason of the unity of the person, that which is proper to one nature is sometimes in Scripture attributed to the person denominated by the other nature (Acts 20:28; John 3:13; 1 John 3:16).

VIII. To all those for whom Christ hath purchased redemption, He doth certainly and effectually apply and communicate the same (John 6:37, 39; 10:15–16); making intercession for them (1 John 2:1–2; Rom. 8:34), and revealing unto them, in and by the Word, the mysteries of salvation (John 15:13, 15; Eph. 1:7–9; John 17:6); effectually persuading them by His Spirit to believe and obey, and governing their hearts by His Word and Spirit (John 14:16; Heb. 12:2; 2 Cor. 4:13; Rom. 8:9, 14; 15:18–19; John 17:17); overcoming all their enemies by His almighty power and wisdom, in such manner, and ways, as are most consonant to His wonderful and unsearchable dispensation (Ps. 110:1; 1 Cor. 15:25–26; Mal. 4:2–3; Col. 2:15).

CHAP. IX.— *Of Free Will.*

I. GOD hath endued the will of man with that natural liberty, that it is neither forced, nor, by any absolute necessity of nature, determined to good, or evil (Matt. 17:12; James 1:14; Deut. 30:19).

II. Man, in his state of innocency, had freedom and power to will and to do that which was good and well pleasing to God (Eccl. 7:29; Gen. 1:26); but yet, mutably, so that he might fall from it (Gen. 2:16–17; 3:6).

III. Man, by his fall into a state of sin, hath wholly lost all ability of will to any spiritual good accompanying salvation (Rom. 5:6; 8:7; John 15:5): so as, a natural man, being altogether averse from that good (Rom. 3:10, 12), and dead in sin (Eph. 2:1, 5; Col. 2:13), is not able, by his own strength, to convert himself, or to prepare himself thereunto (John 6:44, 65; Eph. 2:2–5; 1 Cor. 2:14; Titus 3:3–5).

IV. When God converts a sinner, and translates him into the state of grace, He freeth him from his natural bondage under sin (Col. 1:13; John 8:34, 36); and, by His grace alone, enables him freely to will and to do that which is spiritually good (Phil. 2:13; Rom. 6:18, 22); yet so, as that by reason of his remaining corruption, he doth not perfectly, nor only, will that which is good, but doth also will that which is evil (Gal. 5:17; Rom. 7:15, 18–19, 21, 23).

V. The will of man is made perfectly and immutably free to good alone in the state of glory only (Eph. 4:13; Heb. 12:23; 1 John 3:2; Jude 24).

CHAP. X.— *Of Effectual Calling.*

I. ALL those whom God hath predestinated unto life, and those only, He is pleased, in His appointed and accepted time, effectually to call (Rom. 8:30; 11:7; Eph. 1:10–11), by His Word and Spirit (2 Thess. 2:13–14; 2 Cor. 3:3, 6), out of that state of sin and death, in which they are by nature to grace and salvation, by Jesus Christ (Rom. 8:2; Eph. 2:1–5; 2 Tim. 1:9–10); enlightening their minds spiritually and savingly to understand the things of God (Acts 26:18; 1 Cor. 2:10, 12; Eph. 1:17–18), taking away their heart of stone, and giving unto them an heart of flesh (Ezek. 36:26); renewing their wills, and, by His almighty power, determining them to that which is good (Ezek. 11:19; Phil. 2:13; Deut. 30:6; Ezek. 36:27), and effectually drawing them to Jesus Christ (Eph. 1:19; John 6:44–45): yet so, as they come most freely, being made willing by His grace (Song 1:4; Ps. 110:3; John 6:37; Rom. 6:16–18).

II. This effectual call is of God's free and special grace alone, not from any thing at all foreseen in man (2 Tim. 1:9; Titus 3:4–5; Eph. 2:4–5, 8–9; Rom. 9:11), who is altogether passive therein, until, being quickened and renewed by the Holy Spirit (1 Cor. 2:14; Rom. 8:7; Eph. 2:5), he is thereby enabled to answer this call, and to embrace the grace offered and conveyed in it (John 6:37; Ezek. 36:27; John 5:25).

III. Elect infants, dying in infancy, are regenerated, and saved by Christ, through the Spirit (Luke 18:15–16; Acts 2:38–39; John 3:3, 5; 1 John 5:12; Rom. 8:9), who worketh when, and where, and how He pleaseth (John 3:8): so also are all other elect persons who are uncapable of being outwardly called by the ministry of the Word (1 John 5:12; Acts 4:12).

IV. Others, not elected, although they may be called by the ministry of the Word (Matt. 22:14), and may have some common operations of the Spirit (Matt. 7:22; 13:20–21; Heb. 6:4–5), yet they never truly come unto Christ, and therefore cannot be saved (John 6:64–66; 8:24): much less can men, not professing the Christian religion, be saved in any other way whatsoever, be they never so diligent to frame their lives according to the light of nature, and the laws of that religion they do profess (Acts 4:12; John 14:6; Eph. 2:12; John 4:22; 17:3). And to assert and maintain that they may, is very pernicious, and to be detested (2 John 9–11; 1 Cor. 16:22; Gal. 1:6–8).

CHAP. XI.— *Of Justification.*

I. THOSE whom God effectually calleth, He also freely justifieth (Rom. 8:30; 3:24): not by infusing righteousness into them, but by pardoning their sins, and by accounting and accepting their persons as righteous; not for any thing wrought in them, or done by them, but for Christ's sake alone; nor by imputing faith itself, the act of believing, or any other evangelical obedience to them, as their righteousness; but by imputing the obedience and satisfaction of Christ unto them (Rom. 4:5–8; 2 Cor. 5:19, 21–22, 24–25, 27–28; Titus 3:5, 7; Eph. 1:7; Jer. 23:6; 1 Cor. 1:30–31; Rom. 5:17–19), they receiving and resting on Him and His righteousness by faith; which faith they have not of themselves, it is the gift of God (Acts 10:44; Gal. 2:16; Phil. 3:9; Acts 13:38–39; Eph. 2:7–8).

II. Faith, thus receiving and resting on Christ and His righteousness, is the alone instrument of justification (John 1:12; Rom. 3:28; 5:1): yet it is not alone in the person justified, but is ever accompanied with all other saving graces, and is no dead faith, but worketh by love (James 2:17, 22, 26; Gal. 5:6).

III. Christ, by His obedience and death, did fully discharge the debt of all those that are thus justified, and did make a proper, real, and full satisfaction to His Father's justice in their behalf (Rom. 5:8–10, 19; 1 Tim. 2:5–6; Heb. 10:10, 14; Dan. 9:24, 26; Isa. 53:4–6, 10–12). Yet, in as much as He was given by the Father for them (Rom. 8:32); and His obedience and satisfaction accepted in their stead (2 Cor. 5:21; Matt. 3:17; Eph. 5:2); and both, freely, not for anything in them; their justification is only of free grace (Rom. 3:24; Eph. 1:17); that both the exact justice, and rich grace of God might be glorified in the justification of sinners (Rom. 3:26; Eph. 2:7).

IV. God did, from all eternity, decree to justify all the elect (Gal. 3:8; 1 Peter 1:2, 19–20; Rom. 8:30), and Christ did, in the fulness of time, die for their sins, and rise again for their justification (Gal. 4:4; 1 Tim. 2:6; Rom. 4:25): nevertheless, they are not justified, until the Holy Spirit doth, in due time, actually apply Christ unto them (Col. 1:21–22; Gal. 2:16; Titus 3:4–7).

V. God doth continue to forgive the sins of those that are justified (Matt. 6:12; 1 John 1:7, 9; 2:1–2); and, although they can never fall from the state of justification (Luke 22:32; John 10:28; Heb. 10:14), yet they may, by their sins, fall under God's fatherly displeasure, and not have the light of His countenance restored unto them, until they humble themselves, confess their sins, beg pardon, and renew their faith and repentance (Ps. 89:31–33; 51:7–12; 32:5; Matt. 26:75; 1 Cor. 11:30, 32; Luke 1:20).

VI. The justification of believers under the old testament was, in all these respects, one and the same with the justification of believers under the new testament (Gal. 3:9, 13–14; Rom. 4:22–24).

CHAP. XII.— *Of Adoption.*

ALL those that are justified, God vouchsafeth, in and for His only Son Jesus Christ, to make partakers of the grace of adoption (Eph. 1:5; Gal. 4:4–5), by which they are taken into the number, and enjoy the liberties and privileges of the children of God (Rom. 8:17; John 1:12), have His name put upon them (Jer. 14:9; 2 Cor. 6:18; Rev. 3:12), receive the spirit of adoption (Rom. 8:15), have access to the throne of grace with boldness (Eph. 3:12; Rom. 5:2), are enabled to cry, Abba, Father (Gal. 4:6), are pitied (Ps. 103:13), protected (Prov. 14:26), provided for (Matt. 6:30, 32; 1 Peter 5:7), and chastened by Him as by a Father (Heb. 12:6): yet never cast off (Lam. 3:31), but sealed to the day of redemption (Eph. 4:30); and inherit the promises (Heb. 6:12), as heirs of everlasting salvation (1 Peter 1:3–4; Heb. 1:14).

CHAP. XIII.— *Of Sanctification.*

I. THEY, who are effectually called, and regenerated, having a new heart, and a new spirit created in them, are further sanctified, really and personally, through the virtue of Christ's death and resurrection (1 Cor. 6:11; Acts 20:32; Phil. 3:10; Rom. 6:5–6), by His Word and Spirit dwelling in them (John 17:17; Eph. 5:26; 2 Thess. 2:13): the dominion of the whole body of sin is destroyed (Rom. 6:6, 14), and the several lusts thereof are more and more weakened and mortified (Gal. 4:24; Rom. 8:13); and they more and more quickened and strengthened in all saving graces (Col. 1:11; Eph. 3:16–19), to the practice of true holiness, without which no man shall see the Lord (2 Cor. 7:1; Heb. 12:14).

II. This sanctification is throughout, in the whole man (1 Thess. 5:23); yet imperfect in this life, there abiding still some remnants of corruption in every part (1 John 1:10; Rom. 7:18, 23; Phil. 3:12); whence ariseth a continual and irreconcilable war, the flesh lusting against the Spirit, and the Spirit against the flesh (Gal. 5:17; 1 Peter 2:11).

III. In which war, although the remaining corruption, for a time, may much prevail (Rom. 7:23); yet, through the continual supply of strength from the sanctifying Spirit of Christ, the regenerate part doth overcome (Rom. 6:14; 1 John 5:4; Eph. 4:15–16); and so, the saints grow in grace (2 Peter 3:18; 2 Cor. 3:18), perfecting holiness in the fear of God (2 Cor. 7:1).

CHAP. XIV.— *Of Saving Faith.*

I. THE grace of faith, whereby the elect are enabled to believe to the saving of their souls (Heb. 10:39), is the work of the Spirit of Christ in their hearts (2 Cor. 4:13; Eph. 1:17–19; 2:8), and is ordinarily wrought by the ministry of the Word (Rom. 10:14, 17), by which also, and by the administration of the sacraments, and prayer, it is increased and strengthened (1 Peter 2:2; Acts 20:32; Rom. 4:11; Luke 17:5; Rom. 1:16–17).

II. By this faith, a Christian believeth to be true whatever is revealed in the Word, for the authority of God Himself speaking therein (John 4:42; 1 Thess. 2:13; 1 John 5:10; Acts 24:14); and acteth differently upon that which each particular passage thereof containeth; yielding obedience to the commands (Rom. 16:26), trembling at the threatenings (Isa. 66:2), and embracing the promises of God for this life, and that which is to come (Heb. 11:13; 1 Tim. 4:8). But the principal acts of saving faith are accepting, receiving, and resting upon Christ alone for justification, sanctification, and eternal life, by virtue of the covenant of grace (John 1:12; Acts 16:31; Gal. 2:20; Acts 15:11).

III. This faith is different in degrees, weak or strong (Heb. 5:13–14; Rom. 4:19–20; Matt. 6:30; 8:10); may be often and many ways assailed, and weakened, but gets the victory (Luke 22:31–32; Eph. 6:16; 1 John 5:4–5): growing up in many to the attainment of a full assurance, through Christ (Heb. 6:11–12; 10:22; Col. 2:2), who is both the author and finisher of our faith (Heb. 12:2).

CHAP. XV.— *Of Repentance unto Life.*

I. REPENTANCE unto life is an evangelical grace (Zech. 12:10; Acts 11:18), the doctrine whereof is to be preached by every minister of the Gospel, as well as that of faith in Christ (Luke 24:47; Mark 1:15; Acts 20:21).

II. By it, a sinner, out of the sight and sense not only of the danger, but also of the filthiness and odiousness of his sins, as contrary to the holy nature and righteous law of God; and upon the apprehension of His mercy in Christ to such as are penitent, so grieves for, and hates his sins, as to turn from them all unto God (Ezek. 18:30–31; 36:31; Isa. 30:22; Ps. 51:4; Jer. 31:18–19; Joel 2:12–13; Amos 5:15; Ps. 119:128; 2 Cor. 7:11), purposing and endeavouring to walk with Him in all the ways of His commandments (Ps. 119:6, 59, 106; Luke 1:6; 2 Kings 23:25).

III. Although repentance be not to be rested in, as any satisfaction for sin, or any cause of the pardon thereof (Ezek. 36:31–32; 16:61–63), which is the act of God's free grace in Christ (Hos. 14:2, 4; Rom. 3:24; Eph. 1:7); yet is it of such necessity to all sinners, that none may expect pardon without it (Luke 13:3, 5; Acts 17:30–31).

IV. As there is no sin so small, but it deserves damnation (Rom. 6:23; 5:12; Matt. 12:36); so there is no sin so great, that it can bring damnation upon those who truly repent (Isa. 55:7; Rom. 8:1; Isa. 1:16, 18).

V. Men ought not to content themselves with a general repentance, but it is every man's duty to endeavour to repent of his particular sins, particularly (Ps. 19:13; Luke 19:8; 1 Tim. 1:13, 15).

VI. As every man is bound to make private confession of his sins to God, praying for the pardon thereof (Ps. 51:4–5, 7, 9, 14; 32:5–6); upon which, and the forsaking of them, he shall find mercy (Prov. 28:13; 1 John 1:9); so, he that scandalizeth his brother, or the Church of Christ, ought to be willing, by a private or public confession, and sorrow for his sin, to declare his repentance to those that are offended (James 5:16; Luke 17:3–4; Josh. 7:19; Ps. 51), who are thereupon to be reconciled to him, and in love to receive him (2 Cor. 2:8).

CHAP. XVI.— *Of Good Works.*

I. GOOD works are only such as God hath commanded in His holy Word (Mic. 6:8; Rom. 12:2; Heb. 13:21), and not such as, without the warrant thereof, are devised by men, out of blind zeal, or upon any pretence of good intention (Matt. 15:9; Isa. 29:13; 1 Peter 1:18; Rom. 10:2; John 16:2; 1 Sam. 15:21–23).

II. These good works, done in obedience to God's commandments, are the fruits and evidences of a true and lively faith (James 2:18, 22): and by them believers manifest their thankfulness (Ps. 116:12–13; 1 Peter 2:9), strengthen their assurance (1 John 2:3, 5; 2 Peter 1:5–10), edify their brethren (2 Cor. 9:2; Matt. 5:16), adorn the profession of the gospel (Titus 2:5, 9–12; 1 Tim. 6:1), stop the mouths of the adversaries (1 Peter 2:15), and glorify God (1 Peter 2:12; Phil. 1:11; John 15:8), whose workmanship they are, created in Christ Jesus thereunto (Eph. 2:10), that, having their fruit unto holiness, they may have the end, eternal life (Rom. 6:22).

III. Their ability to do good works is not at all of themselves, but wholly from the Spirit of Christ (John 15:4–6; Ezek. 36:26–27). And that they may be enabled thereunto, besides the graces they have already received, there is required an actual influence of the same Holy Spirit, to work in them to will, and to do, of His good pleasure (Phil. 2:13; 4:13; 2 Cor. 3:5): yet are they not hereupon to grow negligent, as if they were not bound to perform any duty unless upon a special motion of the Spirit; but they ought to be diligent in stirring up the grace of God that is in them (Phil. 2:12; Heb. 6:11–12; 2 Peter 1:3, 5, 10–11; Isa. 64:7; 2 Tim. 1:6; Acts 26:6–7; Jude 20–21).

IV. They who, in their obedience, attain to the greatest height which is possible in this life, are so far from being able to supererogate, and to do more than God requires, as that they fall short of much which in duty they are bound to do (Luke 17:10; Neh. 13:22; Job 9:2–3; Gal. 5:17).

V. We cannot by our best works merit pardon of sin, or eternal life at the hand of God, by reason of the great disproportion that is between them and the glory to come; and the infinite distance that is between us and God, whom, by them, we can neither profit, nor satisfy for the debt of our former sins (Rom. 3:20; 4:2, 4, 6; Eph. 2:8–9; Titus 3:5–7; Rom. 8:18; Ps. 16:2; Job 22:2–3; 35:7–8), but when we have done all we can, we have done but our duty, and are unprofitable servants (Luke 17:10): and because, as they are good, they proceed from His Spirit (Gal. 5:22–23); and as they are wrought by us, they are defiled, and mixed with so much weakness and imperfection, that they cannot endure the severity of God's judgment (Isa. 64:6; Gal. 5:17; Rom. 7:15, 18; Ps. 143:2; 130:3).

VI. Notwithstanding, the persons of believers being accepted through Christ, their good works also are accepted in Him (Eph. 1:6; 1 Peter 2:5; Ex. 28:38; Gen. 4:4; Heb. 11:4); not as though they were in this life wholly unblameable and unreprovable in God's sight (Job 9:20; Ps. 143:2); but that He, looking upon them in His Son, is pleased to accept and reward that which is sincere, although accompanied with many weaknesses and imperfections (Heb. 13:20–21; 2 Cor. 8:12; Heb. 6:10; Matt. 25:21, 23).

VII. Works done by unregenerate men, although for the matter of them they may be things which God commands; and of good use both to themselves and others (2 Kings 10:30–31; 1 Kings 21:27, 29; Phil. 1:15–16, 18): yet, because they proceed not from a heart purified by faith (Gen. 4:5; Heb. 11:4, 6); nor are done in a right manner, according to the Word (1 Cor. 13:3; Isa. 1:12); nor to a right end, the glory of God (Matt. 6:2, 5, 16), they are therefore sinful, and cannot please God, or make a man meet to receive grace from God (Hag. 2:14; Titus 1:15; Amos 5:21–22; Hos. 1:4; Rom. 9:16; Titus 3:15): and yet, their neglect of them is more sinful and displeasing unto God (Ps. 14:4; 36:3; Job 21:14–15; Matt. 25:41–43, 45; 23:3).

CHAP. XVII.— *Of the Perseverance of the Saints.*

I. THEY, whom God hath accepted in His Beloved, effectually called, and sanctified by His Spirit, can neither totally nor finally fall away from the state of grace, but shall certainly persevere therein to the end, and be eternally saved (Phil. 1:6; 2 Peter 1:10; John 10:28–29; 1 John 3:9; 1 Peter 1:5, 9).

II. This perseverance of the saints depends not upon their own free will, but upon the immutability of the decree of election, flowing from the free and unchangeable love of God the Father (2 Tim. 2:18–19; Jer. 31:3); upon the efficacy of the merit and intercession of Jesus Christ (Heb. 10:10, 14; 13:20–21; 9:12–15; Rom. 8:33–39; John 17:11, 24; Luke 22:32; Heb. 7:25), the abiding of the Spirit, and of the seed of God within them (John 14:16–17; 1 John 2:27; 3:9), and the nature of the covenant of grace (Jer. 32:40): from all which ariseth also the certainty and infallibility thereof (John 10:28; 2 Thess. 3:3; 1 John 2:19).

III. Nevertheless, they may, through the temptations of Satan and of the world, the prevalency of corruption remaining in them, and the neglect of the means of their preservation, fall into grievous sins (Matt. 26:70, 72, 74); and, for a time, continue therein (Ps. 51: Title, 14): whereby they incur God's displeasure (Isa. 64:5, 7, 9; 2 Sam. 11:27), and grieve His Holy Spirit (Eph. 4:30), come to be deprived of some measure of their graces and comforts (Ps. 51:8, 10, 12; Rev. 2:4; Song 5:2–4, 6), have their hearts hardened (Isa. 63:17; Mark 6:52; 16:14), and their consciences wounded (Ps. 32:3–4; 51:8); hurt and scandalize others (2 Sam. 12:14), and bring temporal judgments upon themselves (Ps. 89:31–32; 1 Cor. 11:32).

CHAP. XVIII.—*Of the Assurance of Grace and Salvation.*

1. ALTHOUGH hypocrites and other unregenerate men may vainly deceive themselves with false hopes and carnal presumptions of being in the favour of God, and estate of salvation (Job 8:13–14; Mic. 3:11; Deut. 29:19; John 8:41) (which hope of theirs shall perish [Matt. 7:22–23]): yet such as truly believe in the Lord Jesus, and love Him in sincerity, endeavouring to walk in all good conscience before Him, may, in this life, be certainly assured that they are in the state of grace (1 John 2:3; 3:14, 18–19, 21, 24; 5:13), and may rejoice in the hope of the glory of God, which hope shall never make them ashamed (Rom. 5:2, 5).

II. This certainty is not a bare conjectural and probable persuasion grounded upon a fallible hope (Heb. 6:11, 19); but an infallible assurance of faith founded upon the divine truth of the promises of salvation (Heb. 6:17–18), the inward evidence of those graces unto which these promises are made (2 Peter 1:4–5, 10–11; 1 John 2:3; 3:14; 2 Cor. 1:12), the testimony of the Spirit of adoption witnessing with our spirits that we are the children of God (Rom. 8:15–16), which Spirit is the earnest of our inheritance, whereby we are sealed to the day of redemption (Eph. 1:13–14; 4:30; 2 Cor. 1:21–22).

III. This infallible assurance doth not so belong to the essence of faith, but that a true believer may wait long, and conflict with many difficulties, before he be partaker of it (1 John 5:13; Isa. 50:10; Mark 9:24; Ps. 88; 77:1–12): yet, being enabled by the Spirit to know the things which are freely given him of God, he may, without extraordinary revelation, in the right use of ordinary means, attain thereunto (1 Cor. 2:12; 1 John 4:13; Heb. 6:11–12; Eph. 3:17–19). And therefore it is the duty of every one to give all diligence to make his calling and election sure (2 Peter 1:10), that thereby his heart may be enlarged in peace and joy in the Holy Ghost, in love and thankfulness to God, and in strength and cheerfulness in the duties of obedience (Rom. 5:1–2, 5; 14:17; 15:13; Eph. 1:3–4; Ps. 4:6–7; 119:32), the proper fruits of this assurance; so far is it from inclining men to looseness (1 John 2:1–2; Rom. 6:1–2; Titus 2:11–12, 14; 2 Cor. 7:1; Rom. 8:1, 12; 1 John 3:2–3; Ps. 130:4; 1 John 1:6–7).

IV. True believers may have the assurance of their salvation divers ways shaken, diminished, and intermitted; as, by negligence in preserving of it, by falling into some special sin which woundeth the conscience and grieveth the Spirit; by some sudden or vehement temptation, by God's withdrawing the light of His countenance, and suffering even such as fear Him to walk in darkness and to have no light (Song 5:2–3, 6; Ps. 51:8, 12, 14; Eph. 4:30–31; Ps. 77:1–10; Matt. 26:69–72; Ps. 31:22; 88; Isa. 50:10): yet are they never utterly destitute of that seed of God, and life of faith, that love of Christ and the brethren, that sincerity of heart, and conscience of duty, out of which, by the operation of the Spirit, this assurance may, in due time, be revived (1 John 3:9; Luke 22:32; Job 13:15; Ps. 73:15; 51:8, 12; Isa. 50:10); and by the which, in the mean time, they are supported from utter despair (Mic. 7:7–9; Jer. 32:40; Isa. 54:7–10; Ps. 22:1; 88).

CHAP. XIX.— *Of the Law of God.*

I. GOD gave to Adam a law, as a covenant of works, by which He bound him and all his posterity, to personal, entire, exact, and perpetual obedience, promised life upon the fulfilling, and threatened death upon the breach of it, and endued him with power and ability to keep it (Gen. 1:26–27; 2:17; Rom. 2:14–15; 10:5; 5:12, 19; Gal. 3:10, 12; Eccl. 7:29; Job 28:28).

II. This law, after his fall, continued to be a perfect rule of righteousness; and, as such, was delivered by God upon Mount Sinai, in ten commandments, and written in two tables (James 1:25; 2:8, 10–12; Rom. 13:8–9; Deut. 5:32; 10:4; Ex. 24:1): the first four commandments containing our duty towards God; and the other six, our duty to man (Matt. 22:37–40).

III. Beside this law, commonly called moral, God was pleased to give to the people of Israel, as a church under age, ceremonial laws, containing several typical ordinances, partly of worship, prefiguring Christ, His graces, actions, sufferings, and benefits (Heb. 11; 10:1; Gal. 4:1–3; Col. 2:17); and partly, holding forth divers instructions of moral duties (1 Cor. 5:7; 2 Cor. 6:17; Jude 23). All which ceremonial laws are now abrogated, under the new testament (Col. 2:14, 16–17; Dan. 9:27; Eph. 2:15–16).

IV. To them also, as a body politic, He gave sundry judicial laws, which expired together with the State of that people; not obliging any other now, further than the general equity thereof may require (Ex. 21; 22:1–29; Gen. 49:10; 1 Peter 2:13–14; Matt. 5:17, 38–39; 1 Cor. 9:8–10).

V. The moral law doth for ever bind all, as well justified persons as others, to the obedience thereof (Rom. 13:8–10; Eph. 6:2; 1 John 2:3–4, 7–8); and that, not only in regard of the matter contained in it, but also in respect of the authority of God the Creator, who gave it (James 2:10–11). Neither doth Christ, in the Gospel, any way dissolve, but much strengthen this obligation (Matt. 5:17–19; James 2:8; Rom. 3:31).

VI. Although true believers be not under the law, as a covenant of works, to be thereby justified, or condemned (Rom. 6:14; Gal. 2:16; 3:13; 4:4–5; Acts 13:39; Rom. 8:1); yet is it of great use to them, as well as to others; in that, as a rule of life informing them of the will of God, and their duty, it directs and binds them to walk accordingly (Rom. 7:12, 22, 25; Ps. 119:4–6; 1 Cor. 7:19; Gal. 5:14, 16, 18–23); discovering also the sinful pollutions of their nature, hearts, and lives (Rom. 7:7; 3:20); so as, examining themselves thereby, they may come to further conviction of, humiliation for, and hatred against sin (James 1:23–25; Rom. 7:9, 14, 24), together with a clearer sight of the need they have of Christ, and the perfection of His obedience (Gal. 3:24; Rom. 7:24–25; 8:3–4). It is likewise of use to the regenerate, to restrain their corruptions, in that it forbids sin (James 2:11; Ps. 119:101, 104, 128): and the threatenings of it serve to show what even their sins deserve; and what afflictions, in this life, they may expect for them, although freed from the curse thereof threatened in the law (Ezra 9:13–14; Ps. 89:30–34). The promises of it, in like manner, show them God's approbation of obedience, and what blessings they may expect upon the performance thereof (Lev. 26:1–14; 2 Cor. 6:16; Eph. 6:2–3; Ps. 37:11; Matt. 5:5; Ps. 19:11): although not as due to them by the law as a covenant of works (Gal. 2:16; Luke 17:10). So as, a man's doing good, and refraining from evil, because the law encourageth to the one, and deterreth from the other, is no evidence of his being under law; and not under grace (Rom. 6:12, 14; 1 Peter 3:8–12; Ps. 34:12–16; Heb. 12:28–29).

VII. Neither are the forementioned uses of the law contrary to the grace of the Gospel, but do sweetly comply with it (Gal. 3:21); the Spirit of Christ subduing and enabling the will of man to do that freely, and cheerfully, which the will of God, revealed in the law, requireth to be done (Ezek. 36:27; Heb. 8:10; Jer. 31:33).

CHAP. XX.— *Of Christian Liberty, and Liberty of Conscience.*

1. THE liberty which Christ hath purchased for believers under the Gospel consists in their freedom from the guilt of sin, the condemning wrath of God, the curse of the moral law (Titus 2:14; 1 Thess. 1:10; Gal. 3:13); and, in their being delivered from this present evil world, bondage to Satan, and dominion of sin (Gal. 1:4; Col. 1:13; Acts 26:18; Rom. 6:14); from the evil of afflictions, the sting of death, the victory of the grave, and everlasting damnation (Rom. 8:28; Ps. 119:71; 1 Cor. 15:54–57; Rom. 8:1); as also, in their free access to God (Rom. 5:1–2), and their yielding obedience unto Him, not out of slavish fear, but a child-like love and willing mind (Rom. 8:14–15; 1 John 4:18). All which were common also to believers under the law (Gal. 3:9, 14). But, under the new testament, the liberty of Christians is further enlarged, in their freedom from the yoke of the ceremonial law, to which the Jewish Church was subjected (Gal. 4:1–3, 6–7; 5:1; Acts 15:10–11); and in greater boldness of access to the throne of grace (Heb. 4:14, 16; 10:19–22), and in fuller communications of the free Spirit of God, than believers under the law did ordinarily partake of (John 7:38–39; 2 Cor. 3:13, 17–18).

II. God alone is Lord of the conscience (James 4:12; Rom. 14:4), and hath left it free from the doctrines and commandments of men, which are, in any thing, contrary to His Word; or beside it, if matters of faith, or worship (Acts 4:19; 5:29; 1 Cor. 7:23; Matt. 23:8–10; 2 Cor. 1:24; Matt. 15:9). So that, to believe such doctrines, or to obey such commands, out of conscience, is to betray true liberty of conscience (Col. 2:20, 22–23; Gal. 1:10; 2:4–5; 5:1): and the requiring of an implicit faith, and an absolute and blind obedience, is to destroy liberty of conscience, and reason also (Rom. 10:17; 14:23; Isa. 8:20; Acts 17:11; John 4:22; Hos. 5:11; Rev. 13:12, 16–17; Jer. 8:9).

III. They who, upon pretence of Christian liberty, do practice any sin, or cherish any lust, do thereby destroy the end of Christian liberty, which is, that being delivered out of the hands of our enemies, we might serve the Lord without fear, in holiness and righteousness before Him, all the days of our life (Gal. 5:13; 1 Peter 2:16; 2 Peter 2:19; John 8:34; Luke 1:74–75).

IV. And because the powers which God hath ordained, and the liberty which Christ hath purchased, are not intended by God to destroy, but mutually to uphold and preserve one another, they who, upon pretence of Christian liberty, shall oppose any lawful power, or the lawful exercise of it, whether it be civil or ecclesiastical, resist the ordinance of God (Matt. 12:25; 1 Peter 2:13–14, 16; Rom. 13:1–8; Heb. 13:17). And, for their publishing of such opinions, or maintaining of such practices, as are contrary to the light of nature, or to the known principles of Christianity (whether concerning faith, worship, or conversation), or to the power of godliness; or, such erroneous opinions or practices, as either in their own nature, or in the manner of publishing or maintaining them, are destructive to the external peace and order which Christ hath established in the Church, they may lawfully be called to account (Rom. 1:32; 1 Cor. 5:1, 5, 11, 13; 2 John 10–11; 2 Thess. 3:14; 1 Tim. 6:3–5; Titus 1:10–11, 13; 3:10; Matt. 18:15–17; 1 Tim. 1:19–20; Rev. 2:2, 14–15, 20; 3:9), and proceeded against, by the censures of the Church, and by the power of the civil magistrate (Deut. 13:6–12; Rom. 13:3–4; 2 John 10–11; Ezra 7:23, 25–28; Rev. 17:12, 16–17; Neh. 13:15, 17, 21–22, 25, 30; 2 Kings 23:5–6, 9, 20–21; 2 Chron. 34:33; 15:12–13, 16; Dan. 3:29; 1 Tim. 2:2; Isa. 49:23; Zech. 13:2–3).

CHAP. XXI.—*Of Religious Worship, and the Sabbath Day.*

I. THE light of nature showeth that there is a God, who hath lordship and sovereignty over all, is good, and doth good unto all, and is therefore to be feared, loved, praised, called upon, trusted in, and served, with all the heart, and with all the soul, and with all the might (Rom. 1:20; Acts 17:24; Ps. 119:68; Jer. 10:7; Ps. 31:23; 18:3; Rom. 10:12; Ps. 62:8; Josh. 24:14; Mark 12:33). But the acceptable way of worshipping the true God is instituted by Himself, and so limited by His own revealed will, that He may not be worshipped according to the imaginations and devices of men, or the suggestions of Satan, under any visible representation, or any other way not prescribed in the holy Scripture (Deut. 12:32; Matt. 15:9; Acts 17:25; Matt. 4:9–10; Deut. 15:1–20; Ex. 20:4–6; Col. 2:23).

II. Religious worship is to be given to God, the Father, Son, and Holy Ghost; and to Him alone (Matt. 4:10; John 5:23; 2 Cor. 13:14); not to angels, saints, or any other creature (Col. 2:18; Rev. 19:10; Rom. 1:25): and, since the fall, not without a Mediator; nor in the mediation of any other but of Christ alone (John 14:6; 1 Tim. 2:5; Eph. 2:18; Col. 3:17).

III. Prayer, with thanksgiving, being one special part of religious worship (Phil. 4:6), is by God required of all men (Ps. 65:2): and, that it may be accepted, it is to be made in the name of the Son (John 14:13–14; 1 Peter 2:5), by the help of His Spirit (Rom. 8:26), according to His will (1 John 5:14), with understanding, reverence, humility, fervency, faith, love, and perseverance (Ps. 47:7; Eccl. 5:1–2; Heb. 12:28; Gen. 18:27; James 5:16; 1:6–7; Mark 11:24; Matt. 6:12, 14–15; Col. 4:2; Eph. 6:18); and, if vocal, in a known tongue (1 Cor. 14:14).

IV. Prayer is to be made for things lawful (1 John 5:14); and for all sorts of men living, or that shall live hereafter (1 Tim. 2:1–2; John 17:20; 2 Sam. 7:29; Ruth 4:12): but not for the dead (2 Sam. 12:21–23; Luke 16:25–26; Rev. 14:13), nor for those of whom it may be known that they have sinned the sin unto death (1 John 5:16).

V. The reading of the Scriptures with godly fear (Acts 15:21; Rev. 1:3), the sound preaching (2 Tim. 4:2) and conscionable hearing of the Word, in obedience unto God, with understanding, faith, and reverence (James 1:22; Acts 10:33; Matt. 13:19; Heb. 4:2; Isa. 66:2), singing of psalms with grace in the heart (Col. 3:16; Eph. 5:19; James 5:13); as also, the due administration and worthy receiving of the sacraments instituted by Christ, are all parts of the ordinary religious worship of God (Matt. 28:19; 1 Cor. 11:23–29; Acts 2:42): beside religious oaths (Deut. 6:13; Neh. 10:29), vows (Isa. 19:21; Eccl. 5:4–5), solemn fastings (Joel 2:12; Esth. 4:16; Matt. 9:15; 1 Cor. 7:5), and thanksgivings upon special occasions (Ps. 108; Esth. 9:22), which are, in their several times and seasons, to be used in an holy and religious manner (Heb. 12:28).

VI. Neither prayer, nor any other part of religious worship, is now, under the Gospel, either tied unto, or made more acceptable by any place in which it is performed, or towards which it is directed (John 4:21): but God is to be worshipped everywhere (Mal. 1:11; 1 Tim. 2:8), in spirit and truth (John 4:23–24); as, in private families (Jer. 10:25; Deut. 6:6–7; Job 1:5; 2 Sam. 6:18, 20; 1 Peter 3:7; Acts 10:2) daily (Matt. 6:11), and in secret, each one by himself (Matt. 6:6; Eph. 6:18); so, more solemnly in the public assemblies, which are not carelessly or wilfully to be neglected, or forsaken, when God, by His Word or providence, calleth thereunto (Isa. 56:6–7; Heb. 10:25; Prov. 1:20–21, 24; 8:34; Acts 13:42; Luke 4:16; Acts 2:42).

VII. As it is the law of nature, that, in general, a due proportion of time be set apart for the worship of God; so, in His Word, by a positive, moral, and perpetual commandment binding all men in all ages, He hath particularly appointed one day in seven, for a Sabbath, to be kept holy unto Him (Ex. 20:8, 10–11; Isa. 56:2, 4, 6–7): which, from the beginning of the world to the resurrection of Christ, was the last day of the week; and, from the resurrection of Christ, was changed into the first day of the week (Gen. 2:2–3; 1 Cor. 16:1–2; Acts 20:7), which, in Scripture, is called the Lord's Day (Rev. 1:10), and is to be continued to the end of the world, as the Christian Sabbath (Ex. 20:8, 10; Matt. 5:17–18).

VIII. This Sabbath is then kept holy unto the Lord, when men, after a due preparing of their hearts, and ordering of their common affairs before-hand, do not only observe an holy rest, all the day, from their own works, words, and thoughts about their worldly employments and recreations (Ex. 20:8; 16:23, 25–26, 29–30; 31:15–17; Isa. 58:13; Neh. 13:15–19, 21–22), but also are taken up, the whole time, in the public and private exercises of His worship, and in the duties of necessity and mercy (Isa. 58:13; Matt. 12:1–13).

CHAP. XXII.— Of Lawful Oaths and Vows.

I. A LAWFUL oath is a part of religious worship (Deut. 10:20), wherein, upon just occasion, the person swearing solemnly calleth God to witness what he asserteth, or promiseth, and to judge him according to the truth or falsehood of what he sweareth (Ex. 20:7; Lev. 19:12; 2 Cor. 1:23; 2 Chron. 6:22–23).

II. The name of God only is that by which men ought to swear, and therein it is to be used with all holy fear and reverence (Deut. 6:13). Therefore, to swear vainly, or rashly, by that glorious and dreadful Name; or, to swear at all by any other thing, is sinful, and to be abhorred (Ex. 20:7; Jer. 5:7; Matt. 5:34, 37; James 5:12). Yet, as in matters of weight and moment, an oath is warranted by the Word of God, under the new testament, as well as under the old (Heb. 6:16; 2 Cor. 1:23; Isa. 65:16); so a lawful oath, being imposed by lawful authority, in such matters, ought to be taken (1 Kings 8:31; Neh. 13:25; Ezra 10:5).

III. Whosoever taketh an oath ought duly to consider the weightiness of so solemn an act, and therein to avouch nothing but what he is fully persuaded is the truth (Ex. 20:7; Jer. 4:2): neither may any man bind himself by oath to any thing but what is good and just, and what he believeth so to be, and what he is able and resolved to perform (Gen. 24:2–3, 5–6, 8–9). Yet is it a sin to refuse an oath touching any thing that is good and just, being imposed by lawful authority (Num. 5:19, 21; Neh. 5:12; Ex. 22:7–11).

IV. An oath is to be taken in the plain and common sense of the words, without equivocation, or mental reservation (Jer. 4:2; Ps. 24:4). It cannot oblige to sin; but in any thing not sinful, being taken, it binds to performance, although to a man's own hurt (1 Sam. 25:22, 32–34; Ps. 15:4). Nor is it to be violated, although made to heretics, or infidels (Ezek. 17:16, 18–19; Josh. 9:18–19; 2 Sam. 21:1).

V. A vow is of the like nature with a promissory oath, and ought to be made with the like religious care, and to be performed with the like faithfulness (Isa. 19:21; Eccl. 5:4–6; Ps. 61:8; 66:13–14).

VI. It is not to be made to any creature, but to God alone (Ps. 76:11; Jer. 44:25–26): and, that it may be accepted, it is to be made voluntarily, out of faith, and conscience of duty, in way of thankfulness for mercy received, or for the obtaining of what we want, whereby we more strictly bind ourselves to necessary duties: or, to other things, so far and so long as they may fitly conduce thereunto (Deut. 23:21–23; Ps. 50:14; Gen. 28:20–22; 1 Sam. 1:11; Ps. 66:13–14; 132:2–5).

VII. No man may vow to do any thing forbidden in the Word of God, or what would hinder any duty therein commanded, or which is not in his own power, and for the performance whereof he hath no promise of ability from God (Acts 23:12, 14; Mark 6:26; Num. 30:5, 8, 12–13). In which respects, popish monastical vows of perpetual single life, professed poverty, and regular obedience, are so far from being degrees of higher perfection, that they are superstitious and sinful snares, in which no Christian may entangle himself (Matt. 19:11–12; 1 Cor. 7:2, 9; Eph. 4:28; 1 Peter 4:2; 1 Cor. 7:23).

CHAP. XXIII.— *Of the Civil Magistrate.*

I. GOD, the supreme Lord and King of all the world, hath ordained civil magistrates, to be, under Him, over the people, for His own glory, and the public good: and, to this end, hath armed them with the power of the sword, for the defence and encouragement of them that are good, and for the punishment of evil doers (Rom. 13:1–4; 1 Peter 2:13–14).

II. It is lawful for Christians to accept and execute the office of a magistrate, when called thereunto (Prov. 8:15–16; Rom. 13:1–2, 4): in the managing whereof, as they ought especially to maintain piety, justice, and peace, according to the wholesome laws of each commonwealth (Ps. 2:10–12; 1 Tim. 2:2; Ps. 82:3–4; 2 Sam. 23:3; 1 Peter 2:13); so, for that end, they may lawfully, now under the new testament, wage war, upon just and necessary occasion (Luke 3:14; Rom. 13:4; Matt. 8:9–10; Acts 10:1–2; Rev. 17:14, 16).

III. The civil magistrate may not assume to himself the administration of the Word and sacraments, or the power of the keys of the kingdom of heaven (2 Chron. 26:18; Matt. 18:17; 16:19; 1 Cor. 12:28–29; Eph. 4:11–12; 1 Cor. 4:1–2; Rom. 10:15; Heb. 5:4): yet he hath authority, and it is his duty, to take order that unity and peace be preserved in the Church, that the truth of God be kept pure and entire, that all blasphemies and heresies be suppressed, all corruptions and abuses in worship and discipline prevented or reformed, and all the ordinances of God duly settled, administered, and observed (Isa. 49:23; Ps. 122:9; Ezra 7:23, 25–28; Lev. 24:16; Deut. 13:5–6, 12; 2 Kings 18:4; 1 Chron. 13:1–9; 2 Kings 24:1–26; 2 Chron. 34:33; 15:12–13). For the better effecting whereof, he hath power to call synods, to be present at them, and to provide that whatsoever is transacted in them be according to the mind of God (2 Chron. 19:8–11; 2 Chron. 29–30; Matt. 2:4–5).

IV. It is the duty of people to pray for magistrates (1 Tim. 2:1–2), to honour their persons (1 Peter 2:17), to pay them tribute and other dues (Rom. 13:6–7), to obey their lawful commands, and to be subject to their authority, for conscience' sake (Rom. 13:5; Titus 3:1). Infidelity, or difference in religion, doth not make void the magistrates' just and legal authority, nor free the people from their due obedience to them (1 Peter 2:13–14, 16): from which ecclesiastical persons are not exempted (Rom. 13:1; 1 Kings 2:35; Acts 25:9–11; 2 Peter 2:1, 10–11; Jude 8–11), much less hath the Pope any power and jurisdiction over them in their dominions, or over any of their people; and, least of all, to deprive them of their dominions, or lives, if he shall judge them to be heretics, or upon any other pretence whatsoever (2 Thess. 2:4; Rev. 13:15–17).

CHAP. XXIV.— *Of Marriage and Divorce.*

I. MARRIAGE is to be between one man and one woman: neither is it lawful for any man to have more than one wife, nor for any woman to have more than one husband, at the same time (Gen. 2:24; Matt. 19:5–6; Prov. 2:17).

II. Marriage was ordained for the mutual help of husband and wife (Gen. 2:18), for the increase of mankind with a legitimate issue, and of the Church with an holy seed (Mal. 2:15); and for preventing of uncleanness (1 Cor. 7:2, 9).

III. It is lawful for all sorts of people to marry, who are able with judgment to give their consent (Heb. 13:4; 1 Tim. 4:3; 1 Cor. 7:36–38; Gen. 24:57–58). Yet it is the duty of Christians to marry only in the Lord (1 Cor. 7:39). And therefore such as profess the true reformed religion should not marry with infidels, papists, or other idolaters: neither should such as are godly be unequally yoked, by marrying with such as are notoriously wicked in their life, or maintain damnable heresies (Gen. 34:14; Ex. 34:16; Deut. 7:3–4; 1 Kings 11:4; Neh. 13:25–27; Mal. 2:11–12; 2 Cor. 6:14).

IV. Marriage ought not to be within the degrees of consanguinity or affinity forbidden in the Word (Lev. 18; 1 Cor. 5:1; Amos 2:7). Nor can such incestuous marriages ever be made lawful by any law of man or consent of parties, so as those persons may live together as man and wife (Mark 6:18; Lev. 18:24–28). The man may not marry any of his wife's kindred, nearer in blood than he may of his own: nor the woman of her husband's kindred, nearer in blood than of her own (Lev. 20:19–21).

V. Adultery or fornication committed after a contract, being detected before marriage, giveth just occasion to the innocent party to dissolve that contract (Matt. 1:18–20). In the case of adultery after marriage, it is lawful for the innocent party to sue out a divorce (Matt. 5:31–32): and, after the divorce, to marry another, as if the offending party were dead (Matt. 19:9; Rom. 7:2–3).

VI. Although the corruption of man be such as is apt to study arguments unduly to put asunder those whom God hath joined together in marriage: yet, nothing but adultery, or such wilful desertion as can no way be remedied by the Church, or civil magistrate, is cause sufficient of dissolving the bond of marriage (Matt. 19:8–9; 1 Cor. 7:15; Matt. 19:6): wherein, a public and orderly course of proceeding is to be observed; and the persons concerned in it not left to their own wills, and discretion, in their own case (Deut. 24:1–4).

CHAP. XXV.— *Of the Church.*

I. THE catholic or universal Church, which is invisible, consists of the whole number of the elect, that have been, are, or shall be gathered into one, under Christ the Head thereof; and is the spouse, the body, the fulness of Him that filleth all in all (Eph. 1:10, 22–23; 5:23, 27, 32; Col. 1:18).

II. The visible Church, which is also catholic or universal under the Gospel (not confined to one nation, as before under the law), consists of all those throughout the world that profess the true religion (1 Cor. 1:2; 12:12–13; Ps. 2:8; Rev. 7:9; Rom. 15:9–12); and of their children (1 Cor. 7:14; Acts 2:39; Ezek. 16:20–21; Rom. 11:16; Gen. 3:15; 17:7): and is the kingdom of the Lord Jesus Christ (Matt. 13:47; Isa. 9:7), the house and family of God (Eph. 2:19; 3:15), out of which there is no ordinary possibility of salvation (Acts 2:47).

III. Unto this catholic visible Church Christ hath given the ministry, oracles, and ordinances of God, for the gathering and perfecting of the saints, in this life, to the end of the world: and doth, by His own presence and Spirit, according to His promise, make them effectual thereunto (1 Cor. 12:28; Eph. 4:12–13; Matt. 28:19–20; Isa. 59:21).

IV. This catholic Church hath been sometimes more, sometimes less visible (Rom. 11:3–4; Rev. 12:6, 14). And particular Churches, which are members thereof, are more or less pure, according as the doctrine of the Gospel is taught and embraced, ordinances administered, and public worship performed more or less purely in them (Rev. 2–3; 1 Cor. 5:6–7).

V. The purest Churches under heaven are subject both to mixture and error (1 Cor. 13:12; Rev. 2–3; Matt. 13:24–30, 47); and some have so degenerated, as to become no Churches of Christ, but synagogues of Satan (Rev. 18:2; Rom. 11:18–22). Nevertheless, there shall be always a Church on earth to worship God according to His will (Matt. 16:18; Ps. 72:17; 102:28; Matt. 28:19–20).

VI. There is no other head of the Church but the Lord Jesus Christ (Col. 1:18; Eph. 1:22). Nor can the Pope of Rome, in any sense, be head thereof:

but is that Antichrist, that man of sin, and son of perdition, that exalteth himself, in the Church, against Christ and all that is called God (Matt. 23:8–10; 2 Thess. 2:3–4, 8–9; Rev. 13:6).

CHAP. XXVI.— *Of the Communion of Saints.*

I. ALL saints, that are united to Jesus Christ their Head, by His Spirit, and by faith, have fellowship with Him in His grace, sufferings, death, resurrection, and glory (1 John 1:3; Eph. 3:16–19; John 1:16; Eph. 2:5–6; Phil. 3:10; Rom. 6:5–6; 2 Tim. 2:12): and, being united to one another in love, they have communion in each other's gifts and graces (Eph. 4:15–16; 1 Cor. 12:7; 3:21–23; Col. 2:19), and are obliged to the performance of such duties, public and private, as do conduce to their mutual good, both in the inward and outward man (1 Thess. 5:11, 14; Rom. 1:11–12, 14; 1 John 3:16–18; Gal. 6:10).

II. Saints by profession are bound to maintain an holy fellowship and communion in the worship of God, and in performing such other spiritual services as tend to their mutual edification (Heb. 10:24–25; Acts 2:42, 46; Isa. 2:3; 1 Cor. 11:20); as also in relieving each other in outward things, according to their several abilities and necessities. Which communion, as God offereth opportunity, is to be extended unto all those who, in every place, call upon the name of the Lord Jesus (Acts 2:44–45; 1 John 3:17; 2 Cor. 8–9; Acts 11:29–30).

III. This communion, which the saints have with Christ, doth not make them, in any wise partakers of the substance of His Godhead; or to be equal with Christ in any respect: either of which to affirm is impious and blasphemous (Col. 1:18–19; 1 Cor. 8:6; Isa. 42:8; 1 Tim. 6:15–16; Ps. 45:7; Heb. 1:8–9). Nor doth their communion one with another, as saints, take away, or infringe the title or propriety which each man hath in his goods and possessions (Ex. 20:15; Eph. 4:28; Acts 5:4).

CHAP. XXVII.— *Of the Sacraments.*

I. SACRAMENTS are holy signs and seals of the covenant of grace (Rom. 4:11; Gen. 17:7, 10), immediately instituted by God (Matt. 28:19; 1 Cor. 11:23), to represent Christ and His benefits; and to confirm our interest in Him (1 Cor. 10:16; 11:25–26; Gal. 3:27; 3:17): as also, to put a visible difference between those that belong unto the Church and the rest of the world (Rom. 15:8; Ex. 12:48; Gen. 34:14); and solemnly to engage them to the service of God in Christ, according to His Word (Rom. 6:3–4; 1 Cor. 10:16, 21).

II. There is, in every sacrament, a spiritual relation, or sacramental union, between the sign and the thing signified: whence it comes to pass, that the names and effects of the one are attributed to the other (Gen. 17:10; Matt. 26:27–28; Titus 3:5).

III. The grace which is exhibited in or by the sacraments rightly used, is not conferred by any power in them; neither doth the efficacy of a sacrament depend upon the piety or intention of him that doth administer it (Rom. 2:28–29; 1 Peter 3:21): but upon the work of the Spirit (Matt. 3:11; 1 Cor. 12:13), and the word of institution, which contains, together with a precept authorizing the use thereof, a promise of benefit to worthy receivers (Matt. 26:27–28; 28:19–20).

IV. There be only two sacraments ordained by Christ our Lord in the Gospel; that is to say, Baptism and the Supper of the Lord: neither of which may be dispensed by any, but by a minister of the Word lawfully ordained (Matt. 28:19; 1 Cor. 11:20, 23; 4:1; Heb. 5:4).

V. The sacraments of the old testament, in regard of the spiritual things thereby signified and exhibited, were, for substance, the same with those of the new (1 Cor. 10:1–4).

CHAP. XXVIII.—*Of Baptism.*

I. BAPTISM is a sacrament of the new testament, ordained by Jesus Christ (Matt. 28:19), not only for the solemn admission of the party baptized into the visible Church (1 Cor. 12:13); but also, to be unto him a sign and seal of the covenant of grace (Rom. 4:11; Col. 2:11–12), of his ingrafting into Christ (Gal. 3:27), of regeneration (Titus 3:5), of remission of sins (Mark 1:4), and of his giving up unto God, through Jesus Christ, to walk in newness of life (Rom. 6:3–4). Which sacrament is, by Christ's own appointment, to be continued in His Church until the end of the world (Matt. 28:19–20).

II. The outward element to be used in this sacrament is water, wherewith the party is to be baptized, in the name of the Father, and of the Son, and of the Holy Ghost, by a minister of the Gospel, lawfully called thereunto (Matt. 3:11; John 1:33; Matt. 28:19–20).

III. Dipping of the person into the water is not necessary; but Baptism is rightly administered by pouring, or sprinkling water upon the person (Heb. 9:10, 19–22; Acts 2:41; 16:33; Mark 7:4).

IV. Not only those that do actually profess faith in and obedience unto Christ (Mark 16:15–16; Acts 8:37–38), but also the infants of one, or both, believing parents, are to be baptized (Gen. 17:7, 9; Gal. 3:9, 14; Col. 2:11–12; Acts 2:38–39; Rom. 4:11–12; 1 Cor. 7:14; Matt. 28:19; Mark 10:13–16; Luke 18:15).

V. Although it be a great sin to contemn or neglect this ordinance (Luke 7:30; Ex. 4:24–26), yet grace and salvation are not so inseparably annexed unto it, as that no person can be regenerated, or saved, without it (Rom. 4:11; Acts 10:2, 4, 22, 31, 45, 47); or, that all that are baptized are undoubtedly regenerated (Acts 8:13, 23).

VI. The efficacy of Baptism is not tied to that moment of time wherein it is administered (John 3:5, 8); yet, notwithstanding, by the right use of this ordinance, the grace promised is not only offered, but really exhibited, and conferred, by the Holy Ghost, to such (whether of age or infants) as that grace belongeth unto, according to the counsel of God's own will, in His appointed time (Gal. 3:27; Titus 3:5; Eph. 5:25–26; Acts 2:38, 41).

VII. The sacrament of Baptism is but once to be administered unto any person (Titus 3:5).

CHAP. XXIX.— *Of the Lord's Supper.*

I. OUR Lord Jesus, in the night wherein He was betrayed, instituted the sacrament of His body and blood, called the Lord's Supper, to be observed in His Church, unto the end of the world, for the perpetual remembrance of the sacrifice of Himself in His death; the sealing all benefits thereof unto true believers, their spiritual nourishment and growth in Him, their further engagement in and to all duties which they owe unto Him; and, to be a bond and pledge of their communion with Him, and with each other, as members of His mystical body (1 Cor. 11:23–26; 10:16–17, 21; 12:13).

II. In this sacrament, Christ is not offered up to His Father; nor any real sacrifice made at all, for remission of sins of the quick or dead (Heb. 9:22, 25–26, 28); but only a commemoration of that one offering up of Himself, by Himself, upon the cross, once for all: and a spiritual oblation of all possible praise unto God, for the same (1 Cor. 11:24–26; Matt. 26:26–27): so that the popish sacrifice of the mass (as they call it) is most abominably injurious to Christ's one, only sacrifice, the alone propitiation for all the sins of His elect (Heb. 7:23–24, 27; 10:11, 12, 14, 18).

III. The Lord Jesus hath, in this ordinance, appointed His ministers to declare His word of institution to the people; to pray, and bless the elements of bread and wine, and thereby to set them apart from a common to an holy use; and to take and break the bread, to take the cup, and (they communicating also themselves) to give both to the communicants (Matt. 26:26–28; Mark 14:22–24; Luke 22:19–20; 1 Cor. 11:23–26); but to none who are not then present in the congregation (Acts 20:7; 1 Cor. 11:20).

IV. Private masses, or receiving this sacrament by a priest, or any other, alone (1 Cor. 10:6); as likewise, the denial of the cup to the people (Mark 14:23; 1 Cor. 11:25–29), worshipping the elements, the lifting them up, or carrying them about, for adoration, and the reserving them for any pretended religious use; are all contrary to the nature of this sacrament, and to the institution of Christ (Matt. 15:9).

V. The outward elements in this sacrament, duly set apart to the uses ordained by Christ, have such relation to Him crucified, as that, truly, yet sacramentally only, they are sometimes called by the name of the things they represent, to wit, the body and blood of Christ (Matt. 26:26–28); albeit, in substance and nature, they still remain truly and only bread and wine, as they were before (1 Cor. 11:26–28; Matt. 26:29).

VI. That doctrine which maintains a change of the substance of bread and wine, into the substance of Christ's body and blood (commonly called transubstantiation) by consecration of a priest, or by any other way, is repugnant, not to Scripture alone, but even to common sense, and reason; overthroweth the nature of the sacrament, and hath been, and is, the cause of manifold superstitions; yea, of gross idolatries (Acts 3:21; 1 Cor. 11:24–26; Luke 24:6, 39).

VII. Worthy receivers, outwardly partaking of the visible elements, in this sacrament (1 Cor. 11:28), do then also, inwardly by faith, really and indeed, yet not carnally and corporally but spiritually, receive, and feed upon, Christ crucified, and all benefits of His death: the body and blood of Christ being then, not corporally or carnally, in, with, or under the bread and wine; yet, as really, but spiritually, present to the faith of believers in that ordinance, as the elements themselves are to their outward senses (1 Cor. 10:16).

VIII. Although ignorant and wicked men receive the outward elements in this sacrament; yet, they receive not the thing signified thereby; but, by their unworthy coming thereunto, are guilty of the body and blood of the Lord, to their own damnation. Wherefore, all ignorant and ungodly persons, as they are unfit to enjoy communion with Him, so are they unworthy of the Lord's table; and cannot, without great sin against Christ, while they remain such, partake of these holy mysteries (1 Cor. 11:27–29; 2 Cor. 6:14–16), or be admitted thereunto (1 Cor. 5:6–7, 13; 2 Thess. 3:6, 14–15; Matt. 7:6).

CHAP. XXX.— *Of Church Censures.*

I. THE Lord Jesus, as King and Head of His Church, hath therein appointed a government, in the hand of Church officers, distinct from the civil magistrate (Isa. 9:6–7; 1 Tim. 5:17; 1 Thess. 5:12; Acts 20:17–18; Heb. 13:7, 17, 24; 1 Cor. 12:28; Matt. 28:18–20).

II. To these officers the keys of the kingdom of heaven are committed; by virtue whereof, they have power, respectively, to retain, and remit sins; to shut that kingdom against the impenitent, both by the Word, and censures; and to open it unto penitent sinners, by the ministry of the Gospel; and by absolution from censures, as occasion shall require (Matt. 16:19; 18:17–18; John 20:21–23; 2 Cor. 2:6–8).

III. Church censures are necessary, for the reclaiming and gaining of offending brethren, for deterring of others from the like offences, for purging out of that leaven which might infect the whole lump, for vindicating the honour of Christ, and the holy profession of the Gospel, and for preventing the wrath of God, which might justly fall upon the Church, if they should suffer His covenant, and the seals thereof, to be profaned by notorious and obstinate offenders (1 Cor. 5; 1 Tim. 5:20; Matt. 7:6; 1 Tim. 1:20; 1 Cor. 11:27–34; Jude 23).

IV. For the better attaining of these ends, the officers of the Church are to proceed by admonition, suspension from the sacrament of the Lord's Supper for a season; and by excommunication from the Church, according to the nature of the crime, and demerit of the person (1 Thess. 5:12; 2 Thess. 3:6, 14–15; 1 Cor. 5:4–5, 13; Matt. 18:17; Titus 3:10).

CHAP. XXXI.— *Of Synods and Councils.*

I. FOR the better government, and further edification of the Church, there ought to be such assemblies as are commonly called Synods or Councils (Acts 15:2, 4, 6).

II. As magistrates may lawfully call a synod of ministers, and other fit persons, to consult and advise with, about matters of religion (Isa. 49:23; 1 Tim. 2:1–2; 2 Chron. 19:8–11; 29–30; Matt. 2:4–5; Prov. 11:14); so, if magistrates be open enemies to the Church, the ministers of Christ, of themselves, by virtue of their office, or they, with other fit persons upon delegation from their Churches, may meet together in such assemblies (Acts 15:2, 4, 22–23, 25).

III. It belongeth to synods and councils, ministerially to determine controversies of faith, and cases of conscience; to set down rules and directions for the better ordering of the public worship of God, and government of His Church; to receive complaints in cases of maladministration, and authoritatively to determine the same: which decrees and determinations, if consonant to the Word of God, are to be received with reverence and submission; not only for their agreement with the Word, but also for the power whereby they are made, as being an ordinance of God appointed thereunto in His Word (Acts 15:15, 19, 24, 27–31; 16:4; Matt. 18:17–20).

IV. All synods or councils, since the Apostles' times, whether general or particular, may err; and many have erred. Therefore they are not to be made the rule of faith, or practice; but to be used as a help in both (Eph. 2:10; Acts 17:11; 1 Cor. 2:5; 2 Cor. 1:24).

V. Synods and councils are to handle, or conclude, nothing, but that which is ecclesiastical: and are not to intermeddle with civil affairs which concern the commonwealth, unless by way of humble petition in cases extraordinary; or, by way of advice, for satisfaction of conscience, if they be thereunto required by the civil magistrate (Luke 12:13–14; John 18:36).

CHAP. XXXII.—*Of the State of Men after Death, and of the Resurrection of the Dead.*

I. THE bodies of men, after death, return to dust, and see corruption (Gen. 3:19; Acts 13:36): but their souls, which neither die nor sleep, having an immortal subsistence, immediately return to God who gave them (Luke 23:43; Eccl. 12:7): the souls of the righteous, being then made perfect in holiness, are received into the highest heavens, where they behold the face of God, in light and glory, waiting for the full redemption of their bodies (Heb. 12:23; 2 Cor. 5:1, 6, 8; Phil. 1:23; Acts 3:21; Eph. 4:10). And the souls of the wicked are cast into hell, where they remain in torments and utter darkness, reserved to the judgment of the great day (Luke 16:23–24; Acts 1:25; Jude 6–7; 1 Peter 3:19). Beside these two places, for souls separated from their bodies, the Scripture acknowledgeth none.

II. At the last day, such as are found alive shall not die, but be changed (1 Thess. 4:17; 1 Cor. 15:51–52): and all the dead shall be raised up, with the self-same bodies, and none other (although with different qualities), which shall be united again to their souls for ever (Job 19:26–27; 1 Cor. 15:42–44).

III. The bodies of the unjust shall, by the power of Christ, be raised to dishonour: the bodies of the just, by His Spirit, unto honour; and be made conformable to His own glorious body (Acts 24:15; John 5:28–29; 1 Cor. 15:43; Phil. 3:21).

CHAP. XXXIII.—*Of the Last Judgment.*

I. GOD hath appointed a day, wherein He will judge the world, in righteousness, by Jesus Christ (Acts 17:31), to whom all power and judgment is given of the Father (John 5:22, 27). In which day, not only the apostate angels shall be judged (1 Cor. 6:3; Jude 6; 2 Peter 2:4), but likewise all persons that have lived upon earth shall appear before the tribunal of Christ, to give an account of their thoughts, words, and deeds;

and to receive according to what they have done in the body, whether good or evil (2 Cor. 5:10; Eccl. 12:14; Rom. 2:16; 14:10, 12; Matt. 12:36–37).

II. The end of God's appointing this day is for the manifestation of the glory of His mercy, in the eternal salvation of the elect; and of His justice, in the damnation of the reprobate, who are wicked and disobedient. For then shall the righteous go into everlasting life, and receive that fulness of joy and refreshing, which shall come from the presence of the Lord: but the wicked, who know not God, and obey not the Gospel of Jesus Christ, shall be cast into eternal torments, and be punished with everlasting destruction from the presence of the Lord, and from the glory of His power (Matt. 25:31–46; Rom. 2:5–6; 11:22–23; Matt. 25:21; Acts 3:19; 2 Thess. 1:7–10).

III. As Christ would have us to be certainly persuaded that there shall be a day of judgment, both to deter all men from sin; and for the greater consolation of the godly in their adversity (2 Peter 3:11, 14; 2 Cor. 5:10–11; 2 Thess. 1:5–7; Luke 21:7, 28; Rom. 8:23–25): so will He have that day unknown to men, that they may shake off all carnal security, and be always watchful, because they know not at what hour the Lord will come; and may be ever prepared to say, Come, Lord Jesus, come quickly. Amen (Matt. 24:36, 42–44; Mark 13:35–37; Luke 12:35–36; Rev. 22:20).

112

The London Confession (1646)

As expected, the London (Baptist) Confession of 1644 attracted the attention of the paedobaptists shortly after its publication. In particular, Daniel Featley/Fairclough (1578–1645) examined the confession in the last chapter of his pointed book *The Dippers Dipt or; The Anabaptists duck'd and plunged Over Head and Eares, at a Disputation in Southwark* (1645). The disputation mentioned was actually held in 1642. Featley wrote up his notes from that particular exchange while languishing in prison. He had landed in jail because he rejected the Solemn League and Covenant endorsed by Parliament and the Westminster Assembly of Divines in 1643. Featley declined the oath because he was a Royalist and prelatic sympathizer. Parliament charged him with being a "spy" within the assembly and had him imprisoned. When his health failed, he was subsequently released and died shortly thereafter, at Chelsea.

Baptists responded to Featley's attack with the revision of 1646. Signatories included: John Spilsbury (1593–ca. 1668), William Kiffin (1616–1701), Hanserd Knollys (ca. 1599–1691), and Thomas Killcop. Parliament eventually recognized the confession in 1647, and Particular Baptists were granted toleration under the auspices of Oliver Cromwell's (1599–1658) policies. All this was to change dramatically with the Restoration of Charles II (1630–1685) in 1660.

Our text is based on the version printed in E. B. Underhill, *Confessions of Faith, and other Public Documents, Illustrative of the History of the Baptist Churches of England in the 17th Century* (1854), 27–48. This edition inserts the prooftexts within the flow of the articles themselves. We have modified spelling in a few places.

A CONFESSION OF FAITH
OF SEVEN CONGREGATIONS OR CHURCHES OF CHRIST IN LONDON, WHICH ARE COMMONLY (THOUGH UNJUSTLY) CALLED ANABAPTISTS

I.

The Lord our God is but one God (1 Cor. 8:6; Isa. 44:6; 46:9), whose subsistence is in Himself (Ex. 3:14); whose essence cannot be comprehended by any but Himself, who only has immortality (1 Tim. 6:16), dwelling in the light, which no man can approach unto; who is in Himself most holy (Isa. 43:15), every way infinite (Ps. 147:5), in greatness (Deut. 32:3), wisdom (Job 36:5), power (Jer. 10:12), love; merciful and gracious (Ex. 34:6–7), long-suffering, and abundant in goodness and truth, who gives being, moving, and preservation to all creatures (Acts 17:28; Rom. 11:36).

II.

In this divine and infinite being, there is the Father (1 Cor. 1:3), the Word (John 1:1), and the Holy Spirit (John 15:26), each having the whole divine essence (Ex. 3:14), yet the essence undivided; all infinite without any beginning, therefore but one God (1 Cor. 8:6), who is not to be divided in nature, and being, but distinguished by several peculiar relative properties.

III.

God has decreed in Himself, before the world was, concerning all things (Isa. 46:10; Eph. 1:11; Rom. 11:33; Pss. 115:3; 135:6), whether necessary, accidental (Ps. 33:15; 1 Sam. 10:9, 26), or voluntary, with all the circumstances of them, to work, dispose, and bring about all things according to the counsel of His own will, to His glory (yet without being the author of sin, or having fellowship with anything therein); in which appears His wisdom in disposing all things, unchangeableness, power, and faithfulness in accomplishing His decree: and God has before the foundation of the world, foreordained some men to eternal life, through Jesus Christ, to the praise and glory of His grace; and leaving the rest in their sin to their just condemnation, to the praise of His justice (Prov. 21:6; Ex. 21:13; Prov. 16:33; Ps. 144; Isa. 45:7: Jer. 14:22; Matt. 6:28, 30; Col. 1:16–17; Num. 23:19–20; Rom. 3:4; Jer. 10:10; Eph. 1:4–5; Jude 4, 6; Prov. 16:4).

IV.

In the beginning God made all things very good (Gen. 1:1; Col. 1:16; Isa. 45:12); created man after His own image (1 Cor. 15:45–46), filled with all meet perfection of nature, and free from all sin; but long he abode not in this honor (Eccl. 7:29), Satan using the subtlety of the serpent to seduce first Eve (Gen. 3:1, 4–5; 2 Cor. 11:3), then by her seducing Adam; who without any compulsion, in eating the forbidden fruit, transgressed the command of God (1 Tim. 2:14), and fell, whereby death came upon all his posterity (Gal. 3:22), who now are conceived in sin, and by nature the children of wrath, the servants of sin, the subjects of death (Rom. 5:12, 18–19; 6:22; Eph. 2:3), and other miseries in this world, and for ever, unless the Lord Jesus Christ set them free.

V.

God in His infinite power and wisdom (Job 38:11), disposes all things to the end for which they were created (Isa. 46:10–11; Eccl. 3:14), that neither good nor evil befalls any by chance, or without His providence (Matt. 10:29–30; Ex. 21:13; Prov. 16:33); and that whatsoever befalls the elect, is by His appointment, for His glory, and their good (Rom. 8:28).

VI.

All the elect being loved of God with an everlasting love (Jer. 31:3), are redeemed (Eph. 1:3, 7; 2:4, 9; 1 Thess. 5:9), quickened, and saved, not by themselves, nor their own works, lest any man should boast, but, only and wholly by God, of His own free grace and mercy through Jesus Christ (Acts 13:38; 2 Cor. 5:21; Jer. 9:23–24), who is made unto us by God, wisdom (1 Cor. 1:30–31; Jer. 23:6), righteousness, sanctification, and redemption, and all in all, that he that rejoices, might rejoice in the Lord.

VII.

And this is life eternal (John 17:3; Heb. 5:9), that we might know Him, the only true God, and Jesus Christ whom He has sent. And on the contrary, the Lord will render vengeance, in flaming fire, to them that know not God, and obey not the gospel of Jesus Christ (1 Thess. 1:8; John 6:36).

VIII.

The rule of this knowledge, faith, and obedience, concerning the worship of God, in which is contained the whole duty of man, is not men's laws, or unwritten traditions (Col. 2:23; Matt. 15:9, 6), but only the Word of God contained in the Holy Scriptures (John 5:39; 2 Tim. 3:15–17; Isa. 8:20; Gal. 1:8–9; Acts 3:22–23), in which is plainly recorded whatsoever is needful for us to know, believe, and practice, which are the only rule of holiness and obedience for all saints, at all times, in all places to be observed.

IX.

The Lord Jesus Christ, of whom Moses and the prophets wrote (Gen. 3:15; 22:18; 49:10; Dan. 7:13; 9:24–26), the apostles preached, He is the Son of God (Prov. 8:23; John 1:1–3; Heb. 1:8), the brightness of His glory, etc., by whom He made the world, who upholds and governs all things that He has made; who also, when the fullness of time was come (Gal. 4:4), was made of a woman, of the tribe of Judah (Heb. 7:14; Rev. 5:5; Gen. 49:9–10; Rom. 1:3; 9:10; Matt. 1:16; Luke 3:23, 26; Heb. 2:16; Isa. 53:3–5; Heb. 4:15), of the seed of Abraham and David; to wit, of the virgin Mary, the Holy Spirit coming down upon her, the power of the Most High overshadowing her; and He was also tempted as we are, yet without sin.

X.

Jesus Christ is made the Mediator of the new and everlasting covenant of grace between God and man (1 Tim. 2:5; Heb. 9:15; John 14:6), ever to be perfectly and fully the Prophet, Priest, and King of the church of God forevermore (Isa. 9:6–7).

XI.

Unto this office He was appointed by God from everlasting (Prov. 8:23; Isa. 42:6; 49:15); and in respect of His manhood, from the womb called, separated, and anointed most fully and abundantly with all gifts necessary, God having without measure poured out His Spirit upon Him (Isa. 11:2–5; 61:1–2; Luke 4:17, 22; John 1:14, 16; 3:34).

XII.

Concerning His mediatorship, the Scripture holds forth Christ's call to His office; for none takes this honor upon him, but he that is called of God as was Aaron (Heb. 5:4–6); it being an action of God, whereby a special promise being made, He ordains His Son to this office; which promise is, that Christ should be made a sacrifice for sin; that He should see His seed (Isa. 53:10–11), and prolong His days, and the pleasure of the Lord shall prosper in His hand; all of mere free and absolute grace towards God's elect, and without any condition foreseen in them to procure it (John 3:16; Rom. 8:32).

XIII.

This office to be Mediator, that is, to be Prophet, Priest, and King of the church of God, is so proper to Christ, that neither in whole, or any part thereof, it cannot be transferred from Him to any other (1 Tim. 2:5; Heb. 7:14; Dan. 7:14; Acts 4:12; Luke 1:33; John 14:6).

XIV.

This office to which Christ is called, is threefold as prophet (Deut. 18:15; Acts 3:22–23), priest (Heb. 3:1; 4:14–15), and king (Ps. 2:6): This number and order of offices is necessary; for in respect of our ignorance, we stand in need of His prophetical office (2 Cor. 5:20; Acts 26:18). And in respect of our great alienation from God (Col. 1:21), we need His priestly office to reconcile us: and in respect of our averseness and utter inability to return to God, we need His kingly office, to convince (John 16:8), subdue (Ps. 110:3), draw (Song 1:3; John 6:44; Phil. 4:13), uphold, and preserve us to His heavenly kingdom (2 Tim. 4:18).

XV.

Concerning the prophecy of Christ, it is that whereby He has revealed the will of God (John 1:18; 12:49–50; 15; 17:8; Deut. 18:15), whatsoever is needful for His servants to know and obey (Matt. 23:10); and therefore He is called not only a prophet and doctor, and the apostle of our profession (Heb. 3:1), and the angel of the covenant (Mal. 3:1), but also the very wisdom of God (1 Cor. 1:24; Col. 2:3), in whom are hid all the treasures of wisdom and knowledge, who forever continues revealing the same truth of the gospel to His people.

XVI.

That He might be a prophet every way complete, it was necessary He should be God, and also that He should be man; for unless He had been God, He could never have perfectly understood the will of God; and unless He had been man, He could not suitably have unfolded it in His own person to men (John 1:18; Acts 3:22; Deut. 18:15; Heb. 1:1).

Note: That Jesus Christ is God is wonderfully and clearly expressed in the Scriptures. He is called "the mighty God" (Isa. 9:6); "that Word was God" (John 1:1); "Christ, who is God over all" (Rom. 9:5); "God manifested in the flesh" (1 Tim. 3:16). The same is very God (1 John 5:20); He is the first (Rev. 1:8); He gives being to all things, and without Him was nothing made (John 1:2); He forgives sins (Matt. 9:6); He is before Abraham (John 8:58); He was and is, and ever will be the same (Heb. 13:8); He is always with His to the end of the world (Matt. 28:20), which could not be said of Jesus Christ, if He were not God. And to "the Son He saith, Thy throne, O God, is forever and ever" (Heb. 1:8; John 1:18).

Also, Christ is not only perfectly God, but perfect man, made of a woman (Gal. 4:4), made of the seed of David (Rom. 1:3); coming out of the loins of David (Acts 2:30), of Jesse and Judah (Acts 13:23); in that the children were partakers of flesh and blood, He Himself likewise took part with them (Heb. 2:14); "He took not on Him the nature of angels, but the seed of Abraham" (v. 16). So that "we are bone of His bone, and flesh of His flesh" (Eph. 5:30); "so that He that sanctifieth, and they that are sanctified, are all of one" (Heb. 2:11. See Acts 3:22; Deut. 18:15 Heb. 1:1).

XVII.

Concerning His priesthood (John 17:19; Heb. 5:7–9; 10:12; Rom. 5:19; Eph. 5:2; Col. 1:20; Eph. 2:14–16; Rom. 8:34), Christ having sanctified Himself, has appeared once to put away sin, by that one offering of Himself a sacrifice for sin, by which He has fully finished and suffered all things God required for the salvation of His elect, and removed all rites and shadows, etc., and is now entered within the veil into the Holy of Holies, which is the presence of God. Also, He makes His people a spiritual house, a holy priesthood, to offer up spiritual sacrifice acceptable to God through Him. Neither does the Father accept, nor Christ offer to the Father, any other worship or worshippers (Heb. 9:24; 8:1; 1 Peter 2:5; John 4:23–24).

XVIII.

This priesthood was not legal or temporary, but according to the order of Melchizedek (Heb. 7:17), and is stable and perfect, not for a time, but forever (Heb. 7:16, 18–21, 24–25), which is suitable to Jesus Christ, as to Him that ever lives: Christ was the Priest, Sacrifice, and Altar: He was a Priest according to both natures; He was a Sacrifice according to His human nature, whence in Scripture it is attributed to His body (Heb. 5:6), to His blood (Heb. 10:10; 1 Peter 1:18–19; Col. 1:20, 22): yet the effectualness of this sacrifice did depend upon His divine nature; therefore it is called the blood of God. He was the Altar according to His divine nature (Heb. 9:13; Acts 20:28), it belonging to the Altar to sanctify that which is offered upon it, and so it ought to be of greater dignity than the sacrifice itself (Heb. 9:14; 13:10, 12, 15; Matt. 23:17; John 17:19).

XIX.

Concerning His kingly office, Christ being risen from the dead (1 Cor. 15:4; 1 Peter 3:21–22; Matt. 28:18–20; Luke 24:51; Acts 1:1; 5:30–31; John 19:36; Rom. 14:9; John 5:26–27; Rom. 5:6–8; 14:17; Gal. 5:22–23; Mark 1:27; Heb. 1:14; John 16:15; Job 1:8; Rom. 1:21; Eph. 4:17–18; 2 Peter 2), and ascended into heaven, and having all power in heaven and earth, He spiritually governs His church, and exercises His power over all, angels and men, good and bad, to the preservation and salvation of the elect, and to the over-ruling and destruction of His enemies. By this kingly power He applies the benefits, virtue, and fruits of His prophecy and priesthood to His elect, subduing their sins, preserving and strengthening them in all their conflicts against Satan, the world, and the flesh, keeping their hearts in faith and filial fear by His Spirit: by this His mighty power He rules the vessels of wrath, using, limiting and restraining them, as it seems good to His infinite wisdom.

XX.

This His kingly power shall be more fully manifested when He shall come in glory to reign among His saints, when He shall put down all rule and authority under His feet, that the glory of the Father may be perfectly manifested in His Son, and the glory of the Father and the Son in all His members (1 Cor. 15:24, 28; Heb. 9:28; 2 Thess. 1:9–10; 1 Thess. 4:15–17; John 17:21, 26).

XXI.

Jesus Christ by His death did purchase salvation for the elect that God gave unto Him: These only have interest in Him, and fellowship with Him, for whom He makes intercession to His Father in their behalf, and to them alone God by His Spirit applies this redemption; as also the free gift of eternal life is given to them, and none else (Eph. 1:14; Heb. 5:9; Matt. 1:21; John 17:6; Heb. 7:25; 1 Cor. 2:12; Rom. 8:29–30; 1 John 5:12; John 15:13; 3:16).

XXII.

Faith is the gift of God (Eph. 2:8; John 6:29; 4:10; Phil. 1:29; Gal. 5:22), wrought in the hearts of the elect by the Spirit of God; by which faith they come to know and believe the truth of the Scriptures (John 17:17; Heb. 4:11–12; John 6:63), and the excellency of them above all other writings, and all things in the world, as they hold forth the glory of God in His attributes, the excellency of Christ in His nature and offices, and of the power and fullness of the Spirit in its workings and operations; and so are enabled to cast their souls upon His truth thus believed.

XXIII.

All those that have this precious faith wrought in them by the Spirit, can never finally nor totally fall away, seeing the gifts of God are without repentance; so that He still begets and nourishes in them faith, repentance, love, joy, hope (Matt. 7:24–25; John 13:10; 10:28–29), and all the graces of the Spirit unto immortality (1 Peter 1:4–6; Isa. 49:13–16); and though many storms and floods arise, and beat against them, yet they shall never be able to take them off that foundation and rock, which by faith they are fastened upon; notwithstanding through unbelief, and the temptations of Satan, the sensible sight of this light and love, be clouded and overwhelmed for a time, yet God is still the same, and they shall be sure to be kept by the power of God unto salvation, where they shall enjoy their purchased possession, they being engraven upon the palms of His hands, and their names having been written in the book of life from all eternity.

XXIV.

Faith is ordinarily begotten by the preaching of the gospel, or word of Christ (Rom. 10:17; 1 Cor. 1:28), without respect to any power or agency in the creature (Rom. 9:16); but it being wholly passive (Ezek. 16:16; Rom. 3:12), and dead in trespasses and sins, does believe and is converted by no less power than that which raised Christ from the dead (Rom. 1:16; Eph. 1:19; Col. 2:12).

XXV.

The preaching of the gospel to the conversion of sinners, is absolutely free (John 3:14–15; 1:12; Isa. 55:1; John 7:37); no way requiring as absolutely necessary, any qualifications, preparations, or terrors of the law, or preceding ministry of the law; but only and alone the naked soul, a sinner and ungodly (1 Tim. 1:15; Rom. 4:5; 5:8; Acts 5:30–31; 2:36; 1 Cor. 1:22, 24), to receive Christ crucified, dead, and buried, and risen again; who is made a Prince and a Savior for such sinners as through the gospel shall be brought to believe on Him.

XXVI.

The same power that converts to faith in Christ, carries on the soul through all duties, temptations, conflicts, sufferings (1 Peter 1:5; 2 Cor. 12:9); and whatsoever a believer is, he is by grace (1 Cor. 15:10; Phil. 2:12–13; John 15:5; Gal. 2:19–20), and is carried on in all obedience and temptations by the same.

XXVII.

All believers are by Christ united to God (1 Thess. 1:1; John 17:21; 20:17; Heb. 2:11; 1 John 4:16), by which union God is one with them, and they are one with Him; and that all believers are the sons of God (Gal. 2:19–20), and joint heirs with Christ, to whom belong all the promises of this life, and that which is to come.

XXVIII.

Those that have union with Christ, are justified from all their sins by the blood of Christ (1 John 1:7; Heb. 10:14; 9:26; 2 Cor. 5:19; Rom. 3:23; Acts 13:38–39; Rom. 5:1; 3:25, 30); which justification is a gracious and full acquittal of a guilty sinner from all sin, by God, through the satisfaction that Christ has made by His death for all their sins, and this applied (in manifestation of it) through faith.

XXIX.

All believers are a holy and sanctified people (1 Cor. 11; 1 Peter 2:9), and that sanctification is a spiritual grace of the new covenant (Eph. 1:4), and an effect of the love of God manifested in the soul (1 John 4:16; Matt. 28:20), whereby the believer presses after a heavenly and evangelical obedience to all the commands, which Christ as head and king in His new covenant has prescribed to them.

XXX.

All believers through the knowledge of that justification of life given by the Father (2 Cor. 5:19; Rom. 5:9–10), and brought forth by the blood of Christ have as their great privilege of that new covenant (Isa. 54:10; 26:12), peace with God and reconciliation, whereby they that were afar off are made nigh by that blood (Eph. 2:13–14), and have peace passing all understanding (Eph. 4:7); yea, joy in God through our Lord Jesus Christ, by whom we have received atonement (Rom. 5:10–11).

XXXI.

All believers in the time of this life, are in a continual warfare and combat against sin, self, the world, and the devil (Rom. 7:23–24; Eph. 6:10–13); and are liable to all manner of afflictions, tribulations, and persecutions (Heb. 2:9–10; 2 Tim. 3:12), being predestinated and appointed thereunto (Rom. 8:29; 1 Thess. 3:3; Gal. 2:19–20; 2 Cor. 5:7), and whatsoever the saints possess or enjoy of God spiritually, is by faith; and outward and temporal things, are lawfully enjoyed by a civil right by them who have no faith (Deut. 2:5).

XXXII.

The only strength by which the saints are enabled to encounter with all oppositions and trials (John 16:33), is only by Jesus Christ (John 15:5; Phil. 4:11), who is the Captain of their salvation, being made perfect through sufferings; who has engaged His faithfulness and strength to assist them in all their afflictions, and to uphold them in all their temptations, and to preserve them by His power to His everlasting kingdom (2 Tim. 4:18).

XXXIII.

Jesus Christ has here on earth a spiritual kingdom, which is His church (Matt. 11:11; 2 Thess. 1:15; 1 Cor. 1:2; Eph. 1:1), whom He has purchased and redeemed to Himself as a peculiar inheritance; which church is a company of visible saints, called and separated from the world by the word

(Rom. 1:7; Acts 19:8–9; 26:18; 2 Cor. 6:17; Rev. 18:4) and Spirit of God (Acts 2:37; 10:37), to the visible profession of faith in the gospel, being baptized into that faith (Rom. 10:10; Matt. 18:19–20; Acts 2:42), and joined to the Lord, and each other, by mutual agreement in the practical enjoyment of the ordinances commanded by Christ, their Head and King (Acts 9:26; 1 Peter 2:5).

XXXIV.

To this church He has made His promises (Matt. 28:18–20), and gives the signs of His covenant (1 Cor. 11:24; 3:21; 2 Cor. 6:18; Rom. 9:4–5); presence, acceptance, love, blessing (Ps. 133:3), and protection (Rom. 3:7, 10). Here are the fountains and springs of His heavenly graces flowing forth to refresh and strengthen them (Ezek. 47:2).

XXXV.

And all His servants of all estates are to acknowledge Him to be their Prophet, Priest, and King; and called thither to be enrolled among His household servants (Acts 2:41, 47; Isa. 4:3; 1 Cor. 12:6–7, 12, 18; Ezek. 20:37, 40), to present their bodies and souls, and to bring their gifts [that] God has given them, to be under His heavenly conduct and government, to lead their lives in this walled sheepfold, and watered garden (Song 4:12; Eph. 2:19; Rom. 12:4–6; Col. 1:12; 2:5–6, 19), to have communion here with His saints, that they may be assured that they are made meet to be partakers of their inheritance in the kingdom of God (Acts 20:32); and to supply each other's wants, inward and outward; (and although each person has a propriety in his own estate [Acts 5:4], yet they are to supply each other's wants, according as their necessities shall require [Acts 2:44–45; 4:34–35], that the name of Jesus Christ [Luke 14:26; 1 Tim. 6:1] may not be blasphemed through the necessity of any in the church); and also being come, they are here by Himself to be bestowed in their several order, due place, peculiar use, being fitly compact and knit together according to the effectual working of every part, to the edifying of itself in love (Eph. 4:16).

XXXVI.

Being thus joined, every church has power given them from Christ (Acts 1:23, 26; 6:3; 15:22, 25), for their well being, to choose among themselves meet persons for elders and deacons (Rom. 12:7–8), being qualified according to the Word, as those which Christ has appointed in His Testament (1 Tim. 3:2, 6–8; 1 Cor. 12:8, 28; Heb. 13:7, 17; 1 Peter 5:1–3), for the feeding, governing, serving, and building up of His church, and that none have any power to impose either these or any other (1 Peter 4:15).

XXXVII.

That the ministers lawfully called, as aforesaid, ought to continue in their calling and place, according to God's ordinance, and carefully to feed the flock of God committed to them, not for filthy lucre, but of a ready mind (Heb. 5:4; John 10:3–4; Acts 20:28–29; Rom. 12:7–8; Heb. 13:7, 17; 1 Peter 5:1–3).

XXXVIII.

The ministers of Christ ought to have whatsoever they shall need, supplied freely by the church, that according to Christ's ordinance, they that preach the gospel should live of the gospel by the law of Christ (1 Cor. 9:7, 14; Gal. 6:8; Phil. 4:15–16; 2 Cor. 10:4; 1 Tim. 1:9; Ps. 110:3).

XXXIX.

Baptism is an ordinance of the New Testament (Matt. 28:18–19; John 4:1; Mark 16:15–16; Acts 2:37–38; 8:36–38; 18), given by Christ, to be dispensed upon persons professing faith, or that are made disciples; who upon profession of faith, ought to be baptized, and after to partake of the Lord's Supper.

XL.

That the way and manner of dispensing this ordinance, is dipping or plunging the body under water (Matt. 3:6, 16; Mark 1:5, v. 9 reads "into Jordan" in Greek; John 3:23; Acts 8:38; Rev. 2:5; 7:14; Heb. 10:22); it being a sign, [it] must answer the things signified, which is, that interest the saints have in the death, burial, and resurrection of Christ (Rom. 6:3–6; 1 Cor. 15:28–29): And that as certainly as the body is buried under water and risen again, so certainly shall the bodies of the saints be raised by the power of Christ, in the day of the resurrection, to reign with Christ.

Note: The word baptizo signifies to dip or plunge (yet so as convenient garments be both upon the administrator and subject with all modesty).

XLI.

The person designed by Christ to dispense baptism, the Scripture holds forth to be a disciple; it being no where tied to a particular church officer, or person extraordinarily sent, the commission enjoining the administration, being given to them as considered disciples, being men able to preach the gospel (Isa. 8:16; Eph. 3:7; Matt. 28:19; John 4:2; Acts 10:7; 11:20; 1 Cor. 11:24; 10:16–17).

XLII.

Christ has likewise given power to His church to receive in, and cast out, any member that deserves it; and this power is given to every congregation, and not to one particular person, either member or officer, but in relation to the whole body, in reference to their faith and fellowship (Rom. 16:2; Matt. 18:17; 1 Cor. 5:4, 11, 13; 12:6, 2–3; 2 Cor. 2:6–7).

XLIII.

And every particular member of each church, how excellent, great, or learned soever, is subject to this censure and judgment: and that the church ought not without great care and tenderness, and due advice, but by the rule of faith, to proceed against her members (Matt. 18:16–18; Acts 11:2–3; 1 Tim. 5:19–21; Col. 4:17; Acts 15:1–3).

XLIV.

Christ, for the keeping of this church in holy and orderly communion, places some special men over the church who by their office, are to govern, oversee, visit, watch; so likewise for the better keeping thereof, in all places by the members, He has given authority, and laid duty upon all to watch over one another (Acts 20:27–28; Heb. 13:17, 24; Matt. 24:45; 1 Thess. 5:2, 14; Jude 3, 20: Heb. 10:34–35; 12:15).

XLV.

Also, such to whom God has given gifts in the church, may and ought to prophesy, according to the proportion of faith, and so to teach publicly the word of God, for the edification, exhortation, and comfort of the church (1 Cor. 14:3ff.; Rom. 12:6; 1 Peter 4:10–11; 1 Cor. 12:7; 1 Thess. 5:19–21).

XLVI.

Thus being rightly gathered, and continuing in the obedience of the gospel of Christ, none are to separate for faults and corruptions (for as long as the church consists of men subject to failings, there will be difference in the true constituted church) until they have in due order, and tenderness, sought redress thereof (Rev. 2, 3; Acts 15:12; 1 Cor. 1:10; Heb. 10:25; Jude 19; Rev. 2:20, 21, 24; Acts 15:1–2; Rom. 14:1; 15:1–3).

XLVII.

And although the particular congregations be distinct, and several bodies (1 Cor. 4:17; 14:33, 36; 16:1), every one as a compact and knit city within itself (Ps. 122:3; Eph. 2:12, 19: Rev. 21): yet are they all to walk by one rule of truth (1 Tim. 3:15; 6:13–14; 1 Cor. 4:17); so also they (by all means convenient) are to have the counsel and help one of another, if necessity require it, as members of one body, in the common faith, under Christ their Head (Acts 15:2–3; Song 8:8–9; 2 Cor. 8:1, 4, 13–14).

XLVIII.

A civil magistracy is an ordinance of God (Rom. 13:1–4; 1 Peter 2:13–14; 1 Tim. 2:1–3), set up by Him for the punishment of evildoers, and for the praise of them that do well; and that in all lawful things, commanded by them, subjection ought to be given by us in the Lord, not only for wrath, but for conscience's sake; and that we are to make supplications and prayers for kings, and all that are in authority, that under them we may live a quiet and peaceable life, in all godliness and honesty.

Note: The supreme magistracy of this kingdom we acknowledge to be the king and Parliament (now established) freely chosen by the kingdom, and that we are to maintain and defend all civil laws and civil officers made by them, which are for the good of the commonwealth: and we acknowledge with thankfulness that God has made this present king and Parliament honorable in throwing down the prelatical hierarchy, because of their tyranny and oppression over us, under which this kingdom long groaned, for which we are ever engaged to bless God, and honor them for the same. And concerning the worship of God, there is but one Lawgiver, which is able to save and destroy (James 4:12), which is Jesus Christ, who has given laws and rules sufficient in His word for His worship; and for any to make more, were to charge Christ with want of wisdom or faithfulness, or both, in not making laws enough, or not good enough for His house: Surely it is our wisdom, duty, and privilege to observe

Christ's laws only (Pss. 2:6, 9–10, 12). So it is the magistrate's duty to tender the liberty of men's consciences (Eccl. 8:8), (which is the tenderest thing unto all conscientious men, and most dear unto them, and without which all other liberties will not be worth the naming, much less enjoying) and to protect all under them from wrong, injury, oppression, and molestation; so it is our duty not to be wanting in nothing which is for their honor and comfort. And whatsoever is for the well being of the commonwealth wherein we live, it is our duty to do; and we believe it to be our express duty, especially in matters of religion, to be fully persuaded in our minds of the lawfulness of what we do, as knowing "whatsoever is not of faith is sin." And as we cannot do anything contrary to our understandings and consciences, so neither can we forebear the doing of that which our understandings and consciences bind us to do. And if the magistrate should require us to do otherwise, we are to yield our persons in a passive way to their power, as the saints of old have done (James 5:4). And thrice happy shall he be, that shall lose his life for witnessing (though but for the least tittle) of the truth of the Lord Jesus Christ (1 Peter 5; Gal. 5).

XLIX.

But in case we find not the magistrate to favor us herein; yet we dare not suspend our practice, because we believe we ought to go in obedience to Christ (Acts 2:40–41; 4:19; 5:28–29, 41; 20:23; 1 Thess. 3:3; Phil. 1:28–29; Dan. 3:16–17; 6:7, 10, 22–23), in professing the faith which was once delivered to the saints, which faith is declared in the Holy Scriptures, and this our confession of faith a part of them; and that we are to witness to the truth of the Old and New Testament unto the death, if necessity require, in the midst of all trials and afflictions, as His saints of old have done; not accounting our goods, lands, wives, children, fathers, mothers, brethren, sisters; yea, and our own lives dear unto us, so we may finish our course with joy; remembering always, that we ought to obey God rather than men (1 Tim. 6:13–15; Rom. 12:1, 8; 1 Cor. 14:37) who will, when we have finished our course, and kept the faith, give us the crown of righteousness (Rev. 2:20); to whom we must give an account of all our actions, and no man being able to discharge us of the same (2 Tim. 4:6–8; Rom. 14:10, 12; 2 Cor. 5:10; Pss. 49:7; 50:22).

L.

It is lawful for a Christian to be a magistrate or civil officer; and also it is lawful to take an oath, so it is in truth, and in judgment, and in righteousness, for confirmation of truth, and ending of all strife; and that by wrath and vain oaths the Lord is provoked and this land mourns (Acts 8:38; 10:1–2, 35, 44; Rom. 16:23; Deut. 6:13; Rom. 1:9; 2 Cor. 10:11; Jer. 4:2; Heb. 6:16).

LI.

We are to give unto all men whatsoever is their due, as their place, age, estate, requires; and that we defraud no man of anything, but to do unto all men, as we would they should do unto us (1 Thess. 4:6; Rom. 13:5–7; Matt. 22:21; Titus 3; 1 Peter 2:15, 17; 5:5; Eph. 5:21, 23; 6:1, 9; Titus 3:1–3).

LII.

There shall be a resurrection of the dead (Acts 24:15; 2 Cor. 5:10; Rom. 14:12), both of the just and unjust, and everyone shall give an account of himself to God, that every one may receive the things done in his body, according to that he has done, whether it be good or bad.

The Conclusion

Thus we desire to give unto Christ that which is His, and unto all lawful authority that which is their due; and to owe nothing to any man but love; to live quietly and peaceably, as it becomes saints, endeavoring in all things to keep a good conscience, and to do unto every man (of what judgment soever) as we would they should do unto us, that as our practice is, so it may prove us to be a conscionable, quiet, and harmless people (no ways dangerous or troublesome to human society), and to labor and work with our hands that we may not be chargeable to any, but to give to him that needs, both friends and enemies, accounting it more excellent to give than to receive. Also we confess, that we know but in part, and that we are ignorant of many things which we desire and seek to know; and if any shall do us that friendly part to show us from the Word of God what we see not, we shall have cause to be thankful to God and them. But if any man shall impose upon us anything that we see not to be commanded by our Lord Jesus Christ, we should in His strength rather embrace all reproaches and tortures of men, to be stripped of all outward comforts, and if it were possible, to die a thousand deaths, rather than to do anything against the least tittle of the truth of God or against the light of our own consciences. And if any shall call what we have said heresy, then do we with the apostle acknowledge, that after the way they call heresy, worship we the God of our fathers, disclaiming all heresies (rightly so called) because they are against Christ, and to be steadfast and unmovable, always abounding in obedience to Christ, as knowing our labor shall not be in vain in the Lord.

Psalm 74:21–22

Arise, O God, plead thine own cause: remember how the foolish man blasphemeth Thee daily. Oh, let not the oppressed return ashamed, but let the poor and needy praise Thy name.

Come, Lord Jesus, come quickly.

FINIS

113

Benjamin Cox's Baptist Appendix (1646)

Benjamin Cox (ca. 1595–ca. 1663), graduate of Oxford University (1609), was an Anglican minister until 1643, when he rejected infant baptism. He was jailed in Coventry and, on his release, became the pastor of a like-minded group of anti-paedobaptists in that village. The following year found him in London, sponsoring a public debate on infant baptism at Aldermanbury church. His name appears as Benjamin Cockes on the list of signatories for the Confession of the Seven Congregations of London (1646). In November of the same year, his "Appendix" upon the 1644 London Baptist Confession was published. Apparently, some questions had been raised about that confession and Cox wrote on behalf of the subscribers in order to clarify matters. The noteworthy article 19 includes an individualistic view of the function of evangelism. Many Baptist itinerants were induced to spread this brand of the gospel from London and beyond during the Civil War. No church call (or formal ordination to ecclesiastical office) was necessary to this end, merely an inner call—though permission of a congregation was required.

Cox evidently died after 1662. It is likely a spurious suggestion that he initially conformed to the Act of Uniformity of that year, reentered the Church of England, then later reneged for the sake of conscience so as to die a Baptist Nonconformist.

Our text is based on the original 1646 edition, but with some modernization of spelling and verification of the proof texts.

AN APPENDIX TO A CONFESSION OF FAITH

Or, A More Full Declaration of the Faith and Judgment of
Baptized Believers Occasioned by the Inquiry of Some
Well-Affected and Godly Persons in the Country

Declaration of the Faith and Judgment of Baptized Believers:

"Be ready always," says the apostle Peter, "to give an answer to every man that asks you a reason of the hope that is in you, with meekness and fear" (1 Peter 3:15). It is therefore our duty, in meekness and love to give an answer to those godly persons which desire to be fully informed of our judgment concerning religion and the ways of our God. To those, therefore, that have expressed a desire to be so informed, I thus answer.

In a book lately reprinted, entitled, *A Confession of Faith of Several Congregations or Churches of Christ in London, etc.*, is a plain and sincere expression of our judgment in the things therein spoken of, in fifty-two articles: and if our judgment touching some particulars, wherein we seem, or are supposed, to dissent from some others, do not appear clearly enough in that confession, I hope that same shall somewhat more clearly appear in this ensuing Appendix.

1.

We believe that the punishment due to Adam for his first rebellion, and due to all men for their sin in Adam, and for all their sins against the law, was not a lying of the whole person of man in the dust, or grave, eternally without life or sense; for then the punishment of man that sinned, should not have differed from the punishment to the brute beast that sinned not. But the punishment due to man, as aforesaid, was "indignation and wrath, tribulation and anguish," and that eternal: and consequently the redemption which we have by Christ from the curse of the law, is a redemption from eternal misery and torment. This we learn from these places of Scripture compared together (Rom. 2:8–9; Jude 7; Gal. 3:13; Heb. 9:12).

2.

We believe that the eternity of the punishment of the vessels of wrath is an absolute eternity, knowing no end; as well as the eternity of the life of the saints (Matt. 25:46). This we maintain against those that affirm "that all men shall be saved at the last."

3.

Although all the power of the creature to act is from the Creator, and there is a providence of God always extended to every creature, and to every action of the creature; yet we judge that the final corruption of the creature, and the sinfulness of the creature's action, is from the creature, and not from God; and that it is a great sin to say that God is the author of sin (Eccl. 7:29; Hab. 1:13; James 1:13–15: 1 Cor. 14:33; 1 John 2:16). As touching that place which is here objected against us, viz., "Shall there be evil in a city, etc." (Amos 3:6), we conceive that it is either to be rendered according to the last translation in the margin, "Shall there be evil in a city, and shall not the Lord do somewhat?" or else that it is to be understood only of the evil of punishment, and not of the evil of sin.

4.

We teach that they only do or can believe in Jesus Christ, to whom it is given to believe in Him by a special, gracious and powerful work of His Spirit; and that this is (and shall be) given to the elect in the time appointed of God for their effectual calling; and to none but the elect (John 6:64–65; Phil. 1:29; Jer. 31:33–34; Ezek. 36:26; Rom. 8:29–30; John 10:26). This we hold against those that do maintain a free will and sufficient ability in a man to believe, and do deny election.

5.

We affirm, that as Jesus Christ never intended to give remission of sins and eternal life unto any but His sheep (John 10:15; 17:2; Eph. 5:25–27; Rev. 5:9); so these sheep only have their sins washed away in the blood of Christ. The vessels of wrath, as they are none of Christ's sheep, nor ever believe in Him, so they have not the blood of Christ sprinkled upon them, neither are partakers of Him; and therefore have all their sins remaining upon them, and are not saved by Christ from any of them under any consideration whatsoever; but must lie under the intolerable burden of them eternally. The truth of this appears unto us by the light of these Scriptures compared together (Heb. 12:24; 1 Peter 1:2; Heb. 3:14; Matt. 7:23; Eph. 5:6; 1 Tim. 1:9; John 8:24).

6.

Though some of our opponents do affirm that by this doctrine we leave no gospel to be preached to sinners for their conversion; yet through the goodness of God we know and preach to sinners this precious gospel: "God so loved the world, (that is, has been so loving to mankind) that He gave His only begotten Son, that whosoever believeth in Him should not perish, but have everlasting life" (John 3:16); and this faithful saying, worthy of all acceptation, "That Jesus Christ came into the world to save sinners" (1 Tim. 1:15), viz., all those sinners (how vile and grievous soever) not only which already do, but also which hereafter shall believe on Him to life everlasting (1 Tim. 1:16), and that "to Christ all the prophets give witness, that through His name, whosoever believeth in Him shall receive remission of sins" (Acts 10:43). And this is called "The word of the Gospel" (Acts 15:7). This is the gospel which Christ and His apostles preached, which we have received, and by which we have been converted, unto Christ. And we desire to mind what Paul says in Gal. 1:9: "If any man preach any other gospel unto you than that ye have received, let him be accursed."

7.

Though we confess that no man attains unto faith by his own good will (John 1:13), yet we judge and know that the Spirit of God does not compel a man to believe against his will, but powerfully and sweetly creates in a man a new heart, and so makes him to believe and obey willingly (Ezek. 36:26–27; Ps. 110:3). God thus working in us both to will and to do, of His good pleasure (Phil. 2:13).

8.

Though all our workings for life be in vain, irregular, and not accepted of God (Jesus Christ being our life, who is freely given to us of God), yet we believe and know that being made partakers of Jesus Christ, we do, and shall, and must, through Him, and walking in Him, bring forth the fruit of good works, serving God (in true obedience, and love, and thankfulness unto Him), in holiness and righteousness, being "His workmanship, created in Christ Jesus unto good works, which He hath before ordained that we should walk in them" (Eph. 2:10; Luke 1:74–75).

9.

Though we that believe in Christ are not under the law, but under grace (Rom. 6:14); yet we know that we are not lawless, or left to live without a rule; "not without law to God, but under law to Christ" (1 Cor. 9:21). The gospel of Jesus Christ is a law or commanding rule unto us, whereby, and in obedience whereunto, we are taught to live soberly, righteously, and godly in this present world (Titus 2:11–12); the directions of Christ in His evangelical Word, guiding us unto and in this sober, righteous, and godly walking (1 Tim. 1:10–11).

10.

Though we be not now sent to the law as it was in the hand of Moses, to be commanded thereby, yet Christ in His gospel teaches and commands us to walk in the same way of righteousness and holiness that God by Moses did command the Israelites to walk in, all the commandments of the second table being still delivered unto us by Christ, and all the commandments of the first table also (as touching the life and spirit of them) in this epitome or brief sum, "Thou shalt love the Lord thy God with all thine heart, etc.," (Matt. 22:37–40; Rom. 13:8–10).

11.

Though no sin be imputed to those that believe in Christ, nor does any sin totally or fully reign over them, or in them, yet in them "the flesh lusteth against the spirit" (Gal. 5:17); and "in many things they all offend" (James 3:2), where the apostle speaks of offenses that one believer may take notice of in another. Thus "there is not a just man upon earth, that doeth good, and sinneth not" (Eccl. 7:20); and "if we say that we have no sin, we deceive ourselves, and the truth is not in us" (1 John 1:8).

12.

Though there be no condemnation to them that are in Christ Jesus, yet they are taught, and that effectually, to be ashamed of their sins (Rom. 6:21), and to be sorry for them after a godly sort (2 Cor. 7:9–11); yea to loathe themselves for them (Ezek. 36:31); because that sin is an evil and a filthy thing, and in its own nature tends to the provoking and dishonoring of God, being disobedience against God, and a thing which the most holy

God declares Himself to loathe and abhor; so that nothing but the blood of Christ could purge us from our sins and reconcile us to God, whom by sin we had offended. Therefore the saints both are and must be grieved, and must judge themselves, because they have sinned against their holy and glorious God, and merciful and loving Father (1 Cor. 11:31).

13.

Though nothing is hid from God, and God does not impute iniquity to any believer, yet ought we to confess our sins unto God, and to beseech Him to deal with us according to His own promise; viz., to be still gracious and merciful unto us though we have sinned against Him, not being wroth with us, nor rebuking us, nor ceasing to do good unto us because we have sinned (Isa. 54:9; Heb. 8:12; Dan. 9:18–20; Pss. 32:5; 25:7; Ezek. 36:37; James 5:1). Thus according to Christ's direction, we pray unto God to forgive us our sins (Luke 11:4); yet still we are to look upon God as our Father (Luke 11:2); and consequently upon ourselves as His children; and so not short of justification, or under wrath, but washed in Christ's blood from all our sins. In such confession and petitions we show obedience to God, and do also exercise faith towards God, and repentance or godly sorrow for sin, by which we see and confess that we for our parts have deserved wrath.

14.

Though they which are once really engrafted into Christ shall certainly "be kept by the power of God through faith unto salvation" (1 Peter 1:5); yet ought they to "beware, lest being led away with the error of the wicked they fall from their own steadfastness" (2 Peter 3:17). They ought therefore to seek continual support from God. Yea, they ought to seek at God's hand (in prayer, and in the right use and study of His Word, and in the right use of His ordinances), not only continuance, but also growth in grace (2 Peter 3:18). First, because this is God's command. Secondly, because God, who will establish them, will do it in this way; viz., giving them grace to be obedient to this His command, and blessing them in this obedience.

15.

As we mind that our whole salvation is given unto us of the Father by Jesus Christ, and for His sake; so we likewise mind, that the Father's giving Jesus Christ for us, and to us, and so saving us in Him, and for His sake, is the acting and manifesting of that free love of His towards us, which was in Himself from all eternity (John 17:23; Eph. 1:4–5).

16.

Although a true believer, whether baptized or unbaptized, is in the state of salvation, and shall certainly be saved; yet in obedience to the command of Christ every believer ought to desire baptism, and to yield himself to be baptized according to the rule of Christ in His Word. And where this obedience is in faith performed, there Christ makes this His ordinance a means of unspeakable benefit to the believing soul (Acts 2:38; 22:16; Rom. 6:3–4; 1 Peter 3:21). And a true believer that here sees the command of Christ lying upon him, cannot allow himself in disobedience thereunto (Acts 24:16).

17.

Believers baptized ought to agree and join together in a constant profession of the same doctrine of the gospel, and in professed obedience thereunto, and also in fellowship, and in breaking of bread, and in prayers (Acts 2:42). And a company of baptized believers so agreeing and joining together, are a church or congregation of Christ (Acts 2:47).

18.

As the preaching of the gospel, both for the conversion of sinners, and the edifying of those that are converted; so also the right use of baptism, and of the Lord's Supper, ought to be till the end of the world (Matt. 28:19–20; 1 Cor. 11:26).

19.

A disciple gifted and enabled by the Spirit of Christ to preach the gospel, and stirred up to this service by the same Spirit bringing home to his soul the command of Christ in His Word for the doing of this work, is a man authorized and sent by Christ to preach the gospel (see Luke 19:12ff.; Mark 16:15; and Matt. 28:19 compared with Acts 8:4; Phil. 1:14–15; John 17:20). And those gifted disciples which thus preach Jesus Christ who came in the flesh, are to be looked upon as men sent and given of the Lord (1 John 4:2; Rom. 10:15; Eph. 4:11–13). And they which are converted from unbelief and false worship, and so brought into church fellowship by such preachers, according to the will of Christ, are a seal of their ministry

(1 Cor. 9:2). And such preachers of the gospel may not only lawfully administer baptism unto believers, and guide the action of the church in the use of the Supper (Matt. 28:19; Acts 8:5–12; 1 Cor. 10:16), but may also call upon the churches, and advise them to choose fit men for officers, and may settle such officers so chosen by a church, in the places or offices to which they are chosen by imposition of hands and prayer (Acts 6:3–6; 14:23; Titus 1:5).

20.

Though a believer's right to the use of the Lord's Supper immediately flows from Jesus Christ apprehended and received by faith, yet inasmuch as all things ought to be done not only decently, but also in order (1 Cor. 14:40); and the Word holds forth this order, that disciples should be baptized (Matt. 28:19; Acts 2:38), and then be taught to observe all things (that is to say, all other things) that Christ commanded the apostles (Matt. 28:20); and accordingly the apostles first baptized disciples, and then admitted them to the use of the Supper (Acts 2:41–42); we therefore do not admit any in the use of the Supper, nor communicate with any in the use of this ordinance, but disciples baptized, lest we should have fellowship with them in their doing contrary to order.

21.

Although we know that in some things we are yet very dark, and in all things as yet we know but in part, and do therefore wait upon God for further light, yet we believe that we ought in our practice to obey, and serve, and glorify God in the use of that light which He has given us; and not neglect the good using of that light which God has already given us, under pretense of waiting for more (1 Cor. 13:9; Acts 18:25).

22.

As Christ does not teach, nor allow that we should be without natural affection, or unsociable (see Rom. 1:31); so our being made partakers of Christ, does not discharge us from the duties of our relations. Believing servants must perform the duties of servants toward their masters, though unbelieving (1 Tim. 6:1). So believing children must perform the duties of children toward their parents (Col. 3:20); believing wives, the duties of wives toward their husbands (1 Peter 3:1); and believing subjects must be subject to principalities and powers, and obey magistrates (Rom. 13:1ff.; Titus 3:1; 1 Peter 2:13–15). But still they must remember that their fear toward God must not be taught by the precept of men (Isa. 29:13); that these ought to obey God rather than men (Acts 5:29); and that the submission that must be given to men, must be given to them for the Lord's sake (1 Peter 2:14).

Thus I conclude with the apostle's words (in 2 Tim. 2:7) a little varied, but not misapplied: "Consider what we teach: and the Lord give you understanding in all things."

FINIS

114

Westminster Larger
Catechism (1647)

F or background to this document, see the introduction to the Westminster Confession of Faith (1646) in this volume, pp. 231–33. We have printed this version of the original text as published by the Publications Committee of the Free Presbyterian Church of Scotland (1970), 127–283; it appears here with their kind permission. We have inserted the Scripture proofs in the body of the catechism without printing the entire text of the passages, as the Free Presbyterian Church version does.

WESTMINSTER LARGER CATECHISM

Quest. 1. *What is the chief and highest end of man?*
Ans. Man's chief and highest end is to glorify God (Rom. 11:36; 1 Cor. 10:31), and fully to enjoy him for ever (Ps. 73:24–28; John 17:21–23).

Q. 2. *How doth it appear that there is a God?*
A. The very light of nature in man, and the works of God, declare plainly that there is a God (Rom. 1:19–20; Ps. 19:1–3; Acts 17:28); but his word and Spirit only do sufficiently and effectually reveal him unto men for their salvation (1 Cor. 2:9–10; 2 Tim. 3:15–17; Isa. 59:21).

Q. 3. *What is the word of God?*
A. The holy scriptures of the Old and New Testaments are the word of God (2 Tim. 3:16; 2 Peter 1:19–21), the only rule of faith and obedience (Eph. 2:20; Rev. 22:18–19; Isa. 8:20; Luke 16:29, 31; Gal. 1:8–9; 2 Tim. 3:15–16).

Q. 4. *How doth it appear that the scriptures are the word of God?*
A. The scriptures manifest themselves to be the word of God, by their majesty (Hos. 8:12; 1 Cor. 2:6–7, 13; Ps. 119:18, 129) and purity (Pss. 12:6; 119:140); by the consent of all the parts (Acts 10:43; 26:22), and the scope of the whole, which is to give all glory to God (Rom. 3:19, 27); by their light and power to convince and convert sinners, to comfort and build up believers unto salvation (Acts 18:28; Heb. 4:12; James 1:18; Ps. 19:7–9; Rom. 15:4; Acts 20:32): but the spirit of God bearing witness by and with the scriptures in the heart of man, is alone able fully to persuade it that they are the very word of God (John 16:13–14; 1 John 2:20, 27; John 20:31).

Q. 5. *What do the scriptures principally teach?*
A. The scriptures principally teach, what man is to believe concerning God, and what duty God requires of man (2 Tim. 1:13).

WHAT MAN OUGHT TO BELIEVE CONCERNING GOD

Q. 6. *What do the scriptures make known of God?*
A. The scriptures make known what God is (Heb. 11:6), the persons in the Godhead (1 John 5:7), his decrees (Acts 15:14–15, 18), and the execution of his decrees (Acts 4:27–28).

Q. 7. *What is God?*
A. God is a Spirit (John 4:24), in and of himself infinite in being (Ex. 3:14; Job 11:7–9), glory (Acts 7:2), blessedness (1 Tim. 6:15), and perfection (Matt. 5:48); allsufficient (Gen. 17:1), eternal (Ps. 90:2), unchangeable (Mal. 3:6; James 1:17), incomprehensible (1 Kings 8:27), every where present (Ps. 139:1–13), almighty (Rev. 4:8), knowing all things (Heb. 4:13; Ps. 147:5), most wise (Rom. 16:27), most holy (Isa. 6:3; Rev. 15:4), most just (Deut. 32:4), most merciful and gracious, longsuffering, and abundant in goodness and truth (Ex. 34:6).

Q. 8. *Are there more Gods than one?*
A. There is but one only, the living and true God (Deut. 6:4; 1 Cor. 8:4, 6; Jer. 10:10).

Q. 9. *How many persons are there in the Godhead?*
A. There be three persons in the Godhead, the Father, the Son, and the Holy Ghost; and these three are one true, eternal God, the same in sub-

stance, equal in power and glory; although distinguished by their personal properties (1 John 5:7; Matt. 3:16–17; 28:19; 2 Cor. 13:14; John 10:30).

Q. 10. *What are the personal properties of the three persons in the Godhead?*
A. It is proper to the Father to beget the Son (Heb. 1:5–6, 8), and to the Son to be begotten of the Father (John 1:14, 18), and to the Holy Ghost to proceed from the Father and the Son from all eternity (John 15:26; Gal. 4:6).

Q. 11. *How doth it appear that the Son and the Holy Ghost are God equal with the Father?*
A. The scriptures manifest that the Son and the Holy Ghost are God equal with the Father, ascribing unto them such names (Isa. 6:3, 5, 8; John 12:41; Acts 28:25; 1 John 5:20; Acts 5:3–4), attributes (John 1:1; Isa. 9:6; John 2:24–25; 1 Cor. 2:10–11), works (Col. 1:16; Gen. 1:2), and worship (Matt. 28:19; 2 Cor. 13:14), as are proper to God only.

Q. 12. *What are the decrees of God?*
A. God's decrees are the wise, free, and holy acts of the counsel of his will (Eph. 1:11; Rom. 11:33; 9:14–15, 18), whereby, from all eternity, he hath, for his own glory, unchangeably foreordained whatsoever comes to pass in time (Eph. 1:4, 11; Rom. 9:22–23; Ps. 33:11), especially concerning angels and men.

Q. 13. *What hath God especially decreed concerning angels and men?*
A. God, by an eternal and immutable decree, out of his mere love, for the praise of his glorious grace, to be manifested in due time, hath elected some angels to glory (1 Tim. 5:21); and in Christ hath chosen some men to eternal life, and the means thereof (Eph. 1:4–6; 2 Thess. 2:13–14): and also, according to his sovereign power, and the unsearchable counsel of his own will, (whereby he extendeth or withholdeth favour as he pleaseth,) hath passed by and foreordained the rest to dishonour and wrath, to be for their sin inflicted, to the praise of the glory of his justice (Rom. 9:17–18, 21–22; Matt. 11:25–26; 2 Tim. 2:20; Jude 4; 1 Peter 2:8).

Q. 14. *How doth God execute his decrees?*
A. God executeth his decrees in the works of creation and providence, according to his infallible foreknowledge, and the free and immutable counsel of his own will (Eph. 1:11).

Q. 15. *What is the work of creation?*
A. The work of creation is that wherein God did in the beginning, by the word of his power, make of nothing the world, and all things therein, for himself, within the space of six days, and all very good (Gen. 1; Heb. 11:3; Prov. 16:4).

Q. 16. *How did God create angels?*
A. God created all the angels (Col. 1:16) spirits (Ps. 104:4), immortal (Matt. 22:30), holy (Matt. 25:31), excelling in knowledge (2 Sam. 14:17; Matt. 24:36), mighty in power (2 Thess. 1:7), to execute his commandments, and to praise his name (Ps. 103:20–21), yet subject to change (2 Peter 2:4).

Q. 17. *How did God create man?*
A. After God had made all other creatures, he created man male and female (Gen. 1:27); formed the body of the man of the dust of the ground (Gen. 2:7), and the woman of the rib of the man (Gen. 2:22), endued them with living, reasonable, and immortal souls (Gen. 2:7; Job 35:11; Eccl. 12:7; Matt. 10:28; Luke 23:43); made them after his own image (Gen. 1:27), in knowledge (Col. 3:10), righteousness, and holiness (Eph. 4:24); having the law of God written in their hearts (Rom. 2:14–15), and power to fulfil it (Eccl. 7:29), and dominion over the creatures (Gen. 1:28); yet subject to fall (Gen. 3:6; Eccl. 7:29).

Q. 18. *What are God's works of providence?*
A. God's works of providence are his most holy (Ps. 145:17), wise (Ps. 104:24; Isa. 28:29), and powerful preserving (Heb. 1:3) and governing (Ps. 103:19) all his creatures; ordering them, and all their actions (Matt. 10:29–31; Gen. 45:7), to his own glory (Rom. 11:36; Isa. 63:14).

Q. 19. *What is God's providence towards the angels?*
A. God by his providence permitted some of the angels, wilfully and irrecoverably, to fall into sin and damnation (Jude 6; 2 Pet. 2:4; Heb. 2:16; John 8:44), limiting and ordering that, and all their sins, to his own glory (Job 1:12; Matt. 8:31); and established the rest in holiness and happiness (1 Tim. 5:21; Mark 8:38; Heb. 12:22); employing them all (Ps. 104:4), at his pleasure, in the administrations of his power, mercy, and justice (2 Kings 19:35; Heb. 1:14).

Q. 20. *What was the providence of God toward man in the estate in which he was created?*

A. The providence of God toward man in the estate in which he was created, was the placing him in paradise, appointing him to dress it, giving him liberty to eat of the fruit of the earth (Gen. 2:8, 15–16); putting the creatures under his dominion (Gen. 1:28), and ordaining marriage for his help (Gen. 2:18); affording him communion with himself (Gen. 1:26–29; 3:8); instituting the Sabbath (Gen. 2:3); entering into a covenant of life with him, upon condition of personal, perfect, and perpetual obedience (Gal. 3:12; Rom. 10:5), of which the tree of life was a pledge (Gen. 2:9); and forbidding to eat of the tree of the knowledge of good and evil, upon the pain of death (Gen. 2:17).

Q. 21. *Did man continue in that estate wherein God at first created him?*

A. Our first parents being left to the freedom of their own will, through the temptation of Satan, transgressed the commandment of God in eating the forbidden fruit; and thereby fell from the estate of innocency wherein they were created (Gen. 3:6–8, 13; Eccl. 7:29; 2 Cor. 11:3).

Q. 22. *Did all mankind fall in that first transgression?*

A. The covenant being made with Adam as a public person, not for himself only, but for his posterity, all mankind descending from him by ordinary generation (Acts 17:26), sinned in him, and fell with him in that first transgression (Gen. 2:16–17; Rom. 5:12–20; 1 Cor. 15:21–22).

Q. 23. *Into what estate did the fall bring mankind?*

A. The fall brought mankind into an estate of sin and misery (Rom. 5:12; 3:23).

Q. 24. *What is sin?*

A. Sin is any want of conformity unto, or transgression of, any law of God, given as a rule to the reasonable creature (1 John 3:4; Gal. 3:10, 12).

Q. 25. *Wherein consisteth the sinfulness of that estate whereinto man fell?*

A. The sinfulness of that estate whereinto man fell, consisteth in the guilt of Adam's first sin (Rom. 5:12, 19), the want of that righteousness wherein he was created, and the corruption of his nature, whereby he is utterly indisposed, disabled, and made opposite unto all that is spiritually good, and wholly inclined to all evil, and that continually (Rom. 3:10–19;

Eph. 2:1–3; Rom. 5:6; 8:7–8; Gen. 6:5); which is commonly called Original Sin, and from which do proceed all actual transgressions (James 1:14–15; Matt. 15:19).

Q. 26. *How is original sin conveyed from our first parents unto their posterity?*
A. Original sin is conveyed from our first parents unto their posterity by natural generation, so as all that proceed from them in that way are conceived and born in sin (Ps. 51:5; Job 14:4; 15:14; John 3:6).

Q. 27. *What misery did the fall bring upon mankind?*
A. The fall brought upon mankind the loss of communion with God (Gen. 3:8, 10, 24), his displeasure and curse; so as we are by nature children of wrath (Eph. 2:2–3), bond slaves to Satan (2 Tim. 2:26), and justly liable to all punishments in this world, and that which is to come (Gen. 2:17; Lam. 3:39; Rom. 6:23; Matt. 25:41, 46; Jude 7).

Q. 28. *What are the punishments of sin in this world?*
A. The punishments of sin in this world are either inward, as blindness of mind (Eph. 4:18), a reprobate sense (Rom. 1:28), strong delusions (2 Thess. 2:11), hardness of heart (Rom. 2:5), horror of conscience (Isa. 33:14; Gen. 4:13; Matt. 27:4), and vile affections (Rom. 1:26); or outward, as the curse of God upon the creatures for our sakes (Gen. 3:17), and all other evils that befall us in our bodies, names, estates, relations, and employments (Deut. 28:15–18); together with death itself (Rom. 6:21, 23).

Q. 29. *What are the punishments of sin in the world to come?*
A. The punishments of sin in the world to come, are everlasting separation from the comfortable presence of God, and most grievous torments in soul and body, without intermission, in hellfire for ever (2 Thess. 1:9; Mark 9:43, 44, 46, 48; Luke 16:24).

Q. 30. *Doth God leave all mankind to perish in the estate of sin and misery?*
A. God doth not leave all men to perish in the estate of sin and misery (1 Thess. 5:9), into which they fell by the breach of the first covenant, commonly called the Covenant of Works (Gal. 3:10, 12); but of his mere love and mercy delivereth his elect out of it, and bringeth them into an estate of salvation by the second covenant, commonly called the Covenant of Grace (Titus 3:4–7; Gal. 3:21; Rom. 3:20–22).

Q. 31. *With whom was the covenant of grace made?*
A. The covenant of grace was made with Christ as the second Adam, and in him with all the elect as his seed (Gal. 3:16; Rom. 5:15–21; Isa. 53:10–11).

Q. 32. *How is the grace of God manifested in the second covenant?*
A. The grace of God is manifested in the second covenant, in that he freely provideth and offereth to sinners a Mediator (Gen. 3:15; Isa. 42:6; John 6:27), and life and salvation by him (1 John 5:11–12); and requiring faith as the condition to interest them in him (John 3:16; 1:12), promiseth and giveth his Holy Spirit (Prov. 1:23) to all his elect, to work in them that faith (2 Cor. 4:13), with all other saving graces (Gal. 5:22–23); and to enable them unto all holy obedience (Ezek. 36:27), as the evidence of the truth of their faith (James 2:18, 22) and thankfulness to God (2 Cor. 5:14–15), and as the way which he hath appointed them to salvation (Eph. 2:18).

Q. 33. *Was the covenant of grace always administered after one and the same manner?*
A. The covenant of grace was not always administered after the same manner, but the administrations of it under the Old Testament were different from those under the New (2 Cor. 3:6–9).

Q. 34. *How was the covenant of grace administered under the Old Testament?*
A. The covenant of grace was administered under the Old Testament, by promises (Rom. 15:8), prophecies (Acts 3:20, 24), sacrifices (Heb. 10:1), circumcision (Rom. 4:11), the Passover (1 Cor. 5:7), and other types and ordinances, which did all foresignify Christ then to come, and were for that time sufficient to build up the elect in faith in the promised Messiah (Heb. 8, 9, 10; 11:13), by whom they then had full remission of sin, and eternal salvation (Gal. 3:7–9, 14).

Q. 35. *How is the covenant of grace administered under the New Testament?*
A. Under the New Testament, when Christ the substance was exhibited, the same covenant of grace was and still is to be administered in the preaching of the word (Mark 16:15), and the administration of the sacraments of baptism (Matt. 28:19–20) and the Lord's supper (1 Cor. 11:23–25); in which grace and salvation are held forth in more fulness, evidence, and efficacy, to all nations (2 Cor. 3:6–18; Heb. 8:6, 10–11; Matt. 28:19).

Q. 36. *Who is the Mediator of the covenant of grace?*
A. The only Mediator of the covenant of grace is the Lord Jesus Christ (1 Tim. 2:5), who, being the eternal Son of God, of one substance and equal with the Father (John 1:1, 14; 10:30; Phil. 2:6), in the fulness of time became man (Gal. 4:4), and so was and continues to be God and man, in two entire distinct natures, and one person, for ever (Luke 1:35; Rom. 9:5; Col. 2:9; Heb. 7:24–25).

Q. 37. *How did Christ, being the Son of God, become man?*
A. Christ the Son of God became man, by taking to himself a true body, and a reasonable soul (John 1:14; Matt. 26:38), being conceived by the power of the Holy Ghost in the womb of the Virgin Mary, of her substance, and born of her (Luke 1:27, 31, 35, 42; Gal. 4:4), yet without sin (Heb. 4:15; 7:26).

Q. 38. *Why was it requisite that the Mediator should be God?*
A. It was requisite that the Mediator should be God, that he might sustain and keep the human nature from sinking under the infinite wrath of God, and the power of death (Acts 2:24–25; Rom. 1:4; 4:25; Heb. 9:14); give worth and efficacy to his sufferings, obedience, and intercession (Acts 20:28; Heb. 9:14; 7:25–28); and to satisfy God's justice (Rom. 3:24–26), procure his favour (Eph. 1:6; Matt. 3:17), purchase a peculiar people (Titus 2:13–14), give his Spirit to them (Gal. 4:6), conquer all their enemies (Luke 1:68–69, 71, 74), and bring them to everlasting salvation (Heb. 5:8–9; 9:11–15).

Q. 39. *Why was it requisite that the Mediator should be man?*
A. It was requisite that the Mediator should be man, that he might advance our nature (Heb. 2:16), perform obedience to the law (Gal. 4:4), suffer and make intercession for us in our nature (Heb. 2:14; 7:24–25), have a fellowfeeling for our infirmities (Heb. 4:15); that we might receive the adoption of sons (Gal. 4:15), and have comfort and access with boldness unto the throne of grace (Heb. 4:16).

Q. 40. *Why was it requisite that the Mediator should be God and man in one person?*
A. It was requisite that the Mediator, who was to reconcile God and man, should himself be both God and man, and this in one person, that the proper works of each nature might be accepted of God for us (Matt. 1:21,

23; 3:17; Heb. 9:14), and relied on by us, as the works of the whole person (1 Peter 2:6).

Q. 41. *Why was our Mediator called Jesus?*
A. Our Mediator was called Jesus, because he saveth his people from their sins (Matt. 1:21).

Q. 42. *Why was our Mediator called Christ?*
A. Our Mediator was called Christ, because he was anointed with the Holy Ghost above measure (John 3:34; Ps. 45:7); and so set apart, and fully furnished with all authority and ability (John 6:27; Matt. 28:18–20), to execute the offices of prophet (Acts 3:21–22; Luke 4:18, 21), priest (Heb. 5:5–7; 4:14–15), and king of his church (Ps. 2:6; Matt. 21:5; Isa. 9:6–7; Phil. 2:8–11), in the estate both of his humiliation and exaltation.

Q. 43. *How doth Christ execute the office of a prophet?*
A. Christ executeth the office of a prophet in his revealing to the church (John 1:18), in all ages, by his Spirit and word (1 Peter 1:10–12), in divers ways of administration (Heb. 1:1–2), the whole will of God (John 15:15), in all things concerning their edification and salvation (Acts 20:32; Eph. 4:11–13; John 20:31).

Q. 44. *How doth Christ execute the office of a priest?*
A. Christ executeth the office of a priest, in his once offering himself a sacrifice without spot to God (Heb. 9:14, 28), to be a reconciliation for the sins of his people (Heb. 2:17); and in making continual intercession for them (Heb. 7:25).

Q. 45. *How doth Christ execute the office of a king?*
A. Christ executeth the office of a king, in calling out of the world a people to himself (Acts 15:14–16; Isa. 55:4–5; Gen. 49:10; Ps. 110:3), and giving them officers (Eph. 4:11–12; 1 Cor. 12:28), laws (Isa. 33:22), and censures, by which he visibly governs them (Matt. 18:17–18; 1 Cor. 5:4–5); in bestowing saving grace upon his elect (Acts 5:31), rewarding their obedience (Rev. 22:12; 2:10), and correcting them for their sins (Rev. 3:19), preserving and supporting them under all their temptations and sufferings (Isa. 63:9), restraining and overcoming all their enemies (1 Cor. 15:25; Ps. 110:1–2ff.), and powerfully ordering all things for his own glory (Rom. 14:10–11), and

their good (Rom. 8:28); and also in taking vengeance on the rest, who know not God, and obey not the gospel (2 Thess. 1:8–9; Ps. 2:8–9).

Q. 46. *What was the estate of Christ's humiliation?*
A. The estate of Christ's humiliation was that low condition, wherein he for our sakes, emptying himself of his glory, took upon him the form of a servant, in his conception and birth, life, death, and after his death, until his resurrection (Phil. 2:6–8; Luke 1:31; 2 Cor. 8:9; Acts 2:24).

Q. 47. *How did Christ humble himself in his conception and birth?*
A. Christ humbled himself in his conception and birth, in that, being from all eternity the Son of God, in the bosom of the Father, he was pleased in the fulness of time to become the son of man, made of a woman of low estate, and to be born of her; with divers circumstances of more than ordinary abasement (John 1:14, 18; Gal. 4:4; Luke 2:7).

Q. 48. *How did Christ humble himself in his life?*
A. Christ humbled himself in his life, by subjecting himself to the law (Gal. 4:4), which he perfectly fulfilled (Matt. 5:17, 19); and by conflicting with the indignities of the world (Ps. 22:6; Heb. 12:2–3), temptations of Satan (Matt. 4:1–12; Luke 4:13), and infirmities in his flesh, whether common to the nature of man, or particularly accompanying that his low condition (Heb. 2:17–18; 4:15; Isa. 52:13–14).

Q. 49. *How did Christ humble himself in his death?*
A. Christ humbled himself in his death, in that having been betrayed by Judas (Matt. 27:4), forsaken by his disciples (Matt. 26:56), scorned and rejected by the world (Isa. 53:2–3), condemned by Pilate, and tormented by his persecutors (Matt. 27:26–50; John 19:34); having also conflicted with the terrors of death, and the powers of darkness, felt and borne the weight of God's wrath (Luke 22:44; Matt. 27:46), he laid down his life an offering for sin (Isa. 53:10), enduring the painful, shameful, and cursed death of the cross (Phil. 2:8; Heb. 12:2; Gal. 3:13).

Q. 50. *Wherein consisted Christ's humiliation after his death?*
A. Christ's humiliation after his death consisted in his being buried (1 Cor. 15:3–4), and continuing in the state of the dead, and under the power of death till the third day (Ps. 16:10; Acts 2:24–27, 31; Rom. 6:9; Matt. 12:40); which hath been otherwise expressed in these words, *He descended into hell.*

Q. 51. *What was the estate of Christ's exaltation?*
A. The estate of Christ's exaltation comprehendeth his resurrection (1 Cor. 15:4), ascension (Mark 16:19), sitting at the right hand of the Father (Eph. 1:20), and his coming again to judge the world (Acts 1:11; 17:31).

Q. 52. *How was Christ exalted in his resurrection?*
A. Christ was exalted in his resurrection, in that, not having seen corruption in death, (of which it was not possible for him to be held, [Acts 2:24, 27]) and having the very same body in which he suffered, with the essential properties thereof (Luke 24:39), (but without mortality, and other common infirmities belonging to this life,) really united to his soul (Rom. 6:9; Rev. 1:18), he rose again from the dead the third day by his own power (John 10:18); whereby he declared himself to be the Son of God (Rom. 1:4), to have satisfied divine justice (Rom. 8:34), to have vanquished death, and him that had the power of it (Heb. 2:14), and to be Lord of quick and dead (Rom. 14:9): all which he did as a public person (1 Cor. 15:21–22), the head of his church (Eph. 1:20, 22–23; Col. 1:18), for their justification (Rom. 4:25), quickening in grace (Eph. 2:1, 5–6; Col. 2:12), support against enemies (1 Cor. 15:25–27), and to assure them of their resurrection from the dead at the last day (1 Cor. 15:20).

Q. 53. *How was Christ exalted in his ascension?*
A. Christ was exalted in his ascension, in that having after his resurrection often appeared unto and conversed with his apostles, speaking to them of the things pertaining to the kingdom of God (Acts 1:2–3), and giving them commission to preach the gospel to all nations (Matt. 28:19–20), forty days after his resurrection, he, in our nature, and as our head (Heb. 6:20), triumphing over enemies (Eph. 4:8), visibly went up into the highest heavens, there to receive gifts for men (Acts 1:9–11; Eph. 4:10; Ps. 68:18), to raise up our affections thither (Col. 3:1–2), and to prepare a place for us (John 14:3), where himself is, and shall continue till his second coming at the end of the world (Acts 3:21).

Q. 54. *How is Christ exalted in his sitting at the right hand of God?*
A. Christ is exalted in his sitting at the right hand of God, in that as Godman he is advanced to the highest favour with God the Father (Phil. 2:9), with all fulness of joy (Acts 2:28; Ps. 16:11), glory (John 17:5), and power over all things in heaven and earth (Eph. 1:22; 1 Peter 3:22); and

doth gather and defend his church, and subdue their enemies; furnisheth his ministers and people with gifts and graces (Eph. 4:10–12; Ps. 110:1), and maketh intercession for them (Rom. 8:34).

Q. 55. *How doth Christ make intercession?*
A. Christ maketh intercession, by appearing in our nature continually before the Father in heaven (Heb. 9:12, 24), in the merit of his obedience and sacrifice on earth (Heb. 1:3), declaring his will to have it applied to all believers (John 3:16; 17:9, 20, 24); answering all accusations against them (Rom. 8:33–34), and procuring for them quiet of conscience, notwithstanding daily failings (Rom. 5:1–2; 1 John 2:1–2), access with boldness to the throne of grace (Heb. 4:16), and acceptance of their persons (Eph. 1:6) and services (1 Peter 2:5).

Q. 56. *How is Christ to be exalted in his coming again to judge the world?*
A. Christ is to be exalted in his coming again to judge the world, in that he, who was unjustly judged and condemned by wicked men (Acts 3:14–15), shall come again at the last day in great power (Matt. 24:30), and in the full manifestation of his own glory, and of his Father's, with all his holy angels (Luke 9:26; Matt. 25:31), with a shout, with the voice of the archangel, and with the trumpet of God (1 Thess. 4:16), to judge the world in righteousness (Acts 17:31).

Q. 57. *What benefits hath Christ procured by his mediation?*
A. Christ, by his mediation, hath procured redemption (Heb. 9:12), with all other benefits of the covenant of grace (2 Cor. 1:20).

Q. 58. *How do we come to be made partakers of the benefits which Christ hath procured?*
A. We are made partakers of the benefits which Christ hath procured, by the application of them unto us (John 1:11–12), which is the work especially of God the Holy Ghost (Titus 3:5–6).

Q. 59. *Who are made partakers of redemption through Christ?*
A. Redemption is certainly applied, and effectually communicated, to all those for whom Christ hath purchased it (Eph. 1:13–14; John 6:37, 39; 10:15–16); who are in time by the Holy Ghost enabled to believe in Christ according to the gospel (Eph. 2:8; 2 Cor. 4:13).

Q. 60. *Can they who have never heard the gospel, and so know not Jesus Christ, nor believe in him, be saved by their living according to the light of nature?*
A. They who, having never heard the gospel (Rom. 10:14), know not Jesus Christ (2 Thess. 1:8–9; Eph. 2:12; John 1:10–12), and believe not in him, cannot be saved (John 8:24; Mark 16:16), be they never so diligent to frame their lives according to the light of nature (1 Cor. 1:20–24), or the laws of that religion which they profess (John 4:22; Rom. 9:31–32; Phil. 3:4–9); neither is there salvation in any other, but in Christ alone (Acts 4:12), who is the Saviour only of his body the church (Eph. 5:23).

Q. 61. *Are all they saved who hear the gospel, and live in the church?*
A. All that hear the gospel, and live in the visible church, are not saved; but they only who are true members of the church invisible (John 12:38–40; Rom. 9:6; Matt. 22:14; 7:21; Rom. 11:7).

Q. 62. *What is the visible church?*
A. The visible church is a society made up of all such as in all ages and places of the world do profess the true religion (1 Cor. 1:2; 12:13; Rom. 15:9–12; Rev. 7:9; Ps. 2:8; 22:27–31; 45:17; Matt. 28:19–20; Isa. 59:21), and of their children (1 Cor. 7:14; Acts 2:39; Rom. 11:16; Gen. 17:7).

Q. 63. *What are the special privileges of the visible church?*
A. The visible church hath the privilege of being under God's special care and government (Isa. 4:5–6; 1 Tim. 4:10); of being protected and preserved in all ages, notwithstanding the opposition of all enemies (Ps. 115:1–2, 9ff.; Isa. 31:4–5; Zech. 12:2–4, 8–9); and of enjoying the communion of saints, the ordinary means of salvation (Acts 2:39, 42), and offers of grace by Christ to all the members of it in the ministry of the gospel, testifying, that whosoever believes in him shall be saved (Ps. 147:19–20; Rom. 9:4; Eph. 4:11–12; Mark 16:15–16), and excluding none that will come unto him (John 6:37).

Q. 64. *What is the invisible church?*
A. The invisible church is the whole number of the elect, that have been, are, or shall be gathered into one under Christ the head (Eph. 1:10, 22–23; John 10:16; 11:52).

Q. 65. *What special benefits do the members of the invisible church enjoy by Christ?*
A. The members of the invisible church by Christ enjoy union and communion with him in grace and glory (John 17:21; Eph. 2:5–6; John 17:24).

Q. 66. *What is that union which the elect have with Christ?*
A. The union which the elect have with Christ is the work of God's grace (Eph. 1:22; 2:6–8), whereby they are spiritually and mystically, yet really and inseparably, joined to Christ as their head and husband (1 Cor. 6:17; John 10:28; Eph. 5:23, 30); which is done in their effectual calling (1 Peter 5:10; 1 Cor. 1:9).

Q. 67. *What is effectual calling?*
A. Effectual calling is the work of God's almighty power and grace (John 5:25; Eph. 1:18–20; 2 Tim. 1:8–9), whereby (out of his free and special love to his elect, and from nothing in them moving him thereunto (Titus 3:4–5; Eph. 2:4–5, 7–9; Rom. 9:11) he doth, in his accepted time, invite and draw them to Jesus Christ, by his word and Spirit (2 Cor. 5:20; 6:1–2; John 6:44; 2 Thess. 2:13–14); savingly enlightening their minds (Acts 26:18; 1 Cor. 2:10, 12), renewing and powerfully determining their wills (Ezek. 11:19; 36:26–27; John 6:45), so as they (although in themselves dead in sin) are hereby made willing and able freely to answer his call, and to accept and embrace the grace offered and conveyed therein (Eph. 2:5; Phil. 2:13; Deut. 30:6).

Q. 68. *Are the elect only effectually called?*
A. All the elect, and they only, are effectually called (Acts 13:48); although others may be, and often are, outwardly called by the ministry of the word (Matt. 22:14), and have some common operations of the Spirit (Matt. 7:22; 13:20–21; Heb. 6:4–6); who, for their wilful neglect and contempt of the grace offered to them, being justly left in their unbelief, do never truly come to Jesus Christ (John 12:38–40; Acts 28:25–27; John 6:64–65; Ps. 81:11–12).

Q. 69. *What is the communion in grace which the members of the invisible church have with Christ?*
A. The communion in grace which the members of the invisible church have with Christ, is their partaking of the virtue of his mediation, in their justification (Rom. 8:30), adoption (Eph. 1:5), sanctification, and whatever else, in this life, manifests their union with him (1 Cor. 1:30).

Q. 70. *What is justification?*

A. Justification is an act of God's free grace unto sinners (Rom. 3:22, 24–25; 4:5), in which he pardoneth all their sins, accepteth and accounteth their persons righteous in his sight (2 Cor. 5:19, 21; Rom. 3:22, 24–25, 27–28); not for any thing wrought in them, or done by them (Titus 3:5, 7; Eph. 1:7), but only for the perfect obedience and full satisfaction of Christ, by God imputed to them (Rom. 5:17–19; 4:6–8), and received by faith alone (Acts 10:43; Gal. 2:16; Phil. 3:9).

Q. 71. *How is justification an act of God's free grace?*

A. Although Christ, by his obedience and death, did make a proper, real, and full satisfaction to God's justice in the behalf of them that are justified (Rom. 5:8–10, 19); yet in as much as God accepteth the satisfaction from a surety, which he might have demanded of them, and did provide this surety, his own only Son (1 Tim. 2:5–6; Heb. 10:10; Matt. 20:28; Dan. 9:24, 26; Isa. 53:4–6, 10–12; Heb. 7:22; Rom. 8:32; 1 Peter 1:18–19), imputing his righteousness to them (2 Cor. 5:21), and requiring nothing of them for their justification but faith (Rom. 3:24–25), which also is his gift (Eph. 2:8), their justification is to them of free grace (Eph. 1:7).

Q. 72. *What is justifying faith?*

A. Justifying faith is a saving grace (Heb. 10:39), wrought in the heart of a sinner by the Spirit (2 Cor. 4:13; Eph. 1:17–19) and word of God (Rom. 10:14, 17), whereby he, being convinced of his sin and misery, and of the disability in himself and all other creatures to recover him out of his lost condition (Acts 2:37; 16:30; John 16:8–9; Rom. 5:6; Eph. 2:1; Acts 4:12), not only assenteth to the truth of the promise of the gospel (Eph. 1:13), but receiveth and resteth upon Christ and his righteousness, therein held forth, for pardon of sin (John 1:12; Acts 16:31; 10:43), and for the accepting and accounting of his person righteous in the sight of God for salvation (Phil. 3:9; Acts 15:11).

Q. 73. *How doth faith justify a sinner in the sight of God?*

A. Faith justifies a sinner in the sight of God, not because of those other graces which do always accompany it, or of good works that are the fruits of it (Gal. 3:11; Rom. 3:28), nor as if the grace of faith, or any act thereof, were imputed to him for his justification (Rom. 4:5; 10:10); but only as it is an instrument by which he receiveth and applieth Christ and his righteousness (John 1:12; Phil. 3:9; Gal. 2:16).

Q. 74. *What is adoption?*

A. Adoption is an act of the free grace of God (1 John 3:1), in and for his only Son Jesus Christ (Eph. 1:5; Gal. 4:4–5), whereby all those that are justified are received into the number of his children (John 1:12), have his name put upon them (2 Cor. 6:18; Rev. 3:12), the Spirit of his Son given to them (Gal. 4:6), are under his fatherly care and dispensations (Ps. 103:13; Prov. 14:26; Matt. 6:32), admitted to all the liberties and privileges of the sons of God, made heirs of all the promises, and fellowheirs with Christ in glory (Heb. 6:12; Rom. 8:17).

Q. 75. *What is sanctification?*

A. Sanctification is a work of God's grace, whereby they whom God hath, before the foundation of the world, chosen to be holy, are in time, through the powerful operation of his Spirit (Eph. 1:4; 1 Cor. 6:11; 2 Thess. 2:13) applying the death and resurrection of Christ unto them (Rom. 6:4–6), renewed in their whole man after the image of God (Eph. 4:23–24); having the seeds of repentance unto life, and all other saving graces, put into their hearts (Acts 11:18; 1 John 3:9), and those graces so stirred up, increased, and strengthened (Jude 20; Heb. 6:11–12; Eph. 3:16–19; Col. 1:10–11), as that they more and more die unto sin, and rise unto newness of life (Rom. 6:4, 6, 14; Gal. 5:24).

Q. 76. *What is repentance unto life?*

A. Repentance unto life is a saving grace (2 Tim. 2:25), wrought in the heart of a sinner by the Spirit (Zech. 12:10) and word of God (Acts 11:18, 20–21), whereby, out of the sight and sense, not only of the danger (Ezek. 18:28, 30, 32; Luke 15:17–18; Hos. 2:6–7), but also of the filthiness and odiousness of his sins (Ezek. 36:31; Isa. 30:22), and upon the apprehension of God's mercy in Christ to such as are penitent (Joel 2:12–13), he so grieves for (Jer. 31:18–19) and hates his sins (2 Cor. 7:11), as that he turns from them all to God (Acts 26:18; Ezek. 14:6; 1 Kings 8:47–48), purposing and endeavouring constantly to walk with him in all the ways of new obedience (Ps. 119:6, 59, 128; Luke 1:6; 2 Kings 23:25).

Q. 77. *Wherein do justification and sanctification differ?*
A. Although sanctification be inseparably joined with justification (1 Cor. 6:11; 1:30), yet they differ, in that God in justification imputeth the righteousness of Christ (Rom. 4:6, 8); in sanctification his Spirit infuseth grace, and enableth to the exercise thereof (Ezek. 36:27); in the former, sin is pardoned (Rom. 3:24–25); in the other it is subdued (Rom. 6:6, 14): the one doth equally free all believers from the revenging wrath of God, and that perfectly in this life, that they never fall into condemnation (Rom. 8:33–34); the other is neither equal in all (1 John 2:12–14; Heb. 5:12–14), nor in this life perfect in any (1 John 1:8, 10), but growing up to perfection (2 Cor. 7:1; Phil. 3:12–14).

Q. 78. *Whence ariseth the imperfection of sanctification in believers?*
A. The imperfection of sanctification in believers ariseth from the remnants of sin abiding in every part of them, and the perpetual lustings of the flesh against the spirit; whereby they are often foiled with temptations, and fall into many sins (Rom. 7:18, 28; Mark 14:66–72; Gal. 2:11–12), are hindered in all their spiritual services (Heb. 12:1), and their best works are imperfect and defiled in the sight of God (Isa. 64:6; Ex. 28:38).

Q. 79. *May not true believers, by reason of their imperfections, and the many temptations and sins they are overtaken with, fall away from the state of grace?*
A. True believers, by reason of the unchangeable love of God (Jer. 31:3), and his decree and covenant to give them perseverance (2 Tim. 2:19; Heb. 13:20–21; 2 Sam. 23:5), their inseparable union with Christ (1 Cor. 1:8–9), his continual intercession for them (Heb. 7:25; Luke 22:32), and the Spirit and seed of God abiding in them (1 John 3:9; 2:27), can neither totally nor finally fall away from the state of grace (Jer. 32:40; John 10:28), but are kept by the power of God through faith unto salvation (1 Peter 1:5).

Q. 80. *Can true believers be infallibly assured that they are in the estate of grace, and that they shall persevere therein unto salvation?*
A. Such as truly believe in Christ, and endeavour to walk in all good conscience before him (1 John 2:3), may, without extraordinary revelation, by faith grounded upon the truth of God's promises, and by the Spirit enabling them to discern in themselves those graces to which the promises of life are made (1 Cor. 2:12; 1 John 3:14, 18–19, 21, 24; 4:13, 16; Heb. 6:11–12), and bearing witness with their spirits that they are the children

of God (Rom. 8:16), be infallibly assured that they are in the estate of grace, and shall persevere therein unto salvation (1 John 5:13).

Q. 81. *Are all true believers at all times assured of their present being in the estate of grace, and that they shall be saved?*
A. Assurance of grace and salvation not being of the essence of faith (Eph. 1:13), true believers may wait long before they obtain it (Isa. 50:10; Ps. 88:1–3, 6–7, 9–10, 13–15); and, after the enjoyment thereof, may have it weakened and intermitted, through manifold distempers, sins, temptations, and desertions (Ps. 77:1–12; Song 5:2–3, 6; Ps. 51:8, 12; 31:22; 22:1); yet are they never left without such a presence and support of the Spirit of God as keeps them from sinking into utter despair (1 John 3:9; Job 13:15; Ps. 73:15, 23; Isa. 54:7–10).

Q. 82. *What is the communion in glory which the members of the invisible church have with Christ?*
A. The communion in glory which the members of the invisible church have with Christ, is in this life (2 Cor. 3:18), immediately after death (Luke 23:43), and at last perfected at the resurrection and day of judgement (1 Thess. 4:17).

Q. 83. *What is the communion in glory with Christ which the members of the invisible church enjoy in this life?*
A. The members of the invisible church have communicated to them in this life the firstfruits of glory with Christ, as they are members of him their head, and so in him are interested in that glory which he is fully possessed of (Eph. 2:5–6); and, as an earnest thereof, enjoy the sense of God's love (Rom. 5:5; 2 Cor. 1:22), peace of conscience, joy in the Holy Ghost, and hope of glory (Rom. 5:1–2; 14:17); as, on the contrary, sense of God's revenging wrath, horror of conscience, and a fearful expectation of judgement, are to the wicked the beginning of their torments which they shall endure after death (Gen. 4:13; Matt. 27:4; Heb. 10:27; Rom. 2:9; Mark 9:44).

Q. 84. *Shall all men die?*
A. Death being threatened as the wages of sin (Rom. 6:23), it is appointed unto all men once to die (Heb. 9:27); for that all have sinned (Rom. 5:12).

Q. 85. *Death, being the wages of sin, why are not the righteous delivered from death, seeing all their sins are forgiven in Christ?*
A. The righteous shall be delivered from death itself at the last day, and even in death are delivered from the sting and curse of it (1 Cor. 15:26, 55–57; Heb. 2:15); so that, although they die, yet it is out of God's love (Isa. 57:1–2; 2 Kings 22:20), to free them perfectly from sin and misery (Rev. 14:13; Eph. 5:27), and to make them capable of further communion with Christ in glory, which they then enter upon (Luke 23:43; Phil. 1:23).

Q. 86. *What is the communion in glory with Christ, which the members of the invisible church enjoy immediately after death?*
A. The communion in glory with Christ, which the members of the invisible church enjoy immediately after death, is, in that their souls are then made perfect in holiness (Heb. 12:23), and received into the highest heavens (2 Cor. 5:1, 6, 8; Phil. 1:23; Acts 3:21; Eph. 4:10), where they behold the face of God in light and glory (1 John 3:2; 1 Cor. 13:12), waiting for the full redemption of their bodies (Rom. 8:23; Ps. 16:9), which even in death continue united to Christ (1 Thess. 4:14), and rest in their graves as in their beds (Isa. 57:2), till at the last day they be again united to their souls (Job 19:26–27). Whereas the souls of the wicked are at their death cast into hell, where they remain in torments and utter darkness, and their bodies kept in their graves, as in their prisons, till the resurrection and judgement of the great day (Luke 16:23–24; Acts 1:25; Jude 6–7).

Q. 87. *What are we to believe concerning the resurrection?*
A. We are to believe, that at the last day there shall be a general resurrection of the dead, both of the just and the unjust (Acts 24:15): when they that are then found alive shall in a moment be changed; and the selfsame bodies of the dead which were laid in the grave, being then again united to their souls for ever, shall be raised up by the power of Christ (1 Cor. 15:51–53; 1 Thess. 4:15–17; John 5:28–29). The bodies of the just, by the Spirit of Christ, and by virtue of his resurrection as their head, shall be raised in power, spiritual, incorruptible, and made like to his glorious body (1 Cor. 15:21–23, 42–44; Phil. 3:21); and the bodies of the wicked shall be raised up in dishonour by him, as an offended judge (John 5:27–29; Matt. 25:33).

Q. 88. *What shall immediately follow after the resurrection?*
A. Immediately after the resurrection shall follow the general and final judgement of angels and men (2 Peter 2:4, 6–7, 14–15; Matt. 25:46); the day and hour whereof no man knoweth, that all may watch and pray, and be ever ready for the coming of the Lord (Matt. 24:36, 42, 44; Luke 21:35–36).

Q. 89. *What shall be done to the wicked at the day of judgement?*
A. At the day of judgement, the wicked shall be set on Christ's left hand (Matt. 25:33), and, upon clear evidence, and full conviction of their own consciences (Rom. 2:15–16), shall have the fearful but just sentence of condemnation pronounced against them (Matt. 25:41–43); and thereupon shall be cast out from the favourable presence of God, and the glorious fellowship with Christ, his saints, and all his holy angels, into hell, to be punished with unspeakable torments, both of body and soul, with the devil and his angels for ever (Luke 16:26; 2 Thess. 1:8–9).

Q. 90. *What shall be done to the righteous at the day of judgement?*
A. At the day of judgement, the righteous, being caught up to Christ in the clouds (1 Thess. 4:17), shall be set on his right hand, and there openly acknowledged and acquitted (Matt. 25:33; 10:32), shall join with him in the judging of reprobate angels and men (1 Cor. 6:2–3), and shall be received into heaven (Matt. 25:34, 46), where they shall be fully and for ever freed from all sin and misery (Eph. 5:27; Rev. 14:13); filled with inconceivable joys (Ps. 16:11), made perfectly holy and happy both in body and soul, in the company of innumerable saints and holy angels (Heb. 12:22–23), but especially in the immediate vision and fruition of God the Father, of our Lord Jesus Christ, and of the Holy Spirit, to all eternity (1 John 3:2; 1 Cor. 13:12; 1 Thess. 4:17–18). And this is the perfect and full communion, which the members of the invisible church shall enjoy with Christ in glory, at the resurrection and day of judgement.

HAVING SEEN WHAT THE SCRIPTURES PRINCIPALLY
TEACH US TO BELIEVE CONCERNING GOD,
IT FOLLOWS TO CONSIDER
WHAT THEY REQUIRE AS THE DUTY OF MAN.

Q. 91. *What is the duty which God requireth of man?*
A. The duty which God requireth of man, is obedience to his revealed will (Rom. 12:1–2; Mic. 6:8; 1 Sam. 15:22).

Q. 92. *What did God at first reveal unto man as the rule of his obedience?*
A. The rule of obedience revealed to Adam in the estate of innocence, and to all mankind in him, besides a special command not to eat of the fruit of the tree of the knowledge of good and evil, was the moral law (Gen. 1:26–27; Rom. 2:14–15; 10:5; Gen. 2:17).

Q. 93. *What is the moral law?*
A. The moral law is the declaration of the will of God to mankind, directing and binding every one to personal, perfect, and perpetual conformity and obedience thereunto, in the frame and disposition of the whole man, soul and body (Deut. 5:1–3, 31, 33; Luke 10:26–27; Gal. 3:10; 1 Thess. 5:23), and in performance of all those duties of holiness and righteousness which he oweth to God and man (Luke 1:75; Acts 24:16): promising life upon the fulfilling, and threatening death upon the breach of it (Rom. 10:5; Gal. 3:10, 12).

Q. 94. *Is there any use of the moral law to man since the fall?*
A. Although no man, since the fall, can attain to righteousness and life by the moral law (Rom. 8:3; Gal. 2:16); yet there is great use thereof, as well common to all men, as peculiar either to the unregenerate, or the regenerate (1 Tim. 1:8).

Q. 95. *Of what use is the moral law to all men?*
A. The moral law is of use to all men, to inform them of the holy nature and will of God (Lev. 11:44–45; 20:7–8; Rom. 7:12), and of their duty, binding them to walk accordingly (Mic. 6:8; James 2:10–11); to convince them of their disability to keep it, and of the sinful pollution of their nature, hearts, and lives (Ps. 19:11–12; Rom. 3:20; 7:7): to humble them in the sense of their sin and misery (Rom. 3:9, 23), and thereby help them to a clearer

sight of the need they have of Christ (Gal. 3:21–22), and of the perfection of his obedience (Rom. 10:4).

Q. 96. *What particular use is there of the moral law to unregenerate men?*
A. The moral law is of use to unregenerate men, to awaken their consciences to flee from the wrath to come (1 Tim. 1:9–10), and to drive them to Christ (Gal. 3:24); or, upon their continuance in the estate and way of sin, to leave them inexcusable (Rom. 1:20; 2:15), and under the curse thereof (Gal. 3:10).

Q. 97. *What special use is there of the moral law to the regenerate?*
A. Although they that are regenerate, and believe in Christ, be delivered from the moral law as a covenant of works (Rom. 6:14; 7:4, 6; Gal. 4:4–5), so as thereby they are neither justified (Rom. 3:20) nor condemned (Gal. 5:23; Rom. 8:1); yet, besides the general uses thereof common to them with all men, it is of special use, to show them how much they are bound to Christ for his fulfilling it, and enduring the curse thereof in their stead, and for their good (Rom. 7:24–25; Gal. 3:13–14; Rom. 8:3–4); and thereby to provoke them to more thankfulness (Luke 1:68–69, 74–75; Col. 1:12–14), and to express the same in their greater care to conform themselves thereunto as the rule of their obedience (Rom. 7:22; 12:2; Titus 2:11–14).

Q. 98. *Where is the moral law summarily comprehended?*
A. The moral law is summarily comprehended in the ten commandments, which were delivered by the voice of God upon mount Sinai, and written by him in two tables of stone (Deut. 10:4; Ex. 34:1–4); and are recorded in the twentieth chapter of Exodus. The four first commandments containing our duty to God, and the other six our duty to man (Matt. 22:37–40).

Q. 99. *What rules are to be observed for the right understanding of the ten commandments?*
A. For the right understanding of the ten commandments, these rules are to be observed:

1. That the law is perfect, and bindeth every one to full conformity in the whole man unto the righteousness thereof, and unto entire obedience for ever; so as to require the utmost perfection of every duty, and to forbid the least degree of every sin (Ps. 19:7; James 2:10; Matt. 5:21–22).

2. That it is spiritual, and so reacheth the understanding, will, affections, and all other powers of the soul; as well as words, works, and gestures

(Rom. 7:14; Deut. 6:5; Matt. 22:37–39; 5:21–22, 27–28, 33–34, 37–39, 43–44).

3. That one and the same thing, in divers respects, is required or forbidden in several commandments (Col. 3:5; Amos 8:5; Prov. 1:19; 1 Tim. 6:10).

4. That as, where a duty is commanded, the contrary sin is forbidden (Isa. 58:13; Deut. 6:13; Matt. 4:9–10; 15:4–6); and, where a sin is forbidden, the contrary duty is commanded (Matt. 5:21–25; Eph. 4:28): so, where a promise is annexed, the contrary threatening is included (Ex. 20:12; Prov. 30:17); and, where a threatening is annexed, the contrary promise is included (Jer. 18:7–8; Ex. 20:7; Ps. 15:1, 4–5; 24:4–5).

5. That what God forbids, is at no time to be done (Job 13:7–8; Rom. 3:8; Job 36:21; Heb. 11:25); what he commands, is always our duty (Deut. 6:8–9); and yet every particular duty is not to be done at all times (Matt. 12:7).

6. That under one sin or duty, all of the same kind are forbidden or commanded; together with all the causes, means, occasions, and appearances thereof, and provocations thereunto (Matt. 5:21–22, 27–28; 15:4–6; Heb. 10:24–25; 1 Thess. 5:22; Jude 23; Gal. 5:26; Col. 3:21).

7. That what is forbidden or commanded to ourselves, we are bound, according to our places, to endeavour that it may be avoided or performed by others, according to the duty of their places (Ex. 20:10; Lev. 19:17; Gen. 18:19; Josh. 24:15; Deut. 6:6–7).

8. That in what is commanded to others, we are bound, according to our places and callings, to be helpful to them (2 Cor. 1:24); and to take heed of partaking with others in what is forbidden them (1 Tim. 5:22; Eph. 5:11).

Q. 100. *What special things are we to consider in the ten commandments?*
A. We are to consider, in the ten commandments, the preface, the substance of the commandments themselves, and several reasons annexed to some of them, the more to enforce them.

Q. 101. *What is the preface to the ten commandments?*
A. The preface to the ten commandments is contained in these words, *I am the Lord thy God, which have brought thee out of the land of Egypt, out of the house of bondage* (Ex. 20:2). Wherein God manifesteth his sovereignty, as being JEHOVAH, the eternal, immutable, and almighty God (Isa. 44:6); having his being in and of himself (Ex. 3:14), and giving being to all

his words (Ex. 6:3) and works (Acts 17:24, 28): and that he is a God in covenant, as with Israel of old, so with all his people (Gen. 17:7; Rom. 3:29); who, as he brought them out of their bondage in Egypt, so he delivereth us from our spiritual thraldom (Luke 1:74–75); and that therefore we are bound to take him for our God alone, and to keep all his commandments (1 Peter 1:15–18; Lev. 18:30; 19:37).

Q. 102. *What is the sum of the four commandments which contain our duty to God?*
A. The sum of the four commandments containing our duty to God, is, to love the Lord our God with all our heart, and with all our soul, and with all our strength, and with all our mind (Luke 10:27).

Q. 103. *Which is the first commandment?*
A. The first commandment is, *Thou shalt have no other gods before me* (Ex. 20:3).

Q. 104. *What are the duties required in the first commandment?*
A. The duties required in the first commandment are, the knowing and acknowledging of God to be the only true God, and our God (1 Chron. 28:9; Deut. 26:17; Isa. 43:10; Jer. 14:22); and to worship and glorify him accordingly (Ps. 95:6–7; Matt. 4:10; Ps. 29:2), by thinking (Mal. 3:16), meditating (Ps. 63:6), remembering (Eccl. 12:1), highly esteeming (Ps. 71:19), honouring (Mal. 1:6), adoring (Isa. 45:23), choosing (Josh. 24:15, 22), loving (Deut. 6:5), desiring (Ps. 73:25), fearing of him (Isa. 8:13); believing him (Ex. 14:31); trusting (Isa. 26:4), hoping (Ps. 130:7), delighting (Ps. 37:4), rejoicing in him (Ps. 32:11); being zealous for him (Rom. 12:11; Num. 25:11); calling upon him, giving all praise and thanks (Phil. 4:6), and yielding all obedience and submission to him with the whole man (Jer. 7:28; James 4:7); being careful in all things to please him (1 John 3:22), and sorrowful when in any thing he is offended (Jer. 31:18; Ps. 119:136); and walking humbly with him (Mic. 6:8).

Q. 105. *What are the sins forbidden in the first commandment?*
A. The sins forbidden in the first commandment, are, Atheism, in denying or not having a God (Ps. 14:1; Eph. 2:12); Idolatry, in having or worshipping more gods than one, or any with or instead of the true God (Jer. 2:27–28; 1 Thess. 1:9); the not having and avouching him for God, and our God (Ps. 81:11); the omission or neglect of any thing due to him,

required in this commandment (Isa. 43:22–24); ignorance (Jer. 4:22; Hos. 4:1, 6), forgetfulness (Jer. 2:32), misapprehensions (Acts 17:23, 29), false opinions (Isa. 40:18), unworthy and wicked thoughts of him (Ps. 50:21); bold and curious searching into his secrets (Deut. 29:29); all profaneness (Titus 1:16; Heb. 12:16), hatred of God (Rom. 1:30); selflove (2 Tim. 3:2), selfseeking (Phil. 2:21), and all other inordinate and immoderate setting of our mind, will, or affections upon other things, and taking them off from him in whole or in part (1 John 2:15–16; 1 Sam. 2:29; Col. 3:2, 5); vain credulity (1 John 4:1), unbelief (Heb. 3:12), heresy (Gal. 5:20; Titus 3:10), misbelieve (Acts 26:9), distrust (Ps. 78:22), despair (Gen. 4:13), incorrigibleness (Jer. 5:3), and insensibleness under judgments (Isa. 42:25), hardness of heart (Rom. 2:5), pride (Jer. 13:15), presumption (Ps. 19:13), carnal security (Zeph. 1:12), tempting of God (Matt. 4:7); using unlawful means (Rom. 3:8); and trusting in lawful means (Jer. 17:5); carnal delights and joys (2 Tim. 3:4); corrupt, blind, and indiscreet zeal (Gal. 4:17; John 16:2; Rom. 10:2; Luke 9:54–55); lukewarmness (Rev. 3:16), and deadness in the things of God (Rev. 3:1); estranging ourselves, and apostatizing from God (Ezek. 14:5; Isa. 1:4–5); praying, or giving any religious worship, to saints, angels, or any other creatures (Rom. 10:13–14; Hos. 4:12; Acts 10:25–26; Rev. 19:10; Matt. 4:10; Col. 2:18; Rom. 1:25); all compacts and consulting with the devil (Lev. 20:6; 1 Sam. 28:7, 11; 1 Chron. 10:13–14), and hearkening to his suggestions (Acts 5:3); making men the lords of our faith and conscience (2 Cor. 1:24; Matt. 23:9); slighting and despising God and his commands (Deut. 32:15; 2 Sam. 12:9; Prov. 13:13); resisting and grieving of his Spirit (Acts 7:51; Eph. 4:30), discontent and impatience at his dispensations, charging him foolishly for the evils he inflicts on us (Ps. 73:2–3, 13–15, 22; Job 1:22); and ascribing the praise of any good we either are, have, or can do, to fortune (1 Sam. 6:7–9), idols (Dan. 5:23), ourselves (Deut. 8:17; Dan. 4:30), or any other creature (Hab. 1:16).

Q. 106. *What are we specially taught by these words* [before me] *in the first commandment?*
A. These words [*before me*] or before my face, in the first commandment, teach us, that God, who seeth all things, taketh special notice of, and is much displeased with, the sin of having any other God: that so it may be an argument to dissuade from it, and to aggravate it as a most impudent provocation (Ezek. 8:5–6ff.; Ps. 44:20–21): as also to persuade us to do as in his sight, whatever we do in his service (1 Chron. 28:9).

Q. 107. *Which is the second commandment?*

A. The second commandment is, *Thou shalt not make unto thee any graven image, or any likeness of any thing that is in heaven above, or that is in the earth beneath, or that is in the water under the earth. Thou shalt not bow down thyself to them, nor serve them: for I the LORD thy God am a jealous God, visiting the iniquity of the fathers upon the children unto the third and fourth generation of them that hate me; and showing mercy unto thousands of them that love me, and keep my commandments* (Ex. 20:4–6).

Q. 108. *What are the duties required in the second commandment?*

A. The duties required in the second commandment are, the receiving, observing, and keeping pure and entire, all such religious worship and ordinances as God hath instituted in his word (Deut. 32:46–47; Matt. 28:20; Acts 2:42; 1 Tim. 6:13–14); particularly prayer and thanksgiving in the name of Christ (Phil. 4:6; Eph. 5:20); the reading, preaching, and hearing of the word (Deut. 17:18–19; Acts 15:21; 2 Tim. 4:2; James 1:21–22; Acts 10:33); the administration and receiving of the sacraments (Matt. 28:19; 1 Cor. 11:23–30); church government and discipline (Matt. 18:15–17; 16:19; 1 Cor. 5; 12:28); the ministry and maintenance thereof (Eph. 4:11–12; 1 Tim. 5:17–18; 1 Cor. 9:7–15); religious fasting (Joel 2:12–13; 1 Cor. 7:5); swearing by the name of God (Deut. 6:13), and vowing unto him (Isa. 19:21; Ps. 76:11): as also the disapproving, detesting, opposing, all false worship (Acts 17:16–17; Ps. 16:4); and, according to each one's place and calling, removing it, and all monuments of idolatry (Deut. 7:5; Isa. 30:22).

Q. 109. *What are the sins forbidden in the second commandment?*

A. The sins forbidden in the second commandment are, all devising (Num. 15:39), counselling (Deut. 13:6–8), commanding (Hos. 5:11; Mic. 6:16), using (1 Kings 11:33; 12:33), and any wise approving, any religious worship not instituted by God himself (Deut. 12:30–32); tolerating a false religion (Deut. 13:6–12; Zech. 13:2–3; Rev. 2:2, 14–15, 20; 17:12, 16–17); the making any representation of God, of all or of any of the three persons, either inwardly in our mind, or outwardly in any kind of image or likeness of any creature whatsoever (Deut. 4:15–19; Acts 17:29; Rom. 1:21–23, 25); all worshipping of it (Dan. 3:18; Gal. 4:8), or God in it or by it (Ex. 32:5); the making of any representation of feigned deities (Ex. 32:8), and all worship of them, or service belonging to them (1 Kings 18:26, 28; Isa. 65:11); all superstitious devices (Acts 17:22; Col. 2:21–23), corrupting the worship of God (Mal. 1:7–8, 14), adding to it, or taking from it (Deut. 4:2), whether invented and taken up of ourselves (Ps. 106:39), or received by tradition from others (Matt. 15:9), though under the title of antiquity (1 Peter 1:18), custom (Jer. 44:17), devotion (Isa. 65:3–5; Gal. 1:13–14), good intent, or any other pretence whatsoever (1 Sam. 13:11–12; 15:21); simony (Acts 8:18); sacrilege (Rom. 2:22; Mal. 3:8); all neglect (Ex. 4:24– 26), contempt (Matt. 22:5; Mal. 1:7, 13), hindering (Matt. 23:13), and opposing the worship and ordinances which God hath appointed (Acts 13:44–45; 1 Thess. 2:15–16).

Q. 110. *What are the reasons annexed to the second commandment, the more to enforce it?*
A. The reasons annexed to the second commandment, the more to enforce it, contained in these words, *FOR I the LORD thy God am a jealous God, visiting the iniquity of the fathers upon the children unto the third and fourth generation of them that hate me; and showing mercy unto thousands of them that love me, and keep my commandments* (Ex. 20:5–6); are, besides God's sovereignty over us, and propriety in us (Ps. 45:11; Rev. 15:3–4), his fervent zeal for his own worship (Ex. 34:13–14), and his revengeful indignation against all false worship, as being a spiritual whoredom (1 Cor. 10:20–22; Jer. 7:18–20; Ezek. 16:26–27; Deut. 32:16–20); accounting the breakers of this commandment such as hate him, and threatening to punish them unto divers generations (Hos. 2:2–4); and esteeming the observers of it such as love him and keep his commandments, and promising mercy to them unto many generations (Deut. 5:29).

Q. 111. *Which is the third commandment?*
A. The third commandment is, *Thou shalt not take the name of the Lord thy God in vain: for the Lord will not hold him guiltless that taketh his name in vain* (Ex. 20:7).

Q. 112. *What is required in the third commandment?*
A. The third commandment requires, That the name of God, his titles, attributes (Matt. 6:9; Deut. 28:58; Ps. 29:2; 68:4; Rev. 15:3–4), ordinances (Mal. 1:14; Eccl. 5:1), the word (Ps. 138:2), sacraments (1 Cor. 11:24– 25, 28–29), prayer (1 Tim. 2:8), oaths (Jer. 4:2), vows (Eccl. 5:2, 4–6), lots (Acts 1:24, 26), his works (Job 36:24), and whatsoever else there is whereby he makes himself known, be holily and reverently used in thought

(Mal. 3:16), meditation (Ps. 8:1, 3–4, 9ff.), word (Col. 3:17; Ps. 105:2, 5), and writing (Ps. 102:18); by an holy profession (1 Peter 3:15; Mic. 4:5), and answerable conversation (Phil. 1:27), to the glory of God (1 Cor. 10:31), and the good of ourselves (Jer. 32:39), and others (1 Peter 2:12).

Q. 113. *What are the sins forbidden in the third commandment?*
A. The sins forbidden in the third commandment are, the not using of God's name as is required (Mal. 2:2); and the abuse of it in an ignorant (Acts 17:23), vain (Prov. 30:9), irreverent, profane (Mal. 1:6–7, 12; 3:14), superstitious (1 Sam. 4:3–5; Jer. 7:4, 9–10, 14, 31; Col. 2:20–22), or wicked mentioning or otherwise using his titles, attributes (2 Kings 18:30, 35; Ex. 5:2; Ps. 139:20), ordinances (Ps. 50:16–17), or works (Isa. 5:12), by blasphemy (2 Kings 19:22; Lev. 24:11), perjury (Zech. 5:4; 8:17), all sinful cursings (1 Sam. 17:43; 2 Sam. 16:5), oaths (Jer. 5:7; 23:10), vows (Deut. 23:18; Acts 23:12, 14), and lots (Esth. 3:7; 9:24; Ps. 22:18); violating of our oaths and vows, if lawful (Ps. 24:4; Ezek. 17:16, 18–19); and fulfilling them, if of things unlawful (Mark 6:26; 1 Sam. 25:22, 32–34); murmuring and quarrelling at (Rom. 9:14, 19–20), curious prying into (Deut. 29:29), and misapplying of God's decrees (Rom. 3:5, 7; 6:1) and providences (Eccl. 8:11; 9:3; Ps. 39); misinterpreting (Matt. 5:21–48), misapplying (Ezek. 13:22), or any way perverting the word, or any part of it (2 Peter 3:16; Matt. 22:24–31), to profane jests (Isa. 22:13; Jer. 23:34, 36, 38), curious or unprofitable questions, vain janglings, or the maintaining of false doctrines (1 Tim. 1:4, 6–7; 6:4–5, 20; 2 Tim. 2:14; Titus 3:9); abusing it, the creatures, or any thing contained under the name of God, to charms (Deut. 18:10–14; Acts 19:13), or sinful lusts and practices (2 Tim. 4:3–4; Rom. 13:13–14; 1 Kings 21:9–10; Jude 4); the maligning (Acts 13:45; 1 John 3:12), scorning (Ps. 1:1; 2 Peter 3:3), reviling (1 Peter 4:4), or any wise opposing of God's truth, grace, and ways (Acts 13:45–46, 50; 4:18; 19:9; 1 Thess. 2:16; Heb. 10:29); making profession of religion in hypocrisy, or for sinister ends (2 Tim. 3:5; Matt. 23:14; 6:1–2, 5, 16); being ashamed of it (Mark 8:38), or a shame to it, by unconformable (Ps. 73:14–15), unwise (1 Cor. 6:5–6; Eph. 5:15–17), unfruitful (Isa. 5:4; 2 Peter 1:8–9), and offensive walking (Rom. 2:23–24), or backsliding from it (Gal. 3:1, 3; Heb. 6:6).

Q. 114. *What reasons are annexed to the third commandment?*
A. The reasons annexed to the third commandment, in these words, [*The Lord thy God,*] and, [*For the Lord will not hold him guiltless that taketh his name in vain,* (Ex. 20:7)] are, because he is the Lord and our God, therefore his name is not to be profaned, or any way abused by us (Lev. 19:12); especially because he will be so far from acquitting and sparing the transgressors of this commandment, as that he will not suffer them to escape his righteous judgement (Ezek. 36:21–23; Deut. 28:58–59; Zech. 5:2–4), albeit many such escape the censures and punishments of men (1 Sam. 2:12, 17, 22, 24; 3:13).

Q. 115. *Which is the fourth commandment?*
A. The fourth commandment is, *Remember the sabbathday, to keep it holy. Six days shalt thou labour, and do all thy work: But the seventh day is the sabbath of the* LORD *thy God: in it thou shalt not do any work, thou, nor thy son, nor thy daughter, thy manservant, nor thy maidservant, nor thy cattle, nor thy stranger that is within thy gates. For in six days the* LORD *made heaven and earth, the sea, and all that in them is, and rested the seventh day: wherefore the* LORD *blessed the sabbathday, and hallowed it* (Ex. 20:8–11).

Q. 116. *What is required in the fourth commandment?*
A. The fourth commandment requireth of all men the sanctifying or keeping holy to God such set times as he hath appointed in his word, expressly one whole day in seven; which was the seventh from the beginning of the world to the resurrection of Christ, and the first day of the week ever since, and so to continue to the end of the world; which is the Christian Sabbath (Deut. 5:12–14; Gen. 2:2–3; 1 Cor. 16:1–2; Acts 20:7; Matt. 5:17–18; Isa. 56:2, 4, 6–7), and in the New Testament called *The Lord's day* (Rev. 1:10).

Q. 117. *How is the sabbath or the Lord's day to be sanctified?*
A. The sabbath or the Lord's day is to be sanctified by an holy resting all the day (Ex. 20:8, 10), not only from such works as are at all times sinful, but even from such worldly employments and recreations as are on other days lawful (Ex. 16:25–28; Neh. 13:15–22; Jer. 17:21–22); and making it our delight to spend the whole time (except so much of it as is to be taken up in works of necessity and mercy [Matt. 12:1–13]) in the public and private exercises of God's worship (Isa. 58:13; Luke 4:16; Acts 20:7; 1 Cor. 16:1–2; Ps. 92, Title; Isa. 66:23; Lev. 23:3): and, to that end, we are to

prepare our hearts, and with such foresight, diligence, and moderation, to dispose and seasonably dispatch our worldly business, that we may be the more free and fit for the duties of that day (Ex. 20:8; Luke 23:54, 56; Ex. 16:22, 25–26, 29; Neh. 13:19).

Q. 118. *Why is the charge of keeping the sabbath more specially directed to governors of families, and other superiors?*
A. The charge of keeping the sabbath is more specially directed to governors of families, and other superiors, because they are bound not only to keep it themselves, but to see that it be observed by all those that are under their charge; and because they are prone ofttimes to hinder them by employments of their own (Ex. 20:10; Josh. 24:15; Neh. 13:15, 17; Jer. 17:20–22; Ex. 23:12).

Q. 119. *What are the sins forbidden in the fourth commandment?*
A. The sins forbidden in the fourth commandment are, all omissions of the duties required (Ezek. 22:26), all careless, negligent, and unprofitable performing of them, and being weary of them (Acts 20:7, 9; Ezek. 33:30–32; Amos 8:5; Mal. 1:13); all profaning the day by idleness, and doing that which is in itself sinful (Ezek. 23:38); and by all needless works, words, and thoughts, about our worldly employments and recreations (Jer. 17:24, 27; Isa. 58:13).

Q. 120. *What are the reasons annexed to the fourth commandment, the more to enforce it?*
A. The reasons annexed to the fourth commandment, the more to enforce it, are taken from the equity of it, God allowing us six days of seven for our own affairs, and reserving but one for himself, in these words, *Six days shalt thou labour, and do all thy work* (Ex. 20:9): from God's challenging a special propriety in that day, *The seventh day is the sabbath of the Lord thy God* (Ex. 20:10): from the example of God, who *in six days made heaven and earth, the sea, and all that in them is, and rested the seventh day*: and from that blessing which God put upon that day, not only in sanctifying it to be a day for his service, but in ordaining it to be a means of blessing to us in our sanctifying it; wherefore *the Lord blessed the sabbathday, and hallowed it* (Ex. 20:11).

Q. 121. *Why is the word* Remember *set in the beginning of the fourth commandment?*

A. The word *Remember* is set in the beginning of the fourth commandment (Ex. 20:8), partly, because of the great benefit of remembering it, we being thereby helped in our preparation to keep it (Ex. 16:23; Luke 23:54, 56; Mark 15:42; Neh. 13:19), and, in keeping it, better to keep all the rest of the commandments (Ps. 92:title, 13–14; Ezek. 20:12, 19–20), and to continue a thankful remembrance of the two great benefits of creation and redemption, which contain a short abridgement of religion (Gen. 2:2–3; Ps. 118:22, 24; Acts 4:10–11; Rev. 1:10); and partly, because we are very ready to forget it (Ezek. 22:26), for that there is less light of nature for it (Neh. 9:14), and yet it restraineth our natural liberty in things at other times lawful (Ex. 34:21); that it cometh but once in seven days, and many worldly businesses come between, and too often take off our minds from thinking of it, either to prepare for it, or to sanctify it (Deut. 5:14–15; Amos 8:5); and that Satan with his instruments much labour to blot out the glory, and even the memory of it, to bring in all irreligion and impiety (Lam. 1:7; Jer. 17:21–23; Neh. 13:15–23).

Q. 122. *What is the sum of the six commandments which contain our duty to man?*

A. The sum of the six commandments which contain our duty to man, is, to love our neighbour as ourselves (Matt. 22:39), and to do to others what we would have them do to us (Matt. 7:12).

Q. 123. *Which is the fifth commandment?*

A. The fifth commandment is, *Honour thy father and thy mother: that thy days may be long upon the land which the Lord thy God giveth thee* (Ex. 20:12).

Q. 124. *Who are meant by* father *and* mother *in the fifth commandment?*

A. By *father* and *mother*, in the fifth commandment, are meant, not only natural parents (Prov. 23:22, 25; Eph. 6:1–2), but all superiors in age (1 Tim. 5:1–2) and gifts (Gen. 4:20–22; 45:8); and especially such as, by God's ordinance, are over us in place of authority, whether in family (2 Kings 5:13), church (2 Kings 2:12; 13:14; Gal. 4:19), or commonwealth (Isa. 49:23).

Q. 125. *Why are superiors styled* Father *and* Mother?

A. Superiors are styled *Father* and *Mother*, both to teach them in all duties toward their inferiors, like natural parents, to express love and tenderness to them, according to their several relations (Eph. 6:4; 2 Cor. 12:14; 2 Thess. 2:7–8, 11; Num. 11:11–12); and to work inferiors to a greater willingness and cheerfulness in performing their duties to their superiors, as to their parents (1 Cor. 4:14–16; 2 Kings 5:13).

Q. 126. *What is the general scope of the fifth commandment?*

A. The general scope of the fifth commandment is, the performance of those duties which we mutually owe in our several relations, as inferiors, superiors, or equals (Eph. 5:21; 1 Peter 2:17; Rom. 12:10).

Q. 127. *What is the honour that inferiors owe to their superiors?*

A. The honour which inferiors owe to their superiors is, all due reverence in heart (Mal. 1:6; Lev. 19:3), word (Prov. 31:28; 1 Peter 3:6), and behaviour (Lev. 19:32; 1 Kings 2:19); prayer and thanksgiving for them (1 Tim. 2:1–2); imitation of their virtues and graces (Heb. 13:7; Phil. 3:17); willing obedience to their lawful commands and counsels (Eph. 6:1–2, 5–7; 1 Peter 2:13–14; Rom. 13:1–5; Heb. 13:17; Prov. 4:3–4; 23:22; Ex. 18:19, 24); due submission to their corrections (Heb. 12:9; 1 Peter 2:18–20); fidelity to (Titus 2:9–10), defence (1 Sam. 26:15–16; 2 Sam. 18:3; Esth. 6:2), and maintenance of their persons and authority, according to their several ranks, and the nature of their places (Matt. 22:21; Rom. 13:6–7; 1 Tim. 5:17–18; Gal. 6:6; Gen. 45:11; 47:12); bearing with their infirmities, and covering them in love (1 Peter 2:18; Prov. 23:22; Gen. 9:23), that so they may be an honour to them and to their government (Ps. 127:3–5; Prov. 31:23).

Q. 128. *What are the sins of inferiors against their superiors?*

A. The sins of inferiors against their superiors are, all neglect of the duties required toward them (Matt. 15:4–6); envying at (Num. 11:28–29), contempt of (1 Sam. 8:7; Isa. 3:5), and rebellion (2 Sam. 15:1–12) against, their persons (Ex. 21:15) and places (1 Sam. 10:27), in their lawful counsels (1 Sam. 2:25), commands, and corrections (Deut. 21:18–21); cursing, mocking (Prov. 30:11, 17), and all such refractory and scandalous carriage, as proves a shame and dishonour to them and their government (Prov. 19:26).

Q. 129. *What is required of superiors towards their inferiors?*
A. It is required of superiors, according to that power they receive from God, and that relation wherein they stand, to love (Col. 3:19; Titus 2:4), pray for (1 Sam. 12:23; Job 1:5), and bless their inferiors (1 Kings 8:55–56; Heb. 7:7; Gen. 49:28); to instruct (Deut. 6:6–7), counsel, and admonish them (Eph. 6:4); countenancing (1 Peter 3:7), commending (1 Peter 2:14; Rom. 13:3), and rewarding such as do well (Esth. 6:3); and discountenancing (Rom. 13:3–4), reproving, and chastising such as do ill (Prov. 29:15; 1 Peter 2:14); protecting (Job 29:12–17; Isa. 1:10, 17), and providing for them all things necessary for soul (Eph. 6:4) and body (1 Tim. 5:8): and by grave, wise, holy, and exemplary carriage, to procure glory to God (1 Tim. 4:12; Titus 2:3–5), honour to themselves (1 Kings 3:28), and so to preserve that authority which God hath put upon them (Titus 2:15).

Q. 130. *What are the sins of superiors?*
A. The sins of superiors are, besides the neglect of the duties required of them (Ezek. 34:2–4), an inordinate seeking of themselves (Phil. 2:21), their own glory (John 5:44; 7:18), ease, profit, or pleasure (Isa. 56:10–11; Deut. 17:17); commanding things unlawful (Dan. 3:4–6; Acts 4:17–18), or not in the power of inferiors to perform (Ex. 5:10–18; Matt. 23:2, 4); counselling (Matt. 14:8; Mark 6:24), encouraging (2 Sam. 13:28), or favouring them in that which is evil (1 Sam. 3:13); dissuading, discouraging, or discountenancing them in that which is good (John 7:46–49; Col. 3:21; Ex. 5:17); correcting them unduly (1 Peter 2:18–20; Heb. 12:10; Deut. 25:3); careless exposing, or leaving them to wrong, temptation, and danger (Gen. 38:11, 26; Acts 18:17); provoking them to wrath (Eph. 6:4); or any way dishonouring themselves, or lessening their authority, by an unjust, indiscreet, rigorous, or remiss behaviour (Gen. 9:21; 1 Kings 12:13–16; 1:6; 1 Sam. 2:29–31).

Q. 131. *What are the duties of equals?*
A. The duties of equals are, to regard the dignity and worth of each other (1 Peter 2:17), in giving honour to go one before another (Rom. 12:10); and to rejoice in each others gifts and advancement, as their own (Rom. 12:15–16; Phil. 2:3–4).

Q. 132. *What are the sins of equals?*
A. The sins of equals are, besides the neglect of the duties required (Rom. 13:8), the undervaluing of the worth (2 Tim. 3:3), envying the gifts (Acts 7:9; Gal. 5:26), grieving at the advancement or prosperity one of another (Num. 12:2; Esth. 6:12–13); and usurping preeminence one over another (3 John 9; Luke 22:24).

Q. 133. *What is the reason annexed to the fifth commandment, the more to enforce it?*
A. The reason annexed to the fifth commandment, in these words, *That thy days may be long upon the land which the Lord thy God giveth thee* (Ex. 20:12), is an express promise of long life and prosperity, as far as it shall serve for God's glory and their own good, to all such as keep this commandment (Deut. 5:16; 1 Kings 8:25; Eph. 6:2–3).

Q. 134. *Which is the sixth commandment?*
A. The sixth commandment is, *Thou shalt not kill* (Ex. 20:13).

Q. 135. *What are the duties required in the sixth commandment?*
A. The duties required in the sixth commandment are, all careful studies, and lawful endeavours, to preserve the life of ourselves (Eph. 5:28–29) and others (1 Kings 18:4) by resisting all thoughts and purposes (Jer. 26:15–16; Acts 23:12, 16–17, 21, 27), subduing all passions (Eph. 4:26), and avoiding all occasions (2 Sam. 2:22; Deut. 22:8), temptations (Matt. 4:6–7; Prov. 1:10–11, 15–16), and practices, which tend to the unjust taking away the life of any (1 Sam. 24:12; 26:9–11; Gen. 37:21–22); by just defence thereof against violence (Ps. 82:4; Prov. 24:11–12; 1 Sam. 14:45), patient bearing of the hand of God (James 5:7–11; Heb. 12:9), quietness of mind (1 Thess. 4:11; 1 Peter 3:3–4; Ps. 37:8–11), cheerfulness of spirit (Prov. 17:22); a sober use of meat (Prov. 25:16, 27), drink (1 Tim. 5:23), physic (Isa. 38:21), sleep (Ps. 127:2), labour (Eccl. 5:12; 2 Thess. 3:10, 12; Prov. 16:26), and recreations (Eccl. 3:4, 11); by charitable thoughts (1 Sam. 19:4–5; 22:13–14), love (Rom. 13:10), compassion (Luke 10:33–34), meekness, gentleness, kindness (Col. 3:12–13); peaceable (James 3:17), mild and courteous speeches and behaviour (1 Peter 3:8–11; Prov. 15:1; Judg. 8:1–3); forbearance, readiness to be reconciled, patient bearing and forgiving of injuries, and requiting good for evil (Matt. 5:24; Eph. 4:2, 32; Rom. 12:17, 20–21); comforting and succouring the distressed, and protecting

and defending the innocent (1 Thess. 5:14; Job 31:19–20; Matt. 25:35–36; Prov. 31:8–9).

Q. 136. *What are the sins forbidden in the sixth commandment?*
A. The sins forbidden in the sixth commandment are, all taking away the life of ourselves (Acts 16:28), or of others (Gen. 9:6), except in case of public justice (Num. 35:31, 33), lawful war (Jer. 48:10; Deut. 20), or necessary defence (Ex. 22:2–3); the neglecting or withdrawing the lawful and necessary means of preservation of life (Matt. 25:42–43; James 2:15– 16; Eccl. 6:1–2); sinful anger (Matt. 5:22), hatred (1 John 3:15; Lev. 19:17), envy (Prov. 14:30), desire of revenge (Rom. 12:19); all excessive passions (Eph. 4:31), distracting cares (Matt. 6:31, 34); immoderate use of meat, drink (Luke 21:34; Rom. 13:13), labour (Eccl. 12:12; 2:22–23), and recreations (Isa. 5:12); provoking words (Prov. 15:1; 12:18), oppression (Ezek. 18:18; Ex. 1:14), quarrelling (Gal. 5:15; Prov. 23:29), striking, wounding (Num. 35:16–18, 21), and whatsoever else tends to the destruction of the life of any (Ex. 21:18–36).

Q. 137. *Which is the seventh commandment?*
A. The seventh commandment is, *Thou shalt not commit adultery* (Ex. 20:14).

Q. 138. *What are the duties required in the seventh commandment?*
A. The duties required in the seventh commandment are, chastity in body, mind, affections (1 Thess. 4:4; Job 31:1; 1 Cor. 7:34), words (Col. 4:6), and behaviour (1 Peter 2:3); and the preservation of it in ourselves and others (1 Cor. 7:2, 35–36); watchfulness over the eyes and all the senses (Job 31:1); temperance (Acts 24:24–25), keeping of chaste company (Prov. 2:16–20), modesty in apparel (1 Tim. 2:9); marriage by those that have not the gift of continency (1 Cor. 7:2, 9), conjugal love (Prov. 5:19–20), and cohabitation (1 Peter 3:7); diligent labour in our callings (Prov. 31:11, 27–28); shunning all occasions of uncleanness, and resisting temptations thereunto (Prov. 5:8; Gen. 39:8–10).

Q. 139. *What are the sins forbidden in the seventh commandment?*
A. The sins forbidden in the seventh commandment, besides the neglect of the duties required (Prov. 5:7), are, adultery, fornication (Heb. 13:4; Gal. 5:19), rape, incest (2 Sam. 13:14; 1 Cor. 5:1), sodomy, and all unnatural lusts (Rom. 1:24, 26–27; Lev. 20:15–16); all unclean imaginations,

thoughts, purposes, and affections (Matt. 5:28; 15:19; Col. 3:5); all corrupt or filthy communications, or listening thereunto (Eph. 5:3–4; Prov. 7:5, 21–22); wanton looks (Isa. 3:16; 2 Peter 2:14), impudent or light behaviour, immodest apparel (Prov. 7:10, 13); prohibiting of lawful (1 Tim. 4:3), and dispensing with unlawful marriages (Lev. 18:1–21; Mark 6:18; Mal. 2:11–12); allowing, tolerating, keeping of stews, and resorting to them (1 Kings 15:12; 2 Kings 23:7; Deut. 23:17–18; Lev. 19:29; Jer. 5:7; Prov. 7:24–27); entangling vows of single life (Matt. 19:10–11), undue delay of marriage (1 Cor. 7:7–9; Gen. 38:26); having more wives or husbands than one at the same time (Mal. 2:14–15; Matt. 19:5); unjust divorce (Mal. 2:16; Matt. 5:32), or desertion (1 Cor. 7:12–13); idleness, gluttony, drunkenness (Ezek. 16:49; Prov. 23:30–33), unchaste company (Gen. 39:10; Prov. 5:8); lascivious songs, books, pictures, dancings, stage plays (Eph. 5:4; Ezek. 23:14–16; Isa. 23:15–17; 3:16; Mark 6:22; Rom. 13:13; 1 Peter 4:3); and all other provocations to, or acts of uncleanness, either in ourselves or others (2 Kings 9:30; Jer. 4:30; Ezek. 23:40).

Q. 140. *Which is the eighth commandment?*
A. The eighth commandment is, *Thou shalt not steal* (Ex. 20:15).

Q. 141. *What are the duties required in the eighth commandment?*
A. The duties required in the eighth commandment are, truth, faithfulness, and justice in contracts and commerce between man and man (Ps. 15:2, 4; Zech. 7:4, 10; 8:16–17); rendering to every one his due (Rom. 13:7); restitution of goods unlawfully detained from the right owners thereof (Lev. 6:2–5; Luke 19:8); giving and lending freely, according to our abilities, and the necessities of others (Luke 6:30, 38; 1 John 3:17; Eph. 4:28; Gal. 6:10); moderation of our judgements, wills, and affections concerning worldly goods (1 Tim. 6:6–9; Gal. 6:14); a provident care and study to get (1 Tim. 5:8), keep, use, and dispose these things which are necessary and convenient for the sustentation of our nature, and suitable to our condition (Prov. 27:23–27; Eccl. 2:24; 3:12–13; 1 Tim. 6:17–18; Isa. 38:1; Matt. 11:8); a lawful calling (1 Cor. 7:20; Gen. 2:15; 3:19), and diligence in it (Eph. 4:28; Prov. 10:4); frugality (John 6:12; Prov. 21:20); avoiding unnecessary lawsuits (1 Cor. 6:1–9), and suretyship, or other like engagements (Prov. 6:1–6; 11:15); and an endeavour, by all just and lawful means, to procure, preserve, and further the wealth and outward estate of

others, as well as our own (Lev. 25:35; Deut. 22:1–4; Ex. 23:4–5; Gen. 47:14, 20; Phil. 2:4; Matt. 22:39).

Q. 142. *What are the sins forbidden in the eighth commandment?*
A. The sins forbidden in the eighth commandment, besides the neglect of the duties required (James 2:15–16; 1 John 3:17), are, theft (Eph. 4:28), robbery (Ps. 62:10), manstealing (1 Tim. 1:10), and receiving any thing that is stolen (Prov. 29:24; Ps. 50:18); fraudulent dealing (1 Thess. 4:6), false weights and measures (Prov. 11:1; 20:10), removing landmarks (Deut. 19:14; Prov. 23:10), injustice and unfaithfulness in contracts between man and man (Amos 8:5; Ps. 37:21), or in matters of trust (Luke 16:10–12); oppression (Ezek. 22:29; Lev. 25:17), extortion (Matt. 23:25; Ezek. 22:12), usury (Ps. 15:5), bribery (Job 15:34), vexatious lawsuits (1 Cor. 6:6–8; Prov. 3:29–30), unjust inclosures and depopulations (Isa. 5:8; Mic. 2:2); ingrossing commodities to enhance the price (Prov. 11:26); unlawful callings (Acts 19:19, 24–25), and all other unjust or sinful ways of taking or withholding from our neighbour what belongs to him, or of enriching ourselves (Job 20:19; James 5:4; Prov. 21:6); covetousness (Luke 12:15); inordinate prizing and affecting worldly goods (1 Tim. 6:5; Col. 3:2; Prov. 23:5; Ps. 62:10); distrustful and distracting cares and studies in getting, keeping, and using them (Matt. 6:25, 31, 34; Eccl. 5:12); envying at the prosperity of others (Ps. 73:3; 37:1, 7); as likewise idleness (2 Thess. 3:11; Prov. 18:9), prodigality, wasteful gaming; and all other ways whereby we do unduly prejudice our own outward estate (Prov. 21:17; 23:20–21; 28:19), and defrauding ourselves of the due use and comfort of that estate which God hath given us (Eccl. 4:8; 6:2; 1 Tim. 5:8).

Q. 143. *Which is the ninth commandment?*
A. The ninth commandment is, *Thou shalt not bear false witness against thy neighbour* (Ex. 20:16).

Q. 144. *What are the duties required in the ninth commandment?*
A. The duties required in the ninth commandment are, the preserving and promoting of truth between man and man (Zech. 8:16), and the good name of our neighbour, as well as our own (3 John 12); appearing and standing for the truth (Prov. 31:8–9); and from the heart (Ps. 15:2), sincerely (2 Chron. 19:9), freely (1 Sam. 19:4–5), clearly (Josh. 7:19), and fully (2 Sam. 14:18–20), speaking the truth, and only the truth, in matters

of judgement and justice (Lev. 19:15; Prov. 14:5, 25), and in all other things whatsoever (2 Cor. 1:17–18; Eph. 4:25); a charitable esteem of our neighbours (Heb. 6:9; 1 Cor. 13:7); loving, desiring, and rejoicing in their good name (Rom. 1:8; 2 John 4; 3 John 3–4); sorrowing for (2 Cor. 2:4; 12:21), and covering of their infirmities (Prov. 17:9; 1 Peter 4:8); freely acknowledging of their gifts and graces (1 Cor. 1:4–5, 7; 2 Tim. 1:4–5), defending their innocency (1 Sam. 22:14); a ready receiving of a good report (1 Cor. 13:6–7), and unwillingness to admit of an evil report (Ps. 15:3), concerning them; discouraging talebearers (Prov. 25:23), flatterers (Prov. 26:24–25), and slanderers (Ps. 101:5); love and care of our own good name, and defending it when need requireth (Prov. 22:1; John 8:49); keeping of lawful promises (Ps. 15:4); studying and practising of whatsoever things are true, honest, lovely, and of good report (Phil. 4:8).

Q. 145. *What are the sins forbidden in the ninth commandment?*
A. The sins forbidden in the ninth commandment are, all prejudicing the truth, and the good name of our neighbours, as well as our own (1 Sam. 17:28; 2 Sam. 16:3; 1:9–10, 15–16), especially in public judicature (Lev. 19:15; Hab. 1:4); giving false evidence (Prov. 19:5; 6:16, 19), suborning false witnesses (Acts 6:13), wittingly appearing and pleading for an evil cause, outfacing and overbearing the truth (Jer. 9:3, 5; Acts 24:2, 5; Ps. 12:3–4; 52:1–4); passing unjust sentence (Prov. 17:15; 1 Kings 21:9–14), calling evil good, and good evil; rewarding the wicked according to the work of the righteous, and the righteous according to the work of the wicked (Isa. 5:23); forgery (Ps. 119:69; Luke 19:8; 16:5–7), concealing the truth, undue silence in a just cause (Lev. 5:1; Deut. 13:8; Acts 5:3, 8–9; 2 Tim. 4:6), and holding our peace when iniquity calleth for either a reproof from ourselves (1 Kings 1:6; Lev. 19:17), or complaint to others (Isa. 59:4); speaking the truth unseasonably (Prov. 29:11), or maliciously to a wrong end (1 Sam. 22:9–10; Ps. 52:title, 1–5), or perverting it to a wrong meaning (Ps. 56:5; John 2:19; Matt. 26:60–61), or in doubtful or equivocal expressions, to the prejudice of truth or justice (Gen. 3:5; 26:7, 9); speaking untruth (Isa. 59:13), lying (Lev. 19:11; Col. 3:9), slandering (Ps. 50:20), backbiting (Ps. 15:3), detracting (James 4:11; Jer. 38:4), talebearing (Lev. 19:16), whispering (Rom. 1:29–30), scoffing (Gen. 21:9; Gal. 4:29), reviling (1 Cor. 6:10), rash (Matt. 7:1), harsh (Acts 28:4), and partial censuring (Gen. 38:24; Rom. 2:1); misconstructing intentions, words, and actions (Neh. 6:6–8; Rom. 3:8; Ps. 69:10; 1 Sam. 1:13–15; 2 Sam. 10:3); flattering (Ps. 12:2–3),

vainglorious boasting (2 Tim. 3:2), thinking or speaking too highly or too meanly of ourselves or others (Luke 18:9, 11; Rom. 12:16; 1 Cor. 4:6; Acts 12:22; Ex. 4:10–13); denying the gifts and graces of God (Job 27:5–6; 4:6); aggravating smaller faults (Matt. 7:3–5); hiding, excusing, or extenuating of sins, when called to a free confession (Prov. 28:13; 30:20; Gen. 3:12–13; Jer. 2:35; 2 Kings 5:25; Gen. 4:9); unnecessary discovering of infirmities (Gen. 9:22; Prov. 25:9–10); raising false rumours (Ex. 23:1), receiving and countenancing evil reports (Prov. 29:12), and stopping our ears against just defence (Acts 7:56–57; Job 31:13–14): evil suspicion (1 Cor. 13:5; 1 Tim. 6:4); envying or grieving at the deserved credit of any (Num. 11:29; Matt. 21:15), endeavouring or desiring to impair it (Ezra 4:12–13), rejoicing in their disgrace and infamy (Jer. 48:27); scornful contempt (Ps. 35:15–16, 21; Matt. 27:28–29), fond admiration (Jude 16; Acts 12:22); breach of lawful promises (Rom. 1:31; 2 Tim. 3:3); neglecting such things as are of good report (1 Sam. 2:24), and practising, or not avoiding ourselves, or not hindering what we can in others, such things as procure an ill name (2 Sam. 13:12–13; Prov. 5:8–9; 6:33).

Q. 146. Which is the tenth commandment?

A. The tenth commandment is, *Thou shalt not covet thy neighbour's house, thou shalt not covet thy neighbour's wife, nor his manservant, nor his maidservant, nor his ox, nor his ass, nor any thing that is thy neighbour's* (Ex. 20:17).

Q. 147. What are the duties required in the tenth commandment?

A. The duties required in the tenth commandment are, such a full contentment with our own condition (Heb. 13:5; 1 Tim. 6:6), and such a charitable frame of the whole soul toward our neighbour, as that all our inward motions and affections touching him, tend unto, and further all that good which is his (Job 31:29; Rom. 12:15; Ps. 122:7–9; 1 Tim. 1:5; Esth. 10:3; 1 Cor. 13:4–7).

Q. 148. What are the sins forbidden in the tenth commandment?

A. The sins forbidden in the tenth commandment are, discontentment with our own estate (1 Kings 21:4; Esth. 5:13; 1 Cor. 10:10); envying (Gal. 5:26; James 3:14, 16) and grieving at the good of our neighbour (Ps. 112:9–10; Neh. 2:10), together with all inordinate motions and affections to any thing that is his (Rom. 7:7–8; 13:9; Col. 3:5; Deut. 5:21).

Q. 149. *Is any man able perfectly to keep the commandments of God?*
A. No man is able, either of himself (James 3:2; John 15:5; Rom. 8:3), or by any grace received in this life, perfectly to keep the commandments of God (Eccl. 7:20; 1 John 1:8, 10; Gal. 5:17; Rom. 7:18–19); but doth daily break them in thought (Gen. 6:5; 8:21), word and deed (Rom. 3:9–19; James 3:2–13).

Q. 150. *Are all transgressions of the law of God equally heinous in themselves, and in the sight of God?*
A. All transgressions of the law of God are not equally heinous; but some sins in themselves, and by reason of several aggravations, are more heinous in the sight of God than others (John 19:11; Ezek. 8:6, 13, 15; 1 John 5:16; Ps. 78:17, 32, 56).

Q. 151. *What are those aggravations that make some sins more heinous than others?*
A. Sins receive their aggravations,

1. From the persons offending (Jer. 2:8); if they be of riper age (Job 32:7, 9; Eccl. 4:13), greater experience or grace (1 Kings 11:4, 9), eminent for profession (2 Sam. 12:14; 1 Cor. 5:1), gifts (James 4:17; Luke 12:47–48), place (Jer. 5:4–5), office (2 Sam. 12:7–9; Ezek. 8:11–12), guides to others (Rom. 2:17–24), and whose example is likely to be followed by others (Gal. 2:11–14).

2. From the parties offended (Matt. 21:38–39): if immediately against God (1 Sam. 2:25; Acts 5:4; Ps. 51:4), his attributes (Rom. 2:4), and worship (Mal. 1:8, 14); against Christ, and his grace (Heb. 2:2–3; 12:25); the Holy Spirit (Heb. 10:29; Matt. 12:31–32), his witness (Eph. 4:30), and workings (Heb. 6:4–6); against superiors, men of eminency (Jude 8; Num. 12:8–9; Isa. 3:5), and such as we stand especially related and engaged unto (Prov. 30:17; 2 Cor. 12:15; Ps. 55:12–15); against any of the saints (Zeph. 2:8, 10–11; Matt. 18:6; 1 Cor. 6:8; Rev. 17:6), particularly weak brethren (1 Cor. 8:11–12; Rom. 14:13, 15, 21), the souls of them, or any other (Ezek. 13:19; 1 Cor. 8:12; Rev. 18:12–13; Matt. 23:15), and the common good of all or many (1 Thess. 2:15–16; Josh. 22:20).

3. From the nature and quality of the offence (Prov. 6:30–33): if it be against the express letter of the law (Ezra 9:10–12; 1 Kings 11:9–10), break many commandments, contain in it many sins (Col. 3:5; 1 Tim. 6:10; Prov. 5:8–12; 6:32–33; Josh. 7:21): if not only conceived in the heart, but

breaks forth in words and actions (James 1:14–15; Matt. 5:22; Mic. 2:1), scandalize others (Matt. 18:7; Rom. 2:23–24), and admit of no reparation (Deut. 22:22, 28–29; Prov. 6:32–35): if against means (Matt. 11:21–24; John 15:22), mercies (Isa. 1:3; Deut. 32:6), judgements (Amos 4:8–11; Jer. 5:3), light of nature (Rom. 1:26–27), conviction of conscience (Rom. 1:32; Dan. 5:22; Titus 3:10–11), public or private admonition (Prov. 29:1), censure of the church (Titus 3:10; Matt. 18:17), civil punishments (Prov. 27:22; 23:35); and our prayers, purposes, promises (Ps. 78:34–37; Jer. 2:20; 42:5–6, 20–21), vows (Eccl. 5:4–6; Prov. 20:25), covenants (Lev. 26:25), and engagements to God or men (Prov. 2:17; Ezek. 17:18–19): if done deliberately (Ps. 36:4), wilfully (Jer. 6:16), presumptuously (Num. 15:30; Ex. 21:14), impudently (Jer. 3:3; Prov. 7:13), boastingly (Ps. 52:1), maliciously (3 John 10), frequently (Num. 14:22), obstinately (Zech. 7:11–12), with delight (Prov. 2:14), continuance (Isa. 57:17), or relapsing after repentance (Jer. 34:8–11; 2 Peter 2:20–22).

4. From circumstances of time (2 Kings 5:26) and place (Jer. 7:10; Isa. 26:10): if on the Lord's day (Ezek. 23:37–39), or other times of divine worship (Isa. 58:3–5; Num. 25:6–7); or immediately before (1 Cor. 11:20–21) or after these (Jer. 7:8–10; Prov. 7:14–15; John 13:27, 30), or other helps to prevent or remedy such miscarriages (Ezra 9:13–14): if in public, or in the presence of others, who are thereby likely to be provoked or defiled (2 Sam. 16:22; 1 Sam. 2:22–24).

Q. 152. *What doth every sin deserve at the hands of God?*
A. Every sin, even the least, being against the sovereignty (James 2:10–11), goodness (Ex. 20:1–2), and holiness of God (Hab. 1:13; Lev. 10:3; 11:44–45), and against his righteous law (1 John 3:4; Rom. 7:12), deserveth his wrath and curse (Eph. 5:6; Gal. 3:10), both in this life (Lam. 3:39; Deut. 28:15–68), and in that which is to come (Matt. 25:41); and cannot be expiated but by the blood of Christ (Heb. 9:22; 1 Peter 1:18–19).

Q. 153. *What doth God require of us, that we may escape his wrath and curse due to us by reason of the transgression of the law?*
A. That we may escape the wrath and curse of God due to us by reason of the transgression of the law, he requireth of us repentance toward God, and faith toward our Lord Jesus Christ (Acts 20:21; Matt. 3:7–8; Luke 13:3, 5; Acts 16:30–31; John 3:16, 18), and the diligent use of the outward

means whereby Christ communicates to us the benefits of his mediation Prov. 2:1–5; 8:33–36).

Q. 154. *What are the outward means whereby Christ communicates to us the benefits of his mediation?*
A. The outward and ordinary means whereby Christ communicates to his church the benefits of his mediation, are all his ordinances; especially the word, sacraments, and prayer; all which are made effectual to the elect for their salvation (Matt. 28:19–20; Acts 2:42, 46–47).

Q. 155. *How is the word made effectual to salvation?*
A. The Spirit of God maketh the reading, but especially the preaching of the word, an effectual means of enlightening (Neh. 8:8; Acts 26:18; Ps. 19:8), convincing, and humbling sinners (1 Cor. 14:24–25; 2 Chron. 34:18–19, 26–28); of driving them out of themselves, and drawing them unto Christ (Acts 2:37, 41; 8:27–39); of conforming them to his image (2 Cor. 3:18), and subduing them to his will (2 Cor. 10:4–6; Rom. 6:17); of strengthening them against temptations and corruptions (Matt. 4:4, 7, 10; Eph. 6:16–17; Ps. 19:11; 1 Cor. 10:11); of building them up in grace (Acts 20:32; 2 Tim. 3:15–17), and establishing their hearts in holiness and comfort through faith unto salvation (Rom. 16:25; 1 Thess. 3:2, 10–11, 13; Rom. 15:4; 10:13–17; 1:16).

Q. 156. *Is the word of God to be read by all?*
A. Although all are not to be permitted to read the word publicly to the congregation (Deut. 31:9, 11–13; Neh. 8:2–3; 9:3–5), yet all sort of people are bound to read it apart by themselves (Deut. 17:19; Rev. 1:3; John 5:39; Isa. 34:16), and with their families (Deut. 6:6–9; Gen. 18:17, 19; Ps. 78:5–7): to which end, the holy scriptures are to be translated out of the original into vulgar languages (1 Cor. 14:6, 9, 11–12, 15–16, 24, 27–28).

Q. 157. *How is the word of God to be read?*
A. The holy scriptures are to be read with an high and reverent esteem of them (Ps. 19:10; Neh. 8:3–10; Ex. 24:7; 2 Chron. 34:27; Isa. 66:2); with a firm persuasion that they are the very word of God (2 Peter 1:19–21), and that he only can enable us to understand them (Luke 24:45; 2 Cor. 3:13–16); with desire to know, believe, and obey the will of God revealed in them (Deut. 17:10, 20); with diligence (Acts 17:11), and attention to the matter and scope of them (Acts 8:30, 34; Luke 10:26–28); with meditation

(Ps. 1:2; 119:97), application (2 Chron. 34:21), selfdenial (Prov. 3:5; Deut. 33:3), and prayer (Prov. 2:1–6; Ps. 119:18; Neh. 7:6, 8).

Q. 158. *By whom is the word of God to be preached?*
A. The word of God is to be preached only by such as are sufficiently gifted (1 Tim. 3:2, 6; Eph. 4:8–11; Hos. 4:6; Mal. 2:7; 2 Cor. 3:6), and also duly approved and called to that office (Jer. 14:15; Rom. 10:15; Heb. 5:4; 1 Cor. 12:28–29; 1 Tim. 3:10; 4:14; 5:22).

Q. 159. *How is the word of God to be preached by those that are called thereunto?*
A. They that are called to labour in the ministry of the word, are to preach sound doctrine (Titus 2:1, 8), diligently (Acts 18:25), in season and out of season (2 Tim. 4:2); plainly (1 Cor. 14:19), not in the enticing words of man's wisdom, but in demonstration of the spirit, and of power (1 Cor. 2:4); faithfully (Jer. 23:28; 1 Cor. 4:1–2), making known the whole counsel of God (Acts 20:27); wisely (Col. 1:28; 2 Tim. 2:15), applying themselves to the necessities and capacities of the hearers (1 Cor. 3:2; Heb. 5:12–14; Luke 12:42); zealously (Acts 18:25), with fervent love to God (2 Cor. 5:13–14; Phil. 1:15–17) and the souls of his people (Col. 4:12; 2 Cor. 12:15); sincerely (2 Cor. 2:17; 4:2), aiming at his glory (1 Thess. 2:4–6; John 7:18), and their conversion (1 Cor. 9:19–22), edification (2 Cor. 12:19; Eph. 4:12), and salvation (1 Tim. 4:16; Acts 26:16–18).

Q. 160. *What is required of those that hear the word preached?*
A. It is required of those that hear the word preached, that they attend upon it with diligence (Prov. 8:34), preparation (1 Peter 2:1–2; Luke 8:18), and prayer (Ps. 119:18; Eph. 6:18–19); examine what they hear by the scriptures (Acts 17:11); receive the truth with faith (Heb. 4:2), love (2 Thess. 2:10), meekness (James 1:21), and readiness of mind (Acts 17:11), as the word of God (1 Thess. 2:13); meditate (Luke 9:44; Heb. 2:1), and confer of it (Luke 24:14; Deut. 6:6–7); hide it in their hearts (Prov. 2:1; Ps. 119:11), and bring forth the fruit of it in their lives (Luke 8:15; James 1:25).

Q. 161. *How do the sacraments become effectual means of salvation?*
A. The sacraments become effectual means of salvation, not by any power in themselves, or any virtue derived from the piety or intention of him by whom they are administered, but only by the working of the Holy Ghost,

and the blessing of Christ, by whom they are instituted (1 Peter 3:21; Acts 8:13, 23; 1 Cor. 3:6–7; 12:13).

Q. 162. *What is a sacrament?*
A. A sacrament is an holy ordinance instituted by Christ in his church (Gen. 17:7, 10; Ex. 12; Matt. 28:19; 26:26–28), to signify, seal, and exhibit (Rom. 4:11; 1 Cor. 11:24–25) unto those that are within the covenant of grace (Rom. 15:8; Ex. 12:48), the benefits of his mediation (Acts 2:38; 1 Cor. 10:16); to strengthen and increase their faith, and all other graces (Rom. 4:11; Gal. 3:27); to oblige them to obedience (Rom. 6:3–4; 1 Cor. 10:21); to testify and cherish their love and communion one with another (Eph. 4:2–5; 1 Cor. 12:13); and to distinguish them from those that are without (Eph. 2:11–12; Gen. 34:14).

Q. 163. *What are the parts of a sacrament?*
A. The parts of a sacrament are two; the one an outward and sensible sign, used according to Christ's own appointment; the other an inward and spiritual grace thereby signified (Matt. 3:11; 1 Peter 3:21; Rom. 2:28–29).

Q. 164. *How many sacraments hath Christ instituted in his church under the New Testament?*
A. Under the New Testament Christ hath instituted in his church only two sacraments, baptism and the Lord's supper (Matt. 28:19; 1 Cor. 11:20, 23; Matt. 26:26–28).

Q. 165. *What is baptism?*
A. Baptism is a sacrament of the New Testament, wherein Christ hath ordained the washing with water in the name of the Father, and of the Son, and of the Holy Ghost (Matt. 28:19), to be a sign and seal of ingrafting into himself (Gal. 3:27), of remission of sins by his blood (Mark 1:4; Rev. 1:5), and regeneration by his Spirit (Titus 3:5; Eph. 5:26); of adoption (Gal. 3:26–27), and resurrection unto everlasting life (1 Cor. 15:29; Rom. 6:5); and whereby the parties baptized are solemnly admitted into the visible church (1 Cor. 12:13), and enter into an open and professed engagement to be wholly and only the Lord's (Rom. 6:4).

Q. 166. *Unto whom is baptism to be administered?*
A. Baptism is not to be administered to any that are out of the visible church, and so strangers from the covenant of promise, till they profess

their faith in Christ, and obedience to him (Acts 8:36–37; 2:38), but infants descending from parents, either both, or but one of them, professing faith in Christ, and obedience to him, are in that respect within the covenant, and to be baptized (Gen. 17:7, 9; Gal. 3:9, 14; Col. 2:11–12; Acts 2:38–39; Rom. 4:11–12; 1 Cor. 7:14; Matt. 28:19; Luke 18:15–16; Rom. 11:16).

Q. 167. *How is our baptism to be improved by us?*
A. The needful but much neglected duty of improving our baptism, is to be performed by us all our life long, especially in the time of temptation, and when we are present at the administration of it to others (Col. 2:11–12; Rom. 6:4, 6, 11); by serious and thankful consideration of the nature of it, and of the ends for which Christ instituted it, the privileges and benefits conferred and sealed thereby, and our solemn vow made therein (Rom. 6:3–5); by being humbled for our sinful defilement, our falling short of, and walking contrary to, the grace of baptism, and our engagements (1 Cor. 1:11–13; Rom. 6:2–3); by growing up to assurance of pardon of sin, and of all other blessings sealed to us in that sacrament (Rom. 4:11–12; 1 Peter 3:21); by drawing strength from the death and resurrection of Christ, into whom we are baptized, for the mortifying of sin, and quickening of grace (Rom. 6:3–5); and by endeavouring to live by faith (Gal. 3:26–27), to have our conversation in holiness and righteousness (Rom. 6:22), as those that have therein given up their names to Christ (Acts 2:38); and to walk in brotherly love, as being baptized by the same Spirit into one body (1 Cor. 12:13, 25–27).

Q. 168. *What is the Lord's supper?*
A. The Lord's supper is a sacrament of the New Testament (Luke 22:20), wherein, by giving and receiving bread and wine according to the appointment of Jesus Christ, his death is showed forth; and they that worthily communicate feed upon his body and blood, to their spiritual nourishment and growth in grace (Matt. 26:26–28; 1 Cor. 11:23–26); have their union and communion with him confirmed (1 Cor. 10:16); testify and renew their thankfulness (1 Cor. 11:24), and engagement to God (1 Cor. 10:14–16, 21), and their mutual love and fellowship each with the other, as members of the same mystical body (1 Cor. 10:17).

Q. 169. *How hath Christ appointed bread and wine to be given and received in the sacrament of the Lord's supper?*

A. Christ hath appointed the ministers of his word, in the administration of this sacrament of the Lord's supper, to set apart the bread and wine from common use, by the word of institution, thanksgiving, and prayer; to take and break the bread, and to give both the bread and the wine to the communicants: who are, by the same appointment, to take and eat the bread, and to drink the wine, in thankful remembrance that the body of Christ was broken and given, and his blood shed, for them (1 Cor. 11:23–24; Matt. 26:26–28; Mark 14:22–24; Luke 22:19–20).

Q. 170. *How do they that worthily communicate in the Lord's supper feed upon the body and blood of Christ therein?*

A. As the body and blood of Christ are not corporally or carnally present in, with, or under the bread and wine in the Lord's supper (Acts 3:21), and yet are spiritually present to the faith of the receiver, no less truly and really than the elements themselves are to their outward senses (Matt. 26:26, 28); so they that worthily communicate in the sacrament of the Lord's supper, do therein feed upon the body and blood of Christ, not after a corporal and carnal, but in a spiritual manner; yet truly and really (1 Cor. 11:24–29), while by faith they receive and apply unto themselves Christ crucified, and all the benefits of his death (1 Cor. 10:16).

Q. 171. *How are they that receive the sacrament of the Lord's supper to prepare themselves before they come unto it?*

A. They that receive the sacrament of the Lord's supper are, before they come, to prepare themselves thereunto, by examining themselves (1 Cor. 11:28) of their being in Christ (2 Cor. 13:5), of their sins and wants (1 Cor. 5:7; Ex. 12:15); of the truth and measure of their knowledge (1 Cor. 11:29), faith (1 Cor. 13:5; Matt. 26:28), repentance (Zech. 12:10; 1 Cor. 11:31); love to God and brethren (1 Cor. 10:16–17; Acts 2:46–47), charity to all men (1 Cor. 5:8; 11:18, 20), forgiving those that have done them wrong (Matt. 5:23–24); of their desires after Christ (Isa. 55:1; John 7:37), and of their new obedience (1 Cor. 5:7–8); and by renewing the exercise of these graces (1 Cor. 11:25–26, 28; Heb. 10:21–22, 24; Ps. 26:6), by serious meditation (1 Cor. 11:24–25), and fervent prayer (2 Chron. 30:18–19; Matt. 26:26).

Q. 172. *May one who doubteth of his being in Christ, or of his due preparation, come to the Lord's supper?*

A. One who doubteth of his being in Christ, or of his due preparation to the sacrament of the Lord's supper, may have true interest in Christ, though he be not yet assured thereof (Isa. 50:10; 1 John 5:13; Ps. 88; 77:1– 12; Jonah 2:4, 7); and in God's account hath it, if he be duly affected with the apprehension of the want of it (Isa. 54:7–10; Matt. 5:3–4; Ps. 31:22; 73:13, 22–23), and unfeignedly desires to be found in Christ (Phil. 3:8–9; Ps. 10:17; 42:1–2, 5, 11), and to depart from iniquity (2 Tim. 2:19; Isa. 50:10; Ps. 66:18–20): in which case (because promises are made, and this sacrament is appointed, for the relief even of weak and doubting Christians [Isa. 40:11, 29, 31; Matt. 11:28; 12:20; 26:28]) he is to bewail his unbelief (Mark 9:24), and labour to have his doubts resolved (Acts 2:37; 16:30); and, so doing, he may and ought to come to the Lord's supper, that he may be further strengthened (Rom. 4:11; 1 Cor. 11:28).

Q. 173. *May any who profess the faith, and desire to come to the Lord's supper, be kept from it?*

A. Such as are found to be ignorant or scandalous, notwithstanding their profession of the faith, and desire to come to the Lord's supper, may and ought to be kept from that sacrament, by the power which Christ hath left in his church (1 Cor. 11:27–34; Matt. 7:6; 1 Cor. 5; Jude 23; 1 Tim. 5:22), until they receive instruction, and manifest their reformation (2 Cor. 2:7).

Q. 174. *What is required of them that receive the sacrament of the Lord's supper in the time of the administration of it?*

A. It is required of them that receive the Lord's supper, that, during the time of the administration of it, with all holy reverence and attention they wait upon God in that ordinance (Lev. 10:3; Heb. 12:28; Ps. 5:7; 1 Cor. 11:17, 26–27), diligently observe the sacramental elements and actions (Ex. 24:8; Matt. 26:28), heedfully discern the Lord's body (1 Cor. 11:29), and affectionately meditate on his death and sufferings (Luke 22:19), and thereby stir up themselves to a vigorous exercise of their graces (1 Cor. 11:26; 10:3–5, 11, 14); in judging themselves (1 Cor. 11:31), and sorrowing for sin (Zech. 12:10); in earnest hungering and thirsting after Christ (Rev. 22:17), feeding on him by faith (John 6:35), receiving of his fullness (John 1:16), trusting in his merits (Phil. 1:16), rejoicing in his love (Ps. 63:4–5; 2 Chron. 30:21), giving thanks for his grace (Ps. 22:26); in renewing of their covenant with God (Jer. 50:5; Ps. 50:5), and love to all the saints (Acts 2:42).

Q. 175. *What is the duty of Christians, after they have received the sacrament of the Lord's supper?*
A. The duty of Christians, after they have received the sacrament of the Lord's supper, is seriously to consider how they have behaved themselves therein, and with what success (Ps. 28:7; 85:8; 1 Cor. 11:17, 30–31); if they find quickening and comfort, to bless God for it (2 Chron. 30:21–23, 25–26; Acts 2:42, 46–47), beg the continuance of it (Ps. 36:10; Song 3:4; 1 Chron. 29:18), watch against relapses (1 Cor. 10:3–5, 12), fulfil their vows (Ps. 50:14), and encourage themselves to a frequent attendance on that ordinance (1 Cor. 11:25–26; Acts 2:42, 46): but if they find no present benefit, more exactly to review their preparation to, and carriage at, the sacrament (Song 5:1–6; Eccl. 5:1–6); in both which, if they can approve themselves to God and their own consciences, they are to wait for the fruit of it in due time (Ps. 123:1–2; 42:5, 8; 43:3–5): but, if they see they have failed in either, they are to be humbled (2 Chron. 30:18–19; Isa. 1:16, 18), and to attend upon it afterwards with more care and diligence (2 Cor. 7:11; 1 Chron. 15:12–14).

Q. 176. *Wherein do the sacraments of baptism and the Lord's supper agree?*
A. The sacraments of baptism and the Lord's supper agree, in that the author of both is God (Matt. 28:19; 1 Cor. 11:23); the spiritual part of both is Christ and his benefits (Rom. 6:3–4; 1 Cor. 10:16); both are seals of the same covenant (Rom. 4:11; Col. 2:12; Matt. 26:27–28), are to be dispensed by ministers of the gospel, and by none other (John 1:33; Matt. 28:19; 1 Cor. 11:23; 4:1; Heb. 5:4); and to be continued in the church of Christ until his second coming (Matt. 28:19–20; 1 Cor. 11:26).

Q. 177. *Wherein do the sacraments of baptism and the Lord's supper differ?*
A. The sacrament of baptism and the Lord's supper differ, in that baptism is to be administered but once, with water, to be a sign and seal of our regeneration and ingrafting into Christ (Matt. 3:11; Titus 3:5; Gal. 3:27), and that even to infants (Gen. 17:7, 9; Acts 2:38–39; 1 Cor. 7:14); whereas the Lord's supper is to be administered often, in the elements of bread and wine, to represent and exhibit Christ as spiritual nourishment to the soul (1 Cor. 11:23–26), and to confirm our continuance and growth in him

(1 Cor. 10:16), and that only to such as are of years and ability to examine themselves (1 Cor. 11:28–29).

Q. 178. *What is prayer?*
A. Prayer is an offering up of our desires unto God (Ps. 62:8), in the name of Christ (John 16:23), by the help of his Spirit (Rom. 8:26); with confession of our sins (Ps. 32:5–6; Dan. 9:4), and thankful acknowledgement of his mercies (Phil. 4:6).

Q. 179. *Are we to pray unto God only?*
A. God only being able to search the hearts (1 Kings 8:39; Acts 1:24; Rom. 8:27), hear the requests (Ps. 65:2), pardon the sins (Mic. 7:18), and fulfil the desires of all (Ps. 145:18–19); and only to be believed in (Rom. 10:14), and worshipped with religious worship (Matt. 4:10); prayer, which is a special part thereof (1 Cor. 1:2), is to be made by all to him alone (Ps. 50:15), and to none other (Rom. 10:14).

Q. 180. *What is it to pray in the name of Christ?*
A. To pray in the name of Christ is, in obedience to his command, and in confidence on his promises, to ask mercy for his sake (John 14:13–14; 16:24; Dan. 9:17); not by bare mentioning of his name (Matt. 7:21), but by drawing our encouragement to pray, and our boldness, strength, and hope of acceptance in prayer, from Christ and his mediation (Heb. 4:14–16; 1 John 5:13–15).

Q. 181. *Why are we to pray in the name of Christ?*
A. The sinfulness of man, and his distance from God by reason thereof, being so great, as that we can have no access into his presence without a mediator (John 14:6; Isa. 59:2; Eph. 3:12); and there being none in heaven or earth appointed to, or fit for, that glorious work but Christ alone (John 6:27; Heb. 7:25–27; 1 Tim. 2:5), we are to pray in no other name but his only (Col. 3:17; Heb. 13:15).

Q. 182. *How doth the Spirit help us to pray?*
A. We not knowing what to pray for as we ought, the Spirit helpeth our infirmities, by enabling us to understand both for whom, and what, and how prayer is to be made; and by working and quickening in our hearts (although not in all persons, nor at all times, in the same measure) those

apprehensions, affections, and graces which are requisite for the right performance of that duty (Rom. 8:26–27; Ps. 10:17; Zech. 12:10).

Q. 183. *For whom are we to pray?*
A. We are to pray for the whole church of Christ upon earth (Eph. 6:18; Ps. 28:9); for magistrates (1 Tim. 2:1–2), and ministers (Col. 4:3); for ourselves (Gen. 32:11), our brethren (James 5:16), yea, our enemies (Matt. 5:44); and for all sorts of men living (1 Tim. 2:1–2), or that shall live hereafter (John 17:20; 2 Sam. 7:29); but not for the dead (2 Sam. 12:21–23), nor for those that are known to have sinned the sin unto death (1 John 5:16).

Q. 184. *For what things are we to pray?*
A. We are to pray for all things tending to the glory of God (Matt. 6:9), the welfare of the church (Ps. 51:18; 122:6), our own (Matt. 7:11) or others good (Ps. 125:4); but not for any thing that is unlawful (1 John 5:14).

Q. 185. *How are we to pray?*
A. We are to pray with an awful apprehension of the majesty of God (Eccl. 5:1), and deep sense of our own unworthiness (Gen. 18:27; 32:10), necessities (Luke 15:17–19), and sins (Luke 18:13–14); with penitent (Ps. 51:17), thankful (Phil. 4:6), and enlarged hearts (1 Sam. 1:15; 2:1); with understanding (1 Cor. 14:15), faith (Mark 11:24; James 1:6), sincerity (Ps. 145:18; 17:1), fervency (James 5:16), love (1 Tim. 2:8), and perseverance (Eph. 6:18), waiting upon him (Mic. 7:7), with humble submission to his will (Matt. 26:39).

Q. 186. *What rule hath God given for our direction in the duty of prayer?*
A. The whole word of God is of use to direct us in the duty of prayer (1 John 5:14); but the special rule of direction is that form of prayer which our Saviour Christ taught his disciples, commonly called *The Lord's Prayer* (Matt. 6:9–13; Luke 11:2–4).

Q. 187. *How is the Lord's prayer to be used?*
A. The Lord's prayer is not only for direction, as a pattern, according to which we are to make other prayers; but may also be used as a prayer, so that it be done with understanding, faith, reverence, and other graces necessary to the right performance of the duty of prayer (Matt. 6:9; Luke 11:2).

Q. 188. *Of how many parts doth the Lord's prayer consist?*
A. The Lord's prayer consists of three parts; a preface, petitions, and a conclusion.

Q. 189. *What doth the preface of the Lord's prayer teach us?*
A. The preface of the Lord's prayer (contained in these words, *Our Father which art in heaven*, [Matt. 6:9]) teacheth us, when we pray, to draw near to God with confidence of his fatherly goodness, and our interest therein (Luke 11:13; Rom. 8:15); with reverence, and all other childlike dispositions (Isa. 64:9), heavenly affections (Ps. 123:1; Lam. 3:41), and due apprehensions of his sovereign power, majesty, and gracious condescension (Isa. 63:15–16; Neh. 1:4–6): as also, to pray with and for others (Acts 12:5).

Q. 190. *What do we pray for in the first petition?*
A. In the first petition, (which is, *Hallowed be thy name*, [Matt. 6:9]) acknowledging the utter inability and indisposition that is in ourselves and all men to honour God aright (2 Cor. 3:5; Ps. 51:15), we pray, that God would by his grace enable and incline us and others to know, to acknowledge, and highly to esteem him (Ps. 67:2–3), his titles (Ps. 83:18), attributes (Ps. 86:10–13, 15), ordinances, word (2 Thess. 3:1; Ps. 147:19–20; 138:1–3; 2 Cor. 2:14–15), works, and whatsoever he is pleased to make himself known by (Pss. 145; 8); and to glorify him in thought, word (Ps. 103:1; 19:14), and deed (Phil. 1:9, 11): that he would prevent and remove atheism (Ps. 67:1–4), ignorance (Eph. 1:17–18), idolatry (Ps. 97:7), profaneness (Ps. 74:18, 22–23), and whatsoever is dishonourable to him (2 Kings 19:15–16); and, by his overruling providence, direct and dispose of all things to his own glory (2 Chron. 20:6, 10–12; Ps. 83; 140:4, 8).

Q. 191. *What do we pray for in the second petition?*
A. In the second petition, (which is, *Thy kingdom come*, [Matt. 6:10]) acknowledging ourselves and all mankind to be by nature under the dominion of sin and Satan (Eph. 2:2–3), we pray, that the kingdom of sin and Satan may be destroyed (Ps. 67:1, 18; Rev. 12:10–11), the gospel propagated throughout the world (2 Thess. 3:1), the Jews called (Rom. 10:1), the fullness of the Gentiles brought in (John 17:9, 20; Rom. 11:25–26; Ps. 67); the church furnished with all gospel officers and ordinances (Matt. 9:38; 2 Thess. 3:1), purged from corruption (Mal. 1:11; Zeph. 3:9), countenanced and maintained by the civil magistrate (1 Tim. 2:1–2): that

the ordinances of Christ may be purely dispensed, and made effectual to the converting of those that are yet in their sins, and the confirming, comforting, and building up of those that are already converted (Acts 4:29–30; Eph. 6:18–20; Rom. 15:29–30, 32; 2 Thess. 1:11; 2:16–17): that Christ would rule in our hearts here (Eph. 3:14–20), and hasten the time of his second coming, and our reigning with him for ever (Rev. 22:20): and that he would be pleased so to exercise the kingdom of his power in all the world, as may best conduce to these ends (Isa. 64:1–2; Rev. 4:8–11).

Q. 192. *What do we pray for in the third petition?*
A. In the third petition, (which is, *Thy will be done in earth, as it is in heaven,* [Matt. 6:10]) acknowledging, that by nature we and all men are not only utterly unable and unwilling to know and do the will of God (Rom. 7:18; Job 21:14; 1 Cor. 2:14), but prone to rebel against his word (Rom. 8:7), to repine and murmur against his providence (Ex. 17:7; Num. 14:2), and wholly inclined to do the will of the flesh, and of the devil (Eph. 2:2): we pray, that God would by his Spirit take away from ourselves and others all blindness (Eph. 1:17–18), weakness (Eph. 3:16), indisposedness (Matt. 26:40–41), and perverseness of heart (Jer. 31:18–19); and by his grace make us able and willing to know, do, and submit to his will in all things (Ps. 119:1, 8, 35; Acts 21:14), with the like humility (Mic. 6:8), cheerfulness (Ps. 100:2; Job 1:21; 2 Sam. 15:25–26), faithfulness (Isa. 38:3), diligence (Ps. 119:4–5), zeal (Rom. 12:11), sincerity (Ps. 119:80), and constancy (Ps. 119:112), as the angels do in heaven (Isa. 6:2–3; Ps. 103:20–21; Matt. 18:10).

Q. 193. *What do we pray for in the fourth petition?*
A. In the fourth petition, (which is, *Give us this day our daily bread,* [Matt. 6:11]) acknowledging, that in Adam, and by our own sin, we have forfeited our right to all the outward blessings of this life, and deserve to be wholly deprived of them by God, and to have them cursed to us in the use of them (Gen. 2:17; 3:17; Rom. 8:20–22; Jer. 5:25; Deut. 28:15–22); and that neither they of themselves are able to sustain us (Deut. 8:3), nor we to merit (Gen. 32:10), or by our own industry to procure them (Deut. 8:17–18); but prone to desire (Jer. 6:13; Mark 7:21–22), get (Hos. 12:7), and use them unlawfully (James 4:3): we pray for ourselves and others, that both they and we, waiting upon the providence of God from day to day in the use of lawful means, may, of his free gift, and as to his fatherly wisdom shall seem best, enjoy a competent portion of them (Gen. 43:12–14; 28:20;

Eph. 4:28; 2 Thess. 3:11–12; Phil. 4:6); and have the same continued and blessed unto us in our holy and comfortable use of them (1 Tim. 4:3–5), and contentment in them (1 Tim. 6:6–8); and be kept from all things that are contrary to our temporal support and comfort (Prov. 30:8–9).

Q. 194. *What do we pray for in the fifth petition?*
A. In the fifth petition, (which is, *Forgive us our debts, as we forgive our debtors,*[Matt. 6:12]) acknowledging, that we and all others are guilty both of original and actual sin, and thereby become debtors to the justice of God; and that neither we, nor any other creature, can make the least satisfaction for that debt (Rom. 3:9–22; Matt. 18:24–25; Ps. 130:3–4): we pray for ourselves and others, that God of his free grace would, through the obedience and satisfaction of Christ, apprehended and applied by faith, acquit us both from the guilt and punishment of sin (Rom. 3:24–26; Heb. 9:22), accept us in his Beloved (Eph. 1:6–7); continue his favour and grace to us (2 Peter 1:2), pardon our daily failings (Hos. 14:2; Jer. 14:7), and fill us with peace and joy, in giving us daily more and more assurance of forgiveness (Rom. 15:13; Ps. 51:7–10, 12); which we are the rather emboldened to ask, and encouraged to expect, when we have this testimony in ourselves, that we from the heart forgive others their offences (Luke 11:4; Matt. 6:14–15; 18:35).

Q. 195. *What do we pray for in the sixth petition?*
A. In this petition, (which is, *And lead us not into temptation, but deliver us from evil,* [Matt. 6:13]) acknowledging, that the most wise, righteous, and gracious God, for divers holy and just ends, may so order things, that we may be assaulted, foiled, and for a time led captive by temptations (2 Chron. 32:31); that Satan (1 Chron. 21:1), the world (Luke 21:34; Mark 4:19), and the flesh, are ready powerfully to draw us aside, and ensnare us (James 1:14); and that we, even after the pardon of our sins, by reason of our corruption (Gal. 5:17), weakness, and want of watchfulness (Matt. 26:41), are not only subject to be tempted, and forward to expose ourselves unto temptations (Matt. 26:69–72; Gal. 2:11–14; 2 Chron. 18:3; 19:2), but also of ourselves unable and unwilling to resist them, to recover out of them, and to improve them (Rom. 7:23–24; 1 Chron. 21:1–4; 2 Chron. 16:7–10); and worthy to be left under the power of them (Ps. 81:11–12): we pray, that God would so overrule the world and all in it (John 17:15), subdue the flesh (Ps. 51:10; 119:133), and restrain Satan (2 Cor. 12:7–8),

order all things (1 Cor. 10:12–13), bestow and bless all means of grace (Heb. 13:20–21), and quicken us to watchfulness in the use of them, that we and all his people may by his providence be kept from being tempted to sin (Matt. 26:41; Ps. 19:13); or, if tempted, that by his Spirit we may be powerfully supported and enabled to stand in the hour of temptation (Eph. 3:14–17; 1 Thess. 3:13; Jude 24); or when fallen, raised again and recovered out of it (Ps. 51:12), and have a sanctified use and improvement thereof (1 Peter 5:8–10): that our sanctification and salvation may be perfected (2 Cor. 13:7, 9), Satan trodden under our feet (Rom. 16:20; Zech. 3:2; Luke 22:31–32), and we fully freed from sin, temptation, and all evil, for ever (John 17:15; 1 Thess. 5:23).

Q. 196. *What doth the conclusion of the Lord's prayer teach us?*
A. The conclusion of the Lord's prayer, (which is, *For thine is the kingdom, and the power, and the glory, for ever. Amen.*[Matt. 6:13]) teacheth us to enforce our petitions with arguments (Rom. 15:30), which are to be taken, not from any worthiness in ourselves, or in any other creature, but from God (Dan. 9:4, 7–9, 16–19); and with our prayers to join praises (Phil. 4:6), ascribing to God alone eternal sovereignty, omnipotency, and glorious excellency (1 Chron. 29:10–13); in regard whereof, as he is able and willing to help us (Eph. 3:20–21; Luke 11:13), so we by faith are emboldened to plead with him that he would (2 Chron. 20:6, 11), and quietly to rely upon him, that he will fulfil our requests (2 Chron. 14:11). And, to testify this our desire and assurance, we say, *Amen* (1 Cor. 14:16; Rev. 22:20–21).

115

Westminster Shorter
Catechism (1647)

For historical background, see the introduction to the Westminster Confession of Faith (1646) in this volume, pp. 231–33. We have printed this version of the original text as published by the Publications Committee of the Free Presbyterian Church of Scotland (1970), 285–318; it appears here with their kind permission. We have inserted the Scripture proofs in the body of the catechism without printing the entire text of the passages, as the Free Presbyterian Church version does.

THE SHORTER CATECHISM.

Quest. 1. *WHAT is the chief end of man?*
Ans. Man's chief end is to glorify God (1 Cor. 10:31; Rom. 11:36), and to enjoy him for ever (Ps. 73:25–28).

Q. 2. *What rule hath God given to direct us how we may glorify and enjoy him?*
A. The word of God, which is contained in the scriptures of the Old and New Testaments (2 Tim. 3:16; Eph. 2:20), is the only rule to direct us how we may glorify and enjoy him (1 John 1:3–4).

Q. 3. *What do the scriptures principally teach?*
A. The scriptures principally teach what man is to believe concerning God, and what duty God requires of man (2 Tim. 1:13; 3:16).

Q. 4. *What is God?*
A. God is a Spirit (John 4:24), infinite (Job 11:7–9), eternal (Ps. 90:2), and unchangeable (James 1:17), in his being (Ex. 3:14), wisdom (Ps. 147:5),

power (Rev. 4:8), holiness (Rev. 15:4), justice, goodness, and truth (Ex. 34:6–7).

Q. 5. *Are there more Gods than one?*
A. There is but One only, the living and true God (Deut. 6:4; Jer. 10:10).

Q. 6. *How many persons are there in the Godhead?*
A. There are three persons in the Godhead; the Father, the Son, and the Holy Ghost; and these three are one God, the same in substance, equal in power and glory (1 John 5:7; Matt. 28:19).

Q. 7. *What are the decrees of God?*
A. The decrees of God are, his eternal purpose, according to the counsel of his will, whereby, for his own glory, he hath foreordained whatsoever comes to pass (Eph. 1:4, 11; Rom. 9:22–23).

Q. 8. *How doth God execute his decrees?*
A. God executeth his decrees in the works of creation and providence.

Q. 9. *What is the work of creation?*
A. The work of creation is, God's making all things of nothing, by the word of his power, in the space of six days, and all very good (Gen. 1; Heb. 11:3).

Q. 10. *How did God create man?*
A. God created man male and female, after his own image, in knowledge, righteousness, and holiness, with dominion over the creatures (Gen. 1:26–28; Col. 3:10; Eph. 4:24).

Q. 11. *What are God's works of providence?*
A. God's works of providence are, his most holy (Ps. 145:17), wise (Ps. 104:24; Isa. 28:29), and powerful preserving (Heb. 1:3) and governing all his creatures, and all their actions (Ps. 103:19; Matt. 10:29–31).

Q. 12. *What special act of providence did God exercise toward man in the estate wherein he was created?*
A. When God had created man, he entered into a covenant of life with him, upon condition of perfect obedience; forbidding him to eat of the tree of the knowledge of good and evil, upon the pain of death (Gal. 3:12; Gen. 2:17).

Q. 13. *Did our first parents continue in the estate wherein they were created?*
A. Our first parents, being left to the freedom of their own will, fell from the estate wherein they were created, by sinning against God (Gen. 3:6–8, 13; Eccl. 7:29).

Q. 14. *What is sin?*
A. Sin is any want of conformity unto, or transgression of, the law of God (1 John 3:4).

Q. 15. *What was the sin whereby our first parents fell from the estate wherein they were created?*
A. The sin whereby our first parents fell from the estate wherein they were created, was their eating the forbidden fruit (Gen. 3:6, 12).

Q. 16. *Did all mankind fall in Adam's first transgression?*
A. The covenant being made with Adam, not only for himself, but for his posterity; all mankind, descending from him by ordinary generation, sinned in him, and fell with him, in his first transgression (Gen. 2:16–17; Rom. 5:12; 1 Cor. 15:21–22).

Q. 17. *Into what estate did the fall bring mankind?*
A. The fall brought mankind into an estate of sin and misery (Rom. 5:12).

Q. 18. *Wherein consists the sinfulness of that estate whereinto man fell?*
A. The sinfulness of that estate whereinto man fell, consists in the guilt of Adam's first sin, the want of original righteousness, and the corruption of his whole nature, which is commonly called Original Sin; together with all actual transgressions which proceed from it (Rom. 5:12, 19; 5:10–20; Eph. 2:1–3; James 1:14–15; Matt. 15:19).

Q. 19. *What is the misery of that estate whereinto man fell?*
A. All mankind by their fall lost communion with God (Gen. 3:8, 10, 24), are under his wrath and curse (Eph. 2:2–3; Gal. 3:10), and so made liable to all miseries in this life, to death itself, and to the pains of hell for ever (Lam. 3:39; Rom. 6:23; Matt. 25:41, 46).

Q. 20. *Did God leave all mankind to perish in the estate of sin and misery?*
A. God having, out of his mere good pleasure, from all eternity, elected some to everlasting life (Eph. 1:4), did enter into a covenant of grace, to

deliver them out of the estate of sin and misery, and to bring them into an estate of salvation by a Redeemer (Rom. 3:20–22; Gal. 3:21–22).

Q. 21. *Who is the Redeemer of God's elect?*
A. The only Redeemer of God's elect is the Lord Jesus Christ (1 Tim. 2:5–6), who, being the eternal Son of God, became man (John 1:14; Gal. 4:4), and so was, and continueth to be, God and man in two distinct natures, and one person, for ever (Rom. 9:5; Luke 1:35; Col. 2:9; Heb. 7:24–25).

Q. 22. *How did Christ, being the Son of God, become man?*
A. Christ, the Son of God, became man, by taking to himself a true body (Heb. 2:14, 16; 10:5), and a reasonable soul (Matt. 26:38), being conceived by the power of the Holy Ghost, in the womb of the virgin Mary, and born of her (Luke 1:27, 31, 35, 42; Gal. 4:4), yet without sin (Heb. 4:15; 7:26).

Q. 23. *What offices doth Christ execute as our Redeemer?*
A. Christ, as our Redeemer, executeth the offices of a prophet, of a priest, and of a king, both in his estate of humiliation and exaltation (Acts 3:21–22; Heb. 12:25; 2 Cor. 13:3; Heb. 5:5–7; 7:25; Ps. 2:6; Isa. 9:6–7; Matt. 21:5; Ps. 2:8–11).

Q. 24. *How doth Christ execute the office of a prophet?*
A. Christ executeth the office of a prophet, in revealing us, by his word and Spirit, the will of God for our salvation (John 1:18; 1 Peter 1:10–12; John 15:15; 20:31).

Q. 25. *How doth Christ execute the office of a priest?*
A. Christ executeth the office of a priest, in his once offering up of himself a sacrifice to satisfy divine justice (Heb. 9:14, 28), and reconcile us to God (Heb. 2:17); and in making continual intercession for us (Heb. 7:24–25).

Q. 26. *How doth Christ execute the office of a king?*
A. Christ executeth the office of a king, in subduing us to himself (Acts 15:14–16), in ruling (Isa. 33:22) and defending us (Isa. 32:1–2), and in restraining and conquering all his and our enemies (1 Cor. 15:25).

Q. 27. *Wherein did Christ's humiliation consist?*
A. Christ's humiliation consisted in his being born, and that in a low condition (Luke 2:7), made under the law (Gal. 4:4), undergoing the miseries of this life (Heb. 12:2–3; Isa. 53:2–3), the wrath of God (Luke

22:44; Matt. 27:46), and the cursed death of the cross (Phil. 2:8); in being buried (1 Cor. 15:3–4), and continuing under the power of death for a time (Acts 2:24–27, 31).

Q. 28. *Wherein consisteth Christ's exaltation?*
A. Christ's exaltation consisteth in his rising again from the dead on the third day (1 Cor. 15:4), in ascending up into heaven (Mark 16:19), in sitting at the right hand of God the Father (Eph. 1:20), and in coming to judge the world at the last day (Acts 1:11; 17:31).

Q. 29. *How are we made partakers of the redemption purchased by Christ?*
A. We are made partakers of the redemption purchased by Christ, by the effectual application of it to us (John 1:11–12) by his Holy Spirit (Titus 3:5–6).

Q. 30. *How doth the Spirit apply to us the redemption purchased by Christ?*
A. The Spirit applieth to us the redemption purchased by Christ, by working faith in us (Eph. 1:13–14; John 6:37, 39; Eph. 2:8), and thereby uniting us to Christ in our effectual calling (Eph. 3:17; 1 Cor. 1:9).

Q. 31. *What is effectual calling?*
A. Effectual calling is the work of God's Spirit (2 Tim. 1:9; 2 Thess. 2:13–14), whereby, convincing us of our sin and misery (Acts 2:37), enlightening our minds in the knowledge of Christ (Acts 26:18), and renewing our wills (Ezek. 36:26–27), he doth persuade and enable us to embrace Jesus Christ, freely offered to us in the gospel (John 6:44–45; Phil. 2:13).

Q. 32. *What benefits do they that are effectually called partake of in this life?*
A. They that are effectually called do in this life partake of justification (Rom. 8:30), adoption (Eph. 1:5), and sanctification, and the several benefits which in this life do either accompany or flow from them (1 Cor. 1:26, 30).

Q. 33. *What is justification?*
A. Justification is an act of God's free grace, wherein he pardoneth all our sins (Rom. 3:24–25; 4:6–8), and accepteth us as righteous in his sight (2 Cor. 5:19, 21), only for the righteousness of Christ imputed to us (Rom. 5:17–19), and received by faith alone (Gal. 2:16; Phil. 3:9).

Q. 34. *What is adoption?*
A. Adoption is an act of God's free grace (1 John 3:1), whereby we are received into the number, and have a right to all the privileges of the sons of God (John 1:12; Rom. 8:17).

Q. 35. *What is sanctification?*
A. Sanctification is the work of God's free grace (2 Thess. 2:13), whereby we are renewed in the whole man after the image of God (Eph. 4:23–24), and are enabled more and more to die unto sin, and live unto righteousness (Rom. 6:4, 6; Rom. 8:1).

Q. 36. *What are the benefits which in this life do accompany or flow from justification, adoption, and sanctification?*
A. The benefits which in this life do accompany or flow from justification, adoption, and sanctification, are, assurance of God's love, peace of conscience (Rom. 5:1–2, 5), joy in the Holy Ghost (Rom. 14:17), increase of grace (Prov. 4:18), and perseverance therein to the end (1 John 5:13; 1 Peter 1:5).

Q. 37. *What benefits do believers receive from Christ at death?*
A. The souls of believers are at their death made perfect in holiness (Heb. 12:23), and do immediately pass into glory (2 Cor. 5:1, 6, 8; Phil. 1:23; Luke 23:43); and their bodies, being still united to Christ (1 Thess. 4:14), do rest in their graves (Isa. 57:2) till the resurrection (Job 19:26–27).

Q. 38. *What benefits do believers receive from Christ at the resurrection?*
A. At the resurrection, believers being raised up in glory (1 Cor. 15:43), shall be openly acknowledged and acquitted in the day of judgment (Matt. 25:23; 10:32), and made perfectly blessed in the full enjoying of God (1 John 3:2; 1 Cor. 13:12) to all eternity (1 Thess. 4:17–18).

Q. 39. *What is the duty which God requireth of man?*
A. The duty which God requireth of man, is obedience to his revealed will (Mic. 6:8; 1 Sam. 15:22).

Q. 40. *What did God at first reveal to man for the rule of his obedience?*
A. The rule which God at first revealed to man for his obedience, was the moral law (Rom. 2:14–15; 10:5).

Q. 41. *Where is the moral law summarily comprehended?*
A. The moral law is summarily comprehended in the ten commandments (Deut. 10:4; Matt. 19:17).

Q. 42. *What is the sum of the ten commandments?*
A. The sum of the ten commandments is, To love the Lord our God with all our heart, with all our soul, with all our strength, and with all our mind; and our neighbour as ourselves (Matt. 22:37–40).

Q. 43. *What is the preface to the ten commandments?*
A. The preface to the ten commandments is in these words, *I am the Lord thy God which have brought thee out of the land of Egypt, out of the house of bondage* (Ex. 20:2).

Q. 44. *What doth the preface to the ten commandments teach us?*
A. The preface to the ten commandments teacheth us, That because God is the Lord, and our God, and Redeemer, therefore we are bound to keep all his commandments (Luke 1:74–75; 1 Peter 1:15–19).

Q. 45. *Which is the first commandment?*
A. The first commandment is, *Thou shalt have no other gods before me* (Ex. 20:3).

Q. 46. *What is required in the first commandment?*
A. The first commandment requireth us to know and acknowledge God to be the only true God, and our God (1 Chron. 28:9; Deut. 26:17); and to worship and glorify him accordingly (Matt. 4:10; Ps. 29:2).

Q. 47. *What is forbidden in the first commandment?*
A. The first commandment forbiddeth the denying (Ps. 14:1), or not worshipping and glorifying the true God as God (Rom. 1:21), and our God (Ps. 81:10–11); and the giving of that worship and glory to any other, which is due to him alone (Rom. 1:25–26).

Q. 48. *What are we specially taught by these words [before me] in the first commandment?*
A. These words [*before me*] in the first commandment teach us, That God, who seeth all things, taketh notice of, and is much displeased with, the sin of having any other god (Ezek. 8:5–6; Ps. 46:20–21).

Q. 49. *Which is the second commandment?*

A. The second commandment is, *Thou shalt not make unto thee any graven image, or any likeness of any thing that is in heaven above, or that is in the earth beneath, or that is in the water under the earth: thou shalt not bow down thyself to them, nor serve them: for I the Lord thy God am a jealous God, visiting the iniquity of the fathers upon the children unto the third and fourth generation of them that hate me; and shewing mercy unto thousands of them that love me, and keep my commandments* (Ex. 20:4–6).

Q. 50. *What is required in the second commandment?*

A. The second commandment requireth the receiving, observing, and keeping pure and entire, all such religious worship and ordinances as God hath appointed in his word (Deut. 32:46; Matt. 28:20; Acts 2:42).

Q. 51. *What is forbidden in the second commandment?*

A. The second commandment forbiddeth the worshipping of God by images (Deut. 4:15–19; Ex. 32:5, 8), or any other way not appointed in his word (Deut. 12:31–32).

Q. 52. *What are the reasons annexed to the second commandment?*

A. The reasons annexed to the second commandment are, God's sovereignty over us (Ps. 95:2–3, 6), his propriety in us (Ps. 45:11), and the zeal he hath to his own worship (Ex. 34:13–14).

Q. 53. *Which is the third commandment?*

A. The third commandment is, *Thou shalt not take the name of the Lord thy God in vain: for the Lord will not hold him guiltless that taketh his name in vain* (Ex. 20:7).

Q. 54. *What is required in the third commandment?*

A. The third commandment requireth the holy and reverent use of God's names (Matt. 6:9; Deut. 28:58), titles (Ps. 68:4), attributes (Rev. 15:3–4), ordinances (Mal. 1:11, 14), word (Ps. 138:1–2), and works (Job 36:24).

Q. 55. *What is forbidden in the third commandment?*

A. The third commandment forbiddeth all profaning or abusing of any thing whereby God maketh himself known (Mal. 1:6–7, 12; 2:2; 3:14).

Q. 56. *What is the reason annexed to the third commandment?*
A. The reason annexed to the third commandment is, That however the breakers of this commandment may escape punishment from men, yet the Lord our God will not suffer them to escape his righteous judgment (1 Sam. 2:12, 17, 22, 29; 3:13; Deut. 28:58–59).

Q. 57. *Which is the fourth commandment?*
A. The fourth commandment is, *Remember the sabbath-day, to keep it holy. Six days shalt thou labour, and do all thy work: but the seventh day is the sabbath of the Lord thy God: in it thou shalt not do any work, thou, nor thy son, nor thy daughter, thy man-servant, nor thy maid-servant, nor thy cattle, nor thy stranger that is within thy gates: for in six days the Lord made heaven and earth, the sea, and all that in them is, and rested the seventh day: wherefore the Lord blessed the sabbath-day, and hallowed it* (Ex. 20:8–11).

Q. 58. *What is required in the fourth commandment?*
A. The fourth commandment requireth the keeping holy to God such set times as he hath appointed in his word; expressly one whole day in seven, to be a holy sabbath to himself (Deut. 5:12–14).

Q. 59. *Which day of the seven hath God appointed to be the weekly sabbath?*
A. From the beginning of the world to the resurrection of Christ, God appointed the seventh day of the week to be the weekly sabbath; and the first day of the week ever since, to continue to the end of the world, which is the Christian sabbath (Gen. 2:2–3; 1 Cor. 16:1–2; Acts 20:7).

Q. 60. *How is the sabbath to be sanctified?*
A. The sabbath is to be sanctified by a holy resting all that day (Ex. 20:8, 10; 16:25–28), even from such worldly employments and recreations as are lawful on other days (Neh. 13:15–19, 21–22); and spending the whole time in the publick and private exercises of God's worship (Luke 4:16; Acts 20:7; Ps. 92:title; Isa. 66:23), except so much as is to be taken up in the works of necessity and mercy (Matt. 12:1–31).

Q. 61. *What is forbidden in the fourth commandment?*
A. The fourth commandment forbiddeth the omission or careless performance of the duties required (Ezek. 22:26; Amos 8:5; Mal. 1:13), and the profaning the day by idleness (Acts 20:7, 9), or doing that which is

in itself sinful (Ezek. 23:38), or by unnecessary thoughts, words, or works, about our worldly employments or recreations (Jer. 17:24–26; Isa. 58:13).

Q. 62. *What are the reasons annexed to the fourth commandment?*
A. The reasons annexed to the fourth commandment are, God's allowing us six days of the week for our own employments (Ex. 20:9), his challenging a special propriety in the seventh, his own example, and his blessing the sabbath-day (Ex. 20:11).

Q. 63. *Which is the fifth commandment?*
A. The fifth commandment is, *Honour thy father and thy mother; that thy days may be long upon the land which the Lord thy God giveth thee* (Ex. 20:12).

Q. 64. *What is required in the fifth commandment?*
A. The fifth commandment requireth the preserving the honour, and performing the duties, belonging to every one in their several places and relations, as superiors (Eph. 5:21), inferiors (1 Peter 2:17), or equals (Rom. 12:10).

Q. 65. *What is forbidden in the fifth commandment?*
A. The fifth commandment forbiddeth the neglecting of, or doing any thing against, the honour and duty which belongeth to every one in their several places and relations (Matt. 15:4–6; Ezek. 34:2–4; Rom. 13:8).

Q. 66. *What is the reason annexed to the fifth commandment?*
A. The reason annexed to the fifth commandment, is a promise of long life and prosperity (as far as it shall serve for God's glory and their own good) to all such as keep this commandment (Deut. 5:16; Eph. 6:2–3).

Q. 67. *Which is the sixth commandment?*
A. The sixth commandment is, *Thou shalt not kill* (Ex. 20:13).

Q. 68. *What is required in the sixth commandment?*
A. The sixth commandment requireth all lawful endeavours to preserve our own life (Eph. 5:28–29), and the life of others (1 Kings 18:4).

Q. 69. *What is forbidden in the sixth commandment?*
A. The sixth commandment forbiddeth the taking away of our own life, or the life of our neighbour unjustly, or whatsoever tendeth thereunto (Acts 16:28; Gen. 9:6).

Q. 70. *Which is the seventh commandment?*
A. The seventh commandment is, *Thou shalt not commit adultery* (Ex. 20:14).

Q. 71. *What is required in the seventh commandment?*
A. The seventh commandment requireth the preservation of our own and our neighbour's chastity, in heart, speech and behaviour (1 Cor. 7:2–3, 5, 34, 36; Col. 4:6; 1 Peter 3:2).

Q. 72. *What is forbidden in the seventh commandment?*
A. The seventh commandment forbiddeth all unchaste thoughts, words, and actions (Matt. 15:19; 5:28; Eph. 5:3–4).

Q. 73. *Which is the eighth commandment?*
A. The eighth commandment is, *Thou shalt not steal* (Ex. 20:15).

Q. 74. *What is required in the eighth commandment?*
A. The eighth commandment requireth the lawful procuring and furthering the wealth and outward estate of ourselves and others (Gen. 30:30; 1 Tim. 5:8; Lev. 25:35; Deut. 22:1–5; Ex. 23:4–5; Gen. 47:14, 20).

Q. 75. *What is forbidden in the eighth commandment?*
A. The eighth commandment forbiddeth whatsoever doth or may unjustly hinder our own or our neighbour's wealth or outward estate (Prov. 21:17; 23:20–21; 28:19; Eph. 4:28).

Q. 76. *Which is the ninth commandment?*
A. The ninth commandment is, *Thou shalt not bear false witness against thy neighbour* (Ex. 20:16).

Q. 77. *What is required in the ninth commandment?*
A. The ninth commandment requireth the maintaining and promoting of truth between man and man (Zech. 8:16), and of our own and our neighbour's good name (3 John 12), especially in witness-bearing (Prov. 14:5, 25).

Q. 78. *What is forbidden in the ninth commandment?*
A. The ninth commandment forbiddeth whatsoever is prejudicial to truth, or injurious to our own or our neighbour's good name (1 Sam. 17:28; Lev. 19:16; Ps. 15:3).

Q. 79. *Which is the tenth commandment?*
A. The tenth commandment is, *Thou shalt not covet thy neighbour's house, thou shalt not covet thy neighbour's wife, nor his man-servant, nor his maid-servant, nor his ox, nor his ass, nor any thing that is thy neighbours* (Ex. 20:17).

Q. 80. *What is required in the tenth commandment?*
A. The tenth commandment requireth full contentment with our own condition (Heb. 13:5; 1 Tim. 6:6), with a right and charitable frame of spirit toward our neighbour, and all that is his (Job 31:29; Rom. 12:15; 1 Tim. 1:5; 1 Cor. 13:4–7).

Q. 81. *What is forbidden in the tenth commandment?*
A. The tenth commandment forbiddeth all discontentment with our own estate (1 Kings 21:4, 13; 1 Cor. 10:10), envying or grieving at the good of our neighbour (Gal. 5:26; James 3:14, 16), and all inordinate motions and affections to any thing that is his (Rom. 7:7–8; 13:9; Deut. 5:21).

Q. 82. *Is any man able perfectly to keep the commandments of God?*
A. No mere man since the fall is able in this life perfectly to keep the commandments of God (Eccl. 7:20; 1 John 1:8, 10; Gal. 5:17), but doth daily break them in thought, word, and deed (Gen. 6:5; 8:21; Rom. 3:9–21; James 3:2–13).

Q. 83. *Are all transgressions of the law equally heinous?*
A. Some sins in themselves, and by reason of several aggravations, are more heinous in the sight of God than others (Ezek. 8:6, 13, 15; 1 John 5:16; Ps. 78:17, 32, 56).

Q. 84. *What doth every sin deserve?*
A. Every sin deserveth God's wrath and curse, both in this life, and that which is to come (Eph. 5:6; Gal. 3:10; Lam. 3:39; Matt. 25:41).

Q. 85. *What doth God require of us, that we may escape his wrath and curse due to us for sin?*
A. To escape the wrath and curse of God due to us for sin, God requireth of us faith in Jesus Christ, repentance unto life (Acts 20:21), with the diligent use of all the outward means whereby Christ communicateth to us the benefits of redemption (Prov. 2:1–5; 8:33–36; Isa. 55:3).

Q. 86. *What is faith in Jesus Christ?*
A. Faith in Jesus Christ is a saving grace (Heb. 10:39), whereby we receive and rest upon him alone for salvation, as he is offered to us in the gospel (John 1:12; Isa. 26:3–4; Phil. 3:9; Gal. 2:16).

Q. 87. *What is repentance unto life?*
A. Repentance unto life is a saving grace (Acts 11:18), whereby a sinner, out of a true sense of his sin (Acts 2:37–38), and apprehension of the mercy of God in Christ (Joel 2:12; Jer. 3:22), doth, with grief and hatred of his sin, turn from it unto God (Jer. 31:18–19; Ezek. 36:31), with full purpose of, and endeavour after, new obedience (2 Cor. 7:11; Isa. 1:16–17).

Q. 88. *What are the outward means whereby Christ communicateth to us the benefits of redemption?*
A. The outward and ordinary means whereby Christ communicateth to us the benefits of redemption, are his ordinances, especially the word, sacraments, and prayer; all which are made effectual to the elect for salvation (Matt. 28:19–20; Acts 2:42, 46–47).

Q. 89. *How is the word made effectual to salvation?*
A. The Spirit of God maketh the reading, but especially the preaching of the word, an effectual means of convincing and converting sinners, and of building them up in holiness and comfort, through faith, unto salvation (Neh. 8:8; 1 Cor. 14:24–25; Acts 26:18; Ps. 19:8; Acts 20:32; Rom. 15:4; 2 Tim. 3:15–17; Rom. 10:13–17; 1:16).

Q. 90. *How is the word to be read and heard, that it may become effectual to salvation?*
A. That the word may become effectual to salvation, we must attend thereunto with diligence (Prov. 8:34), preparation (1 Peter 2:1–2), and prayer (Ps. 119:18); receive it with faith and love (Heb. 4:2; 2 Thess. 2:10), lay it up in our hearts (Ps. 119:11), and practise it in our lives (Luke 8:15; James 1:25).

Q. 91. *How do the sacraments become effectual means of salvation?*
A. The sacraments become effectual means of salvation, not from any virtue in them, or in him that doth administer them; but only by the blessing of Christ (1 Peter 3:21; Matt. 3:11; 1 Cor. 3:6–7), and the working of his Spirit in them that by faith receive them (1 Cor. 12:13).

Q. 92. *What is a sacrament?*

A. A sacrament is an holy ordinance instituted by Christ; wherein, by sensible signs, Christ, and the benefits of the new covenant, are represented, sealed, and applied to believers (Gen. 17:7, 10; Ex. 22; 1 Cor. 11:23, 26).

Q. 93. *Which are the sacraments of the New Testament?*

A. The sacraments of the New Testament are, Baptism (Matt. 28:19), and the Lord's supper (Matt. 26:26–28).

Q. 94. *What is baptism?*

A. Baptism is a sacrament, wherein the washing with water in the name of the Father, and of the Son, and of the Holy Ghost (Matt. 28:19), doth signify and seal our ingrafting into Christ, and partaking of the benefits of the covenant of grace, and our engagement to be the Lord's (Rom. 6:4; Gal. 3:27).

Q. 95. *To whom is baptism to be administered?*

A. Baptism is not to be administered to any that are out of the visible church, till they profess their faith in Christ, and obedience to him (Acts 8:36–37; 2:38); but the infants of such as are members of the visible church are to be baptized (Acts 2:38–39; Gen. 17:10; Col. 2:11–12; 1 Cor. 7:14).

Q. 96. *What is the Lord's supper?*

A. The Lord's supper is a sacrament, wherein, by giving and receiving bread and wine, according to Christ's appointment, his death is shewed forth; and the worthy receivers are, not after a corporal and carnal manner, but by faith, made partakers of his body and blood, with all his benefits, to their spiritual nourishment, and growth in grace (1 Cor. 11:23–26; 10:16).

Q. 97. *What is required to the worthy receiving of the Lord's supper?*

A. It is required of them that would worthily partake of the Lord's supper, that they examine themselves of their knowledge to discern the Lord's body (1 Cor. 11:28–29), of their faith to feed upon him (2 Cor. 13:5), of their repentance (1 Cor. 11:31), love (1 Cor. 10:16–17), and new obedience (1 Cor. 5:7–8); lest, coming unworthily, they eat and drink judgment to themselves (1 Cor. 11:28–29).

Q. 98. *What is prayer?*

A. Prayer is an offering up of our desires unto God (Ps. 62:8), for things agreeable to his will (1 John 5:14), in the name of Christ (John 16:23), with confession of our sins (Ps. 32:5–6; Dan. 9:4), and thankful acknowledgment of his mercies (Phil. 4:6).

Q. 99. *What rule hath God given for our direction in prayer?*

A. The whole word of God is of use to direct us in prayer (1 John 5:14); but the special rule of direction is that form of prayer which Christ taught his disciples, commonly called *The Lord's prayer* (Matt. 6:9–13; Luke 11:2–4).

Q. 100. *What doth the preface of the Lord's prayer teach us?*

A. The preface of the Lord's prayer (which is, *Our Father which art in heaven* [Matt. 6:9]) teacheth us to draw near to God with all holy reverence and confidence, as children to a father, able and ready to help us (Rom. 8:15; Luke 11:13); and that we should pray with and for others (Acts 12:5; 1 Tim. 2:1–2).

Q. 101. *What do we pray for in the first petition?*

A. In the first petition (which is, *Hallowed be thy name* [Matt. 6:9]) we pray, That God would enable us and others to glorify him in all that whereby he maketh himself known (Ps. 67:2–3); and that he would dispose all things to his own glory (Ps. 83).

Q. 102. *What do we pray for in the second petition?*

A. In the second petition (which is, *Thy kingdom come* [Matt. 6:10]) we pray, That Satan's kingdom may be destroyed (Ps. 68:1, 18); and that the kingdom of grace may be advanced (Rev. 12:10–11), ourselves and others brought into it, and kept in it (2 Thess. 3:1; Rom. 10:1; John 17:9, 20); and that the kingdom of glory may be hastened (Rev. 22:20).

Q. 103. *What do we pray for in the third petition?*

A. In the third petition (which is, *Thy will be done in earth, as it is in heaven* [Matt. 6:10]) we pray, That God, by his grace, would make us able and willing to know, obey, and submit to his will in all things (Ps. 67; 119:36; Matt. 26:39; 2 Sam. 15:25; Job 1:21), as the angels do in heaven (Ps. 103:20–21).

Q. 104. *What do we pray for in the fourth petition?*
A. In the fourth petition (which is, *Give us this day our daily bread* [Matt. 6:11]) we pray, That of God's free gift we may receive a competent portion of the good things of this life, and enjoy his blessing with them (Prov. 30:8–9; Gen. 28:20; 1 Tim. 4:4–5).

Q. 105. *What do we pray for in the fifth petition?*
A. In the fifth petition (which is, *And forgive us our debts, as we forgive our debtors* [Matt. 6:12]) we pray, That God, for Christ's sake, would freely pardon all our sins (Ps. 51:1–2, 7, 9; Dan. 9:17–19); which we are the rather encouraged to ask, because by his grace we are enabled from the heart to forgive others (Luke 11:4; Matt. 18:35).

Q. 106. *What do we pray for in the sixth petition?*
A. In the sixth petition (which is, *And lead us not into temptation, but deliver us from evil* [Matt. 6:13]) we pray, That God would either keep us from being tempted to sin (Matt. 26:41), or support and deliver us when we are tempted (2 Cor. 12:7–8).

Q. 107. *What doth the conclusion of the Lord's prayer teach us?*
A. The conclusion of the Lord's prayer (which is, *For thine is the kingdom, and the power, and the glory, for ever, Amen* [Matt. 6:13]) teacheth us to take our encouragement in prayer from God only (Dan. 9:4, 7–9, 16–19), and in our prayers to praise him, ascribing kingdom, power, and glory to him (1 Chron. 29:10–13). And, in testimony of our desire, and assurance to be heard, we say, *Amen* (1 Cor. 16:16; Rev. 22:20–21).

116

The Cambridge Platform (1648)

In 1646, the Massachusetts General Court summoned a synod at Cambridge in order to provide an authoritative rationale for New England Congregationalism. The initial *sederunt* was September 1, 1646. In the context of the meetings of the Westminster Assembly in London, this defense was in part necessitated by the Presbyterianism proposed by the Assembly's "Form of Government" (1645) and in part by the threat of Parliamentary interference in New England affairs. Richard Mather (1596–1669) of Dorchester, Massachusetts, drafted this justification of the "New England Way" in seventeen chapters. For two years, pastor and elder delegates from the congregational churches in New England discussed and refined the resulting "platform" (second session, June 8, 1647; final sitting, August 15, 1648). Adopted by the synod in 1648, it was published in 1649 with a preface by John Cotton (1585–1657) and ratified by the individual congregations. A confession of faith had been suggested, but the publication of the Westminster Confession in 1647 made that proposal moot. The Calvinism of the Westminster Standards was theologically sufficient for the separated brethren across the Atlantic, even if the church polity of those same brethren was championed (and lost) by the "Five Pillars" of Independency at the Assembly: Thomas Goodwin (1600–1680), Philip Nye (†1672), Sydrach Simpson (ca. 1600–1655), Jeremiah Burroughs (1599–1646), and William Bridge (1600/1601–1671). The Massachusetts General Court adopted the "Platform" in October 1651.

As with all independent (i.e., congregational) formularies, the Platform was to be non-binding, i.e., advisory and hortatory. However, it soon became the distinctive badge of New England Congregationalism, even serving as a "constitution" of their separated society. And herein lies one of the subsidiary motives in its drafting and adoption: the attempt to attenuate civil power in ecclesiastical matters in New England.

One byproduct of the adoption of the Platform was the publication of the following New England congregational apologias: John Cotton's *The Way of the Congregational Churches Cleared, in Two Treatises* (1648); Thomas Hooker's *Survey of the Summe of Church Discipline* (1648); and John Norton's *Responsio* (1648).

Our text is based on the version in Williston Walker, *The Creeds and Platforms of Congregationalism* (1893), 194–237. Spelling, capitalization, and punctuation have been modernized, as well as proof texts that are clearly mistaken.

THE CAMBRIDGE PLATFORM

The Preface

The setting forth of the public confession of the faith of churches has a double end, and both tending to public edification. First the maintenance of the faith entire within itself; secondly the holding forth of unity and harmony, both among and with other churches. Our churches here, as (by the grace of Christ) we believe and profess the same doctrine of the truth of the gospel, which generally is received in all the Reformed churches of Christ in Europe, so especially we desire not to vary from the doctrine of faith and truth held forth by the churches of our native country. For though it is not one native country that can breed us all of one mind; nor ought we to have the glorious faith of our Lord Jesus with respect of persons; yet as Paul, who was himself a Jew, professed to hold forth the doctrine of justification by faith and of the resurrection of the dead, according as he knew his godly countrymen did who were Jews by nature (Gal. 2:15; Acts 26:6,7), so we, who are by nature Englishmen, do desire to hold forth the same doctrine of religion (especially in fundamentals) which we see and know to be held by the churches of England according to the truth of the gospel.

The more we discern (that which we do, and have cause to do with incessant mourning and trembling) the unkind, and unbrotherly, and unchristian contentions of our godly brethren and countrymen in matters of church government, the more earnestly do we desire to see them joined together in one common faith and ourselves with them. For this end, having perused the public confession of faith agreed upon by the reverend assembly of divines at Westminster, and finding the sum and substance thereof (in matters of doctrine) to express not their own judgments only, but ours also; and being likewise called upon by our godly magistrates, to draw up a public confession of that faith, which is constantly taught and generally professed amongst us, we thought good to present unto them, and with them to our churches and with them to all the churches of Christ abroad, our professed and hearty assent and attestation to the whole confession of faith (for substance of doctrine) which the reverend assembly presented to the religious and honorable Parliament of England—excepting only some sections in the twenty-fifth, thirtieth, and thirty-first chapters of their confession, which concern points of controversy in church discipline, touching which we refer ourselves to the draft of church discipline in the ensuing treatise.

The truth of what we here declare may appear by the unanimous vote of the Synod of the Elders and messengers of our churches assembled at Cambridge, the last of the sixth month, 1648. Which jointly passed in these words: This Synod having perused, and considered (with much gladness of heart and thankfulness to God) the Confession of faith published of late by the reverend Assembly in England, do judge it to be very holy, orthodox, and judicious in all matters of faith; and do therefore freely and fully consent thereunto, for the substance thereof. Only in those things which have respect to church government and discipline, we refer ourselves to the platform of church discipline agreed upon by this present assembly; and do therefore think it meet that this confession of faith should be commended to the churches of Christ among us and to the Honored Court as worthy of their due consideration and acceptance. Howbeit, we may not conceal that the doctrine of vocation expressed in Chap. 10. Sec. I., and summarily repeated Chap. 13 Sec. I., passed not without some debate. Yet considering, that the term of vocation, and others by which it is described are capable of a large, or more strict sense and use; and that is not intended to bind apprehensions precisely in point of order or method, there has been a general condescendancy thereunto.

Now by this our professed consent and free concurrence with them in all the doctrines of religion, we hope it may appear to the world that as we are a remnant of the people of the same nation with them, so we are professors of the same common faith and fellowship, fellow heirs of the same common salvation. Yea moreover, as this our profession of the same faith with them will exempt us (even in their judgments) from suspicion of heresy, so (we trust) it may exempt us in the like sort from suspicion of schism. That though we are forced to dissent from them in matters of church discipline, yet our dissent is not taken up out of arrogance of spirit in ourselves (whom they see willingly condescend to learn of them), neither is it carried with uncharitable censoriousness toward them (both which are the proper and essential characters of schism), but in meekness of wisdom, as we walk along with them, and follow them, as they follow Christ. So where we conceive a different apprehension of the mind of Christ (as it falls out in some few points touching church order), we still reserve due reverence to them (whom we judge to be, through Christ, the glorious lights of both nations) and only crave leave (as in spirit we are bound) to follow the Lamb whithersoever He goes and (after the apostle's example), as we believe, so we speak.

And if the example of such poor outcasts as ourselves might prevail if not with all (for that were too great a blessing to hope for), yet with some or other of our brethren in England, so far as they are come to mind and speak the same thing with such as dissent from them, we hope in Christ, it would not only moderate the harsh judging and condemning of one another in such differences of judgment, as may be found in the choicest saints, but also prevent (by the mercy of Christ) the peril of the distraction and destruction of all the churches in both kingdoms. Otherwise, if brethren shall go on to bite and devour one another, the apostle feared (as we also, with sadness of heart do) it will tend to the consuming of them and us all—which the Lord prevent.

We are not ignorant that (besides these aspersions of heresy and schism) other exceptions also are taken at our way of church government, but (as we conceive) upon as little ground.

> As 1. That by admitting none into the fellowship of our church but saints by calling, we rob many parish churches of their best members to make up one of our congregations; which is not only to gather churches out of churches (a thing unheard of in Scripture), but also to weaken the hearts and hands of the best ministers in the parishes by despoiling them of their best hearers.

2. That we provide no course for the gaining and calling in of ignorant and erroneous and scandalous persons, whom we refuse to receive into our churches, and so exclude from the wholesome remedy of church discipline.

3. That in our way, we sow seeds of division and hindrance of edification in every family; while admitting into our churches only voluntaries: the husband will be of one church, the wife of another; the parents of one church, the children of another; the master of one church, the servants of another. And so the parents and masters being of different churches from their children and servants, they cannot take a just account of their profiting by what they hear. Yea by this means the husbands, parents, and masters shall be chargeable to the maintenance of many other churches and church officers besides their own: which will prove a charge and burden unsupportable.

But for answer as to the first. For gathering churches out of churches, we cannot say that is a thing unheard of in Scripture. The first Christian church was gathered out of the Jewish church and out of many synagogues in that church and consisted partly of inhabitants of Jerusalem, partly of the Galileans; who though they kept some parts of public worship with the temple; yet neither did they frequent the sacrifices, nor repair to the Sanhedrin for the determining of their church causes, but kept entire and constant communion with the apostles' church in all the ordinances of the gospel. And for the first Christian church of the Gentiles at Antioch, it appears to have been gathered and constituted partly of the dispersed brethren of the church at Jerusalem (whereof some were men of Cyprus and Cyrene) and partly of the believing Gentiles. Acts 11:20, 21.

If it be said the first Christian church at Jerusalem and that at Antioch were gathered not out of any Christian church, but out of the Jewish temple and synagogues which were shortly after to be abolished; and their gathering to Antioch was upon occasion of dispersion in time of persecution.

We desire, it may be considered:

1. That the members of the Jewish church were more strongly and straitly tied by express holy covenant to keep fellowship with the Jewish church till it was abolished than any members of Christian parish churches

are wont to be tied to keep fellowship with their parish churches. The episcopal canons, which bind them to attend their parish church—it is likely they are now abolished with the Episcopacy. The common law of the land is satisfied (as we conceive) if they attend upon the worship of God in any other church though not within their own parish. But no such like covenant of God, nor any other religious tie lies upon the Jews to attend upon the worship of God in their temple and synagogues.

2. Though the Jewish temple church at Jerusalem was to be abolished, yet that does not make the desertion of it by the members to be lawful till it was abolished. Further abolition is no warrant for present desertion; unless it be lawful in some case while the church is yet in present standing to desert it, to wit, either for avoiding of present pollutions or for hope of greater edification and so for better satisfaction to conscience in either. Further events (or foresight of them) do not resolve present relations. Else wives, children, servants, might desert their husbands, parents, masters, when they are mortally sick.

3. What the members of the Jewish church did in joining to the church at Antioch in time of persecution, it may well be conceived the members of any Christian church may do the like for satisfaction of conscience. Peace of conscience is more desirable than the peace of the outward man; and freedom from scruples of conscience is more comfortable to a sincere heart than freedom from persecution.

If it is said these members of the Christian church at Jerusalem that joined to the church at Antioch removed their habitations together with their relations; which if the brethren of the congregational way would do, it would much abate the grievance of their departure from their presbyterial churches.

We verily could wish them so to do, as well approving the like removal of habitations in case of changing church relations (provided that it may be done without too much detriment to their outward estates) and we for our part have done the same. But to put a necessity of removal of habitation in such a case, it is to foment and cherish a corrupt principle of making civil cohabitation, if not a formal cause, yet at least a proper adjunct of church relation, which the truth of the gospel does not acknowledge. Now to foment an error to the prejudice of the truth of the gospel is not to walk with a right foot according to the truth of the gospel, as Paul judges. Gal. 2:14.

4. We do not think it meet or safe for a member of a presbyterial church forthwith to desert his relation to his church, take himself to the

fellowship of a congregational church, though he may discern some defect in the estate or government of his own.

For 1. Faithfulness of brotherly love in church relation requires that the members of the church should first convince their brethren of their sinful defects and duly wait for their reformation, before they depart from them. For if we must take such a course for the healing of a private brother, in a way of brotherly love, with much meekness, and patience, how much more ought we so to walk with like tenderness toward a whole church.

Again 2. By the hasty departure of sound members from a defective church, reformation is not promoted, but many times retarded and corruption increased. Whereas on the contrary, while sincere members breathing after purity of reformation abide together, they may (by the blessing of God upon their faithful endeavors) prevail much with their elders and neighbors towards a reformation. It may be so much as that their elders in their own church shall receive none to the seals but visible saints; and in the classis shall put forth no authoritative act (but consultative only) touching the members of other churches: nor touching their own, but with the consent (silent consent at least) of their own church: which two things, if they can obtain with any humble, meek, holy, faithful endeavors, we conceive they might (by the grace of Christ) find liberty of conscience to continue their relation with their own presbyterial church without scruple.

5. But to add a word further touching the gathering of churches out of churches, what if there were no express example of such a thing extant in the Scriptures? that which we are wont to answer the Antipaedobaptists may suffice here. It is enough, if any evidence thereof may be gathered from just consequence of Scripture light. Dr. Ames's judgment concerning this case, passes (for aught we know) without exception, which he gave in his fourth book of conscience in answer to question 3, chapter 24. "If any," he says, "wronged with unjust vexation or providing for his own edification or in testimony against sin, depart from a church where some evils are tolerated and join himself to another more pure, yet without condemning the church he leaves, he is not therefore to be held as a schismatic or as guilty of any other sin." Where the tripartite disjunction, which the judicious doctor puts, declares the lawfulness of the departure of a church member from his church, when either through weariness of unjust vexation, or in way of provision for his own edification or in testimony against sin, he joins himself to another congregation more Reformed. Any one of these,

he judges a just and lawful cause of departure though all of them do not concur together. Neither will such a practice despoil the best ministers of the parishes of their best hearers.

For 1. Sometimes the ministers themselves are willing to join with their better sort of hearers in this way of reformation; and then they and their hearers continue still their church relation together, yea and confirm it more straitly and strongly by an express renewed covenant, though the ministers may still continue their wonted preaching to the whole parish.

2. If the ministers do dislike the way of those whom they otherwise count their best members and so refuse to join with them therein, yet if those members can procure some other ministers to join with them in their own way and still continue their dwelling together in the same town, they may easily order the times of the public assembly as to attend constantly upon the ministry of their former church; and either after or before the public assembly of the parish take an opportunity to gather together for the administration of sacraments and censures and other church ordinances among themselves. The first apostolic church assembled to hear the word with the Jewish church in the open courts of the temple, but afterwards gathered together for breaking of bread and other acts of church order from house to house.

3. Suppose presbyterial churches should communicate some of their best gifted members towards the erecting and gathering of another church, it would not forthwith be their detriment, but may be their enlargement. It is the most noble and perfect work of a living creature (both in nature and grace) to propagate and multiply his kind; and it is the honor of the faithful spouse of Christ to set forward the work of Christ as well abroad as at home. The church in Song 8:8–9, to help forward her little sister church, was willing to part with her choice materials, even beams of cedar and such precious living stones as were fit to build a silver palace. In the same book, the church is compared sometimes to a garden, sometimes to an orchard, Song 4:12, 13. No man plants a garden or orchard, but seeks to get the choicest herbs and plants of his neighbors and they freely impart them; nor do they account it a spoil to their gardens and orchards, but rather a glory. Nevertheless, we go not so far. We neither seek nor ask the choice members of the parishes but accept them being offered.

If it is said they are not offered by the ministers nor by the parish churches (who have most right in them) but only by themselves.

It may justly be demanded, what right or what power have either the ministers or parish churches over them? Not by solemn church covenant; for that, though it is the firmest engagement, is not owned, but rejected. If it is by their joining with the parish in the calling and election of a minister to such a congregation at his first coming, there is indeed just weight in such an engagement. Nor do we judge it safe for such to remove from such a minister, unless it be on such grounds as may justly give him due satisfaction. But if the union of such members to a parish church and to the ministry thereof is only by cohabitation within the precincts of the parish, that union, as it was founded upon human law, so by human law it may easily be released. Or otherwise, if a man removes his habitation, he removes also the bond of his relation and the ground of offense.

4. It need not to be feared, that all the best hearers of the best ministers—no, nor most of them—will depart from them upon point of church government. Those who have found the presence and power of the Spirit of Christ breathing in their ministers, either to their conversion or edification, will be slow to change such a ministry of faith and holiness for the liberty of church order. Upon which ground and sundry other such like, there are doubtless sundry godly and judicious hearers in many parishes in England that do and will prefer their relation to their ministers (though in a presbyterial way) above the congregational confederation.

5. But if all or the most part of the best hearers of the best ministers of parishes should depart from them, as preferring in their judgments the congregational way, yet in case the congregational way should prove to be of Christ, it will never grieve the holy hearers of godly ministers that their hearers should follow after Christ; yea many of themselves (upon due deliberation) will be ready to go along with them. It never grieved nor troubled John the Baptist that his disciples departed from him to follow after Christ, John 3. But in case the congregational way should prove to be not the institution of Christ (as we take it) but the invention of men, then doubtless the presbyterial form (if it be of God) will swallow up the other, as Moses' rod devoured the rods of the Egyptians. Nor will this put a necessity upon both the opposite parties to shift for themselves, and to seek to supplant one another, but only will call upon them ἀληθέυειν ἐν ἀγάπῃ to seek and follow the truth in love, to attend in faithfulness each unto his own flock and to administer to them all the holy things of God and their portion of food in due season. And as for others, quietly to forbear them

and yet to instruct them with meekness that are contrary minded, leaving it to Christ (in the use of all good means) to reveal His own truth in his own time and meanwhile endeavoring to keep the unity of the Spirit in the bond of peace. Phil. 3:15, 16; Eph. 4:3.

To the second exception, that we take no course for the gaining and healing and calling in of ignorant and erroneous and scandalous persons, whom we refuse to receive into our churches and so exclude them from the remedy of church discipline.

We conceive the receiving of them into our churches would rather lose and corrupt our churches than gain and heal them. A little leaven laid in a lump of dough will sooner leaven the whole lump than the whole lump will sweeten it. We therefore find it safer to square rough and unhewn stones before they are laid into the building, rather than to hammer and hew them when they lie unevenly in the building. And accordingly, we use two means to gain and call in such as are ignorant or scandalous. (1) The public ministry of the Word, upon which they are invited by counsel and required by wholesome laws to attend. And the Word it is which is the power of God to salvation to the calling and winning of souls. (2) Private conference and conviction by the elders and other able brethren of the church; whom they do the more respectively hearken unto when they see no hope of enjoying church fellowship or participation in the sacraments for themselves or their children till they approve their judgments to be sound and orthodox and their lives subdued to some hope of godly conversation. What can classical discipline or excommunication itself do more in this case?

The third exception wraps up in it a threefold domestic inconvenience and each of them meet to be eschewed: (1) disunion in families between each relation; (2) disappointment of edification for want of opportunity in the governors of families to take account of things heard by their children and servants; (3) disbursements of chargeable maintenance to the several churches whereto the several persons of their families are joined.

All which inconveniences either do not fall out in congregational churches or are easily redressed. For none are orderly admitted into congregational churches but such as are well approved by good testimony to be duly observant of family relations. Or if any otherwise disposed should creep in, they are either orderly healed or duly removed in a way of

Christ. Nor are they admitted unless they can give some good account of their profiting by ordinances before the elders and brethren of the church: and much more to their parents and masters. Godly tutors in the university can take an account of their pupils, and godly householders in the city can take account of their children and servants, how they profit by the Word they have heard in several churches; and that to the greater edification of the whole family by the variety of such administrations. Bees may bring honey and wax into the hive when they are not limited to one garden of flowers, but may fly abroad to many.

Nor is any change expected from wives, children, or servants to the maintenance of congregational churches further than they be furnished with personal estates or earnings, which may enable them to contribute of such things as they have and not of such things as they have not. God accepts not robbery for a sacrifice. And though a godly householder may justly take himself bound in conscience to contribute to any such church whereto his wife or children or servants do stand in relation; yet that will not aggravate the burden of his charge, no more than if they were received members of the same church to which he himself is related.

But why do we stand thus long to plead exemptions from exceptions? The Lord help all His faithful servants (whether presbyterial or congregational) to judge and shame ourselves before the Lord for all our former compliances to greater enormities in church government than are to be found either in the congregational or presbyterial way. And then surely either the Lord will clear up His own will to us and so frame and subdue us all to one mind and one way (Ezek. 43:10, 11) or else we shall learn to bear one another's burdens in a spirit of meekness. It will then doubtless be far from us so to attest the discipline of Christ as to detest the disciples of Christ; so to contend for the seamless coat of Christ as to crucify the living members of Christ; so to divide ourselves about church communion as through breaches to open a wide gap for a deluge of Antichristian and profane malignity to swallow up both church and civil state.

What shall we say more? Is difference about church order become the inlet of all the disorders in the kingdom? Has the Lord indeed left us to such hardness of heart that church government shall become a snare to Zion (as sometimes Moses was to Egypt, Ex. 10:7) that we cannot leave contesting and contending about it till the kingdom is destroyed? Did not the Lord Jesus, when He dedicated His sufferings for His church and His also unto His Father, make it His earnest and only prayer for us in this world that we all might be one in Him? John 17:20–23. And is it possible that He (whom the Father heard always, John 11:42) should not have this last most solemn prayer heard and granted? or shall it be granted for all the saints elsewhere and not for the saints in England; so that among them disunion shall grow even about church union and communion? If it is possible for a little faith (so much as a grain of mustard seed) to remove a mountain, is it not possible for so much strength of faith as is to be found in all the godly in the kingdom to remove those images of jealousy and to cast those stumbling blocks out of the way which may hinder the free passage of brotherly love among brethren? It is true indeed, the National Covenant does justly engage both parties faithfully to endeavor the utter extirpation of the anti-Christian hierarchy and much more of all blasphemies, heresies and damnable errors. Certainly, if the congregational discipline be independent from the inventions of men, is it not much more independent from the delusions of Satan? What fellowship has Christ with Belial? Light with darkness? Truth with error? The faithful Jews did not need the help of the Samaritans to rebuild the temple of God. Yea, they rejected their help when it was offered, Ezra 4:1–3. And if the congregational way is a way of truth (as we believe) and if the brethren that walk in it be zealous of the truth and hate every false way (as by the rule of their holy discipline they are instructed, 2 John 10, 11), then verily there is no branch in the National Covenant that engages the covenanters to abhor either congregational churches or their way which being duly administered, do no less effectively extirpate the anti-Christian hierarchy and all blasphemies, heresies, and pernicious errors than the other way of discipline does which is more generally and publicly received and ratified.

But the Lord Jesus commune with all our hearts in secret: and He who is the King of His church, let Him be pleased to exercise His kingly power in our spirits that so His kingdom may come into our churches in purity and peace. Amen. Amen.

Chapter I

Of the Form of Church Government; and That Is One,
Immutable and Prescribed in the Word of God

1. Ecclesiastical polity or church government or discipline is nothing else but that form and order that is to be observed in the church of Christ upon earth, both for the constitution of it and all the administrations that therein are to be preformed (Ezek. 43:11; Col. 2:5; 1 Tim. 3:15).

2. Church government is considered in a double respect—either in regard of the parts of government themselves or necessary circumstances thereof. The parts of government are prescribed in the Word, because the Lord Jesus Christ, the King and Lawgiver of His church, is no less faithful in the house of God than was Moses (Heb. 3:5–6), who from the Lord delivered a form and pattern of government to the children of Israel in the Old Testament (Ex. 25:40). And the Holy Scriptures are now also so perfect as they are able to make the man of God perfect and thoroughly furnished unto every good work (2 Tim. 3:16); and therefore doubtless to the well-ordering of the house of God.

3. The parts of church government are all of them exactly described in the Word of God, being parts or means of instituted worship according to the second commandment (1 Tim. 3:15; 1 Chron. 15:13; Ex. 20:4): and therefore to continue one in the same unto the appearing of our Lord Jesus Christ as a kingdom that cannot be shaken (1 Tim. 6:13, 16; Heb. 12:27–28), until He shall deliver it up unto God, even the Father (1 Cor. 15:24). So that it is not left in the power of men, officers, churches or any state in the world to add or diminish or alter anything in the least measure therein (Deut. 12:32; Ezek. 43:8; 1 Kings 12:31–33).

4. The necessary circumstances, as time and place, etc., belonging unto order and decency, are not so left unto men as that under pretense of them, they may thrust their own inventions upon the churches (1 Kings 12:28–29; Isa. 29:13; Col. 2:22–23; Acts 15:28): being circumscribed in the Word with many general limitations, where they are determined in respect of the matter to be neither worship itself, nor circumstances separable from worship: in respect of their end, they must be done unto edification (Matt. 15:9;

1 Cor. 11:23, ?34): in respect of the manner, decently and in order, according to the nature of the things themselves—and civil and church custom, does not even nature itself teach you (1 Cor. 14:26, 40; 11:14, 16; 14:12, 19; Acts 15:28)? Yea, they are in some sort determined particularly, namely that they are done in such a manner as all circumstances considered is most expedient for edification: so, as if there is no error of man concerning their determination, the determining of them is to be accounted as if it were divine.

Chapter II

Of the Nature of the Catholic Church in General,
and in Special, of a Particular Visible Church

1. The catholic church is the whole company of those that are elected, redeemed, and in time effectually called from the state of sin and death unto a state of grace and salvation in Jesus Christ (Eph. 1:22–23; 5:25–26, 30; Heb. 12:23).

2. This church is either triumphant or militant. Triumphant, the number of them who are glorified in heaven; militant, the number of them who are conflicting with their enemies upon earth (Rom. 8:17; 2 Tim. 2:12; 4:8; Eph. 6:12–13).

3. This militant church is to be considered as invisible and visible. Invisible, in respect of their relation wherein they stand to Christ, as a body unto the head, being united unto Him by the Spirit of God and faith in their hearts; visible, in respect of the profession of their faith, in their persons and in particular churches—and so there may be acknowledged a universal visible church (2 Tim. 2:19; Rev. 2:17; 1 Cor. 6:17; Eph. 3:17; Rom. 1:8; 1 Thess. 1:8; Isa. 2:2; 1 Tim. 6:12).

4. The members of the militant visible church considered either as not yet in church order or as walking according to the church order of the gospel (Acts 19:1; Col. 2:5; Matt. 18:17; 1 Cor. 5:12). In order, and so besides the spiritual union and communion common to all believers, they enjoy moreover a union and communion ecclesiastical-political. So we deny a universal visible church.

5. The state [of] the members of the militant visible church walking in order was either before the law (Gen. 18:19; Ex. 19:6), economical, that is in families; or under the Law, national: or, since the coming of Christ, only congregational. (The term independent, we approve not.) Therefore neither national, provincial, nor classical.

6. A congregational church is by the institution of Christ a part of the militant visible church, consisting of a company of saints by calling, united into one body by a holy covenant for the public worship of God and the mutual edification one of another in the fellowship of the Lord Jesus (1 Cor. 14:23, 36; 1:2; 12:27; Ex. 19:5–6; Deut. 29:1, 9–15; Acts 2:42; 1 Cor. 14:26).

Chapter III

Of the Matter of the Visible Church, both
in Respect of Quality and Quantity

The matter of a visible church are saints by calling (1 Cor. 1:2; Eph. 1:1; Heb. 6:10; 1 Cor. 1:5; Rom. 15:14; Ps. 50:16–17; Acts 8:37; Matt. 3:6; Rom. 6:17). By saints, we understand:

1. Such as not only have attained the knowledge of the principles of religion and are free from gross and open scandals, but also, together with the profession of their faith and repentance, walk in blameless obedience to the Word, so as that in charitable discretion they may be accounted saints by calling (1 Cor. 1:2; Phil. 1:1; Col. 1:2) (though perhaps some or more of them be unsound and hypocrites inwardly): because the members of such particular churches are commonly by the Holy Ghost called saints and faithful brethren in Christ; and sundry churches have been reproved for receiving and suffering such persons to continue in fellowship among them, as have been offensive and scandalous: the name of God also by this means is blasphemed and the holy things of God defiled and profaned, the hearts of the godly grieved, and the wicked themselves hardened and helped forward to damnation; the example of such does endanger the sanctity of others. A little leaven leavens the whole lump (Eph. 1:1; 1 Cor. 5:2, 13; Rev. 1:14–15, 20; Ezek. 44:7, 9; 23:38–39; Num. 29, 20; Hag. 2:13–14; 1 Cor. 11:27, 29; Ps. 37:21; 1 Cor. 5:6; 7:14).

2. The children of such, who are also holy.

3. The members of churches, though orderly constituted, may in time degenerate and grow corrupt and scandalous, which though they ought not to be tolerated in the church, yet their continuance therein, through the defect of the execution of discipline and just censures, does not immediately dissolve the being of the church, as appears in the church of Israel and the churches of Galatia and Corinth, Pergamum and Thyatira (Jer. 2:21; 1 Cor. 5:12; Jer. 14; Gal. 5:4; 2 Cor. 12:21; Rev. 2:14–15, 21–22).

4. The matter of the church in respect of its quantity ought not to be of greater number than may ordinarily meet together conveniently in one place (1 Cor. 14:21; Matt. 18:17); nor ordinarily fewer than may conveniently carry on church work. Hence when the Holy Scriptures make mention of the saints combined into a church estate in a town or city where there was but one congregation (Rom. 16:1; 1 Thess. 1:1; Rev. 2:8; 3:7), it usually calls those saints the church in the singular number, as the church of the Thessalonians, the church of Smyrna, Philadelphia, and the like. But when it speaks of the saints in a nation or province wherein there were sundry congregations, it frequently and usually calls them by the name of the churches in the plural number, as the churches of Asia, Galatia, Macedonia, and the like (1 Cor. 16:1, 19; Gal. 1:2; 2 Cor. 8:1; 1 Thess. 2:14). This is further confirmed by what is written of sundry of those churches in particular, how they were assembled and met together: the whole church in one place as the church at Jerusalem, the church at Antioch, the church at Corinth, and Cenchrea—though it were more near to Corinth, it being the port thereof, and answerable to a village, yet being a distinct congregation from Corinth, it had a church of its own as well as Corinth had (Acts 2:46; 5:12; 6:2; 14:27; 15:38; 1 Cor. 5:4; 14:23; Rom. 16:1).

5. Nor can it with reason be thought but that every church appointed and ordained by Christ had a ministry ordained and appointed for the same. And yet it is plain that there were no ordinary officers appointed by Christ for any other than congregational churches: elders being appointed to feed, not all flocks but the particular

flock of God over which the Holy Ghost had made them the overseers (Acts 20:28), and that flock they must attend, even the whole flock; and one congregation being as much as any ordinary elders can attend. Therefore there is no greater church than a congregation, which may ordinarily meet in one place.

Chapter IV
Of the Form of a Visible Church and of Church Covenant

1. Saints by calling must have a visible political union amongst themselves or else they are not a particular church (1 Cor. 12:27; 1 Tim. 3:15; Eph. 2:22; 1 Cor. 12:15–17), as those similitudes hold forth, which Scripture makes use of, to show the nature of particular churches: as a body, a building, or house, hands, eyes, feet, and other members must be united; or else, remaining separate, are not a body. Stones, timber—though squared, hewn, and polished—are not a house until they are compacted and united; so saints or believers in judgment of charity are not a church unless orderly knit together.

2. Particular churches cannot be distinguished one from another but by their forms. Ephesus is not Smyrna, [nor is] Pergamum Thyatira (Rev. 1), but each one [is] a distinct society of itself, having officers of their own which did not have the charge of others; virtues of their own, for which others are not praised; corruptions of their own for which others are not blamed.

3. This form is the visible covenant, agreement or consent whereby they give up themselves unto the Lord to the observing of the ordinances of Christ together in the same society which is usually called the church covenant (Ex. 19:5, 8; Deut. 29:12–13; Zech. 11:10; 9:11); for we see not otherwise how members can have church power one over another mutually. The comparing of each particular church unto a city and unto a spouse seems to conclude not only a form, but that that form is by way of a covenant (Eph. 2:19; 2 Cor. 11:2; Gen. 17:7; Deut. 29:12–13; Eph. 2:12, 19). The covenant, as it was that which made the family of Abraham and children of Israel to be a church and people unto God, so it is that which now makes the several societies of Gentile believers to be churches in these days.

4. This voluntary agreement, consent, or covenant (for all these are here taken for the same), although the more express and plain it is, the more it puts us in mind of our mutual duty and stirs us up to it and leaves less room for the questioning of the truth of the church estate of a company of professors and the truth of membership of particular persons. Yet we conceive the substance of it is kept where there is a real agreement and consent of a company of faithful persons to meet constantly together in one congregation for the public worship of God and their mutual edification, which real agreement and consent they do express by their constant practice in coming together for the public worship of God and by their religious subjection unto the ordinances of God there (Ex. 19:5–8; 24:3, 7; Josh. 24:18–24; Ps. 50:5; Neh. 9:38; 10:1; Gen. 17; Deut. 29): the rather if we do consider how Scripture covenants have been entered into, not only expressly by word of mouth, but by sacrifice; by hand writing and seal; and also sometimes by silent consent, without any writing or expression of words at all.

5. This form then being mutual covenant, it follows it is not faith in the heart, nor the profession of that faith, nor cohabitation, nor baptism. (1) Not faith in the heart because that is invisible. (2) Not a bare profession because that declares them no more to be members of one church than of another. (3) Not cohabitation: atheists or infidels may dwell together with believers. (4) Not baptism because it presupposes a church estate, as circumcision in the Old Testament, which gave no being unto the church, the church being before it and in the wilderness without it. Seals presuppose a covenant already in being; one person is a complete subject of baptism, but one person is incapable of being a church.

6. All believers ought, as God gives them opportunity thereunto, to endeavor to join themselves unto a particular church and that in respect of the honor of Jesus Christ in His example and institution, by the professed acknowledgement of and subjection unto the order and ordinances of the gospel (Acts 2:47; 9:26; Matt. 3:13–15; 28:19–20; Pss. 133:2–3; 87:7; Matt. 18:20; 1 John 1:3): as also in respect of their good of communion, founded upon their visible union, and contained in the promises of Christ's special presence in the church: whence they have fellowship with Him and in Him one with another: also for keeping them in the way

of God's commandments and recovering of them in case of wandering (which all Christ's sheep are subject to in this life), being unable to return of themselves (Ps. 119:176; 1 Peter 2:25; Eph. 4:16; John 16:22, 24–25; Matt. 18:15–17); together with the benefit of their mutual edification and of their posterity that they may not be cut off from the privileges of the covenant. Otherwise, if a believer offends, he remains destitute of the remedy provided in that behalf. And should all believers neglect this duty of joining to all particular congregations, it might follow thereupon that Christ should have no visible political churches upon earth.

Chapter V

Of the First Subject of Church Power, or to Whom
Church Power Does First Belong

1. The first subject of church power is either supreme or subordinate and ministerial. The supreme (by way of gift from the Father) is the Lord Jesus Christ. The ministerial is either extraordinary, as the apostles, prophets, and evangelists: or ordinary, as every particular congregational church (Matt. 28:18; Rev. 3:7; Isa. 9:6; John 20:21, 23; 1 Cor. 14:32; Titus 1:5; 1 Cor. 5:12).

2. Ordinary church power is either the power of office, that is such as is proper to the eldership: or power of privilege, such as belongs unto the brotherhood. The latter is in the brethren formally and immediately from Christ, that is, so as it may according to order be acted or exercised immediately by themselves (Rom. 12:4, 8; Acts 12:3; 6:3–4; 14:23; 1 Cor. 12:29–30). The former is not in them formally or immediately and therefore cannot be acted or exercised immediately by them, but is said to be in them in that they design the persons unto office who only are to act or to exercise this power.

Chapter VI

Of the Officers of the Church and Especially
of Pastors and Teachers

1. A church being a company of people combined together by covenant for the worship of God (Acts 14:23), it appears thereby that there may be the essence and being of a church without any officers, seeing there is both the

form and matter of a church which is implied when it is said the apostles ordained elders in every church.

2. Nevertheless, though officers are not absolutely necessary to the simple being of churches when they are called (Rom. 10:17; Jer. 3:15; 1 Cor. 12:28; Eph. 4:11; Ps. 68:18; Eph. 4:8, 11), yet ordinarily they are to their calling, and to their wellbeing. And therefore the Lord Jesus out of His tender compassion has appointed and ordained officers, which He would not have done if they had not been useful and needful for the church (Eph. 4:12–13). Yea, being ascended into heaven, He received gifts for men and gave gifts to men, whereof officers for the church are justly accounted no small part. They are to continue to the end of the world and for the perfecting of all the saints (1 Cor. 12:28; Eph. 4:11; Gal. 1; Acts 8:6, 12, 19; 11:28; Rom. 11:7–8).

3. The officers were either extraordinary or ordinary: extraordinary, as apostles, prophets, evangelists; ordinary, as elders and deacons. The apostles, prophets and evangelists (1 Cor. 4:9), as they were called extraordinarily by Christ, so their office ended with themselves. Whence it is that Paul directing Timothy how to carry along church administrations gives no direction about the choice or course of apostles, prophets or evangelists, but only of elders and deacons (1 Tim. 3:1–7, 8–13; Titus 1:5; Acts 20:17, 28; 1 Peter 5:1–3). And when Paul was to take his last leave of the church of Ephesus, he committed the care of feeding the church to no other but unto the elders of that church (1 Tim. 3:2; Phil. 1:1; Acts 20:17, 28; 1 Tim. 5:17). The like charge does Peter commit to the elders.

4. Of elders (who are also in Scripture called bishops) some attended chiefly to the ministry of the Word, as the pastors and teachers; others attend especially unto rule, who are therefore called ruling elders (Eph. 4:11; Rom. 12:7–8; 1 Cor. 12:8).

5. The office of pastor and teacher appears to be distinct. The pastor's special work is to attend to exhortation and therein to administer a word of wisdom; the teacher is to attend to doctrine and therein to administer a word of knowledge (2 Tim. 4:1–2; Titus 1:9); and either of them to administer the seals of that covenant unto the dispensation whereof they are alike called; as also to execute the censures, being but a kind of application

of the Word, the preaching of which, together with the application thereof, they are alike charged withal (Eph. 4:11–12; 1:22–23).

6. And forasmuch as both pastors and teachers are given by Christ for the perfecting of the saints and edifying of His body, which saints and body of Christ is His church; therefore we account pastors and teachers to be both of them church officers (1 Sam. 10:12, 19–20; 2 Kings 2:3, 15); and not the pastor for the church and the teacher only for the schools, though this we gladly acknowledge that schools are both lawful, profitable and necessary for the training up of such in good literature or learning, as may afterwards be called forth unto the office of pastor or teacher in the church.

Chapter VII
Of Ruling Elders and Deacons

1. The ruling elder's office is distinct from the office of pastor and teacher (Rom. 12:7–9; 1 Tim. 5:17; 1 Cor. 12:28). The ruling elders are not so called to exclude the pastors and teachers from ruling, but because ruling and governing is common to these with the other (Heb. 13:17; 1 Tim. 5:17); whereas attending to teach and preach the Word is peculiar unto the former.

2. The ruling elder's work is to join with the pastor and teacher in those acts of spiritual rule which are distinct from the ministry of the Word and sacraments committed to them. Of which sort, these are as follows (2 Chron. 23:19; Rev. 21:12; 1 Tim. 4:14; Matt. 18:17; 2 Cor. 2:7–8; Acts 2:26):

I. To open and shut the doors of God's house by the admission of members approved by the church; by ordination of officers chosen by the church; and by excommunication of notorious and obstinate offenders renounced by the church; and by restoring of penitents, forgiven by the church.

II. To call the church together when there is occasion and seasonably to dismiss them again (Acts 21:18, 22–23).

III. To prepare matters in private, that in public they may be carried to an end with less trouble and more speedy dispatch.

IV. To moderate the carriage of all matters in the church assembled: as to propound matters to the church, to order the season of speech and silence, and to pronounce sentence according to the mind of Christ with the consent of the church (Acts 6:2–3; 13:15; 2 Cor. 8:10; Heb. 13:7, 17; 2 Thess. 2:10–12).

V. To be guides and leaders to the church in all matters whatsoever pertaining to church administrations and actions.

VI. To see that none in the church live inordinately out of rank and place without a calling, or idly in their calling.

VII. To prevent and heal such offenses in life or in doctrine as might corrupt the church (Acts 20:28, 32).

VIII. To feed the flock of God with a word of admonition (1 Thess. 5:12; James 5:14; Acts 20:20).

IX. And as they shall be sent for, to visit and pray over their sick brethren.

X. And at other times as opportunity shall serve thereunto.

3. The office of a deacon is instituted in the church by the Lord Jesus. Sometimes they are called helps (Acts 6:3, 6; Phil. 1:1; 1 Cor. 12:28; 1 Tim. 3:8–9). The Scripture tells us how they should be qualified: "grave, not double tongued, not given too much to wine, not given to filthy lucre." They must first be proved and then use the office of a deacon being found blameless. The office and work of the deacon is to receive the offerings of the church, gifts given to the church, and to keep the treasury of the church (Acts 4:35; 6:2–3): and therewith to serve the tables which the church is to provide for, as the Lord's Table, the table of the ministers and of such as are in necessity, to whom they are to distribute in simplicity (Rom. 12:8).

4. The office thereof being limited unto the care of the temporal good things of the church (1 Cor. 7:17), it extends not unto attendance upon and administration of the spiritual things thereof, as the Word and sacraments or the like.

5. The ordinance of the apostle and practice of the church commends the Lord's Day as a fit time for the contribution of the saints (1 Cor. 16:1–3).

6. The instituting of all these officers in the church is the work of God Himself (1 Cor. 12:28; Eph. 4:8, 11; Acts 20:28); of the Lord Jesus Christ; of the Holy Ghost, and therefore such officers as He has not appointed are altogether unlawful either to be placed in the church or to be retained therein, and are to be looked at as human creatures, mere inventions and appointments of man, to the great dishonor of Christ Jesus, the Lord of His house, the King of His church, whether popes, patriarchs, cardinals, archbishops, lord bishops, archdeacons, officials, commissaries and the like. These and the rest of that hierarchy and retinue, not being plants of the Lord's planting, shall all certainly be rooted out and cast forth (Matt. 15:13).

7. The Lord has appointed ancient widows (where they may be had) to minister in the church in giving attendance to the sick and to give succor unto them and others in like necessities (1 Tim. 5:9–10).

Chapter VIII
Of the Election of Church Officers

1. No man may take the honor of a church officer unto himself, but he that was called of God, as was Aaron (Heb. 5:4).

2. Calling unto office is either immediate, by Christ Himself (Gal. 1:1; Acts 14:23; 6:3)—such was the call of the apostles and prophets. This manner of calling ended with them, as has been said. Or calling unto office is mediate by the church.

3. It is meet that before any are ordained or chosen officers, they should be tried and proved because hands are not suddenly to be laid upon any and both elders and deacons must be of honest and good report (1 Tim. 5:22; Acts 16:2; 6:3).

4. The things in respect of which they are to be tried are those gifts and virtues which the Scripture requires in men that are to be elected into such

places, viz., that elders must be "blameless, sober, apt to teach" and endued with such other qualifications as are laid down, 1 Tim. 3:2; Titus 1:6–9. Deacons to be fitted, as is directed, Acts 6:3; 1 Tim. 3:8–11.

5. Officers are to be called by such churches whereunto they are to minister (Acts 14:23; 1:23; 6:3–5); of such moment is the preservation of this power that the churches exercised it in the presence of the apostles.

6. A church being free cannot become subject to any but by a free election (Gal. 5:13); yet when such a people do choose any to be over them in the Lord, then do they become subject and most willingly submit to their ministry in the Lord whom they have so chosen (Heb. 13:17).

7. And if the church has power to choose their officers and ministers (Rom. 16:17), then in case of manifest unworthiness and delinquency they have power also to depose them. For to open and shut, to choose and refuse, to constitute in office and remove from office are acts belonging unto the same power.

8. We judge it much conducive to the well-being and communion of churches (Song 8:8–9) that where it may conveniently be done, neighbor churches be advised withal and their help made use of in the trial of church officers, in order to their choice.

9. The choice of such church officers belongs not to the civil magistrates, as such, or diocesan bishops or patrons: for of these or any such like, the Scripture is wholly silent as having any power therein.

Chapter IX
Of Ordination and Imposition of Hands

1. Church officers are not only to be chosen by the church, but also to be ordained by imposition of hands and prayer; with which at ordination of elders, fasting also is to be joined (Acts 13:3; 14:23; 1 Tim. 5:22).

2. This ordination we account nothing else but the solemn putting of a man into his place and office in the church whereunto he had right before

by election, being like the installing of a magistrate in the commonwealth (Num. 8:10; Acts 6:5–6; 13:2–3). Ordination therefore is not to go before but to follow election (Acts 6:5–6; 14:23). The essence and substance of the outward calling of an ordinary officer in the church does not consist in his ordination, but in his voluntary and free election by the church and in his accepting of that election; whereupon is founded the relation between pastor and flock, between such a minister and such a people. Ordination does not constitute an officer, nor give him the essentials of his office. The apostles were elders without imposition of hands by men: Paul and Barnabas were officers before that imposition of hands, Acts 13:3. The posterity of Levi were priests and Levites before hands were laid on them by the children of Israel.

3. In such churches where there are elders, imposition of hands in ordination is to be performed by those elders (1 Tim. 4:14; Acts 13:3; 1 Tim. 5:22).

4. In such churches where there are no elders, imposition of hands may be performed by some of the brethren orderly chosen by the church thereunto (Num. 8:10). For if the people may elect officers, which is the greater and wherein the substance of the office consists, they may much more (occasion and need so requiring) impose hands in ordination, which is the less and but the accomplishment of the other.

5. Nevertheless in such churches where there are no leaders and the church so desires, we see not why imposition of hands may not be preformed by the elders of other churches. Ordinary officers laid hands upon the officers of many churches. The presbytery of Ephesus laid hands upon Timothy, an evangelist. The presbytery at Antioch laid hands upon Paul and Barnabas (1 Tim. 4:14; Acts 13:3).

6. Church officers are officers to one church, even that particular one over which the Holy Ghost has made them overseers (1 Peter 5:2; Acts 20:28). Insomuch as elders are commanded to feed not all flocks, but that flock which is committed to their faith and trust and depends upon them. Nor can constant residence at one congregation be necessary for a minister; no, nor yet lawful, if he be not a minister to one congregation only, but to the church universal: because he may not attend one part only of the church,

whereunto he is a minister, but he is called to attend unto all the flock (Acts 20:28).

7. He that is clearly loosed from his office relation unto that church whereof he was a minister cannot be looked at as an officer, nor perform any act of office in any other church unless he be again orderly called unto office: which when it shall be, we know nothing to hinder; but imposition of hands also in his ordination ought to be used towards him again. For so Paul the apostle received imposition of hands twice at least from Ananias, Acts 9:17 and Acts 13:3.

Chapter X

Of the Power of the Church and Its Presbytery

1. Supreme and lordly power over all the churches upon earth does only belong unto Jesus Christ, who is King of the church and the Head thereof. He has the government upon His shoulders and has all the power given to Him both in heaven and earth (Ps. 2:6; Eph. 1:21–22; Isa. 9:6; Matt. 28:18).

2. A company of professed believers ecclesiastically confederate, as they are a church before they have officers and without them, so even in that estate, subordinate church power under Christ delegated to them by Him, does belong to them in such a manner as is before expressed (chap. 5, sec. 2), and as flowing from the very nature and essence of a church: it being natural to all bodies and so unto a church body to be furnished with sufficient power for its own preservation and subsistence (Acts 1:23; 14:23; 6:3–4; Matt. 18:17; 1 Cor. 5:4–5).

3. This government of the church is a mixed government (and so has been acknowledged long before the term Independency was heard of). In respect of Christ, the Head and King of the church, and the sovereign power residing in Him and exercised by Him, it is a monarchy (Rev. 3:7; 1 Cor. 5:12). In respect of the body or brotherhood of the church and power from Christ granted unto them, it resembles a democracy (1 Tim. 5:17). In respect of the presbytery and power committed to them, it is an aristocracy.

4. The sovereign power which is peculiar unto Christ is exercised: (1) in calling the church out of the world into holy fellowship with Himself; (2) in instituting the ordinances of His worship and appointing His ministers and officers for the dispensing of them (Gal. 1:4; Rev. 5:8–9; Matt. 28:20; Eph. 4:8, 12; James 4:12; Isa. 33:22); (3) in giving laws for the ordering of all our ways and the ways of His house; (4) in giving power and life to all His institutions and to His people by them; (5) in protecting and delivering His church against and from all the enemies of their peace (1 Tim. 3:15; 2 Cor. 10:4–5; Isa. 32:2; Luke 1:51).

5. The power granted by Christ unto the body of the church and brotherhood, is a prerogative or privilege which the church does exercise: (1) in choosing their own officers, whether elders or deacons; (2) in admission of their own members; and therefore there is great reason they should have power to remove any from their fellowship again (Acts 6:3, 5; 14:23; 9:26). Hence in case of offense any one brother has power to convince and admonish an offending brother; and in case of not hearing him, to take one or two more to set on the admonition; and in case of not hearing them, to proceed to tell the church (Matt. 18:15–17). And as his offense may require, the whole church has power to proceed to the public censure of him, whether by admonition or excommunication, and upon his repentance to restore him again unto his former communion (Titus 3:10; Col. 4:17; Matt. 18:17; 2 Cor. 2:7–8).

6. In case an elder offend incorrigibly, the matter so requiring, as the church had power to call him to office, so they have power according to order (the counsel of other churches where it may be had directing thereto) to remove him from office (Col. 4:17; Rom. 16:17). And being now but a member, in case he add contumacy to his sin, the church that had power to receive him into their fellowship also has the same power to cast him out that they have concerning any other member (Matt. 18:17).

7. Church government or rule is placed by Christ in the officers of the church, who are therefore called rulers while they rule with God (1 Tim. 5:17; Heb. 13:17; 1 Thess. 5:12). Yet in case of maladministration, they are subject to the power of the church, according as has been said before. The Holy Ghost frequently, yea always, where it mentions church rule and

church government, ascribes it to elders (Rom. 12:8; 1 Tim. 5:17; 1 Cor. 12:28–29; Heb. 13:7, 17); whereas the work and duty of the people is expressed in the phrase of obeying their elders and submitting themselves unto them in the Lord. So it is manifest that an organic or complete church is a body politic consisting of some that are governors and some that are governed in the Lord.

8. The power which Christ has committed to the elders is to feed and rule the church of God and accordingly to call the church together upon any weighty occasion, when the members so called, without just cause, may not refuse to come (Acts 20:28; 6:2; Num. 16:12; Ezek. 46:10; Acts 13:15); nor when they are come, depart before they are dismissed; nor speak in the church, before they have leave from the elders; nor continue so doing when they require silence; nor may they oppose nor contradict the judgment or sentence of the elders without sufficient and weighty cause because such practices are manifestly contrary unto order and government, and inlets of disturbance, and tend to confusion.

9. It belongs also unto the elders to examine any officers or members before they are received of the church; to receive the accusations brought to the church and to prepare them for the church's hearing (Rev. 2:2; 1 Tim. 5:19; Acts 21:18, 22–23; 1 Cor. 5:4–5). In handling of offenses and other matters before the church, they have power to declare and publish the counsel and will of God touching the same and to pronounce sentence with the consent of the church. Lastly they have power, when they dismiss the people, to bless them in the name of the Lord (Num. 6:23–26).

10. This power of government in the elders does not in any way prejudice the power of privilege in the brotherhood; as neither the power of privilege in the brethren does prejudice the power of government in the elders (Acts 14:15, 23; 6:2; 1 Cor. 5:4; 2 Cor. 2:6–7); but they may sweetly agree together, as we may see in the example of the apostles furnished with the greatest church power who took in the concurrence and consent of the brethren in church administrations. Also that Scripture, 2 Cor. 2:9 and 10:6, declares that what the churches were to act and do in these matters, they were to do in way of obedience and that not only to the direction of the apostles, but also of their ordinary elders (Heb. 13:17).

11. From the premises, namely, that the ordinary power of government belonging only to the elders, power of privilege remains with the brotherhood (as power of judgment in matters of censure and power of liberty in matters of liberty), it follows that in an organic church and right administration, all church acts proceed after the manner of a mixed administration, so as no church act can be consummated or perfected without the consent of both.

Chapter XI
Of the Maintenance of Church Officers

1. The apostle concludes that necessary and sufficient maintenance is due unto the ministers of the Word: from the law of nature and nations, from the law of Moses, the equity thereof, as also the rule of common reason (1 Cor. 9:9, 15: Matt. 9:38; 10:10; 1 Tim. 5:18). Moreover the Scripture does not only call elders laborers and workmen (Gal. 6:6), but also speaking of them does say that the laborer is worthy of his hire (1 Cor. 9:9, 14; 1 Tim. 5:18) and requires that he which is taught in the Word, should communicate to him in all good things; and mentions it as an ordinance of the Lord that they which preach the gospel should live of the gospel; and forbids the muzzling of the mouth of the ox that treads out the corn.

2. The Scriptures allege requiring this maintenance as a bounden duty and due debt, and not as a matter of alms and free gift. Therefore people are not at liberty to do or not to do what and when they please in this matter, no more than any other commanded duty and ordinance of the Lord; but ought of duty to minister of their carnal things to them that labor among them in the Word and doctrine (Rom. 15:27; 1 Cor. 9:14), as well as they ought to pay any other workman their wages or to discharge and satisfy their other debts or to submit themselves to observe any other ordinance of the Lord.

3. The apostle, Gal. 6:6, enjoining that he which is taught communicate to him that teaches in all good things, does not leave it arbitrary, what or how much a man shall give or in what proportion, but even the latter, as well as the former, is prescribed and appointed by the Lord (1 Cor. 16:2).

4. Not only members of churches, but all that are taught in the Word are to contribute unto him that teaches in all good things (Gal. 6:6). In case congregations are defective in their contributions, the deacons are to call upon them to do their duty (Acts 6:3–4). If their call does not suffice, the church by her power is to require it of their members and where church power through the corruption of men does not or cannot attain the end, the magistrate is to see ministry duly provided for as appears from the commended example of Nehemiah (Neh. 13:11). The magistrates are nursing fathers and nursing mothers and stand charged with the custody of both tables (Isa. 49:23); because it is better to prevent a scandal that it may not come and easier also than to remove it when it is given. It is most suitable to rule that by the church's care each man should know his proportion according to rule, what he should do before he does it that his judgment and heart may be satisfied in what he does and just offense prevented in what is done (2 Cor. 8:13–14).

Chapter XII

Of Admission of Members into the Church

1. The doors of the churches of Christ upon earth do not by God's appointment stand so wide open that all sorts of people good or bad may freely enter therein at their pleasure (2 Chron. 23:19; Matt. 13:25; 22:12); but such as are admitted thereto as members ought to be examined and tried first whether they are fit and meet to be received into church society or not. The eunuch of Ethiopia, before his admission, was examined by Philip whether he did believe on Jesus Christ with all his heart (Acts 8:37). The angel of the church at Ephesus is commended for trying such as said they were apostles and were not (Rev. 2:2; Acts 9:26). There is like reason for trying them that profess themselves to be believers. The officers are charged with the keeping of the doors of the church and therefore are in a special manner to make trial of the fitness of such who enter (Rev. 21:12; 2 Chron. 23:19). Twelve angels are set at the gates of the temple, lest such as were ceremonially unclean should enter there.

2. The things which are requisite to be found in all church members are repentance from sin and faith in Jesus Christ (Acts 2:38–42; 8:37). And

therefore these are the things whereof men are to be examined at their admission into the church and which then they must profess and hold forth in such sort as may satisfy rational charity that the things are there indeed. John the Baptist admitted men to baptism, confessing and bewailing their sins: and of others it is said that they came and confessed and showed their deeds (Matt. 3:6; Acts 19:8).

3. The weakest measure of faith is to be accepted in those that desire to be admitted into the church: because weak Christians, if sincere, have the substance of that faith, repentance, and holiness which is required in church members (Rom. 14:1): and such have most need of the ordinances for their confirmation and growth in grace. The Lord Jesus would not quench the smoking flax nor break the bruised reed, but gather the tender lambs in His arms and carry them gently in His bosom (Matt. 12:20; Isa. 40:11). Such charity and tenderness is to be used, as the weakest Christian, if sincere, may not be excluded nor discouraged. Severity of examination is to be avoided.

4. In case any through excessive fear or other infirmity is unable to make their personal relation of their spiritual estate in public, it is sufficient that the elders, having received private satisfaction, make relation thereof in public before the church—they testifying their assents thereunto. This is the way that tends most to edification. But whereas persons are of better abilities, there it is most expedient that they make their relations and confessions personally with their own mouth, as David professes of himself (Ps. 66:16).

5. A personal and public confession and declaring of God's manner of working upon the soul is both lawful, expedient, and useful in sundry respects and upon sundry grounds. Those three thousand (Acts 2:37, 41), before they were admitted by the apostles, did manifest that they were pricked in their hearts at Peter's sermon, together with earnest desire to be delivered from their sins, which now wounded their consciences, and their ready receiving of the word of promise and exhortation. We are to be ready to render a reason of the hope that is in us to every one that asks us (1 Peter 3:15): therefore we must be able and ready upon any occasion to declare and show our repentance for sin, faith unfeigned, and effectual calling, because these are the reason of a well grounded hope (Heb. 11:1; Eph. 1:18). "I have not hidden thy righteousness from the great congregation" (Ps. 40:10).

6. This profession of faith and repentance, as it must be made by such at their admission that were never in church society before, so nothing hinders but the same may also be preformed by such as have formerly been members of some other church; and the church to which they now join themselves as members may lawfully require the same. Those three thousand (Acts 2) who made their confession were members of the church of the Jews before; so were they that were baptized by John (Matt. 3:5–6). Churches may err in their admission: and persons regularly admitted may fall into offense (Gal. 2:4; 1 Tim. 5:24). Otherwise, if churches might obtrude their members or if church members might obtrude themselves upon other churches without due trial, the matter so requiring, both the liberty of churches would hereby be infringed in that they might not examine those concerning whose fitness for communion they were unsatisfied (Song 8:8). And besides the infringing of their liberty, the churches themselves would unavoidably be corrupted and the ordinances defiled, while they might not refuse, but must receive the unworthy—which is contrary unto the Scripture teaching that all churches are sisters and therefore equal.

7. The like trial is to be required from such members of the church as were born in the same or received their membership and were baptized in their infancy, or minority, by virtue of the covenant of their parents, when being grown up unto years of discretion, they shall desire to be made partakers of the Lord's Supper (Matt. 7:6; 1 Cor. 11:27). Unto which, because holy things must not be given to the unworthy, therefore it is requisite that these as well as others should come to their trial and examination and manifest their faith and repentance by an open profession thereof before they are received to the Lord's Supper, and otherwise not to be admitted thereunto. Yet these church members that were so born or received in their childhood before they are capable of being made partakers of full communion have many privileges which others (not church members) have not. They are in covenant with God; have the seal thereof upon them, viz., baptism; and so if not regenerated, yet are in a more hopeful way of attaining regenerating grace and all the spiritual blessings both of the covenant and seal; they are also under church watch and consequently subject to the reprehensions, admonitions, and censures thereof for their healing and amendment, as need shall require.

Chapter XIII

Of Church Members, Their Removal from One Church to Another,
and of Letters of Recommendation and Dismission

1. Church members may not remove or depart from the church and so one from another as they please, nor without just and weighty cause; but ought to live and dwell together, forasmuch as they are commanded not to forsake the assembling of themselves together (Heb. 10:25). Such departure tends to the dissolution and ruin of the body: as the pulling of stones and pieces of timber from the building and of members from the natural body tend to the destruction of the whole.

2. It is therefore the duty of church members, in such times and places when counsel may be had, to consult with the church whereof they are members about their removal, that accordingly they have their approbation, may be encouraged or otherwise desist (Prov. 11:?14). They who are joined with consent should not depart without consent, except forced thereunto.

3. If a member's departure be manifestly unsafe and sinful, the church may not consent thereunto: for in so doing, they should not act in faith and should partake with him in his sin (Rom. 14:23; 1 Tim. 5:22; Acts 21:14). If the case is doubtful and the person not to be persuaded, it seems best to leave the matter unto God and not forcibly to detain him.

4. Just reasons for a member's removal of himself from the church are: (1) if a man cannot continue without partaking in sin (Eph. 5:11); (2) in case of personal persecution, so Paul departed from the disciples at Damascus (Acts 9:25, 29–30; 8:1). Also, in case of general persecution, when all are scattered. (3) In case of real, and not only pretended want of competent subsistence, a door being opened for a better supply in another place, together with the means of spiritual edification (Neh. 13:20). In these or like cases, a member may lawfully remove and the church cannot lawfully detain him.

5. To separate from a church, either out of contempt of their holy fellowship or out of covetousness or for greater enlargements with just grief to the church (2 Tim. 4:10); or out of schism or want of love (Rom. 16:17); and out of a spirit of contention in respect of some unkindness or some evil only

conceived (Jude 19); or indeed, in the church, which might and should be tolerated and healed with a spirit of meekness (Eph. 4:2–3), and of which evil the church is not yet convinced (though perhaps he himself is) nor admonished (Col. 3:13; Gal. 6:1–2): for these or the like reasons to withdraw from public communion in Word or seals or censures is unlawful and sinful.

6. Such members as have orderly removed their habitation ought to join themselves unto the church in order (where they do inhabit) if it may be (Isa. 56:8; Acts 9:26). Otherwise they can neither perform the duties nor receive the privileges of members. Such an example tolerated in some is apt to corrupt others; which if many should follow would threaten the dissolution and confusion of churches, contrary to the Scripture (1 Cor. 14:33).

7. Order requires that a member thus removing have letters testimonial (Acts 18:27) and of dismission from the church whereof he yet is unto the church whereunto he desires to be joined, lest the church should be deluded that the church may receive him in faith and not be corrupted by receiving deceivers and false brethren. Until the person dismissed is received into another church, he ceases not by his letters of dismission to be a member of the church whereof he was. The church cannot make a member no member but by excommunication.

8. If a member is called to remove only for a time where a church is, letters of recommendation are requisite and sufficient for communion with that church in the ordinances and in their watch (2 Cor. 3:1): as Phoebe, a servant of the church at Cenchrea, had letters written for her to the church of Rome that she might be received, as becomes saints (Rom. 16:1–2).

9. Such letters of recommendation and dismission were written for Apollos; for Mark to the Colossians; for Phoebe to the Romans; for sundry others to the churches (Acts 18:27; Col. 4:10; Rom. 16:1). And the apostle tells us that some persons, not sufficiently known otherwise, have special need of such letters, though he for his part had no need thereof (2 Cor. 3:1). The use of them is to be a benefit and help to the party for whom they are written; and for the furthering of his receiving among the saints in the place where he is going; and the due satisfaction of them in their receiving of him.

Chapter XIV
Of Excommunication and Other Censures

1. The censures of the church are appointed by Christ for the preventing, removing, and healing of offenses in the church (1 Tim. 5:20; Deut. 17:12–13; Jude ?23; Deut. 13:11; 1 Cor. 5:6; Rom. 2:24); for the reclaiming and gaining of offending brethren; for the deterring others from the like offenses; for purging out the leaven which may infect the whole lump; for vindicating the honor of Christ and of His church and the holy profession of the gospel (Rev. 2:14–16, 20); and for preventing the wrath of God that may justly fall upon the church, if they should suffer His covenant and the seals thereof to be profaned by notorious and obstinate offenders.

2. If an offense is private (one brother offending another), the offender is to go and acknowledge his repentance for it unto his offended brother, who is then to forgive him; but if the offender neglect or refuse to do it, the brother offended is to go and convince and admonish him of it between themselves privately (Matt. 5:23–24; Luke 17:3–4; Matt. 18:15). If thereupon the offender is brought to repent of his offense, the admonisher has won his brother, but if the offender does not hear his brother, the brother offended is to take with him one or two more (Matt. 18:16), that in the mouth of two or three witnesses every word may be established (whether the word of admonition, if the offender receives it, or the word of complaint, if he refuses it). For if he refuses it, the offended brother is by the mouth of elders to tell the church (Matt. 18:17); and if he hears the church and declares the same by penitent confession, he is recovered and gained. If the church discerns him to be willing to hear, yet not fully convinced of his offense, as in the case of heresy (Titus 3:10), they are to dispense to him a public admonition; which, declaring the offender to lie under the public offense of the church, does thereby withhold or suspend him from the holy fellowship of the Lord's Supper, till his offense is removed by penitent confession. If he still continues obstinate, they are to cast him out by excommunication (Matt. 18:17).

3. But if the offense is more public at first and of a more heinous and criminal nature (1 Cor. 5:4–5, 7), to wit, such as are condemned by the light of nature, then the church without such gradual proceeding is to cast

out the offender from their holy communion for the further mortifying of his sin and the healing of his soul, in the day of the Lord Jesus.

4. In dealing with an offender, great care is to be taken that we are neither overly strict or rigorous, nor too indulgent or remiss (Gal. 6:1); our proceeding herein ought to be with a spirit of meekness, considering ourselves lest we also be tempted and that the best of us have need of much forgiveness from the Lord (Matt. 18:34–35; 6:14–15; Ezek. 13:10; Jer. 6:14). Yet the winning and healing of the offender's soul, being the end of these endeavors, we must not daub with untempered mortar nor heal the wounds of our brethren slightly. On some have compassion, others save with fear.

5. While the offender remains excommunicate, the church is to refrain from all member-like communion with him in spiritual things (Matt. 18:17; 1 Cor. 5:11; 2 Thess. 3:6, 14) and also from all familiar communion with him in civil things, farther than the necessity of natural or domestic or civil relations require; and are therefore to forbear to eat and drink with him that he may be ashamed.

6. Excommunication being a spiritual punishment, it does not prejudice the excommunicate in, nor deprive him of his civil rights; and therefore touches not princes or other magistrates in point of their civil dignity or authority. And, the excommunicate being but as a publican and a heathen, heathens being lawfully permitted to come to hear the Word in church assemblies (1 Cor. 14:24–25), we acknowledge therefore the like liberty of hearing the Word may be permitted to persons excommunicate that is permitted unto the heathen (2 Thess. 3:14). And because we are not without hope of his recovery, we are not to account him as an enemy but to admonish him as a brother.

7. If the Lord sanctify the censure to the offender so as by the grace of Christ he does testify his repentance with humble confession of his sin and judging of himself, giving glory unto God (2 Cor. 2:7–8), the church is then to forgive him and to comfort him and to restore him to the wonted brotherly communion which formerly he enjoyed with them.

8. The suffering of profane or scandalous livers to continue in fellowship and partake in the sacraments is doubtless a great sin in those that have power in their hands to redress it and do it not (Rev. 2:14–15, 20). Nevertheless, inasmuch as Christ and His apostles in their times (Matt. 23:3; Acts 3:1), and the prophets and other godly persons in theirs, did lawfully partake of the Lord's commanded ordinances in the Jewish church and neither taught nor practiced separation from the same, though unworthy ones were permitted therein; and inasmuch as the faithful in the church of Corinth, wherein were many unworthy persons and practices, are never commanded to absent themselves from the sacraments because of the same; therefore the godly in like cases are not presently to separate (1 Cor. 6; ?12:15).

9. As separation from such a church wherein profane and scandalous livers are tolerated is not presently necessary: so for the members thereof, otherwise worthy, hereupon to abstain from communicating with such a church in the participation of the sacraments is unlawful (2 Chron. 30:18; Gen. 18:25). For as it were unreasonable for an innocent person to be punished for the faults of others wherein he has no hand and whereunto he gave no consent, so it is more unreasonable that a godly man should neglect duty and punish himself in not coming for his portion in the blessing of the seals as he ought because others are suffered to come that ought not; especially considering that himself neither consents to their sin nor to the neglect of others who should put them away and do not (Ezek. 9:4): but on the contrary heartily mourns for these things, modestly and seasonably stirs up others to do their duty. If the church cannot be reformed, they may use their liberty as is specified, chapter 13, section 4. But this all the godly are bound unto, even everyone to do his endeavor according to his power and place, that the unworthy may be duly proceeded against by the church to whom this matter pertains.

Chapter XV

Of the Communion of Churches One with Another

1. Although churches are distinct, and therefore may not be confounded one with another; and equal, and therefore do not have dominion one over another (Rev. 1:4; Song 8:8; Rom. 16:16; 1 Cor. 16:19; Acts 15:23; Rev.

2:1): yet all the churches ought to preserve church communion one with another because they are all united unto Christ, not only as a mystical, but as a political head; whence is derived a communion suitable thereunto.

2. The communion of churches is exercised sundry ways. (1) By way of mutual care in taking thought for one another's welfare (Song 8:8). (2) By way of consultation one with another when we have occasion to require the judgment and counsel of other churches touching any person or cause wherewith they may be better acquainted than ourselves. As the church of Antioch consulted with the apostles and elders of the church at Jerusalem about the question of circumcision of the Gentiles and about the false teachers that broached that doctrine (Acts 15:2). In which case, when any church wants light or peace among themselves, it is a way of communion of churches (according to the Word) to meet together by their elders and other messengers in a synod (Acts 15:6) to consider and argue the points in doubt or difference (Acts 15:22–23); and having found out the way of truth and peace, to commend the same by their letters and messengers to the churches, whom the same may concern. But if a church is rent with divisions among themselves or lies under any open scandal and yet refuses to consult with other churches for healing or removing of the same, it is a matter of just offense both to the Lord Jesus and to other churches, as betraying too much want of mercy and faithfulness (Ezek. 34:4), not to seek to bind up the breaches and wounds of the church and brethren; and therefore the state of such a church calls aloud upon other churches to exercise a fuller act of brotherly communion, to wit, by way of admonition.

3. A third way then of communion of churches is by way of admonition, to wit, in case any public offense be found in a church which they either discern not or are slow in proceeding to use the means for the removing and healing (Gal. 2:11–14). Paul had no authority over Peter, yet when he saw Peter not walking with a right foot, he publicly rebuked him before the church. Though churches have no more authority one over another than one apostle had over another, yet as one apostle might admonish another, so may one church admonish another and yet without usurpation. In which case, if the church that lies under offense does not hearken to the church which does admonish her, the church is to acquaint other neighbor churches with that offense which the offending church still lies under (Matt. 18:15–17),

together with their neglect of the brotherly admonition given unto them; whereupon those other churches are to join in seconding the admonition formerly given. And if still the offending church continues in obstinacy and impenitence, they may forbear communion with them and are to proceed to make use of the help of a synod or council of neighbor churches walking orderly (if a greater cannot conveniently be had) for their conviction. If they hear not the synod, the synod having declared them to be obstinate, particular churches, approving and accepting of the judgment of the synod, are to declare the sentence of non-communion respectively concerning them; and thereupon out of a religious care to keep their own communion pure, they may justly withdraw themselves from participation with them at the Lord's table and from such other acts of holy communion as the communion of churches does otherwise allow and require. Nevertheless, if any members of such a church as lies under public offense, do not consent to the offense of the church, but in due sort bear witness against it, they are still to be received to wonted communion. For it is not equal that the innocent should suffer with the offensive (Gen. 18:25). Yea furthermore, if such innocent members after due waiting in the use of all good means for the healing of the offense of their own church shall at last (with the allowance of the council of neighbor churches) withdraw from the fellowship of their own church and offer themselves to the fellowship of another, we judge it lawful for the other church to receive them (being otherwise fit) as if they had been orderly dismissed to them from their own church.

4. A fourth way of communion of churches is by way of participation. The members of one church occasionally coming unto another, we willingly admit them to partake with us at the Lord's table, it being the seal of our communion not only with Christ, nor only with the members of our own church, but also with all the churches of the saints (1 Cor. 12:13). In which regard, we do not refuse to baptize their children presented to us if either their own minister is absent or such a fruit of holy fellowship is desired with us. In like case, such churches as are furnished with more ministers than one do willingly afford one of their own ministers to supply the place of an absent or sick minister of another church for a needful season.

5. A fifth way of church communion is by way of recommendation when a member of one church has occasion to reside in another church (Rom.

16:1), if but for a season, we commend him to their watchful fellowship by letters of recommendation. But if he is called to settle his abode there, we commit him according to his desire to the fellowship of their covenant by letters of dismission (Acts 18:27).

6. A sixth way of church communion is in case of need to minister relief and succor one unto another (Acts 11:22, 29), either of able members to furnish them with officers or of outward support to the necessities of poorer churches: as the churches of the Gentiles contributed liberally to the poor saints at Jerusalem (Rom. 15:26–27).

7. When a company of believers purpose to gather into church fellowship, it is requisite for their safer proceeding and the maintaining of the communion of churches that they signify their intent unto the neighbor churches (Gal. 2:1–2, 9), walking according to the order of the gospel, and desire their presence and help and right hand of fellowship, which they ought readily to give unto them when there is no just cause of excepting against their proceedings.

8. Besides these several ways of communion, there is also a way of propagation of churches. When a church shall grow too numerous, it is a way and fit season to propagate one church out of another (Isa. 40:20; Song 8:8–9) by sending forth such of their members as are willing to remove and to procure some officers to them, as may enter with them into church estate among themselves. As bees, when the hive is too full, issue forth by swarms and are gathered into other hives, so the churches of Christ may do the same upon like necessity, and therein hold forth to the right hand of fellowship both in their gathering into a church and in the ordination of their officers.

Chapter XVI
Of Synods

1. Synods orderly assembled and rightly proceeding according to the pattern, Acts 15, we acknowledge as the ordinance of Christ (Acts 15:2–15). And though not absolutely necessary to the being, yet many times,

through the iniquity of men and perverseness of times, necessary to the well-being of churches, for the establishment of truth and peace therein.

2. Synods being spiritual and ecclesiastical assemblies are therefore made up of spiritual and ecclesiastical causes. The next efficient cause of them under Christ is the power of the churches sending forth their elders and other messengers, who being met together in the name of Christ are the matter of a synod (Acts 15:2–3). And they in arguing, debating, and determining matters of religion according to the Word and publishing the same to the churches whom it concerns, put forth the proper and formal acts of a synod—to the conviction of errors and heresies and the establishment of truth and peace in the churches, which is the end of a synod (Acts 15:6–23, 31; 16:4, 15).

3. Magistrates have power to call a synod by calling to the churches to send forth their elders and other messengers to counsel and assist them in matters of religion (2 Chron. 29:4–11); but yet the constituting of a synod is a church act and may be transacted by the churches even when civil magistrates may be enemies to churches and to church assemblies (Acts 15).

4. It belongs unto synods and councils to debate and determine controversies of faith and cases of conscience; to clear from the Word holy directions for the holy worship of God and good government of the church (Acts 15:1–2, 6–7; 1 Chron. 15:13); to bear witness against maladministration and corruption in doctrine or manners in any particular church and to give directions for the reformation thereof (2 Chron. 29:6–7; Acts 15:24, 28–29); not to exercise church censures in way of discipline nor any other act of church authority or jurisdiction which that presidential synod did forbear.

5. The synod's directions and determinations, so far as consonant to the Word of God, are to be received with reverence and submission; not only for their agreement therewith (which is the principal ground thereof and without which they bind not at all), but also secondarily, for the power whereby they are made as being an ordinance of God appointed thereunto in His Word (Acts 15).

6. Because it is difficult, if not impossible, for many churches to come altogether in one place in all their members universally, therefore they may assemble by their delegates or messengers, as the church of Antioch went not all to Jerusalem, but some select men for that purpose (Acts 15:2). For none are or should be fit to know the state of the churches nor to advise of ways for the good thereof than elders. Therefore it is fit that in the choice of the messengers for such assemblies, they have special respect unto such (Acts 15:2, 22–23). Yet inasmuch as not only Paul and Barnabas, but certain others also were sent to Jerusalem from Antioch, Acts 15, and when they were come to Jerusalem, not only the apostles and elders, but other brethren also do assemble and meet about the matter, therefore synods are to consist both of elders and other church members, endued with gifts and sent by the churches, not excluding the presence of any brethren in the churches.

Chapter XVII

Of the Civil Magistrate's Power in Matters Ecclesiastical

1. It is lawful, profitable, and necessary for Christians to gather themselves into church estate and therein to exercise all the ordinances of Christ according unto the Word (Acts 2:41, 47; 4:1–3); although the consent of the magistrate could not be had thereunto because the apostles and Christians in their time did frequently thus practice, when the magistrates being all of them Jewish or pagan and mostly persecuting enemies, would give no countenance or consent to such matters.

2. Church government stands in no opposition to civil government of commonwealths (John 18:36), nor any way entrenches upon the authority of civil magistrates in their jurisdictions, nor any wit weakens their hands in governing (John 18:36; Acts 25:8); but rather strengthens them and furthers the people in yielding more hearty and conscionable obedience unto them, whatsoever some ill-affected persons to the ways of Christ have suggested, to alienate the affections of kings and princes from the ordinances of Christ—as if the kingdom of Christ in His church could not rise and stand without the falling and weakening of their government which is also of Christ (Isa. 49:23). Whereas the contrary is most true, that

they may both stand together and flourish, the one being helpful unto the other in their distinct and due administrations.

3. The power and authority of magistrates is not for the restraining of churches or any other good works, but for helping in and furthering thereof (Rom. 13:4; 1 Tim. 2:2); and therefore the consent and countenance of magistrates when it may be had is not to be slighted or lightly esteemed, but on the contrary, it is part of that honor due to Christian magistrates to desire and crave their consent and approbation therein; which being obtained, the churches may then proceed in their way with much more encouragement and comfort.

4. It is not in the power of magistrates to compel their subjects to become church members and to partake at the Lord's Table, for the priests are reproved that brought unworthy ones into the sanctuary. Then, as it was unlawful for the priests, so it is as unlawful to be done by civil magistrates (Ezek. 44:7, 9). Those whom the church is to cast out if they were in, the magistrate ought not to thrust into the church nor to hold them therein (1 Cor. 5:11).

5. As it is unlawful for church officers to meddle with the sword of the magistrate, so it is unlawful for the magistrate to meddle with the work proper to church officers (Matt. 20:25–26). The acts of Moses and David, who were not only princes but prophets, were extraordinary; therefore, not imitable. Against such usurpation the Lord witnessed by smiting Uzziah with leprosy for presuming to offer incense (2 Chron. 26:16–17).

6. It is the duty of the magistrate to take care of matters of religion and to improve his civil authority for the observing of the duties commanded in the first, as well as for observing of the duties commanded in the second table. They are called "gods" (Ps. 82:6). The end of the magistrate's office is not only the quiet and peaceable life of the subject in matters of righteousness and honesty, but also in matters of godliness, yea of all godliness (1 Tim. 2:1–2). Moses, Joshua, David, Solomon, Asa, Jehoshaphat, Hezekiah, Josiah are much commended by the Holy Ghost for putting forth their authority in matters of religion. On the contrary, such kings as have been failing this way are frequently taxed and reproved by the Lord and not only the kings of Judah, but also Job, Nehemiah, the king of Nineveh, Darius, Artaxerxes,

Nebuchadnezzar, whom none looked at as types of Christ (though were it so, there were no place for any such objection), are commended in the book of God for exercising their authority this way (1 Kings 15:14; 22:43; 2 Kings 12:3; 14:4; 15:35; 1 Kings 20:42; Job 29:25; 31:26, 28; Neh. 13; Jonah 3:7; Ezra 7; Dan. 3:29).

7. The objects of the power of the magistrate are not things merely inward and so not subject to his cognizance and view, as unbelief, hardness of heart, erroneous opinions not vented, but only such things as are acted by the outward man; neither is their power to be exercised in commanding such acts of the outward man, and punishing the neglect thereof (1 Kings 20:28, 42), as are but mere inventions and devices of men; but about such acts as are commanded and forbidden in the Word; yea such as the Word does clearly determine though not always clearly to the judgment of the magistrate or others, yet clearly in itself. In these he of right ought to put forth his authority though often actually he does it not.

8. Idolatry, blasphemy, heresy, venting corrupt and pernicious opinions that destroy the foundation, open contempt of the Word preached, profanation of the Lord's Day, disturbing the peaceable administration and exercise of the worship and holy things of God and the like, are to be restrained and punished by civil authority (Deut. 13; 1 Kings 20:28, 42; Dan. 3:29; Zech. 13:3; Neh. 13:21; 1 Tim. 2:2; Rom. 13:4).

9. If any church one or more shall grow schismatic, rending itself from the communion of other churches or shall walk incorrigibly or obstinately in any corrupt way of their own contrary to the rule of the Word; in such a case, the magistrate is to put forth his coercive power as the matter shall require. The tribes on this side [of] Jordan intended to make war against the other tribes for building the altar of witness whom they suspected to have turned away therein from following the Lord (Josh. 22).

117

The Geneva Theses (1649)

Alexandre Morus (1616–1670) came to Geneva as a student of theology
in 1636, following some years of study at the Saumur Academy founded
by John Cameron (ca. 1579–1625). At the time of his matriculation, Saumur
was directed by the Triumvirate: Moise Amyraut (Moses Amyrald, 1596–
1664), Josué de la Place (Placaeus, †1655), and Louis Cappel (1585–1658).
After completing his studies, Morus was chosen professor of Greek at the
Academy in Geneva on August 2, 1639. Two years later, the notorious *l'affair
Alexander Morus* began (details may be found in James T. Dennison, Jr., "The
Life and Career of Francis Turretin," in Francis Turretin, *Institutes of Elenctic
Theology*, ed. by James T. Dennison, Jr. [1997], 3:642–58 and the literature
cited there; cf. James T. Dennison, Jr., "The Twilight of Scholasticism: Francis
Turretin at the Dawn of the Enlightenment," in *Protestant Scholasticism:
Essays in Reassessment*, ed. by Carl Trueman [1999], 244–55). As he was a
polished orator, Morus was commended by some members of the Venerable
Company of Pastors for ordination to the ministry.

But there were dissenting voices. Some maintained that Morus favored
Amyraut's doctrine of (hypothetical) universal grace (i.e., that Christ died
for every person provided they themselves do not reject that redemption).
Second, it was alleged that he agreed with de la Place on mediate (as opposed
to immediate) imputation of Adamic transgression (i.e., sinners are not
immediately charged with the guilt of Adam's sin, but are charged with the
guilt of native depravity mediated by their parents). Finally, he was rumored
to be sympathetic with Johannes Piscator's (1546–1635) rejection of the
imputation of the active obedience of Christ in justification (Piscator argued
that the passive obedience of Christ only or His death on the cross was solely
sufficient and necessary for justification; cf. James T. Dennison, Jr., "Johannes
Piscator and the Doctrine of Justification." *The Outlook* 53/10 [December

2003]: 8–11). Though Morus asserted his agreement with the doctrine and catechism of Geneva, he was required to submit to a theological examination by the professors of theology. On January 2, 1642, he was ordained to the ministry. On October 7, 1642, he succeeded Frederic Spanheim (1600–1649) as professor of theology in Geneva.

But in 1646, the rumors of heterodoxy were flying once more over Morus. Once again, he weathered a summons before the Company of Pastors and the Council of Geneva. He survived a brief skirmish with Théodore Tronchin (1582–1657) in 1647. But rumors were circulating in other Reformed centers of Europe (especially Holland) that he was not orthodox. Morus appealed to the Council and the Company of Pastors to address letters of recommendation on his behalf to those detracting from his reputation. The complex tussle back and forth over this request resulted in a draft of thirteen articles plus four general charges against him, dated January 19, 1649. Morus absolved himself of any Amyraldian sympathies with the Council, but not with the Company of Pastors. The hullabaloo was polarizing church and state in Calvin's citadel.

On May 28, 1649, the Council of Geneva commissioned Tronchin and Antoine Léger (1594–1661) to draft the following Theses. On June 1, they were approved by the Company of Pastors and signed on their behalf by the moderator, Joannes Jacobus Sartorius (1619–1690). Morus wanted to alter the Theses before he signed them, but the Company of Pastors refused to allow any change. Morus then signed them on June 11. He departed from Geneva on July 7 in order to serve as pastor to a French-speaking congregation in Middelbourg, Holland.

But the Theses would again become the focal point of controversy in 1669 when Charles Maurice was to be examined by the Company in order to become pastor of a church in France. Francis Turretin (1623–1687) would insist that Maurice sign the Theses and he did. But Turretin would not succeed with Jean-Robert Chouet (1642–1731) (see the discussion in Dennison [1997], cited above). The stage was now set for drafting the Helvetic Consensus of 1675.

A very clear copy of the Latin original was graciously supplied by Paule Hochuli Dubuis, assistante conservatrice, Bibliothèque de Genève (Ms. Fr. 469, folios 2–3v). A blurred and incomplete photostatic copy may also be found on pages 428–31 of Donald D. Grohman's Th.D. dissertation, "The Genevan Reactions to the Saumur Doctrine of Hypothetical Universalism:

1635–1685" (Knox College, Toronto School of Theology, 1971). Unfortunately, no typescript of this original exists, making it difficult to decipher certain forms (seventeenth-century writing convention also makes reading the original a challenge). Grohman's translation (pp. 232–35) is revised, corrected, and (I trust) improved below. In part, this is due to some inadequate and inaccurate non-textual insertions, as well as several textual omissions in his version.

I am including my own transcription of the Latin primary document as well as a freshly revised English translation.

I. De peccato originali

1. Primum Adami παράπτωμα posteris ipsius ex justa Dei ordinatione et judicio imputatur, corruptionisque lues in omnes et singulos naturaliter ex illo oriundos diffussa grassatur. Tria itaque sunt quae hominem constituunt reum coram Deo. 1um. Culpa promanans ex eo quod omnes peccavimus in Adamo. 2. Corruptio quae est poena istius culpae imposita tam Adamo quàm posteris. 3. Peccata quae perpetrant homines adulti.

2. Imputatio peccati Adami et imputatio iustitiae Christi ex adverso sibi in his respondent: verè imputatur peccatum Adami posteris eius verè imputatur electis iustitia Christi. Imputatio peccati Adami praecedit corruptionem. Imputatio iustitiae Christi praecedit sanctificationem.

3. Imputatio peccati Adami et impura generatio sunt quidem derivationis peccati originalis duo modi inter se connexi et planè inseparabiles distincti tamen ut Antecedens et Consequens ut causa et effectum ideò enim corruptio naturae ab Adamo in nos derivatur quia in ipso peccavimus et rei facti sumus.

Reiecto erroris eorum

Qui peccatum Adami posteris imputari negant: qui simulata imputationis adstructione revera destruunt vel labefactant eam corruptione naturali in singulos diffusa priorem non agnoscentes.

II. De praedestinatione

1. Obiectum praedestinationis sunt homines lapsi non tamen ut increduli et rebelles vocationi.

2. Sacra scriptura nonnunquam distinctè proponit electionem ad slautem et ad salutis media, ideoque distinctè possunt considerari: Christus missus et mortuus est secundum consilium Dei patris ex aeterno erga electos amore profectum.

3. Quos Deus ex solo beneplacito in Christo elegit, et eos solos dare filio, iisque dare fidem ut ad vitam aeternam perducerentur decrevit.

4. Singularis Amor et misericordia Dei sola caussa est et missionis filii et satisfactionis ab eo praestitae atque ac collationis fidei et applicationis meriti per eam: quae beneficia disgressi non debent obiectis vel à se invicem divelli.

Reiecto erroris eorum

1. Qui docent in Deo dari aliquam bonam voluntatem eos qui pereunt salvandi sub conditione fidei et poenitentiae.

2. Qui ὀικονομίας obtentu Deo affingunt inclinationem, aut velleitatem, aut habitum, aut affectum, aut amorem minùs vehementem, aut virtutum, aut intentionem, aut desiderium, aut voluntatem, aut consilium, aut decretum, aut foedus, aut misericordiam necessariam vel universalem conditionatam qua omnes et singulos homines salvos fieri velit si in Christum credant.

3. Qui Deo tribuunt propositum electioni praevium quo universi generis humani indeterminatè misereri deliberaverit.

4. Qui Deo duplicem adscribunt misericordiam, illustrem unam seu primam et universalem qua omnes et singulos salvari velit: illustriorem alteram secundam et particularem erga electos.

III. De redemptione

1. Quum finis nonnisi eis destinatus sit quibus destinata media adventus Jesu C. in mundum, mors, satisfactio eius salusque iis tantùm destinantur quibus Deus mero suo beneplacito decrevit ab aeterno dare fidem et

poenitentiam quibus eas reipsa confert in tempore. Gratiae salutaris universalitati refragatur scriptura omniumque seculorum experientia.

2. Christus ex mera εὐδοκία patris destinatus fuit et datus mediator certo hominum numero corpus ipsius mysticum ex Dei electione constituentium.

3. Pro illis ipse Christus vocationis suae optimè conscius voluit et decrevit mori et precio mortis infinito addere efficacissimam et singularem voluntatis intentionem.

4. Universales propositiones quae in scripturis reperiuntur non significant pro omnibus et singulis hominibus Christum mortuum esse, satisfecisse &c. Ex consilio patris et sua voluntate: sed, vel restringendae sunt ad corporis Christi universalitatem vel riferri debent ad illam ὀικονομίαν foederis novi quâ, sublata omni populorum externa distinctione filius adopti adsciunt sibi gentes omnes in haereditatem id. erga quaslibet gentes et populos communitio pro arbitrio gratiam praedicationis aperit et defert ex illis ecclesiam colligit quod est fundamentum praedicationis generalis euangelii.

Reiectio erroris eorum

Qui docent Christum mortuum pro omnibus et singulis sufficienter non tantum pretiis sed etiam intentionis ratione, aut pro omnibus conditionatè si credant, aut qui asserunt scripturam docere Christum mortuisse pro omnibus omnino hominibus et speciatim scripturae loca Ezech. 18.21. &c. et 33.11 . Joh. 3.16. 1. ad Tim. 2 .4 . 2 Pet. 3.9. ad omnes et singulos homines debere extendi iisque probari universalitatem dilectionis et gratiae.

IV. De hominis ad gratiam dispositione

1. Quum requisitae ad salutem conditiones reprobis impossibiles sint salutem eorum conditionatè si credant et poenitentiam agant non intendit Deus nisi statuatur aliqua intentio et voluntas Dei vana, frustranea et inutilis.

2. Luminis naturalis sive subiectivi sive obiectivi bonus usus hominem ad salutem perducere nequit, nequidem impetrare à Deo ullum alium gradum luminis ad salutem ordinati.

Reiectio erroris eorum

1. Qui docent vocationem universalem atque omnibus hominibus communem ad salutem salutisque autorem, omnes et singulos homines credere et salvari posse si velint.

2. Voluntate revelate Deum vellit omnium et singulorum salutem.

V. De promissionibus factis fidelibus eorumque praerogativis

1. Vita cuius promissio legi annexa praestita eius stipulatione non modò terrena et temporalis sed et coelestis et aeterna.

2. Fideles etiam ante Christum natum eundem quem nos mediatorem et servatorem eiusdemque spiritum adoptionis habuit.

Reiectio erroris eorum

1. Qui docent foederis legalis praemium ut officium non aliud quàm naturale et temporarium esse.

2. Qui docent patres veteris testamenti arrhabone spiritus sancti caecuisse.

――――――――

I. Concerning Original Sin

1. The first sin (παράπτωμα) of Adam is imputed to his descendants by the ordination and judgment of the justice of God, and the evil of corruption spreads in each and every one coming into the world naturally descended from that one. For that reason, there are three things which constitute men guilty before God: (1) the guilt flowing from the fact that we have all sinned in Adam; (2) the corruption which is the penalty of this guilt imposed upon both Adam and his descendants; (3) the sins which men commit as adults.

2. The imputation of the sin of Adam and the imputation of the righteousness of Christ correspond to their opposite in this way: as truly as the sin of Adam is imputed to his descendants so truly is the righteousness of Christ imputed to his elect. The imputation of the sin of Adam precedes corruption; the imputation of the righteousness of Christ precedes sanctification.

3. The imputation of the sin of Adam and impure generation, are indeed two ways of deriving original sin, themselves mutually connected and plainly inseparable, nevertheless distinct as antecedent and consequent, as cause and effect; for this reason, the corruption of nature in us is derived from Adam because in him we have sinned and have been made guilty.

Rejection of the error of those:

Who deny that the sin of Adam is imputed to his descendants; who, appearing to establish imputation, in truth destroy or overthrow it, not acknowledging that it has first been diffused into each one by natural corruption.

II. Concerning Predestination

1. Fallen men are the object of predestination, yet not as unbelieving and rebellious to the call.

2. Sacred Scripture occasionally represents election to salvation and to the means of salvation distinctly and for that reason they may be distinctly considered: Christ was sent and died according to the counsel of God the Father, proceeding from His eternal love toward the elect.

3. Those whom God elected in Christ out of His good pleasure alone, and those only, He decreed to give to the Son, and to give them faith in order that they would be brought all the way to eternal life.

4. The matchless love and mercy of God is the sole cause both of the sending of the Son and of the satisfaction appointed beforehand through Him, even the conferring of faith and application of merit through it: which benefits should not be objects of separation or be torn asunder from themselves.

Rejection of the error of those:

1. Who teach that in God there is granted, under the condition of faith and repentance, some good will of saving those who perish.

2. Who, using economy (ὀικονομίας) for an excuse, ascribe to God the inclination or volition or disposition or affection or less ardent love or power or intention or desire or will or counsel or decree or covenant or necessary

or universal conditional loving kindness, by which He wills each and every man to be saved if they believe in Christ.

3. Who assign to God a design previous to election in which He determined to be merciful to the whole human race without limit.

4. Who attribute to God a twofold loving-kindness, one clear or first and universal by which He willed each and every person to be saved: the other more clear, second, and particular towards the elect.

III. Concerning Redemption

1. Because the end has been destined only to those to whom the means have been destined, the advent of Jesus Christ into the world, His death, satisfaction, and salvation are destined only to those whom God decreed from eternity from His mere good pleasure to give faith and repentance, to whom He confers those very things in time. Scripture and the experience of all the ages is opposed to the universality of saving grace.

2. Christ, out of the mere good pleasure (εὐδοκία) of the Father, has been destined and given as a mediator to a certain number of men who make up His mystical body on account of the election of God.

3. For these, Christ Himself, perfectly conscious of His vocation, willed and resolved to die and to add to the infinite value of His death, the most efficacious and singular purpose of His will.

4. The universal propositions which are observed in Scripture do not declare that Christ died, made satisfaction, etc. for each and every person in consequence of the counsel of the Father and His will, but either they are to be restricted to the universality of the body of Christ or ought to be related to that economy (ὄικονομίαν) of the new covenant in which the outward distinction of all people having been canceled, the Son having adopted all nations to Himself, they are joined to His inheritance, i.e., in respect to any nation and people in general without distinction, He opens and offers the grace of preaching according to His will, gathers His church from them because this is the basis of the universal preaching of the gospel.

Rejection of the error of those:

Who teach that Christ died for each and every one sufficiently, not merely by reason of worth, but also by reason of intention; or for all conditionally, if they were to believe; or who assert that Scripture teaches that Christ died for all men universally; and most especially the places of Scripture (Ezek. 18:21 etc. and 31:11; John 3:16; 1 Tim. 2:4; 2 Peter 3:9) ought to be extended to each and every man and by these the universality of love and grace ought to be proved.

IV. Concerning the Disposition of Man to Grace

1. Since the requisite conditions for salvation are impossible to the reprobate, God does not intend the salvation of them conditionally if they believe and repent unless it is supposed that there is an empty, deceptive, and useless intention and will of God.

2. The good use of the light of nature either subjective or objective is unable to draw men over to salvation, not even to gain from God any other measure of light appointed for salvation.

Rejection of the error of those:

1. Who teach a universal and common call to all men to salvation and to the author of salvation; and (who teach) that each and every man, if he wishes, is able to believe and be saved.

2. Who teach that by His revealed disposition, God wills the salvation of each and every one.

V. Concerning Promises Made to Believers and Their Prerogatives

1. Life, of which the promise annexed to the Law is exhibited by its stipulation, is not only earthly and temporal, but also heavenly and eternal.

2. Believers even before Christ was born had the same Mediator and Savior we have and the same spirit of adoption.

Rejection of the error of those:

1. Who teach that the reward of the legal covenant as a duty is no other than natural and temporary.

2. Who teach that the fathers of the Old Testament were blind to the pledge [*arrabon*] of the Holy Spirit.

118

The Principles of Faith (1652)

While the publication and adoption of the Westminster Standards by the Assembly of Divines and the English Parliament ostensibly settled the confession and government of the Church of England by 1648, the polarization within the Puritan ranks began to spill out into the public square. A new and different "game at cards" began in 1647 with Oliver Cromwell (1599–1658) and his New Model Army pitted against Parliament and King Charles I (1600–1649). Much of this tension is traceable to the Independent or Congregational faction, whose resistance to a Presbyterian Church of England created a breach with the Scots and other defenders of the Solemn League and Covenant (1643). Charles, ever the schemer, delayer, and divine right scion, shrewdly endorsed the "Engagement" of December 1647, whereas he had previously refused all compromise in royal or Anglican supremacy and Parliamentary prerogative. But the debates at St. Mary the Virgin Church in Putney (October–November 1647) introduced an element destined to shift power to Cromwell's Army. Radical spirits were "crying up toleration" as a means of attaining "liberty of conscience." John Lilburne ("Free-born John," ca. 1615–1657), William Walwyn (ca. 1600–1681), Richard Overton (fl. 1631–1664), and others were stirring the pot already overflowing.

Cromwell's meteoric rise to power in the army and the maneuverings of the Independent/Congregational faction in Parliament placed an altogether ironic spin on political and ecclesiastical matters. Presbyterian troops, who had crossed the Tweed in 1644 to reinforce Parliament's efforts against the king and become co-belligerents with Cromwell and his comrades, now turned their guns and swords against their former allies with a second Civil War (1648). But Cromwell, his army, and sympathizers in Parliament refused to cede their own future to their now "intolerant" antagonists.

Having routed the Scots at Preston (August 17, 1648), Cromwell purged Parliament of all Presbyterian and Royalist sympathizers (Colonel Thomas Pride's "Purge," December 6, 1648). The so-called Rump Parliament which ensued was dissolved in turn by Cromwell on April 20, 1653. "Old Ironsides" (Cromwell's nickname), commander of the New Model Army ("Ironsides," as it was called), was well on his way to becoming Lord Protector of England (or, some quipped, "Lord Dictator"). The Independent/Congregational faction was only too happy to ride his coattails politically and ecclesiastically.

In any event, the Rump Parliament attempted to deal with the vexed question of tolerance via liberty of conscience, especially in ecclesiastical and theological matters. Indeed, what was essential and what was not to be tolerated in a Christian commonwealth? A Committee for the Propagation of the Gospel was constituted to consider the matter. Not surprisingly, it was stacked with Independents/Congregationalists led by John Owen (1616–1683), Thomas Goodwin (1600–1680), Philip Nye (d. 1672), and Sydrach Sympson/Simpson (ca. 1600–1655). The last three were part of the so-called "Five Pillars of Congregationalism" who stonewalled the Westminster Assembly for months, arguing vociferously against *jure divino* Presbyterianism (cf. Robert Paul, *The Assembly of the Lord* [1985]).[1] On March 31, 1652, Owen's Committee published *The Humble Proposals*.[2] The fifteen proposals of this document provided liberty of conscience to those who embraced the "orthodox…Principles of Christian Religion," but allowed no toleration or liberty to those promulgating "delusions of Sathan."

Parliament apparently took no action on these proposals, for on December 2, 1652, a modified and enhanced version of "Proposals" was

---

1. The other two members of this "gang of five" were Jeremiah Burroughs (1599–1646) and William Bridge (c.1600–1670).

2. The full title is: *The Humble Proposals of Mr. Owen, Mr. Tho. Goodwin, Mr. Nye, Mr. Sympson, and other Ministers, who presented the Petition to the Parliament, and other persons, Febr. 11. under debate by a Committee this 31. of March, 1652. for the furtherance and Propagation of the Gospel in this Nation. Wherein they having had equall respects to all Persons fearing God, though of differing judgements, doe hope also that they will tend to union and peace. With Additional Propositions humbly tendred to the Committee for propagating the Gospel, as easie and speedy means for supply of all Parishes in England with able, godly, and Orthodox Ministers. For, Setling of right constituted Churches, and for preventing persons of corrupt judgements, from publishing dangerous Errours, and Blasphemies in Assemblies and Meetings, by other godly Persons, Ministers and others.* (Thomason # E. 658. [12.]).

published.[3] Appended to the proposals themselves (pp. 1–5) was a catalog of "Principles of Christian Religion" (pp. 5–21), complete with full-length proof texts in support of each doctrinal proposition (discussion of these articles may be found in T. M. Lawrence, "Transmission and Transformation: Thomas Goodwin and the Puritan Project, 1600–1704," Ph.D. diss. [2002] 152–61). Another printed version of these principles appeared on November 2, 1654.[4] Using the 1652 version, these principles are printed below with modern spelling and punctuation. We have reduced the proof texts to citation only, omitting the full quotations.

Once again, it appears Parliament took no action on these matters, due no doubt in part to the dissolution of the Rump the following spring (April 20, 1653). Toleration continued to be a bone of contention as England perched on the brink of Cromwell's Protectorate (December 1653 to September 1658).

THE PRINCIPLES OF FAITH

I.

That the holy Scripture is that rule of knowing God, and living to Him, which whosoever does not believe, but takes himself to any other way of discovering truth and the mind of God instead thereof, cannot be saved (2 Thess. 2:10–15; 1 Cor. 15:1–3; 2 Cor. 1:13; Acts 26:22f.; John 5:39; Ps. 147:19–20; John 4:22; 2 Peter 2:1; 3:1–2).

---

3. *Proposals for the furtherance and propagation of the Gospell in this Nation. As the same were humbly presented to the Honourable Committee of Parliament by divers Ministers of the Gospell, and others. As also, Some Principles of Christian Religion, without the beliefe of which, the Scriptures doe plainly and clearly affirme, Salvation is not to be obtained. Which were also presented in explanation of one of the said proposals.* (Thomason # E. 683. [12.]).

4. *The Principles of Faith, presented by Mr. Tho. Goodwin, Mr. Nye, Mr. Sydrach Simson, and other Ministers, to the Committee of Parliament for Religion, by way of explanation to the Proposals for propagating of the Gospel* (Thomason # E. 234. [5.]). This is a duplicate version (including proof texts) of the December 2, 1652 version. The only difference is in the incorrect numbering of art. 14 and the use of the numeral 15 twice for an article in the 1654 edition (cf. pp. 7–8).

II.

That there is a God who is the Creator, Governor, and Judge of the world, which is to be received by faith and every other way of the knowledge of Him is insufficient (Heb. 11:3, 6; Rom. 1:19–22; 1 Cor. 1:21; 2 Thess. 1:8).

III.

That this God who is the Creator is eternally distinct from all creatures in His being and blessedness (Rom. 1:18, 25; 1 Cor. 8:5–6).

IV.

That this God is one in three persons or subsistences (1 John 5:5–9; John 8:17–19, 21; Matt. 28:19; Eph. 4:4–6; 1 John 2:22–23; 2 John 9–10).

V.

That Jesus Christ is the only mediator between God and man, without the knowledge of whom there is no salvation (1 Tim. 2:4–6; 2 Tim. 3:15; 1 John 2:22; Acts 4:10, 12; 1 Cor. 3:10–11).

VI.

That this Jesus Christ is the true God (1 John 5:29; Isa. 45:21–25; Rom. 14:11–12; Phil. 2:6–12).

VII.

That this Jesus Christ is also true man (1 John 4:2–3; 2 John 7).

VIII.

That this Jesus Christ is God and man in one person (1 Tim. 3:16; Matt. 16:13–18).

IX.

That this Jesus Christ is our Redeemer, who by paying a ransom and bearing our sins, has made satisfaction for them (Isa. 53:11; 1 Peter 2:24–25; 1 Cor. 15:2–3; 1 Tim. 2:4–6; 1 Cor. 6:20).

X.

That this same Jesus Christ is He that was crucified at Jerusalem and rose again and ascended into heaven (John 8:24; Acts 4:10–12; 10:38–43; 1 Cor. 15:2–8; Acts 22:8; 2:36–38).

XI.

That this same Jesus Christ, being the only God and man in one person, remains forever a distinct person from all saints and angels, notwithstanding their union and communion with Him (Col. 2:8–10, 19; 1 Tim. 3:16).

XII.

That all men by nature are dead in trespasses and sins and no man can be saved unless he is born again, repents and believes (John 3:3, 5–7, 10; Acts 17:30–31; 26:17–20; Luke 24:47; Acts 20:20–21; John 5:24–25).

XIII.

That we are justified and saved by grace and faith in Jesus Christ, and not by works (Acts 15:24; Gal. 1:6–9; 5:2, 4–5; Rom. 9:31–33; 10:3–4; 1:16–17; Gal. 3:11; Eph. 2:8–10).

XIV.

That to continue in any known sin, upon what pretense or principle soever, is damnable (Rom. 1:32; 6:1–2, 15–16; 1 John 1:6, 8; 3:3–8; 2 Peter 2:19–20; Rom. 8:13).

XV.

That God is to be worshipped according to His own will; and whosoever shall forsake and despise all the duties of His worship cannot be saved (Jer. 10:15; Ps. 14:4; Jude 18–21; Rom. 10:13).

XVI.

That the dead shall rise; and that there is a day of judgment wherein all shall appear, some to go into everlasting life and some into everlasting condemnation (1 Tim. 1:19–20; 2 Tim. 2:17–18; Acts 17:30–31; John 5:28–29; 1 Cor. 15:19).

119

A New Confession of Faith (1654)

Beginning in 1652, John Owen (1616–1683) was a prominent member of the Rump Parliament Committee for the Propagation of the Gospel. That committee, which featured prominent Independents/Congregationalists, had drafted *The Principles of Faith* (1652; reprinted Nov. 2, 1654). When Oliver Cromwell (1599–1658) dissolved the Rump (April 20, 1653), the first Protectorate Parliament (September 3, 1654) established a committee to determine the limits of toleration in religion. Owen was once again a key member, but Parliament added Presbyterian figures to the Congregational theologians (Owen, Goodwin, Nye, and Simpson)—notably, Richard Vines (1600–1655/56), Thomas Manton (1620–1677), Stephen Marshall (ca. 1594–1655), and Francis Cheynell (1608–1665). Richard Baxter (1615–1691), also a member, remains a quandary due to his Neonomian doctrine of justification and his eclectic ecclesiology. The confession they drafted survives in only one extant copy, which originally belonged to George Thomason (†1666) of "Thomason Tracts" fame. His copy is now in the British Library, sans cover or title page. That deficiency is covered by a manuscript copy of the absent page from Thomason's hand.[1]

As was the case with the Principles of Faith (1652), Parliament took no action to implement this succinct declaration. Perhaps this is due (once more) to the dissolution of a parliamentary body by Cromwell—the Lord Protector dissolved the first Protectorate Parliament on January 22, 1655.

It has been suggested that the motivation for this and the previous 1652 summary of Christian principles was related to the English translation and

---

1. Cf. *Catalogue of the Pamphlets, Books, Newspapers, and Manuscripts Relating to the Civil War, the Commonwealth, and Restoration, Collected by George Thomason, 1640–1661,* 2:1, 1653–1661 (1908), 93 (entry for Dec. 12, 1654; E. 826. [3.]).

publication of the Socinian Racovian Catechism (1652).[2] This would explain the Trinitarian language of these brief post-Westminster declarations. And yet such orthodox language would be generic to any statement of Christian essentials. Perhaps more telling is the language of "ransom" in reference to Christ's atoning death. That term would have been anathema to Socinians, whose exemplaristic view of Christ's death on the cross eschews any notion of propitiation or satisfaction of divine justice.

Why this confession was produced on the heels of the republication of the 1652 Principles a month prior is not clear. Apparently, the committee, now enhanced with Presbyterian brethren, felt a fresh start was necessary. While it uses several clauses from the former document, it also enlarges and adds a number of doctrinal articles and reflections not found in the previous *Principles*. Thus it is indeed a "new confession."

The full title of the work is *A new Confession of Faith, or the first principles of the Christian Religion necessary to bee laid as a foundation by all such as desire to build on unto perfection. Represented by a Committee of Divines... unto the grand Committee for Religion as fitt to be owned by all such Ministers as are or shall be allowed to receive the publique maintenance for their works in the Ministry. Propounded to the Parliament, 12 Dec.* A transcript is found in T. M. Lawrence, "Transmission and Transformation: Thomas Goodwin and the Puritan Project, 1600–1704," PhD diss. (2002), 224–27. We have modernized spelling and punctuation in the version below.

NEW CONFESSION OF FAITH

I. The Holy Scriptures of the Old and New Testament are the Word of God and the only rule of knowing Him savingly, and living unto Him in all holiness and righteousness, in which we must rest; which Scriptures, whoever does not believe but rejects them, does instead thereof take himself to any other way of discovering the mind of God, cannot be saved.

---

2. John Coffey, "The Toleration Controversy During the English Revolution," in Christopher Durston & Judith Maltby, eds., *Religion in Revolutionary England* (2006), 52.

II. There is one only God, who is a Spirit, all-sufficient, eternal, infinite, unchangeable, almighty, omniscient, just, merciful, most holy, good, true, faithful and only wise; working all things according to the counsel of His own will; the creator, governor and judge of the world. The knowledge of God by faith is necessary to salvation and every other way of knowledge of Him is insufficient to salvation.

III. That this God is infinitely distinct from all creatures in His being and blessedness.

IV. That this God is one in three persons or subsistences—Father, Son, and Holy Spirit.

V. God made man upright in His own image to yield obedience to Him, so that the chief end of man is to live to God and enjoy Him forever.

VI. Man who was thus created is fallen into a state of sin and misery; so that our nature is wholly corrupted, disabled to all that is spiritually good, in bondage to sin, at enmity with God, prone to all that is evil; and while we continue in that estate, the wrath of God abides upon us.

VII. That every transgression of the law of God is sin, the wages whereof is eternal death.

VIII. That God out of His love sent Jesus Christ to be the only mediator between God and man, without the knowledge of whom, by the revelation of the gospel, there is no salvation.

IX. That this Jesus Christ is God by nature, the only and eternally begotten Son of the Father, and also true man in one person.

X. That this Jesus Christ is our redeemer and surety, who, dying in our stead, laying down His life a ransom for us and bearing our sins, has made full satisfaction for them.

XI. That this Lord Jesus Christ is He that was crucified at Jerusalem, was buried, rose again and ascended into heaven, and there sits at the right hand of God, making intercession for us, who remains forever a distinct person from all saints and angels, notwithstanding their union and communion with Him.

XII. All true believers are partakers of Jesus Christ and all His benefits freely by grace, and are justified by faith in Him and not by works, He being made of God righteousness unto us.

XIII. That no man can be saved unless he is born again of the Holy Spirit, repents, believes, and walks in holy conversation and godliness.

XIV. That whosoever does not prize and love Jesus Christ above himself and all other things, cannot be saved.

XV. Whosoever allows himself to live in any known sin, upon any pretense or principle whatsoever, is in a state of damnation.

XVI. That God is to be worshipped according to His own will, and that only in and through Jesus Christ.

XVII. That all the dead shall rise again.

XVIII. That in the last day, God will judge the world in righteousness by Jesus Christ and reward every one according to his works.

XIX. That all believers shall be translated into an everlasting state of blessedness and an inheritance of glory in the kingdom of heaven.

XX. That all the wicked and unbelievers shall be cast into everlasting torments with the devil and his angels in hell.

120

The Midlands Confession (1655)

The Midlands Association of Particular (Calvinistic) Baptists was formed in England in 1655. Daniel King (fl. 1640–1672) was likely the leader of this alternative to the dominant General (Arminian) Baptists in the region. King was pastor of the Particular Baptist Church at Warwick and has been labeled the founder of the Midlands Baptist Association. Indeed, the strength of the Baptists was in the Midlands just outside of London.

On May 3, 1655, representatives from churches in Warwick, Moreton-in-the-Marsh, Bourton-on-the-Water, Alcester, Tewkesbury, Hook-Norton, and Derby gathered at Warwick to consider the Articles of Faith. King is regarded as the author of the document that follows.

The extant records of the Midlands Baptist Association indicate a series of twelve meetings from June 26, 1655, at Moreton-in-the Marsh to October 5–6, 1658, at Gloucester.

Our text in found at www.the-faith.org.uk/midlands.html and is used here with the gracious permission of John Cargill.

CONFESSION OF FAITH 1655

1. We believe and profess, that there is only one true God, who is our God, who is eternal, almighty, unchangeable, infinite, and incomprehensible; who is a Spirit, having His being in Himself, and giveth being to all creatures; He doth what He will, in heaven and earth; working all things according to the counsel of His own will.

2. That this infinite Being is set forth to be the Father, the Word, and the Holy Spirit; and these three agree in one. 1 John 5:7.

3. We profess and believe the Holy Scriptures, the Old and New Testament, to be the word and revealed mind of God, which are able to make men wise unto Salvation, through faith and love which is in Christ Jesus; and that they are given by inspiration of God, serving to furnish the man of God for every good work; and by them we are (in the strength of Christ) to try all things whatsoever are brought to us, under the pretence of truth. 2 Tim 3:15–17; Isaiah 8:20.

4. That though Adam was created righteous, yet he fell through the temptations of Satan; and his fall overthrew, not only himself, but his posterity, making them sinners by his disobedience; so that we are by nature children of wrath, and defiled from the womb, being shapen in iniquity and conceived in sin. Ps 51:5; Rom 5:12–15.

5. That God elected and chose, in His eternal counsel, some persons to life and salvation, before the foundation of the world, whom accordingly He doth and will effectually call, and whom He doth so call, He will certainly keep by His power, through faith to salvation. Acts 13:48; Eph 1:2–4; 2 Thess 2:13; 1 Peter 1:2, etc.

6. That election was free in God, of His own pleasure, and not at all for, or with reference to, any foreseen works of faith in the creature, as the motive thereunto. Eph 1:4; Rom 11:5–6.

7. That Jesus Christ was, in the fullness of time, manifested in the flesh; being born of a woman; being perfectly righteous, gave Himself for the elect to redeem them to God by His blood. John 10:15; Eph 5:25–27; Rev 5:9.

8. That all men until they be quickened by Christ are dead in trespasses; and therefore have no power of themselves to believe savingly. But faith is the free gift of God, and the mighty work of God in the soul, even like the rising of Christ from the dead. Therefore [we] consent not with those who hold that God hath given power to all men to believe to salvation. Eph 2:1; John 15:5; Eph 1:19.

9. That Christ is the only true King, Priest, and Prophet of the Church. Acts 2:22–23; Heb 4:14.

10. That every man is justified by Christ, apprehended by faith; and that no man is justified in the sight of God partly by Christ and partly by works. Rom 3:20–30 & 8:33; 1 Cor 6:11; Gal 5:4.

11. That Jesus of Nazareth, of whom the scriptures of the Old Testament prophesied, is the true Messiah and Savior of men; and that He died on the cross, was buried, rose again in the same body in which He suffered and ascended to the right hand of the majesty on high, and appeareth in the presence of God, making intercession for us.

12. That all those who have faith wrought in their hearts by the power of God, according to His good pleasure, should be careful to maintain good works, and to abound in them, acting from principles of true faith and unfeigned love, looking to God's glory as their main end. Titus 3:8; Heb 11:6; 1 Cor 6:10 & 31.

13. That those who profess faith in Christ, and make the same appear by their fruits, are the proper subjects of Baptism. Matt 28:18–19.

14. That this baptizing is not by sprinkling, but dipping of the persons in the water, representing the death, burial, and resurrection of Christ. Rom 6:3–4; Col 2:12; Acts 8:38–39.

15. That persons so baptized ought, by free consent, to walk together, as God shall give opportunity in distinct churches, or assemblies of Zion, continuing in the Apostles' doctrine and fellowship, breaking of bread and prayers, as fellow-men caring for one another, according to the will of God. All these ordinances of Christ are enjoined in His Church, being to be observed till His Second Coming, which we all ought diligently to wait for.

16. That at the time appointed of the Lord, the dead bodies of all men, just and unjust, shall rise again out of their graves, that all may receive according to what they have done in their bodies, be it good or evil.

121

Waldensian Confession (1655)

> "Avenge, O Lord, thy slaughtered saints, whose bones
> Lie scattered on the Alpine mountains cold."
> — John Milton, Sonnet XVIII: "On the Late Massacre in Piemont"

Milton's verse protests while poignantly memorializing the Waldensians of Italy, who were brutally massacred on the "Piedmontese Easter," April 24, 1655. Unless they would embrace the papal faith, Roman Catholic authorities commanded the Vaudois to withdraw from territory they possessed in the Piedmont. It was the Duke of Savoy, Charles Emmanuel II (1634–1675), and his henchman, the Marquis de Pianezza, who betrayed a century-old treaty (the Treaty of Cavour, 1561), forcing the Waldensians out of the villages and valleys into the mountains of the Italian Alps. Five thousand Catholic soldiers were directed to attack the Vaudois that Easter week of 1655. Most of these were French troops on their way to attack the Spanish in Lombardy. They were only too happy to oblige their masters in rape, murder, torture, looting, and worse. Jean Leger (1615–1670), Waldensian pastor and eyewitness to the horrors, launched a personal crusade to inform the administrations of all the Protestant ruling houses in Europe of the carnage. Oliver Cromwell (1599–1658) was outraged and dispatched Sir Samuel Morland (1625–1695) as his envoy to the Savoy in protest. Letters were drafted by Cromwell's secretary, John Milton (1608–1674), and hurried to the European potentates. The result was shame for even the king of France, Louis XIV (1638–1715), and a treaty to protect the Vaudois. Schaff opines that the confession below was penned by Jean Leger, moderator of the churches of the Piedmont, in 1655.

The oldest text of this confession appears in Antoine Leger's 1655 *Relation veritable de ce que s'est passé dans les persecutions & massacres faits cette année, aux eglises reformées de Piemont: avec la refutation des calomnies dont les adversaries de la verité taschent de les noircir.* Bound together with this work are *Suite de la relation veritable contenant une briefe Refutation de l'invective du Marquis de Pianesse contre les Reformés* des Vallées de Piemont… (1655) and *Brieve Confession de Foy des Eglises Reformées de Piemont* (pages 79–84). It does not contain the *Additions à la sus-dite Confession* appended below from Vinay, nor does it have the article titles that have been inserted in the margins of that version. The anathema attached to the *Additions* has caused this confession to be called "The Anathematizing Confession." Some regard it as "the purest expression of Bible doctrine at all times maintained by the Vaudois church." Others have noted its dependence upon the French Confession of 1559 and that of La Rochelle of 1571.

The *Additions* appear in the version printed in Jean Leger, *Histoire générale des églises évangeliques des Vallées de Piémont* (1669), I:115–16. Leger gives the text as found in the 1655 work with only slight variation (pp. 112–15). The page margins of this edition also contain the article titles (the last two of which are obviously misaligned in each version in which they are printed, i.e., Leger and Vinay). These have been re-aligned in our version with brackets to match the proper article (numbers 31 and 32, *not* numbers 32 and 33). Müller's version (pp. 500–505) contains the thirty-three articles plus the *Additions*, but lacks the opening preamble. Valdo Vinay prints the French text of Antoine Leger with a few helpful notes (*La Confessioni di fede dei Valdesi Reformati*, 179–186). He notes the omission of an accusation against the Waldensians in the *Additions* (p. 185 of his text). It would appear after number two in our edition and reads (from the Italian): "That Jesus Christ was not without sin" (cf. our translation of the 1662 version below). Samuel Morland prints an English and Italian version side-by-side in *The History of the Evangelical Churches of the Valley of Piemont* (1658), 61–71. His edition places the omitted accusation about the impeccability of Christ at position number three of the *Additions* and includes the "Anathema" at the end.

There are a number of previous English translations of this confession, the most complete of which appears in Schaff's *Creeds of Christendom*, 3:757–770. Abbreviated versions are found in: W. S. Craig, *Some Old Confessions of Faith* (1926), 67–72; Jean Paul Perrin, *History of the Old Waldenses Anterior to the Reformation* (1847), 293–96; *The Waldenses: Sketches of the Evangelical Christians of the Valleys of the Piedmont* (1853),

385–90, where the confession is dated 1669 (likely based on Leger's edition noted above), and without the "Additions". There is also a side-by-side Italian-French version online at www.chiesavaldese.org (it too lacks the "Additions"). Our translation is from Antoine Leger's 1655 version and retains most of the original punctuation of that rendition.

A BRIEF CONFESSION OF FAITH OF THE REFORMED CHURCHES OF THE PIEDMONT[1]

Because we have understood that our adversaries, not content to have cruelly persecuted us and robbed us of all our goods, to render us more odious, once more spreading many false rumors, which tend not only to defame our persons, but especially to darken by infamous calumnies the holy and salutary doctrine that we profess, we are obliged, to disabuse the mind of those who have been preoccupied by these sinister impressions, to make a short declaration of our faith, as we have done in the past and that we retain still in the present according to the Word of God, so that all the world may see the falsity of these calumnies, and the wrong by which we are hated and persecuted for a doctrine so innocent.

We believe

Of the Holy Trinity. 1. That there is one only God, who is a spiritual essence, eternal, infinite, all wise, all merciful, and all just; in a word all-perfect; and that there are three persons in that sole and simple essence, the Father, the Son, and the Holy Spirit.

How This God is Revealed. 2. That this God has revealed Himself to men by His works, as much by the creation as by providence, and by His Word, revealed from the beginning by oracles in divers ways, then reduced to writing in books which are called the Holy Scriptures.

---

1. Later editions add: "Published with their Manifesto, on the occasion of the horrible massacres of the year 1655."

Of Holy Scripture Itself. 3. That it is necessary to receive, as we do receive, this Holy Scripture as divine and canonical, that is to say, for the rule of our faith and our life, and that it is fully contained in the books of the Old and the New Testament: that in the Old Testament ought to be included only the books which God entrusted to the Jewish church, and which she always approved or acknowledged to be divine, namely the five books of Moses, Joshua, Judges, Ruth, 1 and 2 Samuel, 1 and 2 Kings, 1 and 2 Chronicles or Paralipomenon, one of Ezra, Nehemiah, Esther, Job, Psalms, the Proverbs of Solomon, Ecclesiastes, Song of Songs, the four greater Prophets and the twelve lesser: and in the New, the four Gospels, the Acts of the Apostles, the epistles of Paul, one to the Romans, two to the Corinthians, one to the Galatians, one to the Ephesians, one to the Philippians, one to the Colossians, two to the Thessalonians, two to Timothy, one to Titus, one to Philemon, the epistle to the Hebrews, one of St. James, two of St. Peter, three of St. John, one of St. Jude, and the Apocalypse.

How the Divinity is Recognized. 4. That we acknowledge the divinity of these sacred books, not only by the testimony of the church, but principally by the eternal and indubitable truth of the doctrine which they contain, by the excellence, sublimity and majesty of all divine (matters) which they contain, and by the operation of the Holy Spirit who causes us to receive with respect the testimony which the church renders us for them, who opens our eyes to discover the rays of celestial light which shine in the Scripture, and rectifies our taste to discern that food by the divine savor which it has.

Of Creation Itself. 5. That God has made all things of nothing by His entirely free will, and by the infinite power of His Word.

Of Providence and that God Is not the Author of Sin. 6. That He directs and governs all things by His providence, ordaining and appointing all that happens in the world, without being either the author or cause of evil committed by the creatures, or that the culpability in power or obligation may in any way be imputed to Him.

Of Angels. 7. That the angels were all created pure and holy, but that some of them have fallen into an irreparable corruption and perdition, but that the others have persevered by an effect of the divine goodness which has upheld and confirmed them.

The Fall of Adam. 8. That man who had been created pure and holy in the image of God, deprived himself through his own fault of that blessed estate, giving his consent to the cunning speech of the devil.

And the Corruption of the Whole Human Race. 9. That man has lost by his transgression the righteousness and the holiness which he had received, incurring with the indignation of God, death and captivity under the power of the one who has the empire of death, namely the devil, insomuch that his free will has become a serf and slave to sin, to such a degree that the nature of all men both Jews and Gentiles are children of wrath, dead in their trespasses and sins, and as a consequence incapable of having any good movement towards salvation, nor to fashion any good thought without grace, all their imaginations and thoughts being only evil all the time.

Of Original Sin. 10. That all the posterity of Adam are culpable in him of his disobedience, infected by his corruption and fallen in the same calamity, even small infants from the womb of their mother, from which comes the name original sin.

Of Election. 11. That God redeems from this corruption and condemnation the persons whom He has chosen[2] by His mercy in His Son Jesus Christ, passing by the others by an irreproachable right of His freedom and justice.

Of Redemption by Jesus Christ. 12. That Jesus Christ has been ordained by God in His eternal decree to be the sole Savior and only Head of His body, which is the church; He has redeemed her by His own blood in the fullness of time, and both offers and communicates to her all His benefits by the gospel.

True God and True Man. 13. That there are two natures in Jesus Christ, the divine and the human, truly united in one and the same person, without confusion, without division, without separation, without alteration; each

---

2. The Italian text adds: "before the foundation of the world, not for any disposition, faith or holiness that he foresaw in them, but" (Vinay, p. 181).

nature retaining its distinct properties, and that Jesus Christ is true God and true man all at the same time.

Death for Our Offenses. 14. That God so loved the world that He has given His Son to save us by His most perfect obedience, especially by that which He has demonstrated in suffering the cursed death of the cross, and by the victories which He has obtained over the devil, sin and death.

Why His Sacrifice May not Be Repeated. 15. That Jesus Christ has made complete expiation for our sins by His most perfect sacrifice once offered on the cross, it neither can nor ought to be repeated upon any pretext whatsoever.

How He Acquired Salvation for Us not by Our Works, but by Faith. 16. That the Lord Jesus has fully reconciled us to God by the blood of the cross; it is by His merit only, and not by our works, that we are absolved and justified before Him.

17. That we have union with Jesus Christ, and communion with His benefits by faith, which rests upon the promises of life which have been made to us in His gospel.

The Operation of the Holy Spirit. 18. That this faith comes from the gracious operation and efficacy of the Holy Spirit, who enlightens our souls and enables them to lean on the mercy of God for the application of the merits of Jesus Christ.

Christ the Sole Mediator. 19. That Jesus Christ is our true and only Mediator, not only for redemption, but also for intercession, and by whose merits and intercession we have access to the Father for invoking with holy confidence of being heard, without need to have recourse to any other intercessor than He.

Good Works. 20. That as God has promised us regeneration in Jesus Christ, those who are united to Him by a living faith ought to devote themselves, and do devote themselves in effect, to good works.

Their Necessity. 21. That good works are so necessary to believers that they cannot reach the kingdom of heaven without doing them, seeing that truly

God has prepared them in order that we should walk in them, that thus we should avoid vices, and devote ourselves to Christian virtues, employing fasting and all other means which may conduce to so holy a thing.

Their Fruits. 22. That our good works are not able to merit anything, yet our Lord does not abandon the recompense of life eternal by a compassionate continuation of His grace, and in virtue of the constant immutability of the promises which He has made to us.

And Honor. 23. That those who possess eternal life for their faith and their good works, ought to be considered as saints, and glorified, and to be praised for their virtues, imitated in all the noble actions of their life, but neither worshipped nor invoked, because one ought not to pray except to the one only God through Jesus Christ.

The Church and Its Head. 24. That God has gathered unto Himself one church in the world for the salvation of men, and that she has only one Head and Foundation who is Jesus Christ.

Definition of the Church. 25. That this church is the company of the faithful, who have been elected by God before the foundation of the world, and called by a holy vocation, are united to follow the Word of God, believing that which He teaches us, and living in His awe.

She is not Able to Fail. 26. That this church is not able to fail, or be destroyed, but that she must be perpetual.

That All the Congregation is Ordered. 27. That all things ought to be ordered and held fast in her communion.

Of the Sacraments. 28. That God has not only instructed us by His Word, but that furthermore He has instituted the sacraments to be joined to this Word, as the means to unite us to Jesus Christ, and to communicate His benefits, and that there are only two common to all the members of the church under the New Testament, namely baptism and the Lord's Supper.

Of Baptism. 29. That He has instituted that of baptism for a testimony of our adoption, and that we have been washed from our sins by the blood of Jesus Christ and renewed in holiness of life.

Of the Lord's Supper. 30. That He has instituted that of the Holy Supper or Eucharist for the nourishing of our soul, in order that by a true and living faith by the incomprehensible power of the Holy Spirit, eating effectively His flesh, and drinking His blood, and uniting us most intimately and inseparably to Christ, in whom and by whom we have spiritual and eternal life.

And in order that every one may clearly see our faith on this point, we insert here the very terms which are used in our prayer before communion, in our liturgy or form of celebrating the Holy Supper, and in our public catechism, which are pieces which one may see at the end of our Psalms.

These are the words of our prayer: "And as our Lord not only once offered His body and His blood for the remission of our sins, but also is willing to communicate the same to us for food in life eternal, grant us this grace that with true sincerity of heart and an ardent zeal, we may receive from Him so great a benefit, that is, that in certain faith we partake of His body and His blood, indeed of Him fully, etc." The words of our liturgy are: "First then, let us believe from these promises that Jesus Christ who is the infallible truth has pronounced with His mouth, namely that He truly wishes us to participate in His body and His blood, in order that we may possess Him entirely, in such a manner that He lives in us and we in Him." Those of our public catechism are the same in section 53.

[*Of Pastors.*] 31. That it is necessary that the church have pastors, judges well instructed and of a good life by those who have the right, as much for preaching the Word of God as for administering the sacraments, and watching over the flock of Jesus Christ, following the rules of a good and holy discipline, conjointly with the elders and deacons according to the practice of the ancient church.

[*Of Magistrates.*] 32. That God has established the king and the magistrates to govern the people and that the people ought to be subject to them and obey them by virtue of this arrangement, not only for fear, but for conscience, in all the things which have been conformed to the Word of God, who is the King of Kings and the Lord of Lords.

33. Finally, that it is necessary to receive the Apostles' Creed, the Lord's Prayer, and the Decalogue as fundamental elements of our belief, and of our devotions.

And for the more ample declaration of our belief, we reiterate here the protestation which we caused to be printed in the year 1603. That is that we consent in sound doctrine with all the Reformed churches of France, England, the Low Countries, Germany, Switzerland, Bohemia, Poland and Hungary, and others, as it is set forth in their confessions, and the same as the confession of Augsburg according to the declaration which the author has given. And promising to persevere with the help of God constantly in life and in death, being ready to subscribe that eternal truth of God by our own blood, as was done by our predecessors from the time of the apostles [and] particularly in these last centuries. And we humbly beseech all the Evangelical and Protestant churches to hold us, notwithstanding our poverty and lowliness, to be true members of the mystical body of Jesus Christ, suffering for His holy name; and to continue to us the assistance of their prayers to God and all other good offices of their charity, as we have before abundantly experienced, we give them thanks with all the humility which is possible to us, and pray with all our heart the Lord who is remunerative of the same, pouring on them the most precious blessings of His grace and of His glory, both in this life, and in that which is to come. AMEN.

Additions to the Confessions above

A brief justification touching the points, or articles of faith which the doctors of Rome impute to us in common with all the Reformed churches. Accusing us of believing:

1. That God is the author of sin.
2. That God is not all powerful.
3. That Jesus Christ fell into despair on the cross.
4. That in the works of salvation, when man is moved by the Holy Spirit, he does not cooperate any more than a piece of wood or a rock.
5. That the efficacy of predestination, is of no consequence whether one does good or evil.
6. That good works are not necessary to salvation.
7. That we absolutely reject confession of sin and repentance.

8. That fasting must be rejected, and other mortifications of the flesh, to live in dissolution.

9. That any one can explain the Holy Scripture as it pleases him, and according to the inspirations of his own particular spirit.

10. That the church can fail entirely and be destroyed.

11. That baptism is not a necessity for anyone.

12. That in the sacrament of the Eucharist, we do not have any real communion with Jesus Christ, but only in a figure.

13. That it is not obligatory to obey magistrates, kings, princes, etc.

14. Because we do not invoke the holy virgin, and men already glorified, they accuse us of scorn, when we declare them blessed, worthy both of praise and imitation, and hold above all the holy virgin "blessed among all women."

But all these articles which are so maliciously imputed to us, far from believing or teaching them, we hold to be heretical and damnable, and denounce from all our heart anathema against whoever would maintain them.

(Translated by James T. Dennison Jr.)

122

The Somerset Confession (1656)

The Western or Somerset (Particular) Baptist Association originated November 6–7, 1653 at Wells (western England). The moving spirit was Thomas Collier (†1691). As Oliver Cromwell's (1599–1658) toleration policy permitted many "sectaries" to practice their convictions freely, the Quakers brought their doctrine of the "inner light" to this region in 1564. George Fox (1624–1691) himself toured the territory in 1655, attracting large numbers of Baptists to his new religion.

The Somerset Confession was the response of the Baptists to "guilt by association," both with respect to the Quakers and the suspicions of the London Particular Baptists that the western brethren were not fully orthodox. The statement was approved at the seventh meeting of the association on September 5–6, 1656 at Bridgewater. It is alleged that this confession is based upon a draft dating from about 1653. In any case, it seems clear that Collier was the principal author; he had been named "general superintendent and messenger to all the associated churches" in 1655.

The interesting article 35 on the Jews is a further reflection of Cromwell's policy of toleration. He had welcomed Rabbi Manasseh ben Israel (1604–1657) to London in 1655 and entertained a conference in December of that year that considered the readmission of the Jews (banned officially from England since 1290) under his Protectorate (1653–1658). Cromwell joined several Protestant theologians in anticipating the conversion of Israel as a prelude to the second coming of the Lord Jesus.

Our text is based on the 1656 edition. We have modernized the spelling in a few places, altered capitalization, and revised the format of the proof texts (correcting those obviously misprinted).

A CONFESSION OF THE FAITH OF SEVERAL CONGREGATIONS OF CHRIST IN THE COUNTY OF SOMERSET, AND SOME CHURCHES IN THE COUNTIES NEAR ADJACENT. PRINTED AT LONDON, ANNO 1656

I.

We believe that there is but one God (1 Cor. 8:6), who is immortal, eternal, invisible, only wise (1 Tim. 1:17), holy (Lev. 11:44), almighty (Gen. 17:1) infinite (1 Kings 8:27; Isa. 40:28; Ps. 147:5); a Spirit (John 4:24), glorious in holiness (Ex. 15:11), just, merciful, gracious, long-suffering, abundant in mercy and truth (Ex. 34:6–7), faithful in all things (Deut. 7:9).

II.

That this God, who is so in Himself, did according to His own will in time, create all things, by, and for Jesus Christ (Heb. 1:2; Col. 1:16; John 1:3); who is the Word of God (John 1:1) and upholds all things by the Word of His power (Heb. 1:3).

III.

That God made man after His own image (Gen. 1:27), in an estate of uprightness and human perfection (Eccl. 7:29).

IV.

That God gave Adam a just law, requiring obedience under the penalty of death (Gen. 2:17), which law he broke, and brought himself and his posterity under the guilt and judgment denounced (Gen. 3:6; Rom. 5:12, 17–19).

V.

Man being in this undone estate, God did in the riches of His mercy hold forth Christ in a promise (Gen. 3:15).

VI.

That in process of time God gave forth His laws by the hand of Moses (Ex. 20; John 1:17), to fallen man (Gal. 3:19), not for justification to eternal life

(Gal. 3:17; Rom. 3:20), but that all might appear guilty before the Lord by it (Rom. 3:19; 5:20).

VII.

That out of this condition none of the sons of Adam were able to deliver themselves (Rom. 8:3; Eph. 2:1, 5; Rom. 5:6).

VIII.

That God continued and renewed the manifestation of His grace and mercy in Christ after the first promise made (Gen. 3), in other promises (Gen. 22:18; Gen. 12:3; Gal. 3:16); and in types, as the Passover (Ex. 12:8, 13; 1 Cor. 5:7), and the brazen serpent (Num. 21:9; John 3:14); with the ministry and ministration of Moses and Aaron, the sacrifices, etc., being all figures of Christ (Heb. 7:8; 9); and in prophesies (Isa. 9:6; 11:1–2; 53:6; 1 Peter 2:24; 1 Cor. 15:3).

IX.

That God in His Son did freely, without respect to any work done, or to be done by them as a moving cause, elect and choose some to Himself before the foundation of the world (Eph. 1:3–4; 2 Tim. 1:9), whom He in time has, does, and will call, justify, sanctify, and glorify (Rom. 8:29–30).

X.

That those that were thus elected and chosen in Christ were by nature (before conversion) children of wrath even as others (Eph. 2:3; Rom. 3:9).

XI.

That those that are chosen of God, called, and justified, shall never finally fall from Him, but being born from above are kept by the power of God through faith unto salvation (John 6:39; 10:28; 11:26; 1 Peter 1:5; Ps. 89:30–34; 1 John 3:9; John 14:19; Heb. 12:2; Jer. 31:3; John 10:29; Ps. 37:28; Jer. 32:40; Rom. 8:39; 1 Cor. 1:8–9; Rom. 8:30; Ps. 48:14).

XII.

That when the fullness of time was come, God sent forth His Son, made of a woman (Gal. 4:4–5) according to the promises and prophesies of the

Scriptures; who was conceived in the womb of Mary the virgin by the power of the Holy Spirit of God (Luke 1:35; Matt. 1:20), and by her born in Bethlehem (Matt. 2:11; Luke 2:6–7).

XIII.

We believe that Jesus Christ is truly God (Isa. 9:6; Heb. 1:8; Rom. 9:5) and truly man, of the seed of David (1 Tim. 2:5; Acts 13:23; Rom. 1:3).

XIV.

That after He came to be about thirty years of age, being baptized, He manifested Himself to be the Son of God (Luke 3:21–23; John 2:7, 11), the promised Messiah, by doing such works both in His life and in His death which were proper unto, and could be done by none but the Son of God, the true Messiah (John 1:49; 6:9ff.).

XV.

That this man Christ Jesus suffered death under Pilate, at the request of the Jews (Luke 23:24), bearing the sins of His people on His own body on the cross (1 Peter 2:24), according to the will of God (Isa. 53:6), being made sin for us (2 Cor. 5:21), and so was also made a curse for us (Gal. 3:13–14; 1 Peter 3:18), that we might be made the righteousness of God in Him (2 Cor. 5:21), and by His death upon the cross, He has obtained eternal redemption and deliverance for His church (Col 1:14; Eph. 1:7; Acts 20:28; Heb. 9:12; 1 Peter 1:18–19).

XVI.

That this same Jesus, having thus suffered death for our sins, was buried (Matt. 27:59–60), and was also raised by the power of God (Eph. 1:19) the third day according to the Scriptures (1 Cor. 15:3–4), for our justification (Rom. 4:25).

XVII.

That after He had been seen forty days upon the earth, manifesting Himself to His disciples (Acts 1:3), He ascended into the heavens (Acts 1:9–11; Heb. 4:14), and is set on the right hand of the throne of God (Heb. 8:1;

1:3), whom the heavens must receive until the time of the restitution of all things (Acts 3:21).

XVIII.

That the Father having thus exalted Him, and given Him a name above every name (Phil. 2:9), and has made Him who is Mediator (1 Tim. 2:5), Priest (Heb. 10:21; 8:1), Prophet (Acts 3:22), and King to His people (Ps. 2:6; Rev. 15:3). As He is our priest, so is He our peace and reconciliation (Eph. 2:14–15; Rom. 5:9–10), and being entered into the holy place, even heaven itself, there to appear in the presence of God (Heb. 9:24), making continual intercession for us (Heb. 7:24–25), He is become our advocate (1 John 2:1) by whom we have boldness and access unto the throne of grace with acceptance (Heb. 10:19; Eph. 3:12; Heb. 4:16). As He is our prophet, so He has given us the Scriptures, the Old and New Testament, as a rule and direction unto us both for faith and practice (John 5:39; 1 Peter 1:10–12; 2 Tim. 3:16; 1 Peter 1:20–21; Eph. 2:20; 1 Cor. 14:37; Titus 1:2– 3); and that He has sent, does and will (according to His promise) send His Holy Spirit the Comforter, by whom He leads us into all truth (John 14:26; 16:13); and by His continual presence with us, and in us (John 14:16–17), teaching, opening, and revealing the mysteries of the kingdom, and will of God unto us (1 Cor. 2:10–13; Rev. 2:29; 5:5), giving gifts in His church for the work of the ministry, and edifying the body of Christ (Eph. 4:8, 12; 1 Cor. 12:4–6), that through the powerful teachings of the Lord, by His Spirit in His church, they might grow up in Him (Eph. 4:15), be conformed to His will (Ezek. 36:27; 1 Peter 1:2), and sing praises unto His name (Heb. 2:12; 1 Cor. 14:15). And as He is our Prophet, and King, Lord, and Lawgiver (Isa. 33:22; 55:4), Prince of Life (Acts 3:15), Prince of Peace (Isa. 9:6), Master of His people (Matt. 23:8), Head of His church (Col. 1:18), the Almighty (Rev. 1:8), so He has given rules unto us, by which He rules over us (Luke 6:46; John 10:16; 1 John 2:4; John 14:15; Matt. 28:20), and rules over all things for His church (Eph. 1:22; Rev. 19:16) and by the power of love rules by His Spirit in us (2 Cor. 5:14; 1 John 2:5), making us (in a measure) both able and willing to honor Him (Phil. 4:3; Heb. 13:21; Eph. 6:10; Phil. 2:13), and bow before Him (Ps. 95:6; 110:3; Rev. 4:10–11), submitting ourselves to Him alone in all His commands with joy (John 15:14; Rev. 14:4; 7:15; Ps. 119:2, 47; Rev. 15:3–4).

XIX.

That the Spirit is administered by or through the word of faith preached (Gal. 3:2) which word was first declared by the Lord Himself, and was confirmed by them that heard Him (Heb. 2:3), which word is called the gospel of God's grace (Acts 20:24), the word of reconciliation (2 Cor. 5:19), the sword of the Spirit (Eph. 6:17), the weapon of a Christian (2 Cor. 10:4); a faithful (Rev. 22:6), quick, powerful (Heb. 4:12), plain (Prov. 8:9), comfortable (Rom. 15:4), pure (Ps. 12:6), right, true (Ps. 33:4), sound (Titus 2:8), and wholesome word (1 Tim. 6:3).

XX.

That this spirit of Christ, being administered by the word of faith, works in us faith in Christ (John 3:5; 1 Peter 1:22 Acts 16:14; Gal. 5:22) by virtue of which we come to receive our sonship (John 1:12; Gal. 3:26), and is further administered unto us through faith in the promises of God (Eph. 1:13; Acts 2:38–39; 4:4), waiting on Him in those ways and means that He has appointed in His word (John 14:15–17; Luke 11:9, 13), this faith being the ground of things hoped for, and the evidence of things not seen (Heb. 11:1).

XXI.

That justification is God's accounting and declaring that man justified from the guilt and condemnation of all his sin, who has received Jesus Christ and believes in Him (in truth and power) according to the record given of Him by God in Scripture (Rom. 4:5; 1 John 5:10–11; John 3:36).

XXII.

That justification from the guilt and condemnation of sin is only obtained through faith in that man Jesus Christ, crucified at Jerusalem, and by God raised from the dead (Rom. 5:1, 9; Acts 13:38–39; Rom. 4:25; 10:9). And that those who bring in any other way of justification, do therein make void, and acquit themselves of having any interest in the gospel and grace of Christ (Gal. 2:21; 5:4).

XXIII.

That this faith being wrought in truth and power, it not only interests us in our justification, sonship, and glory, but it produces as effects and fruits, a conformity, in a measure, to the Lord Jesus, in His will, graces and virtues (Rom. 5:3–4; 1 John 3:23–24; 2 Peter 1:5–7; Gal. 5:6; Acts 26:18; 1 Thess 1:3).

XXIV.

That it is the duty of every man and woman, that have repented from dead works, and have faith towards God, to be baptized (Acts 2:38; 8:12, 37–38), that is, dipped or buried under the water (Rom. 6:3–4; Col. 2:12), in the name of our Lord Jesus (Acts 8:16), or in the name of the Father, Son, and Holy Spirit (Matt. 28:19), therein to signify and represent a washing away of sin (Acts 22:16), and their death, burial, and resurrection with Christ (Rom. 6:5; Col. 2:12), and being thus planted in the visible church or body of Christ (1 Cor. 12:3), who are a company of men and women separated out of the world by the preaching of the gospel (Acts 2:41; 2 Cor. 6:17), do walk together in communion in all the commandments of Jesus (Acts 2:42), wherein God is glorified and their souls comforted (2 Thess. 1:11–12; 2 Cor. 1:4).

XXV.

That we believe some of those commandments further to be as follows:

1. Constancy in prayer (Col. 4:2–3).
2. Breaking of bread (1 Cor. 11:23–24).
3. Giving of thanks (Eph. 5:20).
4. Watching over one another (Heb. 12:15).
5. Caring one for another (1 Cor. 12:25) by visiting one another, especially in sickness and temptations (Matt. 25:36).
6. Exhorting one another (Heb. 3:13).
7. Discovering to each other, and bearing one another's burdens (Gal. 6:2).
8. Loving one another (Heb. 13:1).
9. Reproving one another when there is need (Matt. 18:15).
10. Submitting one to another in the Lord (1 Peter 5:5).
11. Administering one to another according to the gift received, whether it is in spirituals, or temporals (1 Peter 4:10).
12. The offender to seek reconciliation, as well as the offended (Matt. 5:23–24).

13. Love our enemies and persecutors, and pray for them (Matt. 5:23–24).

14. Every one to work if he is able, and none to be idle (2 Thess. 3:10–12).

15. The women in the church to learn in silence, and in all subjection (1 Tim. 2:11; 1 Cor. 14:34).

16. Private admonition to a brother offending another; and if not prevailing, to take one or two more; if he hear not them, then to tell it to the church; and if he hear not them, to be accounted as an heathen and publican (Matt. 18:15).

17. Public rebuke to public offenders (1 Tim. 5:20).

18. The brethren in ministering forth their gifts, ought to do it decently and in order, one by one, that all may learn and all may be comforted (1 Cor. 14:31, 40).

19. A special care to assemble together, that their duty to God and the church may not be neglected (Heb. 10:24–25).

20. And all things in the church, done in the name and power of the head, the Lord Christ Jesus (Col. 3:17).

21. That in admitting members into the church of Christ, it is the duty of the church, and ministers whom it concerns, in faithfulness to God, that they are careful they receive none but such as do make forth evident demonstration of the new birth, and the work of faith with power (John 3:3; Matt. 3:8–9; Acts 8:37; Ezek. 44:6–7; Acts 2:38; 2 Cor. 9:14; Pss. 26:4–5; 101:7).

XXVI.

That those that truly repent, and believe, and are baptized in the name of the Lord Jesus, are in a fit capacity to exercise faith, in full assurance to receive a greater measure of the gifts and graces of the Holy Spirit (Acts 2:38–39; Eph. 1:13).

XXVIII. [sic]

That it is the duty of the members of Christ in the order of the gospel, though in several congregations and assemblies (being one in the head) if occasion be, to communicate each to the other, in things spiritual, and things temporal (Rom. 15:26; Acts 11:29; 15:22; 11:22).

XXIX.

That the Lord Christ Jesus being the foundation and cornerstone of the gospel church whereon His apostles built (Eph. 2:20; Heb. 2:3), He gave them power and abilities to propagate, to plant, to rule and order (Matt. 28:19–20; Luke 10:16), for the benefit of His body, by which ministry He did show forth the exceeding riches of His grace, by His kindness towards it in the ages to come (Eph. 2:7), which is according to His promise (Matt. 28:20).

XXX.

That this foundation and ministration aforesaid, is a sure guide, rule, and direction, in the darkest time of the anti-Christian apostasy, or spiritual Babylonian captivity, to direct, inform, and restore us in our just freedom and liberty, to the right worship and order belonging to the church of Jesus Christ (1 Tim. 3:14–15; 2 Tim. 3:15–17; John 17:20; Isa. 59:21; Rev. 2:24; Isa. 40:21; Rev. 2:5; 1 Cor. 14:37; Rev. 1:3; 2 Thess. 3:14; Rev. 2:11; 1 Peter 1:25; 1 John 4:6; 2 Peter 1:15–16; Isa. 58:11–12; 2 Peter 3:2; Isa. 8:20).

XXXI.

That the church of Jesus Christ with its ministry may from among themselves, make choice of such members, as are fitly gifted and qualified by Christ, and approve and ordain such by fasting, prayer, and laying on of hands (Acts 13:3; 14:23), for the performance of the several duties, whereunto they are called (Acts 20:28; Rom. 12:6–8; 2 Tim. 4:2; Acts 6:3).

XXXII.

That such a ministry laboring in the word and doctrine, has a power to receive a livelihood of their brethren, whose duty it is to provide a comfortable subsistence for them, if they are able, to whom for Christ's sake they are servants (1 Cor. 9:4, 7; 1 Tim. 5:17–18). Yet it is commendable in cases of necessity, for them, for example's sake, and that they may be able to support the weak, to labor and work with their hands (Acts 20:24–25).

XXXIII.

That the authority of Christ in an orderly ministry in His church, is to be submitted unto (Heb. 13:17; 2 Thess. 3:14).

XXXIV.

That as it is an ordinance of Christ, so it is the duty of His church in His authority, to send forth such brethren as are fitly gifted and qualified through the Spirit of Christ to preach the gospel to the world (Acts 13:1–3; 11:22; 8:14).

XXXV.

That it is the duty of us believing Gentiles, not to be ignorant of that blindness that yet lies on Israel, that none of us may boast (Rom. 11:25), but to have bowels of love and compassion to them, praying for them (Rom. 10:1), expecting their calling, and so much the rather, because their conversion will be to us life from the dead (Rom. 11:15).

XXXVI.

That it is the will of the Lord, and it is given to the saints not only to believe in Him, but to suffer for His name (John 16:3; Phil. 1:26) and so to pass through many tribulations into the kingdom of God (Acts 14:22; 2 Tim. 3:12; 2:12).

XXXVII.

That the angels of the Lord are ministering spirits, sent forth for the good of those that shall be the heirs of salvation (Heb. 1:14; Ps. 91:11–12; Acts 27:23; Luke 22:43).

XXXVIII.

That the wicked angels (Ps. 78:49) kept not their first estate in which they were created (Jude 6), the prince of whom is called the devil (Matt. 8:28), and the great dragon, and the old serpent, and Satan (Rev. 12:9), and the accuser of our brethren (Rev. 12:10), and the prince of this world (John 14:30), and a prince that rules in the air; a spirit working in the children of disobedience (Eph. 2:2), and our adversary (1 Peter 5:8), whose children the wicked are (Matt. 13:39; John 8:44). To him we ought not to give place (Eph. 4:27), whose power Christ has overcome for us (Heb. 2:14), and for him and his angels everlasting fire is prepared (Matt. 25:41).

XXXIX.

That it is our assured expectation, grounded upon promises, that the Lord Jesus Christ shall the second time appear without sin unto salvation, unto His people, to raise and change the vile bodies of all His saints, to fashion them like unto His glorious body, and so to reign with Him, and judge over all nations on the earth in power and glory (Phil. 3:20–21; Heb. 9:28; Acts 3:19–21; Matt. 19:28; Rev. 2:26–27; 1 Cor. 6:2; Ps. 72:8, 11; Dan. 7:27; Zech. 14:9; Ps. 2:8–9; Jer. 23:5–6; Ezek. 21:26–27; Isa. 32:1; Rev. 11:15; Ps. 82:8; Rev. 5:9–10; 20:6).

XL.

That there is a day appointed, when the Lord shall raise the unjust as well as the righteous, and judge them all in righteousness (John 5:28–29; Acts 24:15), but every man in his own order (1 Cor. 15:23; 1 Thess. 4:16), taking vengeance on them that know not God, and obey not the gospel of our Lord Jesus Christ, whose punishment will be everlasting destruction from the presence of the Lord (2 Thess. 1:7–10; Jude 14–15; Rev. 20:11–14).

XLI.

That there is a place into which the Lord will gather all His elect, to enjoy Him for ever, usually in Scripture called heaven (2 Cor. 5:1; John 14:2–3).

XLII.

That there is a place into which the Lord will cast the devil, his angels and wicked men, to be tormented for ever, from His presence and the glory of His power, usually in Scripture called hell (Mark 9:43–45; Ps. 9:17; Matt. 25:41; 10:28; 23:33; Luke 10:15; 16:23).

XLIII.

That it is both the duty and privilege of the church of Christ (till His coming again) in their fellowship together in the ordinances of Christ, to enjoy, prize, and press after, fellowship through and in the Spirit with the Lord, and each with the other (Acts 2:42; 1 Cor. 11:26; Eph. 2:21–22; 4:3–6; 1 Cor. 12:13; Eph. 3:9; Col. 2:2), which we believe to be attained through the exercise of faith in the death, resurrection, and life of Christ (2 Cor. 5:14–16; Col. 2:12; Phil. 3:9–11; 1 Peter 2:5).

XLIV.

That the ministry of civil justice (being for the praise of them that do well, and punishment of evildoers) is an ordinance of God, and that it is the duty of the saints to be subject thereunto not only for fear, but for conscience sake (Rom. 13:1–5; 1 Peter 2:13–14) and that for such, prayers and supplications are to be made by the saints (1 Tim. 2:1–2).

XLV.

That nothing comes to pass by fortune or chance, but all things are disposed by the hand of God, and all for good to His people (Gen. 45:5; 50:20; Rom. 8:28; Eph. 1:11; Job 14:5; Isa. 4:5–6).

XLVI.

And that a church so believing, and so walking, though despised, and of low esteem, is no less in the account of her Lord and King, than though

> Black, yet comely (Song 1:5).
> Fairest, without spot (Song 4:7).
> Precious (Isa. 43:4).
> Beautiful (Song 7:1).
> Holy, without blemish (Eph. 5:27).
> Pleasant (Song 1:16).
> Whose soul loves Christ (Song 1:7).
> Runners after Christ (Song 1:4).
> Honorable (Isa. 43:4).
> The desire of Christ (Song 7:10).
> Complete in Christ (Col. 2:10).
> Lovers of the Father (John 16:27).
> The blessed of the Father (Matt. 25:34).
> Kept by the Lord (1 Peter 1:5; Isa. 27:3).
> Graven on the palms of His hands (Isa. 49:16).
> Tender to the Lord as the apple of His eye (Zech. 2:8).
> Taught of the Lord (Isa. 54:13).
> One that has obtained mercy (1 Peter 2:10).
> One that has a redemption (Eph. 1:7).
> The gates of hell shall not prevail against it (Matt. 16:18).

In that church be glory unto God by Jesus Christ, throughout all ages world without end. Amen (Eph. 3:21).

123

The Savoy Declaration (1658)

Three weeks after the death of the Lord Protector, Oliver Cromwell (1599–1658), the Puritan Congregationalists met at the Savoy Palace in London on September 29, 1658, to draft a confession of faith favorable to their independent polity. The epigones of the long struggle with the Presbyterian Puritans (not to mention the "popish" Anglicans) were all present: John Owen (1616–1683), Thomas Goodwin (1600–1680), Philip Nye (†1672), William Bridge (1600/1601–1670), Joseph Caryl (1602–1673), and William Greenhill (1591–1671). Charged with either amending the Westminster Confession (the reduced version of the Articles of Religion—i.e., the version Parliament approved in 1648 which exscinded chapters 30 and 31 as well as most of chapter 20, while removing section 4 of chapter 24) or drafting a new confession altogether, the synod chose the latter. However, it is manifest that the ghost of the Westminster Confession creeps out in virtually every chapter of the Savoy Declaration. The epigones and company chose the path of least resistance as the way most expeditious.

Twelve days later (October 12), their work was done (further attesting the use of Westminster as a template), and with surprising unanimity. Appended to the confession proper were thirty articles on church polity and order. In this appendage are the *de jure* marks of classic congregationalism, i.e., absolute local autonomy.

Richard Cromwell (1626–1712), successor Lord Protector (1658–1659), was presented with the result on October 14, 1658. Alas, his own ill-fated destiny mooted Savoy as much as it did Westminster and other Puritan Nonconformist matters with the Restoration of Charles II (1630–1685) in 1660. By the turn of the century, the Savoy Declaration was a forgotten museum piece in the land of its drafting.

But in New England, this document was destined to live on. At Boston, in 1680, the Massachusetts Synod of the Congregational Church adopted it with slight modification. In 1708, at Saybrook in Connecticut, it was once again recognized as the Congregational doctrinal and governmental standard.

Our text is based on the version in Williston Walker, *The Creeds and Platforms of Congregationalism* (1893), 354–408. We have modernized spelling and capitalization in many places.

A DECLARATION OF THE FAITH AND ORDER OWNED AND PRACTICED IN THE CONGREGATIONAL CHURCHES IN ENGLAND.

Chapter I
Of the Holy Scripture

Although the light of nature, and the works of creation and providence, do so far manifest the goodness, wisdom, and power of God, as to leave men inexcusable; yet are they not sufficient to give that knowledge of God and of His will, which is necessary unto salvation. Therefore it pleased the Lord at sundry times, and in divers manners to reveal Himself, and to declare that His will unto His church; and afterwards for the better preserving and propagating of the truth, and for the more sure establishment and comfort of the church against the corruption of the flesh, and the malice of Satan and of the world, to commit the same wholly unto writing: which maketh the Holy Scripture to be most necessary; those former ways of God's revealing His will unto His people, being now ceased.

II. Under the name of Holy Scripture, or the Word of God written, are now contained all the books of the Old and New Testament; which are these:

Of the Old Testament
Genesis, Exodus, Leviticus, Numbers, Deuteronomy, Joshua, Judges, Ruth, 1 Samuel, 2 Samuel, 1 Kings, 2 Kings, 1 Chronicles, 2 Chronicles, Ezra, Nehemiah, Esther, Job, Psalms, Proverbs, Ecclesiastes, The Song of Songs,

Isaiah, Jeremiah, Lamentations, Ezekiel, Daniel, Hosea, Joel, Amos, Obadiah, Jonah, Micah, Nahum, Habakkuk, Zephaniah, Haggai, Zechariah, Malachi.

Of the New Testament
Matthew, Mark, Luke, John, The Acts of the Apostles, Paul's epistle to the Romans, 1 Corinthians, 2 Corinthians, Galatians, Ephesians, Philippians, Colossians, 1 Thessalonians, 2 Thessalonians, 1 To Timothy, 2 To Timothy, To Titus, To Philemon, the epistle to the Hebrews, the epistle of James, the first and second epistles of Peter, the first, second, and third epistles of John, the epistle of Jude, the Revelation.

All which are given by the inspiration of God to be the rule of faith and life.

III. The books commonly called Apocrypha, not being of divine inspiration, are no part of the canon of the Scripture; and therefore are of no authority in the church of God, nor to be any otherwise approved or made use of, than other human writings.

IV. The authority of the Holy Scripture, for which it ought to be believed and obeyed, dependeth not upon the testimony of any man or church; but wholly upon God (who is truth itself) the author thereof; and therefore it is to be received, because it is the Word of God.

V. We may be moved and induced by the testimony of the church, to a high and reverent esteem of the Holy Scripture. And the heavenliness of the matter, the efficacy of the doctrine, the majesty of the style, the consent of all the parts, the scope of the whole, (which is, to give all glory to God) the full discovery it makes of the only way of man's salvation, the many other incomparable excellencies, and the entire perfection thereof, are arguments whereby it doth abundantly evidence itself to be the Word of God; yet notwithstanding, our full persuasion and assurance of the infallible truth and divine authority thereof, is from the inward work of the Holy Spirit, bearing witness by and with the Word in our hearts.

VI. The whole counsel of God concerning all things necessary for His own glory, man's salvation, faith and life, is either expressly set down in Scripture, or by good and necessary consequence may be deduced from

Scripture; unto which nothing at any time is to be added, whether by new revelations of the Spirit, or traditions of men. Nevertheless we acknowledge the inward illumination of the Spirit of God to be necessary for the saving understanding of such things as are revealed in the Word: and that there are some circumstances concerning the worship of God and government of the church, common to human actions and societies, which are to be ordered by the light of nature and Christian prudence, according to the general rules of the Word, which are always to be observed.

VII. All things in Scripture are not alike plain in themselves, nor alike clear unto all: yet those things which are necessary to be known, believed, and observed for salvation, are so clearly propounded and opened in some place of Scripture or other, that not only the learned, but the unlearned, in a due use of the ordinary means, may attain unto a sufficient understanding of them.

VIII. The Old Testament in Hebrew (which was the native language of the people of God of old) and the New Testament in Greek (which at the time of writing of it was most generally known to the nations) being immediately inspired by God, and by His singular care and providence kept pure in all ages, are therefore authentic; so as in all controversies of religion the church is finally to appeal unto them. But because these original tongues are not known to all the people of God, who have right unto and interest in the Scriptures, and are commanded in the fear of God to read and search them; therefore they are to be translated into the vulgar language of every nation unto which they come, that the Word of God dwelling plentifully in all, they may worship Him in an acceptable manner, and through patience and comfort of the Scriptures may have hope.

IX. The infallible rule of interpretation of Scripture, is the Scripture itself; and therefore when there is a question about the true and full sense of any Scripture (which is not manifold, but one) it must be searched and known by other places, that speak more clearly.

X. The supreme judge by which all controversies of religion are to be determined, and all decrees of councils, opinions of ancient writers, doctrines of men and private spirits, are to be examined, and in whose sentence we are to rest, can be no other, but the Holy Scripture delivered by the Spirit; into which Scripture so delivered, our faith is finally resolved.

Chapter II
Of God and of the Holy Trinity

There is but one only living and true God who is infinite in being and perfection, a most pure Spirit, invisible, without body, parts, or passions, immutable, immense, eternal, incomprehensible, almighty, most wise, most holy, most free, most absolute, working all things according to the counsel of His own immutable and most righteous will, for His own glory, most loving, gracious, merciful, long-suffering, abundant in goodness and truth, forgiving iniquity, transgression and sin, the Rewarder of them that diligently seek Him; and withal most just and terrible in His judgments, hating all sin, and who will by no means clear the guilty.

II. God has all life, glory, goodness, blessedness, in, and of, Himself; and is alone, in, and unto Himself, all-sufficient, not standing in need of any creatures, which He has made, nor deriving any glory from them, but only manifesting His own glory in, by, unto, and upon them: He is the alone fountain of all being, of whom, through whom, and to whom are all things; and has most sovereign dominion over them, to do by them, for them, or upon them, whatsoever Himself pleaseth: in His sight all things are open and manifest, His knowledge is infinite, infallible, and independent upon the creature, so as nothing is to Him contingent or uncertain: He is most holy in all His counsels, in all His works, and in all His commands. To Him is due from angels and men, and every other creature, whatsoever worship, service, or obedience, as creatures, they owe unto the Creator, and whatever He is further pleased to require of them.

III. In the Unity of the Godhead there be three persons, of one substance, power, and eternity, God the Father, God the Son, and God the Holy Ghost: the Father is of none, neither begotten, nor proceeding; the Son is eternally begotten of the Father; the Holy Ghost eternally proceeding from the Father and the Son. Which doctrine of the Trinity is the foundation of all our communion with God, and comfortable dependence upon Him.

Chapter III
Of God's Eternal Decree

God from all eternity did by the most wise and holy counsel of His own will, freely and unchangeably ordain whatsoever comes to pass: yet so, as thereby neither is God the author of sin, nor is violence offered to the will of the creatures, nor is the liberty or contingency of second causes taken away, but rather established.

II. Although God knows whatsoever may or can come to pass upon all supposed conditions, yet hath He not decreed anything, because He foresaw it as future, or as that which would come to pass upon such conditions.

III. By the decree of God for the manifestation of His glory, some men and angels are predestinated unto everlasting life, and others foreordained to everlasting death.

IV. These angels and men thus predestinated, and foreordained, are particularly and unchangeably designed, and their number is so certain and definite, that it cannot be either increased or diminished.

V. Those of mankind that are predestinated unto life, God, before the foundation of the world was laid, according to His eternal and immutable purpose, and the secret counsel and good pleasure of His will, hath chosen in Christ unto everlasting glory, out of His mere free grace and love, without any foresight of faith or good works, or perseverance in either of them or any other thing in the creature, as conditions or causes moving Him thereunto, and all to the praise of His glorious grace.

VI. As God hath appointed the elect unto glory, so hath He by the eternal and most free purpose of His will foreordained all the means thereunto. Wherefore they who are elected, being fallen in Adam, are redeemed by Christ, are effectually called unto faith in Christ by His Spirit working in due season, are justified, adopted, sanctified, and kept by His power, through faith, unto salvation. Neither are any other redeemed by Christ, or effectually called, justified, adopted, sanctified, and saved, but the elect only.

VII. The rest of mankind God was pleased, according to the unsearchable counsel of His own will, whereby He extendeth or withholdeth mercy, as He pleaseth, for the glory of His sovereign power over His creatures, to pass by and to ordain them to dishonor and wrath for their sin, to the praise of His glorious justice.

VIII. The doctrine of this high mystery of predestination is to be handled with special prudence and care, that men attending the will of God revealed in His Word, and yielding obedience thereunto, may from the certainty of their effectual vocation be assured of their eternal election. So shall this doctrine afford matter of praise, reverence, and admiration of God, and of humility, diligence, and abundant consolation to all that sincerely obey the gospel.

Chapter IV
Of Creation

It pleased God the Father, Son, and Holy Ghost, for the manifestation of the glory of His eternal power, wisdom, and goodness, in the beginning, to create or make out of nothing the world, and all things therein, whether visible or invisible, in space of six days, and all very good.

II. After God had made all other creatures, He created man, male and female, with reasonable and immortal souls, endued with knowledge, righteousness and true holiness, after His own image, having the law of God written in their hearts and power to fulfill it; and yet under a possibility of transgressing, being left to the liberty of their own will, which was subject unto change. Besides this law written in their hearts, they received a command not to eat of the tree of the knowledge of good and evil; which while they kept, they were happy in their communion with God, and had dominion over the creatures.

Chapter V
Of Providence

God, the great Creator of all things, doth uphold, direct, dispose and govern all creatures, actions, and things from the greatest even to the least by His most wise and holy providence, according unto His infallible foreknowledge, and the free and immutable counsel of His own will, to the praise of the glory of His wisdom, power, justice, goodness, and mercy.

II. Although in relation to the foreknowledge and decree of God, the first cause, all things come to pass immutably and infallibly; yet by the same providence He ordereth them to fall out, according to the nature of second causes, either necessarily, freely, or contingently.

III. God in His ordinary providence maketh use of means, yet is free to work without, above, and against them at His pleasure.

IV. The almighty power, unsearchable wisdom, and infinite goodness of God so far manifest themselves in His providence, in that His determinate counsel extendeth itself even to the first fall, and all other sins of angels and men (and that not by a bare permission) which also He most wisely and powerfully boundeth, and otherwise ordereth and governeth in a manifold dispensation to His own most holy ends; yet so, as the sinfulness thereof proceedeth only from the creature, and not from God, who being most holy and righteous, neither is, nor can be the author or approver of sin.

V. The most wise, righteous, and gracious God doth oftentimes leave for a season His own children to manifold temptations, and the corruption of their own hearts, to chastise them for their former sins, or to discover unto them the hidden strength of corruption, and deceitfulness of their hearts, that they may be humbled; and to raise them to a more close and constant dependence for their support upon Himself, and to make them more watchful against all future occasions of sin, and for sundry other just and holy ends.

VI. As for those wicked and ungodly men, whom God as a righteous judge, for former sins, doth blind and harden, from them He not only withholdeth His grace, whereby they might have been enlightened in their understandings, and wrought upon in their hearts; but sometimes also withdraweth the gifts which they had, and exposeth them to such objects, as their corruption makes occasions of sin; and withal gives them over to their own lusts, the temptations of the world, and the power of Satan;

whereby it comes to pass that they harden themselves, even under those means which God useth for the softening of others.

VII. As the providence of God doth in general reach to all creatures, so after a most special manner it taketh care of His church, and disposeth all things to the good thereof.

Chapter VI
Of the Fall of Man, of Sin, and of the Punishment Thereof

God having made a covenant of works and life, thereupon, with our first parents and all their posterity in them, they being seduced by the subtlety and temptation of Satan did willfully transgress the law of their creation and break the covenant in eating the forbidden fruit.

II. By this sin they, and we in them, fell from original righteousness and communion with God, and so became dead in sin, and wholly defiled in all the faculties and parts of soul and body.

III. They being the root, and by God's appointment standing in the room and stead of all mankind, the guilt of this sin was imputed, and corrupted nature conveyed to all their posterity descending from them by ordinary generation.

IV. From this original corruption, whereby we are utterly indisposed, disabled, and made opposite to all good, and wholly inclined to all evil, do proceed all actual transgressions.

V. This corruption of nature during this life doth remain in those that are regenerated; and although it be through Christ pardoned and mortified, yet both itself and all the motions thereof are truly and properly sin.

VI. Every sin, both original and actual, being a transgression of the righteous law of God, and contrary thereunto, doth in its own nature bring guilt upon the sinner, whereby he is bound over to the wrath of God, and curse of the Law, and so made subject to death, with all miseries, spiritual, temporal, and eternal.

Chapter VII
Of God's Covenant with Man

The distance between God and the creature is so great, that although reasonable creatures do owe obedience unto Him as their Creator, yet they could never have attained the reward of life, but by some voluntary condescension on God's part, which He hath been pleased to express by way of covenant.

II. The first covenant made with man, was a covenant of works, wherein life was promised to Adam, and in him to his posterity, upon condition of perfect and personal obedience.

III. Man by his fall having made himself incapable of life by that covenant, the Lord was pleased to make a second, commonly called the covenant of grace; wherein He freely offereth unto sinners life and salvation by Jesus Christ, requiring of them faith in Him that they may be saved, and promising to give unto all those that are ordained unto life, His Holy Spirit, to make them willing and able to believe.

IV. This covenant of grace is frequently set forth in the Scripture by the name of a testament, in reference to the death Jesus Christ the Testator, and to the everlasting inheritance, with all things belonging to it, therein bequeathed.

V. Although this covenant hath been differently and variously administered in respect of ordinances and institutions in the time of the Law, and since the coming of Christ in the flesh; yet for the substance and efficacy of it, to all its spiritual and saving ends, it is one and the same; upon the account of which various dispensations, it is called the Old and New Testament.

Chapter VIII
Of Christ the Mediator

It pleased God, in His eternal purpose, to choose and ordain the Lord Jesus His only begotten Son, according to a covenant made between them both, to be the Mediator between God and man; the Prophet, Priest, and King, the Head and Savior of His church, the Heir of all things, and Judge of the world; unto whom He did from all eternity give a people to be His seed, and to be by Him in time redeemed, called, justified, sanctified, and glorified.

II. The Son of God, the second person in the Trinity, being very and eternal God of one substance, and equal with the Father, did, when the fullness of time was come, take upon Him man's nature, with all the essential properties and common infirmities thereof, yet without sin, being conceived by the power of the Holy Ghost, in the womb of the virgin Mary of her substance. So that two whole perfect and distinct natures, the Godhead and the manhood, were inseparably joined together in one person, without conversion, composition, or confusion; which person is very God and very man, yet one Christ, the only Mediator between God and man.

III. The Lord Jesus in His human nature, thus united to the divine in the person of the Son, was sanctified and anointed with the Holy Spirit above measure, having in Him all the treasures of wisdom and knowledge, in whom it pleased the Father that all fullness should dwell, to the end that being holy, harmless, undefiled, and full of grace and truth, He might be thoroughly furnished to execute the office of a mediator and surety; which office He took not unto Himself, but was thereunto called by His Father, who also put all power and judgment into His hand, and gave Him commandment to execute the same.

IV. This office the Lord Jesus did most willingly undertake; which that He might discharge, He was made under the Law, and did perfectly fulfill it, and underwent the punishment due to us, which we should have borne and suffered, being made sin and a curse for us, enduring most grievous torments immediately from God in His soul, and most painful sufferings in His body, was crucified, and died, was buried, and remained under the power of death, yet saw no corruption; on the third day He arose from the dead with the same body in which He suffered, with which also He ascended into heaven, and there sitteth at the right hand of His Father, making intercession, and shall return to judge men and angels at the end of the world.

V. The Lord Jesus by His perfect obedience and sacrifice of Himself, which He through the eternal Spirit, once offered up unto God, hath fully satisfied the justice of God, and purchased not only reconciliation, but an everlasting inheritance in the kingdom of heaven, for all those whom the Father hath given unto Him.

VI. Although the work of redemption was not actually wrought by Christ, till after His incarnation; yet the virtue, efficacy, and benefits thereof were communicated to the elect in all ages, successively from the beginning of the world, in and by those promises, types and sacrifices wherein He was revealed and signified to be the Seed of the woman, which should bruise the serpent's head, and the Lamb slain from the beginning of the world, being yesterday and today the same, and forever.

VII. Christ in the work of mediation acteth according to both natures, by each nature doing that which is proper to itself; yet by reason of the unity of the person, that which is proper to one nature, is sometimes in Scripture attributed to the person denominated by the other nature.

VIII. To all those for whom Christ hath purchased redemption, He doth certainly and effectually apply and communicate the same, making intercession for them, and revealing unto them in and by the Word, the mysteries of salvation, effectually persuading them by His Spirit to believe and obey, and governing their hearts by His Word and Spirit, overcoming all their enemies by His almighty power and wisdom, and in such manner and ways as are most consonant to His wonderful and unsearchable dispensation.

Chapter IX
Of Free Will

God hath endued the will of man with that natural liberty and power of acting upon choice, that it is neither forced, nor by any absolute necessity of nature determined to do good or evil.

II. Man in his state of innocency had freedom and power to will and to do that which was good and well pleasing to God; but yet mutably, so that he might fall from it.

III. Man by his fall into a state of sin, hath wholly lost all ability of will to any spiritual good accompanying salvation; so as a natural man being altogether averse from that good, and dead in sin, is not able by his own strength to convert himself, or to prepare himself thereunto.

IV. When God converts a sinner, and translates him into the state of grace, He freeth him from his natural bondage under sin, and by His grace alone enables him freely to will and to do that which is spiritually good; yet so, as that by reason of his remaining corruption, he doth not perfectly nor only will that which is good, but doth also will that which is evil.

V. The will of man is made perfectly and immutably free to good alone in the state of glory only.

Chapter X
Of Effectual Calling

All those whom God hath predestinated unto life, and those only, He is pleased in His appointed and accepted time effectually to call by His Word and Spirit, out of that state of sin and death in which they are by nature, to grace and salvation by Jesus Christ, enlightening their minds spiritually and savingly to understand the things of God, taking away their heart of stone, and giving unto them a heart of flesh, renewing their wills, and by His almighty power determining them to that which is good, and effectually drawing them to Jesus Christ; yet so, as they come most freely, being made willing by His grace.

II. This effectual call is of God's free and special grace alone, not from any thing at all foreseen in man, who is altogether passive therein, until being quickened and renewed by the Holy Spirit he is thereby enabled to answer this call, and to embrace the grace offered and conveyed in it.

III. Elect infants dying in infancy, are regenerated and saved by Christ, who worketh when, and where, and how He pleaseth: so also are all other elect persons who are incapable of being outwardly called by the ministry of the Word.

IV. Others not elected, although they may be called by the ministry of the Word, and may have some common operations of the Spirit, yet not being effectually drawn by the Father, they neither do nor can come unto Christ, and therefore cannot be saved; much less can men not professing the Christian religion, be saved in any other way whatsoever, be they never so diligent to frame their lives according to the light of nature, and the law of that religion they do profess: and to assert and maintain that they may, is very pernicious, and to be detested.

Chapter XI
Of Justification

Those whom God effectually calleth, He also freely justifieth, not by infusing righteousness into them, but by pardoning their sins, and by accounting and accepting their person as righteous, not for anything wrought in them, or done by them, but for Christ's sake alone; nor by imputing faith itself, the act of believing, or any other evangelical obedience to them, as their righteousness, but by imputing Christ's active obedience unto the whole Law, and passive obedience in His death for their whole and sole righteousness, they receiving and resting on Him and His righteousness by faith; which faith they have not of themselves, it is the gift of God.

II. Faith thus receiving and resting on Christ, and His righteousness, is the alone instrument of justification; yet it is not alone in the person justified, but is ever accompanied with all other saving graces, and is no dead faith, but worketh by love.

III. Christ by His obedience and death did fully discharge the debt of all those that are justified, and did by the sacrifice of Himself, in the blood of His cross, undergoing in their stead the penalty due unto them make a proper, real, and full satisfaction to God's justice in their behalf. Yet inasmuch as He was given by the Father for them, and His obedience and satisfaction accepted in their stead, and both freely, not for anything in them, their justification is only of free grace, that both the exact justice and rich grace of God might be glorified in the justification of sinners.

IV. God did from all eternity decree to justify all the elect, and Christ did in the fullness of time die for their sins, and rise again for their justification. Nevertheless, they are not justified personally, until the Holy Spirit doth in due time actually apply Christ unto them.

V. God doth continue to forgive the sins of those that are justified; and although they can never fall from the state of justification, yet they may by their sins fall under God's fatherly displeasure: and in that condition they have not usually the light of His countenance restored unto them, until they humble themselves, confess their sins, beg pardon, and renew their faith and repentance.

VI. The justification of believers under the Old Testament, was in all these respects one and the same with the justification of believers under the New Testament.

Chapter XII
Of Adoption

All those that are justified, God vouchsafeth in and for His only Son Jesus Christ to make partakers of the grace of adoption, by which they are taken into the number, and enjoy the liberties and privileges of the children of God, have His name put upon them, receive the Spirit of adoption, have access to the throne of grace with boldness, are enabled to cry Abba Father, are pitied, protected, provided for, and chastened by Him as by a father, yet never cast off, but sealed to the day of redemption, and inherit the promises as heirs of everlasting salvation.

Chapter XIII
Of Sanctification

They that are united to Christ, effectually called and regenerated, having a new heart and a new spirit created in them, through the virtue of Christ's death and resurrection, are also further sanctified really and personally through the same virtue, by His Word and Spirit dwelling in them; the dominion of the whole body of sin is destroyed, and the several lusts thereof are more and more weakened, and mortified, and they more and more quickened, and strengthened in all saving graces, to the practice of all true holiness, without which no man shall see the Lord.

II. This sanctification is throughout in the whole man, yet imperfect in this life, there abideth still some remnants of corruption in every part, whence ariseth a continual and irreconcilable war, the flesh lusting against the spirit, and the spirit against the flesh.

III. In which war, although the remaining corruption for a time may much prevail, yet through the continual supply of strength from the sanctifying Spirit of Christ, the regenerate part doth overcome, and so the saints grow in grace, perfecting holiness in the fear of God.

Chapter XIV
Of Saving Faith

The grace of faith, whereby the elect are enabled to believe to the saving of their souls, is the work of the Spirit of Christ in their hearts, and is ordinarily wrought by the ministry of the Word; by which also, and by the administration of the seals, prayer, and other means, it is increased and strengthened.

II. By this faith a Christian believeth to be true whatsoever is revealed in the Word, for the authority of God Himself speaking therein, and acteth differently upon that which each particular passage thereof containeth, yielding obedience to the commands, trembling at the threatenings, and embracing the promises of God for this life, and that which is to come. But the principal acts of saving faith are accepting, receiving, and resting upon Christ alone, for justification, sanctification, and eternal life, by virtue of the covenant of grace.

III. This faith, although it be different in degrees, and may be weak or strong, yet it is in the least degree of it different in the kind or nature of it (as is all other saving grace) from the faith and common grace of temporary believers; and therefore, though it may be many times assailed and weakened, yet it gets the victory, growing up in many to the attainment of a full assurance through Christ, who is both the Author and Finisher of our faith.

Chapter XV
Of Repentance unto Life and Salvation

Such of the elect as are converted in riper years, having sometime lived in the state of nature, and therein served divers lusts and pleasures, God in their effectual calling giveth them repentance unto life.

II. Whereas there is none that doth good, and sinneth not, and the best of men may through the power and deceitfulness of their corruptions dwelling in them, with the prevalency of temptation, fall into great sins and provocations; God hath in the covenant of grace mercifully provided, that believers so sinning and falling, be renewed through repentance unto salvation.

III. This saving repentance is an evangelical grace, whereby a person being by the Holy Ghost made sensible of the manifold evils of his sin, doth by faith in Christ humble himself for it with godly sorrow, detestation of it, and self-abhorency, praying for pardon and strength of grace, with a purpose, and endeavor by supplies of the Spirit, to walk before God unto all well-pleasing in all things.

IV. As repentance is to be continued through the whole course of our lives, upon the account of the body of death, and the motions thereof; so it is every man's duty to repent of his particular known sins particularly.

V. Such is the provision which God hath made through Christ in the covenant of grace, for the preservation of believers unto salvation, that although there is no sin so small, but it deserves damnation; yet there is no sin so great, that it shall bring damnation on them who truly repent; which makes the constant preaching of repentance necessary.

Chapter XVI
Of Good Works

Good works are only such as God hath commanded in His Holy Word, and not such as without the warrant thereof are devised by men out of blind zeal, or upon any pretence of good intentions.

II. These good works done in obedience to God's commandments are the fruits and evidences of a true and lively faith, and by them believers manifest their thankfulness, strengthen their assurance, edify their brethren, adorn the profession of the gospel, stop the mouths of the adversaries, and glorify God, whose workmanship they are, created in Christ Jesus thereunto, that having their fruit unto holiness, they may have the end eternal life.

III. Their ability to do good works is not at all of themselves, but wholly from the Spirit of Christ. And that they may be enabled thereunto, besides the graces they have already received, there is required an actual influence of the same Holy Spirit to work in them to will and to do, of His good pleasure; yet are they not hereupon to grow negligent, as if they were not bound to perform any duty, unless upon a special motion of the Spirit, but they ought to be diligent in stirring up the grace of God that is in them.

IV. They who in their obedience attain to the greatest height which is possible in this life, are so far from being able to supererogate, and to do more than God requires, as that they fall short of much, which in duty they are bound to do.

V. We cannot by our best works merit pardon of sin, or eternal life at the hand of God, by reason of the great disproportion that is between them, and the glory to come; and the infinite distance that is between us, and God, whom by them we can neither profit, nor satisfy for the debt of our former sins; but when we have done all we can, we have done but our duty, and are unprofitable servants: and because as they are good, they proceed from His Spirit, and as they are wrought by us, they are defiled and mixed with so much weakness and imperfection, that they cannot endure the severity of God's judgment.

VI. Yet notwithstanding, the persons of believers being accepted through Christ, their good works also are accepted in Him, not as though they were in this life wholly unblameable and unreproveable in God's sight, but that He, looking upon them in His Son, is pleased to accept and reward that which is sincere, although accompanied with many weaknesses and imperfections.

VII. Works done by unregenerate men, although for the matter of them they may be things which God commands, and of good use both to themselves and to others: yet because they proceed not from a heart purified by faith, nor are done in a right manner, according to the Word, nor to a right end, the glory of God; they are therefore sinful, and cannot please God, nor make a man meet to receive grace from God; and yet their neglect of them is more sinful, and displeasing unto God.

Chapter XVII
Of the Perseverance of the Saints

They whom God hath accepted in His beloved, effectually called, and sanctified by His Spirit can neither totally nor finally fall away from the state of grace, but shall certainly persevere therein to the end, and be eternally saved.

II. This perseverance of the saints depends not upon their own free will, but upon the immutability of the decree of election, from the free and unchangeable love of God the Father, upon the efficacy of the merit and intercession of Jesus Christ, and union with Him, the oath of God, the abiding of His Spirit, and of the seed of God within them, and the nature of the covenant of grace, from all which ariseth also the certainty and infallibility thereof.

III. And though they may, through the temptation of Satan, and of the world, the prevalency of corruption remaining in them, and the neglect of the means of their preservation, fall into grievous sins, and for a time continue therein, whereby they incur God's displeasure and grieve His Holy Spirit, come to have their graces and comforts impaired, have their hearts hardened, and their consciences wounded, hurt and scandalize others, and bring temporal judgments upon themselves; yet they are and shall be kept by the power of God through faith unto salvation.

Chapter XVIII
Of the Assurance of Grace and Salvation

Although temporary believers and other unregenerate men may vainly deceive themselves with false hopes, and carnal presumptions of being in the favor of God, and state of salvation, which hope of theirs shall perish; yet such as truly believe in the Lord Jesus, and love Him in sincerity, endeavoring to walk in all good conscience before Him, may in this life be certainly assured that they are in the state of grace, and may rejoice in the hope of the glory of God, which hope shall never make them ashamed.

II. This certainty is not a bare conjectural and probable persuasion, grounded upon a fallible hope, but an infallible assurance of faith, founded on the blood and righteousness of Christ, revealed in the gospel, and also upon the inward evidence of those graces unto which promises are made, and on the immediate witness of the Spirit, testifying our adoption, and as a fruit thereof, leaving the heart more humble and holy.

III. This infallible assurance doth not so belong to the essence of faith, but that a true believer may wait long, and conflict with many difficulties before he be partaker of it; yet being enabled by the Spirit to know the things which are freely given him of God, he may without extraordinary revelation in the right use of ordinary means attain thereunto. And therefore it is the duty of everyone to give all diligence to make his calling and election sure, that thereby his heart may be enlarged in peace and joy in the Holy Ghost, in love and thankfulness to God, and in strength and cheerfulness in the duties of obedience, the proper fruits of this assurance; so far is it from inclining men to looseness.

IV. True believers may have the assurance of their salvation divers ways shaken, diminished, and intermitted, as by negligence in preserving of it, by falling into some special sin, which woundeth the conscience, and grieveth the Spirit, by some sudden or vehement temptation, by God's withdrawing the light of His countenance, suffering even such as fear Him to walk in darkness, and to have no light; yet are they neither utterly destitute of that seed of God, and life of faith, that love of Christ and the brethren, that sincerity of heart and conscience of duty, out of which by the operation of the Spirit this assurance may in due time be revived, and by the which in the meantime they are supported from utter despair.

CHAPTER XIX
Of the Law of God

God gave to Adam a law of universal obedience written in his heart, and a particular precept of not eating the fruit of the tree of knowledge of good and evil, as a covenant of works, by which He bound him and all his posterity to personal, entire, exact, and perpetual obedience, promised life upon the fulfilling, and threatened death upon the breach of it, and endued him with power and ability to keep it.

II. This law so written in the heart, continued to be a perfect rule of righteousness after the fall of man, and was delivered by God upon Mount Sinai in ten commandments, and written in two tables; the four first commandments containing our duty towards God, and the other six our duty to man.

III. Beside this law commonly called moral, God was pleased to give to the people of Israel ceremonial laws, containing several typical ordinances, partly of worship, prefiguring Christ, His graces, actions, sufferings and benefits, and partly holding forth divers instructions of moral duties: All which ceremonial laws being appointed only to the time of reformation, are by Jesus Christ the true Messiah and only Lawgiver, who was furnished with power from the Father for that end, abrogated and taken away.

IV. To them also He gave sundry judicial laws, which expired together with the state of that people, not obliging any now by virtue of that institution, their general equity only being still of moral use.

V. The moral law doth forever bind all, as well justified persons as others, to the obedience thereof; and that not only in regard of the matter contained in it, but also in respect of the authority of God the Creator, who gave it: neither doth Christ in the gospel any way dissolve, but much strengthen this obligation.

VI. Although true believers be not under the law, as a covenant of works, to be thereby justified or condemned; yet it is of great use to them as well as to others, in that, as a rule of life, informing them of the will of God, and their duty, it directs and binds them to walk accordingly, discovering also the sinful pollutions of their nature, hearts and lives, so as examining themselves thereby, they may come to further conviction of humiliation for, and hatred against sin, together with a clearer sight of the need they have of Christ, and the perfection of His obedience. It is likewise of use to the regenerate, to restrain their corruptions, in that it forbids sin, and the threatenings of it serve to show what even their sins deserve, and what afflictions in this life they may expect for them, although freed from the curse thereof threatened in the law. The promises of it in like manner show them God's approbation of obedience, and what blessings they may expect upon the performance thereof, although not as due to them by the law, as a covenant of works; so as a man's doing good, and refraining from evil, because the law encourageth to the one, and deterreth from the other, is no evidence of his being under the law, and not under grace.

VII. Neither are the forementioned uses of the law contrary to the grace of the gospel, but do sweetly comply with it, the Spirit of Christ subduing and enabling the will of man to do that freely and cheerfully, which the will of God revealed in the law required to be done.

CHAPTER XX
Of the Gospel, and of the Extent of the Grace Thereof

The covenant of works being broken by sin, and made unprofitable unto life, God was pleased to give unto the elect the promise of Christ, the seed of the woman, as the means of calling them, and begetting in them faith and repentance: In this promise the gospel, as to the substance of it, was revealed, and was therein effectual for the conversion and salvation of sinners.

II. This promise of Christ, and salvation by Him, is revealed only in and by the Word of God; neither do the works of creation or providence, with the light of nature, make discovery of Christ, or of grace by Him, so much as in a general or obscure way; much less that men destitute of the revelation of Him by the promise or gospel, should be enabled thereby to attain saving faith or repentance.

III. The revelation of the gospel unto sinners, made in divers times, and by sundry parts, with the addition of promises and precepts for the obedience required therein, as to the nations and persons to whom it is granted, is merely of the sovereign will and good pleasure of God, not being annexed by virtue of any promise to the due improvement of men's natural abilities, by virtue of common light received without it, which none ever did make or can so do. And therefore in all ages the preaching of the gospel hath been granted unto persons and nations, as to the extent or straitening of it, in great variety, according to the counsel of the will of God.

IV. Although the gospel be the only outward means of revealing Christ and saving grace, and is as such abundantly sufficient thereunto; yet that men who are dead in trespasses, may be born again, quickened, or regenerated, there is moreover necessary an effectual, irresistible work of the Holy Ghost upon the whole soul, for the producing in them a new spiritual life, without which no other means are sufficient for their conversion unto God.

Chapter XXI
Of Christian Liberty, and Liberty of Conscience

The liberty which Christ hath purchased for believers under the gospel consists in their freedom from the guilt of sin, the condemning wrath of God, the rigor and curse of the law, and in their being delivered from this present evil world, bondage to Satan, and dominion of sin, from the evil of afflictions, the fear and sting of death, the victory of the grave, and everlasting damnation; as also in their free access to God, and their yielding obedience unto Him, not out of slavish fear, but a childlike love and willing mind: all which were common also to believers under the law, for the substance of them; but under the New Testament the liberty of Christians is further enlarged in their freedom from the yoke of the ceremonial law, the whole legal administration of the covenant of grace, to which the Jewish church was subjected, and in greater boldness of access to the throne of grace, and in fuller communications of the free Spirit of God, than believers under the law did ordinarily partake of.

II. God alone is Lord of the conscience, and hath left it free from the doctrines and commandments of men, which are in anything contrary to His Word, or not contained in it; so that to believe such doctrines, or to obey such commands out of conscience, is to betray true liberty of conscience; and the requiring of an implicit faith, and an absolute and blind obedience, is to destroy liberty of conscience, and reason also.

III. They who upon pretence of Christian liberty do practice any sin, or cherish any lust, as they do thereby pervert the main design of the grace of the gospel to their own destruction; so they wholly destroy the end of Christian liberty, which is, that being delivered out of the hands of our enemies, we might serve the Lord without fear, in holiness and righteousness before Him, all the days of our life.

Chapter XXII
Of Religious Worship, and the Sabbath Day

The light of nature showeth that there is a God, who hath lordship and sovereignty over all, is just, good, and doth good unto all, and is therefore to be feared, loved, praised, called upon, trusted in, and served with all the heart, and all the soul, and with all the might. But the acceptable way of worshipping the true God is instituted by Himself, and so limited by His own revealed will, that He may not be worshipped according to the imaginations and devices of men, or the suggestions of Satan, under any visible representations, or any other way not prescribed in the Holy Scripture.

II. Religious worship is to be given to God the Father, Son, and Holy Ghost, and to Him alone; not to angels, saints, or any other creatures; and since the fall, not without a mediator, nor in the mediation of any other but of Christ alone.

III. Prayer with thanksgiving, being one special part of natural worship, is by God required of all men; but that it may be accepted, it is to be made in the name of the Son by the help of His Spirit, according to His will, with understanding, reverence, humility, fervency, faith, love, and perseverance; and when with others in a known tongue.

IV. Prayer is to be made for things lawful, and for all sorts of men living, or that shall live hereafter, but not for the dead, nor for those of whom it may be known that they have sinned the sin unto death.

V. The reading of the Scriptures, preaching, and hearing the Word of God, singing of psalms, as also the administration of baptism and the Lord's Supper, are all parts of religious worship of God, to be performed in obedience unto God with understanding, faith, reverence, and godly fear: solemn humiliations, with fastings and thanksgiving upon special occasions, are in their several times and seasons to be used in a holy and religious manner.

VI. Neither prayer nor any other part of religious worship, is now under the gospel either tied unto, or made more acceptable by any place in which it is performed, or towards which it is directed; but God is to be worshipped everywhere in spirit and in truth, as in private families daily, and in secret each one by himself, so more solemnly in the public assemblies, which are not carelessly nor willfully to be neglected, or forsaken, when God by His Word or providence calleth thereunto.

VII. As it is of the law of nature, that in general a proportion of time by God's appointment be set apart for the worship of God; so by His Word in a positive, moral, and perpetual commandment, binding all men in all ages, He hath particularly appointed one day in seven for a Sabbath to be kept holy unto Him, which from the beginning of the world to the resurrection of Christ was the last day of the week, and from the resurrection of Christ was changed into the first day of the week, which in Scripture is called the Lord's Day, and is to be continued to the end of the world as the Christian Sabbath, the observation of the last day of the week being abolished.

VIII. This Sabbath is then kept holy unto the Lord, when men after a due preparing of their hearts, and ordering their common affairs beforehand, do not only observe an holy rest all the day from their own works, words, and thoughts about their worldly employments and recreations, but also are taken up the whole time in the public and private exercises of His worship, and in the duties of necessity and mercy.

Chapter XXIII
Of Lawful Oaths and Vows

A lawful oath is a part of religious worship, wherein the person swearing in truth, righteousness, and judgment, solemnly calleth God to witness what he asserteth or promiseth, and to judge him according to the truth or falsehood of what he sweareth.

II. The name of God only is that by which men ought to swear, and therein it is to be used with all holy fear and reverence. Therefore to swear vainly, or rashly, by that glorious or dreadful name, or to swear at all by any other thing, is sinful and to be abhorred; yet as in matters of weight and moment an oath is warranted by the Word of God under the New Testament, as well as under the Old; so a lawful oath, being imposed by lawful authority in such matters, ought to be taken.

III. Whosoever taketh an oath warranted by the Word of God, ought duly to consider the weightiness of so solemn an act, and therein to avow nothing but what he is fully persuaded is the truth: neither may any man bind himself by oath to any thing, but what is good and just, and what he believeth so to be, and what he is able and resolved to perform. Yet it is a sin to refuse an oath touching anything that is good and just, being lawfully imposed by authority.

IV. An oath is to be taken in the plain and common sense of the words, without equivocation or mental reservation. It cannot oblige to sin, but in anything not sinful, being taken it binds to performance, although to a man's own hurt; nor is it to be violated, although made to heretics or infidels.

V. A vow, which is not to be made to any creature, but God alone, is of the like nature with a promissory oath, and ought to be made with the like religious care, and to be performed with the like faithfulness.

VI. Popish monastical vows of perpetual single life, professed poverty, and regular obedience, are so far from being degrees of higher perfection, that they are superstitious and sinful snares, in which no Christian may entangle himself.

Chapter XXIV
Of the Civil Magistrate

God, the supreme Lord and King of all the world, hath ordained civil magistrates to be under Him, over the people for His own glory and the public good; and to this end hath armed them with the power of the sword, for the defense and encouragement of them that do good, and for the punishment of evildoers.

II. It is lawful for Christians to accept and execute the office of a magistrate, when called thereunto: in the management whereof, as they ought specially to maintain justice and peace, according to the wholesome laws of each commonwealth; so for that end they may lawfully now under the New Testament wage war upon just and necessary occasion.

III. Although the magistrate is bound to encourage, promote, and protect the professor and profession of the gospel and to manage and order civil administrations in a due subserviency to the interest of Christ in the world, and to that end to take care that men of corrupt minds and conversations do not licentiously publish and divulge blasphemy and errors in their own nature, subverting the faith, and inevitably destroying the souls of them that receive them: yet in such differences about the doctrines of the gospel, or ways of the worship of God, as may befall men exercising a good conscience, manifesting it in their conversation, and holding the foundation, not disturbing others in their ways or worship that differ from them, there is no warrant for the magistrate under the gospel to abridge them of their liberty.

IV. It is the duty of people to pray for magistrates, to honor their persons, to pay them tribute and other dues, to obey their lawful commands, and to be subject to their authority for conscience sake. Infidelity, or difference in religion, doth not make void the magistrates' just and legal authority, nor free the people from their obedience to Him: from which ecclesiastical persons are not exempted, much less hath the pope any power or jurisdiction over them in their dominions, or over any of their people, and least of all to deprive them of their dominions or lives, if he shall judge them to be heretics, or upon any other pretence whatsoever.

Chapter XXV
Of Marriage

Marriage is to be between one man and one woman: neither is it lawful for any man to have more than one wife, nor for any woman to have more than one husband, at the same time.

II. Marriage was ordained for the mutual help of husband and wife, for the increase of mankind with a legitimate issue, and of the church with a holy seed, and for preventing of uncleanness.

III. It is lawful for all sorts of people to marry, who are able with judgment to give their consent. Yet it is the duty of Christians to marry in the Lord, and therefore such as profess the true Reformed religion, should not marry with infidels, papists, or other idolaters: neither should such as are godly, be unequally yoked by marrying with such as are wicked in their life, or maintain damnable heresy.

IV. Marriage ought not to be within the degrees of consanguinity or affinity forbidden in the Word; nor can such incestuous marriages ever be made lawful by any law of man, or consent of parties, so as those persons may live together as man and wife.

Chapter XXVI
Of the Church

The catholic or universal church, which is invisible, consists of the whole number of the elect, that have been, are, or shall be gathered into one under Christ, the Head thereof, and is the spouse, the body, the fullness of Him that filleth all in all.

II. The whole body of men throughout the world, professing the faith of the gospel and obedience unto God by Christ according unto it, not destroying their own profession by any errors everting the foundation, or unholiness of conversation, are, and may be called the visible catholic church of Christ, although as such it is not entrusted with the administration of any ordinances, or have any officers to rule or govern in, or over the whole body.

III. The purest churches under heaven are subject both to mixture and error, and some have so degenerated as to become no churches of Christ, but synagogues of Satan. Nevertheless Christ always hath had, and ever shall have a visible kingdom in this world, to the end thereof, of such as believe in Him, and make profession of His name.

IV. There is no other head of the church but the Lord Jesus Christ; nor can the pope of Rome in any sense be head thereof; but it is that Antichrist, that man of sin, and son of perdition, that exalteth himself in the church against Christ, and all that is called God, whom the Lord shall destroy with the brightness of His coming.

V. As the Lord in His care and love towards his church, has in His infinite wise providence exercised it with great variety in all ages, for the good of them that love Him, and His own glory: so according to His promise, we expect that in the later days, Antichrist being destroyed, the Jews called, and the adversaries of the kingdom of His dear Son broken, the churches of Christ being enlarged, and edified through a free and plentiful communication of light and grace, shall enjoy in this world a more quiet, peaceable, and glorious condition than they have enjoyed.

Chapter XXVII
Of the Communion of Saints

All saints that are united to Jesus Christ their head, by His Spirit and faith, although they are not made thereby one person with Him, have fellowship in His graces, sufferings, death, resurrection, and glory: and being united to one another in love, they have communion in each others' gifts and graces, and are obliged to the performance of such duties, public and private, as do conduce to their mutual good, both in the inward and outward man.

II. All saints are bound to maintain an holy fellowship and communion in the worship of God, and in performing such other spiritual services as tend to their mutual edification; as also in relieving each other in outward things, according to their several abilities and necessities: which communion, though especially to be exercised by them in the relations wherein they stand, whether in families or churches, yet as God offereth opportunity, is to be extended unto all those who in every place call upon the name of the Lord Jesus.

Chapter XXVIII
Of the Sacraments

Sacraments are holy signs and seals of the covenant of grace, immediately instituted by Christ, to represent Him and His benefits, and to confirm our interest in Him, and solemnly to engage us to the service of God in Christ, according to His Word.

II. There is in every sacrament a spiritual relation, or sacramental union between the sign and the thing signified; whence it comes to pass that the names and effects of the one are attributed to the other.

III. The grace which is exhibited in or by the sacraments rightly used, is not conferred by any power in them, neither doth the efficacy of a sacrament depend upon the piety or intention of him that doth administer it, but upon the work of the Spirit, and the word of institution, which contains together with a precept authorizing the use thereof, a promise of benefit to worthy receivers.

IV. There be only two sacraments ordained by Christ our Lord in the gospel, that is to say, baptism and the Lord's Supper; neither of which may be dispensed by any but a minister of the Word lawfully called.

V. The sacraments of the Old Testament, in regard of the spiritual things thereby signified and exhibited, were for substance the same with those of the New.

Chapter XXIX
Of Baptism

Baptism is a sacrament of the New Testament, ordained by Jesus Christ to be unto the party baptized a sign and seal of the covenant of grace, of his ingrafting into Christ, of regeneration, of remission of sins, and of his giving up unto God through Jesus Christ to walk in newness of life; which ordinance is by Christ's own appointment to be continued in His church until the end of the world.

II. The outward element to be used in this ordinance, is water, wherewith the party is to be baptized in the name of the Father, and of the Son, and of the Holy Ghost, by a minister of the gospel lawfully called.

III. Dipping of the person into the water is not necessary, but baptism is rightly administered by pouring or sprinkling water upon the person.

IV. Not only those that do actually profess faith in and obedience unto Christ, but also the infants of one or both believing parents are to be baptized, and those only.

V. Although it be a great sin to contemn or neglect this ordinance, yet grace and salvation are not so inseparably annexed unto it, as that no person can be regenerated or saved without it; or that all that are baptized, are undoubtedly regenerated.

VI. The efficacy of baptism is not tied to that moment of time wherein it is administered, yet notwithstanding, by the right use of this ordinance, the grace promised is not only offered, but really exhibited and conferred by the Holy Ghost to such (whether of age or infants) as that grace belongeth unto, according to the counsel of God's own will in His appointed time.

VII. Baptism is but once to be administered to any person.

Chapter XXX
Of the Lord's Supper

Our Lord Jesus in the night wherein He was betrayed, instituted the sacrament of His body and blood, called the Lord's Supper, to be observed in His churches unto the end of the world, for the perpetual remembrance, and showing forth of the sacrifice of Himself in His death, the sealing of all benefits thereof unto true believers, their spiritual nourishment, and growth in Him, their further engagement in and to all duties which they owe unto Him, and to be a bond and pledge of their communion with Him, and with each other.

II. In this sacrament Christ is not offered up to His Father, nor any real sacrifice made at all for remission of sin of the quick or dead, but only a memorial of that one offering up of Himself by Himself upon the cross once for all, and a spiritual oblation of all possible praise unto God for the same; so that the popish sacrifice of the Mass (as they call it) is most abominable, injurious to Christ's own only sacrifice, the alone propitiation for all the sins of the elect.

III. The Lord Jesus hath in this ordinance appointed His ministers to pray and bless the elements of bread and wine, and thereby to set them apart from a common to a holy use, and to take and break the bread, to take the cup, and (they communicating also themselves) to give both to the communicants, but to none who are not then present in the congregation.

IV. Private Masses, or receiving the sacrament by a priest, or any other alone, as likewise the denial of the cup to the people, worshiping the elements, the lifting them up, or carrying them about for adoration, and the reserving them for any pretended religious use, are contrary to the nature of this sacrament, and to the institution of Christ.

V. The outward elements in this sacrament duly set apart to the uses ordained by Christ, have such relation to Him crucified, as that truly, yet sacramentally only, they are sometimes called by the name of the things they represent, to wit, the body and blood of Christ; albeit in substance and nature they still remain truly and only bread and wine as they were before.

VI. That doctrine which maintains a change of the substance of bread and wine into the substance of Christ's body and blood (commonly called transubstantiation) by consecration of a priest, or by any other way, is repugnant not to Scripture alone, but even to common sense and reason, overthroweth the nature of the sacrament, and hath been, and is the cause of manifold superstitions, yea, of gross idolatries.

VII. Worthy receivers outwardly partaking of the visible elements in this sacrament, do then also inwardly by faith, really and indeed, yet not carnally and corporally, but spiritually, receive and feed upon Christ crucified, and all benefits of His death; the body and blood of Christ being then not corporally or carnally in, with, or under the bread or wine; yet as really, but spiritually present to the faith of believers in that ordinance, as the elements themselves are to their outward senses.

VIII. All ignorant and ungodly persons, as they are unfit to enjoy communion with Christ, so are they unworthy of the Lord's Table, and cannot without great sin against Him, while they remain such, partake of these holy mysteries, or be admitted thereunto; yea whosoever shall receive unworthily, are guilty of the body and blood of the Lord, eating and drinking judgment to themselves.

Chapter XXXI
Of the State of Man after Death, and of the Resurrection of the Dead

The bodies of men after death return to dust, and see corruption, but their souls (which neither die nor sleep) having an immortal subsistence, immediately return to God who gave them, the souls of the righteous being then made perfect in holiness, are received into the highest heavens, where they behold the face of God in light and glory, waiting for the full redemption of their bodies. And the souls of the wicked are cast into hell, where they remain in torment and utter darkness, reserved to the judgment of the great day. Besides these two places for souls separated from their bodies, the Scripture acknowledgeth none.

II. At the last day such as are found alive shall not die, but be changed, and all the dead shall be raised up with the self-same bodies, and none other, although with different qualities, which shall be united again to their souls for ever.

III. The bodies of the unjust shall by the power of Christ be raised to dishonor; the bodies of the just by His Spirit unto honor, and be made conformable to His own glorious body.

Chapter XXXII
Of the Last Judgment

God hath appointed a day wherein He will judge the world in righteousness by Jesus Christ, to whom all power and judgment is given of the Father; in which day not only the apostate angels shall be judged, but likewise all persons that have lived upon earth, shall appear before the tribunal of Christ, to give an account of their thoughts, words, and deeds, and to receive according to what they have done in the body, whether good or evil.

II. The end of God's appointing this day, is for the manifestation of the glory of His mercy in the eternal salvation of the elect, and of His justice in the damnation of the reprobate, who are wicked and disobedient: for then shall the righteous go into everlasting life, and receive that fullness of joy and glory, with everlasting reward in the presence of the Lord; but the wicked who know not God, and obey not the gospel of Jesus Christ, shall be cast into eternal torments, and be punished with everlasting destruction from the presence of the Lord, and from the glory of His power.

III. As Christ would have us to be certainly persuaded that there shall be a judgment, both to deter all men from sin, and for the greater consolation of the godly in their adversity; so will He have that day unknown to men, that they may shake off all carnal security, and be always watchful, because they know not at what hour the Lord will come, and may be ever prepared to say, come Lord Jesus, come quickly. Amen.

Of the Institution of Churches, and the Order
Appointed in Them by Jesus Christ

By the appointment of the Father all power for the calling, institution, order, or government of the church, is invested in a supreme and sovereign manner in the Lord Jesus Christ, as king and head thereof.

II. In the execution of this power wherewith he is so entrusted, the Lord Jesus calleth out of the world unto communion with Himself, those that are given unto Him by His Father, that they may walk before Him in all the ways of obedience, which be prescribeth to them in His Word.

III. Those thus called (through the ministry of the Word by His Spirit) He commandeth to walk together in particular societies or churches, for their mutual edification, and the due performance of that public worship, which He requireth of them in this world.

IV. To each of these churches thus gathered, according unto His mind declared in His Word, He hath given all that power and authority, which is any way needful for their carrying on that order in worship and discipline, which He hath instituted for them to observe with commands and rules, for the due and right exerting and executing of that power.

V. These particular churches thus appointed by the authority of Christ, and entrusted with power from Him for the ends before expressed, are each of them as unto those ends, the seat of that power which He is pleased to communicate to His saints or subjects in this world, so that as such they receive it immediately from Himself.

VI. Besides these particular churches, there is not instituted by Christ any church more extensive or catholic entrusted with power for the administration of His ordinances, or the execution of any authority in His name.

VII. A particular church gathered and completed according to the mind of Christ, consists of officers and members. The Lord Christ having given to His called ones (united according to his appointment in church order) liberty and power to choose persons fitted by the Holy Ghost for that purpose, to be over them and to minister to them in the Lord.

VIII. The members of these churches are saints by calling, visibly manifesting and evidencing (in and by their profession and walking) their obedience unto that call of Christ, who being further known to each other by their confession of the faith wrought in them by the power of God, declared by themselves or otherwise manifested, do willingly consent to walk together according to the appointment of Christ, giving up themselves to the Lord, and to one another by the will of God in professed subjection to the ordinances of the gospel.

IX. The officers appointed by Christ to be chosen and set apart by the church so called, and gathered for the peculiar administration of ordinances, and execution of power or duty which He entrusts them with, or calls them to, to be continued to the end of the world, are pastors, teachers, elders, and deacons.

X. Churches thus gathered and assembling for the worship of God, are thereby visible and public, and their assemblies (in what place soever they are, according as they have liberty or opportunity) are therefore church or public assemblies.

XI. The way appointed by Christ for the calling of any person, fitted and gifted by the Holy Ghost, unto the office of pastor, teacher, or elder in a church, is, that he be chosen thereunto by the common suffrage of the church itself, and solemnly set apart by fasting and prayer, with imposition of hands of the eldership of that church, if there be any before constituted therein; and of a deacon, that he be chosen by the like suffrage, and set apart by prayer, and the like imposition of hands.

XII. The essence of this call of a pastor, teacher, or elder unto office, consists in the election of the church, together with his acceptation of it, and separation by fasting and prayer. And those who are so chosen, though not set apart by imposition of hands, are rightly constituted ministers of Jesus Christ, in whose name and authority they exercise the ministry to them so committed. The calling of deacons consisteth in the like election and acceptation, with separation by prayer.

XIII. Although it be incumbent on the pastors and teachers of the churches to be instant in preaching the Word, by way of office, yet the work of preaching the Word is not so peculiarly confined to them, but that others also gifted and fitted by the Holy Ghost for it, and approved (being by lawful ways and means in the providence of God called thereunto) may publicly, ordinarily, and constantly perform it; so that they give themselves up thereunto.

XIV. However, they who are engaged in the work of public preaching, and enjoy the public maintenance upon that account, are not thereby obliged to dispense the seals to any other than such as (being saints by calling, and gathered according to the order of the gospel) they stand related to, as pastors or teachers; yet ought they not to neglect others living within their parochial bounds, but besides their constant public preaching to them, they ought to enquire after their profiting by the Word, instructing them in, and pressing upon them (whether young or old) the great doctrines of the gospel, even personally and particularly, so far as their strength and time will admit.

XV. Ordination alone without the election or precedent consent of the church, by those who formerly have been ordained by virtue of that power they have received by their ordination, doth not constitute any person a church officer, or communicate office power unto him.

XVI. A church furnished with officers (according to the mind of Christ) hath full power to administer all His ordinances; and where there is want of any one or more officers required, that officer, or those which are in the church, may administer all the Ordinances proper to their particular duty and offices; but where there are no teaching officers, none may administer the seals, nor can the church authorize any so to do.

XVII. In the carrying on of church administration, no person ought to be added to the church, but by the consent of the church itself; that so love (without dissimulation) may be preserved between all the members thereof.

XVIII. Whereas the Lord Jesus Christ hath appointed and instituted as a means of edification, that those who walk not according to the rules and laws appointed by Him (in respect of faith and life, so that just offense doth arise to the church thereby) be censured in His name and authority; every church hath power in itself to exercise and execute all those censures appointed by Him in the way and order prescribed in the gospel.

XIX. The censures so appointed by Christ are admonition and excommunication: and whereas some offenses are or may be known only to some, it is appointed by Christ, that those to whom they are so known, do first admonish the offender in private: in public offenses where [there is] any sin, before all; or in case of non-amendment upon private admonition, the offense being related to the church, and the offender not manifesting his repentance, he is to be duly admonished in the name of Christ by the whole church, by the ministry of the elders of the church; and if this censure prevail not for his repentance, then he is to be cast out by excommunication with the consent of the church.

XX. As all believers are bound to join themselves to particular churches, when and where they have opportunity so to do, so none are to be admitted unto the privileges of the churches who do not submit themselves to the rule of Christ in the censures for the government of them.

XXI. This being the way prescribed by Christ in case of offense, no church members upon any offenses taken by them, having performed their duty required of them in this matter, ought to disturb any church order, or absent themselves from the public assemblies, or the administration of any ordinances upon that pretence, but to wait upon Christ in the further proceeding of the church.

XXII. The power of censures being seated by Christ in a particular church is to be exercised only towards particular members of each church respectively as such; and there is no power given by Him unto any synods or ecclesiastical assemblies to excommunicate, or by their public edicts to threaten excommunication, or other church censures against churches, magistrates, or their people upon any account, no man being obnoxious to that censure, but upon his personal miscarriage, as a member of a particular church.

XXIII. Although the church is a society of men, assembling for the celebration of the ordinances according to the appointment of Christ, yet every society assembling for that end or purpose, upon the account of cohabitation within any civil precincts and bounds, is not thereby constituted a church, seeing there may be wanting among them, what is essentially required thereunto; and therefore a believer living with others in such a precinct, may join himself with any church for his edification.

XXIV. For the avoiding of differences that may otherwise arise, for the greater solemnity in the celebration of the ordinances of Christ, and the opening a way for the larger usefulness of the gifts and graces of the Holy Ghost, saints living in one city or town, or within such distances as that they may conveniently assemble for divine worship, ought rather to join in one church for their mutual strengthening and edification, than to set up many distinct societies.

XXV. As all churches and all the members of them are bound to pray continually for the good or prosperity of all the churches of Christ in all places, and upon all occasions to further it (everyone within the bounds of their places and callings, in the exercise of their gifts and graces), so the churches themselves (when planted by the providence of God, so as they may have opportunity and advantage for it) ought to hold communion amongst themselves for their peace, increase of love, and mutual edification.

XXVI. In cases of difficulties or differences, either in point of doctrine or in administrations, wherein either the churches in general are concerned, or any one church in their peace, union, and edification, or any member or members of any church are injured in, or by any proceeding in censures, not agreeable to truth and order: it is according to the mind of Christ, that many churches holding communion together, do by their messengers meet in a synod or council, to consider and give their advice in, or about that matter in difference, to be reported to all the churches concerned. Howbeit these synods so assembled are not entrusted with any church power, properly so called, or with any jurisdiction over the churches themselves, to exercise any censures, either over any churches or persons, or to impose their determinations on the churches or officers.

XXVII. Besides these occasional synods or councils, there are not instituted by Christ any stated synods in a fixed combination of churches, or their officers in lesser or greater assemblies; nor are there any synods appointed by Christ in a way of subordination to one another.

XXVIII. Persons that are joined in church fellowship, ought not lightly or without just cause to withdraw themselves from the communion of the church whereunto they are so joined. Nevertheless, where any person cannot continue in any church without his sin, either for want of the administration of any ordinances instituted by Christ, or by his being deprived of his due privileges, or compelled to anything in practice not warranted by the Word, or in case of persecution, or upon the account of convenience of habitation; he consulting with the church, or the officer or officers thereof, may peaceably depart from the communion of the church, wherewith he hath so walked, to join himself with some other church, where he may enjoy the ordinances in the purity of the same, for his edification and consolation.

XXIX. Such reforming churches as consist of persons sound in the faith and of conversation becoming the gospel, ought not to refuse the communion of each other, so far as may consist with their own principles respectively, though they walk not in all things according to the same rules of church order.

XXX. Churches gathered and walking according to the mind of Christ, judging other churches (though less pure) to be true churches, may receive unto occasional communion with them, such members of those churches as are credibly testified to be godly, and to live without offense.

FINIS

124

Waldensian Confession (1662)

This confession is essentially that of 1655 (cf. the introductory comments to that document, found earlier in this volume). Vinay's text from 1662 (*La Confessioni di fede dei Valdesi Reformati*, 187–204) contains Leger's preface dated Oct. 5, 1661. The particular difference between the printed versions (1655 compared with 1662) is the proof texts: the 1662 version contains them, while the Vinay/Leger version of 1655 does not. Thus, we are reprinting the confession under this date with the Scripture proofs. We have made slight changes indicated by [ ] and some minor corrections in Scripture citations. Note also the presence of the calumny about the impeccability of Christ at the conclusion of the document (no. 3), which is absent from the 1655 version.

CONFESSION OF FAITH (1662)

To the most reverend and honored brethren in the Lord: pastors, elders, officers, and to the other faithful of Piedmont's valleys.

In His goodness and mercy, God was pleased to employ my ministry in the churches for many years and to make it fruitful by His holy blessing, even though His adorable providence transferred it into another place; yet my deep love for them did not decrease or weaken, for I am constrained to it by birth, and because of my first call and your brotherly affection. I recall that all of Christ's ministers must imitate the great Shepherd of souls, the great Priest of our profession, bearing with Him the names of all Israel's tribes not only on His breast with holy solicitude, but also on

His shoulders, having consideration for the burden imposed on them; as Saint Paul gave an example, being constantly pressed, compelled, and anxious in his heart for the consuming care of all the churches of God, partaking with deep affection into all their afflictions and communicating all the necessary consolations, fighting with them against their enemies and in ardent prayer, correcting their vices with sober and fatherly admonitions, and comforting them with holy exhortation, aflame with zeal for God. And surely, dearest brethren, your perilous state as well as ours requires that we run, fight, and cooperate together with holy vigilance not only against Satan, the world, and vice, but also against error, in order to guard our churches from complete destruction, as we already see a fire burning and the deplorable desolation of many other churches in various places near and far—these God in His just judgment deprived of the light of saving truth because men darkened it with their works. The worst enemies of the church are not those who believe they serve God, persecuting her from without with violence, but the errors and the vices that pollute souls from within by the breathing of the old serpent, father of lies, and an unclean spirit; so, having to fight not against flesh and blood but primarily against evil spirits as Saint Paul said, it is convenient to put on the whole armor of God, that we may stand firm against the wiles of the devil. In fact, these enemies not only go around with violence, calumnies, impostures, and false doctrines, but masquerading themselves intrude in various places, seducing carnal men; and since they appear even among us due to the corruption of our nature, we must double our vigilance against evils from without and from within. The calumnies of evil tongues, which insinuate that the freedom of our religion is just unfettered licentiousness to lasciviousness, will be silenced well and efficaciously with facts and not with words; with our holy conversation rather than a mere attempt to explain the truth. It is not convenient that the sons of light live as the sons of darkness for "the night is far spent, and the day is at hand: let us therefore cast off the works of darkness, and let us put on the armor of light" [Rom. 13:12]. In so doing, we will stop the mouth of fools and the wicked who calumniate our conversation, and encourage those in whom remain some sentiments of equity to glorify God by our good works, which they will see. And even if God wills to put us through the furnace of tribulation and affliction, we should not see it as strange, but we should rather rejoice to be considered worthy to suffer for Christ's sake, being assured that this doctrine we profess and for which we are hated and persecuted by the world is God's eternal truth, and He will not abandon His cause and His church. It was so in the time of Jeremiah: if God did punish the church (for she deserved it because of her sin), He was also her refuge, defense, and sanctuary in Babylon, and later He made her arise from the grave, as we see represented in Ezekiel 37. God did marvelously the same among you from time to time and will continue to do so. Since this confession of faith is wholly taken from holy Scriptures, those who oppose it do not fight against us but against God; and even if the confessors of this truth are killed, they will rise again in the third day because when their body is defeated through death, their faith wins and triumphs (Rev. 11, 12, 13; Rom. 8:15, etc.). Praying with all my heart that our good heavenly Father will be pleased to protect all the sheep of His flock in the shadow of His wings, especially your churches, sustaining you by His Holy Spirit and strengthening you in His grace, causing you to increase in every spiritual and heavenly blessing, I remain always in your charity,

From my study, October 5, 1661,

Most humbly and affectionately your Servant and Brother

ANTONIO LEGERO

Pastor and Professor of the Church and Academy in Geneva

CONFESSION OF FAITH
OF THE REFORMED, CATHOLIC, AND APOSTOLIC CHURCHES OF PIEDMONT, CONFIRMED BY WITNESSES FROM HOLY SCRIPTURE

Having understood that our enemies, not content to have cruelly persecuted us and deprived us of our goods, are still sowing false rumors in order not only to stain our persons to make us more and more detestable, but primarily to denigrate with infamous calumnies our holy and saving doctrine that we confess, we feel compelled to reassure the spirit of those who could be concerned by such sinister impostures by making a brief declaration of our faith that we professed in the past and still hold today as conforming to the Word of God, so that all may see the falsehood of those calumnies and the injustice in which we are detested and persecuted for such an innocent doctrine.

Article I

We believe that there is only one God, who is one spiritual essence: eternal, infinite, wholly wise, merciful, righteous, and perfect in all respects; and that there are three persons in that one and simple essence—Father, Son, and Holy Ghost.

Proofs

Deut. 4:39; Isa. 42:8; 45:5. Therefore it is not lawful to put our faith and hope in creatures, nor pray to the saints, nor worship images or the cross, since these things are not from God (Ex. 20:2; Isa. 40:18, 25). Against this the Romish church represents God dressed in popish garments, even though Saint Paul condemned the Romans and pagans of old because they exchanged the glory of the incorruptible God into images in the likeness of man (Rom. 1:23; John 4:24; Job 11:7; Rom. 11:33; Luke 1:37; 1 Tim. 1:17; 1 Kings 8:39; Acts 15:8; Ps. 106:1; Ex. 34:6; Ps. 103:13). If popish doctors believed in such a God, they would not falsely imagine and teach that God burns His children alive in a most ardent fire in their pretended purgatory for hundreds or thousands of years for sins already pardoned by virtue of Christ's death (Isa. 55:7; Ezek. 33:11; 2 Cor. 1:3). In order to turn men's love from God to creatures, many Romish prelates offer to people God in His righteous only, so that if a sinner desires to have grace, instead of directing him to God the Father of all mercies through Jesus Christ—in whom and by whom we can have mercy and obtain plenary indulgence, namely the forgiveness of all sins—they direct him to the blessed virgin, calling her the mother of mercy, and say that God gave her half of His kingdom (namely, mercy), retaining justice for Himself, as the notorious popish doctor Cassander confesses. The mystery of the holy and adorable Trinity is taught in Holy Scripture (Matt. 28:19; 2 Cor. 13:13[14]; 1 John 5:7).

Article II

That this God revealed Himself to men in His works of creation and providence, and especially in His Word revealed from the beginning with oracles of diverse kinds, which were later inscribed in the books called Holy Scripture.

Proofs

Rom. 1:20; Ps. 19:1, 8; 119:105; Heb. 1:1; 2 Pet. 1:20[–21]; 2 Tim. 3:15–16. Therefore, in matters of religion, we ought not to receive any doctrine invented by men from outside the Word of God, which is fully contained in Holy Scripture.

Article III

That it is convenient to receive, as we do receive, this Holy Scripture as divine and canonical, and as our rule of faith and life, and that it is fully contained in the books of the Old and New Testaments; that in the Old Testament ought to be included only the books God entrusted to the Jewish church, who recognized and approved them as divine, namely, the five books of Moses, Joshua, Judges, Ruth, 1 and 2 Samuel, 1 and 2 Kings, 1 and 2 Chronicles or Paralipomenon, one of Ezra, Nehemiah, Esther, Job, Psalms, the Proverbs of Solomon, Ecclesiastes, the Song of Songs, the four great prophets and the twelve minor; and in the New, the four gospels, the Acts of the Apostles, Paul's epistles, one to the Romans, two to the Corinthians, one to the Galatians, one to the Ephesians, one to the Philippians, one to the Colossians, two to the Thessalonians, two to Timothy, one to Titus, one to Philemon, the epistle to the Hebrews, one of saint James, two of saint Peter, three of saint John, one of saint Jude, and the Revelation.

Proofs

Ex. 2:4[?24:4]; 34:27; 2 Pet. 1:21; Rom. 3:2. However, the apocryphal books, which were never given by God to the Jews, are not God's oracles (Rom. 15.4; 2 Tim. 3:16; 1 Thess. 4:8; Deut. 12:32; Rom. 1:1–2; John 5:39, 45; Acts 17:11; Luke 16:29). We therefore ought to trust the books of Holy Scripture more than a man raised from the dead (Luke 24:44; Isa. 8:20; 1 Cor. 4:6; Gal. 6:16; 3:15). It is not legitimate to change or to add anything to the testament of God contained in Holy Scripture, and confirmed by the death of Christ our Lord (Gal. 1:8). How can the pope add so many things beside Holy Scripture with a good conscience (Rev. 22.18)? John, at the close of Revelation, which is the last book of Holy Scripture, wanted to seal it with this holy declaration, in order to restrain the arrogance and temerity of men.

Article IV

That we recognize the divinity of these sacred books not only because of the testimony of the church, but foremost because of the eternal and indisputable truth they contain, by the excellence, sublimity, and majesty divine they show, and by the work of the Holy Spirit, who makes us receive with reverence the testimony rendered by the church, opening our eyes to discover the rays of celestial light shining in the Scripture, and correcting our taste to discern this food according to its divine flavor.

Proofs

John 4:42. Those who read Holy Scripture with reverence recognize it to be the voice of God and not of man (John 3:31; Luke 24:32; Heb. 4:12; Ps. 12:6; 19:9; 1 Cor. 2:11, 14). All believers have the Spirit of God as taught by Paul (Rom. 8:9; 1 Cor. 10:15; 2 Cor. 1:13; 1 Thess. 5:19–21; 1 John 4:1).

Article V

That God made all things from nothing, with absolute freedom of will, and with infinite power of word.

Proofs

Gen. 1.1; Ex. 20:11; Ps. 33:6; Heb. 11:3[?2]; Col. 1:16.

Article VI

That God guides and governs them all by His providence, ordering and directing all that happens in the world, but without being the author or the cause of the evil of creatures, or that the guilt of it might or ought to be imputed in any way to Him.

Proofs

Deut. 32:4; Ps. 135:6; Eph. 1:11; Acts 17:24–25, 28; Matt. 10:29; Lam. 3:38; Isa. 45:6–7; Amos 3:6; Ps. 45:8[?7]; James 1:13; John 8:44; 1 John 3:8; 2:16; Gen. 45:5; 50:20; Acts 2:23; 4:27.

Article VII

That the angels were all created pure and holy, but some fell in an irreparable corruption and perdition, while the others are preserved by God's goodness, which sustained and confirmed them.

Proofs

Col. 1:16; Jude 6; 2 Pet. 2:4; 1 Tim. 5.21; Matt. 16:27; 25:31; Heb. 1:14. However, God never commanded us to pray to them; nor did any believer ever pray or worship any created angel, who always refused to be worshipped (Rev. 19:10; 22:8[–9]). Worship is due to God alone.

Article VIII

That man, who was created pure and holy in God's image, by his own fault deprived himself of that blessed state, having believed the lying words of the devil.

Proofs

Eccl. 7:29; Gen. 1:26–27; Eph. 4:24; Col. 3:10; 2 Cor. 11:3; 1 Tim 2:14; Rom. 5:12.

Article IX

That in his transgression man lost the righteousness and holiness he received, incurring the wrath of God, death, and captivity under the power of the one who has the power of death, namely the devil; so that his free will became a slave of sin and by nature all men, Jews and Gentiles, are children of wrath, dead in trespasses and sins; and are consequently incapable of anything good toward salvation and indeed of any good thought without grace; for all his thoughts are only evil at all times.

Proofs

Rom. 3:9; 5:12; John 8:34; Rom. 6:17; Eph. 2:1; Rom. 8:7; 1 Cor. 2:14; Gen. 6:5; 8:21; Jer. 17:9; Matt. 7:18; John 6:44; 15:5; 3:5, 27; 1 Cor. 2:11, 14; 12:3; 2 Cor. 3:5.

Article X

That all the posterity of Adam are guilty in him and with him in his disobedience, affected by his corruption and fallen into the same calamity, even small children in the womb of their mothers; hence the name "original sin."

Proofs

Rom. 5:12–19; Job 14:4; 15:14; Ps 5:6; 1 Kings 8:46; Prov. 20:9; Eccl. 7:20; Matt. 15:19; Eph. 2:1–3; 1 Cor. 15:22.

Article XI

That God rescues from that corruption and condemnation those whom He elected before the foundation of the world, not because He foresaw any good disposition to faith or holiness in them, but because of His mercy in Christ Jesus His Son, leaving others to themselves according to His sovereign will, in His irreproachable freedom and justice.

Proofs

1 Cor. 4:7; Eph. 2:3–9; 1:3–6; Titus 3:3, 5; Rom. 3:9; 9:11–24; 2 Tim. 1:9; 2:19; Rom. 8:29–30; John 17:6, 9; Rom. 11:5, 33–36.

Article XII

That Christ Jesus, having been ordained of God in His eternal decree to be the only Savior and the only head of His body (that is the church) has purchased her with His own blood, in the fullness of times; and He communicates to her all His benefits through the gospel.

Proofs

Rom. 3:25; 1 Pet. 1:18–20; Gal. 1:4; Matt. 1:21; John 3:16; 2 Tim. 1:9; Eph. 1:4, 6–7, 21–23; 5:23–26; Acts 20:28; 4:12; John 14:6; 1 Tim. 2:5–6; Titus 2:14; 1 John 1:7.

Article XIII

That there are two natures in Christ Jesus, divine and human, truly united in one person, without confusion, separation, division, change; for each nature maintains its distinct prerogatives so that Christ Jesus is true God and true man!

Proofs

Matt. 1:22–23; Isa. 7:14; Luke 1:35; Rom. 1:3–4; 9:5; John 1:14; 1 Tim. 3:16; Heb. 1:3; Col. 2:9; 1 Cor. 1:30.

Article XIV

That God so loved the world that He gave His Son to save us by His own perfect obedience, especially that which He showed suffering the cursed death of the cross, conquering the devil, sin, and death.

Proofs

John 3:16; Rom. 5:8; John 17:9; Rom. 8:3, 32; 1 John 4:9–10; 2:2; 1:7; Rom. 5:19; Phil. 2:7–8; Gal 4:4; 3:13; Heb. 10:8–10; 2:14–15; 1 Cor. 15:56–57; Rev. 12:10–11.

Article XV

That, as Jesus Christ has made full atonement of our sins through His perfect sacrifice once for all on the cross, it cannot be repeated under any pretext.

Proofs

Rom. 3:24–25; 1 Tim. 2:6; Heb. 9:14; 1 Pet. 1:18; 2:24; 1 John 1:7; 2:2; Heb. 7:24, 27. Note that the true sacrifice of Christ was made once and for all; therefore it cannot be repeated as it is supposed in the Mass. We ought to appeal to His perpetual intercession to obtain the benefits of that one sacrifice that possesses eternal value (Heb. 9:12, 22). Therefore, since Christ's blood is not shed again in the Mass, the Mass does not make remission of sins (Heb. 9:25). Affirming that Christ Jesus offers Himself again and again, the Roman priests contradict the apostle (Heb. 9:26). According to holy, apostolic doctrine, if Christ would offer Himself in sacrifice again and again, He would suffer many times; but Christ does not suffer anymore, He does not die anymore (Rom. 6:9). Therefore, He does not offer Himself anymore (Heb. 9:27–28). Christ's sacrifice is His death, so He does not suffer nor die anymore, since He does not offer Himself many times (Heb. 10:10, 14). Let us therefore cling to this one and true sacrifice of Christ.

Article XVI

That having been fully reconciled to God by the Lord Jesus, with His blood at the cross, only by the virtue of His merit and not because of our works, we are absolved and justified in His sight.

Proofs
Jer. 23:6; Isa. 53:5–6, 11; 2 Cor. 5:20–21; Rom. 5:19; 3:24–25, 28; 4:25; 5:9–10; Eph. 1:7; 2:8–9; Col. 1:19–20; Titus 3:5; 1 John 1:7. There is, therefore, no other purgatory (1 Cor. 1:30; Rom. 8:1).

Article XVII

That we are united to Christ and have communion with all His benefits by faith, which is founded upon the promises of life made unto us in the gospel.

Proofs
Rom. 10:17; 1:16; Eph. 3:16–17; Hab. 2:4; Gal. 2:20; John 1:12; 3:36; 6:35; Rom. 5:1.

Article XVIII

That our faith comes through the gracious and effective operation of the Holy Spirit, who enlightens our souls, bringing them to rely upon God's mercy and making the benefits of Christ its own.

Proofs
Eph. 1:16, 18; 2:1, 8; Matt. 11:25–26; 16:17; 1 Cor. 2:9–10; 12:9; Gal. 5:22; John 6:44; Acts 16:14; Rom. 12:3; Phil. 1:29; 2:13; 2 Cor. 1:21–22; Eph. 1:13–14; Rom. 8:14, 17.

Article XIX

That Jesus Christ is our true and only Mediator, not only in His redemption but also in His intercession; and that by His merits and intercession, we have access to the Father, so that we might pray to Him with the holy confidence that we shall be heard, without having the need to call upon any other intercessor but Him.

Proofs

1 Tim. 2:5–6. Christ is not only Mediator of redemption, having purchased us, but also of intercession, since the apostle is speaking of the prayers of believers offered to God for His name's sake. There is therefore only one Mediator for our redemption and intercession (Heb. 12:22–24). Note that the blood of Christ itself speaks, interceding for us, being the price of our redemption. Hence, only the one who shed His blood to redeem us is our intercessor before God (1 John 2:1). Also, the beloved disciple does not direct us to any other advocate or intercessor, but only to Him who is our Redeemer and purification from iniquity. Christ Himself calls us only to Himself without directing us to any other mediator (Matt. 11:28; John 14:6). Therefore, those who follow other ways do not come to God (Eph. 2:18; 3:12; Heb. 10:19; 4:14, 16; John 14:13; 16:23).

Article XX

That since God promises to us regeneration in Jesus Christ, those who are united to Him by a living faith ought to and really do give themselves to good works.

Proofs

1 Pet. 1:3; John 15:5; Phil. 1:11; Eph. 2:5, 10; 2 Cor. 5:15, 17; Rom. 6:4; Gal. 2:20; Titus 2:11–14; John 3:3–6; Titus 3:3–8; Rom. 6:11–13; Eph. 4:21–24; Matt. 3:8–10; 7:17–20; Gal. 5:6; James 2:17; 1 John 5:18.

Article XXI

Good works are so necessary to believers that they cannot come to the kingdom of heaven without them, since God prepared them so that we walk in them; therefore, we must flee vices and devote ourselves to practice Christian virtues, using fasting and all other means assisting us in things so holy.

Proofs

Eph. 2:10; 1 Thess. 4:3; Heb. 12:14; Rev. 21:27; 1 Cor. 6:9–11; Rom. 8:13; Col. 3:5–6; 1 Cor. 9:27; Titus 2:12; Isa. 58:6; 1 Tim. 4:8.

Article XXII

That even though our good works do not have any merit, the Lord will not omit to remunerate them with eternal life out of a merciful continuance of His grace and by virtue of the immutable steadiness of His promises made unto us.

Proofs

Job 9:2–3; Ps. 143:1–2; Rom. 3:20; Luke 17:10; Job 22:2; Ps. 16:2; Eph. 2:8–9; 2 Tim. 1:9; Titus 3:5; Col. 3:23–24. Note that the prize and the reward promised by God to believers is the children's inheritance and not what is due to them as laborers (Matt. 25:34). So they do not claim it because of their merits but because of the grace and mercy of the Father, who adopted them as His children and blessed them, making them His heirs (Rom. 8:15–18). Note also that the sufferings of holy martyrs [does not] cause them to merit the inheritance of celestial glory, nor can they be compared to it (Rom. 6:22–23). So the apostle teaches that man merits death for his sins as the true reward for his iniquities and retribution for his crimes; however, believers cannot expect eternal life as a reward they earned by their good works—rather, they obtain it as a free gift of God by the merits of Jesus Christ our Savior; and to show this more clearly, the apostle, having said that the wages of sin is death, does not continue as one might expect, adding that the wages of good works is life, but that the gift of God is eternal life.

Article XXIII

That those who have eternal life by faith and by their good works must be considered holy and honored for their virtues, imitated in the noble actions of their life, but not worshiped or called upon, for we must pray but to one God through Jesus Christ.

Proofs

Ps. 116:15; Rev. 14:13; Isa. 57:1–2; Heb. 13:7; 1 Cor. 11:1; John 8:39; Matt. 4:10; Isa. 42:8; 48:11; Joel 2:32; Rom. 10:13–14. The object upon which faith rests is God alone. (Jer. 17:5). God alone therefore should be called upon (Ps. 50:15). We do not find in the whole of Scripture any precept to call upon angels or saints in heaven, nor any promise of grace for those who call upon them, nor any example of believers who did it (Matt. 11:28). Christ does not direct us to saints, and the apostles in their epistles and preaching never entrusted themselves to others—not to the blessed virgin or to the saints of old, but to the one God through Jesus Christ, the only Mediator between God and men. Having been asked by the disciples to teach them how to pray, Jesus did not give them various forms of prayer such as one to God, one to angels, one to saints; but to show them clearly that we must call upon God alone, He prescribes to them only one divine model of prayer, which cannot be addressed to any creature (Luke 11:1). Nor any religious offering to be presented to saints has ever He commanded, nor to any angels must we present the spiritual sacrifice of prayer (Judg. 13:16).

Since angels and saints cannot look into men's hearts, they cannot understand true prayers, namely the thoughts and desires of believers, not mere and fallacious words of human lips (1 Kings 8:39). If saints gathered into God's rest in heaven could see the sins and calamities into which people dear to them fall and, above all, into which the church falls, their happiness would be disturbed. Or if, as we indicated, holy King Josiah could not see the public miseries of God's people, much less can saints know the necessities of all individuals around the whole world, or understand their supplications (Eccl. 9:5–6; cf. Job 14:21; 2 Kings 22:20). And if the holy patriarchs such as Abraham, the friend of God and father of believers, and Israel, who saw God face-to-face, did not know their posterity at the time of Isaiah, how is it possible that other saints understand the supplications of all men (Isa. 63:16)?

Article XXIV

That God has gathered a church in the world to save men and that she has but one head and foundation alone, namely, Jesus Christ.

Proofs

Isa. 4:3; John 10:14–16; 11:51–52; Deut. 7:6; Ps. 33:12; 46:6; 87:1–3; 100:3; 147:2; 148:22–23[sic; 12–13]; Acts 4:11; Matt. 16:18; Eph. 1:22–23; 1 Cor. 3:11; Eph. 2:20–21; 5:23. How is the pope then not ashamed of boasting to be the head and husband of the church? How can we believe that that is the chaste wife of Christ if she recognizes another husband?

Article XXV

That that church is the company of believers who, having been elected before the foundation of the world and called by a holy calling, are united in order to follow God's Word, believing what it teaches and living in the fear of God.

Proofs
Eph. 4:11–13; Rom. 8:29–30; Matt. 22:14; 1 John 2:18–19; 1 Thess. 4:7; Jude 1; 1 Cor. 1:2; John 8:47; 10:3–4; 17:6, 9, 17–21, 24; 2 Tim. 2:19; 1 John 2:3–4; 1 John 3:3.

Article XXVI

That that church cannot come to naught and be reduced to nothing, but that she is perpetual since all the elect are, each in his own time, called of God into the communion of the saints and are preserved and kept by the Spirit in the faith; and persevering in it, they will obtain eternal salvation.

Proofs
Jer. 31:3; 33:35–36[*sic*; 25–26]; 32:38–40; Ps. 46:6; Mal. 3:6; Ps. 102:28–29[27–28]; Hos. 2:19. The holy bond of this spiritual marriage between Christ and His church cannot be broken by men or by demons, for God preserves the faith of His own (John 14:16; Rom. 11:29; Ps. 37:28; 48:15[14]; John 6:37, 47; 10:27–28; Rom. 8:29–32, 38–39; Matt. 24:24). In this last verse, Christ teaches that it is impossible that the elect are led astray, but, being kept by God's grace, they persevere in the faith till death (Luke 22:31–32; John 17:11, 20–21; 1 Cor. 1:7–8).

God works to such an extent in the will of His elect that they want to persevere and they in fact do persevere to the end, so that we can truly say that their will cannot make uncertain their perseverance and that they do not boast to obtain it out of their free will, but by the grace of God (Phil. 1:6; 2:13; 1 John 2:19; 3:9).

Article XXVII

That everyone ought to unite to and have communion with that church.

Proofs

Isa. 4:3. This is the true church of God (Isa. 44:5; Joel 2:32). It follows that to be saved we have to join and comply with the true church, not the synagogue of Satan, nor remain alone in a hermitage or excommunicated (Acts 2:47; Gal. 4:26). Those who therefore do not recognize the church as their mother, obeying the pure preaching of the Word of God, cannot say that God is their Father (Heb. 12:22–23; Matt. 18:17; 2 Cor. 6:14–18). Note that in order to be united to the true church, it is necessary to separate from that which is false.

To discern true pastors from false ones, we have to see if their doctrine complies with Scripture (1 John 5:21; 4:1; 2 John 10). Those who do not separate from the false church make themselves accomplices of her errors and superstitions and are joined to her in her everlasting torment, even if they do not realize it (Rev. 18:4).

Those who therefore do not join the true church are not members of Christ's mystical body. Saint Paul never mentions pontiffs, cardinals, or priests among the ordained officers for the edification of the church; therefore, from whence are they (Ps. 27:4; Eph. 4:11–13)? This is the teaching of the Word of God in the Old and New Testament (Matt. 10:14; Heb. 10:25; 13:7, 17; Acts 5:29; John 8:47).

Article XXVIII

That God does not instruct us only through His Word, but that He has also ordained the sacraments to be joined to the Word, as means to unite us to Christ and to make us partake in His benefits; and that there are only two in common among all the members of the church under the New Testament, namely, the baptism and the Holy Supper.

Proofs

Rom. 1:16; 10:17; 4:11–13; Matt. 28:19–20; Mark 1:1–4; Rom. 6:3–5; 1 Cor. 10:16; 11:23–26; 12:12–13. You see our mystical union with Christ sealed with the two seals of the sacraments of the Christian church, namely baptism and Holy Supper.

Article XXIX

That He ordained baptism as a testimony to our adoption, and that in it we are washed of our sins in the blood of Jesus Christ and renewed in holiness of life.

Proofs

Luke 3:2–3; Mark 16:15–16; Acts 2:38; Gal. 3:27; Rom. 6:3–4; Eph. 5:26–27; Col. 2:11–12; 1 Pet. 3:21; Heb. 10:22.

Article XXX

That He ordained the Holy Supper or Eucharist to nourish our souls in such a way that, through a true and living faith, by the incomprehensible work of the Holy Spirit, really eating His flesh and drinking His blood, in Christ we have spiritual and everlasting life, being tightly and inseparably united to Him; and to show clearly to all what we believe, we add the words in the prayer that precedes the sacrament, in the liturgical form of the Holy Supper and in our catechism, which is found after the Psalms we sing; these are the words of the prayer: *Since our Lord offered His body and His blood for the remission of our sins and moreover desires to communicate them to us as a nourishment to everlasting life, let Him give us grace that we might receive such a great benefit with sincerity of heart and ardent zeal, so that with a firm faith we enjoy His body and blood, that is His whole person.* The words of the liturgy are as follows: *We therefore first believe the promises that Jesus Christ, who is infallible truth, pronounced with His own mouth, namely that He really wants to make us partake of His body and blood so that we have Him fully living in us and we living in Him*; and the words of our catechism are found in Lord's Day 53.

Proofs

Matt. 26:26–29. Note that it does not say that because of transubstantiation this is changed into my body, but this is my body, that is a sacrament—that means a sacred sign of my body, as the cup is the New Testament, namely, the sign and seal of it; and the rock struck by Moses was Christ, as the apostle writes in 1 Cor. 10:4, not in substance but as a type and in its meaning. Note that all who receive the sacred bread ought to partake also in the sacred cup, which cannot be withheld from them without sacrilege (Matt. 26:27). Note that the blood of Christ in the Holy Supper is meant as shed, that is, in His death (Matt. 26:28). As therefore this holy blood was not then shed really in the Supper, so it is not today present in the cup or in the wine when it is shed materially in the celebration of the Holy Supper; but only sacramentally, because faith receives in it Christ as dying for us on the cross. Note that the wine Christ drank in the celebration of the Holy Supper was not transubstantiated into blood but that it was true wine, fruit of the vine (Matt. 26:29).

Luke 22:19. Note that He does not say, "make my body," but "celebrate its memory." As the cup is not changed into a covenant or the New Testament, but it is only its sacrament, in the same way the bread is a sacrament of the body of Christ, that is, a holy sign (Luke 22:20). Note that the apostle as a faithful teacher did but deliver to the church only what he received from Christ; but in the Mass there are many things which are not found in the gospel of Christ (1 Cor. 11:23). Note that in the Holy Supper Jesus Christ gave His broken body for us not really but sacramentally by the breaking of the bread. He was not therefore contained bodily in the bread of the Supper. Note that the Holy Supper was not ordained to sacrifice Christ again, as it is assumed in the Mass, but in order to proclaim the sacrifice of His death made once for all and to receive the saving benefit in the remission of our sins (?Luke 22:25).

Note that coming to Christ and eating His flesh and drinking His blood is to believe in Him; and this is done not with our material mouth, but by faith, which is the mouth of the soul (John 6:35). Therefore, the flesh and the blood of Christ are not received bodily in the holy sacrament, for many hypocrites receive it but without having eternal life (John 6:54). Hence, the eating of the body of Christ is not to be understood materially but spiritually by faith, through which we live in Christ and Christ lives and dwells in us (John 6:63; Gal. 2; Eph. 2–3).

Article XXXI

That it is necessary that the church has pastors who are judged well instructed and living well by those who have a right so to judge, both to preach the Word of God and administer the sacraments, as well as to shepherd the flock of Christ according to the principles of a good discipline, along with elders and deacons, in conformity to the custom of the ancient church.

Proofs

Num. 27:17; Heb. 5:4–5; Jer. 3:15; 28:8–9; 23:21–22; 1 Cor. 12:4, 28. The papacy and cardinalate were not ordained of God. The apostle describes here (Eph. 4:11–13) all the offices established by Christ for the edification of the church, and he would have not forgotten the ordination of popes, cardinals, and priests if Christ had established them.

Elder and bishop are two names of the office of pastors or ministers of the church, who do not lord it over the church, as we read in the following references (John 20:21; Mark 16:15; Matt. 28:19–20; 1 Tim. 3:1–5; 5:17; Titus 1:5–7). Paul, speaking to the elders (that is, to the ministers of the church in Ephesus) calls them bishops (Acts 20:17, 28). We ought to follow our pastors as they follow Christ, the great Shepherd of souls; but if they fall into errors, we must hold to the truth of God rather than the lies of men, as we read in the following references (1 Pet. 5:1–3; 1 Tim. 3:8–10; Heb. 13:17).

They examined daily the sermons of Saint Paul in light of the indisputable rule of Holy Scripture (Gal. 1:8–9; Acts 17:11), as Isaiah exhorted of old and as God Himself did (Deut. 13; Isa. 8:20; Matt. 7:15; 16:6; 1 Tim. 4:1–3). Everyone can see by himself where such evident errors rule today, so that we may flee from them if we desire to save our souls.

2 Thess. 2:3–13; 1 Thess. 5:20–21; 1 John 4:1–3. Note that to discern the spirits to know if they are of God, we are commanded to examine their doctrine according to the rule of holy Scripture, as in John 5:39 and Acts 17:11. Above all, we ought to guard ourselves from those who corrupt the article on the incarnation of Christ—as those who imagine a body of Christ which is in many places at the same time, that is, not only in heaven but everywhere they claim by virtue of the transubstantiation in the wafers in a thousand billion places.

Note that it is not said that we have to see if he is sent and approved by the Roman bishop, but [we have to see] if he teaches the doctrine of Christ (2 John 10). The father of lies never ceases to send out lying spirits into the world who claim to have apostolic authority; but we must not blindly follow them; rather, we have to prove and reprove them (Rev. 2:2). The straw of human inventions is the pasture of brutal spirits, but the children of God nourish themselves with the heavenly wheat of His Word, which is also like a sacred fire that burns the straw of false doctrines (1 Pet. 4:11; 1 Cor. 4:6; 1 Tim. 4:13–16; 2 Tim. 4:1–4; Jer. 23:16–19).

And on the duty and care of pastors to correct vices by a holy discipline (Titus 2:15; 1 Tim. 5:20; Isa. 58:1; Ezek. 3:17–21; Matt. 18:15–17).

Article XXXII

That God established kings, princes, and magistrates to govern people, and that people ought to be subject to them and obedient because of this ordination, not only for wrath but as a matter of conscience in all things that are according to the Word of God, who is the King of Kings and Lord of Lords.

Proofs

Prov. 8:15; Dan. 2:20–21; Job 12:18; 2 Chron. 19:5–7; Rom. 13:1–7; Matt. 6; Luke 11.

Article XXXIII

That we ought to receive the Apostles' Creed, the Lord's Prayer, and the Decalogue as fundamental writings of our faith and of our devotions, as it is clear from the witnesses by which we verified our confession, which in its substance contains the same doctrine.

Proofs

Rom. 1:16; 10:8–9; 2 Tim. 1:13. The Lord's Prayer is prescribed unto us as a most perfect pattern for our prayers, vows, and desires in Matthew 6 and Luke 11.

As for a more lengthy declaration of our beliefs, we refer again to the protest already presented in 1603, according to which we profess the right doctrine along with the Reformed Churches in France, Great Britain, the Low Countries, Germany, Switzerland, Bohemia, Poland, Hungary, and others, as it is professed in the Augsburg Confession according to the declaration of the author. We pledge to persevere faithfully in this doctrine by God's grace, in life and death, being ready to subscribe to this eternal truth of God with our own blood as our fathers did since the times of the apostles, and especially in these last few centuries. We humbly plead with all the Evangelical and Protestant churches to consider us, in spite of our poverty and worthlessness, true members of Christ's mystical body who are suffering for His name, and to continue to help us in your prayers to God and in all other works of your love that we have already experienced; for this reason, we thank them in all humility, praying God with all our heart that He will reward you, pouring upon them the most precious blessings of grace and glory, both in this life and in that to come. AMEN.

The following is a brief apology about those headings we along with other Reformed churches are accused of holding by the doctors of the Roman religion, even if we condemn them as full of ungodliness and worthy to be abhorred by Christians.

We are usually accused of believing that:

1. God is the author of sin;
2. God is not omnipotent;
3. Jesus Christ was not without sin;
4. Jesus Christ fell into despair on the cross;
5. Man is like a piece of wood or a rock in his actions to salvation, being moved by the Spirit of God;
6. Because of predestination it is indifferent if one lives well or amiss;
7. Good works are not necessary for salvation;
8. Among us repentance and confession of sins are condemned;
9. It is convenient to reject fasting and other mortifications to live in debauchery;
10. It is lawful for everyone to explain freely Scripture according to the motions of a peculiar spirit;
11. The church can be reduced to nothing and be extinguished;
12. Baptism avails for nothing;
13. In the sacrament of the Eucharist, there is no real communion with Christ, but only a picture;
14. It is not necessary to submit to and obey kings, princes, and magistrates;
15. Since we do not pray to the virgin and glorified saints, we despise them; while we consider them blessed, worthy of laud, and imitation, and especially we consider the glorious virgin blessed above all women.

These beliefs are imputed to us, while our churches detest them as heresies and declare anathema with the whole heart any who uphold them.

(Translated by Andrea Ferrari)

125

The Formula Consensus Helvetica (1675)

Seventeenth-century Reformed orthodoxy looked to the Synod of Dort (on the Continent) and the Westminster Assembly (of Great Britain) for its confessional pillars. The academy established by John Cameron (ca. 1579–1625) at Saumur in France threatened those pillars. Cameron's academy would be distinguished by the theological system of its greatest student and professor—Moïse/Moyse Amyraut (Amyraldus, 1596–1664). Amyraldian "hypothetical redemptionism" would become the bane of the Reformed Church of France and earn the disdain of the epigones in Calvin's citadel, Geneva. The triumvirs of Saumur—Amyraut, Louis Cappel (Cappelus, 1585–1658), and Josué de la Place (Placaeus, 1596–1665)— resisted the Calvinistic orthodoxy of the Synod of Dort (1618–1619), not only on the divine decree regarding the scope of the atonement (Amyraut), but also on the imputation of Adam's sin to his descendants (de la Place's rejection of immediate for mediate imputation of Adamic transgression). Amyraut was summoned before the synod of the French Reformed Church at Alençon in 1637. His *Brief Traité de la Prédestination et de ses Principales Dépendances* (1634) had earned complaints from Geneva, Pierre du Moulin (1568–1658), and André Rivet (1573–1651). Amyraut weathered this storm with a slap on the wrist; however, he was not suspended from his post as professor and pastor at Saumur. By 1659, the National Synod of Loudun had declared Amyraut fully "orthodox."

The Swiss Reformed reacted: Francis Turretin (1623–1687) in Geneva, Johann Henry Heidegger (1633–1698) in Zurich, and Lucas Gernler (1625–1675) in Basel. Alarmed at the rising popularity of Amyraldianism and the progressivism originating at Saumur, these Helvetian triumvirs proposed a Helvetic Consensus specifically directed against the errors of the three professors of Saumur (cf. the Geneva Theses of 1649 for the background to this concern). Canons I–III were directed against Cappel, whose *Arcanum punctationis revelatum* (1624) had challenged Johann Buxtorf's (1564–1629) endorsement of the Mosaic origin of the Hebrew vowel points (1620). Canons X–XII were aimed at de la Place's mediate view of original sin. Canons IV–IX and XI–XXII were pointed at Amyraut.

Turretin initiated the idea of a Swiss Consensus in a letter to Heidegger on November 6, 1669. He was increasingly at odds with young professors at the academy in Geneva—professors who had been educated at Saumur and were importing Amyraldianism, and worse, into the curriculum and theology of the city. Among his opponents were Louis Tronchin (1629–1705), Philippe Mestrezat (1618–1690), and Jean-Robert Chouet (1642–1731) (cf. James T. Dennison, Jr., "The Life and Career of Francis Turretin," in Francis Turretin, *Institutes of Elenctic Theology*, ed. by James T. Dennison, Jr. [1997], 3:642–58). A draft of the Consensus was composed by Heidegger and approved by the Swiss Evangelical Diet in March 1675. The city of Geneva endorsed it in January 1679.

The authority of the consensus was short-lived. Ironically, the son of its proposer dismantled it, in 1706. Jean-Alphonse Turretin (1671–1737) led the charge to repudiate the Helvetic Consensus as outmoded and unprogressive. Geneva and her epigones were becoming enlightened by a kinder and gentler Christianity. Indeed, Pierre Bayle (1647–1706) and Voltaire (1694–1778) were at the gate (cf. James T. Dennison, Jr., "The Twilight of Scholasticism: Francis Turretin at the Dawn of the Enlightenment," *Protestant Scholasticism: Essays in Reassessment*, ed. Carl Trueman and R. Scott Clark [1999], 244–55).

The Latin text is found in Niemeyer (pp. 729–39), and Müller (pp. 861–70). Our translation is from the pen of Dr. Martin I. Klauber and appears here with his gracious permission; cf. his "The Helvetic Formula Consensus (1675): An Introduction and Translation," *Trinity Journal* 11 (1990): 103–23 (especially 115–23). An older translation is located in A. A. Hodge, *Outlines of Theology* (1883), 656–63. Both Klauber and Hodge omit the introductory preface, which we have included, as translated by Richard Bishop.

THE FORMULA CONSENSUS HELVETICA

Composed in Zürich, AD 1675, by John Henry Heidegger, of Zürich, and assisted by Francis Turretin, of Geneva, and Lucas Gernler, of Basel, and designed to condemn and exclude that modified form of Calvinism, which, in the seventeenth century, emanated from the theological school at Saumur, represented by Amyraut, Placaeus, and Daillé; entitled "Form of Agreement of the Helvetic Reformed Churches Respecting the Doctrine of Universal Grace, the Doctrines Related to It, and Some Other Points."

Preface

The divine apostle to the Gentiles earnestly impressed on his true child (γνησίῳ τέκνῳ) Timothy that he "continue in those things which" ἔμαθε καὶ ἐπιστώθη, that is, "which he had learned and which had been entrusted to him" (2 Tim. 3:14). In these lamentable and exasperating times, it is entirely appropriate that the very same thing frequently enter our recollection and call itself to mind. All the more so since sad experience shows that the faith once delivered to the saints by the Word of God is being perverted from the form of sound words (ὑποτυπώσει) and is contracting no slight blemish from the errors that are cropping up not in one principle division of the truth but on every side.

For our part, since the heavenly Father has honored us (unworthy as we are) with divine grace and goodness to a greater extent than many other nations, it is right that we gratefully put down the following circumstance to that account: he has hitherto endowed our leading men (προεστῶτας), especially the very eminent nobles, the fathers of our country, and the very upright guardians of the church, with the spirit of piety, wisdom and courage. As a result, they religiously guard the store (κειμήλιον) of truth that they received from our forefathers out of the Word of God; they grip it tightly, as they say, in their hands, and they do not allow doctrinal corruption to have any access to our churches. But since constancy is nothing less than to desire to maintain what has been acquired and every day we hear the same angel that cried out to the church in Philadelphia, "Behold, I am coming quickly. Hold fast to what you have so that no one will take your crown" (Rev. 3:11), therefore it is right that we bend our knees to the Father of our Lord Jesus Christ and fervently pray that in these difficult times he might mercifully preserve this special advantage (πλεονέκτημα) and benefit for us, even to the end of the age.

Nevertheless opinions that are inferior in several matters of importance, but especially in the doctrine that concerns the extent of divine grace, could gather strength, infect impressionable young men and thus with the passage of time also infect our churches themselves. Moreover (seeing as how scarcely any crop is more fruitful, more fertile than error) the toleration of these opinions by reason of an excessive leniency could cause other, worse opinions to spring up, as has happened at other times, such as the sad example of Remonstrantism can show. Therefore, it is incumbent upon us, by the authority and instruction of the elders, to give consideration to some effective and sacred barrier.

The canons that deal with the doctrine of universal grace, as well as with several related matters of importance, were born of this consideration, and we have endorsed them by unanimous consent. In adopting a suitable arrangement, we have been particularly concerned that truth should join love in a most welcome synergy (ἡδίστη συζυγία) and contend with uncertainties, as they say, for the palm.

Nor indeed is there a reason for the honorable foreign brothers, whom we otherwise cherish and fraternally esteem as having obtained a faith of equal standing (ἰσότιμον πίστιν λαχόντας), to be angry with us about a disagreement that has been brought to light for good and weighty reasons, or to keep saying that we are furnishing anyone with an opportunity for schism. For on both sides, by the grace of God, the foundation of the faith remains, and in both cases, gold and silver and not a few precious stones have been built upon it out of the Word of God. The unity of the mystical body and of the Spirit is secure, "just as we were called in one hope of our calling; for us there is one Lord, one special faith"—and in that same faith a holy concord and bond of hospitality is to be preserved—"one baptism, one God and Father of all, who is over all things, and in all of us" (Eph 4:4–6). Accordingly, among us the chain and bond of a most tender love will always remain secure, and, by the grace of God, the most sacred obligations of the communion of the saints will remain in a state of good repair.

As to what follows, we will not cease to call upon God, the Father of Lights, in pious petition that he might determine and grant that our instruction be salutary and that he might deign to bless it through Jesus Christ, the only inaugurator and consummator of our faith and salvation.

Canons

Canon I: God, the Supreme Judge, not only took care to have his word, which is the "power of God unto salvation to every one that believes" (Rom 1:16), committed to writing by Moses, the Prophets and the Apostles, but has also watched and cherished it with paternal care from the time it was written up to the present, so that it could not be corrupted by craft of Satan or fraud of man. Therefore the Church justly ascribes to it his singular grace and goodness that she has, and will have to the end of the world (2 Pet 1:19), a "sure word of prophecy" and "Holy Scriptures" (2 Tim 3:15), from which, though heaven and earth pass away, "the smallest letter or the least stroke of a pen will not disappear by any means" (Matt 5:18).

Canon II: But, in particular, The Hebrew original of the OT which we have received and to this day do retain as handed down by the Hebrew Church, "who had been given the oracles of God" (Rom 3:2), is, not only in its consonants, but in its vowels—either the vowel points themselves, or at least the power of the points—not only in its matter, but in its words, inspired by God. It thus forms, together with the Original of the NT the sole and complete rule of our faith and practice; and to its standard, as to a Lydian stone, all extant versions, eastern or western, ought to be applied, and wherever they differ, be conformed.

Canon III: Therefore, we are not able to approve of the opinion of those who believe that the text which the Hebrew Original exhibits was determined by man's will alone, and do not hesitate at all to remodel a Hebrew reading which they consider unsuitable, and amend it from the versions of the LXX and other Greek versions, the Samaritan Pentateuch, by the Chaldaic Targums, or even from other sources. They go even to the point of following the corrections that their own rational powers dictate from the various readings of the Hebrew Original itself—which, they maintain, has been corrupted in various ways; and finally, they affirm that besides the Hebrew edition of the present time, there are in the versions of the ancient interpreters which differ from our Hebrew text, other Hebrew Originals. Since these versions are also indicative of ancient Hebrew Originals differing from each other, they thus bring the foundation of our faith and its sacred authority into perilous danger.

Canon IV: Before the creation of the world, God decreed in Christ Jesus our Lord according to his eternal purpose (Eph 3:11), in which, from the mere good pleasure of his own will, without any prevision of the merit of works or of faith, to the praise of his glorious grace, to elect some out of the human race lying in the same mass of corruption and of common blood, and, therefore, corrupted by sin. He elected a certain and definite number to be led, in time, unto salvation in Christ, their Guarantor and sole Mediator. And on account of his merit, by the mighty power of the regenerating Holy Spirit, [he decreed these elect] to be effectually called, regenerated, and gifted with faith and repentance. So, indeed, God, determining to illustrate his glory, decreed to create man perfect, in the first place, then permit him to fall, and finally pity some of the fallen, and therefore elect those, but leave the rest in the corrupt mass, and finally give them over to eternal destruction.

Canon V: Christ himself is also included in the gracious decree of divine election, not as the meritorious cause, or foundation prior to election itself, but as being himself also elect (1 Pet 2:4, 6). Indeed, he was foreknown before the foundation of the world, and accordingly, as the first requisite of the execution of the decree of election, chosen Mediator, and our first born Brother, whose precious merit God determined to use for the purpose of conferring, without detriment to his own justice, salvation upon us. For the Holy Scriptures not only declare that election was made according to the mere good pleasure of the divine counsel and will (Eph 1:5, 9; Matt 11:26), but was also made that the appointment and giving of Christ, our Mediator, was to proceed from the zealous love of God the Father toward the world of the elect.

Canon VI: Wherefore, we can not agree with the opinion of those who teach: 1) that God, moved by philanthropy, or a kind of special love for the fallen of the human race, did, in a kind of conditioned willing, first moving of pity, as they call it, or inefficacious desire, determine the salvation of all, conditionally, i.e., if they would believe; 2) that he appointed Christ Mediator for all and each of the fallen; and 3) that, at length, certain ones whom he regarded, not simply as sinners in the first Adam, but as redeemed in the second Adam, he elected, that is, he determined graciously to bestow on these, in time, the saving gift of faith; and in this sole act election properly so called is complete. For these and all other similar teachings are in no way insignificant deviations from the proper teaching concerning divine election; because the Scriptures do not extend unto all and each God's purpose of showing mercy to man, but restrict it to the elect alone, the reprobate being excluded, even by name, as Esau, whom God hated with an eternal hatred (Rom 9:11). The same Holy Scriptures testify that the counsel and will of God do not change, but stand immovable, and God in the heavens does whatsoever he will (Ps 115:3; Isa 47:10); for God is infinitely removed from all that human imperfection which characterizes inefficacious affections and desires, rashness, repentance, and change of purpose. The appointment, also, of Christ, as Mediator, equally with the salvation of those who were given to him for a possession and an inheritance that can not be taken away, proceeds from one and the same election, and does not form the basis of election.

Canon VII: As all his works were known unto God from eternity (Acts 15:18), so in time, according to his infinite power, wisdom, and goodness, he made man, the glory and end of his works, in his own image, and, therefore, upright, wise, and just. Having created man in this manner, he put him under the Covenant of Works, and in this Covenant freely promised him communion with God, favor, and life, if indeed he acted in obedience to his will.

Canon VIII: Moreover that promise connected to the Covenant of Works was not a continuation only of earthly life and happiness, but the possession especially of eternal and celestial life, a life, namely, of both body and soul in heaven, if indeed man ran the course of perfect obedience, with unspeakable joy in communion with God. For not only did the Tree of Life prefigure this very thing unto Adam, but the power of the law, which, being fulfilled by Christ, who went under it in our place, awards to us nothing other than celestial life in Christ who kept the same righteousness of the law. The power of the law also threatens man with both temporal and eternal death.

Canon IX: Wherefore we can not agree with the opinion of those who deny that a reward of heavenly bliss was offered to Adam on condition of obedience to God. We also do not admit that the promise of the Covenant of Works was any thing more than a promise of perpetual life abounding in every kind of good that can be suited to the body and soul of man in a state of perfect nature, and the enjoyment thereof in an earthly Paradise. For this also is contrary to the sound sense of the Divine Word, and weakens the power of the law considered in itself.

Canon X: God entered into the Covenant of Works not only with Adam for himself, but also, in him as the head and root with the whole human race. Man would, by virtue of the blessing of the nature derived from Adam, inherit also the same perfection, provided he continued in it. So Adam by his sorrowful fall sinned and lost the benefits promised in the Covenant not only for himself, but also for the whole human race that would be born by the flesh. We hold, therefore, that the sin of Adam is imputed by the mysterious and just judgment of God to all his posterity. For the Apostle testifies that "in Adam all sinned, by one man's disobedience many were made sinners" (Rom 5:12, 19) and "in Adam all die" (1 Cor 15:21–22). But there appears no way in which hereditary corruption could fall, as a spiritual death, upon the whole human race by the just judgment of God, unless some sin of that race preceded, incurring the penalty of that death. For God, the most supreme Judge of all the earth, punishes none but the guilty.

Canon XI: For a double reason, therefore, man, because of sin, is by nature, and hence from his birth, before committing any actual sin, exposed to God's wrath and curse; first, on account of the transgression and disobedience which he committed in the loins of Adam; and, secondly, on account of the consequent hereditary corruption implanted to his very conception, whereby his whole nature is depraved and spiritually dead; so that original sin may rightly be regarded as twofold, imputed sin and inherent hereditary sin.

Canon XII: Accordingly we can not, without harm to the Divine truth, agree with those who deny that Adam represented his posterity by God's intention, and that his sin is imputed, therefore, immediately to his posterity; and under this mediate and consequent imputation not only destroy the imputation of the first sin, but also expose the doctrine of hereditary corruption to grave danger.

Canon XIII: As Christ was elected from eternity the Head, the Leader and Lord of all who, in time, are saved by his grace, so also, in time, he was made Guarantor of the New Covenant only for those who, by the eternal election, were given to him as his own people, his seed and inheritance. For according to the determinate counsel of the Father and his own intention, he encountered dreadful death instead of the elect alone, and restored only these into the bosom of the Father's grace, and these only he reconciled to God, the offended Father, and delivered from the curse of the law. For our Jesus saves his people from their sins (Matt 1:21), who gave his life a ransom for many sheep (Matt 20:24, 28; John 10:15), his own, who hear his voice (John 10:27–28), and he intercedes for these only, as a divinely appointed Priest, and not for the world (John 17:9). Accordingly in expiatory sacrifice, they are regarded as having died with him and as being justified from sin (2 Cor 5:12): and thus, with the counsel of the Father who gave to Christ none but the elect to be redeemed, and also with the working of the Holy Spirit, who sanctifies and seals unto a living hope of eternal life none but the elect. The will of Christ who died so agrees and amicably conspires in perfect harmony, that the sphere of the Father's election, the Son's redemption, and the Spirit's sanctification are one and the same.

Canon XIV: This very thing further appears in this also, that Christ provided the means of salvation for those in whose place he died, especially the regenerating Spirit and the heavenly gift of faith, as well as salvation itself, and actually confers these upon them. For the Scriptures testify that Christ, the Lord, came to save the lost sheep of the house of Israel (Matt 15:24), and sends the same Holy Spirit, the source of regeneration, as his own (John 16:7–8): that among the better promises of the New Covenant of which he was made Mediator and Guarantor this one is pre-eminent, that he will inscribe his law, the law of faith, in the hearts of his people (Heb 8:10); that whatsoever the Father has given to Christ will come to him, by faith, surely; and finally, that we are chosen in Christ to be his children, holy and blameless (Eph. 1:4–5); but our being God's holy children proceeds only from faith and the Spirit of regeneration.

Canon XV: But by the obedience of his death Christ, in place of the elect, so satisfied God the Father, that in the estimate of his vicarious righteousness and of that obedience, all of that which he rendered to the law, as its just servant, during his entire life, whether by doing or by suffering, ought to be called obedience. For Christ's life, according to the Apostle's testimony (Phil 1:8), was nothing but submission, humiliation and a continuous emptying of self, descending step by step to the lowest extreme, even to the point of death on the Cross; and the Spirit of God plainly declares that Christ in our stead satisfied the law and divine justice by His most holy life, and makes that ransom with which God has redeemed us to consist not in His sufferings only, but in his whole life conformed to the law. The Spirit, however, ascribes our redemption to the death, or the blood, of Christ, in no other sense than that it was consummated by sufferings; and from that last definitive and noblest act derives a name indeed, but not in such a way as to separate the life preceding from his death.

Canon XVI: Since all these things are entirely so, we can hardly approve the opposite doctrine of those who affirm that of his own intention and counsel and that of the Father who sent him, Christ died for each and every one upon the condition, that they believe. [We also cannot affirm the teaching] that he obtained for all a salvation, which, nevertheless, is not applied to all, and by his death merited a salvation and faith for no one individually, but only removed the obstacle of divine justice, and acquired for the Father the liberty of entering into a new covenant of grace with all men. Finally, they so separate the active and passive righteousness of Christ, as to assert that he claims his active righteousness as his own, but gives and imputes only his passive righteousness to the elect. All these opinions, and all that are like these, are contrary to the plain Scriptures and the glory of Christ, who is Author and Finisher of our faith and salvation; they make his cross of none effect, and under the appearance of exalting his merit, they, in reality, diminish it

Canon XVII: The call to salvation was suited to its due time (1 Tim 2:6). Since by God's will it was at one time more restricted, at another, more widespread and general, but never completely universal. For, indeed, in the OT God announced his word to Jacob, his statutes and his judgments to Israel; he did not do so with any other nation (Ps 147:19–20). In the NT, peace being made in the blood of Christ and the inner walls of partition broken down, God so extended the limits of the preaching of the Gospel and the external call, that there is no longer any difference between the Jew and the Greek; for the same Lord is over all and is gracious to every one who calls upon him (Rom 10:12). But not even thus is the call universal. For Christ testifies that many are called (Matt 20:14), but not all; and when Paul and Timothy tried to go into Bithynia to preach the Gospel, the Spirit prevented them (Acts 16:7). And there have been and there are today, as experience testifies, innumerable myriads of men to whom Christ is not known even by rumor.

Canon XVIII: Meanwhile God has not left himself without witness (Acts 14:7) to those whom he refused to call by his Word unto salvation. For he provided to them the witness of the heavens and the stars (Deut 4:19), and that which may be known of God, even from the works of nature and Providence, he has shown to them (Rom 1:19), for the purpose of showing his long suffering. Yet it is not true that the works of nature and divine Providence are self-sufficient means which fulfilled the function of the external call, whereby he would reveal unto them the mystery of the good pleasure or the mercy of God in Christ. For the Apostle immediately adds: "For since the creation of the world God's invisible qualities, His eternal power and divine nature, have been clearly seen" (Rom 1:20). So they might learn the mystery of salvation through Christ and be without excuse, because they did not correctly use the knowledge that was left to them, but when they knew God, they did not glorify him as God, neither were they thankful. Wherefore also Christ glorifies God, his Father, because he had hidden these things from the wise and the prudent, and revealed them unto babes (Matt 1:25). And as the Apostle teaches: "God has made known unto us the mystery of His will according to His good pleasure which He has purposed in Christ" (Eph 1:9).

Canon XIX: Likewise the external call itself, which is made by the preaching of the Gospel, is on the part of God also, who earnestly and sincerely calls. For in his Word he most earnestly and truly reveals, not, indeed, his secret will respecting the salvation or destruction of each individual, but our responsibility, and what will happen to us if we do or neglect this duty. Clearly it is the will of God who calls, that they who are called come to him and not neglect so great a salvation, and so he earnestly promises eternal life to those who come to him by faith; for, as the Apostle declares, "It is a trustworthy saying: For if we have died with Him, we shall also live with Him; if we disown Him, He will also disown us; if we are faithless, He will remain faithful, for He cannot disown Himself (2 Tim 2:12–13). Neither is this call without result for those who disobey; for God always accomplishes his will, even the demonstration of duty, and following this, either the salvation of the elect who fulfill their responsibility, or the inexcusableness of the rest who neglect the duty set before them. Certainly the spiritual man in no way determined the eternal purpose of God to produce faith along with the externally offered, or written Word of God. Moreover, because God approved every truth which flows from his counsel, it is correctly said to be his will, that everyone who sees the Son and believes in him may have everlasting life (John 6:40). Although these "all" are the elect alone, and God formed no plan of universal salvation without any selection of persons, and Christ therefore died not for everyone but only for the elect who were given to him; yet he intends this in any case to be universally true, which follows from his special and definite purpose. But that, by God's will, the elect alone believe in the external call which is universally offered, while the reprobate are hardened. This proceeds solely from the discriminating grace of God; election by the same grace to those who believe, but their own native wickedness to the reprobate who remain in sin, who after their hardened and impenitent heart build up for themselves wrath for the Day of Judgment, and revelation of the righteous judgment of God.

Canon XX: Accordingly we have no doubt that they are wrong who hold that the call to salvation is disclosed not by the preaching of the Gospel solely, but even by the works of nature and Providence without any further proclamation. They add that the call to salvation is so indefinite and universal that there is no mortal who is not, at least objectively, as they say, sufficiently called either mediately, meaning that God will provide the light of grace to those who use the light of nature correctly, or immediately, to Christ and salvation. They finally deny that the external call can be said to be serious and true, or the candor and sincerity of God be defended, without asserting the absolute universality of grace. For such doctrines are contrary to the Holy Scriptures and the experience of all ages, and manifestly confuse nature with grace and confuse the things which we can know about God with his hidden wisdom. They further confuse the light of reason with the light of divine Revelation.

Canon XXI: Those who are called to salvation through the preaching of the Gospel are not able to believe or obey the call, unless they are raised up out of spiritual death by that very power that God used to command the light to shine out of darkness, and God shines into their hearts with the glory of God in the face of Jesus Christ (2 Cor 4:6). For the natural man does not receive the things of the Spirit of God for they are foolishness unto him: neither can he know them, because they are spiritually discerned (1 Cor 2:14). And Scripture demonstrates this utter inability by so many direct testimonies and under so many mosaics that scarcely in any other point is it surer. This inability may, indeed, be called moral even in so far as it pertains to a moral subject or object: but it ought to be at the same time called natural because man by nature, and so by the law of his formation in the womb, and hence from his birth, is the child of disobedience (Eph 2:2); and has that inability that is so innate that it cannot be shaken off except by the omnipotent heart-turning grace of the Holy Spirit.

Canon XXII: We hold therefore that they speak inaccurately and dangerously, who call this inability to believe moral inability, and do not say that it is natural, adding that man in whatever condition he may be placed is able to believe if he desires, and that faith in some way or other, indeed, is self-originated. The Apostle, however, clearly calls [salvation] the gift of God (Eph 2:8).

Canon XXIII: There are two ways in which God, the just Judge, has promised justification: either by one's own works or deeds in the law, or by the obedience or righteousness of another, even of Christ our Guarantor. [This justification] is imputed by grace to those who believe in the Gospel. The former is the method of justifying man because of perfection; but the latter, of justifying man who is a corrupt sinner. In accordance with these two ways of justification the Scripture establishes these two covenants: the Covenant of Works, entered into with Adam and with each one of his descendants in him, but made void by sin; and the Covenant of Grace, made with only the elect in Christ, the second Adam, eternal. [This covenant] cannot be broken while [the Covenant of Works] can be abrogated.

Canon XXIV: But this later Covenant of Grace according to the diversity of times has also different dispensations. For when the Apostle speaks of the dispensation of the fulness of times, that is, the administration of the last time (Eph 1:10), he very clearly indicates that there had been another dispensation and administration until the times which the Father appointed. Yet in the dispensation of the Covenant of Grace the elect have not been saved in any other way than by the Angel of his presence (Isa 63:9), the Lamb slain from the foundation of the world (Rev 13:8), Christ Jesus, through the knowledge of that just Servant and faith in him and in the Father and his Spirit. For Christ is the same yesterday, today, and forever (Heb 13:8). And by His grace we believe that we are saved in the same manner as the Fathers also were saved, and in both Testaments these statutes remain unchanged: "Blessed are all they that put their trust in Him," (the Son) (Ps 2:12); "He that believes in Him is not condemned, but he that does not believe is condemned already" (John 3:18). "You believe in God," even the Father, "believe also in me" (John 14:1). But if, moreover, the holy Fathers believed in Christ as their God, it follows that they also believed in the Holy Spirit, without whom no one can call Jesus Lord. Truly there are so many clear exhibitions of this faith of the Fathers and of the necessity of such faith in either Covenant, that they can not escape any one unless one wills it. But though this saving knowledge of Christ and the Holy Trinity was necessarily derived, according to the dispensation of that time, both from the promise and from shadows and figures and mysteries, with greater difficulty than in the NT. Yet it was a true knowledge, and, in proportion to the measure of divine Revelation, it was sufficient to procure salvation and peace of conscience for the elect, by the help of God's grace.

Canon XXV: We disapprove therefore of the doctrine of those who fabricate for us three Covenants, the Natural, the Legal, and the Gospel, different in their entire nature and essence; and in explaining these and assigning their differences, so intricately entangle themselves that they greatly obscure and even impair the nucleus of solid truth and piety. Nor do they hesitate at all, with regard to the necessity, under the OT dispensation, of knowledge of Christ and faith in him and his satisfaction and in the whole sacred Trinity, to speculate much too loosely and dangerously.

Canon XXVI: Finally, both to us, to whom in the Church, which is God's house, has been entrusted the dispensation for the present, and unto all our Nazarenes, and to those who under the will and direction of God will at any time succeed us in our responsibility, in order to prevent the fearful enkindling of dissensions with which the Church of God in different places is disturbed in terrible ways, we earnestly wish the following to be done. That in this corruption of the world, with the Apostle of the Gentiles as our faithful monitor, we all keep faithfully that which is committed to our trust, avoiding profane and vain babblings (1 Tim 6:20); and religiously guard the purity and simplicity of that knowledge which is according to piety, constantly clinging to that beautiful pair, Charity and Faith, unstained. Moreover, in order that no one may be induced to propose either publicly or privately some doubtful or new dogma of faith previously unheard of in our churches, and contrary to God's Word, to our Helvetic Confession, to our Symbolical Books, and to the Canons of the Synod of Dort, and not proved and sanctioned in a public assembly of brothers according to the Word of God, let it also be required: that we not only hand down sincerely in accordance with the divine Word, the special necessity of the sanctification of the Lord's Day, and also impressively teach and fervently urge its observation. In conclusion, that in our churches and schools, as often as occasion demands, we unanimously and faithfully hold, teach, and assert that the truth of the Canons recorded here, is deduced from the indubitable Word of God.

The very God of peace and truth sanctify us wholly, and preserve our whole spirit and soul and body blameless unto the coming of our Lord Jesus Christ! To whom, with the Father and the Holy Spirit be eternal honor, praise and glory. Amen!

126
～⊕～
The London Baptist
Confession (1677)

The London Baptist Confession of 1677 is the Westminster Confession of Faith "baptized" with anti-paedobaptist distinctives. In fact, the Savoy Declaration of 1658 is more fundamental to the confession on account of its Independent church polity, which the Baptists also favored. Forced into Nonconformity by the Restoration of Charles II (1630–1685) in 1660, along with other orthodox Calvinists and Dissenters, the Baptists also suffered under the Great Ejection of 1662 and the ban that the Five Mile Act of 1665 imposed. At the invitation of William Kiffin (1616–1701) and William Collins (†1702), the Particular Baptists sought to demonstrate harmony with other British Dissenters in a declaration of their faith. Collins, pastor of the Petty France congregation in London, along with Nehemiah Coxe (†1688), elder in the congregation, are the alleged editors of the final compilation. The Particular Baptists were indeed demonstrating a measure of solidarity with their Presbyterian and Congregational brethren.

With the Act of Toleration (1689) following the Glorious Revolution of 1688, Baptists were encouraged to declare themselves openly. On July 22, 1689, Kiffin, Hanserd Knollys (ca. 1599–1691), Benjamin Keach (ca. 1640–ca. 1704), and several others invited the Baptist Churches of England and Wales to meet in London on September 3. Until September 12, 107 "messengers" from churches in the two nations perfected and publically endorsed the second edition of the 1677 document. The result is regarded as the most significant and mature of the Particular Baptist confessions (new editions 1699, 1719, 1720, 1791, and 1809).

Our text is based on the original 1677 edition with some modernization of spelling and capitalization. We have also inserted the proof texts (some of which have been corrected) within the body of the confession. Titled *A Confession of Faith. Put Forth by the Elders and Brethren of many Congregations of Christians (Baptized upon Profession of their Faith) in London and the Country* (1677), it was subsequently reprinted in 1688. A third edition appeared in 1699 containing the names of the 1689 signatories on the fly-leaf. We have added these names to the end of our version.

A CONFESSION OF FAITH

Chapter I
Of the Holy Scriptures

1. The Holy Scripture is the only sufficient, certain, and infallible rule of all saving knowledge, faith, and obedience (2 Tim. 3:15–17; Isa. 8:20; Luke 16:29, 31; Eph. 2:20); although the light of nature, and the works of creation and providence do so far manifest the goodness, wisdom, and power of God, as to leave men inexcusable; yet are they not sufficient to give that knowledge of God and His will which is necessary unto salvation (Rom. 1:19–21; 2:14–15; Ps. 19:1–3). Therefore it pleased the Lord at sundry times, and in divers manners, to reveal Himself, and to declare that His will unto His church (Heb. 1:1); and afterward for the better preserving, and propagating of the truth, and for the more sure establishment and comfort of the church against the corruption of the flesh, and the malice of Satan, and of the world, to commit the same wholly unto writing (Prov. 22:19–21; Rom. 15:4; 2 Peter 1:19–20), which makes the Holy Scriptures to be most necessary, those former ways of God's revealing His will unto His people being now ceased.

2. Under the name of Holy Scripture, or the Word of God written, are now contained all the books of the Old and New Testament, which are these:

Of the Old Testament

Genesis, Exodus, Leviticus, Numbers, Deuteronomy, Joshua, Judges, Ruth, 1 Samuel, 2 Samuel, 1 Kings, 2 Kings, 1 Chronicles, 2 Chronicles, Ezra, Nehemiah, Esther, Job, Psalms, Proverbs, Ecclesiastes, The Song of Songs, Isaiah, Jeremiah, Lamentations, Ezekiel, Daniel, Hosea, Joel, Amos, Obadiah, Jonah, Micah, Nahum, Habakkuk, Zephaniah, Haggai, Zechariah, Malachi.

Of the New Testament

Matthew, Mark, Luke, John, the Acts of the Apostles, Paul's Epistle to the Romans, 1 Corinthians, 2 Corinthians, Galatians, Ephesians, Philippians, Colossians, 1 Thessalonians, 2 Thessalonians, 1 Timothy, 2 Timothy, to Titus, to Philemon, the Epistle to the Hebrews, the Epistle of James, the first and second Epistles of Peter, the first, second, and third Epistles of John, the Epistle of Jude, the Revelation.

All of which are given by the inspiration of God, to be the rule of faith and life (2 Tim. 3:16).

3. The books commonly called Apocrypha, not being of divine inspiration, are no part of the canon (or rule) of the Scripture, and, therefore are of no authority to the church of God, nor to be any otherwise approved or made use of, than other human writings (Luke 24:27, 44; Rom. 3:2).

4. The authority of the Holy Scripture, for which it ought to be believed, depends not upon the testimony of any man, or church; but wholly upon God (who is Truth itself) the Author thereof; therefore it is to be received, because it is the Word of God (2 Peter 1:19–21; 2 Tim. 3:16; 2 Thess. 2:13; 1 John 5:9).

5. We may be moved and induced by the testimony of the church of God, to a high and reverent esteem of the Holy Scriptures; and the heavenliness of the matter, the efficacy of the doctrine, and the majesty of the style, the consent of all the parts, the scope of the whole (which is to give all glory to God), the full discovery it makes of the only way of man's salvation, and many other incomparable excellencies, and entire perfections thereof, are arguments whereby it does abundantly evidence itself to be the Word of God; yet, notwithstanding, our full persuasion and assurance of the infallible truth, and divine authority thereof, is from the inward work of the Holy Spirit, bearing witness by and with the Word in our hearts (John 16:13–14; 1 Cor. 2:10–12; 1 John 2:20, 27).

6. The whole counsel of God concerning all things necessary for His own glory, man's salvation, faith, and life, is either expressly set down or necessarily contained in the Holy Scripture: unto which nothing at any

time is to be added, whether by new revelation of the Spirit, or traditions of men (2 Tim. 3:15–17; Gal. 1:8–9).

Nevertheless, we acknowledge the inward illumination of the Spirit of God to be necessary for the saving understanding of such things as are revealed in the Word (John 6:45; 1 Cor. 2:9–12), and that there are some circumstances concerning the worship of God, and government of the church, common to human actions and societies, which are to be ordered by the light of nature and Christian prudence, according to the general rules of the Word, which are always to be observed (1 Cor. 11:13–14; 14:26, 40).

7. All things in Scripture are not alike plain in themselves, nor alike clear unto all (2 Peter 3:16); yet those things which are necessary to be known, believed, and observed for salvation, are so clearly propounded and opened in some place of Scripture or other, that not only the learned, but the unlearned, in a due use of ordinary means, may attain to a sufficient understanding of them (Pss. 19:7; 119:130).

8. The Old Testament in Hebrew (which was the native language of the people of God of old [Rom. 3:2]), and the New Testament in Greek (which at the time of the writing of it was most generally known to the nations), being immediately inspired by God, and by His singular care and providence kept pure in all ages, are therefore authentic; so as in all controversies of religion, the church is finally to appeal to them (Isa. 8:20; Acts 15:15). But because these original tongues are not known to all the people of God, who have a right unto, and interest in the Scriptures, and are commanded in the fear of God to read and search them (John 5:39), therefore they are to be translated into the vulgar language of every nation, unto which they come (1 Cor. 14:6, 9, 11–12, 24, 28), that the Word of God dwelling plentifully in all, they may worship Him in an acceptable manner, and through patience and comfort of the Scriptures may have hope (Col. 3:16).

9. The infallible rule of interpretation of Scripture is the Scripture itself (2 Peter 1:20–21; Acts 15:15–16); and therefore when there is a question about the true and full sense of any Scripture (which is not manifold, but one), it must be searched by other places that speak more clearly.

10. The supreme judge, by which all controversies of religion are to be determined, and all decrees of councils, opinions of ancient writers, doctrines of men, and private spirits, are to be examined, and in whose sentence we are to rest, can be no other but the Holy Scripture delivered by the Spirit, into which Scripture so delivered, our faith is finally resolved (Matt. 22:29, 31–32; Eph. 2:20; Acts 28:23).

Chapter II
Of God and of the Holy Trinity

1. The Lord our God is but one only living and true God (1 Cor. 8:4, 6; Deut. 6:4); whose subsistence is in and of Himself (Jer. 10:10; Isa. 48:12), infinite in being (Ex. 3:14) and perfection, whose essence cannot be comprehended by any but Himself; a most pure spirit (John 4:24), invisible (1 Tim. 1:17; Deut. 4:15–16), without body, parts, or passions, who only has immortality, dwelling in the light which no man can approach unto, who is immutable (Mal. 3:6), immense, eternal (1 Kings 8:27; Jer. 23:23), incomprehensible (Ps. 90:2), almighty (Gen. 17:1), every way infinite, most holy (Isa. 6:3), most wise, most free, most absolute; working all things according to the counsel of His own immutable and most righteous will (Ps. 115:3; Isa. 46:10), for His own glory (Prov. 16:4; Rom. 11:36), most loving, gracious, merciful, long-suffering, abundant in goodness and truth, forgiving iniquity, transgression and sin; the Rewarder of them that diligently seek Him (Ex. 34:6–7; Heb. 11:6), and withal most just and terrible in His judgments (Neh. 9:32–33), hating all sin (Ps. 5:5–6), and who will by no means clear the guilty (Ex. 34:7; Nah. 1:2–3).

2. God, having all life (John 5:26), glory (Ps. 148:13), goodness (Ps. 119:68), blessedness, in and of Himself, is alone in and unto Himself all-sufficient, not standing in need of any creature which He has made, nor deriving any glory from them (Job 22:2–3), but only manifesting His own glory in, by, unto, and upon them; He is the alone fountain of all being, of whom, through whom, and to whom are all things (Rom. 11:34–36), and He has most sovereign dominion over all creatures (Dan. 4:25, 34–35), to do by them, for them, or upon them, whatsoever Himself pleases; in His sight all things are open and manifest (Heb. 4:13), His knowledge is infinite, infallible, and independent upon the creature, so as nothing is to

Him contingent or uncertain (Ezek. 11:5; Acts 15:18); He is most holy in all His counsels, in all His works, and in all His commands (Ps. 145:17); to Him is due from angels and men (Rev. 5:12–14), whatsoever worship, service, or obedience, as creatures they owe unto the Creator, and whatever He is further pleased to require of them.

3. In this divine and infinite Being there are three subsistences (1 John 5:7; Matt. 28:19; 2 Cor. 13:14), the Father, the Word (or Son) and Holy Spirit, of one substance, power, and eternity, each having the whole divine essence (Ex. 3:14; John 14:11; 1 Cor. 8:6), yet the essence undivided: the Father is of none, neither begotten nor proceeding; the Son is eternally begotten of the Father (John 1:14, 18); the Holy Spirit proceeding from the Father and the Son (John 15:26; Gal. 4:6); all infinite, without beginning, therefore but one God, who is not to be divided in nature and being, but distinguished by several peculiar relative properties and personal relations; which doctrine of the Trinity is the foundation of all our communion with God, and comfortable dependence on Him.

Chapter III
Of God's Decree

1. God has decreed in Himself, from all eternity, by the most wise and holy counsel of His own will, freely and unchangeably, all things, whatsoever comes to pass (Isa. 46:10; Eph. 1:11; Heb. 6:17; Rom. 9:15, 18); yet so as thereby is God neither the author of sin nor has fellowship with any therein (James 1:13, 17; 1 John 1:5); nor is violence offered to the will of the creature, nor yet is the liberty or contingency of second causes taken away, but rather established (Acts 4:27–28; John 19:11); in which appears His wisdom in disposing all things, and power and faithfulness in accomplishing His decree (Num. 23:19; Eph. 1:3–5).

2. Although God knows whatsoever may or can come to pass, upon all supposed conditions (Acts 15:18), yet has He not decreed anything, because He foresaw it as future, or as that which would come to pass upon such conditions (Rom. 9:11, 13, 16, 18).

3. By the decree of God, for the manifestation of His glory, some men and angels are predestinated, or foreordained to eternal life through Jesus Christ (1 Tim. 5:21; Matt. 25:34), to the praise of His glorious grace (Eph. 1:5–6); others being left to act in their sin to their just condemnation (Rom. 9:22–23; Jude 4), to the praise of His glorious justice.

4. These angels and men thus predestinated and foreordained, are particularly and unchangeably designed, and their number so certain and definite, that it cannot be either increased or diminished (2 Tim. 2:19; John 13:18).

5. Those of mankind that are predestinated to life, God, before the foundation of the world was laid, according to His eternal and immutable purpose, and the secret counsel and good pleasure of His will, has chosen in Christ unto everlasting glory, out of His mere free grace and love (Eph. 1:4, 9, 11; Rom. 8:30; 2 Tim. 1:9; 1 Thess. 5:9), without any other thing in the creature as a condition or cause moving Him thereunto (Rom. 9:13, 16; Eph. 1:5, 12).

6. As God has appointed the elect unto glory, so He has, by the eternal and most free purpose of His will, foreordained all the means thereunto (1 Peter 1:2; 2 Thess. 2:13); wherefore they who are elected, being fallen in Adam, are redeemed by Christ (1 Thess. 5:9–10), are effectually called unto faith in Christ, by His Spirit working in due season, are justified, adopted, sanctified (Rom. 8:30; 2 Thess. 2:13), and kept by His power through faith unto salvation (1 Peter 1:5); neither are any other redeemed by Christ, or effectually called, justified, adopted, sanctified, and saved, but the elect only (John 10:26, 17:9; 6:64).

7. The doctrine of the high mystery of predestination is to be handled with special prudence and care, that men attending the will of God revealed in His Word, and yielding obedience thereunto, may, from the certainty of their effectual vocation, be assured of their eternal election (1 Thess. 1:4–5; 2 Peter 1:10); so shall this doctrine afford matter of praise (Eph. 1:6; Rom. 11:33), reverence, and admiration of God, and of humility, diligence (Rom. 11:5–6), and abundant consolation to all that sincerely obey the gospel (Luke 10:20).

Chapter IV
Of Creation

1. In the beginning it pleased God the Father, Son, and Holy Spirit (John 1:2–3; Heb. 1:2; Job 26:13), for the manifestation of the glory of His eternal power, wisdom, and goodness (Rom. 1:20), to create or make the world, and all things therein, whether visible or invisible, in the space of six days, and all very good (Col. 1:16; Gen. 1:31).

2. After God had made all other creatures, He created man, male and female (Gen. 1:27), with reasonable and immortal souls (Gen. 2:7), rendering them fit unto that life to God for which they were created; being made after the image of God, in knowledge, righteousness, and true holiness (Eccl. 7:29; Gen. 1:26); having the law of God written in their hearts (Rom. 2:14–15), and power to fulfill it; and yet under a possibility of transgressing, being left to the liberty of their own will, which was subject to change (Gen. 3:6).

3. Besides the law written in their hearts, they received a command not to eat of the tree of knowledge of good and evil (Gen. 2:17; 3:8–10), which while they kept, they were happy in their communion with God, and had dominion over the creatures (Gen. 1:26, 28).

Chapter V
Of Divine Providence

1. God, the good Creator of all things, in His infinite power and wisdom does uphold, direct, dispose, and govern all creatures and things (Heb. 1:3; Job 38:11; Isa. 46:10–11; Ps. 135:6), from the greatest even to the least (Matt. 10:29–31), by His most wise and holy providence, to the end for which they were created, according unto His infallible foreknowledge, and the free and immutable counsel of His own will; to the praise of the glory of His wisdom, power, justice, infinite goodness, and mercy (Eph. 1:11).

2. Although in relation to the foreknowledge and decree of God, the first cause, all things come to pass immutably and infallibly (Acts 2:23); so that there is not anything befalls any by chance, or without His providence (Prov. 16:33); yet by the same providence He orders them to fall out

according to the nature of second causes, either necessarily, freely, or contingently (Gen. 8:22).

3. God, in His ordinary providence makes use of means (Acts 27:31, 44; Isa. 55:10–11), yet is free to work without (Hos. 1:7), above (Rom. 4:19–21), and against them (Dan. 3:27) at His pleasure.

4. The almighty power, unsearchable wisdom, and infinite goodness of God, so far manifest themselves in His providence, that His determinate counsel extends itself even to the first fall, and all other sinful actions both of angels and men (Rom. 11:32–34; 2 Sam. 24:1; 1 Chron. 21:1); and that not by a bare permission, which also He most wisely and powerfully bounds, and otherwise orders and governs (2 Kings 19:28; Ps. 76:10), in a manifold dispensation to His most holy ends (Gen. 50:20; Isa. 10:6–7, 12); yet so, as the sinfulness of their acts proceeds only from the creatures, and not from God, who, being most holy and righteous, neither is nor can be the author or approver of sin (Ps. 50:21; 1 John 2:16).

5. The most wise, righteous, and gracious God does oftentimes leave for a season His own children to manifold temptations and the corruptions of their own heart, to chastise them for their former sins, or to discover unto them the hidden strength of corruption and deceitfulness of their hearts, that they may be humbled; and to raise them to a more close and constant dependence for their support upon Himself; and to make them more watchful against all future occasions of sin, and for other just and holy ends (2 Chron. 32:25–26, 31; 2 Sam. 24:1; 2 Cor. 12:7–9). So that whatsoever befalls any of His elect is by His appointment, for His glory, and their good (Rom. 8:28).

6. As for those wicked and ungodly men whom God, as the righteous judge, for former sin does blind and harden (Rom. 1:24, 26, 28; 11:7–8); from them He not only withholds His grace, whereby they might have been enlightened in their understanding, and wrought upon in their hearts (Deut. 29:4); but sometimes also withdraws the gifts which they had (Matt. 13:12), and exposes them to such objects as their corruption makes occasion of sin (Deut. 2:30; 2 Kings 8:12–13); and withal, gives them over to their own lusts, the temptations of the world, and the power of

Satan (Ps. 81:11–12; 2 Thess. 2:10–12), whereby it comes to pass that they harden themselves, under those means which God uses for the softening of others (Ex. 8:15, 32; Isa. 6:9–10; 1 Peter 2:7–8).

7. As the providence of God does in general reach to all creatures, so after a more special manner it takes care of His church, and disposes of all things to the good thereof (1 Tim. 4:10; Amos 9:8–9; Isa. 43:3–5).

Chapter VI
Of the Fall of Man, of Sin, and of the Punishment Thereof

1. Although God created man upright and perfect, and gave him a righteous law, which had been unto life had he kept it, and threatened death upon the breach thereof (Gen. 2:16–17), yet he did not long abide in this honor; Satan, using the subtlety of the serpent to seduce Eve, then by her seducing Adam, who, without any compulsion, did willfully transgress the law of their creation, and the command given unto them, in eating the forbidden fruit (Gen. 3:12–13; 2 Cor. 11:3), which God was pleased, according to His wise and holy counsel, to permit, having purposed to order it to His own glory.

2. Our first parents, by this sin, fell from their original righteousness and communion with God, and we in them whereby death came upon all (Rom. 3:23): all becoming dead in sin (Rom 5:12ff.), and wholly defiled in all the faculties and parts of soul and body (Titus 1:15; Gen. 6:5; Jer. 17:9; Rom. 3:10–19).

3. They being the root, and by God's appointment, standing in the room and stead of all mankind, the guilt of the sin was imputed, and corrupted nature conveyed, to all their posterity descending from them by ordinary generation (Rom. 5:12–19; 1 Cor. 15:21–22, 45, 49), being now conceived in sin (Ps. 51:5; Job 14:4), and by nature children of wrath (Eph. 2:3), the servants of sin, the subjects of death (Rom. 6:20; 5:12), and all other miseries, spiritual, temporal, and eternal, unless the Lord Jesus set them free (Heb. 2:14–15; 1 Thess. 1:10).

4. From this original corruption, whereby we are utterly indisposed, disabled, and made opposite to all good, and wholly inclined to all evil (Rom. 8:7; Col. 1:21), do proceed all actual transgressions (James 1:14–15; Matt. 15:19).

5. The corruption of nature, during this life, does remain in those that are regenerated (Rom. 7:18, 23; Eccl. 7:20; 1 John 1:8); and although it be through Christ pardoned and mortified, yet both itself, and the first motions thereof, are truly and properly sin (Rom. 7:23–25; Gal. 5:17).

Chapter VII
Of God's Covenant

1. The distance between God and the creature is so great, that although reasonable creatures do owe obedience to Him as their creator, yet they could never have attained the reward of life but by some voluntary condescension on God's part, which He has been pleased to express by way of covenant (Luke 17:10; Job 35:7–8).

2. Moreover, man having brought himself under the curse of the law by his fall, it pleased the Lord to make a covenant of grace (Gen. 2:17; Gal. 3:10; Rom. 3:20–21), wherein He freely offers unto sinners life and salvation by Jesus Christ, requiring of them faith in Him, that they may be saved (Rom. 8:3; Mark 16:15–16; John 3:16); and promising to give unto all those that are ordained unto eternal life, His Holy Spirit, to make them willing and able to believe (Ezek. 36:26–27; John 6:44–45; Ps. 110:3).

3. This covenant is revealed in the gospel; first of all to Adam in the promise of salvation by the seed of the woman (Gen. 3:15), and afterwards by farther steps, until the full discovery thereof was completed in the New Testament (Heb. 1:1); and it is founded in that eternal covenant transaction that was between the Father and the Son about the redemption of the elect (2 Tim. 1:9; Titus 1:2); and it is alone by the grace of this covenant that all the posterity of fallen Adam that ever were saved did obtain life and a blessed immortality, man being now utterly incapable of acceptance with God upon those terms on which Adam stood in his state of innocency (Heb. 11:6, 13; Rom. 4:1–2ff.; Acts 4:12; John 8:56).

Chapter VIII
Of Christ the Mediator

1. It pleased God, in His eternal purpose, to choose and ordain the Lord Jesus, His only begotten Son, according to the covenant made between them both, to be the Mediator between God and man (Isa. 42:1; 1 Peter 1:19–20); the Prophet (Acts 3:22), Priest (Heb. 5:5–6), and King (Ps. 2:6; Luke 1:33); Head and Savior of His church (Eph. 1:22–23), the Heir of all things (Heb. 1:2), and Judge of the world (Acts 17:31); unto whom He did from all eternity give a people to be His seed and to be by Him in time redeemed, called, justified, sanctified, and glorified (Isa. 53:10; John 17:6; Rom. 8:30).

2. The Son of God, the second person in the Holy Trinity, being very and eternal God, the brightness of the Father's glory, of one substance and equal with Him; who made the world, who upholds and governs all things He has made, did, when the fullness of time was come, take unto Him man's nature, with all the essential properties and common infirmities thereof (John 1:14; Gal. 4:4), yet without sin (Rom. 8:3; Heb. 2:14, 16–17; 4:15); being conceived by the Holy Spirit in the womb of the virgin Mary, the Holy Spirit coming down upon her: and the power of the Most High overshadowing her; and so was made of a woman, of the tribe of Judah, of the seed of Abraham and David, according to the Scriptures (Luke 1:27, 31, 35); so that two whole, perfect, and distinct natures were inseparably joined together in one person, without conversion, composition, or confusion; which person is very God and very man, yet one Christ, the only mediator between God and man (Rom. 9:5; 1 Tim. 2:5).

3. The Lord Jesus, in His human nature thus united to the divine, in the person of the Son, was sanctified and anointed with the Holy Spirit above measure (Ps. 45:7; Acts 10:38; John 3:34), having in Him all the treasures of wisdom and knowledge (Col. 2:3); in whom it pleased the Father that all fullness should dwell (Col. 1:19), to the end that being holy, harmless, undefiled (Heb. 7:26), and full of grace and truth (John 1:14), He might be thoroughly furnished to execute the office of a mediator and surety (Heb. 7:22); which office He took not upon Himself, but was thereunto called by His Father (Heb. 5:5); who also put all power and judgment in His hand, and gave Him commandment to execute the same (John 5:22, 27; Matt. 28:18; Acts 2:36).

4. This office the Lord Jesus did most willingly undertake (Ps. 40:7–8; Heb. 10:5–10; John 10:18), which that He might discharge He was made under the law (Gal 4:4; Matt. 3:15), and did perfectly fulfill it, and underwent the punishment due to us, which we should have borne and suffered (Gal. 3:13; Isa. 53:6; 1 Peter 3:18), being made sin and a curse for us (2 Cor. 5:21); enduring most grievous sorrows in His soul, and most painful sufferings in His body (Matt. 26:37–38; Luke 22:44; Matt. 27:46); was crucified, and died, and remained in the state of the dead, yet saw no corruption (Acts 13:37): on the third day He arose from the dead (1 Cor. 15:3–4) with the same body in which He suffered (John 20:25, 27), with which He also ascended into heaven (Mark 16:19; Acts 1:9–11), and there sits at the right hand of His Father making intercession (Rom. 8:34; Heb. 9:24), and shall return to judge men and angels at the end of the world (Acts 10:42; Rom. 14:9–10; Acts 1:11).

5. The Lord Jesus, by His perfect obedience and sacrifice of Himself, which He through the eternal Spirit once offered up unto God, has fully satisfied the justice of God (Heb. 9:14; 10:14; Rom. 3:25–26), procured reconciliation, and purchased an everlasting inheritance in the kingdom of heaven, for all those whom the Father has given unto Him (John 17:2; Heb. 9:15).

6. Although the price of redemption was not actually paid by Christ till after His incarnation, yet the virtue, efficacy, and benefit thereof were communicated to the elect in all ages successively, from the beginning of the world, in and by those promises, types, and sacrifices wherein He was revealed, and signified to be the Seed which should bruise the serpent's head (1 Cor. 4:10; Heb. 4:2; 1 Peter 1:10–11); and the Lamb slain from the foundation of the world (Rev. 13:8), being the same yesterday, and today and for ever (Heb. 13:8).

7. Christ, in the work of mediation, acts according to both natures, by each nature doing that which is proper to itself; yet by reason of the unity of the person, that which is proper to one nature is sometimes in Scripture, attributed to the person denominated by the other nature (John 3:13; Acts 20:28).

8. To all those for whom Christ has obtained eternal redemption, He does certainly and effectually apply and communicate the same, making intercession for them (John 6:37; 10:15–16; 17:9); uniting them to Himself

by His Spirit, revealing unto them, in and by His Word, the mystery of salvation, persuading them to believe and obey (John 17:6; Eph. 1:9; 1 John 5:20), governing their hearts by His Word and Spirit (Rom. 8:9, 14), and overcoming all their enemies by His almighty power and wisdom (Ps. 110:1; 1 Cor. 15:25–26), in such manner and ways as are most consonant to His wonderful and unsearchable dispensation; and all of free and absolute grace, without any condition foreseen in them to procure it (John 3:8; Eph. 1:8).

9. This office of mediator between God and man is proper only to Christ, who is the Prophet, Priest, and King of the church of God; and may not be either in whole, or any part thereof, transferred from Him to any other (1 Tim. 2:5).

10. This number and order of offices is necessary; for in respect of our ignorance, we stand in need of His prophetical office (John 1:18); and in respect of our alienation from God, and imperfection of the best of our services, we need His priestly office to reconcile us and present us acceptable unto God (Col. 1:21; Gal. 5:17); and in respect to our averseness and utter inability to return to God, and for our rescue and security from our spiritual adversaries, we need His kingly office to convince, subdue, draw, uphold, deliver, and preserve us to His heavenly kingdom (John 16:8; Ps. 110:3; Luke 1:74–75).

Chapter IX
Of Free Will

1. God has endued the will of man with that natural liberty and power of acting upon choice, that it is neither forced, nor by any necessity of nature determined to do good or evil (Matt. 17:12; James 1:14; Deut. 30:19).

2. Man, in his state of innocency, had freedom and power to will and to do that which was good and well-pleasing to God (Eccl. 7:29), but yet was unstable, so that he might fall from it (Gen. 3:6).

3. Man, by his fall into a state of sin, has wholly lost all ability of will to any spiritual good accompanying salvation (Rom. 5:6; 8:7); so as a natural man, being altogether averse from that good, and dead in sin (Eph. 2:1, 5)

is not able by his own strength to convert himself, or to prepare himself thereunto (Titus 3:3–5; John 6:44).

4. When God converts a sinner, and translates him into the state of grace, He frees him from his natural bondage under sin (Col. 1:13; John 8:36), and by His grace alone enables him freely to will and to do that which is spiritually good (Phil. 2:13); yet so as that by reason of his remaining corruptions, he does not perfectly, nor only will, that which is good, but does also will that which is evil (Rom. 7:15, 18–19, 21, 23).

5. This will of man is made perfectly and immutably free to good alone in the state of glory only (Eph. 4:13).

Chapter X
Of Effectual Calling

1. Those whom God has predestinated unto life, He is pleased in His appointed, and accepted time, effectually to call (Rom. 8:30; 11:7; Eph. 1:10–11; 2 Thess. 2:13–14), by His Word and Spirit, out of that state of sin and death in which they are by nature, to grace and salvation by Jesus Christ (Eph. 2:1–6); enlightening their minds spiritually and savingly to understand the things of God (Acts 26:18; Eph. 1:17–18); taking away their heart of stone, and giving unto them a heart of flesh (Ezek. 36:26); renewing their wills, and by His almighty power determining them to that which is good, and effectually drawing them to Jesus Christ (Deut. 30:6; Ezek. 36:27; Eph. 1:19); yet so as they come most freely, being made willing by His grace (Ps. 110:3; Song 1:4).

2. This effectual call is of God's free and special grace alone, not from anything at all foreseen in man, nor from any power or agency in the creature co-working with His special grace (2 Tim. 1:9; Eph. 2:8), the creature being wholly passive therein, being dead in sins and trespasses, until being quickened and renewed by the Holy Spirit (1 Cor. 2:14; Eph. 2:5; John 5:25), he is thereby enabled to answer this call, and to embrace the grace offered and conveyed in it, and that by no less power than that which raised up Christ from the dead (Eph. 1:19–20).

3. Elect infants dying in infancy are regenerated and saved by Christ through the Spirit (John 3:3, 5–6); who works when, and where, and how He pleases (John 3:8); so also are all elect persons, who are incapable of being outwardly called by the ministry of the Word.

4. Others not elected, although they may be called by the ministry of the Word, and may have some common operations of the Spirit (Matt. 22:14; 13:20–21; Heb 6:4–5), yet not being effectually drawn by the Father, they neither will, nor can truly come to Christ; and therefore cannot be saved (John 6:44–45, 65; 1 John 2:24–25): much less can men that do not receive the Christian religion be saved; be they never so diligent to frame their lives according to the light of nature and the law of that religion they do profess (Acts 4:12; John 4:22; 17:3).

Chapter XI
Of Justification

1. Those whom God effectually calls, He also freely justifies (Rom. 3:24; 8:30), not by infusing righteousness into them, but by pardoning their sins, and by accounting and accepting their persons as righteous (Rom. 4:5–8; Eph. 1:7); not for anything wrought in them, or done by them, but for Christ's sake alone (1 Cor. 1:30–31; Rom. 5:17–19); not by imputing faith itself, the act of believing, or any other evangelical obedience to them, as their righteousness; but by imputing Christ's active obedience unto the whole law, and passive obedience in His death for their whole and sole righteousness (Phil. 3:8–9; Eph. 2:8–10), they receiving and resting on Him and His righteousness by faith, which faith they have not of themselves; it is the gift of God (John 1:12; Rom. 5:17).

2. Faith thus receiving and resting on Christ and His righteousness, is the alone instrument of justification (Rom. 3:28); yet is not alone in the person justified, but is ever accompanied with all other saving graces, and is no dead faith, but works by love (Gal. 5:6; James 2:17, 22, 26).

3. Christ, by His obedience and death, did fully discharge the debt of all those that are justified; and did, by the sacrifice of Himself in the blood of His cross, undergoing in their stead the penalty due to them, make a proper,

real, and full satisfaction to God's justice in their behalf (Heb. 10:14; 1 Peter 1:18–19; Isa. 53:5–6); yet, inasmuch as He was given by the Father for them, and His obedience and satisfaction accepted in their stead, and both freely, not for anything in them (Rom. 8:32; 2 Cor. 5:21), their justification is only of free grace, that both the exact justice and rich grace of God might be glorified in the justification of sinners (Rom. 3:26; Eph. 1:6–7; 2:7).

4. God did from all eternity decree to justify all the elect (Gal. 3:8; 1 Peter 1:2; 1 Tim. 2:6), and Christ did in the fullness of time die for their sins, and rise again for their justification (Rom. 4:25); nevertheless, they are not justified personally, until the Holy Spirit does in due time actually apply Christ unto them (Col. 1:21–22; Titus 3:4–7).

5. God continues to forgive the sins of those that are justified (Matt. 6:12; 1 John 1:7, 9), and although they can never fall from the state of justification (John 10:28), yet they may, by their sins, fall under God's fatherly displeasure (Ps. 89:31–33); and in that condition they have not usually the light of His countenance restored unto them, until they humble themselves, confess their sins, beg pardon, and renew their faith and repentance (Ps. 32:5; Ps. 51; Matt. 26:75).

6. The justification of believers under the Old Testament was, in all these respects, one and the same with the justification of believers under the New Testament (Gal. 3:9; Rom. 4:22–24).

Chapter XII
Of Adoption

All those that are justified, God vouchsafed, in and for the sake of His only Son Jesus Christ, to make partakers of the grace of adoption (Eph. 1:5; Gal. 4:4–5), by which they are taken into the number, and enjoy the liberties and privileges of the children of God (John 1:12; Rom. 8:17), have His name put on them (2 Cor. 6:18; Rev. 3:12), receive the spirit of adoption (Rom. 8:15), have access to the throne of grace with boldness, are enabled to cry Abba, Father (Gal. 4:6; Eph. 2:18), are pitied (Ps. 103:13), protected (Prov. 14:26), provided for (1 Peter 5:7), and chastened by Him as by a Father (Heb. 12:6), yet never cast off (Isa. 54:8–9; Lam. 3:31), but sealed to the day of redemption (Eph. 4:30), and inherit the promises as heirs of everlasting salvation (Heb. 1:14; 6:12).

Chapter XIII
Of Sanctification

1. They who are united to Christ, effectually called, and regenerated, having a new heart and a new spirit created in them through the virtue of Christ's death and resurrection, are also farther sanctified, really and personally (Acts 20:32; Rom. 6:5–6), through the same virtue, by His Word and Spirit dwelling in them (John 17:17; Eph. 3:16–19; 1 Thess. 5:21–23); the dominion of the whole body of sin is destroyed (Rom. 6:14), and the several lusts thereof are more and more weakened and mortified (Gal. 5:24), and they more and more quickened and strengthened in all saving graces (Col. 1:11), to the practice of all true holiness, without which no man shall see the Lord (2 Cor. 7:1; Heb. 12:14).

2. This sanctification is throughout the whole man (1 Thess. 5:23), yet imperfect in this life; there abides still some remnants of corruption in every part (Rom. 7:18, 23), whence arises a continual and irreconcilable war; the flesh lusting against the Spirit, and the Spirit against the flesh (Gal. 5:17; 1 Peter 2:11).

3. In which war, although the remaining corruption for a time may much prevail (Rom. 7:23), yet, through the continual supply of strength from the sanctifying Spirit of Christ, the regenerate part does overcome (Rom. 6:14); and so the saints grow in grace, perfecting holiness in the fear of God, pressing after an heavenly life, in evangelical obedience to all the commands which Christ as Head and King, in His Word has prescribed to them (Eph. 4:15–16; 2 Cor. 3:18; 7:1).

Chapter XIV
Of Saving Faith

1. The grace of faith, whereby the elect are enabled to believe to the saving of their souls, is the work of the Spirit of Christ in their hearts (2 Cor.

4:13; Eph. 2:8), and is ordinarily wrought by the ministry of the Word (Rom. 10:14, 17); by which also, and by the administration of baptism and the Lord's supper, prayer, and other means appointed of God, it is increased and strengthened (Luke 17:5; 1 Peter 2:2; Acts 20:32).

2. By this faith a Christian believes to be true whatsoever is revealed in the Word for the authority of God Himself (Acts 24:14), and also apprehends an excellency therein above all other writings and all things in the world (Pss. 19:7–10; 119:72), as it bears forth the glory of God in His attributes, the excellency of Christ in His nature and offices, and the power and fullness of the Holy Spirit in His workings and operations: and so is enabled to cast His soul upon the truth thus believed (2 Tim. 1:12); and also acts differently upon that which each particular passage thereof contains; yielding obedience to the commands (John 15:14), trembling at the threatenings (Isa. 66:2), and embracing the promises of God for this life and that which is to come (Heb. 11:13); but the principal acts of saving faith have immediate relation to Christ, accepting, receiving, and resting upon Him alone for justification, sanctification, and eternal life, by virtue of the covenant of grace (John 1:12; Acts 16:31; Gal. 2:20; Acts 15:11).

3. This faith, although it be different in degrees, and may be weak or strong (Heb. 5:13–14; Matt. 6:30; Rom. 4:19–20), yet it is in the least degree of it different in the kind or nature of it, as is all other saving grace, from the faith and common grace of temporary believers (2 Peter 1:1); and therefore, though it may be many times assailed and weakened, yet it gets the victory (Eph. 6:16; 1 John 5:4–5), growing up in many to the attainment of a full assurance through Christ (Heb. 6:11–12; Col. 2:2), who is both the Author and Finisher of our faith (Heb. 12:2).

Chapter XV
Of Repentance unto Life and Salvation

1. Such of the elect as are converted at riper years, having sometimes lived in the state of nature, and therein served divers lusts and pleasures, God in their effectual calling gives them repentance unto life (Titus 3:2–5).

2. Whereas there is none that does good and does not sin (Eccl. 7:20), and the best of men may, through the power and deceitfulness of their corruption dwelling in them, with the prevalency of temptation, fall into great sins and provocations; God has, in the covenant of grace, mercifully provided that believers so sinning and falling be renewed through repentance unto salvation (Luke 22:31–32).

3. This saving repentance is an evangelical grace (Zech. 12:10; Acts 11:18), whereby a person, being by the Holy Spirit made sensible of the manifold evils of his sin, does, by faith in Christ, humble himself for it with godly sorrow, detestation of it, and self-abhorrency (Ezek. 36:31; 2 Cor. 7:11), praying for pardon and strength of grace, with a purpose and endeavor, by supplies of the Spirit, to walk before God unto all well-pleasing in all things (Ps. 119:6, 128).

4. As repentance is to be continued through the whole course of our lives, upon the account of the body of death, and the motions thereof, so it is every man's duty to repent of his particular known sins particularly (Luke 19:8; 1 Tim. 1:13, 15).

5. Such is the provision which God has made through Christ in the covenant of grace for the preservation of believers unto salvation, that although there is no sin so small but it deserves damnation (Rom. 6:23), yet there is no sin so great that it shall bring damnation to them that repent (Isa. 1:16–18; 55:7), which makes the constant preaching of repentance necessary.

Chapter XVI
Of Good Works

1. Good works are only such as God has commanded in His Holy Word (Mic. 6:8; Heb. 13:21), and not such as without the warrant thereof are devised by men out of blind zeal, or upon any pretense of good intentions (Matt. 15:9; Isa. 29:13).

2. These good works, done in obedience to God's commandments, are the fruits and evidences of a true and lively faith (James 2:18, 22); and by them believers manifest their thankfulness (Ps. 116:12–13), strengthen their

assurance (1 John 2:3, 5; 2 Peter 1:5–11), edify their brethren, adorn the profession of the gospel (Matt. 5:16), stop the mouths of the adversaries, and glorify God (1 Tim. 6:1; 1 Peter 2:15; Phil. 1:11), whose workmanship they are, created in Christ Jesus thereunto (Eph. 2:10), that having their fruit unto holiness they may have the end eternal life (Rom 6:22).

3. Their ability to do good works is not all of themselves, but wholly from the Spirit of Christ (John 15:4, 6); and that they may be enabled thereunto, besides the graces they have already received, there is necessary an actual influence of the same Holy Spirit, to work in them to will and to do of His good pleasure (2 Cor. 3:5; Phil. 2:13); yet they are not hereupon to grow negligent, as if they were not bound to perform any duty, unless upon a special motion of the Spirit, but they ought to be diligent in stirring up the grace of God that is in them (Phil. 2:12; Heb. 6:11–12; Isa. 64:7).

4. They who in their obedience attain to the greatest height which is possible in this life, are so far from being able to supererogate, and to do more than God requires, as that they fall short of much which in duty they are bound to do (Job 9:2–3; Gal. 5:17; Luke 17:10).

5. We cannot by our best works merit pardon of sin or eternal life at the hand of God, by reason of the great disproportion that is between them and the glory to come, and the infinite distance that is between us and God, whom by them we can neither profit nor satisfy for the debt of our former sins (Rom. 3:20; Eph. 2:8–9; Rom. 4:6); but when we have done all we can, we have done but our duty, and are unprofitable servants; and because as they are good they proceed from His Spirit (Gal. 5:22–23), and as they are wrought by us they are defiled and mixed with so much weakness and imperfection, that they cannot endure the severity of God's judgment (Isa. 64:6; Ps. 143:2).

6. Yet notwithstanding the persons of believers being accepted through Christ, their good works also are accepted in Him (Eph. 1:6; 1 Peter 2:5); not as though they were in this life wholly unblameable and unreproveable in God's sight, but that He, looking upon them in His Son, is pleased to accept and reward that which is sincere, although accompanied with many weaknesses and imperfections (Matt. 25:21, 23; Heb. 6:10).

7. Works done by unregenerate men, although for the matter of them they may be things which God commands, and of good use both to themselves and to others (2 Kings 10:30; 1 Kings 21:27, 29); yet because they proceed not from a heart purified by faith (Gen. 4:5; Heb. 11:4, 6), nor are done in a right manner according to the Word (1 Cor. 13:1), nor to a right end, the glory of God (Matt. 6:2, 5), they are therefore sinful, and cannot please God, nor make a man meet to receive grace from God (Amos 5:21–22; Rom. 9:16; Titus 3:5), and yet their neglect of them is more sinful and displeasing to God (Job 21:14–15; Matt. 25:41–43).

Chapter XVII
Of the Perseverance of the Saints

1. Those whom God has accepted in the beloved, effectually called and sanctified by His Spirit, and given the precious faith of His elect unto, can neither totally nor finally fall from the state of grace, but shall certainly persevere therein to the end, and be eternally saved, seeing the gifts and callings of God are without repentance, whence He still begets and nourishes in them faith, repentance, love, joy, hope, and all the graces of the Spirit unto immortality (John 10:28–29; Phil. 1:6; 2 Tim. 2:19; 1 John 2:19); and though many storms and floods arise and beat against them, yet they shall never be able to take them off that foundation and rock which by faith they are fastened upon; notwithstanding, through unbelief and the temptations of Satan, the sensible sight of the light and love of God may for a time be clouded and obscured from them (Ps. 89:31–32; 1 Cor. 11:32), yet He is still the same, and they shall be sure to be kept by the power of God unto salvation, where they shall enjoy their purchased possession, they being engraved upon the palm of His hands, and their names having been written in the Book of Life from all eternity (Mal. 3:6).

2. This perseverance of the saints depends not upon their own free will, but upon the immutability of the decree of election (Rom. 8:30; 9:11,16), flowing from the free and unchangeable love of God the Father, upon the efficacy of the merit and intercession of Jesus Christ and union with Him (Rom. 5:9–10; John 14:19), the oath of God (Heb. 6:17–18), the abiding of His Spirit, and the seed of God within them (1 John 3:9), and the nature

of the covenant of grace (Jer. 32:40); from all which arises also the certainty and infallibility thereof.

3. And though they may, through the temptation of Satan and of the world, the prevalency of corruption remaining in them, and the neglect of means of their preservation, fall into grievous sins, and for a time continue therein (Matt. 26:70, 72, 74), whereby they incur God's displeasure and grieve His Holy Spirit (Isa. 64:5, 9; Eph. 4:30), come to have their graces and comforts impaired (Ps. 51:10, 12), have their hearts hardened, and their consciences wounded (Ps. 32:3–4), hurt and scandalize others, and bring temporal judgments upon themselves (2 Sam. 12:14), yet they shall renew their repentance and be preserved through faith in Christ Jesus to the end (Luke 22:32, 61–62).

Chapter XVIII
Of the Assurance of Grace and Salvation

1. Although temporary believers and other unregenerate men may vainly deceive themselves with false hopes and carnal presumptions of being in the favor of God and state of salvation, which hope of theirs shall perish (Job 8:13–14; Matt. 7:22–23); yet such as truly believe in the Lord Jesus, and love Him in sincerity, endeavoring to walk in all good conscience before Him, may in this life be certainly assured that they are in the state of grace, and may rejoice in the hope of the glory of God (1 John 2:3; 3:14, 18–19, 21, 24; 5:13), which hope shall never make them ashamed (Rom. 5:2, 5).

2. This certainty is not a bare conjectural and probable persuasion grounded upon a fallible hope, but an infallible assurance of faith (Heb. 6:11, 19), founded on the blood and righteousness of Christ revealed in the gospel (Heb. 6:17–18); and also upon the inward evidence of those graces of the Spirit unto which promises are made (2 Peter 1:4–5, 10–11), and on the testimony of the Spirit of adoption, witnessing with our spirits that we are the children of God (Rom. 8:15–16); and, as a fruit thereof, keeping the heart both humble and holy (1 John 3:1–3).

3. This infallible assurance does not so belong to the essence of faith, but that a true believer may wait long, and struggle with many difficulties

before he be partaker of it (Isa. 50:10; Pss. 88; 77:1–12); yet being enabled by the Spirit to know the things which are freely given him of God, he may, without extraordinary revelation, in the right use of means, attain thereunto (1 John 4:13; Heb. 6:11–12): and therefore it is the duty of every one to give all diligence to make his calling and election sure, that thereby his heart may be enlarged in peace and joy in the Holy Spirit, in love and thankfulness to God, and in strength and cheerfulness in the duties of obedience, the proper fruits of this assurance (Rom. 5:1–2, 5; 14:17; Ps. 119:32)—so far is it from inclining men to looseness (Rom. 6:1–2; Titus 2:11–12, 14).

4. True believers may have the assurance of their salvation divers ways shaken, diminished, and intermitted; as by negligence in preserving of it (Song 5:2–3, 6), by falling into some special sin which wounds the conscience and grieves the Spirit (Ps. 51:8, 12, 14); by some sudden or vehement temptation (Pss. 116:11; 77:7–8; 31:22), by God's withdrawing the light of His countenance, and suffering even such as fear Him to walk in darkness and to have no light (Ps. 30:7), yet are they never destitute of the seed of God (1 John 3:9) and life of faith (Luke 22:32), that love of Christ and the brethren, that sincerity of heart and conscience of duty out of which, by the operation of the Spirit, this assurance may in due time be revived (Ps. 42:5, 11), and by which, in the meantime, they are preserved from utter despair (Lam. 3:26–31).

Chapter XIX
Of the Law of God

1. God gave to Adam a law of universal obedience written in his heart, and a particular precept of not eating the fruit of the tree of knowledge of good and evil (Gen. 2:17; Eccl. 7:29); by which He bound him and all his posterity to personal, entire, exact, and perpetual obedience (Rom. 10:5); promised life upon the fulfilling, and threatened death upon the breach of it, and endued him with power and ability to keep it (Gal. 3:10, 12).

2. The same law that was first written in the heart of man continued to be a perfect rule of righteousness after the fall (Rom. 2:14–15), and was delivered by God upon Mount Sinai, in ten commandments, and written

in two tables, the four first containing our duty towards God, and the other six, our duty to man (Deut. 10:4).

3. Besides this law, commonly called moral, God was pleased to give to the people of Israel ceremonial laws, containing several typical ordinances, partly of worship, prefiguring Christ, His graces, actions, sufferings, and benefits (Heb. 10:1; Col. 2:17); and partly holding forth divers instructions of moral duties (1 Cor. 5:7), all which ceremonial laws being appointed only to the time of reformation, are, by Jesus Christ the true Messiah and only Lawgiver, who was furnished with power from the Father for that end, abrogated and taken away (Col. 2:14, 16–17; Eph. 2:14, 16).

4. To them also He gave sundry judicial laws, which expired together with the state of that people, not obliging any now by virtue of that institution; their general equity only being of moral use (1 Cor. 9:8–10).

5. The moral law does forever bind all, as well justified persons as others, to the obedience thereof (Rom. 13:8–10; James 2:8, 10–12), and that not only in regard of the matter contained in it, but also in respect of the authority of God the Creator, who gave it (James 2:10–11); neither does Christ in the gospel any way dissolve, but much strengthen this obligation (Matt. 5:17–19; Rom. 3:31).

6. Although true believers be not under the law as a covenant of works, to be thereby justified or condemned (Rom. 6:14; Gal. 2:16; Rom. 8:1; 10:4), yet it is of great use to them as well as to others, in that as a rule of life, informing them of the will of God and their duty, it directs and binds them to walk accordingly; discovering also the sinful pollutions of their natures, hearts, and lives, so as examining themselves thereby, they may come to further conviction of, humiliation for, and hatred against sin (Rom. 3:20; 7:7ff.); together with a clearer sight of the need they have of Christ and the perfection of His obedience; it is likewise of use to the regenerate to restrain their corruptions, in that it forbids sin; and the threatenings of it serve to show what even their sins deserve, and what afflictions in this life they may expect for them, although freed from the curse and unallayed rigor thereof. These promises of it likewise show them God's approbation of obedience, and what blessings they may expect upon the performance

thereof, though not as due to them by the law as a covenant of works; so as man's doing good and refraining from evil, because the law encourages to the one and deters from the other, is no evidence of his being under the law and not under grace (Rom. 6:12–14; 1 Peter 3:8–13).

7. Neither are the aforementioned uses of the law contrary to the grace of the gospel, but do sweetly comply with it (Gal. 3:21), the Spirit of Christ subduing and enabling the will of man to do that freely and cheerfully which the will of God, revealed in the law, requires to be done (Ezek. 36:27).

Chapter XX
Of the Gospel, and of the Extent of the Grace Thereof

1. The covenant of works being broken by sin, and made unprofitable unto life, God was pleased to give forth the promise of Christ, the seed of the woman, as the means of calling the elect, and begetting in them faith and repentance (Gen. 3:15); in this promise the gospel, as to the substance of it, was revealed, and therein effectual for the conversion and salvation of sinners (Rev. 13:8).

2. This promise of Christ, and salvation by Him, is revealed only by the Word of God (Rom. 1:17); neither do the works of creation or providence, with the light of nature, make discovery of Christ, or of grace by Him, so much as in a general or obscure way (Rom. 10:14–15, 17); much less that men destitute of the revelation of Him by the promise or gospel, should be enabled thereby to attain saving faith or repentance (Prov. 29:18; Isa. 25:7; 60:2–3).

3. The revelation of the gospel unto sinners, made in divers times and by sundry parts, with the addition of promises and precepts for the obedience required therein, as to the nations and persons to whom it is granted, is merely of the sovereign will and good pleasure of God (Ps. 147:20; Acts 16:7); not being annexed by virtue of any promise to the due improvement of men's natural abilities, by virtue of common light received without it, which none ever made, or can do so (Rom. 1:18ff.); and therefore in all ages, the preaching of the gospel has been granted unto persons and nations, as to the extent or straitening of it, in great variety, according to the counsel of the will of God.

4. Although the gospel be the only outward means of revealing Christ and saving grace, and is, as such, abundantly sufficient thereunto; yet that men who are dead in trespasses may be born again, quickened, or regenerated, there is moreover necessary an effectual insuperable work of the Holy Spirit upon the whole soul, for the producing in them a new spiritual life (Ps. 110:3; 1 Cor. 2:14; Eph. 1:19–20); without which no other means will effect their conversion unto God (John 6:44; 2 Cor. 4:4, 6).

Chapter XXI
Of Christian Liberty and Liberty of Conscience

1. The liberty which Christ has purchased for believers under the gospel, consists in their freedom from the guilt of sin, the condemning wrath of God, the rigor and curse of the law (Gal. 3:13), and in their being delivered from this present evil world (Gal. 1:4), bondage to Satan (Acts 26:18), and dominion of sin (Rom. 8:3), from the evil of afflictions (Rom. 8:28), the fear and sting of death, the victory of the grave (1 Cor. 15:54–57), and everlasting damnation (2 Thess. 1:10): as also in their free access to God, and their yielding obedience unto Him, not out of a slavish fear (Rom. 8:15), but a child-like love and willing mind (Luke 1:74–75; 1 John 4:18). All which were common also to believers under the law for the substance of them (Gal. 3:9, 14); but under the New Testament the liberty of Christians is further enlarged, in their freedom from the yoke of the ceremonial law, to which the Jewish church was subjected, and in greater boldness of access to the throne of grace, and in fuller communications of the free Spirit of God, than believers under the law did ordinarily partake of (John 7:38–39; Heb. 10:19–21).

2. God alone is Lord of the conscience (James 4:12; Rom. 14:4), and has left it free from the doctrines and commandments of men, which are in any thing contrary to His Word, or not contained in it (Acts 4:19; 5:29; 1 Cor. 7:23; Matt. 15:9). So that to believe such doctrines, or obey such commands out of conscience, is to betray true liberty of conscience (Col. 2:20, 22–23); and the requiring of an implicit faith, and absolute and blind obedience, is to destroy liberty of conscience and reason also (1 Cor. 3:5; 2 Cor. 1:24).

3. They who upon pretence of Christian liberty do practice any sin, or cherish any sinful lust, as they do thereby pervert the main design of the grace of the gospel to their own destruction (Rom. 6:1–2), so they wholly destroy the end of Christian liberty, which is, that being delivered out of the hands of all our enemies, we might serve the Lord without fear, in holiness and righteousness before Him, all the days of our lives (Gal. 5:13; 2 Peter 2:18–21).

Chapter XXII
Of Religious Worship and the Sabbath Day

1. The light of nature shows that there is a God, who has lordship and sovereignty over all; is just, good and does good unto all; and is therefore to be feared, loved, praised, called upon, trusted in, and served, with all the heart and all the soul, and with all the might (Jer. 10:7; Mark 12:33). But the acceptable way of worshipping the true God is instituted by Himself (Deut. 12:32), and so limited by His own revealed will, that He may not be worshipped according to the imagination and devices of men, or the suggestions of Satan, under any visible representations, or any other way not prescribed in the Holy Scriptures (Ex. 20:4–6).

2. Religious worship is to be given to God the Father, Son, and Holy Spirit, and to Him alone (Matt. 4:9–10; John 6:23; Matt. 28:19); not to angels, saints, or any other creatures (Rom. 1:25; Col. 2:18; Rev. 19:10); and since the fall, not without a mediator (John 14:6), nor in the mediation of any other but Christ alone (1 Tim. 2:5).

3. Prayer, with thanksgiving, being one special part of natural worship, is by God required of all men (Pss. 95:1–7; 65:2). But that it may be accepted, it is to be made in the name of the Son (John 14:13–14), by the help of the Spirit (Rom. 8:26), according to His will (1 John 5:14); with understanding, reverence, humility, fervency, faith, love, and perseverance; and when with others, in a known tongue (1 Cor. 14:16–17).

4. Prayer is to be made for things lawful, and for all sorts of men living, or that shall live hereafter (1 Tim. 2:1–2; 2 Sam. 7:29); but not for the dead (2 Sam. 12:21–23), nor for those of whom it may be known that they have sinned the sin unto death (1 John 5:16).

5. The reading of the Scriptures (1 Tim. 4:13), preaching, and hearing the Word of God (2 Tim. 4:2; Luke 8:18), teaching and admonishing one another in psalms, hymns, and spiritual songs, singing with grace in our hearts to the Lord (Col. 3:16; Eph. 5:19); as also the administration of baptism (Matt. 28:19–20), and the Lord's supper (1 Cor. 11:26), are all parts of religious worship of God, to be performed in obedience to Him, with understanding, faith, reverence, and godly fear; moreover, solemn humiliation, with fastings (Esth. 4:16; Joel 2:12), and thanksgivings, upon special occasions, ought to be used in an holy and religious manner (Ex. 15:1ff.; Ps. 107).

6. Neither prayer nor any other part of religious worship, is now under the gospel, tied unto, or made more acceptable by any place in which it is performed, or towards which it is directed; but God is to be worshipped everywhere in spirit and in truth (John 4:21; Mal. 1:11; 1 Tim. 2:8); as in private families (Acts 10:2) daily (Matt. 6:11; Ps. 55:17), and in secret each one by himself (Matt. 6:6); so more solemnly in the public assemblies, which are not carelessly nor willfully to be neglected or forsaken, when God by His Word or providence calls thereunto (Heb. 10:25; Acts 2:42).

7. As it is the law of nature, that in general a proportion of time, by God's appointment, be set apart for the worship of God, so by His Word, in a positive-moral, and perpetual commandment, binding all men, in all ages, He has particularly appointed one day in seven for a Sabbath to be kept holy unto Him (Ex. 20:8), which from the beginning of the world to the resurrection of Christ was the last day of the week, and from the resurrection of Christ was changed into the first day of the week, which is called the Lord's Day (1 Cor. 16:1–2; Acts 20:7; Rev. 1:10): and is to be continued to the end of the world as the Christian Sabbath, the observation of the last day of the week being abolished.

8. The Sabbath is then kept holy unto the Lord, when men, after a due preparing of their hearts, and ordering their common affairs beforehand, do not only observe an holy rest all the day, from their own works, words and thoughts, about their worldly employment and recreations (Isa. 58:13; Neh. 13:15–22), but are also taken up the whole time in the public and private exercises of His worship, and in the duties of necessity and mercy (Matt. 12:1–13).

Chapter XXIII
Of Lawful Oaths and Vows

1. A lawful oath is a part of religious worship, wherein the person swearing in truth, righteousness, and judgment, solemnly calls God to witness what he swears (Ex. 20:7; Deut. 10:20; Jer. 4:2), and to judge him according to the truth or falseness thereof (2 Chron. 6:22–23).

2. The name of God only is that by which men ought to swear; and therein it is to be used, with all holy fear and reverence; therefore to swear vainly or rashly by that glorious and dreadful name, or to swear at all by any other thing, is sinful, and to be abhorred (Matt. 5:34, 37; James 5:12); yet as in matter of weight and moment, for confirmation of truth, and ending all strife, an oath is warranted by the Word of God (Heb. 6:16; 2 Cor. 1:23); so a lawful oath being imposed by lawful authority in such matters, ought to be taken (Neh. 13:25).

3. Whosoever takes an oath warranted by the Word of God, ought duly to consider the weightiness of so solemn an act, and therein to avouch nothing but what he knows to be truth; for that by rash, false, and vain oaths, the Lord is provoked, and for them this land mourns (Lev. 19:12; Jer. 23:10).

4. An oath is to be taken in the plain and common sense of the words, without equivocation or mental reservation (Ps. 24:4).

5. A vow, which is not to be made to any creature, but to God alone, is to be made and performed with all religious care and faithfulness (Ps. 76:11; Gen. 28:20–22); but popish monastic vows of perpetual single life (1 Cor. 7:2, 9), professed poverty (Eph. 4:28), and regular obedience, are so far from being degrees of higher perfection, that they are superstitious and sinful snares, in which no Christian may entangle himself (Matt. 19:11).

Chapter XXIV
Of the Civil Magistrate

1. God, the supreme Lord and King of all the world, has ordained civil magistrates to be under Him, over the people, for His own glory and

the public good; and to this end has armed them with the power of the sword, for defense and encouragement of them that do good, and for the punishment of evil doers (Rom. 13:1–4).

2. It is lawful for Christians to accept and execute the office of a magistrate when called thereunto; in the management whereof, as they ought especially to maintain justice and peace (2 Sam. 23:3; Ps. 82:3–4), according to the wholesome laws of each kingdom and commonwealth, so for that end they may lawfully now, under the New Testament, wage war upon just and necessary occasions (Luke 3:14).

3. Civil magistrates being set up by God for the ends aforesaid; subjection, in all lawful things commanded by them, ought to be yielded by us in the Lord, not only for wrath, but for conscience sake (Rom. 13:5–7; 1 Peter 2:17); and we ought to make supplications and prayers for kings and all that are in authority, that under them we may live a quiet and peaceable life, in all godliness and honesty (1 Tim. 2:1–2).

Chapter XXV
Of Marriage

1. Marriage is to be between one man and one woman; neither is it lawful for any man to have more than one wife, nor for any woman to have more than one husband at the same time (Gen. 2:24; Mal. 2:15; Matt. 19:5–6).

2. Marriage was ordained for the mutual help of husband and wife (Gen. 2:18), for the increase of mankind with a legitimate issue (Gen. 1:28), and the preventing of uncleanness (1 Cor. 7:2, 9).

3. It is lawful for all sorts of people to marry, who are able with judgment to give their consent (Heb. 13:4; 1 Tim. 4:3); yet it is the duty of Christians to marry in the Lord (1 Cor. 7:39); and therefore such as profess the true religion, should not marry with infidels, or idolaters; neither should such as are godly be unequally yoked, by marrying with such as are wicked in their life, or maintain damnable heresy (Neh. 13:25–27).

4. Marriage ought not to be within the degrees of consanguinity or affinity, forbidden in the Word (Lev. 18); nor can such incestuous marriages ever be made lawful, by any law of man or consent of parties, so as those persons may live together as man and wife (Mark 6:18; 1 Cor. 5:1).

Chapter XXVI
Of the Church

1. The catholic or universal church, which (with respect to the internal work of the Spirit and truth of grace) may be called invisible, consists of the whole number of the elect, that have been, are, or shall be gathered into one, under Christ, the head thereof; and is the spouse, the body, the fullness of Him that fills all in all (Heb. 12:23; Col. 1:18; Eph. 1:10, 22–23; 5:23, 27, 32).

2. All persons throughout the world, professing the faith of the gospel, and obedience unto God by Christ according unto it, not destroying their own profession by any errors everting the foundation, or unholiness of conversation, are and may be called visible saints (1 Cor. 1:2; Acts 11:26); and of such ought all particular congregations to be constituted (Rom. 1:7; Eph. 1:20–22).

3. The purest churches under heaven are subject to mixture and error (1 Cor. 5; Rev. 2, 3); and some have so degenerated as to become no churches of Christ, but synagogues of Satan (Rev. 18:2; 2 Thess. 2:11–12); nevertheless Christ always has had, and ever shall have a kingdom in this world, to the end thereof, of such as believe in Him, and make profession of His name (Matt. 16:18; Pss. 72:17; 102:28; Rev. 12:17).

4. The Lord Jesus Christ is the Head of the church, in whom, by the appointment of the Father, all power for the calling, institution, order or government of the church, is invested in a supreme and sovereign manner (Col. 1:18; Matt. 28:18–20; Eph. 4:11–12); neither can the pope of Rome in any sense be head thereof, but is that Antichrist, that man of sin, and son of perdition, that exalts himself in the church against Christ, and all that is called God; whom the Lord shall destroy with the brightness of His coming (2 Thess. 2:3–9).

5. In the execution of this power wherewith He is so entrusted, the Lord Jesus calls out of the world unto Himself, through the ministry of His Word, by His Spirit, those that are given unto Him by His Father (John 10:16; 12:32), that they may walk before Him in all the ways of obedience, which He prescribes to them in His Word (Matt. 28:20). Those thus called, He commands to walk together in particular societies, or churches, for their mutual edification, and the due performance of that public worship, which He requires of them in the world (Matt. 18:15–20).

6. The members of these churches are saints by calling, visibly manifesting and evidencing (in and by their profession and walking) their obedience unto that call of Christ (Rom. 1:7; 1 Cor. 1:2); and do willingly consent to walk together, according to the appointment of Christ; giving up themselves to the Lord, and one to another, by the will of God, in professed subjection to the ordinances of the gospel (Acts 2:41–42; 5:13–14; 2 Cor. 9:13).

7. To each of these churches thus gathered, according to His mind declared in His Word, He has given all that power and authority, which is in any way needful for their carrying on that order in worship and discipline, which He has instituted for them to observe; with commands and rules for the due and right exerting and executing of that power (Matt. 18:17–18; 1 Cor. 5:4–5, 13; 2 Cor. 2:6–8).

8. A particular church, gathered and completely organized according to the mind of Christ, consists of officers and members; and the officers appointed by Christ to be chosen and set apart by the church (so called and gathered), for the peculiar administration of ordinances, and execution of power or duty, which He entrusts them with, or calls them to, to be continued to the end of the world, are bishops or elders and deacons (Acts 20:17, 28; Phil. 1:1).

9. The way appointed by Christ for the calling of any person, fitted and gifted by the Holy Spirit, unto the office of bishop or elder in a church, is, that he be chosen thereunto by the common suffrage of the church itself (Acts 14:23); and solemnly set apart by fasting and prayer, with imposition of hands of the eldership of the church, if there be any before constituted therein (1 Tim. 4:14); and of a deacon that he be chosen by the like suffrage, and set apart by prayer, and the like imposition of hands (Acts 6:3, 5–6).

10. The work of pastors being constantly to attend the service of Christ, in His churches, in the ministry of the Word and prayer, with watching for their souls, as they that must give an account to Him (Acts 6:4; Heb. 13:17); it is incumbent on the churches to whom they minister, not only to give them all due respect, but also to communicate to them of all their good things according to their ability (1 Tim. 5:17–18; Gal. 6:6–7), so as they may have a comfortable supply, without being themselves entangled in secular affairs (2 Tim. 2:4); and may also be capable of exercising hospitality towards others (1 Tim. 3:2); and this is required by the law of nature, and by the express order of our Lord Jesus, who has ordained that they that preach the gospel should live of the gospel (1 Cor. 9:6–14).

11. Although it be incumbent on the bishops or pastors of the churches to be instant in preaching the Word, by way of office, yet the work of preaching the Word is not so peculiarly confined to them but that others also gifted and fitted by the Holy Spirit for it, and approved and called by the church, may and ought to perform it (Acts 11:19–21; 1 Peter 4:10–11).

12. As all believers are bound to join themselves to particular churches, when and where they have opportunity so to do; so all that are admitted unto the privileges of a church, are also under the censures and government thereof, according to the rule of Christ (1 Thess. 5:14; 2 Thess. 3:6, 14–15).

13. No church members, upon any offence taken by them, having performed their duty required of them towards the person they are offended at, ought to disturb any church order, or absent themselves from the assemblies of the church, or administration of any ordinances, upon the account of such offence at any of their fellow members, but to wait upon Christ, in the further proceeding of the church (Matt. 18:15–17; Eph. 4:2–3).

14. As each church, and all the members of it, are bound to pray continually for the good and prosperity of all the churches of Christ (Eph. 6:18; Ps. 122:6), in all places, and upon all occasions to further it (everyone within the bounds of their places and callings, in the exercise of their gifts and graces), so the churches (when planted by the providence of God, so as they may enjoy opportunity and advantage for it) ought to hold communion

among themselves, for their peace, increase of love, and mutual edification (Rom. 16:1–2; 3 John 8–10).

15. In cases of difficulties or differences, either in point of doctrine or administration, wherein either the churches in general are concerned, or any one church, in their peace, union, and edification; or any member or members of any church are injured, in or by any proceedings in censures not agreeable to truth and order: it is according to the mind of Christ, that many churches holding communion together, do, by their messengers, meet to consider, and give their advice in or about that matter in difference, to be reported to all the churches concerned (Acts 15:2, 4, 6, 22–23, 25); howbeit these messengers assembled, are not entrusted with any church-power properly so called; or with any jurisdiction over the churches themselves, to exercise any censures either over any churches or persons; or to impose their determination on the churches or officers (2 Cor. 1:24; 1 John 4:1).

Chapter XXVII
Of the Communion of Saints

1. All saints that are united to Jesus Christ, their head, by His Spirit, and faith, although they are not made thereby one person with Him, have fellowship in His graces, sufferings, death, resurrection, and glory (1 John 1:3; John 1:16; Phil. 3:10; Rom. 6:5–6); and, being united to one another in love, they have communion in each other's gifts and graces (Eph. 4:15–16; 1 Cor. 12:7; 3:21–23), and are obliged to the performance of such duties, public and private, in an orderly way, as do conduce to their mutual good, both in the inward and outward man (1 Thess. 5:11, 14; Rom. 1:12; 1 John 3:17–18; Gal. 6:10).

2. Saints by profession are bound to maintain an holy fellowship and communion in the worship of God, and in performing such other spiritual services as tend to their mutual edification (Heb. 10:24–25; 3:12–13); as also in relieving each other in outward things according to their several abilities and necessities (Acts 11:29–30); which communion, according to the rule of the gospel, though especially to be exercised by them, in the relation wherein they stand, whether in families (Eph. 6:4), or churches (1 Cor. 12:14–27), yet, as God offers opportunity, is to be extended to

all the household of faith, even all those who in every place call upon the name of the Lord Jesus; nevertheless, their communion one with another as saints does not take away or infringe the title or propriety which each man has in his goods and possessions (Acts 5:4; Eph. 4:28).

Chapter XXVIII
Of Baptism and the Lord's Supper

1. Baptism and the Lord's Supper are ordinances of positive and sovereign institution, appointed by the Lord Jesus, the only Lawgiver, to be continued in His church to the end of the world (Matt. 28:19–20; 1 Cor. 11:26).

2. These holy appointments are to be administered by those only who are qualified and thereunto called, according to the commission of Christ (Matt. 28:19; 1 Cor. 4:1).

Chapter XXIX
Of Baptism

1. Baptism is an ordinance of the New Testament, ordained by Jesus Christ, to be unto the party baptized, a sign of his fellowship with Him, in His death and resurrection; of his being engrafted into Him (Rom. 6:3–5; Col. 2:12; Gal. 3:27); of remission of sins (Mark 1:4; Acts 22:16); and of his giving up unto God, through Jesus Christ, to live and walk in newness of life (Rom. 6:2, 4).

2. Those who do actually profess repentance towards God, faith in, and obedience to, our Lord Jesus Christ, are the only proper subjects of this ordinance (Mark 16:16; Acts 8:36–37).

3. The outward element to be used in this ordinance is water, wherein the party is to be baptized, in the name of the Father, and of the Son, and of the Holy Spirit (Matt. 28:19–20; Acts 8:38).

4. Immersion, or dipping of the person in water, is necessary to the due administration of this ordinance (Matt. 3:16; John 3:23).

Chapter XXX
Of the Lord's Supper

1. The Supper of the Lord Jesus was instituted by Him the same night wherein He was betrayed, to be observed in His churches, unto the end of the world, for the perpetual remembrance, and showing forth the sacrifice of Himself in His death (1 Cor. 11:23–26), confirmation of the faith of believers in all the benefits thereof, their spiritual nourishment, and growth in Him, their further engagement in, and to all duties which they owe unto Him; and to be a bond and pledge of their communion with Him, and with each other (1 Cor. 10:16–17, 21).

2. In this ordinance Christ is not offered up to His Father, nor any real sacrifice made at all for remission of sin of the quick or dead, but only a memorial of that one offering up of Himself by Himself upon the cross, once for all (Heb. 9:25–26, 28); and a spiritual oblation of all possible praise unto God for the same (1 Cor. 11:24; Matt. 26:26–27). So that the popish sacrifice of the Mass, as they call it, is most abominable, injurious to Christ's own only sacrifice the alone propitiation for all the sins of the elect.

3. The Lord Jesus has, in this ordinance, appointed His ministers to pray, and bless the elements of bread and wine, and thereby to set them apart from a common to an holy use, and to take and break the bread; to take the cup, and (they communicating also themselves) to give both to the communicants (1 Cor. 11:23–26ff.).

4. The denial of the cup to the people, worshipping the elements, the lifting them up, or carrying them about for adoration, and reserving them for any pretended religious use, are all contrary to the nature of this ordinance, and to the institution of Christ (Matt. 26:26–28; 15:9; Ex. 20:4–5).

5. The outward elements in this ordinance, duly set apart to the uses ordained by Christ, have such relation to Him crucified, as that truly, although in terms used figuratively, they are sometimes called by the names of the things they represent, to wit, the body and blood of Christ (1 Cor. 11:27), albeit, in substance and nature, they still remain truly and only bread and wine, as they were before (1 Cor. 11:26–28).

6. That doctrine which maintains a change of the substance of bread and wine, into the substance of Christ's body and blood (commonly called transubstantiation) by consecration of a priest, or by any other way, is repugnant not to Scripture alone (Acts 3:21; Luke 24:6, 39), but even to common sense and reason, overthrows the nature of the ordinance, and has been, and is, the cause of manifold superstitions, yea, of gross idolatries (1 Cor. 11:24–25).

7. Worthy receivers, outwardly partaking of the visible elements in this ordinance, do then also inwardly by faith, really and indeed, yet not carnally and corporally, but spiritually receive, and feed upon Christ crucified, and all the benefits of His death; the body and blood of Christ being then not corporally or carnally, but spiritually present to the faith of believers in that ordinance, as the elements themselves are to their outward senses (1 Cor. 10:16; 11:23–26).

8. All ignorant and ungodly persons, as they are unfit to enjoy communion with Christ, so are they unworthy of the Lord's table, and cannot, without great sin against Him, while they remain such, partake of these holy mysteries, or be admitted thereunto (2 Cor. 6:14–15); yea, whosoever shall receive unworthily, are guilty of the body and blood of the Lord, eating and drinking judgment to themselves (1 Cor. 11:29; Matt. 7:6).

Chapter XXXI
Of the State of Man after Death and of the Resurrection of the Dead

1. The bodies of men after death return to dust, and see corruption (Gen. 3:19; Acts 13:36); but their souls (which neither die nor sleep) having an immortal subsistence, immediately return to God who gave them (Eccl. 12:7). The souls of the righteous being then made perfect in holiness, are received into paradise where they are with Christ, and behold the face of God in light and glory, waiting for the full redemption of their bodies (Luke 23:43; 2 Cor. 5:1, 6, 8; Phil. 1:23; Heb. 12:23); and the souls of the wicked are cast into hell; where they remain in torment and utter darkness, reserved to the judgment of the great day (Jude 6, 7; 1 Peter 3:19; Luke 16:23–24); besides these two places, for souls separated from their bodies, the Scripture acknowledges none.

2. At the last day, such of the saints as are found alive shall not sleep, but be changed (1 Cor. 15:51–52; 1 Thess. 4:17); and all the dead shall be raised up with the selfsame bodies, and none other (Job 19:26–27); although with different qualities, which shall be united again to their souls forever (1 Cor. 15:42–43).

3. The bodies of the unjust shall, by the power of Christ, be raised to dishonor; the bodies of the just, by His Spirit, unto honor, and be made conformable to His own glorious body (Acts 24:15; John 5:28–29; Phil. 3:21).

Chapter XXXII
Of the Last Judgment

1. God has appointed a day wherein He will judge the world in righteousness, by Jesus Christ (Acts 17:31; John 5:22, 27); to whom all power and judgment is given of the Father; in which day, not only the apostate angels shall be judged (1 Cor. 6:3; Jude 6), but likewise all persons that have lived upon the earth shall appear before the tribunal of Christ, to give an account of their thoughts, words, and deeds, and to receive according to what they have done in the body, whether good or evil (2 Cor. 5:10; Eccl. 12:14; Matt. 12:36; Rom. 14:10, 12; Matt. 25:32ff.).

2. The end of God's appointing this day, is for the manifestation of the glory of His mercy, in the eternal salvation of the elect; and of His justice, in the eternal damnation of the reprobate, who are wicked and disobedient (Rom. 9:22–23); for then shall the righteous go into everlasting life, and receive that fullness of joy and glory with everlasting reward, in the presence of the Lord; but the wicked, who do not know God, and obey not the gospel of Jesus Christ, shall be cast aside into eternal torments (Matt. 25:21, 34; 2 Tim. 4:8), and punished with everlasting destruction, from the presence of the Lord, and from the glory of His power (Matt. 25:46; Mark 9:48; 2 Thess. 1:7–10).

3. As Christ would have us to be certainly persuaded that there shall be a day of judgment, both to deter all men from sin (2 Cor. 5:10–11), and for the greater consolation of the godly in their adversity (2 Thess. 1:5–7), so will He have the day unknown to men, that they may shake off all carnal

security, and be always watchful, because they know not at what hour the Lord will come (Mark 13:35–37; Luke 12:35–36), and may ever be prepared to say, Come, Lord Jesus; come quickly (Rev. 22:20). Amen.

Ending Statement and Signatories

We the ministers, and messengers of, and concerned for upwards of, one hundred Baptized Churches, in England and Wales (denying Arminianisim), being met together in London, from the third of the seventh month to the eleventh of the same, 1689, to consider of some things that might be for the glory of God, and the good of these congregations, have thought meet (for the satisfaction of all other Christians that differ from us in the point of Baptism) to recommend to their perusal the confession of our faith, which confession we own, as containing the doctrine of our faith and practice, and do desire that the members of our churches respectively do furnish themselves therewith.

Hansard Knollys, Pastor Broken Wharf, London
William Kiffin, Pastor Devonshire-square, London
John Harris, Pastor, Joiner's Hall, London
William Collins, Pastor, Petty France, London
Hurcules Collins, Pastor, Wapping, London
Robert Steed, Pastor, Broken Wharf, London
Leonard Harrison,Pastor, Limehouse, London
George Barret, Pastor, Mile End Green, London
Isaac Lamb, Pastor, Pennington-street, London
Richard Adams, Minister, Shad Thames, Southwark
Benjamin Keach, Pastor, Horse-lie-down, Southwark
Andrew Gifford, Pastor, Bristol, Fryars, Som. & Glouc.
Thomas Vaux, Pastor, Broadmead, Som. & Glouc.
Thomas Winnel, Pastor, Taunton, Som. & Glouc.
James Hitt, Preacher, Dalwood, Dorset
Richard Tidmarsh, Minister, Oxford City, Oxon
William Facey, Pastor, Reading, Berks
Samuel Buttall, Minister, Plymouth, Devon
Christopher Price, Minister, Abergayenny, Monmouth
Daniel Finch, Minister, Kgs.worth, Herts
John Ball, Minister, Tiverton, Devon

Edmond White, Pastor, Evershall, Bedford
William Prichard, Pastor, Blaenau, Monmouth
Paul Fruin, Minister, Warwick, Warwick
Richard Ring, Pastor, Southhampton, Hants
John Tomkins, Minister, Abingdon, Berks
Toby Willes, Pastor, Bridgewater, Somerset
John Carter, Pastor, Steventon, Bedford
James Webb, Pastor, Devizes, Wilts
Richard Sutton, Pastor, Tring, Herts
Robert Knight, Pastor, Stukeley, Bucks
Edward Price, Pastor, Hereford City, Hereford
William Phipps, Pastor, Exon, Devon
William Hawkins, Pastor, Dimmock, Gloucester
Samuel Ewer, Pastor, Hemstead, Herts
Edward Man, Pastor, Houndsditch, London
Charles Archer, Pastor, Hock-Norton, Oxon
    In the name of and on the behalf of the whole assembly.

127

The Baptist Catechism (1693)

Mystery surrounds the origin of this catechism for the following reasons: First, there is, in fact, no extant copy of the *editio princeps*. The date of the oldest copy is 1695, though most scholars regard the work as having originated in 1693. Second, although the work is known familiarly as "Keach's Catechism" (at least, it was in the eighteenth century), the 1693 London (Baptist) General Assembly allegedly asked William Collins (†1702), a Particular Baptist pastor at Petty France in London, to draft a catechism. A 1720 edition of the document adds to the puzzle, with a note that both Benjamin Keach (1640–1704) and Collins had a claim (i.e., proprietary right) to it. Keach openly espoused believer's baptism around 1655, at a General Baptist congregation, likely in Winslow, Bucks County. His *Child's Instructor*, released on or before 1664, earned him the pillory, imprisonment, and a stiff fine at Aylesbury. In 1668, he moved to London with his first wife (Jane Grove, †1670) and children. It is recorded that he was ordained pastor of the Tooly Street General Baptist church in London in 1668. Prior to moving this congregation to Horsley Down, Southwark, in 1672, Keach fell under the influence of William Kiffin (1616–1701) and Hanserd Knollys (ca. 1599–1691), not to mention his Calvinistic second wife, Susanna Partridge. Henceforth, his associations were of the Particular (Calvinistic) Baptist variety. He organized a congregation at Goat Street, Horsley Down, where he enthusiastically introduced hymn singing during corporate worship (many of which he wrote himself). His advocacy of hymns precipitated the 1692 split in the Particular Baptist churches of London.

In view of the ambiguous data, perhaps the best solution to the attribution problem is to view Collins *and* Keach as having influenced the final version—Collins as principal author, and Keach as later redactor and/or contributor. In any event, it evidences a heavy dependence on the Westminster Shorter Catechism (as the concluding "Advertisement" testifies—see below). That dependence is substantially altered in the questions and answers about baptism. Questions and answers 97–101 and 103 of this document are significantly different from questions and answers 94–95 of the Shorter Catechism.

Our text is based on the 1695 "fifth edition," printed in London, titled *A Brief Instruction in the Principles of Christian Religion: Agreeable to the Confession of Faith put forth by the Elders and Brethren of many Congregations of Christians (baptized upon Profession of Faith), in London and the Country; owning the Doctrine of Personal Election and Final Perseverance.* We have modernized spelling, punctuation, capitalization, the mode of Scriptural citation, and other minor matters. We have inserted proof texts at the end of phrases and corrected where necessary. James M. Renihan has provided a helpful introduction, as well as reprinted the 1695 text in parallel columns with the Westminster Shorter and Larger Catechisms for purposes of comparison in *True Confessions: Baptist Documents in the Reformed Family* (Owensboro, Ky.: Reformed Baptist Academic Press, 2004), 196–231.

THE BAPTIST CATECHISM

Q. 1. *Who is the first and chiefest being?*
A. God is the first and chiefest being (Isa. 44:6; 48:12).

Q. 2. *Ought everyone to believe there is a God?*
A. Everyone ought to believe there is a God (Heb. 11:6); and it is their great sin and folly who do not (Ps. 14:1).

Q. 3. *How may we know there is a God?*
A. The light of nature in man and the works of God plainly declare that there is a God (Rom. 1:19–20; Ps. 19:1–3; Acts 17:24); but His Word and Spirit only, do it fully and effectually, for the salvation of sinners (1 Cor. 2:10; 2 Tim. 3:15–16).

Q. 4. *What is the Word of God?*
A. The Holy Scriptures of the Old and New Testament are the Word of God, and the only certain rule of faith and obedience (2 Tim. 3:16; Eph. 2:20).

Q. 5. *May all men make use of the Scriptures?*
A. All men are not only permitted, but commanded and exhorted, to read, hear, and understand the Holy Scriptures (John 5:39; Deut.17:18–19; Rev. 1:3; Acts 8:30).

Q. 6. *What things are chiefly contained in the Holy Scripture?*
A. The Holy Scriptures chiefly contain what man ought to believe concerning God, and what duty God requires of man (2 Tim. 1:13; 3:15–16).

Q. 7. *What is God?*
A. God is a Spirit (John 4:24), infinite (Job 11:7–9), eternal (Ps. 90:2), and unchangeable (James 1:17), in His being (Ex. 3:14), wisdom (Ps. 147:5), power (Rev. 4:8), holiness (Rev. 15:4), justice, goodness, and truth (Ex. 34:6–7).

Q. 8. *Are there more gods than one?*
A. There is but one only, the living and true God (Deut. 6:4; Jer. 10:10).

Q. 9. *How many persons are there in the Godhead?*
A. There are three persons in the Godhead, the Father, the Son, and the Holy Spirit; and these three are one God, the same in essence, equal in power and glory (1 John 5:7; Matt. 28:19).

Q. 10. *What are the decrees of God?*
A. The decrees of God are His eternal purpose, according to the counsel of His will, whereby for His own glory, He has foreordained whatsoever comes to pass (Eph. 1:4, 11; Rom. 9:22–23).

Q. 11. *How does God execute His decrees?*
A. God executes His decrees in the works of creation and providence.

Q. 12. *What is the work of creation?*
A. The work of creation is God's making all things of nothing, by the Word of His power, in the space of six days, and all very good (Gen. 1; Heb. 11:3).

Q. 13. *How did God create man?*
A. God created man male and female, after His own image, in knowledge, righteousness, and holiness, with dominion over the creatures (Gen. 1:26–28; Col. 3:10; Eph. 4:24).

Q. 14. *What are God's works of providence?*
A. God's works of providence are His most holy (Ps. 145:17), wise (Ps. 104:24; Isa. 28:29), and powerful preserving (Heb. 1:3) and governing all His creatures, and all their actions (Ps. 103:19; Matt. 10:29–31).

Q. 15. *What special act of providence did God exercise towards man in the estate wherein he was created?*
A. When God had created man, He entered into a covenant of life with him, upon condition of perfect obedience: forbidding him to eat of the tree of the knowledge of good and evil, upon pain of death (Gal. 3:12; Gen. 2:17).

Q. 16. *Did our first parents continue in the estate wherein they were created?*
A. Our first parents, being left to the freedom of their own will, fell from the estate wherein they were created, by sinning against God (Gen. 3:6–8, 13; Eccl. 7:29).

Q. 17. *What is sin?*
A. Sin is any want of conformity unto, or transgression of, the law of God (1 John 3:4).

Q. 18. *What was the sin whereby our first parents fell from the estate wherein they were created?*
A. The sin whereby our first parents fell from the estate wherein they were created, was their eating the forbidden fruit (Gen. 3:6, 12).

Q. 19. *Did all mankind fall in Adam's first transgression?*
A. The covenant being made with Adam, not only for himself but for his posterity, all mankind, descending from him by ordinary generation, sinned in him, and fell with him in his first transgression (Gen. 2:16–17; Rom. 5:12; 1 Cor. 15:21–22).

Q. 20. *Into what estate did the fall bring mankind?*
A. The fall brought mankind into an estate of sin and misery (Rom. 5:12).

Q. 21. *Wherein consists the sinfulness of that estate whereunto man fell?*
A. The sinfulness of that estate whereunto man fell, consists in the guilt of Adam's first sin, the want of original righteousness, and the corruption of his whole nature, which is commonly called original sin, together with all actual transgressions which proceed from it (Rom. 5:12–21; Eph. 2:1–3; James 1:14–15; Matt. 15:19).

Q. 22. What is the misery of that estate whereinto man fell?
A. All mankind, by their fall lost communion with God (Gen. 3:8, 10, 24), are under His wrath and curse (Eph. 2:2–3; Gal. 3:10), and so made liable to all miseries in this life, to death itself, and to the pains of hell forever (Lam. 3:39; Rom. 6:23; Matt. 25:41, 46).

Q. 23. Did God leave all mankind to perish in the estate of sin and misery?
A. God, having out of His mere good pleasure, from all eternity, elected some to everlasting life (Eph. 1:4–5), did enter into a covenant of grace, to deliver them out of the estate of sin and misery, and to bring them into an estate of salvation by a Redeemer (Rom. 3:20–22; Gal. 3:21–22).

Q. 24. Who is the Redeemer of God's elect?
A. The only Redeemer of God's elect is the Lord Jesus Christ (1 Tim. 2:5–6), who being the eternal Son of God, became man (John 1:14; Gal. 4:4), and so was and continues to be God and man, in two distinct natures and one person forever (Rom. 9:5; Luke 1:35; Col. 2:9; Heb. 7:24–25).

Q. 25. How did Christ, being the Son of God, become man?
A. Christ, the Son of God, became man by taking to Himself a true body (Heb. 2:14, 16; 10:5) and a reasonable soul (Matt. 26:38); being conceived by the power of the Holy Spirit in the womb of the virgin Mary and born of her (Luke 1:27, 31, 34–35, 42; Gal. 4:4), yet without sin (Heb. 4:15; 7:26).

Q. 26. What offices does Christ execute as our Redeemer?
A. Christ, as our Redeemer, executes the offices of a prophet, of a priest, and of a king, both in His estate of humiliation and exaltation (Acts 3:22; Heb. 12:25; 2 Cor. 13:3; Heb. 5:5–7; 7:25; Ps. 2:6; Isa. 9:6–7; Matt. 21:5; Ps. 2:8–11).

Q. 27. How does Christ execute the office of a prophet?
A. Christ executes the office of a prophet in revealing to us, by His Word and Spirit, the will of God for our salvation (John 1:18; 1 Peter 1:10–12; John 15:15; 20:31).

Q. 28. How does Christ execute the office of a priest?
A. Christ executes the office of a priest in His once offering up of Himself a sacrifice to satisfy divine justice (Heb. 9:14, 28), and reconcile us to God (Heb. 2:17), and in making continual intercession for us (Heb. 7:24–25).

Q. 29. *How does Christ execute the office of a king?*
A. Christ executes the office of a king in subduing us to Himself (Acts 15:14–16), in ruling (Isa. 33:22) and defending us (Isa. 32:1–2), and in restraining and conquering all His and our enemies (1 Cor. 15:25; Ps. 110).

Q. 30. *Wherein did Christ's humiliation consist?*
A. Christ's humiliation consisted in His being born, and that in a low condition (Luke 2:7), made under the law (Gal. 4:4), undergoing the miseries of this life (Heb. 12:2–3; Isa. 53:2–3), the wrath of God (Luke 22:44; Matt. 27:46), and the cursed death of the cross (Phil. 2:8), in being buried (1 Cor. 15:4), and continuing under the power of death for a time (Matt. 12:40; Acts 2:24–27, 31).

Q. 31. *Wherein consists Christ's exaltation?*
A. Christ's exaltation consists in His rising again from the dead on the third day (1 Cor. 15:4), in ascending up into heaven (Mark 16:19), in sitting at the right hand of God the Father (Eph. 1:20), and in coming to judge the world at the last day (Acts 1:11; 17:31).

Q. 32. *How are we made partakers of the redemption purchased by Christ?*
A. We are made partakers of the redemption purchased by Christ by the effectual application of it to us (John 1:11–12) by His Holy Spirit (Titus 3:5–6).

Q. 33. *How does the Spirit apply to us the redemption purchased by Christ?*
A. The Spirit applies to us the redemption purchased by Christ by working faith in us (Eph. 1:13–14; John 6:37, 39; Eph. 2:8), and thereby uniting us to Christ in our effectual calling (Eph. 3:17; 1 Cor. 1:9).

Q. 34. *What is effectual calling?*
A. Effectual calling is the work of God's Spirit (2 Tim. 1:9; 2 Thess. 2:13–14), whereby, convincing us of our sin and misery (Acts 2:37), enlightening our minds in the knowledge of Christ (Acts 26:18), and renewing our wills (Ezek. 36:26–27), He does persuade and enable us to embrace Jesus Christ freely offered to us in the gospel (John 6:44–45; Phil. 2:13).

Q. 35. *What benefits do they that are effectually called, partake of in this life?*
A. They that are effectually called, do in this life partake of justification (Rom. 8:30), adoption (Eph. 1:5), sanctification, and the several benefits which in this life do either accompany or flow from them (1 Cor. 1:30).

Q. 36. *What is justification?*
A. Justification is an act of God's free grace, wherein He pardons all our sins (Rom. 3:24–25; 4:6–8), and accepts us as righteous in His sight (2 Cor. 5:19, 21), only for the righteousness of Christ imputed to us (Rom. 5:17–19), and received by faith alone (Gal. 2:16; Phil. 3:9).

Q. 37. *What is adoption?*
A. Adoption is an act of God's free grace (1 John 3:1), whereby we are received into the number, and have a right to all the privileges of the sons of God (John 1:12; Rom. 8:14).

Q. 38. *What is sanctification?*
A. Sanctification is a work of God's free grace (2 Thess. 2:13), whereby we are renewed in the whole man after the image of God (Eph. 4:23–24), and are enabled more and more to die unto sin, and live unto righteousness (Rom. 6:4, 6).

Q. 39. *What are the benefits which in this life do accompany or flow from justification, adoption, and sanctification?*
A. The benefits which in this life do accompany or flow from justification, adoption, and sanctification, are assurance of God's love, peace of conscience (Rom. 5:1–2, 5), joy in the Holy Spirit (Rom. 14:17), increase of grace (Prov. 4:18), and perseverance therein to the end (1 John 5:13; 1 Peter 1:5).

Q. 40. *What benefits do believers receive from Christ at their death?*
A. The souls of believers are at their death made perfect in holiness (Heb. 12:23), and do immediately pass into glory (2 Cor. 5:1, 6, 8; Phil. 1:23; Luke 23:43): and their bodies being still united to Christ (1 Thess. 4:14), do rest in their graves (Isa. 57:2) till the resurrection (Job 19:26–27).

Q. 41. *What benefits do believers receive from Christ at the resurrection?*
A. At the resurrection, believers become raised up in glory (1 Cor. 15:43), shall be openly acknowledged and acquitted in the day of judgment (Matt. 25:23; 10:32), and made perfectly blessed both in soul and body in the full enjoyment of God (1 John 3:2; 1 Cor. 13:12) to all eternity (1 Thess. 4:17–18).

Q. 42. *But what shall be done to the wicked at their death?*
A. The souls of the wicked shall at their death be cast into the torments of hell, and their bodies lie in their graves till the resurrection and judgment of the great day (Luke 16:23–24; Acts 1:25; Jude 7; 1 Peter 3:19; Ps. 49:14).

Q. 43. *What shall be done to the wicked at the day of judgment?*
A. At the day of judgment, the bodies of the wicked, being raised out of their graves, shall be sentenced, together with their souls, to unspeakable torments with the devil and his angels forever (John 5:28–29; Matt. 25:41, 46; 2 Thess. 1:8–9).

Q. 44. *What is the duty which God requires of man?*
A. The duty which God requires of man is obedience to His revealed will (Mic. 6:8; 1 Sam. 15:22).

Q. 45. *What did God at first reveal to man for the rule of His obedience?*
A. The rule which God at first revealed to man for his obedience was the moral law (Rom. 2:14–15; 10:5).

Q. 46. *Where is the moral law summarily comprehended?*
A. The moral law is summarily comprehended in the Ten Commandments (Deut. 10:4; Matt. 19:17).

Q. 47. *What is the sum of the Ten Commandments?*
A. The sum of the Ten Commandments is, to love the Lord our God, with all our heart, with all our soul, with all our strength, and with all our mind; and our neighbor as ourselves (Matt. 22:37–40).

Q. 48. *What is the preface to the Ten Commandments?*
A. The preface to the Ten Commandments is, in these words, "I am the Lord thy God, which have brought thee out of the land of Egypt, out of the house of bondage" (Ex. 20:2).

Q. 49. *What does the preface to the Ten Commandments teach us?*
A. The preface to the Ten Commandments teaches us that because God is the Lord, and our God and Redeemer, therefore we are bound to keep all His commandments (Luke 1:74–75; 1 Peter 1:15–19).

Q. 50. *Which is the first commandment?*
A. The first commandment is, "Thou shalt have no other Gods before me" (Ex. 20:3).

Q. 51. *What is required in the first commandment?*
A. The first commandment requires us to know and acknowledge God to be the only true God, and our God (1 Chron. 28:9; Deut. 26:17), and to worship and glorify Him accordingly (Matt. 4:10; Ps. 29:2).

Q. 52. *What is forbidden in the first commandment?*
A. The first commandment forbids the denying (Ps. 14:1) or not worshipping and glorifying the true God, as God (Rom. 1:21) and our God (Ps. 81:10–11); and the giving that worship and glory to any other, which is due unto Him alone (Rom. 1:25–26).

Q. 53. *What are we especially taught by these words, "before me," in the first commandment?*
A. These words, "before me," in the first commandment, teach us, that God who sees all things, takes notice of, and is much displeased with, the sin of having any other God (Ezek. 8:5–18).

Q. 54. *Which is the second commandment?*
A. The second commandment is, "Thou shalt not make unto thee any graven image, or any likeness of anything that is in heaven above, or that is in the earth beneath, or that is in the water under the earth. Thou shalt not bow down thyself to them, nor serve them; for I the Lord thy God am a jealous God, visiting the iniquity of the fathers upon the children, unto the third and fourth generation of them that hate me: and showing mercy unto thousands of them that love me and keep my commandments" (Ex. 20:4–6).

Q. 55. *What is required in the second commandment?*
A. The second commandment requires the receiving, observing, and keeping pure and entire, all such religious worship and ordinances, as God has appointed in His Word (Deut. 32:46; Matt. 28:20; Acts 2:42).

Q. 56. *What is forbidden in the second commandment?*
A. The second commandment forbids the worshipping of God by images (Deut. 4:15–19; Ex. 32:5, 8), or any other way not appointed in His Word (Deut. 12:31–32).

Q. 57. *What are the reasons annexed to the second commandment?*
A. The reasons annexed to the second commandment are God's sovereignty over us (Ps. 95:2–3, 6), His propriety in us (Ps. 45:11), and the zeal He has for His own worship (Ex. 34:13–14).

Q. 58. *Which is the third commandment?*
A. The third commandment is, "Thou shalt not take the name of the Lord thy God in vain: for the Lord will not hold him guiltless that taketh His name in vain" (Ex. 20:7).

Q. 59. *What is required in the third commandment?*
A. The third commandment requires the holy and reverent use of God's names (Matt. 6:9; Deut. 28:58), titles (Ps. 68:4), attributes (Rev. 15:3–4), ordinances (Mal. 1:11, 14), Word (Ps. 138:1–2), and works (Job 36:24).

Q. 60. *What is forbidden in the third commandment?*
A. The third commandment forbids all profaning and abusing of any thing whereby God makes Himself known (Mal. 1:6–7, 12; 2:2; 3:14).

Q. 61. *What is the reason annexed to the third commandment?*
A. The reason annexed to the third commandment is, that however the breakers of this commandment may escape punishment from men, yet the Lord our God will not suffer them to escape His righteous judgment (1 Sam. 2:12, 17, 22, 24, 29; 3:13; Deut. 28:58–59).

Q. 62. *Which is the fourth commandment?*
A. The fourth commandment is, "Remember the Sabbath day to keep it holy. Six days shalt thou labor and do all thy work; but the seventh day is the Sabbath of the Lord thy God: in it thou shalt not do any work, thou, nor thy son, nor thy daughter, thy man-servant, nor thy maid-servant, nor thy cattle, nor thy stranger that is within thy gates: for in six days the Lord made heaven and earth, the sea, and all that in them is, and rested the seventh day: wherefore the Lord blessed the Sabbath day and hallowed it" (Ex. 20:8–11).

Q. 63. *What is required in the fourth commandment?*
A. The fourth commandment requires the keeping holy to God one whole day in seven to be a Sabbath to Himself (Ex. 20:8–11; Deut. 5:12–14).

Q. 64. *Which day of the seven has God appointed to be the weekly Sabbath?*
A. Before the resurrection of Christ, God appointed the seventh day of the week to be the weekly Sabbath (Ex. 20:8–11; Deut. 5:12–14), and the first day of the week ever since, to continue to the end of the world, which is the Christian Sabbath (Ps. 118:24; Matt. 28:1; Mark 2:27–28; 16:2; Luke 24:1, 30–36; John 20:1, 19–21, 26; Acts 1:3; 2:1–2; 20:7; 1 Cor. 16:1–2; Rev. 1:10).

Q. 65. *How is the Sabbath to be sanctified?*
A. The Sabbath is to sanctified by a holy resting all that day (Ex. 20:8, 10), even from such worldly employments and recreations as are lawful on other days (Ex. 16:25–28; Neh. 13:15–19, 21–22), and spending the whole

time in the public and private exercises of God's worship (Luke 4:16; Acts 20:7; Ps. 92:title; Isa. 66:23), except so much as is to be taken up in the works of necessity and mercy (Matt. 12:1–13).

Q. 66. *What is forbidden in the fourth commandment?*
A. The fourth commandment forbids the omission or careless performance of the duties required (Ezek. 22:26; Amos 8:5; Mal. 1:13), and the profaning the day by idleness (Acts 20:7, 9), or doing that which is in itself sinful (Ezek. 23:38), or by unnecessary thoughts, words, or works about worldly employments or recreations (Jer. 17:24–27; Isa. 58:13).

Q. 67. *What are the reasons annexed to the fourth commandment?*
A. The reasons annexed to the fourth commandment are God's allowing us six days of the week for our own lawful employments (Ex. 20:9), His challenging a special propriety in a seventh, His own example, and His blessing the Sabbath day (Ex. 20:11).

Q. 68. *Which is the fifth commandment?*
A. The fifth commandment is, "Honor thy father and thy mother, that thy days may be long upon the land which the Lord thy God giveth thee" (Ex. 20:12).

Q. 69. *What is required in the fifth commandment?*
A. The fifth commandment requires the preserving the honor, and performing the duties, belonging to everyone in their several places and relations, as superiors (Eph. 5:21), inferiors (1 Peter 2:17), or equals (Rom. 12:10).

Q. 70. *What is forbidden in the fifth commandment?*
A. The fifth commandment forbids the neglecting of, or doing anything against the honor and duty which belongs to everyone in their several places and relations (Matt. 15:4–6; Ezek. 34:2–4; Rom. 13:8).

Q. 71. *What is the reason annexed to the fifth commandment?*
A. The reason annexed to the fifth commandment is a promise of long life and prosperity (as far as it shall serve God's glory and their own good) to all such as keep this commandment (Deut. 5:16; Eph. 6:2–3).

Q. 72. *Which is the sixth commandment?*
A. The sixth commandment is, "Thou shalt not kill" (Ex. 20:13).

Q. 73. *What is required in the sixth commandment?*
A. The sixth commandment requires all lawful endeavors to preserve our own life (Eph. 5:28–29) and the life of others (1 Kings 18:4).

Q. 74. *What is forbidden in the sixth commandment?*
A. The sixth commandment absolutely forbids the taking away our own life, or the life of our neighbor unjustly, or whatsoever tends thereunto (Acts 16:28; Gen. 9:6).

Q. 75. *Which is the seventh commandment?*
A. The seventh commandment is, "Thou shalt not commit adultery" (Ex. 20:14).

Q. 76. *What is required in the seventh commandment?*
A. The seventh commandment requires the preservation of our own and our neighbor's chastity, in heart, speech, and behavior (1 Cor. 7:2–3, 5, 34, 36; Col. 4:6; 1 Peter 3:2).

Q. 77. *What is forbidden in the seventh commandment?*
A. The seventh commandment forbids all unchaste thoughts, words, and actions (Matt. 15:19; 5:28; Eph. 5:3–4).

Q. 78. *Which is the eighth commandment?*
A. The eighth commandment is, "Thou shalt not steal" (Ex. 20:15).

Q. 79. *What is required in the eighth commandment?*
A. The eighth commandment requires the lawful procuring and furthering the wealth and outward state of ourselves and others (Gen. 30:30; 1 Tim. 5:8; Lev. 25:35; Deut. 22:1–5; Ex. 23:4–5; Gen. 47:14, 20).

Q. 80. *What is forbidden in the eighth commandment?*
A. The eighth commandment forbids whatsoever does or may unjustly hinder our own or our neighbor's wealth or outward state (Prov. 21:17; 23:20-21; 28:19; Eph. 4:28).

Q. 81. *Which is the ninth commandment?*
A. The ninth commandment is, "Thou shalt not bear false witness against thy neighbor" (Ex. 20:16).

Q. 82. *What is required in the ninth commandment?*
A. The ninth commandment requires the maintaining and promoting of truth between man and man (Zech. 8:16), and of our own and our neighbor's good name (3 John 12), especially in witness bearing (Prov. 14:5, 25).

Q. 83. *What is forbidden in the ninth commandment?*
A. The ninth commandment forbids whatsoever is prejudicial to truth, or injurious to our own, or our neighbor's good name (1 Sam. 17:28; Lev. 19:16; Ps. 15:3).

Q. 84. *Which is the tenth commandment?*
A. The tenth commandment is, "Thou shalt not covet thy neighbor's house. Thou shalt not covet thy neighbor's wife, nor his man-servant, nor his maid-servant, nor his ox, nor his ass, nor any thing that is thy neighbor's" (Ex. 20:17).

Q. 85. *What is required in the tenth commandment?*
A. The tenth commandment requires full contentment with our own condition (Heb. 13:5; 1 Tim. 6:6), with a right and charitable frame of spirit towards our neighbor, and all that is his (Job 31:29; Rom. 12:15; 1 Tim. 1:5; 1 Cor. 13:4–7).

Q. 86. *What is forbidden in the tenth commandment?*
A. The tenth commandment forbids all discontentment with our own estate (1 Kings 21:4; Est. 5:13; 1 Cor. 10:10), envying or grieving at the good of our neighbor (Gal. 5:26; James 3:14, 16), and all inordinate motions and affections to anything that is his (Rom. 7:7–8; 13:9; Deut. 5:21).

Q. 87. *Is any man able perfectly to keep the commandments of God?*
A. No mere man since the fall, is able in this life, perfectly to keep the commandments of God (Eccl. 7:20; 1 John 1:8, 10; Gal. 5:17), but daily breaks them in thought, word, and deed (Gen. 6:5; 8:21; Rom. 3:9–21; James 3:2–13).

Q. 88. *Are all transgressions of the law equally heinous?*
A. Some sins in themselves and by reason of several aggravations, are more heinous in the sight of God than others (Ezek. 8:6, 13, 15; 1 John 5:16; Ps. 78:17, 32, 56).

Q. 89. *What does every sin deserve?*

A. Every sin deserves God's wrath and curse, both in this life, and in that which is to come (Eph. 5:6; Gal. 3:10; Lam. 3:39; Matt. 25:41; Rom. 6:23).

Q. 90. *What does God require of us, that we may escape His wrath and curse, due to us for sin?*

A. To escape the wrath and curse of God due to us for sin, God requires of us faith in Jesus Christ, repentance unto life (Acts 20:21), with the diligent use of all the outward means whereby Christ communicates to us the benefits of redemption (Prov. 2:1–6; 8:33–36; Isa. 55:2–3).

Q. 91. *What is faith in Jesus Christ?*

A. Faith in Jesus Christ is a saving grace (Heb. 10:39), whereby we receive and rest upon Him alone for salvation, as He is offered to us in the gospel (John 1:12; Isa. 26:3–4; Phil. 3:9; Gal. 2:16).

Q. 92. *What is repentance unto life?*

A. Repentance unto life is a saving grace (Acts 11:18), whereby a sinner, out of a true sense of his sin (Acts 2:37–38), and apprehension of the mercy of God in Christ (Joel 2:12; Jer. 3:22), does, with grief and hatred of his sin, turn from it unto God (Jer. 31:18–19; Ezek. 36:31), with full purpose of, and endeavor after, new obedience (2 Cor. 7:11; Isa. 1:16–17).

Q. 93. *What are the outward and ordinary means whereby Christ communicates to us the benefits of redemption?*

A. The outward and ordinary means whereby Christ communicates to us the benefits of redemption are His ordinances, especially the Word, baptism, the Lord's Supper, and prayer; all which means are made effectual to the elect for salvation (Matt. 28:19–20; Acts 2:42, 46–47).

Q. 94. *How is the Word made effectual to salvation?*

A. The Spirit of God makes the reading, but especially the preaching of the Word an effectual means of convincing and converting sinners; and of building them up in holiness and comfort, through faith unto salvation (Neh. 8:8; 1 Cor. 14:24–25; Acts 26:18; Ps. 19:8; Acts 20:32; Rom. 15:4; 1 Tim. 3:15–17; Rom. 10:13–17; 1:16).

Q. 95. *How is the Word to be read and heard that it may become effectual to salvation?*

A. That the Word may become effectual to salvation, we must attend thereunto with diligence (Prov. 8:34), preparation (1 Peter 2:1–2), and prayer (Ps. 119:18), receive it with faith and love (Heb. 4:2; 2 Thess. 2:10), lay it up in our hearts (Ps. 119:11), and practice it in our lives (Luke 8:15; James 1:25).

Q. 96. *How do baptism and the Lord's Supper become effectual means of salvation?*

A. Baptism and the Lord's Supper become effectual means of salvation not for any virtue in them or in him that administers them, but only by the blessing of Christ (1 Peter 3:21; Matt 3:11; 1 Cor. 3:6–7) and the working of the Spirit in those that by faith receive them (1 Cor. 12:13).

Q. 97. *What is baptism?*

A. Baptism is an ordinance of the New Testament instituted by Jesus Christ (Matt. 28:19), to be unto the party baptized a sign of his fellowship with Him in His death, burial, and resurrection; of his being ingrafted into Him (Rom. 6:3–5; Col. 2:12; Gal. 3:27); of remission of sins (Mark 1:4; Acts 2:38; 22:16) and of his giving up himself unto God through Jesus Christ to live and walk in newness of life (Rom. 6:3–4).

Q. 98. *To whom is baptism to be administered?*

A. Baptism is to be administered to all those who actually profess repentance toward God, faith in, and obedience to our Lord Jesus Christ; and to none other (Matt. 3:6; 28:19; Mark 16:16; Acts 2:37–38; 8:36–38).

Q. 99. *Are the infants of such as are professing believers to be baptized?*

A. The infants of such as are professing believers are not to be baptized, because there is neither command or example in the Holy Scriptures, or certain consequence from them, to baptize such.

Q. 100. *How is baptism rightly administered?*

A. Baptism is rightly administered by immersion, or dipping the whole body of the party in water, into the name of the Father, and of the Son, and of the Holy Spirit, according to Christ's institution and the practice of the apostles (Matt. 3:16; John 3:23; Matt. 28:19–20; Acts 8:38; 10:48; Rom. 6:4; Col. 2:12).

Q. 101. *What is the duty of such who are rightly baptized?*
A. It is the duty of such who are rightly baptized to give up themselves to some particular and orderly church of Jesus Christ, that they may walk in all the commandments and ordinances of the Lord blameless (Acts 2:41–42; 5:13–14; 9:26; 1 Peter 2:5; Luke 1:6).

Q. 102. *What is the Lord's Supper?*
A. The Lord's Supper is an ordinance of the New Testament instituted by Jesus Christ, wherein by giving and receiving bread and wine, according to His appointment, His death is shown forth, and the worthy receivers are, not after a corporal and carnal manner, but by faith, made partakers of His body and blood, with all His benefits, to their spiritual nourishment and growth in grace (Matt. 26:26–28; 1 Cor. 11:23–26; 10:16).

Q. 103. *Who are the proper subjects of this ordinance?*
A. They who have been baptized upon a personal profession of their faith in Jesus Christ, and repentance from dead works (Acts 2:41–42).

Q. 104. *What is required to the worthy receiving of the Lord's Supper?*
A. It is required of them that would worthily partake of the Lord's Supper, that they examine themselves, of their knowledge to discern the Lord's body (1 Cor. 11:28–29); of their faith to feed upon Him (2 Cor. 13:5); of their repentance (1 Cor. 11:31), love (1 Cor. 10:16–17), and new obedience (1 Cor. 5:7–8): lest, coming unworthily, they eat and drink judgment to themselves (1 Cor. 11:28–29).

Q. 105. *What is prayer?*
A. Prayer is an offering up of our desires to God (Ps. 62:8), by the assistance of the Holy Spirit (Rom. 6:26) for things agreeable to His will (1 John 5:14), in the name of Christ (John 16:23), believing (Matt. 21:22; James 1:6); with confession of our sins (Ps. 32:5–6; Dan. 9:4) and thankful acknowledgment of His mercies (Phil. 4:6).

Q. 106. *What rule has God given for our direction in prayer?*
A. The whole Word of God is of use to direct us in prayer (1 John 5:14), but the special rule of direction is that prayer which Christ taught His disciples, commonly called the Lord's Prayer (Matt. 6:9–13; Luke 11:2–4).

Q. 107. *What does the preface of the Lord's Prayer teach us?*
A. The preface of the Lord's Prayer, which is, "Our Father, which art in heaven" (Matt. 6:9), teaches us to draw near to God with all holy reverence and confidence, as children to a father, able and ready to help us (Rom. 8:15; Luke 11:13); and that we should pray with and for others (Acts 12:5; 1 Tim. 2:1–2).

Q. 108. *What do we pray for in the first petition?*
A. In the first petition, which is "hallowed be Thy name" (Matt. 6:9), we pray that God would enable us and others to glorify Him in all that whereby He makes Himself known (Ps. 67:2–3), and that He would dispose all things to His own glory (Ps. 83).

Q. 109. *What do we pray for in the second petition?*
A. In the second petition, which is "Thy kingdom come" (Matt. 6:10), we pray that Satan's kingdom may be destroyed (Ps. 68:1, 18), and that the kingdom of grace may be advanced (Rev. 12:10–11); ourselves and others brought into it and kept in it (2 Thess. 3:1; Rom. 10:1; John 17:19–20), and that the kingdom of glory may be hastened (Rev. 22:20).

Q. 110. *What do we pray for in the third petition?*
A. In the third petition, which is, "Thy will be done on earth as it is in heaven" (Matt. 6:10), we pray that God by His grace would make us able and willing to know, obey, and submit to His will in all things (Pss. 67; 119:36; Matt. 26:39; 2 Sam. 15:25; Job 1:21), as the angels do in heaven (Ps. 103:20–21).

Q. 111. *What do we pray for in the fourth petition?*
A. In the fourth petition, which is, "give us this day our daily bread" (Matt. 6:11), we pray that of God's free gift, we may receive a competent portion of the good things of this life and enjoy His blessing with them (Prov. 30:8–9; Gen. 28:20; 1 Tim. 4:4–5).

Q. 112. *What do we pray for in the fifth petition?*
A. In the fifth petition, which is, "and forgive us our debts, as we forgive our debtors" (Matt. 6:12), we pray that God, for Christ's sake, would freely pardon all our sins (Ps. 51:1–2, 7, 9; Dan. 9:17–19); which we are the rather encouraged to ask, because by His grace we are enabled from the heart to forgive others (Luke 11:4; Matt. 18:35).

Q. 113. *What do we pray for in the sixth petition?*
A. In the sixth petition, which is, "and lead us not into temptation, but deliver us from evil" (Matt. 6:13), we pray that God would either keep us from being tempted to sin (Matt. 26:41), or support and deliver us when we are tempted (2 Cor. 12:8).

Q. 114. *What does the conclusion of the Lord's Prayer teach us?*
A. The conclusion of the Lord's Prayer, which is, "for Thine is the kingdom, and the power, and the glory, forever, Amen" (Matt. 6:13), teaches us to take our encouragement in prayer from God only (Dan. 9:4, 7–9, 16–19), and in our prayers to praise Him, ascribing kingdom, power, and glory to Him (1 Chron. 29:10–13); and in testimony of our desire and assurance to be heard, we say, Amen (1 Cor. 14:16; Rev. 22:20–21).

An Advertisement to the Reader

Having a desire to show our near agreement with many other Christians, of whom we have great esteem, we some years since put forth a Confession of our Faith, almost in all points the same with the Assembly and Savoy, which was subscribed by the Elders and Messengers of many churches baptized on profession of their faith; and do now put forth a short account of Christian principles, for the instruction of our families, in most things agreeing with the Shorter Catechism of the Assembly. And this we were the rather induced to because we have commonly made use of that Catechism in our families. And the difference being not much, it will be more easily committed to memory.

Combined Scripture, Name,
and Subject Indices

Scripture Index
Volumes 1-4

Matthew (*continued*)

22:24–31	4.326
22:29	4.160, 4.236, 4.535
22:30	1.15, 3.59, 4.302
22:31	4.236
22:31–32	4.535
22:37	1.25, 2.166, 2.177, 3.330
22:37–39	2.167, 4.321
22:37–40	2.792, 4.255, 4.294, 4.320, 4.359, 4.579
22:39	1.25, 2.794, 4.329, 4.335
22:40	3.571
23	1.615, 1.631, 2.80, 2.84, 2.92, 2.198, 2.383, 2.496, 2.528, 2.533, 2.538, 2.552, 2.555, 2.583, 2.594, 2.638, 2.647, 3.13, 3.57, 3.60, 3.84, 3.103, 3.109, 3.124, 3.140
23:2	2.583, 4.331
23:2–3	2.638, 3.418
23:3	2.733, 2.858, 3.231, 4.253, 4.405
23:4	1.74, 4.331
23:8	4.159, 4.449
23:8–10	4.257, 4.265
23:9	4.323
23:9–10	1.95
23:10	4.188, 4.277
23:13	1.66, 2.278, 4.325
23:13–26	1.67
23:14	4.326
23:15	4.338
23:16	2.303
23:17	4.189, 4.279
23:23	1.327, 2.842, 3.373
23:24	2.303
23:25	4.335
23:33	4.455
23:35–36	2.278
23:37	2.485
24	1.535, 1.565, 1.614, 1.623, 2.89, 2.187, 2.502, 2.558, 2.647, 2.830, 3.16, 3.59, 3.68, 3.82, 3.201
24–25	3.48, 3.94, 3.95, 3.135
24:5	1.89
24:6	3.670
24:10–13	1.314, 3.353
24:11	1.89
24:13	2.751, 4.85
24:14	1.46
24:15	3.352, 4.196
24:23	1.677
24:23–24	3.752, 3.754

24:24	4.35, 4.66, 4.128, 4.509
24:26–27	1.677
24:27	1.70
24:27–30	2.172
24:28	2.304, 2.729
24:29	1.61
24:30	1.293, 2.99, 2.333, 2.751, 2.780, 4.310
24:31	2.99
24:34–35	1.311
24:35	1.78, 4.79, 4.156
24:36	2.333, 2.751, 4.272, 4.302, 4.318
24:42	4.163, 4.318
24:42–44	4.272
24:51	3.332
24:44	3.542, 4.318
24:45	3.757, 4.285
25	1.122, 1.609, 1.623, 1.628, 2.119, 2.391, 2.397, 2.398, 2.647, 2.648, 2.649, 2.830, 3.94, 3.201, 3.298
25:1	4.163
25:1–13	3.59
25:6	2.48
25:10	3.542
25:13	2.333
25:14	2.855
25:15	2.304
25:19	4.163
25:21	2.101, 2.268, 2.317, 4.252, 4.272, 4.551, 4.569
25:21–23	2.687
25:23	2.101, 4.252, 4.358, 4.551, 4.578
25:29	2.648, 4.65, 4.241
25:30	1.304, 2.101, 3.358
25:31	2.49, 2.172, 2.751, 3.309, 3.749, 3.754, 4.302, 4.310, 4.502
25:31–46	1.293, 2.99, 2.333, 4.272
25:32	2.48, 2.49, 2.333
25:32ff	4.569
25:33	4.317, 4.318
25:34	1.45, 1.108, 2.101, 2.499, 2.618, 3.46, 3.82, 3.605, 3.749, 4.318, 4.456, 4.507, 4.537, 4.569
25:34–36	1.763
25:34–40	1.109, 3.348
25:35–36	4.333
25:36	4.451
25:39	3.519
25:40	3.423
25:40–45	1.71
25:41	1.133, 1.337, 2.101, 2.172, 2.243,

Titus (*continued*)
3:4–5 4.247, 4.312
3:4–7 3.312, 4.304
3:5 2.100, 2.254, 2.292, 2.575, 2.669, 2.715, 2.783, 2.785, 2.862, 3.315, 3.346, 3.364, 3.477, 3.488, 3.594, 3.690, 4.37, 4.38, 4.81, 4.160, 4.162, 4.247, 4.266, 4.267, 4.313, 4.342, 4.346
3:5–6 2.172, 3.309, 3.321, 4.310
3:5–7 1.484, 2.172, 3.315, 3.316, 4.252
3:6–7 2.669
3:7 2.173, 2.575, 4.247, 4.313
3:8 2.175, 3.316
3:9 3.118, 4.326
3:10 2.329, 2.743, 2.744, 3.104, 3.134, 3.398, 3.434, 4.258, 4.270, 4.323, 4.339
3:10–11 4.339
3:11 2.542
3:12 2.542
3:14 2.842, 3.214
3:15 4.253

Philemon
Book of 1.174, 2.426, 3.307, 4.90, 4.234, 4.438, 4.459, 4.500, 4.533
1–2 3.756
3 2.46, 2.498
4 3.764
6 3.764, 4.253
18–19 3.759

Hebrews
Book of 1.174, 2.426, 2.533, 2.660, 3.307, 4.90, 4.234, 4.438, 4.459, 4.500, 4.533
1 1.529, 1.559, 1.617, 1.624, 1.626, 1.630, 1.640, 2.219, 2.220, 2.374, 2.375, 2.379, 2.381, 2.384, 2.467, 2.558, 2.612, 2.613, 2.619, 3.16, 3.17, 3.18, 3.22, 3.35, 3.37, 3.39, 3.56, 3.65, 3.67, 3.68, 3.70, 3.76, 3.80, 3.134, 3.151, 3.299, 3.300, 3.304, 3.657, 3.751
1–2 3.17
1:1 2.285, 2.309, 2.774, 3.307, 4.186, 4.188, 4.233, 4.278, 4.500, 4.532, 4.541
1:1–2 2.274, 3.557, 4.307
1:1–4 3.338

1:2 1.473, 1.474, 2.96, 2.97, 2.165, 2.166, 2.243, 2.309, 2.655, 2.884, 3.309, 4.57, 4.186, 4.239, 4.244, 4.446, 4.538, 4.542
1:2–3 2.827, 3.198, 4.60
1:2–5 2.168
1:3 1.18, 1.213, 1.291, 1.308, 2.47, 2.98, 2.170, 2.263, 2.775, 2.776, 2.830, 3.6, 3.25, 3.29, 3.39, 3.73, 3.75, 3.150, 3.309, 3.310, 3.341, 3.749, 4.157, 4.163, 4.240, 4.302, 4.310, 4.354, 4.446, 4.449, 4.504, 4.538, 4.575
1:5 2.97, 3.75, 3.552
1:5–6 4.301
1:7 3.309
1:8 2.259, 4.276, 4.278, 4.301, 4.448
1:8–9 3.75, 4.265
1:9 2.777
1:10 2.166
1:10–12 3.34, 3.75
1:13 1.289
1:14 2.243, 2.820, 3.189, 3.309, 3.753, 4.189, 4.249, 4.279, 4.302, 4.454, 4.502, 4.548
2 1.345, 1.563, 1.616, 1.617, 1.618, 1.619, 1.620, 1.630, 1.640, 2.191, 2.379, 2.380, 2.397, 2.400, 2.472, 2.562, 2.624, 3.79
2–4 3.292
2:1 4.341
2:2 2.309
2:2–3 4.338
2:3 3.755, 4.450, 4.453
2:9 2.170, 2.779, 2.884, 3.664
2:9–10 4.193, 4.282
2:10 1.289
2:11 1.289, 2.47, 2.674, 4.192, 4.278, 4.281
2:12 4.449
2:14 1.211, 2.47, 2.97, 2.282, 2.434, 2.565, 2.884, 3.74, 3.312, 4.158, 4.244, 4.278, 4.306, 4.309, 4.356, 4.454, 4.542, 4.576
2:14–15 3.313, 4.60, 4.504, 4.540
2:14–18 2.773
2:15 4.317
2:16 2.97, 2.828, 3.199, 3.751, 4.60, 4.186, 4.276, 4.278, 4.302, 4.306, 4.356, 4.576
2:16–17 2.778, 4.244, 4.542

4:10	1.87, 2.170, 2.778, 3.312, 4.128
4:11–12	2.284
4:12	2.884
4:13	2.260, 2.786, 3.674, 3.753, 4.159, 4.254, 4.315, 4.554
4:13–14	3.309
4:14–15	1.87
4:15	2.302
4:16	1.21, 2.492, 4.192, 4.237, 4.281, 4.282, 4.315
4:18	4.257, 4.557
4:19	1.21
4:20	1.290
4:21	1.290
5	1.591, 1.596, 1.597, 2.206, 2.461, 2.463, 2.465, 2.513, 2.624, 2.634, 3.15, 3.25, 3.65, 3.66, 3.295
5:1	2.558
5:3	4.64
5:4	4.249
5:4–5	4.250, 4.549
5:5	2.168
5:5–9	4.426
5:7	2.96, 2.99, 2.165, 2.242, 2.429, 2.654, 2.775, 2.883, 3.149, 3.309, 4.156, 4.237, 4.300, 4.301, 4.354, 4.433, 4.499, 4.536, 4.574
5:7–8	3.749
5:8	2.461, 3.64, 3.75, 3.76, 3.129, 3.131
5:9	4.235, 4.533
5:10	2.783, 3.680, 4.250
5:10–11	2.675, 4.450
5:11	2.168, 4.190
5:11–12	4.305
5:12	2.87, 4.247, 4.280
5:13	2.46, 4.254, 4.316, 4.345, 4.358, 4.553, 4.578
5:13–15	4.347
5:14	2.797, 4.259, 4.348, 4.367, 4.558, 4.587
5:16	4.149, 4.259, 4.338, 4.348, 4.364, 4.558, 4.584
5:16–17	2.821
5:17	5.149
5:18	2.261, 3.316, 4.149, 4.506
5:19–20	2.260
5:20	1.307, 2.47, 2.97, 2.675, 2.827, 3.198, 4.244, 4.278, 4.301, 4.544
5:21	1.32, 1.33, 2.848, 3.15, 3.109, 3.318, 3.735, 4.510
5:29	4.426

2 John

Book of	1.174, 2.426, 2.569, 3.307, 4.90, 4.234, 4.438, 4.459, 4.500, 4.533
1	2.544
2	2.221
4	4.336
7	4.426
8	2.268, 2.688
9	2.792, 4.160
9–10	3.308, 4.426
9–11	4.247
10	2.318, 2.329, 2.743, 2.744, 3.434, 3.752, 4.380, 4.510, 4.513
10–11	2.789, 4.258
11	3.739, 4.380

3 John

Book of	1.174, 2.426, 2.569, 3.307, 4.90, 4.234, 4.438, 4.459, 4.500, 4.533
3–4	4.336
10	4.339
12	4.363, 4.584

Jude

Book of	1.174, 2.101, 2.426, 3.307, 4.90, 4.234, 4.438, 4.459, 4.500, 4.533
1	2.499, 2.613, 3.13, 3.31, 3.82, 3.87, 4.509
2–4	3.15
3	3.757, 3.760, 4.196, 4.285
4	3.678, 3.749, 3.750, 4.184, 4.239, 4.274, 4.301, 4.326, 4.537
6	3.38, 3.309, 3.750, 4.184, 4.185, 4.245, 4.271, 4.274, 4.302, 4.454, 4.502, 4.568, 4.569
6–7	4.271, 4.317
7	4.291, 4.304, 4.568, 4.578
8	2.367, 4.338
8–11	4.262
13	3.38
14–15	4.455
15	4.196
16	4.337
18–21	4.427
19	2.613, 3.760, 4.286, 4.402
20	3.757, 4.196, 4.285, 4.314
20–21	4.252
22–23	2.795
23	4.255, 4.270, 4.321, 4.345, 4.403
24	2.613, 4.246, 4.352
24–25	3.764

Name Index
Volumes 1-4

Subject Index
Volumes 1-4